THE LIBERTY PARTY, 1840–1848

ANTISLAVERY, ABOLITION, AND THE ATLANTIC WORLD
R. J. M. Blackett and James Brewer Stewart, Editors

THE LIBERTY PARTY
1840–1848

Antislavery Third-Party Politics
in the United States

REINHARD O. JOHNSON

LOUISIANA STATE UNIVERSITY PRESS
BATON ROUGE

Published by Louisiana State University Press
www.lsupress.org

Copyright © 2009 by Louisiana State University Press
Preface copyright © 2021 by Louisiana State University Press

All rights reserved. Except in the case of brief quotations used in articles or reviews, no part of this publication may be reproduced or transmitted in any format or by any means without written permission of Louisiana State University Press.

Louisiana Paperback Edition, 2021

DESIGNER: Michelle A. Neustrom
TYPEFACE: Mailart Rubberstamp, Minion Pro
TYPESETTER: J. Jarrett Engineering, Inc.

Library of Congress Cataloging-in-Publication Data

Johnson, Reinhard O., 1944–
   The Liberty Party, 1840–1848 : antislavery third-party politics in the United States / Reinhard O. Johnson.
     p. cm. — (Antislavery, abolition, and the Atlantic world)
   Includes bibliographical references and index.
   ISBN 978-0-8071-3393-4 (cloth : alk. paper) 1. Liberty Party (U.S. : 1840–1848) 2. Antislavery movements—United States—History—19th century. I. Title.
   JK2391.L93J64 2009
   324.2732—dc22

                                                                             2008032658

ISBN 978-0-8071-7516-3 (paperback) | ISBN 978-0-8071-7546-0 (pdf) | ISBN 978-0-8071-4263-9 (epub)

The author thanks the editors of the following journals for permission to republish material that originally appeared, in different form, in "The Liberty Party in New Hampshire, 1840–1848: Antislavery Politics in the Granite State," *Historical New Hampshire* 33 (Summer 1978): 123–165; "The Liberty Party in Vermont, 1840–1848: The Forgotten Abolitionists," *Vermont History* 47 (Fall 1979):258–275; "The Liberty Party in Massachusetts, 1840–1848: Antislavery Third-Party Politics in the Bay State," *Civil War History* 28, no. 3 (September 1982): 237–265; "The Liberty Party in Maine, 1840–1848: The Politics of Antislavery Reform" *Maine Historical Society Quarterly* 19 (Winter 1980):135–176.

This book is dedicated to Claudina Reinhard Johnson
and the late Oscar E. Johnson.

CONTENTS

Preface to the Paperback Edition   ix

Acknowledgments   xiii

Introduction: The Liberty Party, 1840–1848   1

1. The Formation of the Liberty Party   5
2. The Liberty Party Takes Shape: Early Development and the Election of 1844   22
3. A Period of Uncertainty and Confusion, 1845–1846   50
4. The Move to Free Soil, 1847–1848   75
5. New England   92
6. The Middle States   137
7. The Old Northwest   164
8. The Liberty Party Appeal   222
9. African Americans and the Liberty Party   242
10. The Liberty Party Membership   264
11. The Garrisonians, the Liberty Party, and the Abolition Movement in the 1840s   292

Afterword   303

Appendix A. Votes in Major Statewide Races, 1840–1848   307

Appendix B. Banner Liberty Counties, 1844   313

Appendix C. National Liberty Party Platform, 1844   315

Appendix D. Liberty Membership   323

Notes   385

Index   487

PREFACE TO THE PAPERBACK EDITION

Except for a few minor changes and corrections of typographical errors, this paperback edition differs little from the original hardback edition in the main text, footnotes, and index. This is not the case, however, with Appendix D, minibiographies of Liberty members mentioned in the body of the book. As I initially worked on the book during the 1980s and 1990s, I kept a list of biographical details of party members and sympathizers. Then, in the late 1990s and early 2000s, I discovered much more material as sources came available on the Internet. Fortunately, I decided to do a last run-through of the members list in 2008, shortly before the final manuscript went to LSU Press. The amount of new material amazed me and helped me fill in many gaps in the biographies.

If I was amazed in 2008, I am now astounded at the number of new sources that I have found online just twelve years later. As a result, I have made additions and corrections to many entries. Some are merely alterations of birth or death dates, but in other cases they are more extensive: deleting less important information, adding more-significant material, or even rewriting the whole entry. Many entries could have been expanded if not for page limitations to the book.

John Cross is a prime example. Over forty years ago, when I began in-depth research on the Liberty Party in Illinois, it soon became obvious that Cross was a very important antislavery figure, not only in Illinois abolitionism but also in the whole movement in the Old Northwest, especially because of his role in setting up routes on the Underground Railroad. I thought that it would be easy to find material on someone who was "One of the Seventy" famous antislavery lecturers, solicited passengers in the newspaper as the "Superintendent of the Underground Railroad," and was sentenced to jail for his antislavery activities by none other than Judge Stephen A. Douglas. Think again. Trying to find biographical material on him, even in 2008, was maddening. I did not even get his birthplace and years of birth and death correct in the original edition. Now, in 2020, there is so much material on Cross and several others that it is difficult to keep their biographies short. Nevertheless, other Liberty supporters still remain shadowy figures, at least until additional resources become more easily accessible.

I have continued to discover supplementary information on the Liberty organization and its members while researching various antislavery topics. John B. Alley (1817–1896) won national office, serving four terms in the U.S. Congress (1859–1867), but he is only one of many who held state and local offices. Many others had prominent roles in institutions of higher learning, especially evangelical colleges that dotted the Midwest and post–Civil War South. These antislavery activists—female and male, black and white—will emerge as they are identified and examined, and if more state and community studies analyze the multifaceted nature of the movement.

Some new research has also enhanced understanding of Liberty history. Stacey M. Robertson, in *Hearts Beating for Liberty* (2010), and Julie Roy Jeffrey ("The Liberty Women of Boston: Evangelicalism and Antislavery Politics," *New England Quarterly* 85, no. 1 [March 2012]: 38–77) add to an appreciation of women in the Liberty movement. Corey M. Brooks, in *Liberty Power: Antislavery Third Parties and the Transformation of American Politics* (2016), and Stanley Harrold, in *American Abolitionism: Its Direct Political Impact from Colonial Times into Reconstruction* (2019), discuss the ongoing impact of Liberty policies and politicians on the national stage. One can only wish that there were more studies of Liberty members like E. Fuller Torrey's *The Martyrdom of Abolitionist Charles Torrey* (2013), which is an excellent biography of a complex and sometimes controversial party leader. Several other studies—such as Kevin Pierce Thornton's article about a black Liberty man of whom I was not aware ("Andrew Harris, Vermont's Forgotten Abolitionist," *Vermont History* 83, no. 2 [Summer/Fall 2015]: 119–56)—discuss individuals who were members of the party but whose Liberty activities were sometimes peripheral to their other interests.

Researchers have done little new work on the Liberty Party or abolitionism during the 1840s in general at the state and local levels. Historians who have recently examined the total antislavery experience have added little to existing knowledge of the Liberty Party; and new state and community studies of the antislavery experience—whether political, economic, religious, social, or intellectual—treat the party as an afterthought at best. Historian Richard J. Ellis, in his very thorough *Old Tip vs. the Sly Fox: The 1840 Election and the Making of a Partisan Nation* (2020), does discuss possible Liberty and abolitionist influences on both the 1840 and 1844 elections, but his quantitative speculations are based on county-level data sets. Political scientist Adam Chamberlain has made the party a centerpiece of two articles ("The Growth of Third-Party Voting: An Empirical Case Study of Vermont, 1840–55," *State Politics and Policy Quarterly* 12, no. 3 [September 2012]: 343–61; "From Pressure Group to Political Party: The Case for the American Anti-Slavery Society and the Liberty Party," *Social Science Quarterly* 99, no. 1 [March 2018]: 246–61). He utilizes township-level returns—as I have done in my articles and dissertation cited in this book. Just as historians can be urged to pay more attention to numbers, particularly regarding the ecological fallacy, social scientists might consider spending a bit more time on historical context.

What still needs to be considered for a better understanding of the Liberty Party, antislavery politics, and the whole abolition movement? The subjects are hardly played out. I am very surprised that no one has done any new work on the small group of political abolitionists who did not migrate to the Free Soil Party and its subsequent manifestations. This would encompass the Liberty League and its many successors, and the neglected election of Gerrit Smith to the U.S. Congress in 1852. Little new research has been done on local abolitionism in general and antislavery politics in particular. More studies with the focus of Tom Campbell's *Fighting Slavery in Chicago: Abolitionists, the Law of Slavery, and Lincoln* (2009) would be welcome.

Instead, many recent writers have made broad interpretive statements—often without adequate supporting arguments and with much textbook-style padding—that have marginalized any systematic analysis of grassroots abolitionism, much less any discussion of multifaceted political activism. As in the past, too many historians continue to overemphasize the role of William Lloyd Garrison and his small groups of followers while neglecting the great body of abolitionists outside his limited areas of influence. We must fully and critically examine these recent historians' writings if we are ever to achieve a more nuanced understanding of what happened to transform the U.S. antislavery movement between 1840 and 1860 from a marginal cult into a major factor in the coming of the Civil War.

Almost fifteen years ago, Richard White wrote an excellent short essay stating that American historians "seem to be united on one thing: a reluctance to debate.... There is a culture of caution, a prickly overprofessionalization, that has begun to influence all of us." ("What Are We Afraid Of?," From the OAH President, *OAH Newsletter* 34, no. 3 [August 2006]: 3). This is still true in antislavery studies. With the exception of a few scholars, such as Stanley Harrold, most writing in the field on antislavery/abolition and convention sessions has devolved into a series of mutually congratulatory comments or state-of-the-field exercises. One can only hope that scholars will engage in more of the constructive, respectful, reciprocal criticism that will lead to a better understanding of the whole movement. Otherwise, we will just continue shifting the deck chairs instead of producing rigorous, meaningful historical writing.

—Reinhard O. Johnson
Brimley, Michigan
August 2020

ACKNOWLEDGMENTS

I owe thanks to many people who have helped me during the research and writing of this book. I have received unfailing help and courtesy from almost every librarian, archivist, and historian whom I have consulted. A special debt of gratitude is due to the researchers whose recent works on antislavery and politics have contributed so much to my understanding of the Liberty environment. I also want to acknowledge the contributions of the many state and local historians who toil on town and county histories, narrowly conceived monographs, and compilations of documents. Their preservation of the "facts" has enriched this study, especially as I sought to trace the lives and environments of Liberty followers. I also want to thank those organizations and individuals that are making them available on the Internet. They have made available materials either out-of-reach or unknown to me.

I have benefited from the advice and encouragement of others more directly involved in the process of research and writing. James Roger Sharp of Syracuse University has been involved in this project from its inception. He has gone far beyond what one could expect from a dissertation advisor. He not only has given me half a lifetime of encouragement, but he also read and made helpful comments on the final draft. Richard Carwardine and Otey Scruggs, who also served on my dissertation committee, suggested several avenues of inquiry as I began to expand the study. As the book neared completion, several other scholars read it and made constructive suggestions. James Brewer Stewart and R. J. M. Blackett, editors of the Antislavery, Abolition, and the Atlantic World series for LSU Press, read and reread the manuscript as they shepherded it to publication. I particularly appreciated Professor Stewart's e-mails of encouragement as he shared his extensive knowledge of politics and antislavery. Frederick Blue gave the manuscript two very careful readings. His comments and advice strengthened the work in many ways. Russell Bright's comments helped to tighten a longer, more unwieldy manuscript. I also want to thank Rand Dotson and his associates at the LSU Press for their prompt, thoughtful, and professional responses to my inquiries. I especially appreciate the work of copy editor Maria denBoer. She has helped immensely in the final preparation of this book.

While most responses from colleagues, librarians and institutions have been wonderful, occasionally I encountered a few darker clouds. I have frequently used libraries around the country to review journals and read my own microfilm. When I attempted to use the library at the University of San Francisco several years ago, however, I was told that I could not gain admittance until I signed up and paid (I think the amount was two hundred dollars) for at least a six-month membership. It did not matter that I had a Ph.D., several publications, and an undergraduate degree from a Jesuit institution, and was a homeowner in the immediate neighborhood. This was a policy put in place by David K. Oyler, and my appeals to the library and the university's administrative offices were unsuccessful. I also pity anyone who has to work under Allan Berg, an administrator at the University of Maryland University College. His constant meddling with courses and teaching schedules, pressure to teach overloads, and a lack of understanding of a scholarly mission could be a case study of poor educational values in an administrator.

I dedicate this work to my parents and also the rest of my family: Claire and the late Cato. I would still like to make a secondary dedication to others who made up the group of gypsy adjuncts and itinerant scholars who have made up the forgotten generation of historians who completed their training during the late 1970s.

THE LIBERTY PARTY, 1840–1848

INTRODUCTION
The Liberty Party, 1840–1848

Since the mid-1960s, the Liberty Party has received increased attention from historians. With the notable exception of Theodore Clarke Smith's *The Liberty and Free Soil Parties in the Northwest*, published in 1897, previous studies of both the antislavery movement and the politics of the 1840s rarely treated it in much detail.[1] Few biographies of prominent Liberty men discussed their party activities in any depth.[2] The field was hardly much richer in unpublished work.[3] The situation began to change by the 1960s, however, with an increasing amount of scholarship on major figures in the party that included much on their Liberty activities—a trend that continues up to the present.[4] A body of scholarship that focuses in whole or part on the Liberty Party now exists. The best comprehensive study of the Liberty Party is Richard Sewell's *Ballots for Freedom: Antislavery Politics in the United States, 1837–1860*, which is a balanced piece of scholarship that deals with the party from a national perspective.[5] At about this time in the mid-1970s, a new group of scholars began examining the Liberty Party on state and local levels and in its relation to evangelical religion.[6] This work and other studies less directly related to the Liberty Party have deeply enriched the understanding of antislavery politics and abolitionism during the 1840s.

Nonetheless, no one has yet written a national study of the Liberty Party. Sewell outlined the development of the party from a national perspective but did not analyze the party on state and local levels except where intrastate matters affected the national party. Vernon Volpe's book, *Forlorn Hope of Freedom: The Liberty Party in the Old Northwest, 1838–1848*, added significantly to the knowledge of the party only in Ohio over that contained in Smith's pioneering 1897 treatment. Still, no study examines the party in all the states where it existed, and most work on abolition or state politics hardly acknowledges its existence.

In actuality, the Liberty Party was a vibrant movement in many places and had its greatest impact on the antislavery movement at the local and state levels. Perhaps the party has been neglected because it developed differently in each state. This study attempts to integrate these diverse state and local aspects of the movement into a national view of the party.

First and foremost this is an examination of the Liberty Party as a political party. I have structured the first part of the work as I would a treatment of the Whigs, Democrats, anti-Masons, or any other political entity, by looking at both national and state developments. The latter part of the book is devoted to the role of the party vis-à-vis various aspects of the larger abolition movement. Throughout the book I have tried to present the options available to Liberty Party members as various situations developed and choices narrowed and, as David Hackett Fischer has stated, "to study historical events as a series of real choices that living people actually made."[7] That most Liberty men were genuinely doing what they thought was best for slaves and free blacks has often been forgotten in discussions of the wide range of philosophies in the antislavery movement. Liberty Party members became willing to compromise their early ideological positions as it became apparent that they had to modify their political strategies to confront slavery more effectively. This led most of them into the Free Soil coalition. The party changed over the eight years of its existence as it responded to the rapidly changing social-political environment during the 1840s. The Liberty Party of mid-1848 was very different from that of mid-1840 or 1841, just as the larger society's views of the slavery question were changing greatly over this eight-year span. The existence of slavery was a non-issue for most citizens in 1840; by 1848, it had become the most volatile issue in the country.

Chapter 1 discusses the Liberty Party's emergence, from its origins in the abolition movement of the 1830s until after the presidential election of 1840. It examines the beginnings of the movement nationally and in states where voting abolitionists debated whether to set up slates of independent electors or pursue some other alternatives. Chapter 2 details how the party put itself on a stronger footing in its first three years, deals with the national Liberty Party convention of 1843, and examines the presidential election of 1844. Chapter 3 looks at the party after the 1844 elections and the various problems party members encountered in devising a consistent political philosophy and attracting voters. These include discussions on the U.S. Constitution and slavery, whether additional planks should be added to the Liberty platform, and to what extent Liberty Party followers should be willing to work politically with those outside the party. Chapter 4 outlines the events leading to the Liberty Party's absorption in the Free Soil Party in 1848 and the formation of the Liberty League by those opposed to the coalition.

Chapters 5, 6, and 7 show party development in the states, broken down by region. I attempt to minimize repetition by mentioning, but not revisiting in detail, events in the state studies that have received extensive treatment in the national chapters. Therefore, there are frequent cross-references to other parts of the study in some of these chapters. In these state studies, I go into considerably more detail on matters that have not been covered elsewhere in the secondary literature. For instance, I summarize the history of the party in Massachusetts, New York, and Ohio—where it has already received considerable treatment—while developing more detail on other states where its history has not been as well documented. This approach shows the variety of Liberty experiences that make it difficult to generalize too particularly about the party. Motives and party philosophy varied from state to state, often being formed by cadres of influential state leaders. For instance, much has been written about the come-outer aspects of "Bible politics" in Upstate New York and the internal bickering among members over the party creed. The party situation there, however, was not representative of it elsewhere. Much has also been written about the coalition-minded Cincinnati Liberty men, but their Liberty philosophy was not accepted by the vast majority of Liberty advocates before 1848, even in their own state. Indeed, the Liberty Party is probably most easily characterized and studied as a loose federation of state parties with certain core beliefs common to all.

Chapter 8 discusses the political appeal of the party, including its religious base and methods of organizing, propagandizing, and electioneering. Chapter 9 deals with the very important relationship between African Americans and other Liberty adherents, including their roles on the Underground Railroad. The Liberty Party was the first party to take any genuine notice of blacks and encourage their involvement. Black voters and those without the vote responded with their participation and assistance in all areas. Chapter 10 examines the Liberty membership, both the leaders and, as far as possible, the grassroots support, including the participation of women in Liberty affairs. Chapter 11 is a discussion of the difficult relationship between the Garrisonian wing of abolition and the Liberty Party. My view is that Garrison and his followers have received too much credit in abolition studies and that the Liberty Party and its attendant organizations became the major vehicle for antislavery protest very early in its history. The study concludes with a short summary afterword.

The four appendixes provide information that would be cumbersome if it was included in the main text. Appendix A contains state returns for all the gubernatorial and presidential elections that the Liberty Party contested along with the 1848 votes for the Free Soil Party in those states. Appendix B lists banner Liberty counties for the 1844 presidential election (counties in which the Liberty

Party received over 10% of the vote or that were the top Liberty county in their state in percentage of support for the Liberty Party). Appendix C is the National Liberty Party Platform for 1844. And Appendix D provides short biographical sketches of all the Liberty members mentioned in the main text.

The aim of this book is to present the Liberty Party's place in the political environment and its role in antislavery reform. My contention is that the party affected both of these on the national and state levels. At the beginning of 1840, the antislavery movement was a bothersome fringe minority that had little real impact on the larger American society and much less on the relatively stable two-party system. Eight years later, the slavery issue permeated many aspects of American life and contributed to sectional feeling and the breakdown of the two-party system. The Liberty Party affected this situation during its more than eight years of existence—it was the longest running national third party until the Socialist Party in the twentieth century—and many of its members played significant roles in subsequent political developments both before and after the Civil War.

I do not use the words *liberal, radical,* or *conservative* in this study unless they are part of a proper title, such as Isaac Hill's Conservative Democrats of New Hampshire or Gerrit Smith's Radical Abolition Party, a successor to the Liberty League. They have little meaning in antislavery studies because they are so rooted in specific contexts. For example, the Liberty Party was considered "radical" by most contemporary observers, but a Garrisonian follower would undoubtedly term it "conservative." Joshua Giddings, the antislavery Whig congressman from Ohio, was viewed as "radical" by many of his fellow party members, but his Liberty Party opponents on Ohio's Western Reserve criticized him for being "tainted by the proslavery Whig party" and his "arguments were rejected as antiabolitionist nonsense."[8] The best way to avoid the relativity of these terms is either to define them very precisely or not to use them at all. I have chosen to omit them.

Some studies also differentiate between the terms *antislavery* and *abolition*. That *antislavery* is more encompassing than *abolition* is axiomatic, but here the terms are used interchangeably, just as the contemporaries of the Liberty Party did. As Theodore Clarke Smith has pointed out, the term *abolitionist* in 1848 "included not only the Garrisonians, but also Liberty men of all shades."[9]

1

THE FORMATION OF THE LIBERTY PARTY

The most pathetic residue of antislavery organization was the little group which had attempted to turn the antislavery impulse toward political action. In 1840, they organized the Liberty Party.

GILBERT HOBBS BARNES, *The Anti-Slavery Impulse*

The Liberty Party came out of the movement for the immediate emancipation of the slave. Repudiation of colonization and gradual schemes for emancipation during the 1820s, the freeing of over one million slaves in the British West Indies beginning in 1831, the increased circulation of abolitionist pamphlets and newspapers, and the emergence of evangelical revivalism gave impetus to immediatism during the 1830s. Twelve men met in Boston in early 1832 to establish an organization devoted to furthering this cause. This New England Anti-Slavery Society grew to over one hundred local auxiliaries by 1835 and eventually reconstituted itself as the Massachusetts Anti-Slavery Society when it became a member of the American Anti-Slavery Society, which had been founded at Philadelphia in December 1833. This national society spread so rapidly across the North that it claimed 1,300 state and local affiliates with approximately 250,000 members by 1838.[1]

No single person or group controlled the whole body of abolitionists. Much of the real power lay in the state and local societies, but certain individuals were recognized as leaders in their regions. Most early antislavery advocates were involved in various reform activities and came to immediate abolition by many routes. A few were longtime veterans of the cause. Some had participated in gradual emancipation and colonization work. Others had developed concern for the slave as a result of religious experiences during the great revivals of the 1820s and 1830s. And a sizable number were converted to abolitionism during the great propaganda campaigns of immediate emancipation during the 1830s.

Perhaps the outstanding characteristic of this antislavery crusade was its intensely religious tone. The turmoil that most denominations experienced before the Civil War demonstrated that a sizable antislavery faction existed within almost every major religious group in the country. In fact, it is difficult to generalize about abolitionists because of their diverse backgrounds and levels of participation in the movement.[2]

During the early years, most state and local societies concentrated on recruitment and propaganda. They published newspapers and innumerable pamphlets, commissioned agents to go on speaking and fundraising tours, and brought in American and English speakers to their meetings and conventions. Partially influenced by the revivalism of the 1830s, their prevailing philosophy of action was "moral suasion," a strategy that emphasized the conversion of the individual as a prelude to basic societal change. "Prejudice and slaveowning, outward manifestations of unrepentant hearts, were to be conquered with the tools of revivalism."[3] Its advocates eschewed violence and coercion and emphasized a person-to-person interaction that made belief in "the power of virtuous agreement to persuade others of the need for emancipation" axiomatic.[4]

Many abolitionists, however, went beyond moral suasion and began to circulate petitions demanding that Congress abolish slavery in the District of Columbia, especially after some Southern postmasters began censoring the U.S. mail of abolitionist literature. In 1836 Southern congressmen, backed by some Northern Democrats, succeeded in passing a "gag rule" that would automatically table antislavery petitions without discussion. This assault on civil liberties, supposedly guaranteed by the First Amendment, incensed many who had not previously been associated with the abolitionists. Those concerned with freedom of speech frequently expressed their sentiments by signing the petitions, which, ironically, increased after the gag rule was approved. The gag rule provided the abolitionists with a national figure, former president John Quincy Adams. Although he refused to allow himself to be characterized as an abolitionist, Adams spoke eloquently against the gag rule from his seat in the U.S. House of Representatives. The gag rule, which would not be permanently discontinued until 1844, strengthened the abolition movement. The controversy won many sympathizers, provided free publicity for the cause, and served as one of the major rallying points among antislavery men of various philosophies.

During the early 1830s, abolitionists were often characterized as misfits and cranks. Few took them seriously. Mobs, sometimes led by "gentlemen of property and standing" in the community, inflicted abuse and injury on abolitionists across the North. Incidents occurred most frequently in states bordering slave territory and least often in the upper New England region. These riots culminated in Alton, Illinois, in November 1837, when abolitionist editor Elijah Lovejoy was shot and killed while defending his press from an unruly crowd. He died at the height of the anti-abolitionist rioting, but from that time on there was a sharp drop in the number and intensity of incidents directed against the abolitionists in the North, although these never entirely disappeared. Average citizens were becoming more concerned about the infringement of civil liberties, and, at the same time, antislavery activists were becoming recognized as legitimate reformers in most Northern communities.

As violent opposition to the antislavery forces declined, however, internal dissension weakened the cohesiveness of the movement. By 1840, many abolitionists spent much of their time raging at one another over a number of issues that were shattering the unity of purpose that had existed just a few years before. Contemporaries and historians have disagreed over what actually caused the famous 1840 split in the American Anti-Slavery Society, the most serious of all the disputes, but all commentators agree that William Lloyd Garrison played a central role in the controversy.[5]

Garrison had become a dominant figure in New England abolitionism. Born into an undistinguished Newburyport, Massachusetts, family in 1806, he led a journeyman printer's life until an 1828 meeting with Benjamin Lundy, editor of an abolitionist newspaper, the *Genius of Universal Emancipation,* changed his life. Although Garrison had been interested in various reforms before he met Lundy, he had not committed himself fully to any particular cause before his exposure to abolition. Shortly after their 1828 meeting, he joined Lundy's newspaper in Baltimore. Once there, he found himself promptly convicted of libel for his condemnation of a slave carrier from his hometown of Newburyport, Massachusetts. After Arthur Tappan, a wealthy New York philanthropist, paid his fine, Garrison left Baltimore and the temporarily defunct *Genius of Universal Emancipation* to go to Boston, where he planned to publish an abolitionist weekly. On January 1, 1831, the young printer published the first issue of the *Liberator,* a newspaper that soon became the most famous antislavery sheet in the land. He worked tirelessly in a variety of abolition activities, helped found both the New England Anti-Slavery Society and the American Anti-Slavery Society, and became one of the leading figures in the American antislavery movement.

By the late 1830s, Garrison had embraced a series of reform positions that extended the principles that had spurred his devotion to antislavery to other causes. He adopted a nonresistance philosophy that opposed force and evolved into a rejection of the state and a refusal to vote. Although he initially did not quarrel with those who wished to exercise their political franchise, he was adamantly opposed to direct political action in the form of an antislavery third party. At the same time, he was becoming more critical of many in the clergy for their refusal to dissociate from churches that would not take strong antislavery stands. Garrison also became more insistent on equal rights for women, particularly for their participation in antislavery meetings. The line between Garrison and his critics was not clear, however, because many agreed with him on some issues while disagreeing on others. Eventually, he became the major issue.

Events in the Massachusetts Anti-Slavery Society in 1839 presaged a May 1840 division in the American Anti-Slavery Society. Shortly after a contentious 1839 meeting of the national society, problems in Massachusetts developed when a sizable group of abolitionists rebelled against Garrison's domination of the state society. Henry Brewster Stanton, the official agent of the American Anti-Slavery Society, aided these insurgents because he disliked Garrison's opposition to political involvement and his power in the state society. Among the issues that brought Garrison's opponents together were the role of politics in antislavery action, the nature of female participation in the society, the introduction of other causes into the organization, and Garrison's harsh public persona, particularly with regard to the clergy and religious organizations.

Garrison easily routed his opponents at the annual meeting of the state society at which all present, including women, could vote. The losers withdrew, founded the Massachusetts Abolition Society, and prepared to issue their own newspaper, the *Massachusetts Abolitionist*. Elizur Wright, an antislavery lecturer and former mathematics professor at Western Reserve (Ohio) College, became its editor.[6] Within eight months a large number of county and town societies affiliated with the new society. Sometimes a local antislavery organization would break its ties with the older society and then join the newer group. In other cases a separate organization would be in competition with the Massachusetts Anti-Slavery Society. These events served as a rehearsal for the division in the national society a year later.[7]

Garrison and his many supporters (including many women) packed the annual national convention of the American Anti-Slavery Society in New York in May 1840, even chartering a special boat to bring Garrison's followers to the meeting.[8] When their votes placed Abby Kelley, a leading female Garrisonian, on the business committee, a large portion of the dissenting minority withdrew to form the American and Foreign Anti-Slavery Society.[9] These New Organization abolitionists had mixed motives for breaking with the old society. Liberty Party leaders Joshua Leavitt, Elizur Wright, and Henry B. Stanton agreed with Garrison on the woman question, but they strongly disagreed with him on political action. Lewis Tappan, Arthur's brother, agreed with Garrison that direct political action was inexpedient, but he differed with him on the role of women. James G. Birney, a former slaveholder and presidential candidate for the Liberty Party, was at odds with Garrison on both women and politics. These and other dissidents came together on one major point: they believed that William Lloyd Garrison was forcing his ideas and personality on the American Anti-Slavery Society to such an extent that they needed to break away to form another society. Nonetheless, some of those who disagreed with Garrison on individual points remained in the Old Organization. For instance, Samuel Sewall, Boston lawyer and seven-time Liberty Party gubernatorial candidate in Massachusetts, did not accept Garrison's position on politics. Nonetheless, he remained in the Old Organization while serving on the Liberty Party's state central committee because he wished to emphasize his belief in the primacy of moral suasion in the antislavery struggle.

Delegates from New England and the Middle Atlantic states dominated this May 1840 meeting. The geographic distribution of the 906 delegates was:

Maine	14
New Hampshire	16
Vermont	14
Massachusetts	449 (352 males, 97 females)
Rhode Island	29
Connecticut	71 (at least 3 females)
New York	165 (at least 8 females)
New Jersey	56
Pennsylvania	68 (at least 16 females)
Delaware	4 (1 male, 3 females)[10]

That there was no proportional representation and everyone present could vote in these meetings precluded some larger states from having much influence. This was particularly true for the region known as the Old Northwest. Delegates from Ohio, Michigan, Illinois, Indiana, and the territories had difficulty making trips to the East. Also, the national society was not as important to these westerners, whose abolitionism was largely independent of direct eastern influence. The religious revivals of the 1820s and 1830s produced a talented group of persons, many of whom were ministers from Lane Seminary in Ohio. Led by Theodore Dwight Weld, these reformers traveled widely on speaking tours.[11] As these men spread out from Ohio, they had enormous impact on the antislavery of the region. Since Garrison and the national society had little influence in this area, these abolitionists were not directly involved in the breakup of the American Anti-Slavery Society. Some individuals did join the new American and Foreign

Anti-Slavery Society, but the state-oriented societies did not wish to become embroiled in a power struggle that had torn apart the national society and was wreaking havoc within many state and local organizations in the Northeast. This split in the American Anti-Slavery Society was a watershed in American abolitionism. Frequently overlooked, however, are the many state and local societies that wanted nothing to do with the controversy. Several state societies pursued a neutral course by withdrawing from the Old Organization but refusing to affiliate with the American and Foreign Anti-Slavery Society.[12]

Although many of the issues dividing abolitionists in 1840—nonresistance, women's rights, anticlericalism, Garrison's personality—were usually confined to the East, where Garrison had influence, antislavery men across the whole North argued about the expediency of third-party nominations. Political activity was nothing new to the abolition movement. Politics had been deemed an appropriate sphere for antislavery work from the beginning of the immediatist movement. In the first year, both the New England Anti-Slavery Society and the American Anti-Slavery Society explicitly endorsed political activism.[13] As early as 1836, Ohio abolitionists became involved in state politics when the *Philanthropist*, a Cincinnati newspaper then edited by former slaveholder James G. Birney, urged antislavery men not to vote for a particular Ohio congressional candidate because he opposed the elimination of slavery in the District of Columbia.[14] The whole question of voting was not a controversial issue in the Old Northwest because the nonresistance philosophy was not popular there and the region had a tradition of political participation. As the leading nineteenth-century commentator on antislavery politics in this area has stated: "So generally was the duty of voting taken by the western abolitionists at this time, that it was seldom discussed, and such individual societies as did mention the matter invariably went contrary to the Garrisonian position."[15]

Soon most antislavery voters carried their involvement in politics further with the "questioning system," following the precedent that English abolitionists had developed so successfully.[16] After abolition societies formally questioned candidates about their positions on slavery topics, members would decide which candidate(s) gave satisfactory answers. If no candidate responded appropriately, voting abolitionists were urged to abandon the major-party nominees and to "scatter" their votes among various write-in antislavery men. This protest vote was especially effective in New England, where a candidate running for office had to receive a simple majority of all votes cast in order to be elected. If no person received the required majority, all the candidates could remain in the runoff elections until someone collected over 50% of the vote. Occasionally, it became apparent that no one was going to be elected, and an office would remain vacant until the next regularly scheduled election.[17] Antislavery voters attempted the questioning system across the North during the late 1830s with decidedly mixed results.

Most abolitionists finally admitted that questioning was a failure. Antislavery voters soon discovered that some candidates were less than candid in their replies. When the Ohio legislature passed a fugitive slave law at the behest of two Kentucky slaveholders in 1839, abolitionists scrutinized the behavior of certain legislators who had responded favorably to their inquiries the previous fall. They found that candidates had been less than truthful in their statements.[18] New York abolitionists speculated that their endorsement seemed less than worthless because politicians who had made statements favorable to antislavery sometimes had lost votes. Sometimes they even put up independent tickets when dissatisfied with the responses from major-party candidates.[19]

The strategy was most useful in the upper four New England states, but even there its effectiveness varied from state to state. In Vermont, it appears that it was an advantage to have abolitionist backing, but in some parts of New Hampshire and Massachusetts, particularly in port towns with a lively trade with the South, it was not. Politicians who courted the abolitionists sometimes reneged on their promises, and occasionally an abolition endorsement seemed to hurt a candidate more than it helped him. Enough problems existed, according to a leading abolitionist years later, "to render the 'questioning of the candidates' a farce."[20] When some local voters in such different states as Michigan, New Hampshire, and New York put up independent slates of candidates in a few races in the 1830s, they did it without any intention of setting up a permanent party. Little enthusiasm existed for a separate political party in any area of the country as the decade drew to a close. As late as July 1838, Henry B. Stanton, Elizur Wright, and James G. Birney—three men who would be prominent in the early Liberty Party—wrote to Gerrit Smith that they opposed the formation of a third party.[21]

Interest in a third party developed because existing antislavery political tactics had produced such poor results that abolitionists found themselves considering alternatives. They carried on an informal debate on a third party in private correspondence, the abolition press, and antislavery meetings. Opponents, who initially had the support of the antislavery press and the vast majority of abolitionists, developed arguments based on principle and expedience. Many took the position that the idealism of the cause would be lost in the general scramble for public office. Nathaniel P. Rogers from New Hampshire maintained that "[w]e should not see abolitionists prostitute their name or their influence on votes to the promotion of party ambition or office-seeking. We would not see them seeking office or political power for themselves as a distinct third party . . . Mere political partyism might reduce abolitionists to the same level with them [politicians] . . . It is by other measures than voting or state making, that the chains of the land are to be broken. We don't want to turn politicians . . . If they can't act *with* party *against* slavery . . . they should quit party."[22]

Those interested in remaining within the two major parties argued that a third party would be ineffective. Despite the failure of the questioning system, they still believed that the only way to produce a truly potent political force was to work with Democrats and Whigs. They quickly pointed out that this was the way emancipation had been achieved in England. The *Philanthropist*, now edited by Dr. Gamaliel Bailey, argued that entering politics would compromise abolition principles. Convinced that the U.S. Constitution permitted no interference with slavery in the slave states, he declared that "a political party contemplating as its object the extinction of State slavery is manifestly an absurdity, for it can act by no political means."[23]

Many of these points were consolidated in the *National Anti-Slavery Standard*, the New York newspaper that replaced the *Emancipator* as the official mouthpiece of the American Anti-Slavery Society after the 1840 split.

> If we take our true religious and moral position, our fulcrum is another world; beyond the power of this to disturb; and thence we obtain a power to move it, as it were with a single hand. By exchanging this position for a political one, we make the aid of numbers the one consideration, while by the same movement we expose and increase our numerical weakness . . . The man who runs the political gauntlet for his seat, will find that his moral power has so oozed away in the process, that he cannot sit in it steadily.[24]

The advocates of a distinct antislavery political party also marshaled a battery of arguments. One of the earliest was that slavery was a political as well as a moral evil.[25] As such, it required both a political and a moral solution. If this could be done within the existing political structure, as had been done in England, well and good; but if existing institutions failed to respond, then duty would drive voting abolitionists to establish alternate means of political expression. Some even looked on this as an opportunity to ennoble the corrupt political system. Pro-third-party men appealed to the expedience of adopting this new tactic. They believed that they could hold the balance of power between the two major parties and pressure at least one of them into assuming an antislavery character. This use of independent political nominations as a pressure tactic was a potential problem particularly for the Whigs, who correctly believed that they had the most to lose by such a strategy. This tactic would be especially effective in New England, where even a small third party might have a considerable impact. Elizur Wright summed up the reasons for a third party in a late 1839 letter to Henry B. Stanton. He advocated a third party for three basic reasons. First, it would encourage action by abandoning nonresistance and promoting the crusade to purify politics. Second, it would cause "[t]error [to be] struck to the hearts of the South" because abolitionists would be using the franchise in their attempts to eliminate the peculiar institution. And third, it would lead to consistency by infusing the antislavery spirit into all aspects of American life.[26]

Supporters injected moral righteousness into their justification for direct political action, but an awareness of the power realities of American politics existed beneath the rhetoric. William Goodell's newspaper, the *Utica* (N.Y.) *Friend of Man*, served as a forum for discussion in late 1839 and early 1840 on the possibilities for a third party. While his own editorials expressed a yearning for a return to a simple, rural republicanism, which he imagined existed in the past, Goodell and other commentators on both sides of the question demonstrated a sophisticated knowledge of politics. For instance, Goodell disagreed with those who thought that abolitionists should work through the two major parties as in Britain. Although he still refused to endorse a new party, he pointed out some differences in the politics of the two countries. He believed that party politics in the United States were "more corrupt and *corrupting* than in Great Britain" for two reasons: "Party Machinery has become more perfect and party control over *individual conscience* has become more complete."[27]

Although religious references and moralistic pronouncements colored their language, many of these men had acute political sensibilities and understood power. Most of those urging a third party originally believed that it would be a temporary vehicle with which to express protest. They believed that they could generate enough support to force one of the major parties to adopt antislavery principles. Some of these men were new to political activity, but most who favored independent nominations voted regularly, often were active in one of the major parties, and sometimes had been candidates or had held public office. In general, they accepted American political institutions as they existed in 1840, but they felt that they had to form a separate party to purify the political process by presenting an antislavery alternative to the Whigs and Democrats.

The small pro-third-party group received its most forceful leadership from two Upstate New York abolitionists, Alvan Stewart and Myron P. Holley. Stewart was a well known, witty lawyer who was one of the first persons to declare that slavery was unconstitutional. He was a founder of the state antislavery society and was an early advocate of a separate party.[28] Holley had been a state legislator as early as 1816 and had served as canal commissioner for the Erie Canal. They had spent much of 1839 agitating for third-party action. In February 1839 Stewart proposed establishing a separate antislavery party to the executive committee of the New York State Anti-Slavery Society.[29] Almost five hundred delegates from across the North attended a July 31 national antislavery convention in Albany at which Stewart presided. It refused to sanction national antislavery candidates and left the nomination of independent candidates to local organizations.[30] The convention, however, did receive encouragement in a letter from Thomas Morris of Ohio, a former Democrat in the U.S. Senate who was now proscribed by his party for his antislavery actions. He wrote that his health prevented his attendance, but he declared his support for independent nominations because "[i]f the Ballot Box, then, is honestly and independently used, it alone will produce the extinguishment of slavery in our country."[31] William Goodell noted that many abolitionists now favored a third party.[32]

Holley then organized a group of fourteen men to meet in Rochester at the Monroe County antislavery convention in September. This small group adopted pro-third-party resolutions and recommended the nomination of an antislavery presidential ticket.[33] Holley prepared an address arguing that the questioning system had failed and the major parties had either ignored abolitionists or bargained with them in bad faith.[34] He traveled to Cleveland for a convention of the American Anti-Slavery Society on October 23 to promote his views. This convention of over four hundred abolitionists, most of them from Ohio, received him well and made him president pro tem of the convention. After a lively debate, many delegates came out for political action but against independent nominations. They rejected the pro-third-party resolutions because they believed they were politically inexpedient and not something that the society should rule on.[35] The rejection of Holley's proposals at Cleveland effectively ended the attempt to turn the American Anti-Slavery Society into a political organization. Holley, Stewart, and their colleagues, however, were a determined group. Three weeks later they called a convention in Warsaw, New York, under the ostensible auspices of the New York State Anti-Slavery Society to make formal nominations of a national ticket. After a lengthy discussion, the delegates nominated a ticket of James G. Birney and Dr. Francis Julius LeMoyne, a physician from western Pennsylvania.[36] Both nominees, neither of whom had been present, quickly declined the offers as premature.[37] Thus, the movement for a new political party seemed to have died.

The nominations of William Henry Harrison and Virginia slaveholder John Tyler at the Whig convention in December to oppose incumbent Democrat

Martin Van Buren, however, angered many abolitionists, causing them to reassess their positions and ponder alternatives. Some were going to abstain from voting; others, such as Gamaliel Bailey of the *Philanthropist*, could accept Harrison, but a few more began leaning toward independent nominations. The third-party group gained a powerful ally in late 1839, when Joshua Leavitt, editor of the *Emancipator* (still the official newspaper of the American Anti-Slavery Society), became convinced that direct political action was necessary. He was so outspoken in his views that the executive committee of the society told him to keep quiet on the subject of independent nominations, and he acquiesced temporarily.[38]

In addition, some important abolitionists who had previously opposed separate nominations began to waver. Gerrit Smith, while still worried about the purity of the movement, dropped his opposition because the questioning system was a failure and he was "convinced that all further attempts to restrain the leading abolitionists of the state from the organization of an independent political party must be futile." Elizur Wright, editor of the *Massachusetts Abolitionist*, came down on the side of independent nominations by late autumn 1839, when he approved the sentiments of the Warsaw convention. John Greenleaf Whittier, poet and editor of the *Pennsylvania Freeman* as well as a former member of the Massachusetts legislature, remained opposed, but he said he would not criticize those who supported it. Austin Willey, influential editor of the (Augusta, Maine) *Advocate of Freedom*, became increasingly outspoken in favor of the third party. And William Goodell bent somewhat when he editorialized that "*[w]e go for independent nominations*, but AGAINST 'a party.'"[39] Nonetheless, prospects for the venture were inauspicious. As late as February 1840, Henry B. Stanton, who favored the project, privately expressed misgivings about setting up a ticket for the 1840 election. The arguments of Smith, Holley, and William L. Chaplin persuaded a large January antislavery convention in Arcade, New York, to approve the call for a national nominating convention. They were unsuccessful at similar gatherings in Farmington and West Bloomfield, New York, where Garrisonian James C. Jackson spoke forcefully against them. Myron Holley refused to be discouraged, and he was instrumental in his county society's issuing a call for a convention to be held in Albany on April 1.[40]

Alvan Stewart chaired this meeting of 121 individuals from 6 northeastern states—104 from New York alone—that met to again debate the merits of independent political action. A substantial number of these men were heartily opposed to the independent movement and characterized the meeting as the "April Fools' Convention."[41] Letters of support were read from prominent abolitionists who could not attend.[42] The opposition also spoke. The Reverend S. S. Beman of

Troy, New York, ridiculed the movement "with such a lightning of wit," according to Elizur Wright, "that if the question of nominating had been voted on immediately after he sat down, the Convention would have been a failure and a joke worthy of the date."[43] Effective speeches by Stewart, Holley, Leavitt, and Professor Beriah Greene of Oneida Institute changed many minds. A resolution approving an independent slate of nominees for a presidential ticket passed 44–33 with many abstentions. The convention then proceeded to nominate Birney for president with Thomas Earle, a Quaker lawyer, former Democrat, and longtime antislavery activist from Philadelphia, as his running mate.[44] Both accepted in letters that discussed the necessity for independent political action. The convention urged state and local societies to call conventions and set up independent slates for the fall elections.[45] William Goodell, who served on the committee of correspondence at the convention but did not vote, was so impressed by the quality of the discussion that he was now undecided about a permanent third party.[46] Although the new party was known by a number of names—Human Rights Party, People's Party, Abolition Party, Freemen's Party, Liberty Party—until the formal adoption of its permanent name at the 1841 national convention, the Albany gathering effectively marked the beginning of the Liberty Party.[47] Nonetheless, many prominent abolitionists did not welcome the new party. Both John Greenleaf Whittier and Gamaliel Bailey wrote to Birney saying that they considered the nominations premature and that most abolitionists would not support the ticket.[48] Their doubts echoed in many state and local meetings up to the election.

The split in the American Anti-Slavery Society and the disagreements over independent nominations left the antislavery movement more splintered than ever. The different positions taken by state groups on these matters reflected the general uncertainty. Just as state and local organizations varied on national affiliations, the response was mixed as voting abolitionists in individual states debated the proper course. Despite no national direction, all the Northern states except Indiana and Connecticut—where the (Hartford, Conn.) *Charter Oak*, opposed the Albany convention and the nominations by the "malcontents of Western New York"[49]—that eventually would support ongoing, active Liberty Party organizations put up slates of independent electors for the 1840 presidential contest. New Jersey made a futile attempt to establish a statewide ticket, but local groups held meetings and supported the Birney-Earle slate.[50] Rhode Island "was partially organized in 1840, but it was soon after completely absorbed in the Dorr Controversy."[51] Other states made uneven progress in organizing campaigns.

Responses to independent political nominations varied in the upper four New England states. Massachusetts was the most organized state in favor of the nominations, but even there the efforts were only rudimentary. A small convention met on May 27 to endorse the Birney-Earle nominations. It selected a statewide ticket of William Jackson for governor and Roger Leavitt, Joshua Leavitt's father, for lieutenant-governor. Jackson, a former U.S. congressman for the Anti-Masonic Party, declined the nomination because he felt that it was premature to be making independent nominations.[52] After Roger Leavitt died during the summer, the many unsuccessful attempts to find a gubernatorial candidate demonstrated the problems within the small group. Garrison must have looked on in glee when no one wanted the dubious honor of being a candidate. After weeks of coaxing, George Washington Jonson, a former Whig, reluctantly allowed his name to appear on the ballot.[53] The group had difficulty organizing support in 1840. Although the state had a central committee, it seems that leaders did not do much work at the grassroots level beyond lecturing at antislavery rallies. Late in the summer, the no longer silent Joshua Leavitt urged organization at the school district level, but there was little indication of much activity.[54] Although the Massachusetts men had done more work for independent nominations than any other state, they were not optimistic about their electoral chances.[55]

Maine, Vermont, and New Hampshire antislavery voters were slow to set up an independent slate of electors. After an October meeting of the Somerset County Anti-Slavery Society defeated a proposal for a set of Maine electors supporting the independent candidates, about twenty men met separately in Bloomfield to nominate their own ticket of Birney-Earle electors.[56] In Vermont, the *Voice of Freedom* was an early opponent of an independent party, and the influential Jonathan P. Miller opposed it because he hoped that the Whig Party would become the antislavery party.[57] When the Albany convention of April 1, 1840, set up the party, only two abolitionists from nearby Vermont voted for it, and only fourteen people attended a June 18 meeting that set up a presidential electoral slate.[58] They attempted to gain support for their movement, chiefly through their newspaper, the *Banner of Liberty*. Few in New Hampshire favored the new party although the state's abolitionists had been among the first, and most successful, in placing an earlier independent antislavery slate. John Greenleaf Whittier, looking back in 1840, recalled that in 1838 "*two thousand* legal voters of that state broke away from their slavery ridden parties—and rallied under the free banner of an independent nomination."[59] The apolitical leanings of *Herald of Freedom* editor Nathaniel P. Rogers and the New Hampshire Abolition Society's many members who wished to maintain their party allegiances hurt organizing efforts. No one attended or sent a letter of support to the April 1, 1840, Albany convention. Those sympathetic to an antislavery party waited until September 1840, when they met and set up a Birney-Earle ticket, but they did little other work.[60]

The only state approaching Massachusetts in effort was New York. The Empire State had capable leaders in Holley, Stewart, Smith, and, by the summer, William Goodell. They were energetic organizers who gave direction to the new movement and, in Smith's case, much needed financing.[61] After an August 5 state convention in Syracuse selected Gerrit Smith and Charles O. Shepard as a gubernatorial ticket, local antislavery meetings made nominations until the week before the election.[62] Little was done in Pennsylvania. The Pennsylvania State Anti-Slavery Society was two organizations; both the eastern and western branches opposed the Albany nominations. Voting abolitionists met separately and selected electors committed to Birney and fellow Pennsylvanian Earle. A few antislavery groups even nominated candidates for local elections, but the *Pennsylvania Freeman*, although reluctantly endorsing the Birney-Earle ticket, was willing to stay with the questioning system and endorsed those who responded satisfactorily. Most who supported local independent nominations did so only after the questioning system was not able to produce an adequate candidate.[63]

Although abolitionists in the Old Northwest tended to be politically active, advocates of independent nominations had a difficult time setting up Birney-Earle slates for the fall election. Michigan was the only state in the Northwest where there was any significant enthusiasm for a third party or independent nominations. A state nominating convention on August 5 endorsed the Birney-Earle ticket and some local conventions selected candidates for the state elections. Generally, the state was not well organized except for the Jackson area, home of the *Michigan Freeman*. The Whig-dominated state antislavery society was opposed to independent nominations.[64] In Ohio the opposition of *Philanthropist* editor Gamaliel Bailey and other state leaders to the new course and the loyalty of the antislavery-oriented Western Reserve area to Whig congressman Joshua Giddings, who supported Harrison, retarded the progress of independent nominations. Bailey reversed his position during the summer, however, and helped organize a state convention of abolitionists in Fort Hamilton on September 1. This meeting endorsed the Birney-Earle ticket by a narrow 57–54 vote and drew up a slate of presidential electors.[65] A few local meetings made nominations for lower-level races, but no real state party apparatus developed. Illinois did even less. The July 4 meeting of the Illinois Anti-Slavery Society passed a resolution condemning both Van Buren and Harrison. Then those favorable to independent nominations met and set up a slate of Birney-Earle electors throughout the state, but they did nothing toward setting up any local organization except for one congressional nomination.[66]

The attempts at independent nominations upset other abolitionists more than Whigs and Democrats. Many abolitionists viewed entrance into the political realm as one more divisive issue. Veteran major-party loyalists realized that the independent slates would have little effect on the election because the last-minute efforts were poorly organized and sporadic. Additionally, political antislavery was a volatile issue that both parties ignored. Although most believed that Whigs far outnumbered Democrats in antislavery ranks, third-party politicos usually balanced their tickets with Whigs and Democrats. No one still knows how much each party lost to the independent nominees in 1840, but most contemporary and subsequent analysts believed antislavery voters with an earlier political identification were mostly Whigs. Pro-third-party spokesmen upset many abolitionists. Elizur Wright lost almost half the subscribers to the *Massachusetts Abolitionist* after he came out for independent nominations.[67] Some members of the executive committee of the Michigan State Anti-Slavery Society attempted to end its support for Treadwell's *Michigan Freeman* because it had "become the advocate and champion of the third party."[68] Both the *Utica Friend of Man* and the *Philanthropist* also suspended operations temporarily.

The situations in the states on the eve of the 1840 presidential election demonstrated that the independent party was not yet a functioning political party. Only New York and Massachusetts had a minimally effective state organization, and little effort went into the campaign itself. Presidential candidate Birney was out of the country from May 11 until November 24 as a delegate to the World Anti-Slavery Convention in London, and Thomas Earle restricted his activity to a few appearances near his home. Their supporters did not formally outline a set of political principles and made no effort to work together nationally. The independent ticket was an alternative to the two major parties, and even those sympathetic to it were expecting little success at the polls. In fact, the new party did not even have a name. It was called the Freeman's Party, the Abolition Party, and other names. What third-party slates did accomplish was to provide antislavery voters a consolidated opposition ballot to bring to the polls. These "tickets" could be made up ahead of time and eliminated the necessity for these individuals to make their opinions known by only scattering their votes.

In an election in which the turnout was the highest for any presidential election in American history, the antislavery candidates fared poorly, picking up as

Table 1. 1840 Presidential Vote

	WHIG	DEMOCRAT	LIBERTY
Massachusetts	72,874 (57.6%)	51,954 (41.1%)	1,618 (1.3%)
Maine	46,612 (50.1%)	46,201 (49.7%)	194 (0.2%)
Vermont	32,445 (63.9%)	18,009 (35.5%)	319 (0.6%)
New Hampshire	26,297 (44.4%)	32,801 (55.4%)	126 (0.2%)
Connecticut	31,598 (55.5%)	25,283 (44.4%)	57 (0.1%)
Rhode Island	5,213 (61.3%)	3,263 (38.3%)	34 (0.4%)
Pennsylvania	144,018 (50.0%)	143,675 (49.9%)	343 (0.1%)
New York	226,013 (51.2%)	212,736 (48.2%)	2,943 (0.7%)
New Jersey	33,351 (51.7%)	31,351 (51.7%)	69 (0.1%)
Michigan	22,933 (51.7%)	21,096 (47.6%)	321 (0.7%)
Ohio	148,043 (54.3%)	123,944 (45.4%)	903 (0.3%)
Illinois	45,576 (48.9%)	47,443 (50.9%)	159 (0.2%)

Source: W. Dean Burnham, Presidential Ballots, 1836–1892 (Baltimore: Johns Hopkins Press, 1955) and occasionally other sources for the Liberty vote. This is the main source for presidential votes unless noted in the state studies in chapters 5, 6, and 7. There were undoubtedly some scattering votes and third-party votes that were not tabulated. Such scattering votes are not included in the above totals.

much as 1% of the vote only in Massachusetts. Henry B. Stanton's prediction that "19/20ths" of the abolitionists were opposed to separate candidates was correct.[69] Voters were not willing to abandon their parties in one of the most emotionally charged contests in history.

William Henry Harrison (Whig)	1,274,624 (52.9%)
Martin Van Buren (Democrat)	1,127,781 (46.8%)
James G. Birney (Liberty)	6,225 (0.3%)

State-by-state returns in the North bore out Stanton's assessment (see table 1). Many studies cite these results to show the futility of the whole Liberty movement. This view of the impact of the new party needs to be modified because of the party's extensive growth and development before the next presidential contest. The election of 1844 would more accurately reflect the strength of the Liberty Party.

After the election, party leaders began to make plans to establish a stronger organization. Alvan Stewart, in his role as chairman of the national committee of correspondence, immediately circulated a lengthy address that promoted a plan of party organization and outlined basic party tenets in language replete with religious exhortations. Stewart asked each state to call a convention for mid-

January 1841 to select delegates to a May national convention in New York City. He urged that they alter the constitutions of their antislavery societies to "cast their suffrages at the ballot-box for such rulers, and for such only, in all stations, as will be 'just, ruling in the fear of God' . . . 'proclaiming liberty throughout all the land, to all the inhabitants thereof.'" He encouraged organization at the county and local levels, support of local newspapers, and the nomination of "real abolition te-totalers, or abstainers from all intoxicating drinks."[70] The new party would gather momentum in early 1841.

2

THE LIBERTY PARTY TAKES SHAPE
Early Development and the Election of 1844

> The Liberty Party had no grass-roots organization, no ward campaigners.
> AILEEN KRADITOR, "The Liberty and Free Soil Parties."

After the 1840 election, the whole idea of a separate antislavery political party could have been forgotten. Most abolitionists voted and took part in the political process, but a few abolitionists, such as Garrison and the nonresistants and certain religious groups, had chosen to avoid politics altogether. Others preferred to follow the British model and work through the major parties. If the questioning method produced no satisfactory candidate, abolitionist voters could write in antislavery candidates, make temporary independent nominations, or not vote. Some favored independent nominations but opposed a distinct party. Nevertheless, abolitionists in several states began laying the groundwork for an antislavery political party.

Soon the new party began to develop into a genuine political organization. Over the next eight years, the Liberty Party would undergo modifications brought about by internal conflicts and outside pressure. There never was, however, a cohesive national Liberty Party. Differences over policies and the absence of strong central leadership resulted in several fairly unique Liberty groups organized along state and local lines. Regional differences existed, but they have been overstated and were not consistent within each region. Except for infrequent conventions and a weak national corresponding committee, there was little nationwide control. The national committee met only at convention time, and the members of the committee carried on irregular correspondence on Liberty matters. The Liberty Party had no national publication until 1847 and no national campaign fund or central financing. Since the party had no patronage, even a united leadership would have had no means of bringing recalcitrant members into line. Therefore, there was limited national direction for the new party, and Liberty platforms often varied from state to state. Sometimes Liberty pronouncements within a state were different, usually occurring where state leadership was divided over some matter. The absence of strong central control is crucial to an understanding of the dynamics of the Liberty effort.[1] The occasional national conventions expressed basic tenets to which most members could subscribe, but each state developed its own character. The speed and thoroughness of party organization varied from state to state, but events followed a similar pattern. By early 1841, third-party advocates in most Northern states either called a state convention or attempted to decide the question of an independent party at a meeting of the state antislavery society. Normally, a sizable number of local societies or conventions would express feelings on political matters before the subject reached the state level. Opinions in these meetings ranged from outright opposition to wholehearted approval of a new party.

A discernible change in the tone of these meetings took place by late 1841. A three-stage pattern usually developed. First, there was an almost uniform opposition to establishing an antislavery party and reluctance to introduce the subject of political duty. Second, political abolitionists became more forceful in denouncing the two major parties and opposing those politicians who would countenance slavery. And third, support for a third party grew. The time it took to stabilize the third party also varied from state to state. The upper New England region was the earliest area of the country to accept and implement the idea of a distinctly antislavery party. The large number of abolitionists, town elections to the lower houses of the state legislatures, and annual statewide elections encouraged New Englanders to make decisions on whether or not to run a third-party ticket almost immediately after the 1840 election. Most states in the Old Northwest and Middle Atlantic region did not have major elections until 1842 and were able to delay making a commitment to a new party.

Some national coordination began at the national convention in May 1841. That New York and New England abolitionists dominated this convention in New York City is not surprising. Travel could be difficult at that time of year, and some states do not seem to have had any organizational meetings during the winter. Only a handful of delegates represented Ohio, and the Michigan delegates, who were selected at a spring meeting, never arrived. A supportive Illinois antislavery meeting voted not to send delegates, but "measures were taken to have our sentiments duly made known to that body."[2] As in the abolitionist meetings of the 1830s, all could vote. On the first day the delegates easily nominated Birney as the party standard-bearer for 1844 and chose Thomas Morris, the former Democratic U.S. senator from Ohio, for the second spot on the ticket.[3]

The convention spent the second day devising a plan of political action. It established a national corresponding committee and approved a basic plan for political organization that became the model for the party throughout its existence. Its format was similar to that employed by the two major parties, although the formal national committee was new to American politics. Delegates agreed that candidates should be nominated for all offices at every level and a series of interlocking committees should be established from the school district to the national level. These committees were to be the heart of the party's organizational scheme.

> Each Committee will communicate with their next superior committee once a year, or oftener if required, and will meet at such a time and place, not less than a month, as shall be agreed upon between them and their superior committee. It shall be the duty of Township and Ward Committees to canvass their respective Townships and Wards, and ascertain as far as practicable, how many of the legal voters will vote the Liberty Ticket; and transmit the number to their superior committee, and so on until the information reaches the National Committee.[4]

Trying to implement this plan frustrated Liberty leaders, but, even when it went into operation, communication almost always stopped at the state level. The national committee, chaired by Alvan Stewart, did not meet again until the next convention in August 1843. The convention formally adopted the name Liberty Party and adjourned for two years, not meeting again until called by the national committee.

The convention outlined the party's basic beliefs in an "Address . . . To the Citizens of the United States."[5] Perhaps the most surprising thing about this document was that it avoided much of the religious rhetoric and imagery that characterized so much third-party writing and emphasized its more secular positions. Third-party supporters clearly meant their message to serve as a political justification for abandoning the two major parties and setting out on an independent course. The lengthy document stated that "[w]e find that the general government of the United States, as a matter of existing fact, is under the control of the slave power," and it pointed out that slaveholders had held the presidency for forty out of fifty-two years. This resulted in many of the internal problems of the country, such as the tariff and the bank issue, which were being manipulated by the South for its own aggrandizement. Party theoreticians would develop Slave Power arguments as key parts of the Liberty propaganda efforts for the party's entire existence.[6] The address claimed that political parties "not avowedly and openly *anti*-slavery in their character, are, and for ever must be, *pro*-slavery," until they change their ways. Any political connection with these parties "must be wrong in principle and disastrous in practice."

The address then explained the necessity for running candidates in local elections, arguing that "[t]o defer nominating in the hope that one or both the present political parties will nominate friends of liberty, would be to hope not only without, but against evidence." It stated that local offices "are the most successful instruments of seduction, and that through their influence, chiefly, the friends of liberty, have been led to cast their votes in favor of a slaveholder for Vice President," a reference to John Tyler, who had recently assumed the presidency. These "nominations and votes are among the most effectual measures for carrying the discussion of anti-slavery principles into the minute ramifications of society—the most retiring and remote corners of the community." To the objection that the party was too narrow in its focus, it answered that every political party "has its *paramount* objects—its *test* questions" and the Liberty Party's were "emancipation, abolition, human freedom, instead of the price of cotton? Suppose 'tariff,' 'Bank,' 'sub-treasury,' and other topics of doubtful disputation among our wisest and best men, should be left open for future consideration?" It clearly designated "the redress of the slave's wrongs, in the first place, as the great and paramount object of our political endeavors."[7]

The address was an appeal directed to the political sensibilities that were made in a very different tone from those associated with "Bible politics." It was a style that would characterize some large national and regional gatherings, whereas a more religious spirit surrounded many state and local Liberty meetings. It also demonstrated the Liberty commitment to go beyond the tactics of the 1830s and enter the American political system as a full-fledged participant. By the time the more representative national convention met in Buffalo in August 1843, diversity within the party would become more apparent. Differences were not so noticeable in 1841, but trends developed thereafter that would result in a Liberty Party with several state and local identities by 1843.

After the 1841 convention, party members still had not developed a consensus on anything except the antislavery nature of their enterprise. The meeting deliberately avoided endorsing a platform of party dogma, and the question of leadership in many of the states was unstable. At least one member from each state was designated an officer of the convention and it was expected that he would be a leader in his state. Some of these individuals—Alvan Stewart of New York, Austin Willey of Maine, and Joshua Leavitt of Massachusetts—did become driving forces in their state parties, but others were rarely heard from afterward. Because there was no national leadership and state leaders had little contact with spokesmen from other areas, it was not surprising that each state party operated in a unique manner and grew at a different rate.

The two years after the 1841 convention were very encouraging to Liberty men. Although a critic predicted that Birney was more likely to become "a perfume peddlar in Hayti, or a shoeblack in Timbuctoo, than President of the United States," the party grew rapidly in many states as functional state organizations emerged.[8] At the time of the 1841 convention, most states had not committed themselves to the nomination of state tickets. By the time of the 1843 national meeting, however, the Liberty Party had state tickets and supported newspapers in all the Northern states except New Jersey and Rhode Island.[9] The party enjoyed steady increases in support, grassroots organizations, and votes.

Perhaps the most important event aiding the Liberty Party in these early years was an event over which they had no control: the death of William Henry Harrison. Many Whig abolitionists had opposed the Birney-Earle ticket because they feared the reelection of Martin Van Buren. These Whigs were shocked when Harrison died on April 4, 1841. John Tyler, a Virginia slaveholder, succeeded to the presidency, demonstrating to many the folly of staying in the major parties. Though Birney-Earle supporters had not emphasized this possibility in pre-election statements—no president had ever died in office—Liberty men soon commented that many ostensible abolitionists had vote for a ticket that put a hard-line, pro-slavery president in the White House.[10] Tyler's subsequent actions reinforced the Liberty position. The Whig Party lost many of its antislavery members to the Liberty Party even though it virtually disowned Tyler. Liberty leaders Salmon P. Chase, Samuel Fessenden, and many others came into the party from the Whigs during the spring and summer of 1841.[11] These defections presaged the loss of Whig votes to the new party over the next few years. The Liberty gains from year to year were high in 1842 and 1843 as the new party grew in all the states where it had even a rudimentary organization.

The Liberty success in lower-level elections was an indicator of the party's electoral improvement. Not surprisingly, the Liberty Party had the greatest impact in areas where there were able leaders and some degree of local financing and organization. Many commentators on the party have pointed out the lack of Liberty electoral success, but to define success merely in terms of winning and losing major elections neglects the third-party dynamic of building up a constituency and the role of a third party as a spoiler and pressure group. While a political party in a two-party system should win at least 45% to 50% of the vote with some consistency to remain competitive, a 30% total in a three-party system normally will make a party competitive. In most states a party could win with slightly less than 34% of the vote. Add to this the requirement of a simple majority being necessary for election in Maine, Massachusetts, New Hampshire, Vermont, and Connecticut, and the criteria for electoral success change. This did not mean that the Liberty Party had great success, but it had much greater impact on the political system, particularly below the national level, than has been acknowledged.

Liberty men won a few seats in state legislatures in the upper four New England states during these early years, and one or two candidates were victorious in Connecticut. While this was only a small portion of the contested seats, it showed there were areas in which the antislavery party candidate could get more than half the total vote. Additionally, Liberty votes prevented any party in these states from getting a majority in many elections, thereby causing hundreds of seats to be left temporarily or permanently empty. This meant that many towns could send no representative to the state legislature, some districts sent no state senator, and even some U.S. congressional districts sent no congressman until additional elections took place. And, of course, the new party gave committed antislavery voters an organized political outlet.

Liberty candidates also won many victories in contests of purely a local nature, such as sheriff, board of supervisors, coroner, and town clerk. Eventually, the Liberty Party would capture some of these offices in almost all the Northern states, but in the first few years these triumphs were particularly evident in New England, Michigan, some areas of Ohio, and New York—states with local party apparatuses. For instance, the success in New York State was most apparent in the Madison County area north of Syracuse, where Gerrit Smith's money and enthusiasm helped the Liberty Party create a strong local organization with its own newspaper, James C. Jackson's *Madison County Abolitionist*.[12] Victories in Michigan were even more widespread as a result of the party's vigorous local activity, and it won numerous local offices as it spread across parts of the more populous lower half of the state. Other pockets of Liberty strength were in areas of the Ohio Western Reserve, parts of Illinois, and other communities in every state.

Many factors not directly related to abolitionist intensity show why the party did relatively well in certain areas. Some Liberty men had experience and knew how to run a political operation. Several had served in Washington. Thomas Morris and Dr. Alexander Campbell of Ohio had been U.S. senators, and David Potts of Pennsylvania and William Jackson of Massachusetts had served in the U.S. House of Representatives. Every state where the Liberty Party became established had some leaders with extensive experience in state and especially local government. Party leaders in most states were not politically naïve. They usually selected former Whigs as candidates for governor in most states in 1841, 1842, and 1843 because they correctly perceived that dissatisfied Whigs were the major source of the party's early strength. Nevertheless, they often made sure that they balanced tickets by finding former Democrats for second spots or other important offices to attract members of both parties and to insulate themselves from accusations that they were tools of either major party. In local races they tended to nominate former Whigs in Whig areas of strength and former Democratic antislavery men in Democratic strongholds, although they occasionally would court members of the minority party, hoping to secure the bulk of its votes. Sometimes a major party would drop its own candidate in a local race and give at least tacit support to the Liberty nominee with whom it was aligned on other issues. This helps to explain why the Liberty vote almost always increased as elections became more local. Occasionally, Democrats and Whigs united on a candidate to defeat the Liberty Party where there was a great deal of Liberty strength.

Liberty leaders made special efforts to find attractive candidates, although some Liberty men thought certain leaders might be going too far in their quest for popular support. Seymour B. Treadwell of Michigan complained that he had "witnessed with considerable pain, too great an eagerness . . . among some of our most valued liberty friends throughout the country to *solicit* men of *some popularity,* but who have not been *publicly* known as outspoken, *fearless,* liberty party men."[13] Accusations of collaboration with the opposition party frequently flowed against the Liberty Party from both major parties. There was some substance to these statements in some lower-level elections, but Liberty men did not make it a practice to work with either major party in statewide or congressional races before 1845.

Candidates were not policymakers in some state parties, but elsewhere—most notably New York, Vermont, Illinois, and, later, Wisconsin and Iowa—they were usually among the real party leaders. The nomination of candidates not deeply involved in the movement caused some difficulties in the early years. Occasionally, a Liberty convention would select a person who would refuse the nomination and sometimes even express publicly his opposition to the new party.[14] These incidents decreased as the state parties matured. Liberty candidates did not openly work for nominations but waited to be called to service. Once a Liberty man received a nomination, he usually did not campaign actively. The candidate himself rarely made direct appeals for votes, especially before 1844. He might speak at Liberty Party meetings and prepare an address to the voters, but he left the appeal for votes to his supporters in the Liberty organizations and newspapers.

An important factor in the Liberty effort was the burgeoning number of Liberty presses. In November 1841 Elizur Wright published a list of eighteen newspapers specifically committed to the Liberty Party.[15] Sometimes newspapers were short-lived, but new ones usually took their places, especially in the weeks prior to an election. The Liberty press was one of the most important instruments for party success because the new party lacked exposure from other newspapers. Those controlled by the Whig or Democratic parties paid scant attention to it before 1844, and anti-political or politically neutral antislavery sheets did not give the party favorable treatment. Liberty newspapers transmitted decisions from party leaders, announced party functions, and reported antislavery news. The number and quality of Liberty sheets increased as the party matured. Some eventually became all-purpose newspapers, furnishing business information, travel schedules, general news, and literary entertainment. No central agency coordinated press efforts, however, and the party did not have a national newspaper until Gamaliel Bailey established the *National Era* in Washington, D.C., in 1847. Most Liberty newspapers served only one state or portion of a state, although some—including the *Philanthropist*, the *Emancipator*, and the *Chicago Western Citizen*—had greater influence.

Occasionally the Liberty Party played an important role in a significant political event. The most famous case in the early years was the series of events that followed the autumn state elections in Massachusetts in 1842. This was one of the most hotly contested elections of the decade, and the one in which the Liberty Party first made its potential felt in Massachusetts politics. The party increased its gubernatorial vote by about 82% over 1841, prevented elections in several U.S. congressional districts, and caused havoc in the elections for state and local offices, causing Elizur Wright to exclaim that "[t]hey must look for the young giant hereafter."[16] The popular vote for governor was extremely close in an election marked by a very high turnout.

> Marcus Morton (Democrat)   56,491 (47.9%)
> John Davis (Whig)   54,939 (46.6%)
> Samuel Sewall (Liberty)   6,382 (5.4%)
> Scattering   180 (0.2%)[17]

In its third state election, the Liberty Party had prevented any gubernatorial candidate from receiving the required majority. The state senate, therefore, had to select the governor from two candidates picked by the lower house; but Liberty voters also had prevented the election in sixteen of the forty state senate seats. The task of filling these seats fell to a convention of the elected senators and representatives. Six Liberty representatives had been elected and held the balance of power. In addition, these Liberty representatives could determine who would be the powerful and prestigious Speaker of the House. The *Liberator* correctly pointed out that "their votes were sufficient to determine the political character of the state government."[18]

The Liberty members failed, however, in their attempts at political manipulation in the joint legislative convention. Sources agree that the Liberty representatives endorsed a ticket of six Democrats and ten Whigs, a combination that would have equally divided the forty senate seats and enhanced the possibility of manipulating Samuel Sewall into the governor's chair. The same sources disagree on why the scheme failed. The *Liberator* claimed that "[i]n voting in convention, five of the Liberty party men, who had formerly belonged to the Whig party, adhered to the arrangement, and the other three voted the entire democratic ticket. The effect of this treachery will account for the five extra votes which the six democrats above alluded to received in the convention, above their colleagues."[19] The *Emancipator*, in reply to a letter accusing the Liberty Party of making Democrat Marcus Morton governor, stated that the Liberty men followed the plan; the scheme failed because a Whig member of the lower house switched and voted with the Democrats, thus filling the state senate with Democrats.[20] This was probably the case, in light of an editorial in the Whig *Boston Daily Advertiser* arguing that it would be better to have Morton as governor than an abolitionist. Leading Whigs expressed concern over the possibility of electing a governor who had nowhere near a majority of the voters backing him.[21] Their fears were not groundless. John Greenleaf Whittier wrote to his brother that Sewall "came within a hair's breadth of being governor."[22]

Liberty attempts to maneuver the lower house into electing a third-party member as speaker also failed when the Liberty candidate, a former Democrat, was reluctant to work for the office because of his political inexperience.[23] The abolitionist Whig Daniel P. King was elected by "an amalgamation of Whig and abolitionists," a solution that caused differences among Liberty followers.[24] Arguments over this type of situation had implications that would continually bother Liberty men. They could never agree on if they could work with members of the major parties without compromising their principles and bargain with politicians who allowed slaveholders in their parties. The tactics in the Massachusetts legislature, particularly the willingness of Liberty representatives to vote for non-Liberty men to fill the state senate vacancies and for some to vote for a Whig speaker, resulted in criticism of the Massachusetts leadership for political expediency. The *Liberator* took the lead in chastising Liberty representatives for voting for men still affiliated with the major parties, something the *Emancipator* and Liberty leadership had condemned but now seemed to condone.[25]

Criticism also came from inside the party. James C. Jackson spoke for many party members when he used his newly founded (Utica, N.Y.) *Liberty Press* to scold Massachusetts Liberty men for their willingness to work with members of the major parties. Joshua Leavitt, who acknowledged a division of opinion within the state, denied any inconsistency in policy. He claimed that there was a difference between voting for someone in the state legislature and voting for the same person in a general election. He specifically pointed out that he refused to endorse Daniel P. King in an upcoming runoff election for a seat in the U.S. Congress.[26] Leavitt argued that when the choice became narrowed to certain constitutional candidates in an internal legislative election, Liberty men should be free to vote for an outsider if a Liberty member was not available. He did not comment on a situation where a reluctant Liberty man was available.

Whittier, who was never an opponent of political cooperation with the major parties, maintained that voting for a non-Liberty candidate was acceptable as long as the man was antislavery.[27] In a letter to the *Emancipator*, he reacted strongly in both defending the actions of the Liberty representatives and expressing his unwillingness "to submit the Liberty Party of this State to foreign and self-constituted overseeism."[28] Even Leavitt, who had been one of the strongest opponents of working with a major party in an election, was undertaking efforts to repeal the gag rule with major-party members in the U.S. Congress. He often had kind words for such men as Joshua Giddings, William Slade, and John Quincy Adams. He and Henry B. Stanton also worked as lawyers with major-party abolitionists on the *Amistad* case.[29] Appropriate behavior for Liberty men in cooperating with major-party members in various political situations was never resolved on a national level. States and various units within states either would either work out accommodations or not allow the issue to disrupt party harmony. Only in post-1844 New York State would it become a divisive issue.

The Massachusetts situation after the 1842 elections not only demonstrated the potential importance of the third party, but also made Liberty men face some difficult policy questions. Some Ohio Liberty men in the Cincinnati area already had been examining some of these questions. Their conclusions had national implications because they resulted in an effort to mold the party into something very different from some early leaders had intended.[30] Most Liberty supporters across the North believed that the party was a great moral crusade against the evils of slavery. These Ohio Liberty leaders felt that the great evil was the political power of the slave states, with religious motives relegated to a less prominent position in public declarations. They gained control of the Ohio party early, but most of the state's Liberty men did not subscribe to their opinions. Ohio had one of the most internally divided state Liberty organizations in the country, and honest differences of opinion and petty jealousies all eventually contributed to some bad feelings.[31] The state party, however, was able to unite at election time.

Nonetheless, the controlling faction of the Ohio party worked to broaden the electoral base of the party by adopting more restrained antislavery principles and rhetoric that would not alienate less committed voters. Its spokesmen were Gamaliel Bailey, editor of the *Philanthropist,* and Salmon P. Chase, an ambitious Cincinnati lawyer who had supported Harrison in 1840. Their intrastate influence was out of proportion to their numbers, but they had great energy and controlled the widely read *Philanthropist.* They sought to relieve Liberty men of the charge of fanaticism by taking an explicit states' rights position on the existence of slavery in the slave states. When some Liberty men began claiming that slavery in the slave states might be unconstitutional, Chase feared that this view might "prejudice against us many worthy and sensible people." Instead, he proposed "to direct all the energies of our political action against the unconstitutional encroachments of the Slave Power and against slavery itself wherever it may exist without constitutional sanction."[32] The Ohio state convention of late December 1841 adopted this view when it ran its first statewide ticket.[33]

A letter from the Ohio Liberty leaders to Joshua Leavitt highlighted important differences between the majority of Liberty men, including most in Ohio who put their emphasis on abolition principles, and the Cincinnati group, who made political strength the primary party value. Leavitt was so shocked by the tone and implications of the letter that he delayed publishing it in the *Emancipator* for almost two months. The letter began by proposing an almost revolutionary change in the party's policy.

> It will be seen that we regard as the proper end of a Liberty Party the deliverance of the government from the control of the slave power; not the emancipation of slaves in the slave States ... If slavery should cease tomorrow, this great aim would still remain, and to accomplish it would be the duty and work of successive generations.
>
> It is almost universally conceded that the general government cannot act directly on slavery in the states. It seems to us that this concession should be frankly made, and that we disclaim all purpose of getting the political power of the country with a view to use it for the abolition of slavery in the states ...

Let us leave, then, to the philanthropists the work of promoting the general cause of abolition by appeals and arguments addressed to the conscience and judgment of those who have the decision on the question of emancipation. Let us, as philanthropists concur in such appeals. —But let us beware of seeming to desire to use political power to effect emancipation in the States. And to avoid the appearance of evil, let the political conventions of the Liberty Party avoid arguments and appeals of this character. Let them be left to individuals and associations formed for such purpose . . .

We shall look with much anxiety for the proceedings of your convention, and shall hope to find them accordant with our own, free from every thing of an ecclesiastical character, saying nothing in praise or censure of ecclesiastical action.[34]

Almost all Liberty members in other states either rejected or ignored these suggestions. At the time most agreed that the federal government could not interfere directly with slavery in the slave states, but they were not willing to make emancipation secondary or forbear from "saying nothing in praise or censure of ecclesiastical action."[35] The disagreement over the role of moral reform in formulating Liberty Party policy and rhetoric continued to plague the party. The Chase-Bailey faction wished to downplay the moral factor and to eliminate party positions endorsing the outright abolition of slavery. Instead, they wished to emphasize the political and economic power of the South. Liberty leaders in other states, however, were not reluctant to condemn slavery as a sin and to urge churches to take action against it because many of these persons were either ministers or had a deep, fervent interest in religion. Differences over the major thrust of the party existed in a few states in these early years, but only in Ohio was the more secular philosophy so powerful among influential state leaders.

These intra-party conflicts were understandable. Many of the most visible Ohio Liberty leaders lived in the Cincinnati area, a place that had a mixture of eastern and Southern immigrants, where violence over racial matters was not rare, and which was across the Ohio River from the slave state of Kentucky. The disfranchised blacks here faced legal discrimination and a stigma of inferiority. This social-political environment was different from that in most Liberty areas of influence. Other Liberty pockets of strength in the Old Northwest—Michigan, the northeastern part of Illinois, the strong Quaker counties in Indiana—were more insulated from these pressures because they contained a greater proportion of abolitionists or were farther from hostile border regions. Even in some places near Southern states—such as Ripley, Ohio, and Quincy, Illinois—there were less compromising tones because these were tightly knit abolitionist communities.

Because Ohio was one of the states where a plurality of all votes was sufficient for election, the temptation to compromise in order to expand the party's base was greater than in New England. Liberty leaders there also wanted to appeal to the type of antislavery that existed in some of the border areas, especially the sentiments developed by Kentuckian Cassius Marcellus Clay.[36] All these conditions affected the thinking of some of the Ohio men as they worked for a less strident political party. Practical considerations also caused many Liberty men to greet these proposals with coolness. Eastern Liberty men were the constant targets of committed abolitionists who were unsympathetic to the third party. Ohio Liberty men in these formative years did not have to contend with antislavery presses such as the *Liberator*, the *Vermont Telegraph*, the (N.H.) *Herald of Freedom*, the *Pennsylvania Freeman*, or the *National Anti-Slavery Standard* that were quick to ridicule compromises by the third party.[37] The attempt to soften antislavery declarations in order to make the party more appealing to the mass of voters caused one New Yorker to claim that it was "a direct and bold attempt to sell the abolitionists of Ohio to one of the political parties, and we cry, Beware!!"[38]

Chase was not just content to make Liberty positions more appealing to the average voter. He was constantly searching for a more attractive presidential candidate than James G. Birney. He favored a well-known person, such as John Quincy Adams, William Seward, or William Jay.[39] When he communicated these ideas to Birney, the presidential nominee wrote back that he thought it "strange . . . that any abolitionist conversant with our cause could have thought, at this stage of it, of going *out* of our ranks for candidates for any office."[40] Joshua Leavitt, who had received a similar letter from the Ohio leader, was more critical of Chase. He wrote to Birney that "I should have been astonished at the want of *taste*—to say nothing more, of such a letter by a raw recruit, addressed to *you* . . . with the idea that there is very little practical wisdom among those who raised the Liberty Standard while he was worshipping the Log Cabin [an allusion to Chase's support for Harrison in 1840]."[41] The Ohio leaders made Thomas Morris so uncomfortable as the vice presidential nominee that he, "unsupported by the party paper of his own place of residence [the *Philanthropist*], has withdrawn his name."[42]

In short, serious disagreements over strategy hampered the young party. Ultimately, these issues would have to be resolved, but these disagreements did not fundamentally endanger the party unity because the basic orientation of most Liberty men was toward an antislavery political outlet. They were aware that they had a national image to project, but were content to let that image remain general antislavery principles. As Joshua Leavitt pointed out, most Liberty men were willing to let any national pronouncements "rest until the fall of 1843 or the spring of 1844."[43] Therefore, no national control was exercised over the state parties in the eighteen months before the August 1843 national convention in Buffalo, and uniform party development and philosophy suffered.

The Liberty Party made satisfactory progress by mid-1843. It was firmly established in most of the Northern states and contested elections at all levels. State and local groups called an increasing number of conventions, set up political organizations and machinery, and propagandized the cause through pamphlets and newspapers. States that had lagged behind in the first two years, such as Illinois and Connecticut, began serious efforts to match some of their more organized neighbors.[44] Party tactics were an amalgam of techniques employed by the old antislavery societies and those of the major parties. Election returns for local, state, and off-year congressional elections showed that the new party was attracting new voters rapidly, though it rivaled the major parties in only a few locales. In addition, national circumstances seemed favorable to future success. The gag rule had alienated many persons from their party loyalties because they were concerned with civil liberties. Rumblings on the annexation of Texas were beginning to concern those worried about the expansion of slavery into new territories. More important, many Whigs were disgusted with the course of their party since Tyler had succeeded Harrison. And some Democrats, particularly in abolition-oriented New England, were beginning to get uneasy with their party's pro-Southern stance. As a result, there were many reasons for the optimism that pervaded the Liberty delegates as they assembled in the national convention in Buffalo in August 1843.

Liberty leaders chose Buffalo for their first genuinely national convention because of its central location and relative ease of access by both land and water. That the date of the convention had to be changed twice on account of the possibility of ice in Lake Erie and elections in some of the states was indicative of the poor national party coordination.[45] State organizations selected delegates by various means, with all the free states except New Hampshire being represented in Buffalo. Despite the buoyant atmosphere resulting from the rapid growth of the Liberty vote in state and local elections, the party faced potentially divisive problems. Differences in party philosophy between some in the Ohio leadership and most of the party were becoming more obvious, and members worried that this might prevent building a consensus on the nature of the party. The talented New York and Massachusetts delegations did not dominate the proceedings as easily as they had two years earlier in New York City. These eastern leaders were not sure what to expect from some of the states that had been absent or poorly represented at the earlier meeting. Most delegates agreed with Gerrit Smith's position that he wished the convention to avoid issues that might cause confusion or were extraneous to the party's immediate needs.[46] They did not want to make this national gathering a battleground that could seriously cripple the whole movement.

The convention of over two thousand attendees, "of whom a considerable portion were female," opened on August 30.[47] Even such a hostile Liberty critic as the Garrisonian Stephen S. Foster acknowledged that "[i]t was in my judgment the most earnest, devoted, patriotic, and practically intelligent political body which has ever met on this continent."[48] It began by adopting the procedural rules that Whigs had used at their 1840 national convention, each state being allowed as many voting delegates as its representatives in both houses of Congress. Some states did not have the maximum number, but the stipulation would mitigate the advantage of those states that were nearby or had easy access to the convention. This was an indication that the open abolition conventions of the 1830s were ending as the party moved toward a more traditional political approach. As a sign of solidarity, Leicester King of Ohio was made president of the convention, and Salmon P. Chase joined Alvan Stewart, William Goodell, and Henry B. Stanton as the most important individuals on the business committee, the group responsible for formulating party positions and resolutions. With all viewpoints represented, there was less chance of an open fight on the convention floor and more chance for agreement.

The first potential stumbling block to a national Liberty consensus was whether to ratify the Birney-Morris nominations of the 1841 New York gathering. Disagreements on this question cut across state lines. It was known that Chase and some of his fellow Ohioans, the delegation most opposed to Birney, had been working on an effort to replace him. They received an assist from Thomas Morris, when he resigned his vice presidential nomination because of internal state pressures in Ohio. He had "come to the conclusion to decline it, in order that another Convention, representing the greater number which now compose and are continually joining the Liberty Party, might have an opportunity to act upon it."[49] The hint that Birney should do the same was obvious. The idea of deserting Birney enraged Joshua Leavitt, and only the calming influence of John G. Whittier and Stanton prevented him from publicly scolding the Ohio men. Nonetheless, considerable support for replacing Birney also existed elsewhere, especially in Massachusetts. Stating that he was a "Birney man," Stanton confidentially reported to Gerrit Smith that "[popular Massachusetts Liberty gubernatorial candidate Samuel] Sewall is strong for [William] Jay; & [I] suspect that [Massachusetts reformer and poet John] Pierpont & Wm. Jackson [two other Massachusetts leaders] are. I think, too, that Whittier inclines the same way."[50] It soon became apparent that to push for Birney's removal from the ticket would seriously divide the party. Birney's reluctance to withdraw unconditionally, the unavailability of another candidate with suitable appeal, and a genuine desire to avoid a serious split resulted in the Birney-Morris ticket being unanimously nominated.[51]

After dispensing with the nomination, the business committee began to work on a party platform. This was something relatively new in American politics, as only the Democratic Party in 1840 had adopted formal party stands. A wide range of sentiments existed on the leading issues.[52] The platform emphasized opposition to slavery to the exclusion of all other matters with the exception of resolutions in favor of general education (Resolution 24) and support for Daniel O'Connell, the Irish patriot who had asked Irish Americans to become involved in antislavery efforts (Resolution 40).[53] The remaining thirty-eight substantive resolutions attacked slavery from many angles, but the platform was a compromise that generally avoided both the strong secular approach and heavy religious rhetoric. The evangelical tones that characterized many Liberty conventions in the Northeast, Illinois, and Michigan were absent. It did call for "restoration of equality of rights" (Resolution 2) and "cordially welcome[d] our coloured fellow citizens to fraternity with us" (Resolution 36), this being the first national political convention with black delegates. While the document did not mention the unconstitutionality of slavery in the slave states, it did come out strongly for the unconstitutionality of slavery in the District of Columbia, in Florida Territory, and on the high seas (Resolution 11). The document emphasized the preponderant influence of the South in the economic and political life of the North, particularly emphasizing how products of free labor were hurt by the competition with slave labor (Resolutions 13–23). Except for these resolutions on the dominance of the Slave Power, which all states emphasized in their propaganda, the platform showed few of the features of the many Liberty Party conventions that regularly employed biblical language and references.

A notable exception was Resolution 37, which Ohio editor Gamaliel Bailey dryly reported "was introduced, not by the Business Committee, but by Mr. Pierpont, and was adopted, we are obliged to think, without mature consideration."[54] Unhappiness with Pierpont was not confined to Ohio, however, as Henry B. Stanton did not like the constitutional implications of the resolution, and Theodore Foster viewed it as "a serious and permanent hindrance to the progress of the party."[55] Nonetheless, it expressed the aspirations of many who wanted to come out with more frank avowals of party principle in relation to the federal government and slavery. It attacked the section of the U.S. Constitution that had been used as a justification for returning fugitive slaves to the South. Following a long, moralistic argument, it concluded: "considering that the strength of our cause lies in its righteousness—and our hope for it in conformity to the LAWS OF GOD, and our respects for the RIGHTS OF MAN, we owe it to the Sovereign ruler of the Universe, as proof of our Allegiance to Him to regard and treat the third clause of the second section of the fourth article of that instrument, as utterly null and void, and consequently as forming no part of the Constitution of the United States, wherever we are called upon, or sworn, to support it." This was the type of statement that Chase and others had long feared could come back to haunt them.[56] Its passage foreshadowed a problem that would divide the party after 1844.

Although the platform was too mild in many of its antislavery positions for some and contained a few statements that others considered too inflammatory, it presented an outline of party policy with which most Liberty men could agree. There were denunciations of slavery, criticisms of the South, and a definite adherence to the principle of equal rights for blacks. While the platform did not reflect the precise character of any of the smaller units of the Liberty organization, it did show general agreement on a broad conception of the party. It emphasized the one idea of opposition to slavery in all its ramifications, and it demonstrated the Liberty commitment to racial equality. Perhaps most surprising was the omission of any mention of the possible acquisition of Texas, but the convention took place fourteen months before the election and "at the time the platform was adopted that question had not risen into prominence."[57]

This was the most important gathering in the history of the party. Not only did it outline a set of basic beliefs that clearly defined the party, but it also was unique in other respects. Several African Americans were accredited delegates, the first time in American political history that they had participated in a national gathering. Several served on committees, and Henry Highland Garnet, a minister from Troy, New York, and an early Liberty supporter, gave an impressive address. And, for the first time in history, a woman addressed a national political gathering. Abby Kelley, a Garrisonian nonresistant and foe of the Liberty Party, was permitted to discuss the principles of the American Anti-Slavery Society.[58] She can be given some credit for the refusal of the convention to pass a resolution critical of nonvoting abolitionists.

Initially, the national convention seemed to be a great success. Shortly afterward, Henry Highland Garnet reported that the National Convention of Colored People in Rochester, New York, adopted the principles of the Liberty Party almost unanimously, although a later New York convention claimed this was not a representative gathering.⁵⁹ Liberty followers welcomed this endorsement because they were being criticized by Frederick Douglass, Charles Remond, and William Wells Brown—three blacks who strongly opposed the Liberty Party. Also, many abolitionists who had remained committed to the Garrison brand of antislavery activity were now coming into the Liberty ranks. In addition, Lewis Tappan, who had publicly remained aloof from the party, now made his endorsement and financial resources available.⁶⁰ The convention made a further attempt to nationalize the party when it authorized Leicester King to appoint a national corresponding committee, a task that he completed by mid-December.⁶¹ Unlike the earlier committee, all the members of this group were important state leaders. Delegates returned to their homes with hope and optimism. Chase was not entirely happy, but he reluctantly admitted, "the thing is as it is & we must take the best of it."⁶² The party had held its national convention with a minimum of bloodletting, but basic problems in the party were merely suppressed, not resolved. These difficulties would resurface during the upcoming campaign and, especially, in the years after the 1844 election.

The immediate effects of the convention were felt in the state elections of 1843. Party activity increased almost everywhere. Most Liberty newspapers quickly endorsed the national ticket, and Liberty men built up the state parties as a prelude to the national election. The Liberty Party had existed in most Northern states at the time of the Buffalo convention, but even the best state organizations were barely adequate. Ohio with its talented leaders had not developed a workable statewide system, and even some states that were able to garner a respectable vote, such as New Hampshire, had little grassroots machinery. Recent Liberty gains plus the impetus of the approaching presidential contest brought about a surge of optimism that translated itself into practical activity as Liberty men anticipated gains for the party. The immediate beneficiaries of these efforts were candidates of late 1843 and early 1844 in state and local elections.⁶³ In fact, most states made their greatest Liberty electoral gains in these contests.

While levels of activity varied greatly among the states, the paths of party development progressed in similar ways. States that had already set up a party structure increased its efficiency, and those with little organization began to evolve a state party structure. Still, this progress was hardly uniform. The New York Liberty Party employed seven agents, and Gerrit Smith planned forty-three meetings in Madison County in the first week of November 1843 alone. At the same time, Connecticut and Illinois were still having trouble establishing county auxiliaries.⁶⁴ While Henry B. Stanton was trying to find one Liberty contact person for each town in Massachusetts in the fall of 1843, the eastern part of Pennsylvania was still without a regular Liberty newspaper or a minimally effective third-party organization.[65]

The states of the Old Northwest, again with the exception of Michigan, were slower to organize locally than those in the East, but even within states there was much variability. A territorial ticket even appeared when a convention in Wisconsin Territory nominated an unwilling candidate for territorial delegate to Congress only twelve days before the election.[66] He did poorly in the race, but the Wisconsin Territorial Anti-Slavery Society endorsed the Liberty Party as the "only one which aims at the entire extermination of the slave power through the constitutional agency of the General Government." It concluded, "every freeman is under the highest political obligation to support [it]," which led to the establishing of a party newspaper, nominations of local tickets, and the formation of a local Liberty Association in Milwaukee.[67]

Immediately after the Buffalo convention, Vermont men turned out in sufficient numbers to send the gubernatorial election to the state legislature. Although the seven Liberty members of the lower house did not have sufficient strength to influence the election (as the party had done in Massachusetts the year before) because of Whig dominance in the state, the third party again showed how it could cause problems in upper-level state politics.[68] Almost two thousand Illinois Liberty Party voters nearly doubled the party's 1842 gubernatorial vote in just one congressional district race in 1843, even though the party was in its formative stage, and Chicago elected the party's first officeholder by electing its candidate to a minor city office in early 1844.[69] Liberty successes continued, particularly in the more highly organized areas of Maine, Massachusetts, Michigan, and New York.[70] Of course, the Liberty rate of success was small compared to the total number of contests, and some of the local victories were a result of a major party throwing its support to a Liberty man. Nonetheless, the Liberty Party was an electoral factor in many places, and the new party gave the major parties, particularly the Whigs, cause for concern as they neared the 1844 presidential election.

Unlike 1840, when Birney was in England for almost the entire time between his nomination and the election, the presidential candidate took an active part in the 1844 campaign. He began in October 1843 with a speaking tour through northern New England. Then he traveled from New Haven, Connecticut, through the Burned-Over District of Albany, Peterborough, and Rochester to his new home in the rough frontier area near the current Bay City, Michigan, where he spent the winter before embarking on another long lecturing tour during the summer and fall of 1844.[71] Birney received more attention from his opponents than he had in 1840, and some of the weaknesses of the new party soon became apparent. He found himself in some awkward situations when questioned on positions other than slavery. Birney was a forthright man, not used to making innocuous statements or hiding his opinions, and his opponents saw that his answers could be used against him. For instance, his reply to the question of the chairman of the Western Pennsylvania Liberty Committee—that a "tariff for revenue to meet the ordinary expenditures of the government will have to be the *rule*"—could hardly have pleased the Liberty men of that area where "[e]very man . . . is a Tariff man . . . We have many sincere Abolitionists, here, who would vote with us, only for this Tariff."[72] Birney's taking stands on a whole range of issues—tariffs, banks, Masonry, pacifism, distribution of public lands, federally financed internal improvements, postal reform, Catholicism, and the naturalization of aliens—concerned some party members.

Birney believed that Congress had the power to establish a national bank, but he was opposed to it while slavery existed. He opposed distribution of public lands to the states. He believed that if Congress could abolish slavery in times of war, then it could do so in times peace. And he maintained that Congress could stop the domestic slave trade between the states.[73] Some of these were quite strong positions that varied from many state and local conventions around the country, particularly in the degree of congressional control over slavery. Some local Liberty organizations that had developed their own political philosophy found that their presidential candidate might hold different views. This confusion showed the lack of national consensus on several topics and revealed the absence of a national mechanism whereby these issues could be resolved or avoided.

The nomination of Thomas Morris for vice president exposed more party problems. Some were upset by rumors of his earlier opposition to black suffrage, even though he had proved himself an ardent abolitionist by sacrificing his career in the U.S. Senate and in the Democratic Party on account of his antislavery convictions.[74] Many men also knew that Birney had preferred Dr. Francis Julius LeMoyne of Pennsylvania for second spot on the ticket.[75] Gamaliel Bailey refused to endorse the national ticket in the *Philanthropist* for almost six months after the convention because of personal pique toward Morris. The situation illustrated a power struggle in the Ohio party and, perhaps more important, divergent views as to the character of the Liberty Party. Chase and Bailey counseled moderation, but Morris "was for pushing ultra doctrines."[76] Even after Bailey finally gave his endorsement in February 1844, Morris considered declining the nomination, and he continued to foment discord in Ohio by his "strong expressions and ultra opinions and peculiarities of expression."[77] Although Bailey's acquiescence permitted the party a show of unanimity, his reluctance indicated that all was not well.[78]

The party became more united in the spring of 1844, however, after the Democrats dumped Martin Van Buren for the expansionist pro-slavery Southerner James K. Polk and the Whigs nominated Henry Clay, who had taken a series of confusing positions on the now potent issue of Texas annexation. When expansionists took control of the Democratic national convention and included in its platform a declaration that "the reoccupation of Oregon and the re-annexation of Texas at the earliest practicable period are great American measures," the issue was out in the open. The Liberty Party, as the only party united in its opposition to annexation, tried to make political capital out of the issue during the summer. Although there was much criticism of the Democrats, Liberty men saved their harshest word for Henry Clay and the uncertain stand of the Whigs. Since most Liberty men at this time were former Whigs, they took particular delight in taking aim at members of their old party:

> Lo! All the world for Birney now,
>   Hurrah! Hurrah! Hurrah!
> See! As he comes the parties bow,
>   Hurrah! Hurrah! Hurrah!
> No iron mixed with mirey clay,
> Will ever do the people say,
>   Hurrah! Hurrah! Hurrah![79]

Birney himself prepared a pamphlet, *Headlands in the Life of Henry Clay*, which catalogued the Whig nominee's participation in the slave system.[80] Beriah Green, a professor who had been head of the Oneida (N.Y.) Institute, wrote a campaign biography of Birney that was widely distributed along with Birney's many writings.[81]

The major parties reacted strongly to this criticism by attacking the Liberty Party and attempting to prevent defections from their own ranks. Whig newspapers declared that the new party took its strength from the Whigs, while the Democratic press claimed just the opposite. This was understandable because each party press directed its editorials at members of its own party, and a primary function of the party newspaper was to get out the vote and minimize defections. As the campaign progressed, however, denunciations of the Liberty Party became particularly heated from the Whigs. Critics attacked Birney for many reasons, ranging from his supposed sympathy with Catholicism (one of his sons attended a Catholic school in Cincinnati) to false charges that he sold his former slaves for a profit and defrauded his creditors and that he was the pawn of British abolitionists.[82] This type of behavior was expected in an American political campaign of the 1840s, and Liberty publications were also less than charitable toward their opponents.

The Liberty Party conducted a presidential campaign that was well within the conventional tradition of party behavior. Liberty men in most areas added a strong religious tone as they carried on a campaign with political rallies, speeches, campaign editions of newspapers, pamphlets, and, in more highly organized states, poll watchers. Party presses describe an increase of Liberty rallies, local conventions, speeches, and printed material, such as almanacs and songbooks. It was probably the high point of the party's energy and national unity of purpose. The Liberty Party was not prepared, however, for two events that cost them an inestimable number of votes. The first was an inexcusable political blunder by Birney, and the second was a "dirty trick" that has become known as the "Garland Forgery."

Late in the summer of 1844, Birney attended a local political meeting in Saginaw County, Michigan, before embarking on a speaking tour that would keep him away from home until the election.[83] Birney was active in this nonpartisan meeting, which was investigating corruption by both Democrats and Whigs. Members of both major parties approached him afterward and expressed a desire to put his name in nomination for a seat in the state legislature. Birney articulated a willingness to serve and claimed, "I should regard my election as proof that the people intended to put an end to pernicious party contests."[84] Then, after he had left on his party-sponsored national tour, the Democrats nominated him for the state legislature (that there was no Liberty organization in Saginaw County was not unusual in frontier areas). The Saginaw frontiersmen made the nomination with no thought to its impact on national politics. In fact, leading Democrats were worried about its effect on their fellow party members in the South.[85] Of course, the Whigs seized upon such political naïveté to label the Liberty Party and Birney as willing tools of the Democrats. Horace Greeley's *New York Tribune* wrote:

> The Loco-Focos [Democrats] have exhibited a just sense of Mr. Birney's services to their cause during the past year. No man has labored so hard or effectively to secure the electoral vote of Michigan to Mr. Polk. It was right therefore that he should receive from them this mark of their confidence and gratitude.
>
> His present mission to the East, we have also reason to believe, has

been undertaken at the instance of leading Loco Focos as well as abolitionists of New York . . . Leading Loco Focos in this city [New York] have at any rate openly exulted over his New York mission at this crisis.

We did not need this additional evidence of Mr. Birney's sympathies with Loco-Focoism in the Presidential struggle; but others did, and their eyes will now be opened. Whig abolitionists will not, we predict, consent to be made Mr. Birney's catspaws in such a game for the exclusive benefit of the Loco Foco party, when they come to see this last conclusive proof of his position. They will not follow their Presidential candidate into the camp of Loco-Focoism.[86]

This was a masterful statement designed both to fuel the fears of Whig abolitionists who were contemplating a move to the third party and to cause former Whigs to wonder if they wished to remain in the Liberty Party camp.

Letters immediately poured in to Birney from Liberty Party leaders across the country who were surprised by the allegations.[87] Birney was able to satisfy most leaders that he was not engaged in a political bargain, but his unthinking act undoubtedly cost him many votes from former Whig Liberty men and prospective Whig converts.[88] Many Liberty leaders, however, agreed with normally mild-mannered John Greenleaf Whittier's later assessment that "it was more than a crime—it was a blunder."[89] Birney was eventually vindicated after the election, but a wiser politician would never have gotten himself into a situation where his motives and actions might be so misinterpreted. Back in Saginaw, the Democrats withdrew the nomination during the commotion.

Few blamed the Whigs for taking advantage of Birney's blunder, even if they stretched the truth, because Birney had put himself in a precarious position. This whole chain of events, however, led directly to a more serious incident that had an even greater impact on the election. The infamous Garland Forgery was released against Birney shortly before the election and went far beyond accepted campaign practices. Theodore Foster later characterized it as "the greatest political forgery in the annals of the nation."[90] It was a letter in which Birney allegedly accepted the Democratic nomination from Saginaw County to the Michigan state legislature and stated his reasons for doing so. The letter, purportedly signed by Birney and supposedly published in a *Genesee County* (Mich.) *Democrat* Extra on October 21, stated that he was running for the presidency "ELSE A DUELLIST and GAMBLER [Henry Clay] will soon fill the seat . . . I have concluded to accept the nomination of Representative to the State Legislature . . . The Democracy of the country must be satisfied that I am rendering them more effectual service by advocating Abolition principles, than if I were

OPENLY A DEMOCRAT . . . [I]n case I should be elected to the office of Representative . . . [I] will forgo the agitation of the slavery question in our State Legislature."[91]

Birney's collusion with the Democrats and willingness to abandon antislavery would, of course, have a particularly strong effect on Whigs who had considered voting for him. Ostensibly, Jerome F. Garland, a Saginaw County man who was involved in some political dealings with Birney, released the letter. It first appeared on October 29, but it was carefully withheld from cities in which Birney was speaking until after he had departed, thus preventing an early denial. He did not discover its existence until he was on the last leg of his campaign, when it was too late to respond. While Whigs were almost unanimous in their condemnation of the fraud after the election, none were too concerned about the veracity of the document before voters went to the polls. A long, involved investigation after the election exonerated Birney, Garland, and the *Genesee County Democrat* from any participation in the deception. A Whig press actually published the Extra edition.[92] The forgery served its purpose for the Whigs. It fed the fears of Whig abolitionists who were thinking about voting for Birney as a protest against Henry Clay, and it undoubtedly caused some Liberty men to return to their former party.

Birney's indiscretion and this "dirty trick" hurt his support among Whig abolitionists, but it is difficult to estimate the actual damage. Newspapers ran lists of former Liberty men who were returning to the Whig Party because of the Saginaw nomination or Birney's positions on the issues, which more resembled those of the Democrats.[93] The Garland Forgery reinforced this sentiment and also caused some Liberty men not to vote at all. William Birney wrote to his father that the "Garland letter lost us about 3,000 votes [in Ohio] . . . Hundreds staid [sic] away from the polls and many voted for Clay."[94] His comments were indicative of the trend as many state parties poured large amounts of money and effort into the campaign. The party financed Birney's speaking tours and several state parties mounted great campaign efforts. Henry B. Stanton reported that in Massachusetts six or seven Liberty lecturers had done "Herculean tasks" by lecturing almost every day in the month before the election.[95] The presidential vote reflected the uncertainty:

Henry Clay (Whig)	1,300,097 (48.1%)
James K. Polk (Democrat)	1,338,464 (49.6%)
James G. Birney (Liberty)	61,999 (2.3%)

The Liberty Party had a recorded presence in twelve states (see table 2). The

Table 2. 1844 Presidential Vote

	WHIG	DEMOCRAT	LIBERTY
Massachusetts	67,521 (51.8%)	52,146 (40.0%)	10,815 (8.3%)
Maine	34,378 (40.4%)	45,719 (53.8%)	4,836 (5.7%)
Vermont	26,770 (55.0%)	17,994 (37.0%)	3,894 (8.0%)
New Hampshire	17,866 (36.3%)	27,160 (55.2%)	4,161 (8.5%)
Connecticut	32,832 (50.8%)	29,841 (46.2%)	1,943 (3.0%)
Pennsylvania	160,384 (48.4%)	167,394 (50.6%)	3,152 (1.0%)
New York	232,452 (47.8%)	237,588 (48.9%)	15,814 (3.3%)
New Jersey	38,318 (50.5%)	37,495 (49.4%)	131 (0.2%)
Michigan	24,185 (43.5%)	27,737 (49.9%)	3,638 (6.5%)
Ohio	155,091 (49.7%)	149,127 (47.8%)	8,083 (2.6%)
Illinois	45,931 (42.4%)	58,982 (54.4%)	3,433 (3.2%)
Indiana	67,866 (48.4%)	70,183 (50.1%)	2,108 (1.5%)

Liberty vote dropped from previous highs in many eastern states, and the momentum, which had been present during the rapid growth of the previous two or three years, died. New Hampshire was the banner Liberty Party state in the nation with 8.5% of the vote, but the Granite State still dropped from its 5,767 gubernatorial votes in the March state election to 4,161 in the November presidential contest. The Vermont Liberty Party lost 1,600 votes between the September state elections and November. Maine's Liberty vote dropped from 5,527 (7.0%) for the September governor's race to 4,836 (5.7%) in the presidential contest. Even many devoted Liberty men were thrown off balance and did not know quite how to respond to the situation.[96] Liberty followers found some causes for optimism in the election because the party showed growth in every state of the Old Northwest except Ohio, where the party received slightly fewer votes than it had in the 1844 state races. The Liberty Party made its most impressive gains in Illinois, a latecomer to the Liberty cause, where it increased its vote by over 75%, made great strides in its state organization, and developed a skillfully edited antislavery newspaper, the *Chicago Western Citizen*. In fact, Illinois could boast the banner county and two of the four counties in the country that gave the Liberty Party over 20% of their vote—DeKalb (25.4%) and Putnam (23.1%) joining Lamoille, Vermont (24.8%), and Grant, Indiana (20.2%).

Whigs blamed the Liberty Party for Clay's losses in New York, Michigan, and Indiana, although the claims for Michigan and Indiana are doubtful. In New York, the state's Liberty organization had worked tirelessly. Gerrit Smith and the Tappans had spent much money to get out a large vote, and presidential candidate Birney spent more time campaigning in New York than in any other state.

Despite these efforts, the Liberty Party could not shake the specter of Birney's actions and the Garland Forgery. The party lost almost one thousand votes from its 1843 efforts. Nonetheless, the party was at least indirectly responsible for Polk's winning the presidency, with his narrow victory in New York being the decisive margin. If just one-third of Birney's 15,814 voters had cast their ballots for Henry Clay, the Kentuckian would have been in the White House. Nonetheless, as Vernon Volpe has pointed out, "[t]hose 15,814 Liberty party votes in New York were simply no longer Clay's to lose; most had defected before the 1844 canvas."[97]

Contemporaries and later historians have agreed that the overwhelming majority of Liberty voters in New York and elsewhere for the 1844 election were former Whigs who had joined the party in 1841, 1842, or 1843.[98] Therefore, many have attributed the expansionist Polk's victory to the Whigs who had defected to the Liberty Party (assuming that these abolitionists would have voted for one of the major parties and not scattered their votes or sat out the election). These counterfactual arguments neglect the fact that these voters were lost to the Whigs before the 1844 presidential election. As Lee Benson has stated, "The Liberty Party's gains had actually been scored *between presidential years,* and the party's *numerical* vote remained relatively stable between 1843 and 1847."[99] Volpe is correct in stating that "Liberty party supporters had gone to great length to renounce their former political ties . . . Liberty party converts were not likely to backslide to embrace what they considered a proslavery political party headed by the nation's most prominent, if somewhat moderate, slaveholder."[100] Indeed, Liberty men were to hear this charge frequently in the next few years as the Polk administration took the United States to war with Mexico over Texas annexation.[101]

Liberty men were ambivalent and restrained in their reactions to the election. They had no love for Henry Clay against whom they had campaigned so energetically, but they also realized that his policies on slavery-related matters, particularly regarding new territories in the West, would have been more favorable to abolitionists than the ones that Polk would pursue. They were more concerned that the growing Liberty strength had come to a standstill in most states and that many former Whigs might return to their old party because of a belief that Liberty votes had made Polk president and concern over the Democratic tinge of much Liberty rhetoric. Party leaders and editors were surprised that they had not done better in 1844, but these spokesmen resolved to bear their disappointments stoically and to convey a mood of optimism for the future.

While the national election disconcerted Liberty men, they felt some satisfaction at having done so much in a little more than four years. By the mid-1840s, the Liberty organization was the major vehicle for serious abolitionist sentiment in every state. William Lloyd Garrison and the American Anti-Slavery

Society had lost most of their followers within a few years after the 1840 split, and most members of the American and Foreign Anti-Slavery Society were either Liberty Party members or moving toward it. A measure of the declining Garrisonian influence is the almost total absence of comment about them in the Liberty press and private correspondence by the middle of the decade despite the almost ceaseless criticism of Liberty affairs. Most abolitionists, both male and female, belonged to societies and organizations that worked closely with the Liberty Party. Most state societies that originally remained aloof from recommending a political course of action endorsed the Liberty efforts by the mid-1840s. The abolition press overwhelmingly sympathized with the Liberty Party. By the time of the 1844 election, all except four or five of the thirty to forty abolition papers in the country endorsed the Liberty Party. Some, such as the *Oberlin Evangelist*, were not Liberty newspapers per se, but they endorsed the party and its principles at election time.[102]

Even though the central organization of the party was poor, Liberty followers built up independent state organizations. These state groups were the heart of the Liberty movement. People in these state machines gained an education in the ways of state and local politics from their own experiences and the veteran politicians among them. They learned the intricacies of political life and developed political philosophies that would impact the Liberty Party and carry over to careers in the Free Soil and Republican parties. This political savvy was partially responsible for the local successes that boosted Liberty morale. By 1845, Liberty candidates had served in all the state legislatures in the upper four New England states and Connecticut. Gubernatorial races were defeated in Connecticut, Massachusetts, and Vermont. Liberty men won local offices in every state where the party existed.

The party also needed to address other serious problems in addition to party stagnation and the threat of former Whigs renewing their old allegiances. Perhaps the chronic lack of funds was the most serious and nagging problem. All but a few newspapers had financial problems. Liberty agents and lecturers often could not get enough money even to pay their own small salaries and expenses. Most Liberty men were not wealthy, and there were no patronage jobs for minor party adherents. Presidential candidate Birney was in such financial straits that he left Cincinnati for the Michigan frontier. There he built a cabin with his own hands in a location that was sixteen miles up the Saginaw River from the nearest post office and could only be reached by boat or on the ice.[103] A few wealthy party members and philanthropists—Arthur and Lewis Tappan, Leicester King, Gerrit Smith, Seth May, and Ebenezer Dole of Maine, Joel Hayden of Massachusetts, and a few others—bore much of the financial burden of the new party. Gerrit

Smith's correspondence in particular reveals a man who contributed freely to Liberty men in financial predicaments even when he was on the verge of bankruptcy.

Financial problems hurt Liberty vote-getting efforts because it cost money to publish campaign literature, bring in speakers, rent halls, and conduct an intense political campaign. Much of the Liberty vote in the 1844 presidential race in Madison County, New York (14.9%—1,311 of 8,842 votes), was attributable, in large part, to the energy and bankroll of Gerrit Smith, who organized a campaign blitz in the weeks before the election. This Liberty vote is impressive because no other county in the state could even collect 10% of the vote. Unfortunately, for the Liberty Party, it did not have these resources elsewhere. Financial problems would hinder the party for the rest of its existence.

Between 1840 and 1844, the Liberty Party made the transition from protest group to a genuine political party. Nonetheless, lack of effective central leadership, differing political philosophies, poor finances, and a stagnating voter base still hampered their effort. The future appeared uncertain to most Liberty men as they pondered their difficulties after the 1844 election.

3

A PERIOD OF UNCERTAINTY AND CONFUSION, 1845–1846

> The Liberty Party in running Birney, simply committed a political crime, evil in almost all its consequences.
>
> THEODORE ROOSEVELT, *Thomas H. Benton*

Shortly after the 1844 election, an editorial in the *Philanthropist*—"Where Are We?"—reflected the thoughts of many in the Liberty Party.[1] The discouraging results of the presidential election prompted Liberty men to reevaluate their basic outlook on the party. They came up with several, and sometimes contradictory, solutions. As historian Ronald G. Walters has observed, "[t]he lines of conflict crisscrossed in complicated ways and, as usual, personality conflicts figured in."[2] As in the early 1840s, debates on the nature of the party took place primarily on the state level, and the national Liberty Party emerged only in preparation for a national election. A hastily called national Liberty convention met in Albany in early December 1844, but most representatives were from New York, Connecticut, and Massachusetts. A friend wrote to Gamaliel Bailey, "[W]e could only regret our *Western* friends were not represented."[3] Given the expense of travel and the difficulty with the weather in December, their absence was not surprising. The delegates decided that it was too soon to make nominations for 1848, but they reaffirmed their commitment to abolition politics.

Birney soon made it clear that he was not a candidate for 1848 and "wish[ed] now to be considered as merged in the mass, and as no other than one of the rank and file of that party."[4] The question of his candidacy became superfluous during the summer of 1845, when he suffered a physically disabling stroke after a fall from his horse.[5] The other half of the ticket, Thomas Morris, died shortly after the election. Birney's inability to be the standard-bearer and Morris's death eliminated two sources of bickering for Liberty men, but the party no longer had a titular head, and no one person ever managed to fill this vacuum satisfactorily.

By the time the party nominated its next presidential candidate, it was looking beyond the field of strictly Liberty men to those who had not been aligned with the party in 1844. In fact, the most attractive candidate who was a party member was William Jay, who had not even been a formal member of the party until February 1843.

During the three years following the presidential election, the various states concentrated their efforts on local, state, and regional meetings with little thought of national coordination. Sometimes a few easterners were present at important conventions in the Old Northwest, and northwestern Liberty men occasionally attended gatherings in the East; but state parties developed along individual state lines.[6] Internal disagreements among Liberty men, however, were not along geographic lines. Differences appeared in regional gatherings, in some state meetings, and even within local organizations. Lack of consensus was an outstanding feature of the Liberty Party after 1844. A small elite generally determined state policy and then submitted its decisions to a convention for approval. Such states as Vermont, Connecticut, Illinois, and, to a lesser extent, Maine reached agreement easily, but policymakers in New York, Massachusetts, and Michigan frequently aired disagreements on convention floors. No similar forum existed nationally. A caustic but perceptive commentator wrote in the *Niles' National Register,* "Certain it is, that there now exists not only all three parties we have named [The Abolition Party, The Anti-Slavery Party, The Liberty Party], but at least three other subdivisions, each claiming to be true grit—real orthodox emancipationists."[7] The national Liberty Party organization was a weak confederation, and almost all the power was in the state and local units.

Party leaders attempted to define the party and chart its future. They organized three large regional conventions between June 1845 and June 1846: first, the Southern and Western Convention of the Friends of Constitutional Liberty at Cincinnati on June 11–12, 1845; then the Great Convention of the Friends of Freedom in the Eastern and Middle States in Boston on October 1–3, 1845; and, finally, the North-Western Liberty Convention in Chicago on June 24–26, 1846. These gatherings have been generally neglected or underrated in discussions of the development of political antislavery strategy during the mid-1840s.[8] They were important for several reasons. They moved beyond state meetings in an attempt to develop regional bases for the party. Although these meetings were clearly set up by the Liberty Party, organizers made some attempts to reach out to non-Liberty members whose antislavery zeal fell short of Liberty standards. All were forums where Liberty members discussed new directions for the party in order to increase its appeal and effectiveness. All were rallies to keep up the spirits and revitalize the commitment of Liberty followers, and each had a few participants from outside the region. The issues discussed in them reflected undercurrents of dissatisfaction and disagreements over a number of issues among the membership.

The Southern and Western Convention of the Friends of Constitutional Liberty was the first of the three meetings. Despite Charles Dexter Cleveland's claim that "the call embraced all who were resolved to act against Slavery... It was not therefore exclusively a Convention of the Liberty party," Liberty men composed most of the two thousand delegates from Ohio, Michigan, Indiana, the Wisconsin and Iowa territories, Massachusetts, New York, Pennsylvania, Rhode Island, western Virginia, and Kentucky.[9] Liberty leaders from outside the region included former U.S. congressman William Jackson and John Pierpont from Massachusetts. James G. Birney returned to the site of many of his earlier antislavery struggles to preside over the convention in what was to be his last major public appearance. He was still the titular head of the party, but Ohio leaders Salmon P. Chase, Samuel Lewis, and Gamaliel Bailey did most of the preparatory work and set the agenda for the meeting.[10] They were determined to reach out to other groups, particularly disaffected members of the Democratic Party, but they received little response, although William Seward and Cassius Clay sent sympathetic letters. Southerners took part in the proceedings. Sixty Virginians signed the call, and John Fee, an antislavery Congregational minister from Kentucky, attended.[11]

Chase continued his attempt to move the party toward some sort of coalition politics and away from the moralistic, religious-tinged approach that characterized many Liberty pronouncements in a long and cogently argued "Address to the People of the United States." Chase included passages in an early draft that that some "thought would be interpreted as overtures to the Democratic party for coalition."[12] James G. Birney previewed these passages and referred them to a committee that persuaded Chase to remove the most offensive passages, although Chase still characterized the Liberty Party "as the true Democratic Party of the country."[13] The document became a major propaganda tool of the party. It was ultimately published in pamphlet form and "not less than ONE HUNDRED THOUSAND in all were printed and distributed."[14] An early Chase biographer said that it was "perhaps the best work that fell from Chase's pen during this period."[15]

The address emphasized the economic and political threat resulting from the institution of slavery, not the moral and religious ramifications of the system. Chase began by tracing the relation of the government to slavery from the time of the American Revolution. He insisted "that from the assembling of the First Congress in 1774, until its final organization under the existing constitution in 1789, the American Government was anti-slavery in its character and policy." He concluded "that slaveholding in the States can have no rightful sanction or support from national authority, but must depend wholly upon State law for existence and continuance." Chase then cited several founding fathers and the actions of some states to show that "it was supposed to be certain that the Union would ultimately embrace at least fourteen Free states, and that slavery would be excluded from all territory thereafter acquired by the nation, and from all States created out of such territory." He lamented "how sadly different are the facts of history." He detailed "the encroachments of the Slave power, which originated in the three-fifths rule of the Constitution designed perhaps, as a censure upon slavery . . . [but which] has had a very different practical effect." Instead of discouraging slaveholding, "the slaveholders, by making the protection and advancement of their peculiar interests the price of their political support, have generally succeeded in controlling all."

Chase proposed to remedy this "by repealing all legislation, and discontinuing all action, in favor of slavery, at home and abroad" where there was national jurisdiction. Nonetheless, he distanced himself from those who viewed the Constitution as an antislavery document, who wanted the Declaration of Independence to "be regarded as the common law of America," or who held to the higher law doctrine "that slaveholding is contrary to the supreme law of the Supreme Ruler." He made it clear that he spoke for those who "deprecate the dissolution of the Union as a dreadful political calamity." He clearly rejected the new interpretations of the Constitution that were becoming popular in abolitionist circles and held the belief that slavery in the states existed by virtue of state law and could not be directly interfered with by the national government.

Chase indicted the Democratic Party for not being true to its principles and the Whig Party because "[i]ts natural position is conservative." He urged voters to support the Liberty Party because it was the only one that espouses "the great cardinal principle of true Democracy and of true Christianity . . . [Its] members agree to regard the extinction of slavery as the most important end which can, at this time, be proposed to political action." He appealed to the non-slaveholders of the slave states because "the continuance of slavery depends on your suffrages." Stating that slavery "paralyzes your industry and enterprise" and "degrades and dishonors labor," he made appeals to the workingman. Noticeably absent from his treatise were the moralistic and religious sentiments that punctuated so much Liberty writing.[16] Perhaps this was not so surprising because he was a deacon in an Episcopal church and did not share the religious enthusiasms of so many of his fellow Liberty men.[17]

The address was not highly original. Most of its ideas had been in currency for some time, especially on the influence of the Slave Power. Chase's arguments on the power of the national government over slavery in the states probably reflected the feelings of a sizable number of Liberty followers, although some theorists were developing new theories of the constitutional power over slavery that were quickly becoming popular. Probably the most significant aspect of the address and the convention itself was the secular tone. Religious feelings were not so much absent as muted. The address was an articulate exposition of the ideas in one segment of the party. It would be a mistake, nonetheless, to interpret its message as a national consensus on the character of the Liberty Party. The tones of regional meetings in Boston later that year and in Chicago in 1846 would be decidedly different and more illustrative of core Liberty thought.

Liberty leaders in the East issued the call for the Great Convention of the Friends of Freedom in the Eastern and Middle States in August 1845.[18] The convention met in Boston on October 1–3 with three thousand in attendance, including a few participants from the Old Northwest.[19] Venerable Maine abolitionist Samuel Fessenden was made president, heading a list of some of the leading Liberty men in the region. Several non–Liberty Party members declined invitations and watched developments with interest, but the spirit of the meeting was much less conciliatory than that of the Cincinnati gathering. As a participant wrote years later, "High moral principles pervaded the convention."[20] The convention placed emphasis on the plight of the slave and dealt with matters relating to the condition of free blacks in the North. Resolution 8 "rejoice[d] to see so many signs that the cruel and mean prejudice of color is giving way before the light of reason, and especially the noble examples of magnanimity and talent displayed by men of color who have traversed the free States as advocates of liberty." It set up a committee to examine the requests by African Americans in Detroit and Elmira for help in establishing educational institutions.

Gerrit Smith prepared an address on slavery that was so popular that Boston Liberty men enlisted him to give five more lectures as they approached their state elections.[21] Samuel Sewall headed a committee that wrote a report strongly denouncing the acquisition of Texas. A religious spirit pervaded the convention, and it passed a series of resolutions written by Amos A. Phelps on the "moral and Biblical bearings of our cause" that convention organizer Henry B. Stanton thought were correct but "rather out of place."[22] The convention clearly opposed any dilution of principle and went on record in Resolution 6 that "it involves no sacrifice of principle to belong to a political party having but 'one idea.'" Nonetheless, the convention tabled a resolution asserting that Congress had the power to abolish slavery within the slave states.[23] In fact, the convention was not markedly different from many other Liberty gatherings in the Northeast, although it served the very functional purpose of bringing Liberty leaders together in a regional meeting for the first time.

The North-Western Liberty Convention met June 24–26, 1846, in Chicago and proved to be the liveliest and largest of the three regional meetings. An estimated six thousand attendees met in a convention that was very different from the Cincinnati gathering a year earlier.[24] None of the Ohio leaders were present.[25] In fact, the only Ohioan who participated to any extent was antislavery Whig Edward S. Hamlin, who had been a Whig member of Congress (1844–1845) and was the founder of the (Cleveland, Ohio) *True Democrat*. Even though he was not a Liberty Party member, he participated in the sessions and was appointed to the prestigious business committee.[26] James G. Carter, a well-known educational reformer and Liberty Party congressional candidate from Massachusetts, was selected to preside over the meeting. This convention was more typical of state and local conventions in the region than the Cincinnati meeting a year earlier and more in tune with the religious and moral spirit of the Boston gathering. The meeting opened with prayers, and George W. Clark and the interracial, mixed-gender Liberty Choir of Chicago sang during breaks in the sessions. Fugitive slave Henry Bibb addressed the convention and participated fully in its sessions. Delegates passed strong resolutions decrying "the prejudice against the colored man" and "the laws of the several States making an invidious distinction in political rights, on the ground of color." As in Boston, ministers participated heartily in the sessions and served on numerous committees, urging their principles on the churches as well as the political system.

The convention also aired more controversial matters. Guy Beckley brought ideas on broadening the Liberty platform that he, Theodore Foster, and James G. Birney had been developing in Michigan. The convention gave the expanded platform a cool reception and essentially affirmed the one-idea concept.[27] This discouraged Foster, who soon reported to Birney that "[t]he Liberty party . . . [is] determined to be no party at all . . . My visit to Chicago fully convinced me of this. The ministers . . . are mostly opposed to venturing out politically: they will not do it: and they will keep the men with them."[28] George W. Clark's proposal to endorse women's suffrage met with a similar fate. More successful was Charles V. Dyer's move "to establish a National Anti-Slavery Press at Washington city as soon as possible." This set the process in motion for the founding of the *National Era* in Washington, D.C., in early 1847.

All three regional gatherings had many positive effects for the Liberty Party. Perhaps the most apparent result was the reinvigoration of the party. Members became more cognizant of what was happening outside their own states. Fringe states and areas such as Rhode Island and Iowa Territory began to show evidence of activity. Most of the other states showed increases in their percentage of the statewide vote after the conventions, but the increases were not great enough to prevent many in the party from seeking to clarify party policy and to attain greater electoral success. These attempts accentuated differences that had existed in the party but had been smoothed over for party unity. Now they began to damage party unity.

Three broad questions troubled Liberty men in almost every area after 1844. First: Was the U.S. Constitution an antislavery document that could be used to abolish slavery where it already existed? Second: Should the party adhere to the one idea of antislavery, or should it broaden the platform to make the Liberty Party a more general reform organization? And third: Should Liberty men fuse or coalesce with elements from either or both of the major parties if the opportunity was available?[29] These issues had been present since the founding of the party, but after 1844 they became serious as Liberty men engaged in heated and sometimes acrimonious debates over them.

The debate over the relationship between the U.S. Constitution and slavery had been going on in abolitionist circles since the 1830s, and antislavery thinkers developed numerous theories on slavery vis-à-vis the Constitution.[30] William Lloyd Garrison and many of his associates, most notably the Boston lawyer Wendell Phillips, gradually developed the idea that the Constitution was a pro-slavery document and it was the duty of moral men to annul it. Although many Liberty men acknowledged that the Constitution protected slavery in the states, the bulk of Liberty men did not wish to be associated with "disunionist" ideas of the Garrisonians. Soon after the founding of the Liberty Party, it became clear that Liberty men must define their position on this question more clearly. An antislavery political party had to have a position on what, if any, constitutional powers the federal government possessed to eliminate slavery in the slave states. They devised numerous theories, with the focal point being how much the federal government could interfere with slavery in the states where it already existed. Some of these were clearly reasoned, articulate expositions, while others were no more than statements with little regard for legal arguments. Henry B. Stanton admitted to Salmon P. Chase that "when the mass of the community feel about slavery & southern arrogance as you & I do, they will find as few constitutional impediments as they will have conscientious scruples, against its abolition by political action."[31] In short, theory often followed conviction.

Before 1844, most Liberty men held that the federal government had no power to interfere with slavery in the slave states because the U.S. Constitution relegated exclusive authority over this matter to the individual states. They believed that the peculiar institution was a gross defect and a blot on human systems, but it was legal. Chase was a leading exponent of this position that slavery could be eliminated in the slave states only by constitutional amendment. He preferred "to direct all the energies of our political action against the unconstitutional encroachments of the Slave Power and against Slavery itself wherever it may exist without constitutional sanction."[32] This would include the territories and the District of Columbia, and also prohibition of the interstate slave trade. In brief, squeeze slavery to death by every means except going into the slave states, and "SHUT UP SLAVERY IN THE STATES, *where alone it is tolerated by the* CONSTITUTION; and both the INTEREST and the SAFETY of these states WOULD REQUIRE ITS IMMEDIATE ABOLITION."[33] Some Ohio Liberty leaders went so far as to redirect the focus of party agitation so that "the proper end of a Liberty Party [is] the deliverance of the government from the control of the slave power, not the emancipation of slaves in the slave states."[34] While most Liberty men were not willing to subscribe to the Ohioans' hierarchy of goals, they were not yet prepared to assert that the federal government had the power to abolish slavery.

A second general theory—that the U.S. Constitution was an antislavery document—had been articulated by a few Liberty followers and been endorsed by some conventions before the 1844 presidential election.[35] However, it became so popular after 1844 that it became a troublesome issue in the party's ongoing attempt to define itself. The corollary to this view was that the federal government had the power to abolish slavery in the slave states. As one newspaper observed, "This difference of opinion is . . . *radical.*"[36] As early as 1838, Alvan Stewart, widely recognized as a fine lawyer with an acute legal mind, proposed that the American Anti-Slavery Society should strike out the clause in its constitution that recognized a state's exclusive control over slavery within its boundaries. While earlier abolitionists had claimed that the Constitution was not a pro-slavery document, William Goodell later wrote that "Alvan Stewart was the first to elaborate a compact argument in defence of the doctrine that the Federal Government had constitutional power to abolish slavery in the slave States."[37] Goodell recalled that Stewart had first proposed these ideas in September 1837 at the annual meeting of the New York State Anti-Slavery Society and he based his arguments on the due process clause of the Fifth Amendment of the U.S. Constitution.[38] His position caused him some serious problems in New York, where William Jay's harsh response contributed to a long-term rivalry between them.[39]

Other important Liberty men, however, espoused the antislavery nature of the Constitution.[40] Vice presidential candidate Thomas Morris disagreed with most of his colleagues from Ohio when he wrote that his opinion had "long been settled, that by the Declaration of Independence, followed by the Constitution of the United States, Slavery, by the legal force and fair construction of these instruments, is for ever abolished throughout our country."[41] As early as 1838, he wrote that "[i]t is upon this false position, that a person can be converted by law into a thing, that slavery rests its whole claim—a position at war with the Constitution of the United States, and which ought not to be sustained in our courts of justice."[42] James Appleton, Maine Liberty candidate for governor, implied an antislavery construction in his letter of acceptance for the 1842 nomination. While declaring that he "would not be supposing that Congress has the power to abolish slavery in the states," he wondered, "is slavery consistent with a republican form of government?" He thought that it was not, but he believed that the question ought to be adjudicated by the U.S. Supreme Court.[43] A year later the former chief justice on the Vermont Supreme Court and Liberty gubernatorial candidate, Titus Hutchinson, delivered an address asserting the unconstitutionality of slavery even more explicitly. He maintained that the framers had expected slavery to exist only a few years and slavery's existence in the 1840s was contrary to the spirit and intent of the Constitution and, therefore, unconstitutional.[44] Liberty supporter George Washington F. Mellen, an eccentric Boston chemist, published the first book on the subject, *An Argument on the Unconstitutionality of Slavery*, in 1841.[45] His colorful, unstable personality and his lack of legal training resulted in this work having little influence.[46]

A few local conventions endorsed the idea that the Constitution was an antislavery document, but they generally did not go into long, legal reasoning. Instead, they simply affirmed the unconstitutionality of slavery and proclaimed its illegality. The resolutions of a congressional district Liberty convention in Calais, Maine, were typical: "Resolved . . . under that Constitution according to its letter and spirit no person can be born or held a slave. Resolved, That we regard every person born under the constitution of the U.S. as a citizen, and as such, entitled to all the rights and privileges of citizenship—and that the constitution every where regards Africans and their descendants as persons."[47] These men and conventions were a minority before the 1844 election. Although Liberty men in all areas continued to protest the encroachment of the Slave Power in every aspect of American life, they usually denied any intention to interfere with slavery in the slave states or avoided the issue.

This attitude began to change in many Liberty circles after 1844. Discouraged by the stagnation of the party in most areas and criticized by the Garrisonians for working in a system established by a pro-slavery document, more Liberty men became converts to the view that the Constitution was an antislavery document. This trend was hastened by the publication of two very influential books—William Goodell's *Views of American Constitutional Law* (1844) and Lysander Spooner's *The Unconstitutionality of Slavery* (1845)—which argued in various ways that the U.S. Constitution was antislavery. Goodell, who was not a trained lawyer, proposed that laws must be interpreted according to the "spirit of the Constitution," which was "liberty." Slavery was antagonistic to liberty. Therefore, slavery must be unconstitutional. For those who would cite specific sections, with claims that these upheld slavery, Goodell replied: "What if it *were* so, that the *letter* of the Constitution could not rightfully be claimed as a guaranty of such a specific form of 'republican government,' as excludes slavery—does not the living '*spirit* of the Constitution' and of the provision afford such a guaranty? . . . Is 'the *spirit* of the Constitution' to be satisfied with the mere outward shell, without the vital essence of a republic?"[48]

Lysander Spooner, who never joined the Liberty Party, was a lawyer as well as a powerful pamphleteer. His arguments were closer to conventional legal reasoning than were Goodell's, but he directed his appeal to a wide audience. He placed great weight on the fact that neither state constitutions nor the U.S. Constitution recognized slavery, and he claimed that there was no validity for it in law. With an emphasis on natural rights, he concluded that the Constitution "not only does not recognize or sanction slavery, as a legal institution, but that, on the contrary, it presumes all men to be free; that it positively denies the right of property in man; and that it, of *itself,* makes it impossible for slavery to have a legal existence in any of the United States."[49] The Spooner and Goodell books were enormously popular among Liberty supporters and went through several printings. Many Liberty men were moving away from the view that all the federal government could do was to put pressure on the slave states to abolish slavery.[50]

Alvan Stewart, meanwhile, was determined to make the position that the Constitution was an antislavery document into party creed. As chairman of the Liberty Party executive committee, he sent a letter to Liberty newspapers in June 1844 in which he claimed that the U.S. Constitution was an antislavery document because it guaranteed to every state a republican form of government. He declared that "Congress is most imperatively required to give each slave State a Republican form of Government, and this can be done by Congress declaring each State Constitution or State law upholding slavery as contrary to the *form* of a Republican Government, and therefore null and void."[51] In May 1845 Stewart brought his ideas to the New Jersey Supreme Court, where he was only able to convince one justice that a New Jersey slave born into slavery was free. He argued that constitutional precedent, natural rights, and the Fifth Amendment's due process clause made the U.S. Constitution an antislavery document.[52] In his reply to the defense's legal team, he stated what he believed was the Liberty Party position:

> The liberty party holds the Constitution of the United States to be, when properly interpreted, an anti-slavery document, replete with tendencies in favor of freedom; but that the slaveholding portion of this country have seized upon the reins of government and perverted the Constitution's high intent . . . and have violated the Constitution by employing it to sanction slavery in many ways . . . The liberty party Abolitionists mean to employ the Constitution, and in pursuance of its authority, and not contrary thereto, to overthrow slavery in every way, and by all lawful means.[53]

More Liberty men began to take position that the federal government could constitutionally abolish slavery in the states. James G. Birney, Gerrit Smith, and Theodore Foster of Michigan, Austin Willey of Maine, and Elizur Wright and Joshua Leavitt of Massachusetts were only a few of the leaders who moved toward this view after 1844, and they reflected what was happening in conventions at all levels.[54] Vermont became the first state to go on record for this interpretation. It passed a resolution at its large July 1845 convention stating that "slavery is a palpable violation, not only of the law of God, but of the constitution of the United States, and the entire structure of our national government."[55] More important, perhaps, was the resolution of the Great Liberty Convention of the Eastern and Middle States in October 1845 that vaguely claimed the Constitution "contains clauses which cannot be maintained in force without resulting in the abolition of slavery."[56] An October 1847 meeting of the New York State Anti-Slavery Society also passed a resolution affirming the antislavery nature of the U.S. Constitution.[57] By this time most New York Liberty men accepted this position.[58]

Liberty men elsewhere did not necessarily accept this antislavery constitutional theory. It had its greatest strength in Vermont, Massachusetts, New York, and Wisconsin Territory; it had some supporters in Michigan, Maine, and Connecticut; and it had little support in Illinois, Indiana, Pennsylvania, and New Hampshire. Ohio was divided with the Western Reserve Area and some other locations accepting the antislavery interpretation. Two-time Liberty congressional candidate Joel Tiffany from Lorain County, Ohio, developed his own theories that he based on natural law and the concepts of equality and protection of slaves as citizens of native birth.[59] Some Ohio leaders, however, were most vehement in their opposition to the antislavery interpretation. Led by Salmon P. Chase, Stanley Matthews, and Gamaliel Bailey, they consistently reaffirmed their earlier states' rights position. When Bailey established the first national Liberty newspaper, the *National Era*, in Washington, D.C., in early 1847, one of the first things he did was make his position on the relationship between the Constitution and slavery clear. He said that "where [slavery] exists by the law and within the jurisdiction of the State, it leaves its members in that State to resort to the State legislature or judicial action for its removal."[60] Liberty newspapers carried heated exchanges of opinion on this question. The antislavery interpretation theorists who did not join the Liberty League stopped pushing their position when they joined the Free Soil coalition.

A second question over which Liberty men quarreled after 1844 was whether to broaden the party platform to include positions on matters not related to slavery or to remain committed to a policy of limiting statements to the single topic of antislavery. Some members had conceived of the party as a "human rights" party as early as 1840. Before the 1841 national Liberty convention formally adopted the name Liberty Party, several local organizations had called it the Human Rights Party. Nonetheless, most conventions went on record as adhering to the single principle of antislavery. This "one idea," as Liberty men called it, was more a theory than a reality even before 1844, particularly where the temperance issue was involved. Temperance was strong among all elements of the American antislavery movement, and it became almost a test of Liberty Party membership in many states.[61] Massachusetts Liberty men made temperance a corollary to antislavery from the beginning. Hiram Cummings, publisher of the *Emancipator*, asserted that candidates were "staunch temperance men—as is every other Liberty man within the state."[62] Charles T. Torrey stated that "this [was] not from policy, but from principle."[63] This temperance position was never challenged in Massachusetts. Maine Liberty advocates were carbon copies of Bay State men on this question. John Godfrey, a Liberty editor in Maine, claimed that "[i]f the Liberty party had nominated, or should nominate, anti-temperance men, we should be among the last to advocate adherence to its nomination."[64]

The temperance strain was present everywhere. Few Liberty newspapers even accepted advertisements from hotels or eating establishments that were not temperance houses, and hardly anyone ever objected to the use of the Liberty Party for temperance purposes.[65] Virtually all Liberty leaders seem to have been temperance persons during these years, and few Liberty supporters drank alcoholic beverages. The Liberty Party sought, and sometimes received, the endorsement of temperance organizations on the basis of temperance, not antislavery. In Michigan temperance meetings were often held at the same time as Liberty gatherings, and some Liberty men began identifying themselves as

"Washingtonian Abolitionists."⁶⁶ Not all temperance men were Liberty men, however, because many temperance advocates preferred to work within the two major parties or to put up their own non-Liberty slates in elections.⁶⁷ That the temperance emphasis in the party was so axiomatic undoubtedly restricted the potential Liberty constituency in a country where hard drinking was a part of life for many, but there is little evidence that this was any concern to the party.

Individual candidates and local conventions did introduce some other extraneous issues—a pro-tariff orientation in western Pennsylvania, for instance—but most party members before 1844 believed that the introduction and emphasis on other issues as party creed would fragment the already small vote. In reality many Liberty newspapers endorsed a variety of other causes. For instance, Joshua Leavitt's *Boston Morning Chronicle* advertised itself as a general family reform paper that supported two-cent postage, the Liberty Party, temperance, no work on the Sabbath, and American principles in England.⁶⁸ The causes might vary, but Liberty newspapers that backed them rarely insisted that they be grafted onto the Liberty Party. Additionally, voters in state and local elections were generally well acquainted with the views of Liberty candidates on certain issues because of their pre-Liberty positions or because they gave their opinions on other issues. Liberty conventions were astute enough to select candidates who would not alienate support because of unpopular stands on non-slavery issues. The presidential campaign in 1844, however, brought into focus the problem of seeking general electoral appeal while not taking a formal party stand on important issues of the day. When Birney began to take public positions on almost every issue, the intra-party controversies revealed the diversity within the party on other matters.

Many Liberty men reassessed their positions on the one-idea principle following the 1844 elections. They were probably thinking along the lines of the Maine central committee, which warned its constituency that "all history demonstrates that for any reform in its earliest stages of existence to remain stationary is *certain death*."⁶⁹ Some leaders came to the conclusion that the party was doomed unless it made an effort to appeal to voters who were not willing to break with the old parties on the issue of slavery alone. Two prominent Liberty editors and tacticians, William Goodell in New York and Theodore Foster in Michigan, independently reached the conclusion that the Liberty Party had to expand its platform and quietly began to sound out others in the spring and summer of 1845. They realized that they were espousing a potentially volatile proposal. Foster, an editor of the *Signal of Liberty*, confided to James G. Birney that he "intend[ed] to broach [the expanded platform idea] in the Signal, not suddenly, but gradually and judiciously so as to shock our one idea brethren as little as possible."[70] Initially, his plan did not entail a national party doctrine but merely having lower-level conventions take stands on other issues while "making them always subordinate to the abolition of Slavery, and preserving *that* as the *only test* question of membership."[71] At the same time, Goodell was expounding similar ideas to his New York allies with mixed results. He found some support, but most New York Liberty leaders agreed with Gerrit Smith that the party "would shut its doors against ten thousands of voting abolitionists, were it to multiply its objects, and exact subscriptions to uniform views about Bank and Tariffs and other financial questions."[72]

Despite considerable opposition in both states, the movement picked up momentum during the summer of 1845. Goodell delivered an address at a specially called state Liberty meeting in Port Byron, New York, in June. He traced the history of the Liberty Party and the growth of equal rights sentiment and came to the conclusion that they all belonged under the same political banner. The new multi-reform movement gradually gained important support. James G. Birney agreed that the party should expand its platform to encompass the important issues of the day because, among other things, he had found so much difficulty in separating party stands from personal predilections during his campaign of the previous year. He agreed with Foster and Goodell that the party should become identified with more reform positions. Both Foster and Goodell began to develop general reform ideologies that would appeal to Democrats and displease Whigs. Foster wrote to Birney later in the year that

> it must be apparent to you that the line of action chalked out by Goodell in his Address and by you in your late letter to me will give the antislavery ship a new and most important tack, making her head directly *against* manufacturing, protective, conservative, aristocratic Whiggery, and bringing it directly *along side* of radical, reformatory Young Democracy. The charge, however, is a good one, if we are determined to be a permanent party. We must appeal *to the masses*. We shall not succeed well in *trading* with Seward and Co.

He agreed with Birney's "idea of going for the rights of the *white* man" in gaining "us a vantage ground in contending with the other parties which we have never had yet."[73] While taking less reformist positions, Salmon P. Chase and Gamaliel Bailey also argued for an ideological move toward the Democrats and the development of a "True Democracy" in Ohio.[74] And William Elder was trying to forge a union with workingmen Democrats in Pittsburgh. He believed that a political party "must grow out of interests—all the interests which Government is concerned about . . . that a party of one idea has no proper political capabilities."[75]

The multi-reform movement emphasized reforms under three general headings: human rights, the political system, and economy in government. Its main appeals were for abolition of slavery and equal political rights for all, direct election of all state and national offices, a reform of the judicial system, a gradual reduction in the army and navy, and decreased salaries for governmental workers. Most also adopted at least moderate free trade principles and called for a low tariff for revenue only (a position that would upset the Liberty men who agreed with a Whig philosophy of higher tariffs). These were general beliefs, although individual leaders soon proposed additional causes. For instance, the (Pittsburgh) *Spirit of Liberty* wanted to espouse free public lands for the poor and a ten-hour day for industrial workers.[76]

Many of these reformers were looking back to an earlier day and a simple, rural republicanism that gave the individual much more immediate control over events. These hopes received an articulate exposition in William Goodell's *Utica Friend of Man* in early 1840 when abolitionists were debating the merits of a third party. He continued this line of thinking during 1846 in his *Perry* (N.Y.) *Impartial Countryman*.[77] A desire for these idyllic times ignored the increasingly complex world of industrial America in the mid-1840s. This was not the case with many other Liberty men, however, who were in the vanguard of the new economy and expansion westward. These individuals were leaders of the party in many areas but have been neglected because they left few written records, either because they did not put their theories down on paper or their written records have been lost.

In fact, the general reform movement within the party was a minority movement. Those in favor of a general reform platform managed to achieve real influence only in New York, Wisconsin Territory, and, to a lesser extent, Michigan. At the 1846 state meeting in Wisconsin, "the resolution embracing the comprehensive idea . . . was discussed at length, and passed almost unanimously."[78] In Michigan, several local conventions and Liberty leaders supported the multi-reform package, but opposition from many former Whigs, including Seymour B. Treadwell and Charles H. Stewart, resulted in no concerted state action on the new proposals.[79] Instead, official pronouncements tended to ignore the question. For example, a March 1846 address from the state central committee avoided these issues and concentrated on the party's need for funds.[80] Most Liberty men decisively rejected a broadened platform. The three large regional Liberty conventions all refused to endorse an expanded platform, and most state and local organizations either ignored it or passed resolutions to oppose it. The New

York advocates of the expanded platform, however, were not as willing to let the matter die as easily as those in Wisconsin and Michigan. The New York situation concerned at least one Michigan correspondent, who knew that intra-party feuding was a way of life among New York Liberty men. He wrote that he hoped "you New York Abolitionists won't turn cannibals and eat one another up."[81] Nonetheless, the New Yorkers soon were quarreling over multi-reform and cooperation with the major parties.

William Goodell was clearly the leader of this new direction for antislavery politics. He gradually came to the conclusion that his ideas were going to have little impact on the existing Liberty structure. He introduced the idea of an expanded platform at the previously mentioned June 1845 New York State Liberty convention in Port Byron.[82] His proposals met with some support, particularly from *Albany Patriot* editor James C. Jackson, but Lewis Tappan and Samuel Ringgold Ward, a black Liberty leader, led the opposition and convinced the convention to indefinitely postpone action on the proposals.[83] Tappan was worried that "they will shipwreck themselves if not run the cause aground."[84] Nonetheless, Goodell and his cohorts formed a Liberty League in June 1846, but they did it "[i]n order to secure a more thorough organization of Liberty men, and a more efficient prosecution of the Liberty cause," not to break with the Liberty Party.[85] Finally, he issued a call for a separate convention to meet in Macedon Lock, New York, in June 1847. He gained support from *Albany Patriot* editor James C. Jackson, educator Beriah Greene, recently converted Gerrit Smith, Dr. Francis J. LeMoyne, and James G. Birney. The seventy persons present at the gathering nominated Gerrit Smith for president and Elihu Burritt, a Massachusetts reformer best known for his work in the peace movement, for vice president. They adopted a platform that endorsed among its nineteen planks that the U.S. Constitution was an antislavery document, abolition of the army and navy, repeal of all tariffs, and virtually free public lands.[86]

This movement remained quite small and was generally confined to New York. Burritt, who was overseas at a peace convention, quickly declined the nomination.[87] A Congregational minister who was very active in the Underground Railroad in Michigan, Charles C. Foote, eventually replaced Burritt as Smith's running mate. Even in New York, only the *Albany Patriot,* the *Cortland True American,* and Goodell's *Perry Impartial Countryman* were sympathetic to the fourth party. Others—including the (Utica, N.Y.) *Liberty Press* editor Wesley Bailey, who criticized those "who will not vote the fetters of the slave off unless he can at the same time vote himself a farm!"—were openly hostile.[88] Elizur Wright's *Boston Daily Chronotype* was the only other newspaper to endorse the new party, although other individuals also supported it.[89] While the Liberty

League did take some of the most active and idealistic men out of the regular Liberty Party in New York, its effect on the Liberty Party in most areas was negligible.

The debate on fusion and coalition tactics was the third major area of disagreement among Liberty men. This had always been an issue threatening party unity. Elizur Wright, John G. Whittier, Henry B. Stanton, William Elder, Gamaliel Bailey, and Salmon P. Chase were among those who had always viewed the party as a temporary expedient. They wanted the party to act as a pressure group to force at least one of the two major parties to adopt a strong antislavery position.[90] Whittier acknowledged that he agreed with the sentiments of Abraham Pennock, a Quaker Liberty man from Pennsylvania, that "where existing parties nominate an advocate for liberty, for their candidate, he may have our votes."[91] Whittier once went so far as to drop out of a race when it seemed he might win and, in another case, he supported an antislavery Democrat against the Liberty nominee.[92] Elizur Wright was clear on the need to use the Liberty Party as a pressure vehicle so that "the great political parties of our country will soon deem it important to secure the support of abolitionists, for their favorite candidates, as they now do the support of the slaveholders."[93] Some Liberty men in Wayne County, Michigan, and on Ohio's Western Reserve already had shown this in their praise for Joshua Giddings and their willingness to work for such major-party candidates. Factions in favor of working with the major parties gained control of the state parties only in parts of Ohio and, later, in New Hampshire. The Cincinnati group was the most active nationally. Chase and Bailey were constantly trying to maneuver the Liberty Party into a union with Whigs or, especially, Democrats.[94] Chase was so concerned about the party being labeled as extremist that he proposed changing the name from Liberty Party to "True Democrat."[95] Despite their tireless efforts, the Ohio group never had much influence on the other state parties or even in many areas of their own state until shortly before the Free Soil merger.

Joshua Leavitt, on the other hand, was more typical of Liberty sentiment. He usually spoke out unequivocally against any semblance of fusion or coalition. Other parties were free to endorse Liberty candidates, but Liberty men were to avoid any involvement with other parties. To a great extent, he based his rationale on the come-outer argument.[96] Nonresistants had urged people to leave a corrupt government, and well-known abolitionists Stephen S. Foster and Parker Pillsbury had been continually preaching the necessity of abandoning churches that would not condemn slavery. Leavitt and others argued that individuals should come out of the pro-slavery parties in order to purify the whole political process. Leavitt regarded the Liberty Party as a "temporary instrumentality," but only temporary in that it would "disappear with the first successful result of the nomination," a time when antislavery forces would have a majority that would push all parties into antislavery positions.[97] Unlike Whittier and Wright, Leavitt dealt harshly with those Liberty men who courted favor with the major parties. In 1843, a Liberty nominee for state senator in Massachusetts gave a pledge to a Democratic caucus that he would vote for Marcus Morton, the Democratic candidate for governor, if the race had to be decided in the state legislature. Leavitt publicly scolded him in the *Emancipator* and supported the decision to strike his name from the Liberty ballot.[98] Leavitt himself, however, briefly endorsed the idea of fusion with the temperance advocates of Berkshire County, Massachusetts, in local elections in early 1844, but he quickly reversed himself after he received some sharp criticism.[99]

The policy of avoiding alliances with non-Liberty men was the general public policy of the Liberty Party before 1846, but local practices varied. While Liberty candidates for national and high state offices were independent of other parties in almost all races after 1840, fusion increased in lower-level elections. The question of the Liberty Party's relation with the two major parties became an important issue in some states shortly after 1845. Circumstances peculiar to Maine, New York, and New Hampshire caused Liberty men to disagree on whether to break party lines and vote for non-Liberty men or to run their own candidates.

The rise of the temperance issue in Maine politics presented Liberty men with a great temptation to work with members of the major parties. Temperance had been, and would continue to be, a central issue in Maine politics. The issue became particularly explosive during the mid-1840s. Temperance-minded Whigs and Democrats often were willing to abandon their own party's nominee because he was not sufficiently strong on temperance. They were not so willing to cast their votes for Liberty candidates, all temperance men, because the third party was causing so much confusion in state politics, but they were amenable to working with Liberty men to set up independent slates containing members of all three parties. This presented the Liberty Party with a difficult dilemma: on the one hand, Liberty men did not wish to be responsible for the defeat of temperance, but, on the other hand, they did not want to be accused of dealing with members of pro-slavery organizations. Liberty responses varied. The *Emancipator* warned its neighbor against such action; Austin Willey's *Liberty Standard* maintained an unaccustomed silence; and John E. Godfrey, reformist lawyer and editor of the *Bangor Gazette*, urged Liberty men to set the party aside temporarily when the temperance issue was at stake.[100] In spite of the criticism from Leavitt and the *Emancipator*, Maine Liberty men did not get very upset about the fusion question. Nevertheless, their acting outside the party set a precedent that would lead to more serious problems a few months later when the state party would debate the feasibility of following the coalition tactics of New Hampshire.

The problem in New York over maintaining the purity of the party was more serious. Difficulty developed during the early part of 1846 when it came time to select delegates for a convention to revise the state constitution. Liberty men were worried about whether the new constitution would permit African American men to have an unrestricted vote. Some, led by Alvan Stewart and the editors of the *Liberty Press* and the *Herkimer Freeman*, believed that Liberty men should vote for delegates who favored unrestricted black suffrage irrespective of party and began to call conventions to this end.[101] The other group, led by mostly future Liberty Leaguers and the *Albany Patriot*, declared that Liberty men should not cast their votes for any but Liberty Party men.[102] James C. Jackson correctly wrote that the disagreement "marks a wide difference of radical principle among us, which sooner or later must produce collision."[103] The result was a bitter division in the Liberty Party of New York. Gerrit Smith, who had been an opponent of multi-reform, began to cooperate with Liberty Leaguers more closely. He refused to attend Liberty Party meetings and became disillusioned with the party because it "has subscribed to the doctrine of voting for pro-slavery men . . . to construct the fundamental and organic law of the State of New York."[104] Later, admitting that the New York "Liberty Party was torn to pieces by our Convention question," Smith was to join the Liberty League and founded the National Liberty Party in June 1848 partly to avoid the compromising principles of the regular Liberty Party. Disillusion with the perceived loss of principle in the New York Liberty Party was an important factor in the Liberty League's entering politics.[105]

Problems in Maine and New York, as well as minor intrastate disputes in a few other states, affected only the states or locales involved. New Hampshire Liberty men, however, took actions that had an impact on the party across the North. They were the first to openly support candidates in major elections who were not exclusively Liberty men.[106] Cooperation with one or the other of the major parties had existed in a few local elections, but the party backed its own candidates in national and statewide races. New Hampshire Democratic congressman John P. Hale rebelled against the dictates of the Democratic-dominated state legislature in 1844 when it ordered him to support the annexation of Texas. Democratic leaders soon purged him from the state ticket at a special convention instigated by the state Democratic chairman, Franklin Pierce. While most Democrats, and even Hale himself, accepted the party decision, some Democrats, Liberty men, and Whigs applauded Hale. They decided that he should not be sacrificed without a fight. Motives varied from sincere anti-extension sentiment to political opportunism, but a movement to keep him in Congress soon developed. Whigs, who were much more antislavery than Democrats, were happy to see the internal dissension that might give them a chance to upset their foe, and Liberty men applauded Hale's courage.[107]

Dissident Democrats provided the leadership for the movement to keep Hale in Congress. They established an Independent Democratic organization to work for Hale and called numerous conventions. They did not appeal directly for Whig and Liberty votes, although they expected to gain some support from them.[108] Liberty men initially were reluctant to vote for Hale. Remembering his support for Polk in the fall, the *Granite Freeman* urged them to "stand firm" for their own candidates. While expressing admiration for Hale, it felt that voting for him would be a dilution of party principle.[109] Prominent antislavery men from neighboring Massachusetts, however, were giving active encouragement to Hale. John G. Whittier wrote a laudatory letter to Hale and composed a poem in his honor.[110] Supposedly apolitical William Lloyd Garrison persuaded the Massachusetts Anti-Slavery Society to send its agents into New Hampshire to work for Hale.[111] In the spring elections of 1845, Hale managed to prevent the Democratic Party's candidate from getting the needed majority, thus necessitating a runoff election.

While the Liberty Party did not specifically endorse Hale in the fall runoff, it quietly dropped its candidate, leaving the way open for Liberty men to support Hale. Pro-Hale forces narrowly prevented a Democratic victory in the September runoff but improved their position in a November election. Democrats, becoming aware that their hegemony in the state would be threatened in the spring 1846 state elections, brought all the pressure of their vaunted party machine, reputed to be the most effective in the nation, on wavering Democrats. State senator Charles Lane, the vitriolic editor of the *Belknap Gazette,* made comments revealing some of the underlying racism that was partially responsible for Democratic policy. He wrote that "[t]wo Whig papers and one Abolition have openly, wantonly, and evidently with malice aforethought, accused us of want of *dignity* in condemning our paper! Well, we have never made pretensions to dignity—it takes a person who can yoke up with *a blubber-lipped darkey,* and *snuff the sweet scented secretions* with the most perfect *sang-froid,* to make a real '*dyed in the wool*' dignified editor. We can never *stomach* that, so we throw *dignity* to the wind."[112]

Democrats were worried because Hale had conducted a vigorous speaking tour during the fall and winter. Independents worked closely with the Liberty men to win enough town representative seats to enable them to bargain with Whigs in the state legislature. This cooperation between Liberty men and Independent Democrats became explicit at the Liberty Party's state convention in Concord on January 8, 1846. Former Whig Daniel Hoit declined the Liberty nomination for governor, and former Democratic Judge Nathaniel S. Berry became the Liberty candidate. Independent Democrats met in Concord on the same afternoon and also nominated Judge Berry.[113] Liberty men also bargained with amenable Whigs and Independent Democrats for local offices.

The heated March elections produced a large turnout, and Democrats failed to get a simple majority in the state senate, in the state house, or in the vote for governor. Therefore, when the state legislature met in June 1846, an alliance of Whigs, Independent Democrats, and Liberty men negotiated for the spoils of the Democratic defeat. The three groups arrived at a bargain. John P. Hale was to go to the U.S. Senate for a full term to begin in 1847. Whig Anthony Colby was to be governor. And Joseph Cilley, a Liberty man who had left the Whig Party, was to fill the one year of a U.S. Senate term brought about by the elevation of Levi Woodbury to the Supreme Court.[114] The open bargain embarrassed the *Granite Freeman*, which realized that Liberty men had never before cooperated with non-Liberty men so openly. It weakly stated that there was "no amalgamation" with Whigs in the state legislature, but individual party members were merely voting their own consciences. The editor conceded that the Liberty men and Independent Democrats were working closely together.[115]

Soon Independent Democrats and Liberty men moved to cement the alliance. The *Granite Freeman* abandoned its lukewarm approval of Hale and began to extol his virtues. Hale, in turn, spoke at Liberty meetings throughout the summer. On September 12 the Liberty men and Independent Democrats met in joint convention in New Market and formed one organization. The coalition was primarily a political maneuver, with issues other than the restriction of slavery not mentioned. John G. Whittier and Henry B. Stanton came as observers from Massachusetts, and the harmonious proceedings fueled their hopes for an expanded national movement.[116] From this time on, participants agreed to act as one party. Gradually, the two organizations combined, and the merger of the *Independent Democrat* and *Granite Freeman* into the *Independent Democrat and Granite Freeman* by May 1847 signaled the completion of the operation.

Reactions to the New Hampshire situation varied among Liberty men across the country. Some believed that the New Hampshire Liberty Party was compromising its principles for the sake of political power, but most Liberty observers adopted a wait-and-see attitude. The Independents were criticized for allying with the Liberty men because it might taint them with extremism. Commenting on such accusations, John P. Hale revealed much about the mutual admiration of the two parties to the merger.

> Whigs and Democrats looked on us with indifference ... while on the other hand the Liberty party men, abandoning for awhile their own organization, and the man of their choice, rallied around me and sustained me by their votes and their sympathies at a time when I and the cause were in the greatest peril ... In one word were we to refuse the cooperation of those who were ready to work with us, for fear of the odium attached to a name mainly on account of the manliness, independence, and self-sacrificing spirit of those who had borne it?[117]

When Gerrit Smith finally broke with the regular Liberty organization in early 1848, he issued a public letter that was very harsh toward New Hampshire Liberty men for allowing themselves to abandon the political come-outer philosophy to support candidates belonging to major parties. His privately published letter was meant to be not only a rebuke to New Hampshire policies but also to those following them elsewhere.

> When, for the sake of securing the election to the Senate of the United States of a member of your own party [Joseph Cilley], you consented to vote for members of those other Parties, you were guilty of breaking faith with your associates in the Liberty Party, and of dealing treacherously with its vital and fundamental principle ... [Y]our Alliance went far to debauch the Liberty Party, and to turn it away from its sacred, stern, disinterested regard for its principles, to follow the vulgar and corrupting attraction of numbers and victories ... there was scarcely a Liberty Party Newspaper in the land, that did not exult over, or at least, acquiesce in your betrayal of Liberty Party principles.[118]

Similar disagreements caused a brief problem in Maine when Whig and Liberty supporters began to discuss cooperation for the September 1846 state elections. Austin Willey's *Liberty Standard* declared that this would mean "the destruction of the Liberty party in Somerset" and criticized the *Bangor Gazette*, the other Liberty newspaper, because it "censured us and ... those in that county who were resisting the insidious attack."[119] This dispute was eventually smoothed over with mutual apologies, but most Liberty leaders in Maine and elsewhere did not agree with the editor of the *Bangor Gazette*, who proclaimed, "We wish to see Maine New Hampshirized, and New York, and every other state in this glorious Union."[120]

In at least one other state, cooperation existed in higher-level contests. In the Indiana congressional elections in 1847, "there was a general return to fusion and the old system of interrogation," but "[t]his election has had peculiar interest as the only one in the Northwest in which the Liberty party turned its back on the usual programme and gave itself up to coalition."[121] This was not done, however, without the strong opposition of Liberty leader Benjamin Stanton, editor of the (New Garden) *Free Labor Advocate*. He warned that if the Liberty Party failed to nominate candidates, he would "act by myself, nominate a ticket for myself, and vote it myself."[122]

This basic disagreement within the party over strategy would have to be resolved, but most Liberty men were mild in their criticism of the New Hampshire tactics. Most preferred to wait. Of the Liberty men who had taken a strong position, the delight of Chase and Bailey in Ohio was matched by the horror of the Liberty Leaguers. Many regular Liberty Party men realized that the party was floundering without a national figure, and they realized that John P. Hale was a respected public figure who had the additional advantage of having a national forum when he entered the U.S. Senate. Adopting Hale, however, meant that Liberty followers would have to change their outspoken antislavery principles significantly. Instead of becoming more strident in their abolition pronouncements, as many had been doing since 1844, they would have to do two things. First, they would have to accept the anti-extension of slavery in place of outright, aggressive abolition efforts as the party's main feature. And second, they would have to support a candidate without superior abolition credentials to be the titular head of their party. In return, Liberty men could look forward to greater electoral success that would place Liberty men in positions where they could influence direct change.

Circumstances in the North were favorable for coalition with dissatisfied segments of the major parties. Democrats had become identified as a party controlled by the South, and Whigs did not seem to be much of an alternative because they feared losing their substantial Southern support. The annexation of Texas and the Mexican War further troubled them. The extension of slavery became an important public issue when Democratic congressman David Wilmot of Pennsylvania moved to amend an appropriations bill with his famous proviso that stated: "as an express and fundamental condition to the acquisition of any territory from the Republic of Mexico . . . neither slavery nor involuntary servitude shall ever exist."[123] With such sentiment in the North building toward anti-extension, many Liberty men willingly toned down their antislavery principles in the search for political strength. The alternative was to become a fringe participant in a debate that they had helped to bring into the political arena in 1840.

With the founding of the *National Era* in Washington, D.C., in early January 1847, the Liberty merger forces had a major propaganda tool.[124] This was the first truly national antislavery and Liberty newspaper. The *Liberator* and *Na-*

tional Anti-Slavery Standard were never truly national sheets, and even the best of the many Liberty publications had no more than regional influence. There had been calls for establishing a national Liberty organ since at least early 1842.[125] The major force behind the project was Lewis Tappan, whose biographer has claimed that it was "his most important contribution to political antislavery."[126] His own financial resources and influence in the American and Foreign Anti-Slavery Society provided a strong base for the endeavor. He was instrumental in the selection of former *Philanthropist* editor Gamaliel Bailey over the more acerbic Joshua Leavitt as editor of the newspaper.[127] Bailey ran the newspaper, drawing correspondents from across the North, including John Greenleaf Whittier and Amos A. Phelps from Massachusetts and Linnaeus P. Noble from New York, and placing agents even in the Deep South. He was especially fortunate to get John G. Whittier as a corresponding editor because he was an experienced journalist on friendly terms with all antislavery factions. This first attempt to establish a national Liberty Party newspaper did not receive enthusiastic approval from all Liberty men, especially those opposed to coalition tactics and those who believed the U.S. Constitution was an antislavery document. Some feared that a national newspaper would kill off many small Liberty sheets, but it is difficult to attribute the folding of any Liberty newspaper after 1847 directly to the *National Era*. Many of them had a short lifespan even before a national paper existed.[128]

The rate of party growth varied from state to state after 1844. It did not decline and die after 1844, but its increase was limited. The party's activity lessened somewhat in New York, which was "in ruins" following the fight over delegates to the constitutional convention and the Liberty League proposals.[129] Some states—most notably Illinois and Maine—showed substantial gains in major elections, and there was an increase in Liberty strength in all states in the Old Northwest except Michigan. The party continued to control many local offices and increased its local strength in Maine, Vermont, Illinois, Ohio, and New Hampshire. The party grew in the Wisconsin Territory, and abolitionists organized activities in the Iowa Territory and nominated a full ticket for state offices in Rhode Island for the first time. An American and Foreign Anti-Slavery Society report listed fifty-three abolitionist newspapers (thirty-six Liberty, five Old Organization, and twelve unable to be classified), and several of these had large subscription lists. The *Green Mountain Freeman* had the largest circulation of any newspaper in Vermont, and the *Chicago Western Citizen*'s more than three thousand subscribers made it the largest weekly in the state.[130]

Nonetheless, it was undeniable that the Liberty cause had slowed since 1844 and could not match its early growth. The last national convention had occurred in 1843, and the three major conventions—in Cincinnati and Boston in 1845 and in Chicago in 1846—were primarily regional gatherings that accomplished little except to bring large numbers of people together for rallies that boosted morale. Liberty men began to sense that there were limits to their growth. The loss by a margin of 223,834 to 85,306 on a referendum proposing unrestricted black suffrage in New York was convincing evidence that the party as then constituted could not succeed at the polls, there or in most other states (as similar votes in Illinois and Wisconsin would soon show). If an electorate was not willing to give the black man the unrestricted vote, it certainly was not going to support a distinctly antislavery political party. Liberty voters had to make a choice between acting as a narrow pressure group or changing their approaches in order to achieve greater electoral success.

# 4

THE MOVE TO FREE SOIL, 1847–1848

> The liberty party was conceived in frustration and self-delusion, acted out a farce, and died by betrayal.
>
> AILEEN S. KRADITOR, "The Liberty and Free Soil Parties"

The Liberty Party underwent dramatic changes affecting its basic political philosophy in 1847, and these changes made it easy, almost unavoidable, for it to be part of the Free Soil movement. Liberty men could have resisted coalition and maintained party integrity in 1848, as some did through the Liberty League, but compromises in 1847 prepared the way for a merger with dissident Whigs and Democrats. The basic change in 1847 was Liberty's acceptance of the anti-extension of slavery as its political creed. This meant that some party members would abandon the philosophical position that the U.S. Constitution was an antislavery document and that party rhetoric would have to de-emphasize the former Liberty goal of the direct abolition of slavery throughout the United States.

This scenario developed when the Liberty men accepted John P. Hale as the titular head of the party. Hale's dislike of slavery had not caused him to join any abolition society in the late 1830s or early 1840s, and he had even supported James K. Polk in 1844. His expulsion from the Democratic ticket and subsequent popularity in New Hampshire came from his anti-extension sentiments and willingness to oppose the state party machine, not from any strong abolition pronouncements. When the Liberty Party selected him as its presidential candidate in late 1847, it had to accept his more restrained positions on antislavery action. This crucial shift in Liberty thinking cleared the way for Liberty participation in the later Free Soil coalition.

At the beginning of 1847, the Liberty Party had no effective national leadership and no nominee for the presidency in 1848. Its central committee, set up by the Buffalo convention in 1843, never operated effectively. A disgruntled Ohio editor declared that "[t]he Committee has never acted as such. It has had no meetings—no mutual consultation. Mr. Stewart has put forth some articles, which he signs as Chairman, but these were never passed upon by the Committee, and probably were not shown before publication to any member of it."[1] When Alvan Stewart tried to poll the committee on some issues in the spring of 1847, he either could not reach the members or could not elicit responses from some of them.[2] This was not Stewart's fault. He devoted much time and energy to the Liberty Party. Besides his work in his home state of New York, he traveled many miles in harsh conditions for the cause and helped to organize the Connecticut and New Jersey Liberty parties and was the lead lawyer in the famous 1846 New Jersey case on the unconstitutionality of slavery.[3] All this time he suffered recurring bouts of "Inflammatory Rheumatism" and was continually caring for "his wife [who, a correspondent wrote to James G. Birney in 1844,] has been *insane* for three months."[4]

The party also lacked any national identity beyond its basic opposition to slavery. Liberty men had no national strategy, and state party philosophies varied widely, ranging from New Hampshire's limiting slavery to where it already existed and cooperating with elements of the major parties to the belief that slavery was unconstitutional and the federal government could eliminate it everywhere. Political practices ranged from outright coalition in New Hampshire to calls for party purity in some others. The behavior of U.S. senator Joseph Cilley of New Hampshire caused further consternation in the party. Cilley, who left the Whig Party to run as the Liberty congressional candidate in 1846, had been selected by the New Hampshire coalition to fill an unexpired term in the U.S. Senate. When he took his seat in the U.S. Senate, he went against most Liberty thinking by voting with the Whigs, refusing to submit dissolution of the Union petitions—behavior too reminiscent of the gag rule to some Liberty supporters—and supporting the war with Mexico.[5] Several states were undergoing crises of their own. Massachusetts Liberty men were struggling with their responses to the "Conscience Whig" and workingmen's movements. Michigan Liberty men were undergoing serious disagreements on party philosophy. New Yorkers had to deal with the Liberty League, land reform, the anti-rent movement, and the emerging Barnburner faction in the Democratic Party. And divisions in the Ohio Liberty Party became more apparent after *Philanthropist* editor Gamaliel Bailey's departure to Washington, D.C., to edit the *National Era*. Party members everywhere pondered whether to remain committed to the one idea of antislavery or to branch into multi-reform politics. These debates took place in local, state, and regional gatherings and through the party press.

A major problem was indecision over the national ticket for 1848. Unlike 1840 and 1844, no general agreement developed on who would head the party. Former standard-bearer Birney had taken himself out of the race. Although he still maintained a base of support, he would have had little chance for the nomination even if healthy because many remembered his mistakes in the 1844 campaign, and some were concerned over his endorsement of multi-reform.[6] Liberty newspapers endorsed a number of candidates by mid-May 1847. The (Maine) *Liberty Standard* and *Chicago Western Citizen* endorsed Hale; the *Emancipator* urged consideration of Samuel Fessenden of Maine; the *Albany Patriot*, after stating a preference for Birney or Gerrit Smith, finally endorsed Salmon P. Chase; and the *Cincinnati National Press*, successor of the *Philanthropist*, suggested that Ohioan Sam Lewis be considered.[7]

Meanwhile, two interrelated forces were at work in the Liberty Party throughout the remainder of 1847. First, there was a move away from the harsh abolition pronouncements that had characterized the party toward the milder anti-extension position of John P. Hale. And second, some party members wanted to involve the Liberty Party in coalition politics. A powerful opponent of a more relaxed antislavery stance and a critic of fusion or coalition politics was Joshua Leavitt, who used the *Emancipator* to articulate his hard-line defense of the old party positions. He had recently taken an even stronger abolition stand when he became a convert to the belief that the U.S. Constitution was an antislavery document, a position that he supported when the Massachusetts state convention endorsed it in January 1847.[8] He was under pressure from Chase, Bailey, Stanton, and Whittier to reconsider his views on Hale and the whole Liberty philosophy.

To accept Hale would be an obvious break from past policy because Independent Democrat Hale was not a member of the Liberty Party, and his public pronouncements did not go beyond anti-extension. He was even reluctant to acknowledge the constitutionality of the abolition of slavery in the District of Columbia and the prohibition of the interstate slave trade.[9] In addition to his milder antislavery commitments, some were concerned that he did not have the evangelical piety that characterized most Liberty candidates.[10] Nonetheless, Hale's popularity had been growing rapidly during 1846 and early 1847, partly because he was willing to speak at so many local Liberty gatherings in New England. Even though Hale's antislavery philosophy fell far short of the positions advocated by the 1847 Massachusetts state convention and the *Emancipator* had already endorsed Fessenden, Lewis Tappan, Fessenden, Stanton, and Whittier persuaded Leavitt to join them in extending Hale an invitation to visit them in

Boston in July.¹¹ Hale accepted their invitation and left his hosts with the belief that he would reluctantly accept a draft.¹² Hale impressed them at the meeting, and the *Emancipator* endorsed his candidacy shortly thereafter.¹³

Soon more Liberty newspapers began to urge that Hale head the Liberty ticket. While a few Liberty men were unhappy with the prospect of Hale's candidacy, he was generally acceptable to most elements of the party except the Liberty Leaguers, who had formed their own organization in Macedon Lock in June 1846. The loss of the Liberty League advocates smoothed the way for coalition politics by eliminating a vocal and uncompromising segment from party influence, although they continued to participate in Liberty conventions in an attempt to reform the regular Liberty Party. The increased acceptance of Hale by many holdouts signaled an end to the old, hard-line resistance that had been Liberty policy toward non-party candidates. The basis of the Liberty Party was still antislavery, but it was obvious that it had gone in a new direction and was again in the process of redefining itself.

Most Liberty men, however, were not yet prepared to accept the strategies of the faction that sought a broader base of popular support than Hale could deliver. Under the tireless leadership of Chase and Bailey, this smaller group continued to seek coalition with dissatisfied members of the two major parties while most Liberty men either opposed a merger or were biding their time.¹⁴ These Liberty men were different from most of their counterparts in most other states because they paid more attention to national developments than to state tactics. This group was aware of the latent coalition sentiment present in some areas, especially among less prominent Liberty leaders who had faithfully supported the party and allowed their names to be put in nomination. There was little doubt that some had been involved in fusion tactics in lower-level elections and in some state legislatures, particularly after the success of coalition in New Hampshire. A widening gap between the Liberty rhetoric and reality on not participating in politics with non-Liberty men was becoming more apparent. This willingness to work with non-party members locally was one more indication that the Liberty Party was changing its character from a political protest movement with a religious tone to a more traditional party interested in electoral success.

The Chase-Bailey group and New Hampshire Liberty men were more firmly committed to coalition politics in mid-1847 than other Liberty groups. Differences became clear during the summer of 1847, when a dispute erupted over the date for holding the national Liberty nominating convention for the 1848 presidential election. The pro-coalition forces wanted the convention delayed until the late spring or summer of 1848 to maximize the chances for a merger with unhappy Whigs and Democrats. They feared that major-party dissidents would not be prepared to commit to a coalition until after the two major parties had held their nominating conventions. The old-line Liberty men, on the other hand, still desired to maintain party integrity despite the shift from abolition to antiextension implicit in their acceptance of John P. Hale as their standard-bearer. They preferred a fall 1847 meeting.

According to procedures agreed upon at the 1843 Buffalo convention, the party's national corresponding secretary, Joshua Leavitt, was to poll the national committee concerning the date for calling a national nominating convention. When the *National Era* took a poll of Liberty newspapers in early 1847, it reported a majority in favor of a late spring 1848 meeting.[15] When Leavitt conducted his poll of committee members, it showed a large majority in favor of the fall of 1847.[16] The *National Era* responded by criticizing the committee in harsh terms, stating that "Independent men will repudiate any political party which substitutes *popular* usage and control by party despotism."[17] When party members themselves voted in state and local conventions, the results were often inconclusive.[18] Cooler heads, such as John G. Whittier, prevented further escalation of the controversy, and the *National Era* reluctantly acquiesced in the committee decision.[19] The convention was called for October 20, 1847, in Buffalo. Coalitionists failed to get the meeting postponed, but they did not give up entirely. Chase lobbied in the intervening months to get the actual nomination delayed until the spring, a time he hoped would be more favorable to an agreement with disaffected members of the major parties. He had little success in the state parties. Differences between his faction and most important Liberty men in other states were apparent in local conventions throughout 1847.

Lack of consensus on the fusion-coalition issue was present in almost every state. This caused problems in state races in Maine, and a noticeable increase in fusion tickets took place in the fall 1847 elections in the Old Northwest and Vermont, a state that generally maintained firm party lines.[20] A few longtime leaders also changed their positions. Guy Beckley, former editor of the *Signal of Liberty*, expressed his willingness to vote for a person of good character against a Liberty candidate when "other things being equal, he has the best chance of success."[21] Henry B. Stanton, still a high-ranking Liberty leader, wrote that "I shall not go with the Liberty Party . . . provided either of the other parties, or any considerable portion of both or either, bring forward a Wilmot Proviso candidate."[22] Pressure in Indiana became so intense that three Liberty congressional candidates withdrew in order to strengthen Whig candidacies.[23] Most Liberty men were unwilling to go so far so fast, but the unmistakable drift in party opinion was in the direction of fusion and coalition politics. Two or three years earlier someone like John P. Hale would not have had a chance for the nomination, but by the fall of 1847 he was the favorite. This reflected a basic change in Liberty Party political philosophy that had been developing since the 1844 election.

The Liberty Party's national nominating convention that met in Buffalo on October 20, 1847, reflected this change. Decisions made at this important gathering put the Liberty Party on a course that would lead it directly into the Free Soil coalition within ten months. Four to five hundred delegates and observers attended the gathering at which, in a throwback to earlier abolitionist conventions, any Liberty man could participate in some aspects of the meeting.[24] Every free state and territory except Iowa Territory sent formal representatives, although New York and nearby Ohio and Pennsylvania had the greatest number in attendance. All three major strains of the Liberty movement were well represented: the strong coalitionists, the one-idea advocates, and the multi-reform Liberty League. The roll of official delegates included the following numbers:

Maine	8
New Hampshire	3
Vermont	2
Massachusetts	12
Connecticut	6
Rhode Island	3
New Jersey	1
New York	35
Pennsylvania	26
Ohio	23
Michigan	5
Indiana	4
Illinois	8
Wisconsin Territory	3

The Liberty League sent a contingent headed by Gerrit Smith, who co-chaired the New York delegation with non–Liberty Leaguer Lewis Tappan. Leaders wanted to keep the Leaguers in the party if possible, and the meeting proceeded harmoniously. Smith's address and the Liberty League proposals concerning the unconstitutionality of slavery and the multi-reform platform received a respectful hearing but met overwhelming defeat.[25] The meeting took more restrained stands on slavery issues than many of the state and local gatherings. Although the convention declared that the eventual goal of the Liberty Party was "the establishment of peaceful emancipation throughout the Union," the antislavery sentiments were milder than the 1844 platform. Delegates called for the repeal of both the slave code in the District of Columbia and of the Fugitive Slave Act of 1793 and opposed the extension of slavery into the territories. They made a statement "to withdraw the support of the government from slavery and to array the powers of the general government on the side of Liberty and Free Labor."

After Chase's resolution to postpone the nomination until the spring lost 128–37, delegates proceeded with the selection of candidates. They nominated John P. Hale over Gerrit Smith by 103–44 and then selected a former justice of the Ohio Supreme Court, Leicester King, as his running mate. The coalition forces had not prevented the fall nomination, but they had gotten a moderate platform and two candidates who were willing to withdraw if a broader movement developed. Chase and his friends succeeded in laying the groundwork for eventual Liberty participation in a larger coalition, and, perhaps more important, Liberty League supporters met a decisive defeat. They refused to endorse Hale or the party positions, and none of them was included on the national corresponding committee.[26] The convention was a watershed in the evolution of the Liberty Party, as the overwhelming majority of the members tempered their former party positions sufficiently to open the way for future cooperation with antislavery Whigs and Democrats. The Liberty move into the Free Soil coalition varied from state to state and sometimes reflected idiosyncrasies in state and local politics.[27]

Most Liberty men responded favorably to the Hale-King ticket, but approval was not unanimous. The (Wis.) *American Freeman* reluctantly put the ticket at the top of its columns with the disclaimer that it did "not wish to be considered pledged."[28] Although the Wisconsin Liberty Association approved the ticket by a 2–1 margin, the state convention in April refused to endorse Hale because he was not an orthodox Liberty man.[29] Francis Julius LeMoyne, the Liberty gubernatorial candidate in Pennsylvania, echoed the beliefs of some when he recommended nominating abolitionists of long-standing instead of relatively new converts.[30] Some Michigan men were hesitant, but both the state antislavery society and the Liberty conventions endorsed Hale.[31] The Garrisonians tossed a few barbs at the new direction of the party, with Edmund Quincy characterizing it as "The Suicide of the Liberty Party," yet he considered it a wise move.[32]

Liberty Leaguers met in Auburn, New York, in late January to reaffirm the Smith-Foote ticket and to again endorse the Liberty League platform.[33] Outside New York they had little support. There were some rumblings in Wisconsin in favor of the multi-reformers. Former important Liberty leader Elizur Wright and his *Boston Daily Chronotype* endorsed the League. James G. Birney, who resigned his vice presidency in the American and Foreign Anti-Slavery Society because of its endorsement of Hale, supported the new group. And George Bradburn, who had broken with the Old Organization in Massachusetts and come over to the Liberty Party, participated in League meetings.[34] The Auburn convention symbolized their rejection of the old Liberty Party, which they saw as "pretty much shattered to pieces by the ridiculous Hale movement which will itself explode and go to attoms [sic] as soon as the next election is over."[35] Despite its numerical insignificance, the League remained a constant irritant as it verbally assaulted the Liberty Party while almost completely ignoring the two major parties.[36]

Events in 1848 fulfilled the coalitionists' hopes. Dissension among Democrats was particularly serious because of the Southern orientation of their party and intra-party struggles in New York. Whig unhappiness also existed, especially on the Ohio Western Reserve and among the Conscience Whig element in Massachusetts.[37] Major-party dissidents made no important moves in early 1848 for at least two reasons: there was no national leader uniting all the unhappy elements, and most of these veteran politicos retained deep emotional and practical attachments to their parties. Leadership for a coalition also was a problem. The deaths of former New York Democratic governor Silas Wright and former president John Quincy Adams by February 1848 left those contemplating separation with no spokesman of sufficient national stature in either party able to unite all the factions into a viable coalition. Hale was the most visible rallying point, but he was a political maverick who lacked national experience. Antislavery Democrats and Whigs spoke admiringly of him but showed little enthusiasm for him as a leader of a new anti-extension coalition. As it became probable that Lewis Cass, a Michigan man with strong Southern support, would become the Democratic presidential nominee, and that Zachary Taylor, a Louisiana slaveholder and Mexican War hero, would receive the Whig nomination, antislavery men in both parties became more deeply concerned. Their frustrations culminated at the national nominating conventions of the two major parties.[38]

The Democratic national convention in Baltimore at the end of May was a stormy affair in which the Southerners and their Northern allies beat back the challenges of the anti-extensionists. They nominated Cass and William O. Butler, a Kentucky slaveholder and war hero, on a platform that came out against "the efforts of the Abolitionists or others made to induce Congress to interfere with questions of slavery, or to take incipient steps in relation thereto."[39] This clearly put the party on record as against both anti-extension and the Wilmot Proviso. The highlight of the convention was a floor fight over which of the two New York warring factions should be seated. The convention agreed to let both delegations sit and share the state's votes, but this was unacceptable to one of the two groups, which then watched the proceedings in silence before walking out. This segment became known as the "Barnburners" because, like the farmer who had burned down his barn to drive out the rats, they were willing to destroy the Democratic Party rather than accede to the domination of their rivals, the Hunkers. The paramount issue in this struggle was internal New York politics, but Barnburners, led by Martin Van Buren's son, John, were more sympathetic to the Wilmot Proviso than the Hunkers. The Barnburners were not strong anti-extensionists, however, and would not have broken with the party if they had been recognized by the convention as having hegemony in New York. They possessed able leaders in Preston King and John Van Buren, the former president's son. Martin Van Buren himself publicly remained out of the disagreement while serving as a consultant for his son.[40] After bolting the national convention at Baltimore, they issued a call for their own nominating convention at Utica for June 22 while closely watching the developments at the Whig convention in Philadelphia during the first week of June.

Several of the Conscience Whigs of Massachusetts had already let it be known that they would not support Taylor or anyone not specifically opposed to the extension of slavery.[41] When the tumultuous Philadelphia convention nominated Taylor and Millard Fillmore of New York, the Conscience element refused to support them. The convention endorsed no party platform for 1848 because of its likely divisive effects. Liberty coalitionists watched the situation unfold and encouraged the development of a national movement out of the troubles in the two major parties.

Action took place on many fronts during the next month. Barnburners took the lead at their June 22 convention in Utica. Although Martin Van Buren declared his unavailability for candidacy, he wrote a letter so favorable to the new movement that the convention made him the presidential nominee with Senator Henry Dodge, a strong Wilmot Proviso Democrat from Wisconsin, as his running mate. When Dodge declined, it opened the possibility for broadening the base of the movement by offering the vice presidential spot to a Liberty man or dissident Whig. Martin Van Buren realized that any hope for success hinged upon the participation of these two groups, and this view prevailed in a call for an August 9 convention in Buffalo. Conscience Whigs organized many rallies, most notably attracting five thousand persons in Worcester, Massachusetts, and received the support of many Liberty men. John G. Whittier wrote that the Liberty men were "willing that the [Whigs] shall be the leaders and standard-bearers, while they fall into the ranks of the common soldiers of freedom."[42] In the Old Northwest Chase led Liberty men in the People's Convention in Columbus, Ohio, on June 21 and urged that a convention be held in Buffalo.[43]

In general, little resistance developed among Liberty men to the drift toward coalition politics. Except for Liberty League newspapers, only the (Wis.) *American Freeman* took a strong position against reducing the Liberty antislavery position to the principles of the Wilmot Proviso.[44] This was not a shift in their personal feelings toward slavery but a move toward practical politics. Liberty men knew that they would have to join a coalition if one developed or they would virtually disintegrate as a party. They were aware that Hale was willing, perhaps even anxious, to resign in favor of a larger movement. Anti-extension with the hope for political success was sufficient for most Liberty men. It was obvious that there was no hope for electoral success by eschewing coalition and going it alone. The choice was between political purity and political influence. Political influence won out.

Nevertheless, most Liberty followers were very unhappy with Martin Van Buren's candidacy. Many had deviated sharply from past practice the previous fall in endorsing Hale, but Van Buren was too much for many to accept. They had not forgotten his tie-breaking vote as vice president in the U.S. Senate in 1834 that suspended abolition literature in the South, his presidential opposition to the abolition of slavery in the District of Columbia, and his endorsement of the gag rule. The American and Foreign Anti-Slavery Society, which Lewis Tappan had recently rejuvenated, continued its support for Hale and issued an address from the executive committee directed against Van Buren. Without naming him, it stated the belief that Liberty men would not vote "for a politician who has, when in power, professed his aid to the slavocracy of the country and the world, and who has not envisaged any desire that the record should be expunged." They left an opening for his nomination, nonetheless, if "he adopts the distinguishing principles of the Liberty Party."[45] Even the coalition-minded Whittier, who had been working for Liberty participation in a larger movement, believed that "Van Buren is too old a sinner to hope for his conversion."[46]

Stanton and Chase, nonetheless, saw the inevitability of the Van Buren nomination and began to work to make him acceptable to Liberty men.[47] As the date for the Buffalo convention approached, Martin Van Buren was the favorite because his rejection would probably cost the movement the support of the Barnburner Democrats,[48] but most Liberty men were still strong for Hale. Few went so far as the *Cincinnati Weekly Herald* in a warm acceptance of Van Buren as the nominee of an anti-extension convention, but Liberty Party members spent their summer becoming accustomed to its likelihood.[49] Throughout July anti-extensionists called state and local Free Soil conventions across the North to select delegates to the August 9 Buffalo convention. Liberty men participated in these gatherings and usually received one-third of the delegates. These conventions usually avoided being specific on endorsing candidates or articulating positions other than the basic opposition to the extension of slavery into the territories because those present did not wish to introduce divisive issues.[50]

Hardcore Liberty Leaguers were not about to be swept up in the Free Soil frenzy. They held another convention, this time in Rochester, New York, on May 31–June 1 to affirm the nomination of Charles C. Foote as Smith's running mate. Few from outside New York attended. The assemblage also elected a state ticket headed by William Goodell. Not many well-known antislavery leaders were present except for those from the Burned-Over District of Upstate New York. The party's candidate for lieutenant-governor was so obscure that the *Albany Patriot* did not know his first name.[51] Another convention dominated by Gerrit Smith met two weeks later in Buffalo and formed the National Liberty Party with the same nominees as the Liberty League convention. The two groups finally joined forces officially at a late September convention in Canastota, New York. Liberty Leaguers did hold a few conventions, but their effect over the next few months was minimal.[52]

The national Free Soil convention that met in Buffalo on August 9 was comprised of an unusual assortment of former adversaries.[53] One newspaper forecast that it "will be a motley and heterogeneous assemblage, having no parallel since the convention which met at Babel, B.C. 2247. Not only all varieties of opinion but almost every shade of *color* will have its representatives there. The credentials required will be a certificate that the bearer *has bolted*, from what party and for what purpose it matters not."[54] Approximately twenty thousand persons attended the meeting. Each state was allotted six at-large delegates and three for each congressional district, thus permitting an equal division of representatives among the three parties present. Many of the major decisions, however, were reached apart from the main convention proceedings. Salmon P. Chase was a central figure in these backroom negotiations.[55] He worked for Liberty support for major-party nominees in return for major-party backing on a Liberty-oriented platform. Many planks that had nothing to do with slavery were designed to appeal to some of the larger groups present at the convention, but the major emphasis of the document would be an opposition to the extension of slavery. The platform emerged as Democratic in tone—cheap postage, retrenchment in the federal government, and a tariff for revenue only—but a Whig plank for federal expenditures for internal improvements was included. It also contained homestead legislation, proposing a "FREE GRANT TO ACTUAL SETTLERS," to appeal to the Land Reformers present. Despite the different interests among those present, the key issue was anti-extension. Conscience Whig Charles Francis Adams, who had been elected president of the convention, stated in his introductory remarks that the delegates were assembled "out of pure devotion to a principle . . . I regard the Wilmot Proviso as, in substance, a struggle between right and wrong. As a contest between truth and falsehood, between the principle of Liberty and the rule of slavery."[56]

The platform reflected the centrality of the antislavery issue, even though the planks were milder than the 1844 National Liberty Platform. The bulk of the platform was an articulation of the anti-extension issue. It "*Resolved,* THAT IT IS THE DUTY OF THE FEDERAL GOVERNMENT TO RELIEVE ITSELF FROM ALL RESPONSIBILITY FOR THE EXISTENCE OR CONTINUANCE OF SLAVERY WHEREVER THAT GOVERNMENT POSSESS CONSTITUTIONAL POWER TO LEGISLATE ON THAT SUBJECT, AND IS THUS RESPONSIBLE FOR ITS EXISTENCE." This meant "[n]o more slave states and no more slave territories." The delegates and the general convention ratified the platform by acclamation.

While these were bold antislavery planks for dissident Whigs and Democrats, it was a considerably weaker platform than most Liberty men had been accustomed to accepting. State conventions in Vermont, Massachusetts, New York, and Wisconsin—as well as many smaller conventions across the North—had declared the U.S. Constitution an antislavery document and called for the immediate abolition of slavery by the federal government. Even Liberty men who did not go this far had condemned both the fugitive slave laws and the three-fifths clause of the Constitution, called for equal rights and full suffrage for blacks, and emphasized the sinfulness of slavery. None of these positions were present in the Free Soil platform. That this was truly a Liberty platform, as many would later claim, was questionable.

Each of the three parties had its favorite candidate for president: Democrats with Martin Van Buren, Liberty men with John P. Hale, and Whigs with John McLean, a Supreme Court justice from Ohio who had shown interest in the Whig nomination in 1844 and 1848. McLean's wavering course had cost him much support, and Salmon P. Chase announced that McLean wished his name withdrawn. This left only Van Buren and Hale as realistic possibilities. In the balloting for the presidential spot, Chase and Henry B. Stanton, who was now part of the New York delegation, helped deliver sufficient Liberty and Whig votes to select Van Buren. Nonetheless, the closeness of the vote and the large number who voted for Hale are noteworthy. On the "informal" ballot for the presidential nomination, Van Buren managed to secure a majority of only twenty-one. An examination of the state totals shows that Hale commanded considerable strength despite the maneuverings of Chase and Stanton (see table 3).[57] Heavy New York support assured Van Buren of his majority. Henry Stanton undoubt-

Table 3. The Informal Vote for the Free Soil Presidential Candidate

	VAN BUREN	HALE	OTHER
Maine	5	6	0
New Hampshire	0	15	0
Vermont	7	11	0
Massachusetts	20	11	4
Connecticut	11	6	0
Rhode Island	3	3	0
New York	72	29	2
New Jersey	12	6	2
Pennsylvania	34	32	10
Ohio	37	31	10
Indiana	14	14	5
Illinois	16	6	5
Michigan	8	6	1
Wisconsin	9	3	1
Iowa	0	1	0
Delaware	1	2	0
Maryland	4	0	0
Virginia	1	1	0
Total	254	183	40

Source: Dyer, *Phonographic Report of the Proceeding of the National Free Soil Convention,* 881. Dyer's totals give Van Buren 244, but the column adds up to 254. A letter from Ohio in *National Era,* September 14, 1848, says Ohio only gave 27 to Van Buren, probably accounting for Dyer's discrepancy.

edly brought some of his fellow Liberty men from New York delegation with him to Van Buren's side, particularly since the absence of many Liberty Leaguers from the delegation lessened the opposition to coalition politics.[58] It is not surprising that many former Whigs could not bring themselves to back Van Buren, at least on an informal ballot, and would cast their votes for Joshua Giddings, Charles Francis Adams, or even Hale, who enjoyed some popularity among Whigs. The overwhelming majority of Liberty men seem to have stayed with Hale. That Hale might have been the nominee if he had pursued it more diligently is possible, but it almost certainly would have cost the movement the support of the Barnburners. The informal vote made it apparent that Van Buren was the winner. Joshua Leavitt's motion to make the vote for Van Buren unanimous carried easily. Delegates turned to an antislavery Whig for the vice presidency. After an Ohio delegate withdrew Joshua Giddings's name, the convention chose Charles Francis Adams by acclamation. The whole convention then listened to antislavery orations and adopted "Free Soil, Free Speech, Free Labor, Free Men" as the motto of the new party. Members returned home to make hurried preparations for the state and national elections.

Almost all the Liberty state organizations and presses embraced the Free Soil movement. The *Emancipator* argued that "[t]he Barnburners have their choice for the Presidency, the Conscience Whigs theirs for the Vice Presidency, and the Liberty men have the principles—the platform."[59] Nonetheless, many Liberty men briefly delayed their approval because of Van Buren's nomination. Despite Joshua Leavitt's eloquent speech at Buffalo—which Richard Henry Dana said moved many listeners to tears—and his articles praising the nominations, they hesitated until Van Buren gave his written acceptance of the nomination with his pledge to run on the positions articulated in the Free Soil platform.[60] Once Van Buren agreed to the platform, almost all Liberty men except the Liberty Leaguers rallied under the Free Soil banner. Even Elizur Wright abandoned his earlier endorsement of the Liberty League and supported the Free Soil Party as the only national party that did not neglect "a whole part of the population."[61] The (Wis.) *American Freeman,* mouthpiece for some of the strongest opposition to coalition politics, did a complete turnabout by strongly supporting Van Buren and changing its name to the *Wisconsin Freeman.*[62] Some Liberty newspapers changed their names to reflect the new affiliation, while others kept their old names and endorsed the new party. These former Liberty sheets became major propaganda tools for the Free Soil Party in 1848. Non-Liberty abolitionist presses also tended to support it. Liberty Party foe, the ardent Garrisonian Edmund Quincy, while claiming "a strenuous maintenance of our Nonjuring Unionism," gave his approval in the pages of the *Liberator* because "[i]ts direction is the same as ours. Our relations are not incompatible with mutual respect, sympathy, and, to a degree, cooperation."[63]

State Liberty parties contributed their political organizations to the Free Soil effort. These operations varied in effectiveness from the highly useful Massachusetts and western Pennsylvania structures to fragmentary local efforts in Connecticut, eastern Pennsylvania, and badly divided New York, where the Barnburners had their own machine. By mid-September, practically the whole Liberty apparatus combined with the grassroots organizations of dissident major-party factions to create a workable, if somewhat unsophisticated, political network. Liberty men did not just surrender their presses and political machines and then disappear from the Free Soil state parties. Former Liberty men played important roles in the Free Soil Party at all levels. That many men appeared on state tickets as presidential electors is not too surprising because these positions were largely honorary,[64] but many Liberty men became Free Soil candidates. Gubernatorial candidates in two states, Oscar L. Shafter in Vermont and Samuel Fessenden in Maine, had been longtime Liberty Party members, and Seth Gates was the candidate for lieutenant-governor in New York. Liberty men were candidates in lower-level elections and served as presidential electors wherever the old party had been established. In fact, the Democratic, Whig, and Free Soil candidates for a congressional seat in an abolition section of Wisconsin were all members of the Wisconsin Liberty Association.[65]

The new party carried on an active, issue-oriented campaign based on the reform principles in its platform. The results of the state elections in Vermont in early September were encouraging. With less than four weeks to prepare, Oscar L. Shafter received almost 15,000 votes, and Free Soilers displaced the Democrats as the second party in the state, causing the *Green Mountain Freeman* to exult that the results were "beyond our most sanguine hopes."[66] This success carried over into the state legislature where the Free Soilers captured 2 (of 30) senate seats and elected 82 (of 223) representatives to the lower house, far better than any Liberty performance.[67] The September elections in Maine, however, should have had a sobering effect on Free Soil expectations for the November presidential contest. Fessenden's percentage only increased from his 11.5% of 1847 to 15.1%. Free Soilers elected only thirteen state representatives, and Democrats continued their state domination. The new party would have had a greater impact on these elections except for the recent passage of a new state law, prompted by earlier Liberty successes, that eliminated the simple majority requirement in gubernatorial and state representative races.[68]

So much success in such a brief time encouraged Free Soilers as they prepared their campaign drive for the November presidential contest. They held rallies, printed campaign editions of the growing number of Free Soil newspapers, and buried many of their longstanding differences in the common effort. It was a heady time to be involved in antislavery politics. Disappointment came in November.

The new party won no electoral votes and was the second party only in Massachusetts, New York and Vermont (see table 4). Zachary Taylor (Whig) won with 47.3% of the vote (1,360,967 votes); Lewis Cass (Democrat) was second, with 42.5% (1,222,342 votes); and Martin Van Buren (Free Soil) trailed with 10.2% (294,719 votes). The Free Soil Party managed to receive as much as one-quarter of the vote only in one other state, Wisconsin. Then the vote fell off markedly to the next highest Free Soil vote, Michigan with below 16%. Many states did only slightly better than the Liberty Party had done the previous year. Van Buren received only about 10% of the vote nationally, and less than 15% in the free states. Free Soilers claimed twelve seats in the U.S. House of Representatives, including

Table 4. 1848 Presidential Returns in Major Liberty States

	FREE SOIL	WHIG	DEMOCRAT
Massachusetts	38,058 (28.3%)	61,070 (45.4%)	35,281 (26.2%)
Maine	12,096 (13.9%)	35,125 (40.3%)	39,830 (45.9%)
Vermont	14,337 (29.6%)	23,122 (47.8%)	10,948 (22.6%)
New Hampshire	7,560 (15.1%)	14,781 (29.5%)	27,763 (55.4%)
Connecticut	5,029 (8.1%)	30,318 (48.6%)	27,051 (43.4%)
Rhode Island	729 (6.5%)	6,780 (60.8%)	3,636 (32.6%)
Pennsylvania	11,273 (3.1%)	185,423 (50.2%)	172,704 (46.8%)
New York*	120,510 (26.4%)	218,603 (47.9%)	114,320 (25.1%)
New Jersey	926 (2.3%)	40,009 (51.4%)	36,880 (47.4%)
Michigan	10,393 (16.0%)	23,947 (36.8%)	30,742 (47.2%)
Ohio	35,523 (10.8%)	138,656 (42.1%)	154,782 (47.1%)
Illinois	15,791 (12.7%)	52,853 (42.4%)	55,915 (44.9%)
Indiana	8,060 (5.3%)	70,300 (46.0%)	74,558 (48.8%)
Iowa†	1,216 (4.4%)	11,064 (43.3%)	12,093 (47.4%)
Wisconsin	10,423 (26.6%)	13,747 (35.1%)	15,001 (38.3%)

*New York reported 2,545 (0.6%) for the Liberty League.
†Iowa had a scattering vote of 1,241 (4.9%).

New Hampshire coalition member Amos Tuck and former Liberty man Charles Durkee of Wisconsin. Ohio Free Soilers in the state legislature bargained and maneuvered Salmon P. Chase into a U.S. Senate seat, where he joined John P. Hale.[69] The party did not win any gubernatorial races, but it won many seats in state legislatures and numerous local offices.

The Liberty League was not a factor. Gerrit Smith received only 2,733 (0.056%) of the vote nationally, and only 188 of those were from outside New York. Liberty Leaguers did not even engage in a very spirited campaign and were discouraged by the direction that most political abolitionists were taking. Smith received, however, the support of James G. Birney, Beriah Greene, and Francis J. LeMoyne, along with former New York Liberty League opponents Lewis Tappan and William Jay.[70] William Goodell fared even more poorly than Smith in the New York gubernatorial race.[71]

The great majority of former Liberty Party men voted for Van Buren in 1848.[72] The increasing number of Democrats who were joining the Liberty Party in its last few years welcomed the Van Buren candidacy, and former Whigs who were in the Liberty Party had no viable alternative to Van Buren if they wished to express themselves politically. Having painfully wrenched themselves out of their old party once, they were unlikely to return to vote for slaveholder Zachary

Taylor. Besides, the vice presidential candidate was Charles Francis Adams, and several former Whigs held important positions in the new party. Therefore, few Liberty men returned to either of the major parties in 1848. Overall, the composition of the Free Soil Party varied from state to state, with Democrats contributing proportionally more support than the Whigs, even if the New York Barnburners are discounted.[73]

The electoral power envisioned by Liberty leaders when they joined the coalition never materialized. Although the Free Soil Party would hold substantial power in some states, usually by working with Democrats, the national coalition formed at Buffalo soon came apart. When the New York Barnburners rejoined the main body of the Democratic Party, the party lost its most powerful component and its titular head. The experiment in coalition politics meant the demise of the Liberty Party. Four years later, Free Soil presidential candidate John P. Hale drew over 135,000 votes less than Van Buren's 1848 total. The Liberty League hung on in Upstate New York, and Gerrit Smith did win a term in the U.S. Congress in a complicated 1852 race.

Many Liberty Party members remained in politics at the local, state, and national levels. Many of these men received their first taste of public life as Liberty men. They had grown up politically as the party itself evolved. The Liberty Party had begun as a small protest movement, primarily interested in giving political expression to views that were avoided by the two major parties. It became a movement increasingly concerned with electoral success. As the party matured, it gradually accepted traditional American political values and adopted the political style of a contemporary party. This caused Liberty supporters to tone down their rhetoric, dilute their earlier political stands, and, ultimately, become involved with a broader-based movement that they hoped would bring electoral success. The Free Soil movement soon began to lose its strength in many states, and former Liberty members drifted in various political directions. Almost all Liberty men, however, would ultimately gather together under the banner of the Republican Party.

5

NEW ENGLAND

The Liberty Party established itself most quickly in New England for several reasons. New England was the most antislavery region in the country, and annual gubernatorial and legislative elections provided frequent opportunities for antislavery men to vote. That winning candidates had to obtain a simple majority for election in all races meant that even a small third party could have an impact. And most states had committed abolitionists who carried their principles into politics.

MASSACHUSETTS

The Whig Party controlled Massachusetts during most of the 1830s and 1840s, losing annual gubernatorial elections only in 1839 and 1842, but state politics were generally competitive. Voters were apathetic until the 1840 campaign, when participation in state politics increased.[1] Massachusetts was the leading state of the region in the development of the third party. Abolitionists in the Bay State were a contentious group, however, and politics was just one of the factors that had led to the split between the followers of William Lloyd Garrison and his opponents.

In the competitive political environment of the early 1840s, the Massachusetts Liberty Party played a significant role in state politics and was probably the most effective statewide Liberty organization in the country.[2] In the early years the state's Liberty men proselytized in nearby states, and many of them eventually would carry the party message to other areas of the country. Many aspects of the state's antislavery history and the party's early growth have been detailed earlier in this work because of their national implications. Massachusetts was the only state that made even a small attempt to organize for the 1840 presidential election, and this rudimentary effort was rewarded by the highest state Liberty percentage in 1840 with 1,618 votes (1.3%).[3]

The state central committee, which was selected by early party meetings, took control of attempts to organize the party in every area of the state. It wrote party platforms and statements, set the gubernatorial nominations and the slate of presidential electors, and even nominated some candidates for state and congressional offices in areas where a local party was not yet organized.[4] Party organization was always a problem, but the state was blessed with able leaders and an active press. By the early 1840s, Joshua Leavitt, Henry B. Stanton, Elizur Wright, Charles T. Torrey, Amos Phelps, lawyer Samuel Sewall, poets John Greenleaf Whittier and John Pierpont, and others were all working for the party. These leaders were most active in the months leading up to the annual fall elections when they held numerous rallies, printed electoral tickets, distributed Extra editions of newspapers and tracts, and lectured constantly.[5] The newspapers were particularly important to the party's efforts. After leaving the *Massachusetts Abolitionist*, Elizur Wright edited the *Boston Free American*, which merged with Joshua Leavitt's *Emancipator* in December 1841 after its move from New York to Boston. Leavitt even began a daily newspaper, the *Boston Morning Chronicle*, in early 1844. These papers were the conduits for Liberty news and strategy far beyond the immediate Boston area. Several other journals in the state would eventually support the party.

These efforts resulted in early electoral progress. Party gubernatorial support increased in the first three years after the 1840 election.

YEAR	LIBERTY VOTE	LIBERTY %
1840	1,081	0.88
1841	3,488	3.14
1842	6,382	5.42
1843	8,903	7.34
1844	9,734	7.25[6]

The number of scattering votes, or write-in ballots, was negligible, numbering between 180 and 246.[7] Voting abolitionists either remained true to a major party or voted Liberty tickets. One hundred twenty votes were given to Garrisonian Wendell Phillips in 1841 (along with 113 other scattering votes), indicating that only about two hundred voters followed the Garrisonian philosophy for voting abolitionists. Part of the reason for this was that Samuel Sewall, a Liberty man who temporarily remained in the Old Organization, served on the party's state central committee and was the Liberty gubernatorial nominee in every election after 1841.[8] Liberty men were encouraged by their progress. After George Washington Jonson's reluctant candidacy in 1840, Lucius Boltwood, secretary of the board of trustees at Amherst College, increased the Liberty vote by 223% in 1841. Then Sewall increased the total by 83% in the hotly contested election of 1842 that almost catapulted him into the governor's chair.[9] He made further progress in 1843 with a 40% increase over his 1842 totals. But then the progress halted. The party added only slightly over 831 (9.3%) voters in the 1844 gubernatorial contest, and its percentage of the total electorate actually dropped slightly.

The party did better at the local level. It usually elected five to ten representatives to the General Court, the lower house of the state legislature. Occasionally, a major party would not run a candidate or drop out of a runoff election so that a town would have representation in the General Court. Other times a major party would nominate the same candidate as the Liberty Party based on the candidate's known views on other issues. Sometimes temperance advocacy seems to have carried a Liberty candidate into office over a "wet" candidate. Frequently the Liberty Party would put up a respected local figure who would collect enough votes to win by sheer personality and strength of character.[10] Once in a while Democrats and Whigs would unite to defeat the Liberty Party. This happened in Georgetown, a very strong Liberty town, in the race for state representative in 1842.[11] Liberty candidates entered strictly local races including constables, town boards, sheriffs, and county offices. Perhaps as important as actual wins were the numerous races that were defeated and required runoff elections. In 1842 and 1843 the gubernatorial contest had to go to the state legislature because no candidate had a simple majority. The impact was even greater in races for the General Court where approximately one hundred towns were involved in runoff elections in 1842, further increasing the party's exposure.[12]

Most of these early Liberty voters were former Whigs.[13] In Massachusetts this would begin to change by 1844 as more Democrats would enter the new party while some former Whigs would go back to their old party. This trend was evident in the 1844 presidential contest when Whigs began courting their old political allies who had abandoned their original party to join the third party. Birney's dalliance with the Democrats in his home state of Michigan, his Democratic-leaning philosophy, and the Garland Forgery gave credibility to these efforts. As Whig newspapers began publishing lists of their former party members who were returning to their old party, Liberty men declared that these Liberty defectors were never real Liberty supporters.[14] There was more stability in the leadership and the candidate group, which suffered few defections during the life of the party. Liberty men usually balanced statewide tickets. All gubernatorial candidates were former Whigs, while their running mates often were former anti-Masons and Democrats. The early leadership in Massachusetts had many ordained ministers, but the candidates generally came from non-clerical sources. They were often lawyers, doctors, or businessmen who had had experience in public affairs, often in elective office. They were respected leaders in their communities, they were usually involved in other reforms, and they all believed in temperance. William Jackson, a regular candidate for several offices, had served in the state legislature and two terms in the U.S. Congress. Many other candidates had held state and local offices.

Liberty men focused their attention on the 1844 presidential race. When Henry Brewster Stanton took charge of the campaign, he organized speakers and conventions, wrote articles, and traveled in his own district where he was running for the U.S. Congress.[15] Other Liberty men lectured several times a week in the months leading up to the election.[16] While both the Whigs and Democrats lost strength from their gubernatorial totals, Birney gained over one thousand votes and 1 percentage point despite a strong Whig campaign against him.

> Henry Clay (Whig)   67,521 (51.8%)
> James K. Polk (Democrat)   52,146 (40.0%)
> James G. Birney (Liberty) 10,815 (8.3%)[17]

The party enjoyed steady if not spectacular growth, but other forces in the state would soon complicate the picture.

Despite its growth and the energy in the 1844 campaign, the party fell into a period of malaise in 1845. Liberty men took the lead in the Texas anti-annexation movement and hosted the successful Great Convention of the Friends of Freedom in the Eastern and Middle States in October 1845, but the party still appeared disorganized.[18] Sewall again received the gubernatorial nomination, but Elihu Burritt—a reformer and peace advocate who had consented to run for the state senate on the Liberty ticket in 1844—refused the second spot, throwing the party into last-minute disarray.[19] Normally mild-mannered John Greenleaf Whittier was surely not alone in his frustration with the mismanagement shortly before an election.

> What does it mean? The last "Emancipator" comes out on the 16th inst. With Dr. [John] Brewster for Lieutenant-Governor, and in the *same paper*, under date of the 10th is a call for a meeting of the State Liberty Committee to nominate somebody else in his place! Is that your way of doing business? For Heaven's sake, let us know here what you have concluded upon. The "Transcript" here had [Elihu] Burritt week before last; last week it had Brewster, and this week nobody! All this looks like

child's play—or rather, that for want of due energy at headquarters our election is going by default.[20]

State politics became more confused with the rise of two minor parties—a small Workingman's Party and a much more significant nativist American Republican Party. The former had little effect on the election, but the latter almost matched the Liberty vote. The minor parties prevented George Briggs from getting the necessary majority, but he won in the state legislature. The new parties did not greatly impact the Liberty vote (8,316—7.9%).[21] Nonetheless, the first decline in the Liberty vote, 2,499 (23.1%) from the Birney totals, upset Massachusetts Liberty men, even though they lost a smaller percentage of their vote than did the Whigs or Democrats. A discouraged Henry B. Stanton wrote to Gerrit Smith, "I derive but little consolation from the fact that the other parties also fell off, & that we made a relative gain." He came to the conclusion that the slaves would only be freed by war.[22]

Nevertheless, Massachusetts Liberty men went all out in an attempt to increase their numbers in 1846. Delegates to an 1846 state Liberty convention renewed efforts to set up a thorough and functional statewide organization. They established a central committee of twenty-five members who would be part of an interlocking series of stages down to a member in every school district. Town committees were to make up a list that included anyone who had ever voted for the Liberty Party, and vigilance committees were to report Liberty and opposition votes and distribute Liberty literature. The central committee would raise its own money and incur no debts, leaving the towns and counties free to raise their own operational funds without having to fund the state organization. It would be the duty of the committee to see that the state was organized and to call state conventions. The convention then renominated the Sewall-Brewster ticket.[23] Unlike some other years, Liberty men followed through on their resolutions in 1846. A year later Caleb Swan, chairman of the central committee, reviewed this plan and the subsequent activities in the state during 1846. He drew a picture of an energetic state central committee that distributed a circular to every town in the state with the plan of organization. Several committee members even made a special trip to Springfield in May to meet with leaders in western Massachusetts. A Liberty man made a study of voting patterns in every town, and the committee followed this up by commissioning Hiram Cummings to travel throughout the state.[24] Many local conventions selected well-known educators and public figures to serve as candidates, several for the first time.[25]

The campaign and election itself are difficult to analyze. The annexation of Texas, the Wilmot Proviso, John P. Hale's Independent Democratic movement in New Hampshire, and the looming possibility of war with Mexico led to confusion among Massachusetts Democrats. At the same time, an antislavery Conscience element was developing within the Whig Party.[26] Some Liberty men broke ranks and split their tickets in lower-level races. Elizur Wright's willingness to endorse candidates outside the party, particularly his endorsement of John Gorham Palfrey over Liberty man James G. Carter, a well-known educator, for the U.S. Congress, presaged a split that would grow harsher in 1847.[27] Nonetheless, Sewall gained 20.2% in the raw vote (9,997) and increased the Liberty percentage to 9.8%, the party's highest percentage ever in a Massachusetts gubernatorial race. Although Briggs did win reelection outright, two congressional and many state legislative races failed to elect a clear winner. Liberty men were pleased to be regaining some of their strength, but they still had not reached the raw level that they had attained in the 1844 presidential contest. They were also aware of problems.

The year 1847 was a key year for the Liberty Party in Massachusetts. Philosophical differences and reactions to developments in the major parties contributed to a turbulent year that eventually culminated in the Free Soil coalition. This involved dual, and somewhat contradictory, approaches to the Liberty creed. The party began taking bolder stands on some issues at the same time that some Liberty men were calling for greater cooperation with dissident elements in the major parties. Before 1844, most Massachusetts Liberty followers agreed with the view that the U.S. Constitution protected slavery in the slave states. Few disagreed with Joshua Leavitt's assertion that the objective of political antislavery action was "*not* to abolish slavery in the South—for the best of all reasons—we have no political power by the constitution which can reach that evil."[28] Occasionally a local convention would go further, but few agreed with Elizur Wright who denied that the U.S. Constitution could be used to protect slavery from federal interference.[29] Nonetheless, views changed sufficiently by January 1847 so that the state convention could resolve "[t]hat the Constitution of the United States does not establish slavery nor give it any legal existence; nor does it by any fair interpretation, sanction it within the States."[30]

Disagreements over constitutional interpretations were not as destructive to party harmony as disputes over multi-reform and collaboration with the major parties. By mid-1847, a split developed between Leavitt, who believed in the one-idea principle and opposed political collaboration, and Wright, who wished to expand the Liberty platform and to work with antislavery elements in the major parties. Leavitt won the early battles, as most local conventions supported adhering to the one idea of antislavery and refused to endorse candidates outside the party. By early 1847, Wright decided to take a more aggressive course. Always independent and somewhat of a Liberty outsider by the mid-1840s, he had gone in a different direction than the main body of the party, especially in his more secular stances and criticism of much of organized religion. His newspaper, the *Boston Daily Chronotype*, remained supportive of the Liberty Party, but it did not hold with the party line in many cases. Wright criticized the state convention for rejecting multi-reform and opposing the endorsement of antislavery major-party candidates. He carried his reformist convictions to an approval of Gerrit Smith and the new Liberty League after its June 1847 convention, and he served as an officer at Smith's National Liberty Party convention a year later.[31] He became so estranged from the state Liberty Party leadership that he was amazed when he discovered that "[t]hey have placed our names in their honourable list [for state senator in the fall 1847 elections], even though our columns have made it somewhat notorious that we go for the nineteen propositions of the Macedon Lock Convention."[32]

Antagonism between Wright and Leavitt had been building ever since Wright had endorsed Whig John Gorham Palfrey for Congress the previous fall.[33] Wright was not alone in abandoning the notion of the Liberty Party as a protest movement and seeking ways to bring about electoral success. Henry B. Stanton and John Greenleaf Whittier were among the leaders of those who were eager to join a movement that promised more electoral success. The rise of the Conscience Whig element, the introduction of the Wilmot Proviso bill, and the success of John P. Hale and the Independent Democrats in neighboring New Hampshire only whetted their appetites for political success. Whittier was particularly important. He always had been open to major-party antislavery candidates, and he began suggesting the practicality of coalition politics in his position as a corresponding editor of the *National Era*.[34]

The move toward coalition politics in the Bay State began in earnest in the mid-summer of 1847. Despite the fact that the *Emancipator* had already endorsed Samuel Fessenden for president, John P. Hale's previously discussed visit to the Bay State impressed Liberty leaders so much that by September 1 the *Emancipator* had removed Fessenden's name from its masthead and thrown its support to Hale. Liberty conventions in the state generally embraced Hale, but most still did not wish to endorse multi-reform planks.[35] At the same time Liberty men continued their work for the fall 1847 elections. In the spring Hiram Cummings published *The Liberty Man's Book*, which the *Emancipator* reported "is designed expressly for Liberty town and district committees, and will be found of great use in effecting a more thorough organization."[36] Despite the efforts, the Liberty vote declined slightly (9,157—8.7%). The party won some local races, but it became apparent that the party as constituted would grow very little even if Lib-

Table 5. Massachusetts Presidential and Gubernatorial Vote, 1848

PARTY	PRESIDENTIAL RACE		GUBERNATORIAL RACE	
	CANDIDATE	VOTES (%)	CANDIDATE	VOTES (%)
Whig	Zachary Taylor	61,070 (45.4%)	George Briggs	61,640 (49.7%)
Democratic	Lewis Cass	35,281 (26.2%)	Caleb Cushing	25,323 (20.4%)
Free Soil	Martin Van Buren	38,058 (28.3%)	Stephen C. Phillips	36,011 (29.0%)
Workingman's			Frederick Robinson	475 (0.4%)
Others				606 (0.5%)

erty men campaigned energetically. The choice was either to remain a relatively small although vocal group or to be a part of a larger coalition. Most Massachusetts Liberty men concluded that a broadened reform platform would not do this. Instead, they moved comfortably into the Free Soil movement.

The nominations of Lewis Cass by the Democrats and Zachary Taylor by the Whigs aided those seeking an antislavery coalition. The Conscience Whigs took the lead in Massachusetts. When a Conscience Whig convention met in Worcester in June 1848, Whittier wrote to Charles Sumner that the Liberty men were anxious to cooperate. He declared that "nay more, they are willing that the latter [Conscience Whigs] shall be leaders and standard-bearers, while they [Liberty men] fall into the ranks of the common soldiers of freedom."[37] The *Emancipator* dropped its original opposition to the national Free Soil convention and finally concluded that Liberty delegates should attend it and support Hale over Van Buren.[38] Liberty men comprised one-third of the Massachusetts delegation to Buffalo, and most of them voted for Hale in the informal poll before the real vote.[39] No great objections were voiced against Van Buren, however, in the convention. More important, Joshua Leavitt's move to make his candidacy—with Massachusetts Conscience Whig Charles Francis Adams as his running mate—unanimous was significant in Massachusetts because he had voiced so many reservations about the movement and especially with Van Buren as its standard-bearer.[40] He returned to Massachusetts and threw himself wholeheartedly into the campaign. Most Liberty men joined him behind the Free Soil ticket and participated in setting up a state ticket; some ran in local races and for the state legislature under the Free Soil banner.[41] Elizur Wright abandoned the Liberty League and endorsed the new party as being the only national party that did not neglect "a whole part of the population."[42] There was a large turnout in both the state and national races (see table 5).

To analyze the 1848 election and the political roots of the Massachusetts Free Soil Party in 1848 is difficult. It seems clear that the Liberty voters cast virtually all their support for Free Soil, and the Free Soil Party picked up more than 25,000 votes from the major parties.[43] Democrats lost varying amounts to Free Soil, but Whigs were not very effective in rallying consistent support for their candidates. Although they remained stable or made gains in most towns, they suffered severe losses in others. In other words, the Free Soil Party had very deep pockets of former Whig supporters in some areas while these losses are masked by statewide totals. The most troublesome aspect of the vote is the drop in the Democratic vote (by almost ten thousand) from the presidential to the gubernatorial tallies. The historian of the Democratic Party in Massachusetts, Arthur P. Darling, offers the plausible explanation that "[a]s a former Whig, Cushing was unsatisfactory to many Jacksonian Democrats; and as he, more than Cass, was committed to 'Southern principles,' many Democrats, who favored Van Buren yet were willing to leave their own party could vote for Cass while in deference to their opinions they could not vote for Cushing."[44] The repudiation of the pro-Southern stand of the state party so disturbed Democratic leaders that they made an outspoken antislavery Democrat, Robert Rantoul, their future candidate in an attempt to win back nonvoting and Free Soil Democrats.

The Massachusetts Liberty Party made an impact on politics and became the major vehicle for antislavery protest in the Bay State during the 1840s. The party leadership and candidates evolved as the party moved away from the highly moralistic rhetoric of the early years toward a more secular orientation, but the moral fervor was never lost. The voter base underwent a great change after 1844 as former Democrats entered the Liberty ranks while some former Whigs returned to their original party. The success of the party in preventing a simple majority for election caused politicians to examine election laws and eventually adopt a plurality system. More important, it injected the slavery issue directly into the state's politics.

MAINE

Neighboring Maine had the same type of political system as Massachusetts, but its political environment was very different. From 1829 to 1854 the Democrats lost only two of the annual gubernatorial races (1837 and 1840) and the presidential contest only in 1840. During these few years when the two-party system was more competitive, turnout was consistently around 80%.[45] Although many persons believed that the state "was bound to the South by political and commercial bands of steel," there was substantial antislavery activity.[46] Three state men attended the founding of the American Anti-Slavery Society in 1833, and a state society was founded as an auxiliary to it in October 1834. By the end of the decade, abolitionists had established many local societies, made converts, and founded the (Augusta, Maine) *Advocate of Freedom* as the state newspaper. Maine abolitionism had a crusading religious tone that was continually emphasized by its leaders, most of whom were ministers or important laymen in major Protestant denominations. With the exception of the Free Will Baptists, who were totally antislavery, denominations were divided in their attitudes toward slavery. As a general rule, state's Congregationalists and Baptists were more sympathetic to abolitionism while Methodists were more hostile, but all denominations contributed to its leadership.

Maine abolitionists suffered little internal strife, and anticlericalism and nonresistance never gained a foothold in Maine. The women's rights controversy caused few problems in the state because Maine women were content to work through their own antislavery societies in sponsoring sewing bees and bazaars and taking secondary roles in larger antislavery gatherings. William Lloyd Garrison was not an issue because he was almost universally disliked for his anticlericalism and aggressive manner.[47] There was, however, a period of uncertainty on political action. Initially, most antislavery men preferred to work within the existing two-party system, and this pressure tactic seemed to bring about some positive results. In 1838 the lower house of the Maine legislature passed a resolution opposing the annexation of Texas and the continuance of slavery in the District of Columbia by an 85–30 vote. Although Democrats defeated these resolutions 11–10 in the state senate, it demonstrated that some Democrats and Whigs could be persuaded to take mildly antislavery positions.[48] By early 1840, county antislavery conventions and the state society had debated political action and decided that an abolitionist should not vote for a candidate who was not against slavery, but they refused to take positions on a third party.[49] By the time of the April 1, 1840, national convention in Albany, Austin Willey, the new editor of the *Advocate of Freedom,* was more sympathetic to an independent political movement. Reflecting on the failure of questioning candidates and scattering ballots if no regular candidate could be found, Willey wrote, "it is worthy of serious consideration whether the danger to our cause is not vastly more while we hold our present position as prey to all parties, liable to be bought and sold to the highest bidder. We shall never accomplish any thing in our present scattered Indian mode of warfare. It is in vain to expect it. It is opposed to human nature to expect it."[50] A few weeks later, under pressure from some Maine abolitionists, he hedged somewhat, and the Maine Anti-Slavery Society refused to send any delegates to the convention despite a direct appeal from Charles T. Torrey, a Massachusetts leader of the movement for a third party.[51] Ichabod Codding attended as a private individual, was elected a vice president of the convention, and voted in favor of the new party.⁵²

In September Willey announced that he was returning to the questioning method and voting for Whig gubernatorial candidate Edward Kent in the September elections, subsequently claiming that the rare Whig success in this election was due to abolitionist votes.⁵³ Friends of independent nominations finally managed to set up an electoral ticket for the November presidential election. After an October meeting of the Somerset County Anti-Slavery Society defeated a proposal for an antislavery set of electors supporting Birney, about twenty men met separately at Bloomfield and nominated a slate. Few efforts were made to publicize the nominations or circulate printed ballots, and the new electoral ticket drew only 194 votes (0.2%) in November.⁵⁴

Maine abolitionists shook off their reluctance to participate in the new party during the first half of 1841 and set up a primitive party network by the time of the state elections in September. Pressure for an independent political party began in the local antislavery societies. After the February meeting of the Maine Anti-Slavery Society declared its autonomy from both feuding national organizations, those favorable to a third party reconvened, appointed delegates to the New York convention, and elected a committee to issue a call for a state convention to be held on July 1.⁵⁵ These men then returned to their homes and quickly organized county and town meetings.⁵⁶ A convention in Kent's Hill, Kennebec County, even managed to nominate a candidate for the U.S. Congress in the March elections. The hundreds of votes that this candidate received were signs of the increasing popularity of independent nominations. Delegates attended the national Liberty Party convention and returned home to organize the party on July 1.⁵⁷

The attendance and enthusiasm at the convention was remarkable compared to the apathy of the previous fall. The elevation of slaveholder John Tyler to the presidency after William Henry Harrison's death and the reluctance of Governor Kent to push antislavery measures caused many abolitionists to rethink their positions. This convention followed the same basic pattern as earlier Maine abolitionist gatherings with all those attending able to take part fully (Maine women attended but did not attempt to participate). The convention passed highly moralistic resolutions framed in religious terms, made plans for the distribution of tracts and pamphlets, and commissioned lecturers and agents to work within the state. Members agreed on a rudimentary political organization and established the *Liberty Standard* as the party organ with Joseph Lovejoy, a Universalist minister and brother of Illinois antislavery martyr Elijah Lovejoy, as editor. They nominated Jeremiah Curtis, a former Democrat, for governor, and selected district chairmen to organize the party locally. The new party attacked Democratic gubernatorial candidate John Fairfield for supporting slavery and criticized incumbent Governor Kent for his inaction.

Much Liberty activity took place before the September elections, including employing Austin Willey as an agent and a merger of the new party paper with the *Advocate of Freedom*.[58] Liberty efforts met with some success. While Democrats easily won, the Liberty vote increased to 1,662 (1.9%) and prevented either major party from obtaining the necessary majority in three state senate races and thirty-three seats in the lower house.[59] Election results were particularly bitter for the Whigs, who saw their growth in the state and their hold on the governor's chair end. They blamed their troubles on the Liberty Party, which was primarily composed of former Whigs in these early years.[60]

Few substantive changes in strategy or tactics took place in the two years following the 1841 elections except for replacing former Democrat Curtis with James Appleton, a former Federalist and Whig state legislator and temperance advocate. Although the state society still did not endorse the party, the leadership of both organizations was made up of most of the same people.[61] The local antislavery societies in the towns and counties varied in their response to the new party. Some endorsed the party with little or no debate, but the more frequent practice was to establish a Liberty organization parallel to the local society. Both groups usually held their meetings on successive days at the same location, often in conjunction with women's societies, Christian antislavery groups, and other activities. The relationship between the party and the Maine Anti-Slavery Society was so close that outspoken Liberty man Austin Willey was the society's sole agent in 1842 and 1843.[62]

Liberty men intensified their efforts in 1842 and 1843, but they made few changes in strategy, tactics, or political style. Despite Willey's recollection that there were "attempts to enroll every Liberty voter," the party accomplished only sporadic grassroots organization in these years. Liberty men continued to use the tactics of the 1830s, not the more sophisticated political techniques that they would develop later. They circulated large numbers of tracts, sent agents and lecturers, including the famous former slaves Lewis Clarke and Lunsford Lane, on tours throughout the state, and continued to pressure the churches to take strong antislavery positions.[63] Liberty men in Maine did not adopt the conventional style of American politics. They gave only lip service to setting up a political machine, and little space in the party press was devoted to electioneering. Instead, the party existed as a vehicle of political protest that many members looked upon as a temporary expedient until one or both major parties adopted antislavery positions.[64]

Nonetheless, Liberty men were concerned how they fared in elections, and their methods were successful in solidifying the party's existence.

YEAR	LIBERTY VOTE	LIBERTY %
1841	1,662	1.9
1842	4,080	5.7
1843	4,962	10.0
1844	5,527	7.0

The party increased annually by 145.5% (1842), 21.6% (1843), and 11.4% (1844), reaching a peak of 10% of the total vote in 1843. The Liberty men were encouraged and increased organizational activities for the 1844 presidential contest.[65] Democrats continued to dominate gubernatorial races as Appleton drew off antislavery Whig voters, but the new party made its presence felt in the local races. Even though it elected few representatives in 1842 and 1843, the Liberty candidates frequently captured enough votes to prevent any candidate from obtaining a majority.[66] For instance, no candidate obtained a simple majority for four of the seven U.S. congressional seats in 1843, and Liberty men prevented so many elections for the Maine legislature in 1842 and 1843 that some legislators began proposing that a plurality be sufficient for election.[67] Voters for the new party came from all over this huge state with the exception of sparsely populated frontier areas. The movement became so established in the eastern sections that another Liberty newspaper, the *Bangor Gazette* with lawyer John E. Godfrey as editor, came into existence in 1842. A little more than a year later, there was a brief attempt to publish a daily newspaper.[68]

The party attracted voters by nominating highly respected men. They came from a variety of backgrounds. For example, the seven Liberty candidates for the U.S. Congress in 1843 consisted of a judge, two lawyers, two physicians, a farmer, and a minister. The head of the ticket was James Appleton, "a mechanic working daily at blow-pipe and watchspring."[69] Their religiosity was particularly pronounced, and it would be difficult to find a Liberty follower who was not deeply involved in religion. These people were outspoken about their support for temperance, claiming that their "candidates are, and will be, temperance men."[70] Liberty appeals in these early years emphasized the moral duty of participating in antislavery politics, and Maine Liberty men believed the party "must be based upon the highest principles of truth & Christian philosophy."[71]

The heady optimism of the early years crashed in the 1844 presidential election.

>   Henry Clay (Whig)   34,378 (40.4%)
>   James K. Polk (Democrat)   45,719 (53.8%)
>   James G. Birney (Liberty)   4,836 (5.7%)

The Liberty Party lost 691 votes (a 12.5% decline) between the September and November elections. This was only 5.7% of the total vote and below the number of votes for governor in 1843 with a turnout of over 35,000 more. The drop in total numbers was the most significant figure because it meant that former Liberty voters were leaving the party. Austin Willey attributed the loss of "at least one thousand votes" to the Garland Forgery and the other false rumors against Birney.[72] The Liberty Party's steady growth temporarily ceased.

The discouraging results of 1844 continued into 1845. Although there were many Liberty and antislavery conventions, a Liberty leader admitted that "political interest in 1845 was small . . . No general agencies had been in the field."[73] James Appleton turned down the nomination for governor, and the party selected former Whig Samuel Fessenden, a respected and popular lawyer, for its gubernatorial candidate. In a year when the Whigs lost almost 9,500 votes and the Democrats lost over 14,000 votes from the 1844 presidential tally, Fessenden was able to not only recoup the losses of 1844 but to increase the vote slightly to 5,592 (9.8%). The party won a few representative seats and some local races and caused many runoff elections. Commenting on the party's stagnation shortly after the election, the state central committee issued a warning that "all history demonstrates that for any reform in its early stages of existence to remain stationary is *certain death.*"[74]

Party unity was high because differences over the antislavery nature of the U.S. Constitution and whether it was proper to support non-Liberty candidates never seriously affected party strength.[75] James Appleton had brought up the question on the antislavery construction of the Constitution in his letter accepting the Liberty gubernatorial nomination in 1842. Before 1844, however, the state central committee declared that "POLITICALLY, we claim no right, and have no intention, of interfering with Slavery in the States," but stated that its goal was to "SHUT SLAVERY UP IN THE STATES, where alone it is tolerated by the CONSTITUTION."[76] The situation changed during 1844 and 1845 to where several local and at least one state convention subscribed to the idea that the Constitution was an antislavery document.[77] By late 1845, the party newspaper acknowledged that the Liberty Party "maintains a radically new construction of the constitution."[78] This position could have caused problems for the party because two of its leading lawyers, gubernatorial candidate Samuel Fessenden and congressional candidate Seth May, strongly believed that the federal government could not interfere with slavery in the slave states. They felt that enough outside pressure could be applied to bring about abolition.[79] The party was able to keep this from becoming divisive and maintained party harmony by avoiding a statewide position and "without determining what may be the utmost limits of the power of the constitution against slavery."[80] This noncommittal stance allowed local Liberty meetings to follow their own predilections without forcing their decisions on the larger membership as party dogma. This was a typical example of how Maine Liberty men maintained harmony and avoided the brutal internal struggles that characterized the party in some other states.

The problem on the extent to which Liberty men could cooperate politically with non-Liberty men was not so easily resolved. Many of those against fusion and coalition believed that political association with members of other parties would contaminate Liberty principles and bring an end to the party as an independent political movement. Party differences on this began during the early party years and continued until the Free Soil coalition, and these disagreements sometimes resulted in hot public exchanges that were atypical of the general harmony pervading the state's Liberty movement. Occasional incidents caused problems in the early 1840s when there was some fusion when local Liberty groups supported major-party antislavery candidates.[81] In fact, Whigs and Democrats sometimes united to prevent a Liberty candidate from causing a deadlock in an election, sometimes even agreeing to elect a Whig in one year and a Democrat at the next election.[82] As previously mentioned, even the emergence of the temperance issue in Maine politics did not have lasting repercussions for the party.

Few members in the state became noticeably upset by these difficulties, however, but when John P. Hale and his alliance of Independent Democrats, Whigs, and Liberty men scored their stunning victory in the spring 1846 elections in New Hampshire, the debate over party tactics became much more acrimonious. To accept the New Hampshire formula in Maine would entail significant changes in party ideology. The Maine Liberty Party would be transformed from a moral reform agency to a more secular organization containing less militant antislavery Whigs and Democrats. This would be a difficult transition for those members of the Maine Liberty Party who had been developing a reputation for their uncompromising views. The *Bangor Gazette*, whose editors and backers had already shown an orientation toward practical politics, confronted the issue directly in an editorial that advocated the tactics of the New Hampshire Liberty men and declared that "[w]e wish to see Maine New Hampshirized."[83] The paper encouraged the visit of Joshua Gidding, the famous Whig antislavery congressman from Ohio, and Liberty leaders in the Bangor area were instrumental in persuading John P. Hale to campaign for Liberty candidates in the eastern part of the state.[84] Nevertheless, most Maine Liberty men took issue with coalition and fusion. The internal disagreements became public when Whigs and Liberty men in Somerset County discussed cooperation for the September 1846 elections. Willey's *Liberty Standard* declared that this would mean "the destruction of the Liberty Party in Somerset" and that the *Bangor Gazette* "censured us and . . . those in that county who were resisting the insidious attack."[85] The dispute was eventually smoothed over with mutual apologies, but it was indicative of a basic disagreement in the party.[86] The annual state Liberty gathering supported the *Liberty Standard* position in its January 1847 convention by endorsing Fessenden, an anti-coalition advocate for president, over Hale.[87]

Despite these problems, Maine Liberty men developed a more sophisticated, productive political organization by the 1846 state elections. The primary vehicle to accomplish this was the Maine Liberty Association with its county and town auxiliaries. After some success with the concept at the local level by 1844, the annual state Liberty convention on January 6, 1846, founded the Maine Liberty Association and adopted a detailed constitution.[88] The annual membership fee was one dollar, and life memberships were available for ten dollars. The organization was to aid in the dissemination of antislavery literature, assist in the prosecution of the cause, and, perhaps most important, provide another source of revenue for the chronically depleted Liberty coffers. One hundred fifty delegates immediately became members, and the organization's rolls grew to over seven hundred members by the end of the year. Almost all this money went into town, county, and congressional races. Unlike the lip service urging local organization that was a part of many Liberty organizations, the Maine Liberty Party actually set up an effective grassroots base. It employed an agent, former Whig lawyer Woodbury Davis, and printed a monthly magazine, the *Flag of Freedom*, which Austin Willey claimed had a circulation of 15,000 in 1846.[89] These actions plus Hale's efforts on behalf of Liberty candidates in southeastern Maine resulted in unparalleled Liberty successes in the September state elections.

The Liberty Party reached its high point in 1846. Fessenden received almost four thousand more votes (9,343) than a Liberty gubernatorial candidate had obtained in any previous election. His 13% of the vote deprived a major-party candidate of the necessary majority, so Democrat John Dana had to await the meeting of the state legislature in the spring before he could claim victory. Liberty candidates also did well in the lower house, where their ten representatives doubled the party's previous high. As usual, many state and local offices remained empty because no candidate had received a simple majority of the vote. The Liberty agent reported that the elections for four congressional seats, nineteen state senators, and more than sixty state representatives were defeated at the first ballot.[90] Most of these 1846 gains came at the expense of the Democrats.[91] The state Democratic organization had not sufficiently dissociated itself from national policy, and some had seen the success of Democrat-led coalition politics in New Hampshire and began to work for a similar situation in Maine. Liberty men attributed their improved performance to their more sophisticated organization and Hale's endorsement of many of their candidates.[92]

Liberty men looked forward to 1847 because they believed that the party was on its way to greater success. At its first annual meeting in early 1847, the Maine Liberty Association passed resolutions calling for a three thousand-dollar subscription fund and the financing of five Liberty agents.[93] Five agents did cover the state, and a leading Liberty man in the state declared that "[t]he cause of freedom in the state that summer was prosecuted with unusual efficiency."[94] The political situation in New Hampshire, the Wilmot Proviso, and the war with Mexico created a heated political environment that the Liberty men attempted to exploit. They concentrated their efforts on a series of conventions near July 4 that held rallies and "complete Liberty tickets were made for all offices."[95] They were disappointed by the results of the September 13 election. Democrats braved the weather and almost maintained their 1846 totals in winning the race for governor outright. The Whigs lost over 4,500 votes, and Liberty (7,517—11.5%) declined over 1,800 on a day when "[o]ne of the heaviest rain storms known on the coast poured down in torrents all day, and roads were very nearly impassable."[96] At least part of the Liberty problem had to do with the continuing problem of cooperation with the major parties.

A highly publicized local dispute over a state senate seat in Maine was a microcosm of a basic disagreement that Liberty men were confronting in conventions across the country. Austin Willey's *Liberty Standard* had removed the name of a Mr. Wadsworth from its approved candidate list for the state senate from Lincoln County because he had openly supported the Whig F. H. Morse for the U.S. Congress. The *Liberty Standard* claimed that Wadsworth "had acted in close concert with the leaders of that party in efforts to induce Liberty men to abandon their first organic element as a party." The *Bangor Gazette* and other Liberty newspapers chastised the *Liberty Standard* people for deleting a nomination made by a duly constituted convention and attempting to dominate the party. The *Liberty Standard* denied this accusation, saying that it "omitted his name, *not* on *their tickets,* but on *our list,*" an act that it claimed as a journalistic prerogative. Willey acknowledged that there were vital differences within the factions of the party that were irreconcilable.[97]

Most important men in the Maine Liberty Party—including Willey, Samuel

Fessenden, and most old-line Liberty leaders—still viewed the party as a vehicle for moral reform that could not compromise its guiding principles without undermining its basic foundation.[98] They repeatedly declared that there could be "[n]o voting for slave-holders, or those in political fellowship with them."[99] Although they were applying conventional vote-getting techniques and had gone so far as to support John P. Hale after he had toured the state, they were unwilling to compromise the integrity of the party any further in bargaining for votes. Others, on the other hand, were much more oriented toward immediate political success. Most of them did not figure prominently in state and national Liberty proceedings. They tended to work on the local level, and some were recent converts to the party. They did not believe in the rigidity of party lines, possessed a spirit of compromise, and were practical politicians who were willing to mute their principles and party solidarity in order to take a few steps toward their goal of political power. These men also accepted John P. Hale, and they were eager for a wider-based movement including Whigs and Democrats. The question was not over which faction disliked slavery more. Rather, it was a search for the best means to reach a goal.

The move into the Free Soil coalition dominated the remainder of the Maine Liberty Party's existence. Paradoxically, the views and strategies of the coalition-oriented minority came to dominate the party as the hard-line, one-idea, anti-coalition forces quickly became convinced that they would have to acquiesce if they hoped to have any chance of achieving effective political opposition to slavery. The conversion of the old-line Liberty men did not come about because they were persuaded by arguments but because they had no viable alternative.[100] The turning point for these Liberty men came in late July 1847, when Willey traveled to Boston for the aforementioned meeting with John P. Hale. He came away from the meeting impressed by Hale, and he quickly reached the conclusion that "his principles and objects were those of the Liberty Party."[101] Soon he declared that Maine Liberty men were willing to waive their preference for Fessenden because "we know of no man whose nomination on the whole is likely to be so useful to the cause as that of *John P. Hale.*"[102] Maine Liberty men formalized this in supporting Hale at the October 1847 national convention. Nonetheless, two factions remained within the Maine party, as the larger group favored union with Hale as the presidential candidate on the principle of the non-extension of slavery and the minority were willing to make more accommodations.[103]

After the nomination of Cass and Taylor, Fessenden and Willey moved directly into the coalition camp. The Liberty group became the power in the Free Soil movement in Maine because, unlike many other states, adequate leadership was not forthcoming from disgruntled Whigs and Democrats. Liberty men still held out for Hale and expressed distaste for the old foe of abolitionism, Martin Van Buren.[104] They made sure, however, that Whigs, Democrats, and Liberty men would be equally represented at the August convention.[105] At the Buffalo convention, the Maine delegation cast six votes for Hale, five for Van Buren, with one vote unaccounted for, but they accepted Van Buren despite their earlier protests "if he will consecrate the *remainder* of his life to freedom."[106] Willey changed the name of the *Liberty Standard* to the *Free Soil Republican*, and the grassroots Liberty organization served as the basis for the Free Soil Party.[107]

Liberty men joined dissatisfied Whigs and Democrats at a hastily called Free Soil state convention. They set up a state ticket, headed by Samuel Fessenden, which included many Liberty men.[108] A massive rally of an estimated three thousand people, attended by Hale and Stephen C. Phillips, the Free Soil candidate for governor in Massachusetts, met in Lewiston on September 8. A Portland convention on September 27 selected the Free Soil electors for president and listened to speeches by Hale, John Van Buren, and Charles Sumner.[109] The effect of these efforts was minimal improvement over previous Liberty levels in the September elections or the later presidential contest.

GOVERNOR—1848
Elijah Hamlin (Whig)	30,026 (37.9%)
John W. Dana (Democrat)	37,310 (47.0%)
Samuel Fessenden (Free Soil)	11,978 (15.1%)

PRESIDENT—1848
Zachary Taylor (Whig)	35,125 (40.3%)
Lewis Cass (Democrat)	39,830 (45.8%)
Martin Van Buren (Free Soil)	12,096 (13.9%)

The Free Soilers gained only 128 votes between the two contests and their percentage of the vote dropped from 15.1% to 13.9% because of greater turnout. In the state races, they elected thirteen state representatives and defeated the election of over half of the state senators, but the Democrats continued their domination of the state by winning the governor and presidential votes plus five out of seven congressional seats. The Free Soil Party would have had an even greater impact on the state elections except for a new state law, prompted by Liberty success, making a plurality sufficient for election in races for state representatives.[110]

The Maine Liberty Party was the focal point for the antislavery movement in the state during the 1840s. It espoused a highly moralistic approach to politics, but it remained a multi-denominational movement that avoided the harsher religious stands of many abolitionists in Upstate New York and Massachusetts. It developed a statewide organization with a highly effective Liberty Association and elected many state representatives, garnered up to 13% of the state's gubernatorial vote, and so disrupted the state's politics that electoral laws were changed. Many Liberty men later drew on their experiences of the 1840s as members of both the Prohibition and Republican parties.

VERMONT

Vermont's political environment was nearly the opposite of that in Maine. Vermont Whigs dominated the state, but Democrats remained strong enough to provide enough competition so that voter participation was over 80% by 1840.[111] Beneath the veneer of a Whig-dominant two-party system, however, there was an independent electorate that had given the Anti-Masonic Party control of the state from 1831 to 1835. Vermont also had a reputation for being the most antislavery state in the nation.[112] It "had practically no commercial dealings with the South, almost no social intercourse with that section, and no shipping interests that would profit by the slave trade."[113] The state constitution of 1777 made it the first state to forbid slavery, and state legislative bodies and Vermont representatives in the U.S. Congress consistently took leadership roles in opposition to slavery from the colonial period through the 1830s.[114] James G. Birney acknowledged this in 1837 when he declared "I have never seen our cause stand on such high ground among political men as it does among those of the Vermont Legislature."[115] Vermont antislavery also assumed other forms. Vermont colonizationists were active, and more militant abolitionism took place during the 1830s. After the founding of the American Anti-Slavery Society in 1833, the Vermont Anti-Slavery Society became its first auxiliary, claiming eighty-nine local chapters throughout the state by 1837.[116] Although there were a few protests against abolitionists, strong opposition was minimal. One correspondent to the *Liberator* wrote that "mobs are quite out of fashion in Vermont," and Henry B. Stanton recalled that Vermont was the only state in which he could not recall an anti-abolition mob.[117]

The movement for immediate emancipation, however, lost momentum toward the end of the decade. Abolitionists began questioning candidates in 1838 in an attempt to promote stronger antislavery politics, but results were disappointing. Candidates of both major parties usually gave adequate answers but often did not follow through to the degree promised.[118] Sentiment for an antislavery political party grew slowly in Vermont, a state not plagued by severe internal dissension among its abolitionists. The "woman question" did not exist in the state, and women participated fully in every aspect of the Vermont Anti-Slavery Society.[119] Although the state's abolitionists were divided in their attitudes to William Lloyd Garrison, there is no evidence to suggest that this disagreement hurt the state society. Nine out of thirteen Vermont representatives to the May 1840 meeting of the American Anti-Slavery Society chose to secede to the new American and Foreign Anti-Slavery Society.[120] Initially, the Vermont Anti-Slavery Society took an independent stance after leaving the parent society in early 1841.[121] Although ardent Garrisonians, such as *Vermont Telegraph* editor Orson Murray, signed a statement disagreeing with the move, they continued to work and hold positions in the society.[122] The formation of an antislavery party did not threaten the stability of the state society. No one was proscribed for advocating independent nominations, and there seems to have been no mass exodus of those opposed when the society later went on record in favor of direct political action in 1842. Initial efforts, however, were not very successful. Only about forty persons appeared at an August 1840 meeting, and they decided not to run a state ticket because the September state elections were too close. The *Banner of Liberty*, begun as a third-party newspaper, folded the next month, and the independent Birney electors only gathered 319 votes (0.6%) in the presidential election.[123]

In early 1841 the Liberty movement gained momentum. The state society moved from its noncommittal position on politics to declare that its members were "bound to carry out principles wherever we go, and permit them to govern our conduct in whatever we do, whether in the exercise of our ecclesiastical, our political, or our personal rights."[124] Approximately one hundred people attended a March 1 convention that selected candidates for the spring elections and delegates to the May national convention in New York City.[125] A statewide meeting after the national convention showed confusion in the new movement as it selected its state ticket. The nominations of Charles K. Williams, the Whig chief justice of the state supreme court, and Paul Dillingham Jr., a young Democrat who had been his party's nominee for governor in 1840, were appealing, but both eventually declined. Party leaders hurriedly replaced Williams with Titus Hutchinson, a popular former Whig chief justice of the state supreme court. Alvah Sabin, a Baptist minister and former Democrat, took the spot vacated by Dillingham.[126] The hastily arranged ticket did well in the September election. Hutchinson's 3,039 votes (6.3%) deprived either major party of a majority, and the Liberty Party claimed nine seats in the lower house of the Vermont legislature.[127] This relatively strong showing in 1841 established the Liberty Party as a significant factor in Vermont politics. After the elections, antislavery conventions either endorsed no one or approved the entire Liberty ticket. Whig leaders, correctly believing that they had lost many votes to Hutchinson, took a harder line toward the new party. They stripped Chauncy Knapp, who had written editorials in support of Hutchinson, of his position as secretary of state. They had retained him the previous year even though he had not supported William Henry Harrison, but the strength of the Liberty Party in the state elections resulted in a stricter enforcement of party loyalty by the Whigs.[128]

The success in the state elections convinced many wavering abolitionists that the third party could be an effective instrument against slavery. Former abolition leaders who had eschewed political involvement (most notably *Vermont Telegraph* editor Orson Murray) lost much of their influence during the early 1840s. The state society soon became superfluous, broke up, and ceased publication of its newspaper after 1843. In 1845 a correspondent sympathetic to Garrison wrote to him: "The antislavery of this State is mostly under the influence of the third party."[129] The strength that the new party showed in 1841 made it easier for them to recruit candidates. In 1842 Judge Williams accepted the gubernatorial nomination, and his running mate, Edward Barber, had been the Democratic nominee for the same position the year before. When the Democrats made Barber their nominee—although he had made it clear that he "was entirely separated from all [Democratic] party associations"—Vermont Liberty men did not object.[130] Nonetheless, the Liberty gubernatorial vote declined by 32.3% in the election to 2,093 (3.9%). Barber only tallied 25,154 with his dual candidacy, a gain of only 1,024 over the Democratic gubernatorial candidate, indicating that a large number of Whigs who voted for Williams refused to vote for Barber. This demonstrated that many Liberty voters did not entirely discard their old party loyalties. Noteworthy was the low number of scattering votes (35), an indication of the weakness of Garrisonians in the state.

The 1842 election revealed weaknesses that would plague the party. A report on why the party declined in Vermont in 1842 emphasized three problems. First, the party had become a vehicle through which elements in the major parties could show dissatisfaction in their own ranks, not necessarily a strict abolitionist commitment. Second, the party lacked a strong leadership and effective statewide machinery. And third, lack of an adequate party newspaper hampered party propaganda and communication efforts.[131] Liberty leaders acknowledged that they had benefited from internal problems in the Whig Party that caused many Whigs to leave their party temporarily to vote for Liberty candidates, especially former Whigs.[132] This led to state Liberty tickets being headed by former Whigs and resulted in special appeals to Whigs by Liberty men. Liberty men finally set up a state central committee and undertook more thorough propagandizing for the 1843 elections, and their efforts were rewarded. Judge Williams increased his 1842 vote by 80% (3,766—7.5%) and caused the gubernatorial election again to be decided in the state legislature.

Whig U.S. congressman William Slade then led a movement within the Vermont Whig Party to give his party a stronger antislavery identification.[133] The revolt succeeded, and Slade, who had a national reputation for his antislavery work in Congress, became the annual gubernatorial nominee from 1844 to 1846. This change in the Vermont Whig Party after 1843 had repercussions for the Liberty Party. Although the leadership was not significantly affected, the party lost much of its former Whig grassroots support.[134] There was a corresponding rise in former Democratic support, however, as antislavery Democrats became more disgusted with the static behavior of the Vermont Democracy and the increasingly pro-Southern stance of the national Democratic Party. Liberty leaders noticed these trends, and more former Democrats began appearing on Liberty tickets. In 1844 Charles K. Williams gave way to a former Democratic state assemblyman, William R. Shafter (whose son Oscar L. Shafter also ran on the Liberty ticket for Congress). This produced immediate results. The party increased its vote by over 49% in the 1844 race for governor (5,618—10.2%). The Liberty newspaper observed that

> [m]uch of the larger part of our [Liberty Party] increase in this election is from the ranks of the sham democracy. In LaMoille county, which was the strongest seat of that party in the State, only six representatives are elected: two Liberty men and four Democrats. In this town [Montpelier] the Democratic majority for representative was 142—this year only 20. It seems as though the false and senseless cry that "the Liberty party are in league with the 'Locos,'" must now cease.[135]

A drop-off in Whig support can be seen from the drop in the Liberty vote between the state elections and the presidential contest two months later. In the presidential race the Liberty Party lost over 30% from its September total:

Henry Clay (Whig)	26,770 (55.0%)
James K. Polk (Democrat)	17,994 (37.0%)
James G. Birney (Liberty)	3,894 (8.0%)

Nevertheless, LaMoille County gave Birney 24.8% of its vote, the second highest county vote in the country (after DeKalb County, Illinois's 25.4%).

The period immediately after the 1844 presidential election was crucial for the Liberty Party in Vermont. From this point the state's Liberty men would work to make their party the strongest in the country. Perhaps the most important factor in the Liberty resurgence after the national election was the founding of the *Green Mountain Freeman*. By 1847, it had a greater circulation than any newspaper in the state.[136] The major force behind the paper was Joseph Poland, who became its sole editor in May 1846.[137] A young man of already much antislavery experience, he had founded the *Voice of Freedom* in 1839 at the age of twenty-one, and the leading historian of the Underground Railroad has said that Poland was "for more than a score of years the principal Underground operator in Montpelier."[138] His revamped newspaper spurred Liberty men to establish local organizations and set up a network of communication among the members.

Liberty men also worked on a grassroots organization. They designed a plan to make the Green Mountain Liberty Association, which had filled the void created by the demise of the Vermont Anti-Slavery Society, an effective antislavery organization. Modeled after the Liberty Association in Maine, the emphasis was on distributing literature, sending agents into the field, and collecting dues (one dollar). The party began to set up this statewide organization, but financial problems still troubled the party.[139] Nonetheless, former Democrat William R. Shafter continued to build on the base that he had established in 1844, added over nine hundred votes (to 6,534) and increased his percentage more than 3% to 13.5%. The third party, as it would for the remainder of the decade, forced the selection of the governor into the state legislature, where Slade won. This increase in the Liberty vote in 1845 encouraged further refinement in the state organization. Although it never totally abandoned lecturing and distributing literature, the party became more intent on localizing these efforts. By the spring of 1846, Liberty men concentrated on implementing the grassroots strategy of the "Massachusetts Plan" that advocated establishing a series of interlocking county committees, town committees, and school district vigilance persons.[140] This and the continuing success of the *Green Mountain Freeman* helped reinvigorate the party. Its most important strength was a unity that was lacking in some states. Once the membership arrived at a decision on an issue, the consensus prevailed throughout the party. In fact, there was usually little disagreement before it reached a decision. The January conventions that set the yearly strategy were excellent examples of the ongoing harmony. The nominations for the state central committee were easily adopted, establishing continuity in leadership. Likewise, the resolutions were easily passed and the proceedings took on the tone of a religious revival more than a political meeting. As Poland noted, "[T]he groundwork of the liberty organization was deep toned *religious* sentiment."[141] This tone pervaded the Liberty press and gatherings, and religious meetings often were held immediately before or after Liberty conventions. The political meetings themselves rocked to spiritual hymns and popular antislavery songs, often sung by the famous Hutchinson Family singing group from neighboring New Hampshire.

The Vermont party's unyielding moral tone resulted in its state party platforms being the most outspoken in the nation, particularly on the question of the relationship between the U.S. Constitution and slavery. In 1843 former state supreme court chief justice and a Liberty gubernatorial candidate, Titus Hutchinson, delivered an address asserting the unconstitutionality of slavery.[142] Characteristically, however, the appeal to a "higher law" was more popular in the state than the legalistic approach. At the state Liberty Party convention in July 1845, a reported two to three thousand persons (men and women) resoundingly affirmed this in a resolution that would represent Liberty position in the state until shortly before the Free Soil merger. They resolved "[t]hat to say that the Constitution secures general liberty, and at the same guarantees local slavery, or even compromises or permits its existence, is to affirm the greatest of moral absurdities—to deny self evident truths—to falsify human history—to libel the unity of human nature, and to deny the connection which exists between moral cause and effect."[143] By 1847, Vermont Liberty Party conventions were so extreme that the editors of the *National Era* refused to publish their strong antislavery resolutions concerning abolishing slavery in the slave states.[144] The state party and most of its auxiliary organizations did not tone down their positions until the merger into the Free Soil movement became imminent. Then the Liberty men backtracked to the more conventional Liberty position of pledging not to interfere with slavery in the slave states.[145]

Consensus in the Vermont Liberty Party extended beyond constitutional interpretation to a general unanimity on other policies. Fusion and coalition were not divisive issues, although it seems that some fusion took place in lower elections. This issue did not mean as much to Vermont Liberty men as it did in some states, perhaps because an antislavery tone pervaded all the parties in the state. Although some discussion on expanding the party platform took place, the one-idea principle prevailed.[146] The temperance issue arose at conventions and the *Green Mountain Freeman* was sympathetic to it, but it never seems to have been made an article of faith, perhaps because many believed Liberty men necessarily supported temperance. The multi-reform ideas of the Liberty League received scant attention. Poland strongly opposed broadening the platform because he thought that it would be impractical and "inevitably result in the speedy downfall of the Liberty organization."[147] He criticized the *Emancipator* for advocating free trade, Sabbatarianism, postal reform, and other causes. He predicted "let it have two ideas, and it would have but half its original strength, and so on in the same ratio," and he opposed the Liberty League for the same reasons.[148] The most serious disputes that seem to have affected the Liberty Party in the state were Joseph Poland's mild criticism of new Liberty newspapers within the state. When his old partner on the *Green Mountain Freeman,* C. C. Briggs, founded the *Burlington Gazette,* Poland was unhappy because he felt that this would take subscribers away from the *Green Mountain Freeman.*[149] These were personal matters, however, and there was no attempt to use the state party machinery to squelch competitors.

Vermont Liberty Party men saw themselves engaged in "moral warfare."[150] Although the state central committee ran the party, candidates who ran for office were generally popular politicians who had left a major party. The Vermont party in 1846 and 1847 had more success than any other Liberty contingent in any statewide election. In 1846 the Liberty Party's gubernatorial candidate, St. Albans businessman and former Democrat Lawrence Brainerd, received 7,118 votes (14.6%), the highest gubernatorial percentage anywhere in party history. This 8.9% increase over the previous year was acceptable but somewhat disappointing to the Liberty men after all their efforts. The party elected approximately a dozen members to the lower house and continued to have some success in town races, but Whigs still dominated the state.[151] The year 1847 was similar to 1846. The party changed little and the election results were almost identical for the three parties, with Liberty candidate receiving 6,926 votes (14.4%).[152] Liberty men were becoming aware that their growth was nearly at an end, especially since the major parties were nominating candidates with greater antislavery credentials.

Vermont Liberty men wholeheartedly entered the Free Soil movement. They combined with dissident Democrats and some Whigs to make the Vermont Free Soil Party one of the strongest in the nation and a powerful force in state politics. The Free Soil movement gained momentum rapidly during the summer of 1848. Little opposition to the merger developed in the Vermont Liberty Party. Poland wrote that "[w]e are no sticklers for party; only let the country be rid of the guilt of slavery and political thralldom, and we care not how or by whom the work is done."[153] Another Liberty newspaper in the state wrote that "we have no wish to lose our identity as a party ... [A]t the same time, we ought not to turn a cold shoulder to those who are willing to break away from the old parties."[154] The major stumbling block for a coalition was the unwillingness of Vermont Liberty men to accept the possible candidacy of Martin Van Buren. Poland wrote, "[S]hould Van Buren be the nominee of that convention ... then the Liberty Party is bound by every consideration of moral principle, consistency and true expediency to retain its present organization and candidates."[155] The state convention in July unanimously approved the nomination of John P. Hale for president. There were some disagreements on the expediency of sending delegates to the national Free Soil convention, but more restrained resolutions on the constitutionality of slavery and the existence of slavery in the slave states indicated that Liberty men were willing to negotiate and compromise.[156]

The Whig convention in the state declared its opposition to the extension of slavery but angered more militant antislavery Whigs by approving the nomination of Zachary Taylor. No major split developed in the party, although a few important Whigs—William Slade, Horatio Everett, and Edward Stansbury—soon became involved with the Free Soil Party. The nomination of Lewis Cass by the Democratic national convention caused a greater rift among Vermont Democrats, who had already been losing support to the Liberty Party. Although antislavery Democrats had succeeded in getting a state platform opposed to the extension of slavery, they walked out when the convention supported Lewis Cass for president.[157] The dissident Democrats were the primary organizers of a state Free Soil convention that met August 1. Joseph Poland, who was selected as secretary for the convention, reported that "[t]he convention was composed, we should judge, in the greatest proportion of seceding Democrats—the movement originating with, and convention called by them; notwithstanding a good number of prominent Whigs were present . . . we were glad to see a goodly number of Liberty men present . . . Liberty men have ever professed a willingness to extend a hand of fellowship to such as would take antislavery grounds; and hence their presence, their sympathy, and action upon this occasion."[158]

The convention demonstrated this catholicity in its slate of nominees for state offices. Oscar L. Shafter, the former Democrat who had been a Liberty candidate for the U.S. Congress in 1844, was nominated for governor. Luke W. Poland, a Democrat, received the nomination for second spot on the ticket and Edward A. Stansbury, an antislavery Whig, was selected as the candidate for treasurer. The convention set up a state central committee, a committee of correspondence, and organizations down to the school district level, and it recommended that a Free Soil League be founded in each town.[159] The distinctly Democratic tinge of the Liberty leadership and voter base after 1844 was an important factor in the cooperation between Democrats and Liberty men in Vermont. Former Democrats had headed state Liberty tickets since 1844 and its voter base was increasingly former Democrats.[160]

At the Buffalo Free Soil convention, the Vermont delegates supported Hale 11–7 over Van Buren despite much pressure from the neighboring New York Barnburner contingent. Nonetheless, Vermont Liberty men quickly became resigned to Van Buren's candidacy and comforted themselves with the fact that he would be running on a Liberty-approved platform.[161] The *Green Mountain Freeman* immediately put the Free Soil nomination of Van Buren and Charles

Francis Adams on its masthead; and when Lawrence Brainerd returned from Buffalo and formally resigned as Liberty nominee for governor, Poland endorsed the Free Soil state ticket with a strong editorial.[162] Despite the fact that the new party had very little time to prepare for the September state elections, Free Soil candidates did well at all levels, prompting Poland to report that the gubernatorial vote was "beyond our most sanguine hopes."[163]

Carlos Coolidge (Whig)	22,007 (43.7%)
Paul Dillingham (Democrat)	13,420 (26.6%)
Oscar L. Shafter (Free Soil)	14,931 (29.6%)
Other	47 (0.1%)

This success carried over into the state legislature where the Free Soilers captured 2 of 30 senate seats and elected 82 of 223 representatives.[164] They also caused three-quarters of the congressional seats to be rerun, soon resulting in a change in the state law making a plurality sufficient for election.[165] These results buoyed Free Soil hopes for the November presidential contest, but the party did not even match its earlier totals.

Zachary Taylor (Whig)	23,122 (47.8%)
Lewis Cass (Democrat)	10,948 (22.6%)
Martin Van Buren (Free Soil)	14,337 (29.6%)

The party may have been helped by some Democrats who were sympathetic to the Barnburner movement in neighboring New York, but Van Buren's candidacy undoubtedly hurt Free Soil chances among possible Whig converts. David Ludlum has even speculated that it may have cost them the state, speculating that "[a]nother candidate, unburdened by a political past, might have carried the state in 1848."[166] A subsequent analysis posits that "the Free Soil movement was composed primarily of Liberty men and dissident Democrats."[167]

Vermont was the most antislavery state in the country, and the Liberty Party's percentage in Vermont was the strongest in the country. It built on an early Whig base and added much Democratic support later. It exhibited a high moral tone and singularity of purpose. It did not have, however, the energetic and talented leaders who would give unstinting devotion to the cause. There was not a real professional reformer in the state. This does not denigrate the membership because many of the Liberty men were hardworking and put countless hours into the cause. It is just that they had lives to lead outside of the movement, and the Vermont Liberty Party did not have anyone like a Joshua Leavitt, Henry B. Stanton, Gerrit Smith, Alvan Stewart, Salmon P. Chase, Owen Lovejoy, James G. Birney, Austin Willey, or other states' leaders. As a result, the party may never have reached its full potential. It prepared the foundations, however, for the Free Soil Party that would soon become the dominant element in state politics during the early 1850s and the Republican Party later in the decade. Former Liberty men Charles K. Williams became governor, Lawrence Brainerd a U.S. senator, and both Alvah Sabin and Chauncy L. Knapp U.S. congressmen. Other Liberty men continued their interests in state and local affairs and the learned professions.

NEW HAMPSHIRE

New Hampshire had a unique political environment in which not only the governor and presidential electors but also congressmen (until 1846) were chosen on a general ticket. This produced a "winner take all" situation that enhanced the necessity for a strong state organization. Voters turned out in great numbers for the spring state elections, often surpassing those voting in presidential elections. The statewide orientation had the dual effect of lessening the importance of the town and county as political units and making one-party domination of the state easier. During the 1830s, Jacksonians made the New Hampshire Democratic Party the strongest state political organization in the North. They lost only one state election between 1829 and 1854, and in 1837 party co-founder Isaac Hill was elected governor with 91% of the vote. Democrats established an efficient political machine and developed an ideology that fit well within the traditional framework of Jacksonian Democracy: hostility to banks, industry, and railroad construction. The Depression of 1837, internal squabbles, and a revitalized Whig Party made the state somewhat more competitive by 1840.[168]

New Hampshire Democrats were not sympathetic to the abolition movement. Part of the Jacksonian ideology was the states' rights position, disapproving interference in the internal affairs of another state. Slavery had been outlawed in New Hampshire by a judicial interpretation of the state constitution, but Democrats were opposed to attempts to end slavery. They did not want to offend Southerners, who were important to the trade and shipping interests of New Hampshire's seacoast areas. They were frequent allies in the U.S. Congress as New Hampshire congressmen took the lead in restricting abolitionist activities. Charles Atherton sponsored the infamous gag rule by which antislavery petitions were automatically tabled, and the state's congressional delegation repeatedly showed that it was the most united Northern state delegation in attempts to restrict abolition propaganda.[169]

The state was not devoid of antislavery sentiment, however, and clashes with anti-abolitionists were the most numerous and intense in northern New England. Antislavery forces were often led by clergymen who played important roles in the New England Anti-Slavery Society and in founding the state society in 1834. Increased interest in abolition during the mid- and late 1830s bothered the Democrats. Isaac Hill criticized abolition as "a Congregational-Federalist plot," and abolitionist lecturers were subjected to more incidents of abuse in New Hampshire than elsewhere in New England.[170] Nonetheless, abolitionism progressed quickly, with local societies reporting a total of over three thousand members by 1837.[171] The state also possessed one of the most outspoken antislavery newspapers in the country, Nathaniel P. Rogers's *Herald of Freedom*, which claimed a circulation of more than 1,400 weekly papers by the end of the 1830s.[172] While the Democratic Party and much of the populace were hostile to the movement, there remained a strong abolition sentiment with a religious orientation that was actively working for immediate emancipation. Adversity and minority status did not unite the state's abolitionists, however, and the New Hampshire Anti-Slavery Society was plagued by more internal dissension than in any state except Massachusetts.

Repercussions from the 1839 split in the Massachusetts Anti-Slavery Society were felt among abolitionists in the New Hampshire because of the close ties between the two state organizations. The controversy resulted from many of the same disagreements as in Massachusetts: Garrison's alleged attempts to add other causes to antislavery; complete and full acceptance of women in the society; hostility to Garrison's domination and anticlericalism; and the question of political action. Garrison's denunciations of the clergy for being insufficiently committed to antislavery brought a particularly strong reaction from New Hampshire.[173] Jonathan Curtis, a Congregational minister and president of the New Hampshire Anti-Slavery Society, saw Garrison as the culprit. He demanded that "whenever he [Garrison] or any one else attempts to attach to the anti-slavery cause, already a burden quite as much as we can carry, *non-resistance, or the abolition of all government*, or *women's rights to do wrong*, or any other absurd or impractical vagary, or any matter foreign to the great subject; I say off with your unhallowed hands. Away with your lumber from a cause so sacred as this."[174] He joined those who broke with Garrison to become a charter member of the American and Foreign Anti-Slavery Society. He soon found that he was somewhat out of line with his own state society, however, when a motion to exclude women from equal participation lost 197–57 with all 30 women voting with the majority.[175]

Soon afterward, when resolutions on political action were sent to committee, Curtis resigned his presidency, delivered a protest, and joined many others of the minority in forming the New Hampshire Abolition Society as an auxiliary to the American and Foreign Anti-Slavery Society.[176] Unlike Massachusetts, where a companion female society was established, New Hampshire women stayed out of the New Organization until the mid-1840s, although they did form non-Garrisonian local societies.[177] The leaders in the new society quickly contacted the Massachusetts Abolition Society and requested that Alanson St. Clair and Amos A. Phelps, agents of the Massachusetts Abolition Society, be allowed to come into New Hampshire.[178] They established the (Concord, N.H.) *Abolition Standard* as their official newspaper, and Jonathan Curtis led members on an active recruiting campaign among the local societies. Their efforts met with some success. One of them declared "[w]e have got the clergy and WE shall get the people in course," and the subscriptions to the old society's *Herald of Freedom* dropped after the controversy and the appearance of the *Abolition Standard*.[179] The new society refused to endorse the Birney-Earle presidential ticket. The old society had come out strongly against independent nominations, and the New Hampshire Abolition Society had decided "to stand uncommitted on the question," because not all its members favored independent political action.[180] There was no driving force behind a third party in the state during the summer 1840. Supporters did little until shortly before the election, resulting in a low vote of 126 (0.2%) in the presidential election.

Not discouraged by the small turnout, a small band of Liberty men issued a call for a Liberty Party convention in Concord on December 23 to make nominations for the state elections in the spring.[181] One hundred sixty-five men from twenty-five towns signed the roll in support of the convention. They decided to employ an agent to organize the state, recommended that local Liberty affiliates be set up, and selected a Liberty ticket for major offices. The choice for governor was a popular former Whig, Daniel Hoit, an experienced politician who had served in the state legislature as early as 1807.[182] A few local Liberty conventions met, but the response was not heartening.[183] Nonetheless, Hoit made a surprisingly good showing in the spring elections with 1,273 votes (2.5%).[184] He received over 1,100 more votes than Birney had the previous November. Perhaps more significant, the low number of scattering votes (only 10 where there had been 504 in 1840 when the same 2 major-party candidates ran) showed that politically interested antislavery men were aligning with the Liberty Party instead of following the Old Organization's advice to scatter their votes. This confirmed the suspicion that the Garrisonians were losing support. Early in January 1841 the *Herald of Freedom* acknowledged that it had to switch publishers because it had lost so many subscribers to the New Organization.[185] These abolitionists did not necessarily go directly into the Liberty Party. The New Hampshire Abolition Society, which was increasing its membership, had not yet established close ties with the new party and still contained many voters who supported the major parties.

The next three years were a growth period. Buoyed by their gains in the spring 1841 elections, Liberty men sent three men to the May 1841 national Liberty convention in New York City.[186] They issued a call for a state convention shortly after returning from New York. The two-day meeting in June attracted forty-two participants from twenty-five towns. It renominated Hoit for governor, established the *People's Advocate*, edited by Methodist minister F. P. Tracy, as the party paper, and urged members to organize their counties and towns.[187] Nonetheless, the party remained disorganized and unsophisticated until after the presidential election of 1844. Liberty men were unable to make the transition from the party as a protest vehicle to the party as a political organization. Instead, they adopted earlier abolition tactics (pamphlets, tracts, and agents) without adding the political techniques that were being employed with some sophistication by the party elsewhere. The *People's Advocate* was in constant financial trouble and did not provide the leadership that the Liberty presses did in many other states. It was a low-quality publication that reported national Liberty news and on party activities in other states but contained little information on New Hampshire.[188] A neighboring Liberty editor commented that the Liberty vote in the spring 1843 election would have been greater "had it not been for the embarrassments of the Liberty paper in that state."[189] By 1843, the New Hampshire Abolition Society had begun cooperating with the Liberty Party. The New Organization began holding its meetings just before Liberty conventions, and many of its leaders became involved in Liberty affairs by 1844. By this time the Liberty Party was becoming a more dominant antislavery agency, but members continued to use the abolitionist techniques of the 1830s.

Perhaps the most surprising thing about the Liberty Party was the amount of success it enjoyed in the state during these early years despite minimal organization or recruitment efforts. Gubernatorial candidate Hoit increased his vote every year against the backdrop of continued Democratic domination in the state.

YEAR	LIBERTY VOTE (%)	% INCREASE
1841	1,273 (2.5%)	
1842	2,756 (5.7%)	116.5
1843	3,416 (7.7%)	23.9

This was even more remarkable because a fourth party, the Conservative Democrats, ran a candidate from 1842 to 1844. In addition, the Liberty Party claimed ten seats in the lower house of the state legislature by 1843.[190] Most of these early electoral gains were at the expense of the Whigs, who, after a brief resurgence in the late 1830s to near parity with the Democrats, managed to collect only 25.8% of the gubernatorial vote in 1842 and 28.2% in 1843. This trend was also evident in town elections, where the Whig organization would sometimes support Liberty candidates who were sympathetic to Whig positions on matters not related to slavery. There was also evidence of collusion among Whigs, Conservative Democrats, and Liberty men to elect candidates against the powerful regular Democratic machine.[191]

Since New Hampshire was firmly controlled by Democrats, Liberty tactics were somewhat different from those employed in other New England states, where the party was often able to hold the balance of power between the two major parties. Democratic control of New Hampshire was so extensive, however, that the only hope for political success often was in a combination of all the disparate elements that were opposed to the regular Democratic nominee. While the New Hampshire Liberty Party was able to maintain a distinct identity in statewide elections, this sometimes broke down on the local level. Liberty men lacked the cohesiveness of the party elsewhere. They met in state convention once or twice a year, renominated Daniel Hoit for governor by an overwhelming majority, and then adjourned with little subsequent local party activity. This began to change after the 1843 national Liberty convention discussed plans for state and local organization. New Hampshire did not send a delegation, but state leaders were aware of what transpired. In late 1843 the *People's Advocate* scolded Liberty men in a harsh editorial, "The Liberty Party in New Hampshire. Where Is It?" The article pointed out the poor party organization, lack of Liberty agents, poor support for the newspaper, and absence of leadership from the state central committee.[192]

The year 1844 was crucial in the development of the party in New Hampshire. The National Democratic Party's stand in favor of the annexation of Texas, New Hampshire Democratic congressman John P. Hale's opposition to the gag rule and slavery extension, and the Liberty Party's increased appeals to Democratic voters brought large numbers of Democrats into the Liberty ranks.[193] This laid the basis for a coalition that would be a forerunner of the 1848 Free Soil movement. There was a noticeable decline in clerical influence in the party, particularly after the departure of Alanson St. Clair and the failure of the debt-ridden *People's Advocate*. The (Concord) *Granite Freeman* soon took its place, attracting enough subscribers to become self-sufficient by late September.[194] While the New Hampshire Abolition Society was becoming more closely aligned with the Liberty Party, the Old Organization was becoming so internally divided that it was no longer an effective alternative. It voted to discontinue the *Herald of Freedom* as the society's newspaper because of editor Nathaniel Rogers's extreme nonresistance views.[195] The old society quickly fell apart. Looking back in 1845, Old Organization sympathizer Parker Pillsbury reflected that "[t]hree years of the last five, are green all over with laurels. But the last two have scarcely an oasis on which the eye fastens with delight."[196] Declining opposition left Liberty men free to concentrate on political matters and less on abolitionist infighting.

The spring elections encouraged the reenergized party. Hoit increased his vote to 5,737, 11.7% of the total and an increase of 67.9% from the previous year. This spurred efforts during the summer and fall for the presidential campaign. In addition to founding the *Granite Freeman* as a campaign sheet, county organizations were established, held rallies, and made sure that party ballots were distributed to the towns—the first time that there was so much local activity in the state. Election results, however, disappointed Liberty men even though New Hampshire was the banner Liberty state in the country:

James K. Polk (Democrat)	27,160 (55.2%)
Henry Clay (Whig)	17,866 (36.3%)
James G. Birney (Liberty)	4,161 (8.5%)

The Liberty vote dropped 27.5% from the spring elections, a total loss of 1,576 votes. Birney suffered particularly among the new Democratic accessions because of a strong campaign by the state Democratic organization to hold its voters by emphasizing Birney's Federalist-Whig antecedents.[197] In addition, Hale, who had broken party ranks to speak against the gag rule and the annexation of Texas, endorsed Polk and campaigned for him throughout the summer and fall.[198] This left Liberty men wondering about the future of their party.

The New Hampshire Liberty Party after 1844 had a unique history. It went from a poorly organized group that received scant attention from outside the state to a model for those interested in a broader approach to antislavery politics. It embarked on coalition politics at a time when most state Liberty organizations opposed cooperation with anyone outside the party. Its success caught the attention of party members everywhere. The year 1845, however, did not begin with the sense that something important was about to happen. Disappointed by the presidential results, New Hampshire Liberty men worked on their state organization in preparation for the spring elections. Although they were far behind most other states, the increased number of county and congressional district meetings contrasted with the apathy of the earlier years.[199]

Meanwhile, signs of unrest over slavery surfaced outside the Liberty structure itself. Hale began his break with the Democratic organization and became an important figure in antislavery politics. In 1845 Liberty men and Hale's Independent Democrats began to explore mutual cooperation. In the spring elections the *Granite Freeman* urged Liberty voters to "stand firm" with their own candidates, and it appears that they did on the gubernatorial level. Hoit ran over 1,300 votes ahead of Birney's totals a few months before and gathered the highest Liberty percentage yet (5,464—12.0%). More important, Hale's Independent candidacy prevented the election of one of the regular Democrats and forced a series of runoff elections in which the Liberty Party did not run a candidate.[200] This began a cooperative venture that would lead to a Liberty–Independent Democrat alliance. It continued at a January 1846 Liberty state convention when former Whig Hoit stepped down in favor of former Democratic Liberty man Nathaniel S. Berry, who then received the Independent Democratic nomination. Cooperation soon extended into local races for the spring 1846 elections, and more voters came to the polls than at any time since the 1840 presidential contest. For the first time, Democrats failed to control either house or win the governor's race. The changing situation can be seen in the gubernatorial contest and the races for state legislature. Berry almost doubled Hoit's total of the previous year with 10,406 votes (18.8%), and the state legislature changed composition drastically. Six state senate seats remained unfilled with the Democrats holding four and the Liberty-Independent group with two.[201] The combined forces of Whigs, Independent Democrats, and Liberty men held a bare majority of seats in the lower house, with the combination of Whigs (102), Liberty (14), and Independent Democrats (22) outnumbering the Democrats (122).[202]

Historian Richard H. Sewell has concisely described the situation that then evolved between the March elections and the meeting of the state legislature in June.

> Whatever the channels of this Allied diplomacy, not long after March election the tacit agreement of several months standing hardened: the Whigs would support Hale's election to the [U.S.] Senate [by the state legislature] if the Independent Democrats agreed to make [Whig] Colby governor. Nathaniel Berry . . . had removed himself as a gubernatorial possibility. Hale men pledged themselves to vote for the Whig candidates when the legislature met to elect state senators from the six districts that had made no choice in March. The Allies also agreed to cooperate in the election of other state officials annually chosen by the legislature.[203]

The participants carried out the bargain. When the newly elected state legislature met in June, it filled the six state senate vacancies with Whigs and elected John P.

Hale to the U.S. Senate for a six-year term to begin in 1847. It then selected Whig Anthony Colby to be governor, a choice particularly difficult for Liberty men because of his long hostility to their party. They were somewhat mollified, however, when the state legislature elected Joseph Cilley, a former Whig who was a Liberty congressional candidate in 1846, to fill out the one year left in a vacancy in the U.S. Senate created when Levi Woodbury became a U.S. Supreme Court justice. The coalition had an impact on politics beyond slavery matters. The legislature passed laws that would make the one-party dominance of the 1830s and early 1840s more difficult to achieve. Coalition legislation eliminated the general ticket system for congressional elections and filled many appointive offices with coalition members. It also enacted a number of laws and resolutions of a distinctly antislavery nature. Legislators selected Hale, who was awaiting the beginning of his U.S. Senate term, as Speaker of the House. They then passed joint resolutions asking their congressmen to work for the exclusion of slavery from the territories, end the domestic slave trade, and abolish slavery in the District of Columbia. They also passed a personal liberty law making it illegal for a private citizen to aid in the capture of fugitive slaves and rejected a Democratic resolution in support of the Mexican War.

Coalition leaders looked for ways to maintain their power in the spring 1847 election. The Whig Party was the big question mark in the coalition. Independent Democrats and Liberty men had been working together smoothly since the previous year, but Whigs only joined them in full force at the state legislative session in June. Differences between Whigs and some Independent Democrats over economic policy along with Liberty hostility to Governor Colby made the alliance tenuous.[204] Colby worked to heal the breach with the Liberty men by taking some strongly antislavery positions as governor, but the pro-business Whig attitudes were opposed to the economic philosophy that many Independent Democrats brought with them from their old party.[205] The result was that Whigs would cooperate in legislative assembly and some elections but were not yet ready for full-fledged coalition with Independent Democrats and Liberty men. They also irritated Independent and Liberty followers by trumpeting the 1846 victory as a Whig triumph, causing the *Granite Freeman* to reprint an article from the *Albany Patriot* stating the Whigs "have been and will remain a minority in that state."[206]

Independent Democrats and Liberty men, however, made moves to cement their alliance. The *Granite Freeman* abandoned its former lukewarm approval of Hale and began extolling his virtues. Hale, in turn, spoke at Liberty meetings throughout the summer. On September 12, 1846, the Liberty men and Independents formed one organization at a joint convention in New Market that eventually led to the merger of the two newspapers of the group in early May 1847. This subjected them to some criticism from other Liberty advocates outside the state.[207] This disapproval was mild, however, compared with the assaults from the regular Democratic Party. Aware that the merger formed a basis for a united opposition, the *New Hampshire Patriot* launched a smear campaign equating the new party with the disunionist Garrisonians. It asked its readers "to judge for themselves whether these political abolitionists and Garrison are not banded together to effect one object—A DISSOLUTION OF OUR GLORIOUS UNION."[208] As political realists, however, Democrats could sense the changing voter sentiment on slavery. The New Hampshire Democratic Party's decision to go on record in mid-1846 as opposing the further extension of slavery stole some of the new party's appeal and helped bring the regular Democrats back into power in the spring 1847 elections.[209]

Nonetheless, the New Hampshire Liberty-Independent movement had spread across the state by the time of the spring 1847 election.[210] Former Liberty man Nathaniel Berry again was the Independent candidate, but the Whigs decided to run their own ticket headed again by Anthony Colby. Despite much Independent-Liberty activity and a rigorous statewide campaign by Hale, the new party's strenuous opposition to the Mexican War and the recent anti-extension stand of the state's Democrats led to a regular Democrat resurgence. They won the governor's race and both houses of the state legislature as they exploited their efficient party machine. In an election where turnout increased over the previous year by over 5,000 and set a new high of over 60,000 votes they won with a simple majority. Berry lost almost 2,000 votes (8,531—14.1%), while the Whigs gained over 3,500 ballots and the Democrats increased their total by almost 4,000. To assess where the Independent-Liberty support went in the confused New Hampshire situation is difficult, but some former Whigs were returning to a revitalized Whig Party because of the Democratic orientation of the base of the Independent-Liberty movement.[211] When the Whigs worked with Independent-Liberty men, as in the election of Amos Tuck and James Wilson to Congress in 1847 runoff elections, the old coalition had some success, but mutual suspicions between former Whigs and former Democrats hurt at the polls.[212] The situation was not helped by the conduct of U.S. Senator Joseph Cilley, the former Liberty candidate elected by the state legislature. His views on the Mexican War and his refusal to submit disunion petitions angered many, and he eventually joined the Whigs in Congress.[213]

Nonetheless, over three hundred persons attended the September 30 state convention, where they appointed a full delegation under Amos Tuck to the national Liberty convention, endorsed Hale for president, and renominated

Nathaniel Berry for governor.[214] The disastrous defeat in the spring election had shocked the Whigs into closer contact with the Independent-Liberty people. Viewing the successful results of electing Tuck and Wilson, the Whigs saw that their only hope for political survival lay in working with the third party. In their convention, they passed several strong antislavery and anti-extension resolutions and nominated Berry for governor after Colby stepped aside.[215] Optimism faded to gloom after the 1848 spring elections.[216] Democratic Governor Jared Williams defeated Berry in the first two-party race in the state since 1840. Over 61,000 voters, another high turnout in New Hampshire up to that time, cast their ballots, and Berry (28,819—46.9%) did not even match the Independent-Liberty-Whig total of the previous year.[217] The Democrats strengthened their hold on the state legislature, but their opposition still held two congressional seats and John P. Hale was becoming an important member of the U.S. Senate. The Senate's gain was the coalition's loss because Hale's presence in the state had been a cohesive force in the confused party situation. After Hale's departure for Washington, there was no one to fill the leadership void at home. The party began to disintegrate because of intra-party bickering that was apparent in lower-level races where Whigs did not join their allies.

The Free Soil movement in New Hampshire moved haltingly toward the presidential election. The *Independent Democrat and Granite Freeman* and the state delegates to the Free Soil convention in Buffalo unanimously supported Hale on the preliminary ballot before throwing their support to the Van Buren–Adams ticket. They had little success when they returned to New Hampshire. The Democratic machine worked with its accustomed efficiency, and Cass swamped his divided opponents in an election that attracted over ten thousand fewer voters than the spring elections.

Zachary Taylor (Whig)	14,781 (29.5%)
Lewis Cass (Democrat)	27,763 (55.4%)
Martin Van Buren (Free Soil)	7,560 (15.1%)

Cass received almost 5,500 more votes than the combined numbers of Taylor and Van Buren. The Free Soil movement was not dead in New Hampshire, and Hale and Tuck remained in Washington until 1853. It would continue as the Free Democracy before most members eventually went into the Republican Party, including Nathaniel S. Berry, who became governor in 1861.

The Liberty Party in New Hampshire had a unique development and underwent more changes than any other state party. In the early years there was a distinct clerical influence in the Liberty Party, but this declined after 1844. Moralistic language in conventions and party newspapers softened as the relationship with the Independent Democrats developed. In the early years there was a Whig orientation in the party, but this became increasingly Democratic after 1844. The national implications of the Liberty men's coalescing with the Independent Democrats cannot be underestimated. The New Hampshire success in 1846 and the subsequent acceptance of Hale as a Liberty presidential candidate broke down much anti-coalition fervor in many other state Liberty organizations, making it easier for them to join the Free Soil movement.

CONNECTICUT

By the late 1830s, Connecticut had a competitive two-party system where voter participation from 1837 to 1848 wavered from slightly over 60% to 80%.[218] Whigs won eight of these annual contests, but the state was so competitive that three of the races were decided in the state legislature. Abolitionism was not strong in the state during the 1830s. Only thirty-nine towns started antislavery societies before the Connecticut Anti-Slavery Society was founded in early 1838, and the total membership was only about 1,700 men and women.[219] There was no attempt to introduce a formal questioning system, and political activity was limited to antislavery petitions that were summarily rejected by the state legislature. The state had strong commercial ties to the South, and African Americans were not welcome. Future Liberty congressional candidate John Hooker recalled that freed blacks were "generally held in contempt" and that one of his prominent relatives warned him about being identified with the abolitionists because "they were so unpopular that it would severely injure my chances of getting into business."[220] Prudence Crandall's school for young black girls was destroyed in an infamous 1837 anti-abolitionist incident. As late as December 1839, "the friends of slavery" burned a Congregational meeting house in Wolcott that had held an antislavery rally.[221] Nonetheless, a core of committed white and black abolitionists continued to work for the cause but were reluctant to take sides in the internal disputes within the movement. After the acrimonious May 1840 meeting of the American Anti-Slavery Society, the Connecticut Anti-Slavery Society chose not to affiliate with either the Old or New organizations.[222] The state's abolitionists were also hesitant to move toward independent nominations. Only one Connecticut man participated in the April 1, 1840, Albany convention that set up the Liberty Party, and there appears to have been no effort to field a ticket for the presidential contest.[223] In fact, the newspaper of the state society, the (Hartford, Conn.) *Charter Oak*, was strongly opposed to the nominations by the "malcontents of Western New York."²²⁴ Nonetheless, some abolitionists voted the Birney-Earle ticket in the election.²²⁵

The situation changed in 1841. Sherman Miller Booth, a Yale senior, was instrumental in calling a state convention in Hartford that set up a state ticket for the spring elections. Subsequently, the annual meeting of the Connecticut Anti-Slavery Society in May placed on the table a motion disapproving of an independent party.²²⁶ Then in September a state convention met in Hartford, organized a Liberty Party, and nominated a ticket for the spring 1842 state elections that was headed by Francis Gillette, a former Whig who had been elected to the Connecticut legislature in 1832 and 1838.²²⁷ In the election two Liberty men were elected as representatives, and Gillette managed to take enough votes (1,989— 3.8%) away from the major parties so neither had the required majority, sending the election to the state legislature, where the Democrats won for the first time in five years. This caused the Whigs to move in a more antislavery direction, and they subsequently nominated Roger Baldwin, an abolitionist who had served as a lead attorney for the African captives in the famous *Amistad* case.²²⁸

The time between the 1842 and 1843 state elections was the key period in the history of the Connecticut Liberty Party. Immediately after the 1842 election, Alvan Stewart and Beriah Green came from New York for a state convention in New Haven, helped set up another ticket, again led by Gillette, and recommended an organizational plan for the state.²²⁹ By the end of the year, the political abolitionists had taken effective control of the Connecticut Anti-Slavery Society, and its executive committee established the *Christian Freeman* as the society's newspaper. Two of its editors, Congregational minister Ichabod Codding and Sherman Booth, were strong Liberty men, and they received authorization to work for the Liberty Party.²³⁰ Although the state society remained officially independent, it had turned toward antislavery politics in general and the Liberty Party in particular. This was also true for some of its auxiliaries.²³¹ The *Christian Freeman*'s inaugural issue contained a lengthy article on the "Political Obligations of Christians" and ran the state Liberty ticket that had been nominated at the May convention. The newspaper urged Liberty followers to set up local organizations and made special efforts to see that election ballots were distributed.²³² Garrison's followers did not yield without a fight. John A. Collins attempted to rally loyalists in a series of letters about the state society's new orientation. They were immediately answered by Booth and Codding, with Codding finally asserting that "Mr. Collins must be crazy."²³³ Finally, the few Old Organization adherents set up their own organization, the Connecticut American Anti-Slavery Society, and called "for the immediate dissolution of the union."²³⁴ The movement toward the Liberty Party caused some non-Liberty voting abolitionists to leave the Connecticut Anti-Slavery Society because they objected to its Liberty projects.[235]

Liberty leaders attempted to expand the party's nonpolitical base during 1843. Alvan Stewart once again traveled from New York to help set up a Liberty Association in Hartford that included both men and women, and he urged intensified local efforts.[236] At the same time, Whig attempts to bring their former cohorts back from the Liberty Party met with some success.[237] Therefore, Liberty results stagnated in 1843 as the party lost votes (1,872—3.4%) and began to develop pockets of strength in certain towns.[238] Although the party elected only one representative, once again it prevented any candidate from a gubernatorial majority and prevented an election for twenty-nine seats in the state legislature.[239] The Democrats again won the race in the state legislature, angering many Whig antislavery men and delighting some Liberty men who agreed that the Liberty Party had prevented the abolitionist Baldwin from being elected governor.[240]

In 1844 Gillette increased his vote by less than one hundred (1,971—3.2%) while turnout rose over six thousand.[241] Baldwin and the Whigs finally recaptured the state legislature and the governorship, although the gubernatorial election was again decided in the state legislature. Whigs won back some Liberty voters, and some Democrats switched to the Whig or Liberty Party.[242] The Liberty Party elected only one representative and defeated thirty-five legislative races.[243] Baldwin's actions as governor further solidified his base of abolition support as he continued to work for antislavery and the rights of African Americans. Despite attempts to increase the number of Liberty Associations, establish a Tract Society, and develop a more thorough grassroots organization during 1844, the presidential contest made it clear that the party was stagnating. Its results changed little from the spring contest.

Henry Clay (Whig)	32,832 (50.8%)
James K. Polk (Democrat)	29,841 (46.2%)
James G. Birney (Liberty)	1,943 (3.0%)

Once again, some former Democrats voted for the Liberty Party, and some former Whigs were returning to their old party.[244] Some of these former Whigs were influenced by the increased antislavery orientation of the state Whig Party, but others were undoubtedly made uneasy by Birney's campaign statements that had a Democratic tinge to them, his acceptance of a Democratic nomination in his home state, and the Garland Forgery.[245] As the year ended, the state society and its newspaper were in financial trouble. Many who left the Connecticut Anti-Slavery Society because of its identification with the Liberty Party were among its greatest financial backers.[246] Some Connecticut Liberty supporters attended national Liberty gatherings, but only editors Booth, Codding, and William Burleigh had had much impact beyond Connecticut's borders with the notable exception of the hastily called December 1844 national convention immediately after the 1844 election.[247]

The Connecticut Liberty Party grew little after 1844 and changed little in its philosophy or leadership. Efforts to more completely organize the state were not successful, especially after Ichabod Codding and Sherman Booth left the state. Alanson Work, just back in Middletown, Connecticut, from Missouri where he had served three and a half years in prison for aiding fugitives on the Underground Railroad, complained that "I hear of no Liberty meeting—no concerts—no prayer meetings."[248] The *Christian Freeman* bemoaned the lack of organization in its home city of Hartford. Although the paper claimed 1,750 subscriptions in early 1845, it suffered from non-payments and financial difficulties. By the end of the year, the controlling partnership dissolved and the paper closed for "a little breathing spell" that actually signaled its demise.[249]

The party continued to hold state conventions and set up tickets that were similar every year. Gillette declined the nomination for 1846, but he was quickly persuaded to reconsider and remained the party's only gubernatorial candidate for its entire existence.[250] He usually received about two thousand votes, which was usually about 3% of the total. Liberty men would sometimes claim one or two representatives to the state legislature, but those probably won with collusion or cooperation by a major party because Gillette never came close to getting 50% of the vote in any town. More important, many competitive state representative seats went unfilled in every election because no candidate could get a simple majority. This changed early in 1845, when the state legislature "passed an act declaring that in a second trial for the election of representatives, the candidate receiving a *plurality* of all the votes cast, shall be elected."[251] This blunted the effects of the party in such years as 1846, when the Liberty Party again prevented either major party from gaining a gubernatorial majority. Among the stable leadership were several African Americans—such as James W. C. Pennington and Jehiel T. and Amos Gerry Beman—even though they could not vote. There also seems to have been some changes in the voter base. Most analysts agree that the early Liberty Party was primarily Whig based and that it made its major incursions into the Whig Party in 1842 and 1843.[252] If former Whigs did go back to their old party with antislavery Whig Roger Baldwin's candidacy, then perhaps disgruntled Democrats entered the Liberty Party and canceled out these losses. It seems clear, however, that most Connecticut Liberty men welcomed the move into the Free Soil movement.

The party quickly accepted John P. Hale and suggested that he be paired on a ticket with Salmon P. Chase, but they readily accepted the Hale-King ticket at the October 1847 Buffalo convention.[253] This was in keeping with the state policy of less militant antislavery party stances than many neighbors in New York and Massachusetts, correctly realizing that ideological conflict would further thin its ranks. At the Free Soil convention a year later, the Liberty men seem to have stayed with Hale in the initial ballot while eleven other Connecticut delegates voted Van Buren (showing a definite Democratic tinge to the Connecticut delegation). Nonetheless, the state's Liberty men seem to have wholeheartedly accepted his nomination despite some earlier misgivings.[254] Free Soiler Van Buren almost tripled Gillette's spring vote, but his totals were still unimpressive.

Zachary Taylor (Whig)	30,318 (48.6%)
Lewis Cass (Democrat)	27,051 (43.4%)
Martin Van Buren (Free Soil)	5,029 (8.1%)

His increase over the 1,773 votes that Gillette had received seems to have come from the Democrats.[255] As in the earlier Liberty gubernatorial races, the third-party vote was spread over the whole state without having any specific county stand out, although there were certain towns that did exhibit more strength.[256]

Connecticut was a rough place to be an abolitionist even in the mid- and later 1840s, and the threat of violence did not help Liberty recruitment. Levi Yale, the Liberty nominee for lieutenant-governor, and two of his friends who voted the Liberty ticket suffered in their town. "The two were manufacturers, and their shop in the west part of Meriden was burned by incendiaries, incited thereto by the pro-slavery men. All sorts of opprobrium was heaped on Mr. Yale."[257] As late as 1848, William Burleigh, editor of the *Charter Oak,* received a "mob visitation" of about three hundred for joking about some military pageantry.[258] Unsuccessful efforts to promote the suffrage for African Americans demonstrated the anti-black attitudes that permeated the populace. An amendment to the state constitution to eliminate the racial restriction for voting failed miserably, 19,148–5,353, in a referendum in the autumn of 1847 despite the strong approval of Roger Baldwin and some antislavery Whigs and virtually all Liberty voters.[259] The core Liberty membership, especially those in particularly hostile areas, showed courage and resolve under trying conditions in supporting the abolition party year after year. Some of them—most notably Francis Gillette and Joseph R. Hawley—would rise to prominence in national and state politics later in their careers, and several others became prominent in the Republican Party.

RHODE ISLAND

There was no organized Liberty Party in Rhode Island before 1846.[260] In early 1846, after the Dorr War, antislavery voters began to establish a Liberty Party in the state. They confronted obvious difficulties. Beyond the fact that the state's shipping industry had close ties with the South and abolitionism was not popular, Whigs had captured the loyalties of most abolitionists and African Americans when they delivered on their promise to enfranchise African Americans. Nonetheless, efforts to organize a Liberty Party were begun in early 1846, when Joshua Leavitt and some other Massachusetts Liberty men helped organize a convention and set up a ticket for statewide offices.[261] Apparently there were no local organizations and the ticket just provided an electoral outlet for sympathetic voters. The gubernatorial candidate received 160 votes statewide, but held the balance of power in the election.[262]

Similar state conventions followed in January 1847 and March 1848.[263] The core group of organizers was small and changed little, although they managed to establish a weekly newspaper, the (Providence and Woonsocket) *Liberty Advocate*, in early 1847.[264] They formed the heart of the party, served on the state central committee, and rotated candidacies among themselves. A few members would attend important Liberty gatherings, but it is difficult to find accounts of their activities in the Liberty press.[265] They endorsed the Hale-King ticket and continued their support of Hale at the 1848 national Free Soil convention in Buffalo.[266] Nonetheless, the Free Soil Party did not do well in Rhode Island in the presidential election.

Zachary Taylor (Whig)	6,780 (60.8%)
Lewis Cass (Democrat)	3,636 (32.6%)
Martin Van Buren (Free Soil)	729 (6.5%)

In an election where total turnout was over one thousand votes less than in 1844, Whigs continued to dominate the state. As in Connecticut, historian Frederick Blue has said about Rhode Island in the presidential election itself, "the Free Soil vote was too small to be indicative of any clear trend."[267] Nonetheless, it is probably safe to say that the few voters who had left their old parties to vote the Liberty ticket before 1848 voted for Free Soil in the fall and continued into the Republican Party later.

The New England states shared a town-oriented governmental system with annual elections for statewide offices. The Liberty Party had pockets of considerable strength across the upper four New England states, with much less strength in Connecticut and practically none in Rhode Island. The situation was different in the Middle States, where there were less frequent statewide elections and the Liberty strength was concentrated in certain well-defined areas.

6

THE MIDDLE STATES

Politicians in the Middle States worked in a different electoral environment from that in New England. Gubernatorial elections were not annual, and a simple plurality was sufficient for election in all races. These states had diverse geographic, social, and economic characteristics that separated them from each other as well as the rest of the country. In this section of the country, the Liberty Party had a real presence only in parts of New York and a few areas of Pennsylvania.

NEW YORK

An historian of comparative state politics during this period has observed that "[i]n contrast to the relatively simple style of politics that characterize New England, New York politics baffled contemporary observers, as well as later students, by their extraordinary complexity."[1] By the late 1830s, the state's highly organized, competitive two-party system had a high voter turnout, and the 1840s would see several minor parties emerge. New York also had a strong antislavery movement. Abolitionists were numerically strongest in the Upstate region known as the Burned-Over District, which ran along the Erie Canal from Albany to Buffalo, but there was also considerable antislavery activity in the New York City area, where the American Anti-Slavery Society was founded in 1833 and maintained its headquarters.[2] After a mob disrupted an October 1835 convention in Utica that had been called to establish a state society, members reassembled and moved the meeting to Gerrit Smith's nearby home. Smith was so outraged by the mob behavior that he abandoned the colonization movement for the new group.[3] He would become the most important abolitionist in the state.

Soon the issue of antislavery political action was introduced into the society with Upstate abolitionists as the driving force. At a fall 1837 convention, they made it an explicit policy of the state society to question a candidate's positions on slavery-related matters and pledged to withhold their support from those who did not give satisfactory responses. Unfortunately, the strategy backfired the following year when the one candidate who gave favorable antislavery responses seemed to lose votes in the state elections.[4] In some cases abolitionists even set up independent antislavery tickets so they would not have to vote for unsympathetic major-party candidates.[5] By early 1840, Gerrit Smith and most New York abolitionists were convinced that the questioning system was a failure.[6] This added impetus to the attempts of Myron Holley, Alvan Stewart, and others to establish an independent antislavery political party.[7]

Upstate New York leaders of the Liberty Party founded the party, provided some of its most outspoken and articulate leadership, became its moral conscience, and helped to provide its most significant national impact in the election of 1844. At the same time, they quarreled with each other over party dogma and tactics to such an extent that the party seemed to be in almost constant flux. Many Downstate abolitionists, led by William Jay and businessmen Arthur and Lewis Tappan, remained aloof from early party involvement. Even after the untimely death of Myron Holley in early 1841, Upstate still had very capable leadership with Smith, Goodell, Stewart, and William Chaplin, along with African American supporters led by Henry Highland Garnet and Samuel Ringgold Ward. Liberty Party politics in this region have been accurately characterized as "Bible politics," but the Liberty men of Upstate New York were unique in their approaches to politics.

Liberty men gradually developed a rudimentary party organization and made nominations in the months before the November 1840 presidential election. Their efforts produced the largest number of raw votes for the Birney-Earle ticket of any state, 2,943 (0.7%). Most of these votes came from the Burned-Over District, with Madison and Oneida counties accounting for 633 votes. Little statewide activity took place after the 1840 elections until the May 1841 national Liberty convention in New York City. Nonetheless, some Upstate abolitionists held town and county conventions and nominated candidates for local offices, such as alderman, sheriff, and coroner.[8] The party made an important convert when Gerrit Smith persuaded James C. Jackson to give up his opposition to the party and become founding editor of the *Madison County Abolitionist*, a newspaper bankrolled by Smith.[9] Liberty men received an additional boost before the fall elections when the annual meeting of the state antislavery society in September approved the Birney-Morris nomination.[10] Their efforts were rewarded in the fall state elections when Liberty candidates for state senator received at least 5,936 votes and held the balance of power in some counties.[11]

The party continued its advances in 1842. Gerrit Smith hosted the New York

State Liberty Party convention in Peterboro in February. After Smith had unsuccessfully urged sitting Whig antislavery congressman Seth Gates to accept the gubernatorial nomination and refused his own nomination, the convention settled on a Liberty ticket of Alvan Stewart and a former state legislator, Charles O. Shepard. Stewart managed 7,264 votes (1.8%), a 22.4% increase over the totals in the state senate races a year earlier, while both major parties lost votes and the Democrats regained the governor's chair.[12] The relatively modest increase did not discourage Liberty men as the party moved toward the presidential election of 1844. In fact, 1843, a year in which there was no statewide race, would provide the party with its most significant period of growth. The year also saw the accession of William Jay and Lewis Tappan, which would give the party more credibility among Downstate antislavery forces. New York Liberty men had been courting Jay since the party's inception. He brought impeccable antislavery and personal credentials and carried the name of one of the country's founding fathers. Gerrit Smith persuaded him to overcome his reluctance, and he endorsed the Birney-Morris ticket shortly after the Buffalo convention.[13] Tappan had been a problem for Liberty men. He opposed formation of the party in 1840, and anti-Liberty abolitionists continued to invoke his name in arguing against the third party.[14] Even though Tappan quietly voted for Birney, Gerrit Smith chided him that Harrison's election would be his fault because of his "influential and unhappy opposition to independent abolition nominations."[15] Tappan finally gave his endorsement to the Liberty Party and began participating in its affairs by the fall of 1843.[16]

The state party made its most notable gains in the spring 1843 elections. In Gerrit Smith's bailiwick of Smithfield, "it was determined by a handful of individuals, that the town of Smithfield . . . be carried for the slave."[17] They succeeded admirably there and in other local races. Smith and James C. Jackson were elated when the Liberty vote more than tripled from the 580 of the previous year in Madison County with the party winning several local races in Smithfield. Jackson rejoiced that "[t]he day is ours. Smithfield is *redeemed*," and Smith pointed to the importance of town organization as the key to success.[18] The enthusiasm continued as New York hosted the highly successful national Liberty convention in Buffalo in August.

New York Liberty men followed this rousing meeting with their own state convention in Canastota in mid-September. After making plans to erect a monument to deceased party founder Myron Holley and reaffirming support for the Birney-Morris ticket for 1844, the meeting turned contentious. Gerrit Smith had persuaded William Jay to become a party member and then began orchestrating a move to make him the party's gubernatorial nominee for 1844.[19] Despite the endorsement of the *Albany Weekly Patriot,* things did not go the way that Smith had planned.[20] His attempt to nominate Jay set off a heated debate in the convention. As a Liberty newspaper from outside the state observed, "the principle [sic] objection to Judge Jay was that he had never yet demonstrated he was a liberty party man by attending a single Liberty meeting."[21] Alvan Stewart spoke against Jay's nomination and was supported by a large majority. Stewart was renominated with 159 votes over Jay (35) and William Chaplin (42). Shepard again received the nod for lieutenant-governor with 148 votes over Chaplin (27) and Smith (2).[22] Smith was bitter at the rejection of his ideas. He said the behavior of those at the convention "[has] somewhat diminished my expectation of its success. There was immodest self-advancement there—there was slander there—there was perfidy there: and, what is most alarming, the Liberty Party State Convention assembled there voted, if not a sanction of these indecent and guilty exhibitions, certainly no rebuke of them."[23] While these disagreements did not immediately injure the party's unity of purpose, they were a harbinger of difficulties.

Despite his unhappiness, Smith continued to pour his considerable financial resources into an effort to turn out a large vote in Madison County, and he commissioned seven agents to give forty-three lectures during the first week of November. Liberty men elsewhere worked to build on their successes of the spring in the elections for state senators and representatives, efforts that were noticed by some outside the state. Their efforts were rewarded by 16,097 votes statewide, a 121.6% increase from the gubernatorial race a year earlier.[24] Madison was the banner Liberty county with 1,755 votes (26.1%), a 205.7% increase, but other counties in the region showed significant gains, usually at the expense of the Whigs. Six counties gave more than 10% of their vote to Liberty, and seven counties registered more than a 100% gain between 1842 and 1843.[25]

Signs that the Liberty Party may have peaked, however, appeared by early 1844. Gerrit Smith noticed a decline from the November elections in the town meeting in Madison County. He saw a loss of over 200 votes to 1,522, and an increase in only 3 of 14 towns, including his, and he noted that the major parties sometimes combined against the Liberty Party. He urged Liberty men to compete at every level and not to let local concerns distract them from the primary issue of slavery. Despite noticeable drop in party growth, Liberty men continued to contest for local offices with some success.[26]

In 1844 the situation in New York became more confused with the possibility of Texas annexation. When the Democratic Party spurned New York favorite son Martin Van Buren for James K. Polk, a rebellion began brewing in the state. Some Democrats considered bolting to the third party. At the same time,

New York Whigs worked to lure back former Whigs from the Liberty Party by playing up the Texas issue. In mid-summer their efforts were blunted by Henry Clay's Alabama Letters, which caused even Seth Gates to give up hope for the Whigs and to switch his allegiance to the Liberty Party.[27] Some Liberty men did return to the Whig Party because they feared Polk's election, were uneasy with Birney's Democratic-leaning positions on many issues, or questioned his loyalty because of events in Michigan and the Garland Forgery.[28] Some Democrats, on the other hand, could not tolerate Polk's candidacy. Over one hundred Madison County Democrats publicly crossed over to the Liberty Party. Encouraged by Gerrit Smith, leading Democrat John G. Curtis organized a convention and rallied Democrats to support Birney.[29]

Democrats narrowly won the most controversial election in New York history.

Henry Clay (Whig)	232,452 (47.8%)
James K. Polk (Democrat)	237,588 (48.9%)
James G. Birney (Liberty)	15,814 (3.3%)

In an intensely fought election with a high turnout the Liberty raw vote only increased by 245 from the previous November elections.[30] Whigs blamed the Liberty Party for electing Polk, but closer examination of the election returns suggests many unusual factors in the vote. Most important, as Lee Benson and others have pointed out, "[t]he Liberty Party's gains had actually been scored *between presidential years*," not as a result of any massive switch in the 1844 election itself.[31] Nevertheless, the raw statewide vote gives a misleading picture of the stability of the Liberty vote because there was considerable movement among Liberty voters. An examination of the top three Liberty counties of 1843 shows a significant decline in both their numerical and proportional votes between the state senate election in 1843 and the 1844 presidential contest in Madison (1,755 of 6,715 votes—26.1% to 1,311 of 8,842—14.8%), Clinton (716 of 3,224—22.2% to 410 of 4,547—9.0%), and Wyoming (497 of 4,349—11.4% to 442 of 5,298—8.3%) counties.[32] This decline of 805 votes in the three 1843 banner counties alone while the statewide Liberty totals remained constant indicates change at the local level that goes beyond disaffected Democrats replacing former Whigs returning to their old party.

Consistent patterns across the state are difficult to discern, but Liberty men were obviously able to attract sufficient voters—whether dissident Democrats, Whigs, or unaffiliated voters—to hold their numbers statewide despite complaints about poor organization in the eastern Downstate area.[33] Some Democrats undoubtedly voted for Birney, but it is difficult to determine their number or constancy, particularly since the highly respected Silas Wright, who had rejected second spot on the presidential ticket with Polk, ran over 3,500 votes ahead of Polk in the gubernatorial contest. An astute contemporary observer has suggested that some Democrats may just have sat out the presidential election.[34] Nevertheless, the perception among many Whigs was that the Liberty Party had cost Clay the state and the presidency. Whig editor Horace Greeley, who had labored so hard for Clay that "he broke out with a rash of boils at the close of the campaign," was nearly apoplectic and unforgiving. William Birney later recalled that "Mr. Greeley gave orders that Mr. Birney's name should not be mentioned in the [New York] 'Tribune' thereafter . . . His malice only ended with Mr. Birney's death."[35]

This criticism did not bother New York Liberty men. No sooner were the election results tabulated than they issued a call for a national Liberty convention to meet in Albany in December that Liberty men from New York, Massachusetts, and Connecticut dominated. The convention formulated anti-Texas petitions and passed an anti-nativist resolution, but did not attempt to make any nominations.[36] New York delegates undoubtedly had no idea how turbulent the next four years would be.

The history of the Liberty Party in New York after 1844 was the most complex of any state, with the possible exception of New Hampshire. The diverse and quarrelsome factions of the state party worked in a New York political scene that contained nativists, national reformers, and anti-rent activists in a competitive two-party system within which Democrats and Whigs had their own internal divisions. Whigs were especially bitter at the Liberty men, holding them responsible for Henry Clay's loss in the recently completed presidential contest. Nonetheless, there was no dramatic drop in the Liberty vote despite the organizational and ideological problems. It remained almost constant numerically and actually increased its proportion because of a drop in the total turnout. The party also had a large, if not particularly thriving, number of newspapers.[37]

The year 1845 was an interim year when there was no statewide election in New York. Nevertheless, the Liberty Party encountered some problems that would trouble them in subsequent years. Perhaps most important, William Goodell first made a formal proposal to expand the Liberty platform to include non-slavery-related reforms at a Liberty convention in Port Byron in late June.[38] Upstate Liberty leaders had been discussing these ideas for several months and were divided on the issue, with Alvan Stewart and Gerrit Smith opposing and James C. Jackson favoring expansion.[39] Goodell's presentation provoked a long discussion. Ultimately, it "was not adopted by the Convention, but was printed and circulated, and gained adherents."[40] The oft-heated situation in New York was noticed by many outside the state because of the important persons involved. A Michigan correspondent chided them: "Hope you New York Abolitionists won't turn cannibals and eat one another up . . . Be careful, or we Wolverines will have to 'stir you up with a long pole.'"[41] For the time being, though, all remained in the Liberty Party and vigorously campaigned in the 1845 local elections. Local campaigning was a great strength of the Liberty Party in New York. There were fairly independent islands of Liberty strength that contained strong leadership. Where many other states' gatherings had relatively uniform structures and resolutions, New York Liberty meetings exhibited a variety of procedures and positions on issues. The intense activity paid off in the fall elections for the state legislature. With 15,754 votes for state senators, the party came within 60 votes of the presidential total a year earlier and actually gave the party its highest statewide percentage (4.7%) ever.[42]

A new problem that struck at the heart of the Liberty ideology, however, accelerated divisions in 1846 and shoved disagreements over expanding the party into the background temporarily. New York Liberty men, particularly those Upstate, were some of the most outspoken on matters of party purity in refusing to cooperate with major-party politicians because they tolerated slaveholders in their membership. Upstate New York was a home to the come-outer and Union Church movements, and these abolitionists transferred their views on ecclesiastical matters to the political realm. "No union with slaveholders or those in political fellowship with them" served as a battle cry for their politics, but political realities forced Liberty men to reassess their positions in the light of unforeseen circumstances. The issue was suffrage for New York African Americans.[43] New York blacks could not vote unless they met a two hundred fifty-dollar property qualification, which relatively few of them could. The question became whether Liberty men should cooperate with Whigs and Democrats who might be in favor of eliminating this restriction. Liberty men stood little chance of being elected on their own, and, even more alarming, their candidates might divide the pro-suffrage vote and result in the election of candidates who were against expanding black suffrage.

Liberty men divided on the question, especially after many of their African American allies urged an alliance with pro-suffrage advocates in the major parties. This put Liberty followers in a very difficult position. As the *Albany Patriot* accurately foresaw, the issue "marks a wide difference of radical principle among us, which sooner or later must produce collision."[44] Liberty leaders, newspapers, and conventions divided on the issue. Smith, Goodell, Jackson and the *Albany Patriot*, and most future Liberty Leaguers saw it as a matter of principle and held firm against any electoral cooperation with those outside the party. Alvan Stewart, Wesley Bailey, the *Liberty Press,* the *Herkimer Freeman,* and many African Americans were willing to support pro-suffrage candidates of any political affiliation.[45] Purists were disappointed that some Liberty men stepped aside for Whig candidates.[46] The results left Liberty men discouraged. Smith lamented that "the Liberty Party of this County [Madison] is ruined . . . In flinging away its principles, it has flung away its power for good. It has chopped off its own hands and feet. It lies a monument of suicidal madness and folly, exposed to the jeers and scorn of every passer-by."[47] The *Albany Patriot* declared that "'the Liberty party is in ruin,' so far as the State of New York is concerned."[48] This was not entirely true, but individual relations would never be as harmonious as they once were.

New York Liberty men, though, were resilient. They quickly regrouped, continued their debates over whether to extend their platform, organized for the fall gubernatorial election, and worked to extend the vote to all African Americans on the same basis as white citizens in a referendum set up by the constitutional convention. Those intent on making the Liberty Party a general reform organization continued to work to expand the party platform at the same time as the dispute erupted over whether to cooperate with outsiders in selecting delegates to the constitutional convention. Their position on the antislavery interpretation of the U.S. Constitution was not controversial, however, because it had become virtually a part of the Liberty creed in the state after 1844.[49] Future Liberty Leaguers accepted this interpretation along with their most vocal critic, Alvan Stewart, who was one of its architects and earliest proponents. Conventions in the state did not always follow the same, or sometimes any, legal reasoning, but most adopted an antislavery interpretation that allowed the federal government to abolish slavery in the states.

More troubling to some were the additional reforms that the expansionists wished to graft onto the party.[50] A year after their initial meeting in Port Byron, they met at a Liberty Party convention in Farmington to put their group on a more formal footing. They formed a "Liberty League," but it should be emphasized that they considered it an internal reform founded "to secure a more thorough organization of Liberty men and a more secure prosecution of the Liberty cause."[51] They lamented the losses during the confusion over the selection of delegates to the constitutional convention. The *Albany Patriot* published an editorial that argued "that all who would value the liberation either of *white* men or of *colored* men, should unite with us in resuscitating our 'scattered and peeled' Liberty party, 'terrible from the beginning hitherto,' and wielding it for the overthrow of *all aristocracies,* and the consequent freedom and security of all men."[52]

The convention approved a series of positions very similar to those proposed by Goodell a year earlier and more recently by Theodore Foster, Guy Beckley, and James G. Birney in Michigan. It urged Liberty Leaguers to set up auxiliaries in each town, and soon James C. Jackson and Charles C. Foote, a Presbyterian minister from Michigan, made plans to tour the state as Liberty League agents.[53] Several important Liberty leaders were still strongly opposed to the changes. Alvan Stewart, Wesley Bailey, William Jay, and Lewis Tappan continued to oppose moving away from one-ideaism, and Gerrit Smith continued to believe "that the time is not yet come to attempt it."[54]

All the elements of the party again pulled together as the 1846 gubernatorial election approached. They gathered in their state convention in Canastota on September 9 to select candidates and prepare for the upcoming election. Gerrit Smith was unable to attend, but he sent a letter endorsing William Jay for governor.[55] The differences within the party showed in the vote for the gubernatorial nominee. Six candidates received at least six votes on the first ballot before Henry Bradley, a Penn Yan merchant not directly involved in the internal disputes, increased his totals over three ballots before the convention nominated him unanimously on the fourth. William L. Chaplin, a Liberty League sympathizer who also sympathized with the anti-rent movement, received the nomination for lieutenant-governor. The convention recommended that the black suffrage question be referred to the people separate from the new constitution. It also went on record favoring a discussion of all issues in Liberty Party newspapers. Slavery was still the "paramount" issue, but "we by no means lose sight of *other questions.*"[56] Bradley and Chaplin received an additional endorsement from the National Reform Association, a group of utopian land reformers led by George Evans, when they gave satisfactory answers to a series of questions.[57]

The election results were disappointing for the Liberty candidates despite an active campaign. In an election complicated not only by major-party internal squabbles but also nativist and anti-rent interests, the Liberty gubernatorial candidate received 12,844 votes (3.2%), almost 3,000 less than in the 1844 presidential contest.[58] There was a shifting in the Liberty base of support, however, as declines in former areas of Liberty strength were matched by gains in new areas.[59] More upsetting for Liberty men was the vote on the suffrage referendum. That voters soundly defeated equal suffrage 224,336–85,406 must have had a chilling effect on the Liberty men who had recently called for the popular vote on the issue in their state convention.[60] They became aware, perhaps for the first time, of the widespread depth of anti-black sentiment in the state and that their beliefs were probably doomed to minority status.

Gerrit Smith pondered the events since the 1844 election and gradually came to agree with the Liberty Leaguers. Coalition politics in New Hampshire, the increasing popularity of John P. Hale as a possible Liberty presidential candidate, and the willingness of many New York Liberty men to break party ranks to unite with major-party candidates on specific issues caused Smith to reconsider his earlier position.[61] He moved from his former position that the Liberty Party was a temporary organization to a belief that it had to be considered a permanent party.[62] Goodell, however, saw the problem clearly. He realized that the Liberty Party would be "superseded" by another party if it did not expand its voter base. He preferred to maintain party integrity and broaden its ideological base.[63] In the spring of 1847 the Liberty League was not yet a separate political party but considered itself still a part of the Liberty Party. For instance, the *Albany Patriot*, the leading newspaper in favor of the League philosophy, endorsed Salmon P. Chase for president. Chase's views on the antislavery nature of the Constitution and on cooperating with antislavery elements in the major parties were further from Liberty League ideals than those of almost any party leader.[64] Even when Goodell and Jackson issued the call for the historic convention in Macedon Lock, William L. Chaplin, a Liberty League stalwart, did not agree with its move directly into politics "as to its timeliness or necessity."[65]

This convention in Macedon Lock in early June put the Liberty League on a formal footing as a political party. Both Goodell and Jackson urged Birney to become the party's nominee. He declined for health reasons but assured them that he would support the convention and its nominee.[66] The convention reiterated stands taken the previous year in Farmington and formally set up a political organization separate from the Liberty Party. It nominated a presidential ticket of Gerrit Smith, who had just recently been converted, and Elihu Burritt, a peace advocate from Massachusetts, who was out of the country (he immediately declined).[67] A key issue in the break from the main body of the Liberty Party was the concern over the permanence of an uncompromising antislavery party. Smith was converted when he finally accepted Goodell's arguments that the Liberty Party was heading toward an absorption in a larger movement. The Liberty League considered itself to be a permanent party not interested in coalition or wooing the likes of John P. Hale as its candidate. The new permanent party wanted to go beyond abolition to change the political system and reform the social-economic environment.

Liberty Leaguers did not, however, nominate candidates against regular Liberty nominees, and they continued to participate in some local, state, and national Liberty Party meetings and conventions. They tried to bring the party around to their way of thinking, but they were able to convince only a minority (perhaps 20%) in New York and very few elsewhere. Of the state's Liberty newspapers, only the *Albany Patriot*, the (Cortland) *True American*, and Goodell's *Christian Investigator* supported the new party in New York, and most Liberty men and newspapers actively opposed it.[68] Except for its few prominent leaders, most strong supporters of the party were not well known outside their own areas.[69] Little evidence exists of strictly Liberty League activity.

Divisions between Liberty Leaguers and mainline Liberty Party members existed in New York, and often became very personal. Beriah Green, the intelligent but irascible former head of Oneida Institute, had a particular problem with Alvan Stewart, the popular and hardworking national Liberty chairman. Stewart's criticism of his views stung him, and his resentment came out in a letter to James G. Birney describing his treatment at a meeting of the New York State Anti-Slavery Society. He complained that "Mr. Pierpont [poet and Liberty activist from Massachusetts] was invited, I presume by Mr. Stewart, to employ his power in putting me down. The whole meeting with its various arrangements was, apparently, *managed*, with reference to this design . . . When I spoke, once especially, Mr. S., tho' chairman, turned away, so as to present his imposing rump, affecting to sleep or read a newspaper! . . . They [the actions] show, however, the state of things among us."[70] Green and other Liberty Leaguers were moving out of the mainstream of the national Liberty Party and becoming a splinter group of an already small party. They were relevant to Liberty Party development only in New York, and the vast majority of Liberty men everywhere held the one-idea concept. When Green berated the respected James G. Carter, who had been president of the North-Western Liberty Convention in Chicago, for allowing non-Liberty men to participate in it, he showed how far his views were from most Liberty men. Carter shot back that he resented Green's attempt "somewhat rudely, to swing your party lash over me."[71] Most Liberty newspapers outside New York either ignored the Leaguers or mentioned them only in passing, and in Upstate New York the *Liberty Press* even refused to publish the Liberty League proceedings and agenda.[72]

Once again, however, Liberty voters still came together at election time. A September 29, 1847, state Liberty convention at Syracuse nominated a candidate for lieutenant-governor (the only statewide race), again selecting Charles O. Shepard, who was not clearly aligned with any faction. It also appointed both Gerrit Smith and Alvan Stewart as delegates to the October national convention.[73] Aided by support from the National Reformers and some anti-rent groups, Shepard ran ahead of the rest of the Liberty ticket, and his 13,429 votes (4.1%) actually improved the Liberty vote over Henry Bradley's gubernatorial total a year earlier.[74]

The split between the Liberty League sympathizers and the regular New

York Liberty Party grew wider after the 1847 national Liberty convention rejected League positions, endorsed a watered-down Liberty platform, and resoundingly nominated John P. Hale over Gerrit Smith for president. It became even more serious when the main body of Liberty men, encouraged by Henry B. Stanton, who had recently moved his law practice from Massachusetts to New York, began to work closely with the Barnburner wing of the New York Democratic Party. By the late spring of 1848, Liberty Leaguers became more aggressive in divorcing themselves from the main body of the party. In a series of meetings and conventions they made it clear that they could not support a ticket headed by someone whom they did not consider a true abolitionist. Their movement proceeded upon two parallel lines: the original Liberty League held gatherings and a Gerrit Smith–dominated group acted along a similar but separate political path.

Smith soon began to make a formal break from the regular Liberty Party.[75] He viewed the Hale nomination as a tactic "to draw off scores of thousands of votes" from the major parties and, as a result, cause the party to abandon some of its strong positions on the antislavery nature of the U.S. Constitution and against supporting non–Liberty Party members.[76] He declined Lewis Tappan's request that he contribute money to help send Henry B. Stanton and John Greenleaf Whittier to Washington, D.C., "to cooperate with Messrs. Hale, Palfrey, Giddings and Tuck in the promotion of the antislavery cause" because he disagreed with their positions on the constitutionality of slaveholding and on working with members of the major parties.[77] He was harsher in his criticism of the New Hampshire Liberty Party for its "treason to Liberty Party principles." He supported a meeting in Auburn, New York, in January 1848 that called for a June convention in Buffalo and reiterated his endorsement of the convention in his privately published letter on New Hampshire. He declared that the meeting would nominate a presidential ticket and outline "the principles of a true Civil Government and a true Liberty Party."[78]

The Liberty League held its own meeting in Rochester two weeks before the Buffalo convention and formally nominated Charles C. Foote to run with Smith on a presidential ticket and set up a state ticket headed by William Goodell.[79] Two weeks later, 104 delegates of what became known as the National Liberty Party met in Buffalo.[80] New Yorkers dominated the convention, although a few attendees came from Ohio, Michigan, and Massachusetts.[81] There were also a number of observers, including several New York Barnburners.[82] The meeting began with nominations for the presidential ticket. Smith received 99 of the 104 first ballot votes, and his selection was quickly made unanimous. Nine individuals initially received support for vice president, including 5 votes for Lucretia Mott and 12 for African American Samuel Ringgold Ward, but Charles C. Foote was elected unanimously on the second ballot, thus duplicating the national ticket selected at the Liberty League convention.

Convention resolutions took aim at Liberty men working for coalition with the antislavery elements of the major parties, especially Ohioans Salmon P. Chase, Samuel Lewis, Stanley Matthews, and Gamaliel Bailey, along with special criticism for the *National Era* and the *Emancipator.* They were singled out for their betrayal of Liberty principle in the 1847 national convention "that virtually abandoned the Liberty Party, by its nomination to the Presidency of John P. Hale, who holds not a single one of the distinctive principles of that Party." The convention declared that the party "has not been organized for any temporary purpose" and "has not been organized merely for the overthrow of slavery . . . but will also carry out the principles of equal rights into all their practical consequences and applications." It endorsed land reform, opposed the "infernal war" with Mexico, and supported the "unwillingness to use the products of slave labor."

The convention address was an explication of what has come to be known as "Bible politics." It described the duty of government to protect the rights that "all come from Him, who is the Author, both of Civil Government and of our being," including in these women's property rights and suffrage. It made clear that they believed the suffrage was "to select under the Divine Guidance, the ruler. But it is not to control the ruler . . . [who] is to rule in the fear, not of men, but of God—not as the tool of men but as 'the minister of God.' Hence the absurdity and atheism of the popular doctrine, that the ruler is bound by the will of his constituents. He is to do right, whether they consent, or no; and he is never to take it for granted, that the voice of the people is the voice of God." The two strands—the Liberty League and the National Liberty Party—of these Bible politics finally came together in a single organization at a September 28 convention in Canastota, where "they adopted documents defining the platform of the Liberty League, which has not, since that time, maintained a separate organization."[83] This circle of true believers had virtually no impact outside the state, and they were a small minority, probably never more than 20%, of the former Liberty voters in New York.[84]

Most other Liberty voters moved easily into the Free Soil coalition. Former Liberty men were not as prominent in the Free Soil movement in New York as in some other states because its backbone was the ready-made Barnburner Democratic machine with its favorite son presidential candidate. Most Liberty men and newspapers in the state had supported the Hale-King ticket, and they continued to do so at the beginning of the Free Soil convention. Twenty-nine delegates backed the Hale nomination on the preliminary ballot, but almost all the non–Liberty League members eventually supported and campaigned for the Van Buren–Adams ticket in November. On September 13 the regular Liberty Party met in Utica for its last convention at the same time that the state Free Soil convention was meeting there. Under the leadership of their frequent candidate for lieutenant-governor, Charles O. Shepard, all except three delegates voted to support Van Buren, commenting that "it would be unjust to judge of men who we now find standing upon our noble platform."[85] They adjourned and walked down the street to the Free Soil convention, where they saw one of their own, former Whig congressman and Liberty convert Seth Gates, nominated for lieutenant-governor.[86]

Van Buren received 120,510 votes (26.4%), over 41% of his national total.

Zachary Taylor (Whig)	218,603 (47.9%)
Lewis Cass (Democrat)	114,320 (25.1%)
Martin Van Buren (Free Soil)	120,510 (26.4%)
Gerrit Smith (Liberty League)	2,545 (0.6%)
Other	73

The Free Soil vote came chiefly from Democrats, most of those still remaining in the regular Liberty Party, and relatively few antislavery Whigs, most of whom remained with William Seward and supported Taylor and New York vice presidential candidate Millard Fillmore.[87] Gerrit Smith did retain 2,545 Liberty votes, but most of the rest supported Van Buren and did not sit out the election. Former Democrats soon healed their breach with their intrastate rivals in the Democratic Party. By 1852, the Free Democrats, as third-party followers were now known, retained barely one in five of their 1848 totals and were "reduced to the old Liberty element plus Whigs who joined in 1848 or 1852."[88]

The New York Liberty Party and its members continues to be the most studied of the state parties, but it was not representative of the party elsewhere. Its large Upstate contingent was one of the most uncompromising abolition groups in the country, and even there its many talented leaders were often divided among themselves. Too often, however, the philosophy and actions of this segment of Liberty men has been seen as a microcosm of the party nationally. Instead, the intensely introspective, uncompromising nature of its members made them a devoted but unique element in the Liberty movement. After the decline of the Free Soil movement, most eventually made their way into the Republican Party.

In the interim some remained in antislavery politics and even contributed to the election of Gerrit Smith to the U.S. Congress.

PENNSYLVANIA

Pennsylvania's party system was fully developed by 1840. Although the Democrats captured the gubernatorial races in 1838 and 1841, Harrison had carried the state in the presidential election of 1840 by only 350 votes. Democrats continued to win gubernatorial races, but presidential races remained very competitive.[89]

The state also had a long history of antislavery activity. The antislavery writings of John Woolman and others predated the incorporation of the Pennsylvania Abolition Society in 1789 with Benjamin Franklin as its first president.[90] The American Anti-Slavery Society itself had been formed in Philadelphia in 1833, and the state had one of the country's best and longest-lived antislavery newspapers in the *Pennsylvania Freeman*.[91] Pennsylvania abolitionism then developed into two distinct movements divided along regional lines. The Pennsylvania Anti-Slavery Society, which had been formed in 1837, soon split into eastern and western districts. The subsequent Liberty organizations evolved along the same regional lines, and the result would be two very different types of organizations. The eastern Liberty group was never very successful and would probably have been nonexistent if it did not have a few committed leaders. The western group was a more vibrant organization with talented leaders, a female journalist, a base of African American non-voting support, and a few pockets of deep support.

Abolitionists were not involved in electoral politics during the 1830s. There was no concerted questioning of candidates for office, perhaps because a substantial number of abolitionists were non-voting Quakers or African Americans, who lost the vote with the 1838 state constitution. This frustrated *Pennsylvania Freeman* editor John Greenleaf Whittier, who criticized voters who refused to break with party candidates who were not antislavery. He said, "[T]hey undo on the day of election all which they have done for the bondsmen in the other 364 days of the year . . . The unfaithfulness of so many of our number neutralizes in a great degree even the moral influence of the honest and upright."[92] Most Pennsylvania abolitionists opposed a third party. Several local conventions came out against independent nominations.[93] Pennsylvanian Francis J. LeMoyne had refused the vice presidential nomination of the November 1839 Warsaw (N.Y.) convention. He felt that "[o]ur enterprise is emphatically religious. The means we employ ought to be consistent, and in perfect keeping. At all events our *principal* ought to have that character."[94] The *Pennsylvania Freeman*, now under new editors, published the call for the April 1 Albany convention, but it stated that the executive committee "does not desire to exercise any official influence on the subject, and we do not even know the views of the majority of its members."[95] No Pennsylvanian participated in the Albany convention, although Thomas Earle sent a letter of support.[96] Earle was nominated for vice president on the national ticket, but waited almost two months before accepting because he wanted to make sure that the movement had a wider base of support.[97] The independent ticket met almost immediate opposition in Pennsylvania. Approximately two hundred members attending the annual meeting of the eastern branch of the Pennsylvania Anti-Slavery Society voted down the Albany nominations by a 3–1 margin. An editor's assessment that "[t]he voice of South Eastern Pennsylvania, then, is almost unanimous against the third party" was probably accurate.[98] Particular attention was given to Thomas Earle. He was the butt of a poem because of his political activities.

> Thomas Earle, Thomas Earle
> Oh, cast not the pearl
> Of our cause in the partisan's trough,
> When the people discern
> The truth clearly, they'll turn
> From political slops and such stuff.
> Thomas Earle!
> From political slops and such stuff.[99]

Nonetheless, there was some activity. Philadelphia third-party men met in early June, and independent nominating conventions also met elsewhere and set up electoral tickets.[100] By mid-October there was an electoral ticket and a Pennsylvania senatorial ticket.[101] Some voting abolitionists were trying a questioning system, but independent nominations gained more support as the election neared. *Pennsylvania Freeman* publisher James Miller McKim announced his support and participated in political meetings to make arrangements for the election.[102] Nevertheless, a lively debate continued in the pages of the *Pennsylvania Freeman* throughout the fall.

Not surprisingly, the independent ticket fared poorly. The party received at least 343 votes (0.1%) spread across 25 counties, including 107 in Philadelphia.[103] Most of the remainder came from the western region. Liberty men had to decide if they were going to take steps to make the party permanent. In the eastern part, it appeared that any action was going to have to take place outside the Pennsylvania Anti-Slavery Society. There was a strong segment within it opposed to either political action or the Liberty Party. Even Thomas Earle took the position that the state society should not become involved in governmental affairs.[104]

Nevertheless, Liberty men decided to put the party on a more stable basis. They received an important endorsement from Dr. Francis Julius LeMoyne, a physician from western Pennsylvania, who "had become convinced that the procedure was sound, and was throwing in his fortunes with the party."[105] He would serve as the party's gubernatorial candidate in 1841, 1844, and 1847, a congressional candidate in 1843, a newspaper editor, and an active lecturer in the western part of the state.

Most Liberty activity took place in the west. A Liberty Party did exist in the East, but it had little organization and had no regular newspaper. The disapproval of *Pennsylvania Freeman* editor C. C. Burleigh and the lukewarm support of publisher James Miller McKim hampered its development. McKim continued to "advocate the concentration of votes . . . in the great elections which bring out the strength of the whole state," but not "to embark as political partizans, or to organize themselves into a distinct party."[106] The *Pennsylvania Freeman* would sometimes endorse Liberty candidates, but it denied that it was a Liberty Party newspaper.[107] Voting abolitionists instituted a sporadic questioning system that had little success.[108] A few strong Liberty advocates—Earle, merchant Samuel D. Hastings, and educator Charles Dexter Cleveland—kept the party alive in the east; but internal bickering between Old and New organizations, declining antislavery activism among Philadelphia African Americans, and continuing disagreements over political methods resulted in a weak Liberty effort.[109] Eastern and western Liberty men shared party control. They split electoral tickets and had equal input on other offices, but the real leadership for the state party was in the west. For instance, when leaders pushed some anti-tariff positions in the eastern convention, LeMoyne refused to accept the gubernatorial nomination until they were dropped.[110]

Voting strength for the Liberty Party was concentrated in a few western areas where the party was more firmly established and developed a unique organization with talented leaders. Perhaps most important was the founding of the (Pittsburgh) *Spirit of Liberty* by the executive committee of the Western Pennsylvania Anti-Slavery Society with Edward Smith, a Methodist minister, as editor. Ostensibly, it "professe[d] not to identify itself with the third party," but it in effect became a Liberty paper.[111] Although they did not have the franchise, members of the Pittsburgh African American community and their newspaper, the (Pittsburgh) *Mystery* under young Martin Delany, supported the Liberty effort.[112] While the leaders in the east were older, established professionals, those in the west were a blend of experience and youth.[113] In addition to LeMoyne, the west had a hardworking leadership that included politically experienced former Whig officeholder and physician Dr. William Elder, Reese C. Fleeson of the *Spirit of Liberty*, prominent Pittsburgh physician Dr. Joseph Gazzam, and

Delany. The chairman of the western state committee was Russell Errett, who was beginning a long career in newspaper work and politics that would eventually see him serving three terms in the U.S. Congress.

The Pennsylvania Liberty Party did not reach its peak until 1844. In the 1841 gubernatorial race, LeMoyne only received 763 of 250,763 votes statewide, although the party did make some advances in the west. Only twenty-three scattering votes indicated that abolitionists voted Liberty, stayed with a major party, or sat out the election.[114] The party achieved its greatest increases in the next gubernatorial election, which took place in 1844 shortly before the presidential contest. This was the result of a concerted effort in both parts of the state. A convention in each section met on February 22, 1844, and coordinated their meetings to nominate LeMoyne for governor and Cleveland for the U.S. Senate.[115] The western group encouraged local nominations. The eastern party was not inactive, as Professor Cleveland wrote a lengthy address to the voters of the state that went through three printings of twenty thousand copies apiece and was distributed throughout the entire state.[116] It was more secular in tone than many Liberty publications with only a few references to religious themes. It contained harsh denunciations of Polk and Clay, praised Birney and Morris, reviewed the outstanding character of LeMoyne, and developed a long argument on the power of the South in the national government. Stating that the "GREAT OBJECT OF THE LIBERTY PARTY . . . in the words of the Constitution, 'TO ESTABLISH JUSTICE, TO SECURE THE BLESSINGS OF LIBERTY,'" the party demanded the "ABSOLUTE AND UNQUALIFIED DIVORCE OF THE GENERAL GOVERNMENT FROM ALL CONNECTION WITH SLAVERY."[117] Later the eastern men held other conventions and eventually nominated and "put in nomination a complete ticket, from Congressmen down to Auditor, [and] appointed a vigilance committee in every town." Among the nominees for Congress was David Potts, who had served four terms in the U.S. House of Representatives (1831–1839).[118] Shortly after another eastern convention on August 13, the Liberty men established a newspaper, the *Liberty Herald*, in time for the campaign.[119]

Organizational efforts were much more intense and successful in the west, but the western segment of the party also developed along different ideological lines.[120] In addition to the African American component and its (Pittsburgh) *Mystery*, the region supported at least three other Liberty newspapers—the (Pittsburgh) *Spirit of Liberty*, the (Indiana, Pa.) *Clarion of Freedom*, and the former Whig *Mercer Luminary*.[121] Unlike many of their fellow party men in other areas, however, western Pennsylvania Liberty men strongly supported a high tariff and made it their official Liberty policy. A Liberty convention for Allegheny County in Pittsburgh declared "we have no sympathy with the free trade doctrines" or "confidence in the fluctuating, uncertain, imperfect and compromising revenue policy of the Whig Party." It stated that "such protection as our industry requires ... must be neither incidental nor accidental, but positive, certain, permanent and direct, based upon the principle of protection."[122] This could cause some problems for James G. Birney, who was rumored to be in favor of a low tariff. When Russell Errett queried him because the issue was so important in his area, which "is a Tariff region," that "[o]ne of the greatest men in Pennsylvania,—nay one of the first men of this age—a whole souled Liberty man—[former U.S. Senator and Secretary of the Treasury] *Walter Forward,* will not go with us now, solely on account of his devotion to the Tariff."[123] Birney's reply that "a tariff for revenue to meet the ordinary expenditures of the government will have to be the rule" was not well received. Errett withheld it from publication because "there are many men enlisted under one banner, conscientious men, who might be offended, or estranged."[124]

During the summer the western party, chiefly under the leadership of William Elder, began to forge alliances with the remnant of the workingmen's movement in Pittsburgh. Elder, an early Liberty organizer and an original thinker, was not comfortable with many of the old-line abolitionists and Liberty leaders. In a letter to Salmon P. Chase, he complained that "[i]f they were forced to choose between their antislavery sentiments and their anti-Irish prejudices [they] would sooner send the niggers to Hell than go to Heaven with the catholics."[125] Westerners worked hard before the election. Errett toured through twenty-nine counties, and LeMoyne gave many speeches and distributed over three thousand antislavery tracts.[126] LeMoyne also combined upward revision of the tariff with an appeal to workingmen, asking them to "[j]udge then a just judgment betwixt the Liberty party & the other parties in this matter which may claim your suffrage as the true friends of the protection of *home industry.*"[127] Westerners were optimistic. Chairman Errett estimated that "Western Pa. Hitherto, most of it, uncultivated Liberty ground, will give 5000 votes for us."[128] He was too optimistic, as the party barely drew half of that statewide. LeMoyne received 2,576 votes (0.8%), including 10 for "J. J. LeMoyne." Birney only increased that to 3,152.[129]

Henry Clay (Whig)	160,384 (48.4%)
James K. Polk (Democrat)	167,394 (50.6%)
James G. Birney (Liberty)	3,152 (1.0%)

While this disappointed Liberty men, it was a substantial increase over the 763 votes that LeMoyne had received in 1841. The results showed that the Liberty strength was concentrated in the west. Eleven western, two northeastern, and two southeastern counties that gave the third party at least 50 votes. These 15 of 58 counties totaled 2,578 of 3,152 Birney-Morris votes, showing that there were pockets of strength instead of the Liberty vote being evenly distributed. This was true within counties as well. With the exception of the two northeastern counties—which were probably influenced by the antislavery activity in the Burned-Over District of New York directly to their north—the party had little strength elsewhere.

After 1844, the Native American Party further complicated Pennsylvania electoral politics. The day before the state nativist convention, the Liberty Party held its own convention for eastern Pennsylvania. Delegates quickly distanced themselves from the anticlericalism and disunionism of the Garrisonians and the *Pennsylvania Freeman* that were strong in that area. Delegates requested "an intelligent community to decide between us, who are seeking the emancipation of the slave by legal and peaceful means, and them whose labors are directed, with whatever object, to the overthrow of the Union and the Constitution and who bitterly denounce the ministers and churches of the land."[130] After briefly discussing Negro and women's suffrage, the convention's discussions critical of nativism "were received with cheers intermingled with dissent."[131] Gubernatorial candidate LeMoyne had already condemned the anti-Catholic Philadelphia riots of 1844 and gone on record as opposed to nativism, and western Pennsylvania Liberty leader Elder spoke of them with disdain.[132] The convention asserted that the use of the ballot box for antislavery ends was "moral action of the highest order," and established the *American Citizen*, with Lucius C. Matlack as editor, as a Liberty newspaper for the eastern part of the state.[133] Alvan Stewart came from New York for the convention and rejoiced that the eastern Pennsylvania Liberty men had finally broken with the nonresistant Old Organization.[134] This emphatic repudiation of the Old Organization's cherished principles and the founding of a competitive newspaper caused a much more open split in eastern Pennsylvania abolition. Thomas Earle's denunciation of disunionism received a reply from *Pennsylvania Freeman* editor Charles C. Burleigh, who subsequently refused to publish Earle's rebuttal or Joseph Gibbons's defense of Earle.[135] Then the Eighth Meeting of the Eastern Pennsylvania Anti-Slavery Society on August 11 supported a disunionist position by a 442–188 vote, driving most Liberty men from the society.[136]

The real strength of the Liberty Party continued to be in western Pennsylvania with its eclectic programs and talented leadership. The party's candidate for canal commissioner, an important statewide race in 1845, was William Larimer, a businessman from Allegheny County, who gave the Pennsylvania Liberty Party the highest percentage that it would ever achieve despite finishing fourth in the statewide tally with a mere 2,851 votes (1.2%).[137] The Liberty Party held its totals better than the major parties, but it was becoming obvious that the party had limited appeal in the Quaker State. Its leaders faced a formidable task with a geographically divided party in a confused political environment. This became obvious in 1846, when they lost over seven hundred votes in the election for canal commissioner the following year.[138]

Pennsylvania Liberty men confronted the same major problems as their colleagues did nationally in trying to develop a consistent party creed. The question of the nature of the U.S. Constitution on the powers over slavery, however, did not cause debate among Liberty men in the state. The party in both sections went on record as wanting to divorce the national government from slavery, "leaving it as it ought to be, if it exists at all, merely a local, State institution."[139] No movement to declare the Constitution an antislavery document seems to have developed. Attitudes toward expanding the platform were more mixed. Responding to the "Michigan Circular" of (Mich.) *Signal of Liberty* editors Guy Beckley and Theodore Foster that sought to broaden the platform, the *Washington Patriot* and the *American Citizen* came out firmly against it.[140] The *Spirit of Liberty*, on the other hand, was not only for it but wished it expanded even further to include distribution of public lands to the landless and "to unite the friends of reform, on the true Democratic platform—'*Equal Rights to* ALL.'"[141] These views, however, did not cause any disruption in party unity.

More troublesome was the continuing willingness of some Liberty leaders to work with the major parties. Although some form of collusion took place in lower-level races in many states, the Pennsylvania Liberty Party occasionally questioned major-party candidates. When a Liberty meeting in Pittsburgh in late February 1847 set up a committee to interrogate nominees of the Whigs and Democrats before the state Liberty convention in Harrisburg, it received a rebuke from some Liberty men outside the state. When Pittsburgh was suggested as a good place for a national Liberty convention, the *Emancipator* objected "because a convention lately held there, has indicated a disposition to offer the Liberty Party up to the Whigs, provided they will only nominate Northern candidates, who are willing to give proper answers to certain inconclusive questions."[142]

Whatever the intentions of the Liberty men in Pittsburgh, the major parties did not take their offer very seriously. When the state Liberty Party convention met in Harrisburg in early June, the delegates found that all but one candidate rejected their overtures, and he gave unsatisfactory answers.[143] The convention came out strongly against the Mexican War and renominated LeMoyne for governor for the fall 1847 election. A vote on the proper time for holding a national convention split the party almost right down the middle between hard-line Liberty men desiring a late 1847 convention and those who wished to expand the party's base preferring a meeting in the spring of 1848. The presence of both the Native American and Liberty parties makes the results of the election difficult to analyze.¹⁴⁴ The Democratic Party rebounded from a stunning Whig performance in 1846. The Native American Party lost over 50% of its vote from the previous year, and the Liberty Party continued the decline that had begun in 1846, losing over one-third of its total since its peak 1845 performance and receiving only 1,861 votes (0.6%).¹⁴⁵

By the end of the year, it was clear that the Liberty Party was in poor shape. The state's Liberty newspapers had financial difficulties, even in the west, where the party had some strength. In 1847 William Elder moved to Philadelphia to start the *Liberty Herald* to replace the defunct *American Citizen*, and by January 1848 both the *Spirit of Liberty* and the *Mystery*, the African American publication, were no longer in business.¹⁴⁶ The (Pittsburgh) *Albatross* succeeded the *Spirit of Liberty* in the fall of 1847 under the auspices of antislavery writer and poet Charles S. Shiras.¹⁴⁷ Then Jane Grey Swisshelm, who had written occasional pieces for the *Spirit of Liberty*, founded the (Pittsburgh) *Saturday Visiter* to fill the void left by the short-lived *Albatross*.¹⁴⁸

Pennsylvania Liberty adherents were ready for a larger movement. The convention of the Liberty Party in the eastern part of the state showed this when, after endorsing John P. Hale for president, its resolutions approved the possibility for participation in a larger movement. Liberty men participated actively in the Free Soil Buffalo convention, where the Pennsylvania delegation narrowly selected Van Buren over Hale as the presidential nominee 34–32 with 10 "other" votes. William Elder became a Free Soil leader in Philadelphia, and Swisshelm put her *Saturday Visiter* firmly behind the Free Soil Party, temporarily hired two Free Soil editors, and supported the party through the election. The Free Soil Party did not participate, however, in the state gubernatorial election. Even with Free Soiler David Wilmot supporting the Democratic candidate, the Whigs narrowly captured the election by 297 votes.¹⁴⁹ Abolitionist voters scattered a few votes for Edward Gazzam (48), Earle (7), and LeMoyne (6).¹⁵⁰

Most Liberty men seem to have joined some dissident Democrats and gone into the Free Soil coalition for the presidential race, but the Whig Party, which had a strong antislavery wing that included Thaddeus Stevens, won the state in November.

Zachary Taylor (Whig)	185,423 (50.2%)
Lewis Cass (Democrat)	172,704 (46.8%)
Martin Van Buren (Free Soil)	11,273 (3.1%)¹⁵¹

Longtime Liberty gubernatorial candidate LeMoyne was one of the few leaders who refused to endorse the Free Soil presidential ticket because he saw support for Van Buren as a betrayal of the cause.[152] Even the Pennsylvania Garrisonians were happy to see the new developments, stating that "while abolitionists cannot join in the party nor vote with them, they do rejoice in the great breach in the pro-slavery parties."[153]

The Liberty Party in Pennsylvania had little effect on state politics. Its proportion of the vote was never high and it seems to have had little impact on local races. Nonetheless, it served an important function as a political outlet for antislavery voters who could not accept the disunionist attitudes that pervaded much of Pennsylvania abolitionism. In the western part of the state, the party was more highly organized with a more talented leadership, important African American supporters, and pockets of electoral strength. In fact, the party in the west was probably unique. Its talented leadership toyed with many different electoral solutions and provided some of the important leadership of the future Republican Party.

NEW JERSEY

New Jersey was a state with a relatively homogeneous population and a stable political environment. By 1840, the state had developed a competitive two-party system marked by a turnout of over 80% in 1840 and 1844.[154] Abolitionists did not fare well in New Jersey. The state was near the South, had a slave population estimated in 1846 to be three to four thousand, and enjoyed commercial relations with the South.[155] Nonetheless, African Americans (and women) had had the vote until the franchise was restricted in 1807. There was some antislavery sentiment in the state, but political abolition of any kind had little support. An August 11, 1840, convention of voting abolitionists decided 12–11 against presidential and congressional tickets. The minority met and set up an electoral slate, but some nominees had not been consulted and declined.[156] There was some support for the new party in 1840 and 1841, but there was little formal organization.[157] In the 1840 presidential contest the party received only 69 votes (0.1%).

New Jersey voting abolitionists made another effort for 1844. Led by Quaker physician Dr. John Grimes, they began in June by setting up the (Boonton, Morris County) *New Jersey Freeman* as a Liberty Party newspaper that supported the Birney-Morris presidential ticket and total abstinence. It declared that "we do not believe in separating moral suasion from political action. The BALLOT BOX, is an instrument of great power for good or for evil, and we cannot agree to give the enemies of truth the exclusive benefit of it ... Moral suasion is incomplete without political action." A state Liberty convention on May 21 established a state central committee and endorsed the Liberty presidential ticket.[158] Their newspaper published irregularly (only eight were issued in 1844), but it showed that there was some political antislavery sentiment in the state. New Jersey abolitionists separated Liberty activities from general antislavery agitation. Many participated in both the party and the state antislavery society, but some, such as Theodore Dwight Weld, took part in only the general antislavery conventions. Even non-Liberty antislavery meetings without specifically endorsing the Liberty Party declared that "we are pointed for efficient political action to the Ballot Box."[159] By mid-July the *Freeman* was running a list of nine presidential electors, and by mid-August Liberty men were moving to put the small party on a firmer footing by calling for a state and several local conventions in September.[160]

The state Liberty Party convention met in Newark on September 25 and nominated Jonathan Parkhurst for governor. Local conventions also met and made nominations for two U.S. congressional seats and set up local slates for several state senate and state assembly races as well as for some local offices.[161] Scattered rallies took place, including one at Boonton just before the election that "Ladies and Gentlemen of all parties are invited to attend."[162] The election returns were disappointing, with the party receiving only 131 votes (0.2%). As in many areas where the party was small, Liberty leaders claimed that many of their votes were not being counted.[163] The *New Jersey Freeman* complained that the major parties, "the Whig portion especially," wooed the Liberty voters before the election, but "after the election we cannot find out through their papers even that there is such a party." It admitted, however, that "[o]ur voice is small in New Jersey . . . owing to a want of organization, only four or five counties in the State having a regular ticket."[164] The voice was small, but the state's antislavery newspaper was definitely a Liberty Party sheet and carried a greater percentage of party news than most Liberty newspapers. It culled much of its material from Liberty newspapers on its exchange list, published important Liberty documents, and paid attention to the progress of the party in some other states, such as Virginia and Rhode Island, where the Liberty Party struggled. It carried correspondence on Liberty efforts from around the state, and probably was the fulcrum of the New Jersey Liberty movement.

The small band of Liberty supporters more clearly defined their party after the 1844 elections. They set up a Liberty Association in Boonton, Morris County—the hub of Liberty activity and the home of the *New Jersey Freeman*—that met on the first Friday of every month. It elected officers and ran announcements of its meeting in the *New Jersey Freeman* through May 1846.[165] The party took virtual control of the New Jersey Anti-Slavery Society at its sixth annual meeting in Jersey City. A series of resolutions—probably written by New York guest Alvan

Stewart, who was put on the business committee—committed the organization to support the Liberty Party and "were adopted without a dissenting voice."[166] The party was close to its counterpart in Upstate New York in its orientation. Temperance was a major part of its creed. Temperance organization news and articles often surpassed political news in the party newspaper, and many of the same individuals served as officers in both the Liberty and temperance organizations, although there were temperance advocates whose names never appear associated with any antislavery activities. Although the monthly newspaper was occasionally late or delayed in coming out, it made good use of its exchange list in keeping its readers abreast of Liberty activities nationally and in some individual states. It was more political during this period than many Liberty publications in other states. Abolitionists from outside the state frequently attended both Liberty conventions and meetings of the New Jersey Anti-Slavery Society. These visitors were always strong Liberty supporters, and included Henry Highland Garnet, Lewis Tappan, Luther Lee, and William Elder, but Alvan Stewart was the main outside influence. He attended several meetings and provided legal services in the New Jersey slave cases, in which he argued that the New Jersey Constitution of 1844 abolished slavery in the state.[167]

The New Jersey Anti-Slavery Society continued to be supportive of the Liberty Party. At its August meeting it resolved that "the Ballot box is one of our most effectual resorts for its [slavery] abolition, and should be used chifley [sic] to that end," and it "highly approve[d] of the Great Convention of the Eastern and Middle States in Boston.[168] Its Quarterly Meeting in Patterson on November 12, 1845, recommended that its members subscribe to Liberty newspapers and passed a resolution that not only expressed the feelings of the New Jersey Liberty voters but also of loyal Liberty men wherever they had no realistic chance of making a political impact. It passed a resolution declaring

> *Resolved, 5,* That whether the Liberty Party as such, ever reaches a majority as will enable it directly to wield the civil power of the nation or not, is not a question which is to decide the past, present, and future usefulness of the Liberty Party; inasmuch as we believe, that most if not all of what the other parties have done, and are doing for human liberty, either by legislation or otherwise, they are driven to by the influence of the principles enforced at the ballot box by the Liberty Party.[169]

Despite the unhappiness of leaders over the limited extent of Liberty activity and organization, the party made some gains in the local elections in the fall.[170]

Party enthusiasm waned in 1846 despite the higher-profile congressional races. The Boonton Liberty Association ceased its monthly meetings, the limited statewide party activity centered in the New Jersey Anti-Slavery Society, and there was little local activity except for the perfunctory nominations at election time. The fall elections were discouraging to the loyal few. The editor of the *New Jersey Freeman* wrote that Liberty leaders "presume that our state has fallen off from last year . . . not from any turning back on the part of Liberty men but from an apathy which has been general among all parties. Fourteen Liberty men did not go to the polls in Boonton alone."[171] If the party had a problem getting its supporters to the polls in Boonton, it must have been very difficult elsewhere. This lack of vitality continued through 1847. The January meeting of the state society at Trenton was more interested in the New Jersey slave cases than grassroots Liberty politics.[172] The state was not affected by some of the changes taking place in the party elsewhere. Used to its politically impotent status, it clung to the franchise as a protest tool and opposed any dilution of principle. The *New Jersey Freeman* decried the criticism of the Liberty League movement even as it continued its support of the main Liberty Party. Nonetheless, it endorsed Gerrit Smith for president and objected to John P. Hale as a Liberty candidate until he proved himself worthy of Liberty support by his actions in the Senate.[173] The party continued to run candidates in 1847 with even less success.[174]

After the October 1847 national convention in Buffalo, the state's party members were less than enthusiastic about Hale's nomination, but the annual meeting of the New Jersey Anti-Slavery Society endorsed him, probably at the urging of Alvan Stewart, who again attended the gathering.[175] If Hale received a lukewarm approval from New Jersey Liberty men, the possibility of Martin Van Buren heading a new antislavery coalition was chilling. Nonetheless, Liberty men participated in the call for Free Soil conventions, joined in the proceedings, and served as candidates.[176] Most of the Liberty delegates to the Buffalo national Free Soil convention seem to have remained loyal to Hale on the preliminary ballot but joined in supporting the Van Buren–Adams ticket. Prominent Liberty men do not seem to have been in the upper echelon of the Free Soil Party in New Jersey, but they served loyally in local contests in some areas. For instance, three of the four nominees for the state assembly from Morris County were longtime Liberty leaders.[177] Still, some important individuals did not embrace the Free Soil presidential candidate. Dr. John Grimes, editor of the *New Jersey Freeman*, declared that "[w]e do not like the nominee of the Convention."[178] He endorsed the ticket grudgingly only after Van Buren accepted the platform and "because our doctrine is 'principles not men.'" He was also unhappy with the tenor of a state Free Soil meeting in Morristown where Benjamin Butler gave a speech that he felt was much too kind to Zachary Taylor.[179]

New Jersey voters gave the Free Soil Party its lowest percentage in any Northern state.

Zachary Taylor (Whig)	40,009 (51.4%)
Lewis Cass (Democrat)	36,880 (47.4%)
Martin Van Buren (Free Soil)	849 (1.1%)
Other	77 (0.1%)

The source of the small Free Soil vote is difficult to analyze, especially with the "other" vote, which has an antislavery protest character to it.[180] The election of 1848 effectively ended antislavery politics in the state. The *New Jersey Freeman* limped along for several more issues, but its columns contained virtually no political or antislavery news. Instead, the newspaper emphasized temperance, educational reform, and medical speculation. Within a year Alvan Stewart was dead. He had helped organize and maintain the Liberty Party in the state, attended numerous meetings there, and provided the legal resources for the New Jersey slave cases. In the 1852 presidential election, the Free Democrats, the Free Soil successor, garnered only 347 votes and had no real organization.

The Liberty Party had little impact in New Jersey. Still, this small band of men and women who publicly espoused their antislavery ideals, marched under the Liberty banner in patriotic parades, and clung to their ideals in an unsympathetic environment typified small Liberty minorities across the North that let their communities know that everything was not politics as usual.

Except for the Upstate New York area and a few pockets of strength elsewhere in New York and Pennsylvania, the Liberty Party did not have much of a presence in the Middle States. Nonetheless, it did provide a political outlet for antislavery voters unhappy with the major parties. There was more Liberty strength in the Old Northwest, but it too was concentrated in certain areas of these states.

7

THE OLD NORTHWEST

The Old Northwest contained a diverse population that affected both its state politics and attitudes toward abolitionism. Some areas were settled primarily by Southerners, while other places seem almost to have been transplanted New England towns or immigrants from Upstate New York. This reflected the region's attitude toward slavery, especially along the borders with Southern states. Areas of Southern sympathy often surrounded pockets of abolitionism.

MICHIGAN

Party alignments in Michigan were virtually nonexistent during most of its territorial period, but the Democratic Party became dominant soon after statehood in 1837. Although Whigs won narrow victories in the 1839 gubernatorial and 1840 presidential contests, Democrats overwhelmed them in the 1841 governor's race and did not lose a statewide contest again until 1854.[1] They also dominated the state legislature, peaking in 1844, when they swept the state senate and won a large majority of the lower house. Lewis Cass, territorial governor for eighteen years and a trusted advisor of Andrew Jackson, dominated the state party in his long political career that culminated in his Democratic presidential nomination in 1848. At the same time, Michigan was the most antislavery state in the Old Northwest. It had no common border with a slave state, and much of its population came from abolition-friendly New York and New England. Local antislavery societies developed as early as 1832. By the time abolitionists formed a state society in November 1836, several local organizations were already in existence.[2]

Michigan abolitionists were also pioneers in political antislavery, both in questioning major-party candidates and in setting up independent nominations. Seymour Boughton Treadwell, a former Whig antislavery author and editor, recalled that in 1836 he had taken a political stand "above, and independent of both parties."³ The Michigan State Anti-Slavery Society made the questioning of candidates an official policy at its October 1838 meeting, and members soon posed questions to Whig and Democratic candidates for the 1838 U.S. Senate race. The Democratic nominee won despite being more hostile to abolitionism than the Whig. More troubling was the 1839 gubernatorial contest in which Whig William Woodbridge was decidedly anti-abolition and anti-black. His victory, the last state victory for a Whig, caused antislavery men to question the questioning system.⁴ Abolitionists in Jackson County had been so discouraged by the situation, however, that they made independent nominations in 1839, a course that the executive committee of the state antislavery society soon disowned.⁵ As elsewhere, these early efforts were not encouraging. The effect of the questioning system on voting abolitionists, according to a sympathetic contemporary, "entirely disheartened them. Some of the candidates would not answer at all; some avowed themselves entirely hostile to the objects of the interrogators; while of the few who avowed a conformity of sentiment, scarcely any came up to that standard of action which the questioners had fondly anticipated when they gave their suffrages."⁶ Abolitionists' interest in political action and their inability to work with the established parties were two major reasons that Michigan became the most successful Liberty state in the region before the 1844 election. Upset by Woodbridge's victory and a presidential choice between Harrison and Van Buren, discussions of independent political action grew heated during early 1840. The Fifth Anniversary of the state antislavery society in Jackson in mid-February carried on a lengthy debate on independent political action that resulted in the question being laid on the table and indefinitely postponed.⁷

During the summer, Seymour B. Treadwell published a call in the *Michigan Freeman* for an August 5 convention in Jackson that was signed by sixty-five voters.⁸ This convention formed a presidential ticket for Birney and Earle and nominated a candidate for the U.S. Congress. Treadwell acknowledged that "all of the members of the Board [of the state antislavery society] located at this place except the Editor are rank Harrison and Tyler men."⁹ Thereupon, Whigs on the executive committee voted to discontinue the *Michigan Freeman* as the society's newspaper, an action that a majority of the board later declared "null and void."¹⁰ Shortly thereafter, antislavery Whigs left the state society, and it virtually became a Liberty organization. By its annual meeting in February 1841, the 102 delegates' "vote to withdraw from the old American Anti-Slavery Society, and to become auxiliary to the American and Foreign Anti-Slavery Society, passed without a dissenting voice and with only one voice raised against a third party."¹¹

As Whigs were leaving the state organization, the new party began to take shape.¹² Treadwell and Theodore Foster, who also stood as a candidate for state senator, wrote an "Address to the Electors of Michigan." Freemen's conventions in Jackson and Calhoun counties not only nominated congressional, state legislative, and electoral candidates, but also set up third-party slates for all elections down to coroner.[13] Soon leading abolitionists encouraged their brethren to abandon their former allegiances and join the new party.[14] Nonetheless, there was little time before the election to distribute tickets and campaign very widely. As elsewhere, the new party's vote was small, but the Michigan percentage (321 votes—0.7%) was the highest in the Old Northwest and second only to Massachusetts (1.3%) in the nation.[15] Not surprisingly, the greatest number of votes came from areas where there had been some third-party activity, but many areas that would soon develop a healthy Liberty following cast no votes for the party in 1840.

The Liberty Party began its major period of growth in 1841. Immediately after the February 1841 state meeting of the Michigan State Anti-Slavery Society, Liberty activists met in Jackson, nominated candidates for some state races, and selected a statewide ticket headed by Jabez S. Fitch, a prominent architect and builder from Marshall. They set up a state central committee and encouraged local organization. The new party's mouthpiece, the (Ann Arbor) *Signal of Liberty*, was founded by the executive committee of the Michigan State Anti-Slavery Society and replaced the under-funded *Michigan Freeman*. Guy Beckley, an antislavery Methodist minister, and Theodore Foster, a farmer-businessman, became the editors. It was one of the best Liberty sheets in the country, covering events in other states as well as becoming the voice of the Michigan Liberty Party.[16] The efforts produced positive results in the fall election. Fitch's vote (1,223—3.2% of the vote) was a 288% increase over Birney's vote of a year earlier, and the Whigs lost the governor's chair, "attribut[ing] it, to a considerable extent, to the existence of the Liberty party."[17] The party in Michigan progressed faster than any in the region, and it received an added boost late in the year when presidential candidate Birney relocated to the frontier area near the present Bay City. He would be a major resource for the state party.

Liberty strength continued to grow in 1842 and 1843. The *Signal of Liberty* reported news of national interest, printed local tickets and ballots, circulated antislavery petitions (particularly on getting the suffrage for the state's African Americans), reported on general politics, and provided a forum for debating Liberty strategy and tactics. Because of Beckley's role in the Wesleyan secession and in antislavery in the churches, it had much news on religious matters and gave much space to temperance. By early 1843, its subscription list had grown from the 400 inherited from the *Michigan Freeman* to about 1,150 in 24 counties. The paper combined a highly moralistic tone with an appreciation for practical politics and organization. It editorialized on such subjects as "Adultery Legalized," published comprehensive lists of town nominees and local meetings, and printed voter ballots to a greater extent than many Liberty newspapers.[18]

The party refined its organization between statewide elections during the early years. It expanded its base and made nominations for the spring local elections. Detroit Liberty men, including a number of influential African Americans, began to organize support for the new party and set up a complete city ticket, although its proportion of the total city electorate remained quite small.[19] Other areas held meetings and nominated tickets for local elections, and several Liberty candidates were victorious, sometimes after being added to major-party tickets.[20] Jackson County continued as the heart of the movement in the fall 1842 and spring 1843 elections with its vote often exceeding 15%. Liberty candidates steadily increased their totals, won many local races, and even controlled some towns.[21]

At the same time, the state antislavery society became totally identified with the Liberty Party. Garrisonians, never an important element in the state's abolition, were hardly ever discussed after mid-1843.[22] Whig members of the society had departed and left it under the control of the Liberty sympathizers. This hurt the society's resources because some of these Whigs were among the most generous financial backers of the organization.[23] In early 1844 a few of them reappeared at the annual meeting to object to its Liberty orientation, possibly because they realized the effect that it might have on their already weakened party in the 1844 presidential contest.[24] Whigs were correct in being concerned. Contemporary estimates and subsequent analyses all emphasize the Whig base to the Michigan Liberty Party before 1844. A mid-1843 *Signal of Liberty* editorial stated that "[t]he existence of the Liberty party diminishes the number of Whig votes . . . The Whigs, as now organized cannot succeed in Michigan until the Liberty Party shall be destroyed."[25] Election returns for 1842 and 1843 show that Whigs suffered after the advent of the new party. Even the editors of the *Signal of Liberty* were surprised by the Democratic domination in the fall 1842 state legislative races in which they swept the state senate and captured 38 out of 43 seats in the lower house.[26] Estimates placed the vote for Liberty candidates between 1,500 and over 2,000.[27]

Whig fortunes declined even more in the 1843 fall elections. The Liberty Party held a lively convention in Ann Arbor on February 9, 1843. Delegates turned to new resident James G. Birney for its nominee for governor and vowed to continue the work on local organizations. This meeting also showed the movement of the party toward more conventional political practices. Instead of the open convention of the earlier years, the Liberty Party now used a delegate system based on lower house representation.[28] By this time the party had a functioning state central committee with a hardworking chairman, Charles H. Stewart, a former Whig who was a well known Detroit attorney. He published a five-part series in the *Signal of Liberty* criticizing Whigs for accepting the gag rule and the Harrison-Tyler ticket in 1840 and took particular aim at the Whig *Detroit Advertiser* for its subservience to the South.[29] Birney and other leaders led rallies in the spring and summer.[30] They were rewarded when the gubernatorial election showed another substantial increase in the Liberty total and further decline in Whig support. Birney's totals (2,776—7.1%) showed a Liberty increase of 127.0% over 1841. The election marked the nadir of the Whig Party in Michigan until 1848 with 38.1% of the vote.[31]

Feelings between Whigs and Liberty followers had been frayed since the beginning, especially in the Detroit area, where Whigs and Democrats were closely balanced.[32] The *Detroit Advertiser* realized this and carried on a heated battle with the *Signal of Liberty* and the Liberty Party. Whigs were especially upset when Liberty conventions selected antislavery Whigs as nominees without the candidates' knowledge or acquiescence.[33] These embarrassments did not soften Liberty attacks on the Whigs. An October 3, 1842, Wayne County Liberty convention criticized Whigs and the *Detroit Advertiser* while attempting to entice them into more pronounced antislavery positions. In a move with which most Liberty men statewide or nationally would not agree, it resolved that if they "shall send to Congress a Giddings, as their representative, we will cheerfully coincide with that respected and talented gentleman in the inexpediency of a third party—but until then, never."[34]

Nonetheless, Michigan Whigs began to move in an antislavery direction to lure former Whigs back to their old party.[35] They were partially successful. Several Liberty men publicly announced their support for Henry Clay because they perceived him as more opposed to the annexation of Texas than the expansionist James K. Polk.[36] During the summer, Birney engaged in a heated debate with antislavery Whig Zephaniah Platt. As a former Michigan attorney general and a vice president in the American Anti-Slavery Society, Platt brought impressive political and antislavery credentials to a debate in which he accused Birney of being a tool of the Democrats.[37] Hostility grew very personal as the *Detroit Advertiser* characterized Birney as "a Polkat in the skin of a mink." As Theodore Clarke Smith has observed, these recriminations "reached an acute stage in Michigan sooner than in any other Northwestern State."[38] As the election neared, Whigs capitalized on Birney's blunder in accepting a local nomination from the Democrats, and they were responsible for the Garland Forgery.[39]

The Whigs were almost rewarded in the election, but they could only take some satisfaction in that they had prevented the Democrats from claiming a simple majority.

> Henry Clay (Whig) 24,185 (43.5%)
> James K. Polk (Democrat) 27,737 (49.9%)
> James G. Birney (Liberty) 3,638 (6.5%)

Despite the Garland Forgery and his own missteps, Birney actually increased his total vote from the previous year by 31.1%, although his proportion of the total vote dropped. Whigs believed that the Liberty votes could have swung Michigan to Clay. Such reasoning neglected the facts that the Liberty gains had come in earlier elections and would have required almost every Liberty vote to have been cast for slaveholder Clay. They subjected the state's Liberty men to harsher criticism than anywhere else in the North except New York.[40] Despite being at the forefront of the Liberty movement in the Old Northwest, Michigan Liberty men were disappointed by the results of the election and soon began to consider new strategies to increase their strength.

After the energy of the first four years, the party fell into a numbing lassitude in 1845. A July state convention renominated Birney for governor, and Liberty men seemed optimistic about continued progress. Then Birney fell from his horse in August and subsequently suffered a physically disabling stroke. When it became doubtful that he would recover his health, he resigned his candidacy in early September. This threw the party into consternation just as the campaign was beginning. *Signal of Liberty* editor Theodore Foster and other leaders, unaware of the severity of Birney's condition, were taken aback by his "entirely unexpected communication," and urged him to reconsider. They argued "that the resignation of Mr. B. would throw the party into confusion, diminish the vote, and operate to his personal disadvantage, by the use which would be made of it by the Whigs . . . for the sake of the cause, he *must* remain the candidate."[41] Birney complied, but was never able to campaign or speak publicly again.

Whigs, meanwhile, blamed the Liberty Party for their losses in the state and nation in the recent presidential contest, but the practical result of the furor for them was a move much closer to antislavery principles, and there were "indications of a coming over to abolitionism among them." The Whig Party was in flux and not united. Foster believed the Whig gubernatorial ticket was "regarded everywhere as a tacit acknowle[d]gment of anticipated defeat . . . [T]he party will not make much of a fight this year."[42] At the same time some Liberty men were doing little to hold or attract those with Whiggish principles. They embraced ideas not related to slavery that had a definite Democratic tinge, giving credence to Whig charges that Liberty men were in league with the Democrats. Foster admitted as much in wishing to "give the antislavery ship an important tack, making her head directly *along side* of radical, reformatory Young Democracy."[43] Low morale among Whigs, continued fallout from the Garland incident, and a lackluster Liberty campaign contributed to an easy Democratic victory in a gubernatorial election in which Birney received 3,023 votes (7.7%).[44] Liberty numerical vote declined by 16.9%, but the party lost less than the major parties and actually reached its highest percentage.

The static vote since 1843 reinforced some Michigan leaders in their attempt to "have some other motives to present to people, which will appeal directly to their own interests." Echoing what he had read in the *Philanthropist*, Foster declared "*a new and small party cannot long remain stationary*: if it does not advance, it must necessarily recede."[45] Their solution was to implement their discussions and local activities of the previous year and articulate positions for the Liberty Party on a variety of issues. During the last part of 1845, they had discussed these ideas internally and at local meetings. After speculating on several alternatives, Foster would "let the Liberty men express their opinions in Convention by resolutions or otherwise, upon every subject of interest," but he emphasized "that the question of Slavery is the *paramount* question, and the *only test* of party membership." He intended "to broach [these ideas] in the Signal, not suddenly, but gradually and judiciously, so as to shock our one idea brethren as little as possible."[46] Birney agreed. He believed "[w]hilst the black man constitutes the first object of our consideration, the *white* must not be neglected ... We must be prepared to take on ourselves *all* the administering of government or *none* of it."[47] Foster presented his set of ideas at a Washtenaw County convention in September, and "a resolution approving it, after a long discussion, was passed."[48]

By the end of December, Birney and Foster worked on a set of positions that they submitted to the state society at its annual meeting in early February. Their individual plans differed in some respects, but they both would move the party in the same direction. Beyond abolition both wanted a general reform of government and the reduction and ultimate abolition of the army and navy, and to lessen the overall expense of government. Birney went further than Foster and was more specific in his recommendations. He would "diminish the power, the patronage, and of course, the salary of the President" and "reduce the daily allowance paid to members of Congress at least one half." He advocated that "*free trade* shall be established—the United States leading the way." Foster emphasized political reform with "[e]qual political rights of all [presumably male] citizens" and a more direct democracy, including the "election of many National and State offices, including Post masters," and the "single district system of electing Legislators."[49] Guy Beckley, an editor and important financial backer of the *Signal of Liberty*, agreed with their new direction for the party. They felt this would put the Liberty Party on track to be a permanent party, not a temporary "John the Baptist party."[50] The annual meeting did not go the way that Foster and Birney expected.[51] After the executive committee brought a favorable recommendation to the floor, some heavy criticism resulted in a committee of five to be appointed to consider the expanded platform.[52] They brought out a report recommending against expansion. After a spirited discussion, the approximately one hundred delegates rejected the expansion.[53]

Foster quickly published his views in the *Signal of Liberty* and requested that the committee's five members do the same. Individual committeemen sent a confused set of replies. Charles H. Stewart backtracked and approved the platform except for the abolition of the navy and the tariff positions.[54] Other members softened their criticism or stated that they could run on any platform as long as slavery was the overriding issue. The tariff issue caused the biggest problem because this was a major-party issue that usually separated Whigs from Democrats and clearly caused some uneasiness with those who believed in a protective tariff.[55] The final committee report was against the expansion of the platform, but "the final decision was to be left to the majority of Liberty men who would decide what was the best policy to follow."[56] Throughout the spring and summer there was much correspondence in the *Signal of Liberty* over the proposals.

At the same time, Foster was taking his proposals nationally.[57] He wrote Birney a revealing and confidential note discussing his efforts and their results. Since only one newspaper had republished Birney's January 1 letter from the *Signal of Liberty*, "I judge that it is not well liked." Beckley and he had printed their "views in a condensed form, and sent one to each of the 36 Liberty papers." Only one, the (Pittsburgh) *Spirit of Liberty* (later joined by the *Albany Patriot*), favored them. Foster was particularly troubled that "the action of the State Convention is every where quoted against us out of state." Despite some support "from the log-houses in the backwoods," he was "not sanguine at all in my expectations." He knew what the problem was. He declared "that more of our leaders and political speakers have been and are *ministers*—not statesmen or politicians. Hence their blindness to anything but one idea."[58] He clearly believed that the party should be moving in a different direction.

Most leading abolitionists and party newspapers outside of Michigan were opposed to the expanded platform. Lewis Tappan expressed the general feeling to Birney that "[b]y introducing other topicks [sic] I cannot but think we shall weaken rather than strengthen *our* party."[59] Gerrit Smith was so upset that he published an article maintaining "that the time is not yet come to attempt it."[60] Even among supporters there was debate over which reforms the new party should encompass. For instance, the *Spirit of Liberty* was concerned with workingmen's rights and the ten-hour day, positions the *Signal of Liberty* opposed because it favored limiting governmental influence.[61] The real difficulty, of course, was how to get former Whigs and Democrats to agree on policies that had originally divided them.

Nevertheless, Birney, Foster, and Beckley continued to refine their positions and were determined to bring their ideas to the floor at the North-Western Liberty Convention in Chicago in late June.[62] Beckley and Foster both attended and served in official capacities, but Seymour B. Treadwell, evangelical minister Marcus Harrison, and former slave Henry Bibb were also in the Michigan delegation, and they opposed the expanded platform.[63] The convention debated expanding beyond the one-idea concept and voted it down decisively. Foster and Beckley came back discouraged. Foster believed "[t]he Liberty party... [is] no party at all. They are intent on political suicide" and presciently predicted that it would happen "either generally, by a national antislavery union, or locally, after the fashion of New Hampshire." Again, he blamed the ministers who "are mostly opposed to venturing out politically... and they will keep the men with them."[64]

Foster said he would continue to labor on and try to get out the vote for the congressional campaign in the fall, but it was clear that he thought the party had reached a turning point. Most local conventions throughout the autumn were similar to those of previous years and avoided bringing in other issues or taking positions on expanding the platform. Stewart's central committee address attempted to rally the voters by repeating familiar arguments on how slavery affected American life. It did not mention expanding the platform.[65] Foster continued to hope for some change, but the death knell of the expanded platform was sounded by the annual meeting of the state antislavery in early February when a motion to expand the platform on the basis of Foster's principles was unanimously rejected.[66] The party continued to run candidates as it always had, but correspondence and the tone of meetings as reported in the *Signal of Liberty* do not convey the excitement of the early years, as if the debates had wearied the participants. In the spring and fall 1846 elections, Liberty candidates did not do significantly poorer than previous elections, but they did not make any improvement. In the fall election the three Liberty congressional candidates totaled a little less than three thousand votes.

If 1846 was the year of the debate over an expanded platform for the Michigan Liberty Party, the year 1847 brought a different effort for some Liberty men to expand their influence—cooperation with antislavery elements of the major parties. Against a backdrop of John P. Hale's coalition in New Hampshire, the Wilmot Proviso, and the Mexican War, the Whig Party in the state developed a strong antislavery wing.[67] Even Foster, whose political philosophy was closer to that of the Democrats, was "satisfied that when the time comes, our friends in this state will readily unite with the Whigs *locally*, in state affairs or *nationally*."[68] Michigan Liberty men had always accepted endorsements from a major party in local elections and often selected candidates who would be likely to win endorsements, but these actions allowed them to maintain their party integrity. Now Foster began encouraging them to "unite and cooperate with men and parties which are not all that we could wish them."[69] By early 1847, he was urging Liberty men to elect candidates that "*will do the things which need to be done*" regardless of party as long as they espoused certain basic antislavery principles.[70] Although his requirements were quite stringent, his position was far from that upheld by most strict Liberty men of having nothing to do with candidates who remained in major parties that maintained political fellowship with slaveholders. Nonetheless, he mentioned his opinions quietly and they seem to have caused little stir among Michigan Liberty men. A spring Liberty convention went on record as regretting "that many devoted friends of the slave, in their zeal for individuals, presented on pro-slavery tickets, have voted in fact for principles and parties most repugnant to those of Liberty."[71]

Then Guy Beckley dropped a bombshell that shocked Liberty men inside and outside the state. Beckley had impeccable antislavery credentials—an editor (until the previous year) and financier of the *Signal of Liberty*, a frequent antislavery lecturer, a Methodist Episcopal minister who left the sect to found a Wesleyan Methodist church in Ann Arbor in 1843, and a charter member in the founding of the *National Era* in Washington, D.C.[72] His mid-March 1847 letter to the *Signal of Liberty* was an outspoken departure from earlier Liberty policy. After tracing the history of the party from "confining of its early efforts *mainly* to the propagation of the 'one idea'" and remarking on the "stern rebuff" that met efforts to expand the platform, he defined the type of candidate he would support. He would demand that a potential candidate "be a man of ability and of good moral character" and adhere to five basic characteristics.

1. Equal Political Rights to all men.
2. The passage of a law similar to those of New Hampshire, Vermont, and Massachusetts making it penal for any officer or citizen of this State to aid in the arrest of fugitive slaves.

3. The repeal of all laws of the Federal Government that sustain, sanction or regulate Slavery, including those that uphold it in the District of Columbia and the Territories, and the law of 1793.
4. No more slaveholding states or territories to be received into the Union.
5. To support no man for office, who is a slaveholder, or who would in any manner, directly or indirectly, use his official power or influence for the elevation or appointment of slaveholders to office.

Unlike Foster earlier, however, Beckley broke with past Liberty practice. He made it clear that he did "not choose to *amalgamate*, but . . . *cooperate*," thus maintaining his Liberty independence. He explicitly stated that he would abandon a Liberty nominee if an acceptable candidate was "*the man* who is right according to the above standard, and has the best chance of success, by whomever he may have been nominated, or whatever party he may belong." If no one came up to his standards, "our course of action is plain—put in nomination men who are worthy of our support, and give them our suffrage." This was the first time that a prominent Liberty leader had made a so unequivocal public break with precedent as he declared that "this is the policy, as an individual I shall pursue until something more feasible offers itself." Beckley was a blunt man, and he articulated what many others may have been pondering.[73] James G. Birney, who had marched shoulder to shoulder with Beckley in the Michigan Liberty Party and in the efforts to expand the Liberty platform, quickly challenged him. He addressed several questions to Beckley. If someone whom he supports is a Democrat or Whig,

> is he not in the wrong place, for have we not said, up to this time, that both these parties are pro-Slavery and corrupt? . . . If the Whig and Democratic parties are pro-Slavery, is not your Liberty man a traitor or false to them? . . . [D]o you expect that such a Liberty man will be honest, *after* election—*after* he has got your vote . . . [Do you not believe] [t]hat to vote for any nominee of a party is to vote, really for the party and its principles? . . . [What if an acceptable candidate] is found in each of the other parties? . . . Are we bound to lower our principles, till men will accept them?[74]

Beckley responded unequivocally that, "other things being equal," he would vote for a major-party candidate over a Liberty nominee if "he has the best chance of success, and my vote might place him, *at once*, in a position to do all I ask."[75] He found few allies in the state. In an article on "The Liberty Party in Michigan," a writer noted the steady decline of votes since 1844 and blamed it on apathy, estimating that there should be four thousand Liberty voters in the state. He called for moving slowly and encouraged cool, levelheaded debate.[76] Birney believed that the Beckley plan was "calculated, at once, to break up the Liberty Party." It did not break up the party in Michigan, but it contributed to its losing much of its spirit. A correspondent of the *Signal of Liberty* observed that "the Liberty Party at present is in 'rather a bad fix.' It is obvious that unless some favorable change occur the next election will find us greatly reduced in number, and the subsequent one annihilate us."[77]

Nonetheless, the party faithful slogged on and seemed to sleepwalk through the rest of the year. About seventy delegates attended a late June state convention in Jackson and nominated non-controversial St. Joseph lawyer Chester Gurney and Detroit merchant Horace Hallock as the party's gubernatorial ticket. While rejecting cooperation with other parties, the convention avoided any statements on expanding the platform or on an antislavery interpretation of the U.S. Constitution.[78] They repeated these sentiments at another Jackson convention in September. They resolved to support "such men only as will publicly avow themselves members of the Liberty party ... [M]en should not yield their support to men for mere anti-slavery professions, and that nothing but open and consistent action with the Liberty party should secure our confidence and support."[79] Most conventions and rallies during the fall did not mention these divisive issues. Taking into account the party's internal problems and the fact that both major parties put up candidates who were in the antislavery wings of their parties, the Liberty Party did not lose as many votes as might have been expected. It declined only 14.5% from its 1845 totals to 2,585 votes (5.6%).[80] Increased turnout, however, meant that the Liberty Party received its lowest proportion of the vote in a statewide election since 1841.

The party was reduced to its basic core and, more important, was losing its traditional leadership. Having fulfilled his five-year commitment to edit the *Signal of Liberty*, Foster announced that he was closing it because he could no longer afford to keep it operating.[81] The ailing Birney became interested in observing national policies, the formation of the Liberty League, and developing arguments on the antislavery nature of the U.S. Constitution. He played no role in state Liberty affairs.[82] And Beckley, already marginalized because of his views, died in December 1847. Still, the state party labored on. The sixty-five to seventy delegates to the Michigan State Anti-Slavery Society on February 3 and the Liberty Party convention the following day endorsed the Hale-King ticket after lively discussion, and they took up a collection to help underwrite a successor to the *Signal of Liberty*.[83] Erastus Hussey, a Battle Creek Quaker merchant and former Liberty congressional candidate, filled the journalistic void two months later when he began printing the *Michigan Liberty Press*. The Hale-King ticket immediately appeared on the masthead.[84] The editor soon made it clear that the one idea of slavery was the newspaper's focus and other issues were "minor considerations."[85]

Michigan Liberty men did not hesitate to join the rapidly emerging Free Soil coalition. All of the leaders except Birney supported it, and most Liberty voters smoothly transferred their allegiances to the new party. As one-third of the delegation to the Buffalo convention, they remained true to Hale on the initial ballot but quickly acquiesced in the Van Buren–Adams ticket. Upon returning, they called a Liberty convention for August 16 that recommended disbanding the Liberty Party in favor of Free Soil.[86] Hussey put the Free Soil ticket on the masthead and ran the prospectus for a new paper, the *Free Soil Campaigner*.[87] Michigan Liberty men were not as important in the Free Soil Party as they were in some states. Dissident Democrats took leadership roles, but Whigs contributed much support and joined in bargains in lower-level elections. In fact, most analysts conclude that the new party hurt the Whigs in Michigan more than it did in many states. Democratic voters seemed to hold their party lines better than elsewhere, probably because of the candidacy of favorite son Lewis Cass.[88]

Zachary Taylor (Whig)	23,947 (36.8%)
Lewis Cass (Democrat)	30,742 (47.2%)
Martin Van Buren (Free Soil)	10,393 (16.0%)

The Michigan's Free Soil vote trailed only Wisconsin in the Old Northwest and New York and Vermont in the nation. The election was just a beginning of political change that would lead the state to be one of the early strong Republican Party states. Liberty men contributed to this movement, but, with a few exceptions, they did not do it as candidates or party leaders.[89] Perhaps because so many Liberty leaders were ministers, physicians, and businessmen—not lawyers—they did not enter higher-level public life later. Their major personal efforts were in their professions. Many continued to work in lower-level politics, however, and contributed to the formation of the Republican Party.

The Liberty Party in Michigan was the strongest in the region during the early 1840s, but it lost much of its energy after 1844 as the unanimity in the movement broke down. Its leaders were citizen-reformers who worked in Liberty affairs while carrying on successful careers outside of politics. It had pockets of deep strength across the more settled southern part of the state, where a core of strong community leaders held the party together even as disagreements fragmented the leadership. They helped make Michigan the state most supportive of antislavery activity in the Northwest.

OHIO

From the late 1830s until 1848, Ohio had a competitive two-party system characterized by enthusiastic voter participation that reached nearly 85% in the 1840 presidential election. Both parties were highly organized and its politics were among the most complex in the country.[90] The state's population came from all areas of the country, and its attitudes toward race and abolition reflected this variety. As a border state with many Southern immigrants, black laws and periodic racial violence indicated anti-black sentiment. Racial beliefs affected party politics, and a leading Ohio historian has concluded "the differences between Whigs and Democrats on the question of race were striking and significant." An earlier commentator wrote that the "negro question in Ohio was never extraneous, as it was in Massachusetts and Vermont."[91] Whigs were much more sympathetic to African Americans and slaves, while Democrats were so hostile to blacks and abolitionists that they did not hesitate to proscribe antislavery members.[92]

Nonetheless, many Ohioans worked for black rights and abolition. The Western Reserve area in the northeastern part of the state was almost a little New England or Upstate New York in its population and antislavery fervor, but pockets of abolition existed even along Ohio's border with slave-state Kentucky in Cincinnati and along the Ohio River. One of the earliest calls for immediate emancipation in the country came from John Rankin of Ripley, Ohio, who had been calling for immediate emancipation for ten years before William Lloyd Garrison took up his work in Boston. Many years later Garrison called himself Rankin's "anti-slavery disciple and humble co-worker in the cause of emancipation." The state's abolitionists formed the Ohio Anti-Slavery Society in 1835, when Theodore Dwight Weld assembled representatives of older local societies.[93] They soon became involved in political activities and realized that a relatively small bloc of voters could have an impact in the highly competitive Ohio environment, and they took their antislavery principles into the political realm more quickly than many states.

James G. Birney moved to Cincinnati from Kentucky, became editor of the *Philanthropist,* and urged political involvement as early as 1836. He clearly meant to go beyond petitioning and influencing legislation to becoming involved the electoral process. Birney persuaded the Ohio Anti-Slavery Society to send political antislavery lecturers into the Western Reserve in 1836 and 1837, and he himself spoke in many towns. They included political messages in their talks, encouraged questioning candidates, and urged voters to carry their antislavery principles to the polls.[94] Initially, these efforts seemed to have succeeded. By 1838, abolitionists claimed to have influenced elections in the Western Reserve and helped elect antislavery Whig Joshua Giddings to Congress.[95] At the same time, Whig Governor Joseph Vance alienated antislavery voters when he ordered the extradition of John B. Mahan to Kentucky for aiding an escaped slave in Ohio.[96] When the Whigs suffered a crushing defeat in the election, abolitionists across the North exulted in their newly discovered political power. Gamaliel Bailey wrote to Birney, who was working in New York, that "I am astonished myself. Tell our friends at New York, that Ohio abolitionists know how to vote . . . I do believe we have done better so far as political action is concerned than any state, except Vermont and Massachusetts."[97] The abolitionists' elation was short-lived, however, as they angered many antislavery Whigs and received no appreciation from the Democrats. In fact, the Democrats soon refused to reelect Thomas Morris to the U.S. Senate because of his antislavery predilections.[98] In addition, the Ohio legislature passed a tough fugitive slave law in early 1839 with the support of a Whig who had been elected as an ostensible opponent of slavery.[99] Whig Benjamin Wade suffered so much in an 1839 race that "[f]or years thereafter he strove to separate himself from the political stigma of abolitionism."[100]

These events caused consternation among Ohio's abolitionists, but they agreed about the necessity for political action. Although some Quakers or other abolitionists may have been nonpolitical, they were definitely a small minority and did not attempt to discourage others from political action. In fact, Ohio abolitionists were quite willing to carry their beliefs to the polls. At a September 11, 1839, meeting of the Lorain County Anti-Slavery Society, one thousand members unanimously voted that they would "not vote for any man for President or Vice President of the United States, or for Congress, who is not in favor of the immediate abolition of slavery in the District of Columbia and in the United States territory, and of the abolition of the internal slave trade, and who is not opposed to the admission of new slave states into the Union."[101] The real question for most abolitionists was how they could best carry their antislavery principles into the political realm, and they could not reach a consensus on this. The state society refused to commit itself on a specific political course except to say that individuals should act politically. Most of these abolitionists voted Whig and held out the hope that the Whig Party would eventually become the party of abolition.[102]

As the 1840 presidential contest approached, most of Ohio's abolitionists opposed any move toward independent nominations. Nonetheless, a movement toward independent nominations began in the early summer of 1840.[103] Perhaps the most important convert to the idea of an independent party was *Philanthropist* editor Gamaliel Bailey. After initially opposing the third party, he moved from privately supporting independent nominations to a public endorsement of the Birney-Earle ticket.[104] By early July, he encouraged the selection of presidential electors and called for abolitionists to meet in Hamilton on September 1 to discuss political activities. In the meantime, third-party men organized some local conventions to select electors and nominate candidates.[105] The convention at Hamilton was a contentious gathering in which many argued against a third party.[106] Joshua Leavitt made the long trip from the East Coast, and it was fortunate for third-party supporters that he did. A participant maintained that Leavitt made "the [most] forceable speech in the convention ... His speech carried many with him."[107] The speech included elements on the financial and political power of slaveholders as well as the usual moral strictures against slavery.[108] They needed every vote as a resolution supporting independent nominations narrowly passed 57–54. After the vote, "nearly half the members of the convention left. A good deal of anger was exhibited by those that left." The convention adopted the name Liberty Party and supported the Birney-Earle ticket by acclamation.[109]

Many anti-third-party abolitionists did not accept the results and continued to work for the Whig ticket.[110] Perhaps the most important of these was John Rankin. He backed Harrison and argued in a series of letters to Bailey in the *Philanthropist* that a vote for Birney was in effect a vote for Democrat Martin Van Buren.[111] Many agreed with him. The anti-third-party group continued its opposition in several local conventions. Sometimes the gatherings made endorsements by questioning candidates, sometimes third-party motions were defeated (with the losers promptly meeting separately to set up an electoral slate), and sometimes the meetings made no recommendations.[112] Liberty efforts met with poor results as Ohio's antislavery Whigs worked hard to hold voters.

Bailey remained publicly confident that Birney would receive at least one-third of the estimated voting abolitionists in the state.[113] He was overly optimistic. An overwhelming majority of Ohio abolitionist leaders and rank and file remained with Harrison and the Whigs in the election, with Birney only receiving 903 votes (0.3%). Future Liberty leaders Salmon P. Chase, Leicester King, Samuel Lewis, and Edward Wade all openly supported Harrison. Most other abolitionists did the same or stayed at home.[114] The leading historian of political antislavery believes that "so solidly did Whig abolitionists stick by their party that in the West, at least, more former Democrats than Whigs seem to have cast ballots for Birney."[115] Nevertheless, several important men attached themselves to the new party. In addition to Bailey and Morris, former U.S. senator Alexander Campbell, General James H. Paine, Dyer Burgess, and future U.S. congressman John Hutchins took early leadership roles in the new party.

Liberty men soon began their work. A large convention in Akron recommended the nomination of Thomas Morris for governor even though the election was more than two years away.[116] In mid-December Bailey issued a call for a state antislavery convention to meet in Columbus on January 20 to "agree upon some rational, effective plan of anti-slavery political action." He made it clear that it was not just a third-party convention and all were welcome.[117] This Columbus convention established the Liberty Party as an ongoing part of the Ohio political scene. More than two hundred men and women from thirty-six counties endorsed independent political action at all levels. Women participated in a convention that rejected the questioning system and voted 101–16 "that abolitionists nominate candidates for office in all places where they are not perfectly assured, that one or both of the existing parties will nominate candidates, for whom they can consistently vote."[118] This was particularly important because it endorsed Liberty nominations before those of the major parties but still left room for a local major party to become sufficiently antislavery to warrant Liberty votes. Antislavery Whigs were still strong but many soon changed their views. William Henry Harrison disappointed antislavery Whigs with his friendliness toward the South and his hostility toward abolitionists.[119] Disappointment turned to horror when he died shortly after his inauguration and was succeeded by ardent Southern slaveholder John Tyler.[120] His death was a boost to the Liberty Party because it brought into its ranks many new capable leaders. By the end of the year, Salmon P. Chase, Samuel Lewis, Leicester King, and a whole group of Oberlin abolitionists who had supported Harrison were in the new party.[121]

The year 1841 was a transitional one for the Ohio Liberty Party. Even though there were no statewide elections, the Liberty Party established many local organizations and developed grassroots strength. A state convention held in conjunction with the annual meeting of the Ohio Anti-Slavery Society made nominations for the state legislature, and some local conventions met to set up candidate lists. This began a process that one historian has estimated resulted in over two thousand votes in the fall elections, still a small percentage of the total but over a 100% increase in one year.[122] The progress continued into 1842. A state Liberty convention in Columbus on December 29, 1841, nominated state justice and former state senator Leicester King for governor in 1842 and went on record to "expressly disclaim, in behalf of the General Government, all rights to interfere with Slavery in the states where it exists." This reflected the involvement of newcomer Salmon P. Chase. He wrote the call for the meeting, served on three committees, composed most of the address and resolutions, and even suggested William Seward or John Quincy Adams as presidential candidates for 1844.[123] The "Columbus convention," as it was subsequently referred to, was the defining event in Ohio Liberty Party history. It began a more rigorous organization of the party and clearly identified such Liberty leaders as Chase, King, the popular state superintendent of public instruction, Samuel Lewis, and a future U.S. congressman, Norton W. Townshend.[124]

A difficult decision for Liberty men came quickly. In late March, Joshua Giddings, a Whig congressman from the Western Reserve, was censured in the U.S. House of Representatives for his antislavery actions.[125] He promptly resigned his seat and left for home to stand for reelection. This presented Liberty men with a dilemma. They had to decide whether to forgo running a candidate and give at least tacit support to Giddings, or to maintain party lines and run their own candidate against a popular Whig who had taken a courageous stand in Congress. Most Liberty men did not take long to resolve the dilemma. They did not run their own candidate and many openly supported Giddings, including General James H. Paine, one of the earliest Liberty leaders on the Western Reserve.[126] Even Garrison's *Liberator*, an avowed critic of the American political system, was enthusiastic and urged his reelection "by an overwhelming (it ought to be unanimous) vote."[127] Giddings easily won reelection over his Democratic challenger, 7,469–3,943, and Chase believed that Giddings received the votes of "a thousand Liberty men."[128] He spurned Liberty overtures to join the new party, however, so Liberty men on the Western Reserve would continue to have to make the choice between running a committed Liberty man or lining up behind Giddings.

In the meantime Liberty men concentrated on the fall 1842 gubernatorial contest. With a popular candidate and capable leadership, Liberty men threw themselves energetically into the 1842 campaign. Party organizers arranged speaking engagements, distributed campaign circulars, held rallies, and formed "Liberty Clubs."[129] Their efforts were rewarded by almost six times the number of votes (5,134—2.1%) since 1840. Not only did the Liberty vote increase substantially, but the Whigs also suffered a defeat for which they blamed the new party. The third party clearly held the balance of power, and the Western Reserve area contributed proportionately the largest number of Liberty voters.[130] Despite the presence of such significant Democratic defectors as Thomas Morris, George W. Ells, and John Hutchins, the bulk of the Liberty vote in 1842 seems to have come from Whig sources.[131]

Although there was no statewide election in 1843, Liberty men continued their efforts because all the Ohio seats in the U.S. Congress were contested in the fall. Problems in the state legislature over apportionment and redistricting had prevented the normal even-year elections. The party made nominations in most districts and increased the vote by approximately 30%.[132] A major problem developed for Liberty men in the district where Joshua Giddings was running for reelection. Ohio Liberty men were conducting ongoing internal debates about whether the party should support antislavery candidates of other parties. They received criticism from outside the state because of their willingness to break party lines. Gerrit Smith had been scolding the Ohio abolitionists since 1840 for their support of Harrison and willingness to temper antislavery principles and support major-party candidates. The issue became so heated that Gamaliel Bailey eventually broke off communications with Smith.[133] Liberty men reversed themselves in 1843 and ran their own candidate, Edward Wade. Giddings easily held onto his seat, but Wade made a credible showing with 797 votes (7.5%). Some Liberty men still broke ranks there and elsewhere to vote Whig.[134] As crossover voting continued, Liberty leaders began to harden their position. By mid-1842, Bailey had changed his mind and concluded that the Liberty Party should have its own candidates and agenda, and by the following year he was joined by John Rankin, who finally gave up his Whig allegiances to go with the new party.[135]

The party continued, however, to be bothered by ideological matters and personality clashes. In addition to debating the degree of cooperation permissible with the major parties, the aforementioned efforts of Chase and Bailey to replace Birney and Morris as the party's standard-bearers for 1844 caused conflict, particularly with Morris himself. Bailey and Chase had pressured Morris, a blunt and somewhat irascible political veteran, to give up the vice presidential nomination of the 1841 National Liberty convention, and Bailey refused to put the new 1843 Buffalo ticket on the masthead of the *Philanthropist*. In addition, he would not publish Morris's controversial views on the U.S. Constitution and other antislavery matters.[136] Morris's unsuccessful attempt to control the Liberty Party in the Cincinnati area reached a crisis in early 1844, when he publicly criticized Bailey and cancelled his subscription to the *Philanthropist*. Philosophical differences also separated Morris from Bailey and Chase. As William Birney reported to his father, "Mr. Morris was for pushing ultra doctrines. Mr. Chase thought moderation would better insure success."[137] Chase believed "it not advisable to incur any unnecessary odium" and "believe[d] that political bodies have nothing to do with ecclesiastical organization." He wanted to make a distinction between abolition and the Liberty Party, which would "direct all the energies of our political action against the unconstitutional encroachment of the Slave Power and against Slavery itself where it may exist without constitutional sanction." He maintained that one "who severs himself from the slavery parties is a good Liberty Man. We are not anxious that he should take upon himself any other name [i.e., abolitionist] than that of Liberty Man unless he pleases."[138] Although Chase claimed that "the aim of a Liberty Party, reaching far beyond the mere abolition of slavery, should be to establish Liberty," his views encompassed a narrower view of antislavery political duties than many were willing to accept.[139]

This philosophy put him and Bailey at odds with Morris and most Liberty followers outside the Cincinnati area. Although Morris lost most of his battles in his home area, he prevailed at the state convention in Columbus in early February 1844 (Chase was not present). One hundred sixteen delegates condemned slavery in the South, affirmed the Birney-Morris ticket, renominated Leicester King for governor, urged complete nominations at all levels, and passed spirited antislavery resolutions that went beyond those of earlier state meetings.[140] That this happened is not too surprising. The Chase-Bailey group's domination of many conventions was disproportionate to its numbers. Bailey and particularly Chase had great energy and organizational skills. Chase wrote and shepherded his addresses and resolutions through virtually every meeting in which he participated. This energy and productivity made it appear that they spoke for many more people than they really did. The party outside the Cincinnati area was much more militant in its antislavery resolve and positions than the Bailey-Chase faction. (Warren, Ohio) *Liberty Herald* editor L. L. Rice, Western Reserve antislavery groups, and the Oberlin abolitionists were more similar to their eastern counterparts and more accurately represented the true spirit of the Ohio Liberty Party. They usually did not make overtures to or accept them from major-party candidates, and there was a more highly moralistic tone to their pronouncements. They took more daring positions in their resolutions on such matters as the antislavery nature of the U.S. Constitution and the regulation of slavery and the slave trade.

Nevertheless, Ohio Liberty men came together for the 1844 campaign. By early 1844, Texas annexation was a major issue, and James K. Polk's unabashed support for acquiring Texas caused many Ohio Democrats with antislavery or anti-Southern leanings to question whether they could support the Democratic presidential ticket.[141] Whigs, on the other hand, used the annexation issue to show themselves as more friendly to antislavery interests in an effort to bring former Whigs back from the Liberty Party. Major-party leaders knew that the election would be close and the role of the third party might be crucial. A leading Democrat wrote to Polk that "[t]he two great parties are so nicely balanced that a straw may decide the fight . . . If the abolitionists stand firm . . . we shall carry the state—but everything now depends upon them."[142] Anti-annexation sentiment was strong in Ohio, and state Democrats stayed away from the issue and necessarily ran a subdued campaign. Whigs, meanwhile, argued that a vote for the Liberty Party could elect Polk. In the October state elections, the Democrats failed to hold onto the governor's chair. Liberty men campaigned hard and made a 73.3% increase in their totals over their 1842 totals with 8,898 votes (3.0%).

Democrats and Liberty men then both suffered a real and proportional loss in the presidential race a month later with the Whigs registering a gain.

Henry Clay (Whig)	155,091 (49.7%)
James K. Polk (Democrat)	149,127 (47.8%)
James G. Birney (Liberty)	8,083 (2.6%)

Liberty strength concentrated on the Western Reserve. Lorain (473 Liberty of 4,222 total) and Ashtabula (537 of 5,048) gave over 10% to the Liberty Party, while Hamilton, including Cincinnati, contributed less than 2% (298 of 16,482). While it would be difficult to argue with the energy of the Cincinnati group, their vote-getting ability in their home area was weak.

No one has yet done a systematic study of the total Ohio Liberty vote below the county level, but it seems probable that there was a shift of some former Whig Liberty voters back to their old party. Some Democrats may not have been able to stomach Polk and annexation and voted Liberty or stayed at home. If some went to Liberty, they did not make up for other losses. The Liberty Party lost over 800 votes in one month even though the total turnout increased by over 12,000. It seems clear that the Garland Forgery hurt the Liberty Party and helped the Whigs. Although William Birney's assertion that in Ohio "Mr. Birney lost several thousand votes, most of which went to Mr. Clay" because of the forgery was probably an exaggeration, there is no doubt that uncertainty over the allegations caused some Liberty men to support Clay or sit out the presidential contest.[143] How many left the party is difficult to gauge because there may have been Democratic accessions in both the gubernatorial and presidential contests that countered the defections to the Whigs. The elder Birney's policy statements and behavior may have made him more acceptable to Democrats, and Salmon P. Chase had already begun a courtship of antislavery and anti-annexation Democrats that would accelerate after 1844.

Much of the Ohio Liberty story after 1844 played out on the national scene with the attempts of the Chase-Bailey group to move the Liberty Party toward some sort of union with the Democrats. The party continued to grow in Ohio in the two years after the 1844 elections despite concerted efforts by Whigs in northern

Ohio to win back former supporters. They pointed out the condemnation of the annexation of Texas in the Whig-controlled state legislature and their efforts in trying to repeal Ohio's notorious black laws. Exchanges between the two camps often grew bitter as Whigs blamed the Liberty men for putting Polk in the White House, and Liberty men criticized Whigs for being inconsistent and unreliable in their antislavery pronouncements. Even though Joshua Giddings promised by 1846 never to support a slaveholder again, Liberty men continued to distrust him and his motives. Although there may have been a two-way movement in some areas, as former Whigs returned to their old party and were replaced by new Democratic converts, the Liberty Party held its own or made slight gains in the 1845 local elections following the Great Southern and Western Convention.[144]

Liberty men worked hard on the 1846 elections. A December 31, 1845, state convention nominated Samuel Lewis for governor, and he soon embarked on an extensive seven-month speaking tour that carried him to all parts of the state.[145] The 1846 election was also significant for antislavery politics because Edward Wade again challenged Giddings for his congressional seat, indicating that the strongest antislavery sentiment on the Western Reserve still was not willing to accept Giddings.[146] Of less immediate importance, Chase's candidacy in another district was his first attempt at federal office. Both major parties were aware that the antislavery vote might be critical. Whig candidate William Bebb talked strong anti-black law rhetoric on the Western Reserve, but told a different story in southern Ohio. There he stated "that he was opposed to equal political or educational advantages, and suggest[ed] that a good way to keep negroes out of the State would be to lay a special tax on their land."[147] Democrat David Tod remained silent.

Lewis campaigned hard for antislavery measures. Bebb won a narrow victory, and the Lewis campaign effort—probably the most intense by any statewide Liberty candidate anywhere—resulted in the Liberty Party attaining its highest vote ever in Ohio. He increased the Liberty total by over 1,900 votes (to 10,799—4.4%) from its previous high (the 1844 gubernatorial race), a 21.4% increase numerically and 1.8% more than Birney's proportion of 2.6% in 1844. Giddings easily recaptured his congressional seat, but he and the Democratic candidate lost 3,500 and 2,422 votes respectively while Liberty man Edward Wade gained 86 votes and 12.9% of the total. In another district on the Western Reserve, Liberty candidate Joel Tiffany increased his percentage of the total from 6.1% to 11.5%. He gained 517 votes while his Whig and Democrat opponents lost 1,515 and 1,980. He held the balance of power both years. This demonstrated the uncompromising abolition strength on the Western Reserve, where 1 out of 8 voters did not find Joshua Giddings sufficiently antislavery and Joel Tiffany increased his vote by 35.1%. This did not bode well for the type of antislavery union that Chase and Bailey envisioned.

Ohio Liberty men had shown that they could function with internal differences, but they could not have foreseen the difficulties of the next two years. The disintegration of the Ohio Liberty press hurt the state party. Gamaliel Bailey's departure to Washington, D.C., to edit the *National Era* left the party without its well-known state newspaper. Bailey capably produced a nationally recognized sheet that reached all of Ohio with its list of four to five thousand subscribers.[148] He declared that "*Philanthropist*" would be dropped from its title when he left, but that "every subscriber to the Philanthropist will be considered a subscriber to the National Era." The subscription list for the successor newspaper was only four to five hundred, and its editor constantly was appealing for these to pay their bills. The new editor, twenty-three-year-old lawyer Stanley Matthews, only intended to stay for a few weeks, but he shepherded the paper much longer as it subsequently became the *Weekly Herald* and then the *Cincinnati National Press and Weekly Herald*.[149] More discouraging was L. L. Rice's *Liberty Herald* closing because of fire, and the fact that the "*Cleveland American* was in disarray."[150]

Lack of effective statewide leadership contributed to a decentralization of the state party, but it is difficult to assess how much this affected antislavery fervor or Liberty power as these elements became more localized.[151] Chase was working for a union with the Democrats, and he remained influential in the party, but the old Liberty organization in his area had lost much of its talented leadership by 1847. Thomas Morris was dead; Bailey was in Washington, D.C., with the *National Era*; and William Birney was in Europe, where he would be a teacher and journalist until the 1850s. Stanley Matthews partially filled this void, but much talent and a whole web of state and national connections were gone. Matthews stayed close to his mentor Chase's philosophy of viewing the federal government as having no direct power over slavery within the states, searching for a wider base for the party, and avoiding the moralistic and religiously charged pronouncements of many Liberty leaders elsewhere in the state. For example, he was one of the very few Liberty men anywhere to criticize linking temperance to the Liberty agenda. When a Liberty meeting in New Lisbon passed a resolution stating that it would only support candidates in favor of total abstinence, he harshly commented that "[s]uch a resolution, it seems to us, is entirely out of place in a Liberty Convention. It is travelling out of the record, unless it is intended to go the entire figure of the Liberty League, in which event the other eighteen points ought not to have been omitted."[152]

The party developed differently from this in most Liberty areas of Ohio.[153]

George Bradburn, recently arrived from Massachusetts, was so strongly in favor of making the antislavery interpretation a party test for Liberty candidates that he proposed at the October 1847 national convention that no one who did not think slavery unconstitutional should be approved as a Liberty nominee.[154] The 1844 and 1846 Liberty congressional candidate from Lorain County, Joel Tiffany, agreed with this basic constitutional interpretation. He was preparing his arguments for *A Treatise on the Unconstitutionality of American Slavery; Together with the Powers and Duties of the Federal Government in Relation to That Subject*, which would be published in 1849.[155] Asa Mahan, the president of Oberlin, took similar ground in his debate with William Lloyd Garrison in 1847.[156] Lack of central control affected the overall vigor and success of the party in the state after 1846. With no statewide or congressional elections, the party held no state convention in 1847 and local parties went in more directions than usual. In some areas party discipline broke down and Liberty men returned to questioning candidates.[157] New groups sometimes developed from previous Liberty organizations. A convention in Hudson on the Western Reserve renamed itself the Northern Ohio Liberty Association so that it would include counties south of the Reserve.[158] This united the major area of Ohio's Liberty strength, but its effectiveness would only be tested in local races in 1847. In some races, the Liberty Party actually made increases in its proportion of the vote despite difficulty in getting their tickets in the hands of voters and bad weather holding down the total turnout.[159] Another group went in a different direction. George Bradburn of the *Cleveland American* actively opposed Hale's nomination for president because he was not a genuine Liberty Party man.[160]

The year 1848 marked the move of the overwhelming majority of Liberty men into the Free Soil coalition.[161] The leading Liberty man in the state movement was Salmon P. Chase. While many believed that the Whig Party would be the basis for antislavery union, Chase became convinced that the future of an antislavery union rested with the Democratic Party.[162] He had been considering this possibility since at least 1843 despite his earlier association with the Whig Party, supporting Harrison in 1840, urging presidential candidacies for John Quincy Adams and William Seward, and exploring alliances with such Whigs as Joshua Giddings. After 1844, he directed most of his efforts toward national politics, however, and his influence on the vast majority of Ohio Liberty supporters was not great as the Cincinnati group lost much of its power.[163] No one filled the void, so when the Free Soil movement began to develop, Chase and his Cincinnati group regained control of the Liberty element without much difficulty.

Stanley Matthews attended the Whig national convention and participated in meetings with those who protested Taylor's candidacy.[164] He joined Chase and

Lewis along with some Whigs and Democrats in a call for a People's Convention to meet in Columbus on June 21.[165] The Chase group also called for a state Liberty convention to immediately precede the People's Convention (later changed to immediately following it).[166] Chase did much of the work for the People's Convention and was highly satisfied with the results. Although "[n]ot a great many prominent politicians & hardly any of the leaders of the old political parties were with us . . . Whigs & Democrats met with Liberty men on a common platform & resolved to bury all differences in a common effort."[167] Chase prepared most of the resolutions and arranged for various men to present them at the meeting. The convention made opposition to the extension of slavery its credo and called for a national Free Soil convention in Buffalo in August.[168] Immediately after the People's Convention, Liberty men gathered to reaffirm the support for the Hale-King ticket but left the decision of future actions up to the newly appointed state central committee. More important, they decided not to run a Liberty gubernatorial ticket "in view of the transcendent importance of united, harmonious, and vigorous action in support of the candidates for the Presidency and Vice Presidency."[169] These were the last actions of the Liberty Party in Ohio. With Chase in constant contact with the Barnburner Democrats in New York, the Ohio Liberty men moved ineluctably into the Free Soil coalition. The *Cincinnati Weekly Herald and Philanthropist* quickly expressed its willingness to support Van Buren on an anti-extension platform and then removed the Hale-King ticket from its masthead.[170]

A large Ohio contingent attended the Free Soil convention in Buffalo, and several of its Liberty men were prominent in the proceedings. General James H. Paine, longtime Ohio abolitionist and Liberty man who had recently moved to Wisconsin, opened the meeting. Chase was instrumental in much of the behind-the-scenes negotiations and presided at the nominating convention at a nearby Universalist church. Samuel Lewis and Asa Mahan gave speeches, and Reverend Edward Smith, Austin A. Guthrie, and Norton S. Townshend served on committees.[171] Perhaps the most significant thing about the participants was that they came from all parts of the geographic and ideological spectra in the state. Most Ohio Liberty men remained true to their commitment to Hale in the preliminary voting by a margin of 31–27 over Van Buren with 10 "other" votes.[172] Liberty men then fell in line and supported the eventual Van Buren–Adams ticket. Lewis and Chase began campaigning on their way back from Buffalo and continued to make extensive speaking engagements right up to the presidential election. Other Liberty men soon joined them, and John Van Buren, the presidential candidate's popular son, joined them for one week in October.[173] The *Cincinnati Weekly Herald* changed its name to the *Cincinnati Weekly Globe* and along with about twenty other newspapers, including all the Liberty sheets, supported the Free Soil Party.

The regular Whig Party members clung to their own candidates and worked hard across the state. They were very disappointed in the results of the October state elections, however, because their candidate barely won despite receiving most of the Free Soil vote. As historian Stephen Maizlish has written, "[I]t was immediately clear that without Free-Soil support Ford would not have had a chance. Few could now doubt that Van Buren's Free-Soil candidacy would doom Taylor's Ohio campaign."[174] Free Soilers captured eight seats in the lower house of the state legislature, including former Liberty man Dr. Norton S. Townshend, from the Lorain County district encompassing Oberlin College.[175]

The fears of the Whigs were realized in the national contest.

Zachary Taylor (Whig)	138,656 (42.1%)
Lewis Cass (Democrat)	154,782 (47.1%)
Martin Van Buren (Free Soil)	35,523 (10.8%)[176]

Analysts agree that the bulk of the Free Soil vote came from Whig and Liberty sources.[177] In the two Liberty counties that gave over 10% of their vote to the Liberty Party in 1844, this certainly was the case. Ashtabula was the banner Free Soil county in the state with 55.6% of the vote. The progress from the 1844 election shows these county votes assuredly came from former Whig and Liberty voters (see table 6). The same trend is true in Lorain, the 1844 banner Liberty county. This holds especially true for the Western Reserve counties, where popular Whig congressmen Joshua Giddings and Joseph Root joined the third party, although the Whig defections are less apparent in many other parts of the state.

Ohio's Liberty men fared better than in other states, sending Chase to the U.S. Senate and Townshend to the U.S. Congress after much difficult negotiating. Over the next few decades, former Liberty men held many major positions in federal, state, and local governments. Chase, of course, is the best known. He became a U.S. senator, governor of Ohio, Lincoln's secretary of the treasury, and chief justice of the U.S. Supreme Court. Stanley Matthews followed as U.S. senator and a justice on the U.S. Supreme Court. It is less well known that Townshend, John Hutchins, Edward Wade, John Mercer Langston, James Monroe, and Ralph Plumb became members of the U.S. Congress. The number of former Ohio Liberty men who served in state and local public life was large.

The Ohio Liberty Party was made up of a diverse group of individuals. In the Western Reserve area it was similar to many of its organizations in New York

Table 6. Votes in Ashtabula and Lorain Counties (Ohio), 1844–1848

	1844 PRESIDENT	1848 GOVERNOR	1848 PRESIDENT
Ashtabula County			
Whig	3,388 (67.1%)	3,405 (78.4%)	1,124 (25.2%)
Democrat	1,123 (22.2%)	936 (21.6%)	878 (19.6%)
Liberty	537 (10.6%)		
Free Soil			2,467 (55.2%)
Lorain County			
Whig	1,956 (46.3%)	2,155 (58.6%)	647 (17.3%)
Democrat	1,793 (42.5%)	1,521 (41.4%)	1,473 (39.4%)
Liberty	473 (11.2%)		
Free Soil			1,616 (43.3%)

and New England. Elsewhere, a small group of Liberty men around Cincinnati developed an orientation and strategy that had a lasting impact on the breakup of the second American party system. And there were pockets of Liberty abolitionists in other scattered areas—such as near Ripley, Ohio—that were loyal to the party. Despite the presence of a small Garrisonian element during the 1840s, the vast majority of antislavery activities took place under the aegis of the Liberty Party. The long-term effects of party members are also noteworthy, as it contributed more national statesmen to public life than any other state, and many of its members carried their ideals into other areas of the country during westward expansion. Many of those remaining in Ohio continued their involvement in state and local affairs.

ILLINOIS

During the 1830s, Illinois Democrats developed a dominant political machine that resulted in their control of the state until the coming of the Republican Party. The only serious Whig challenge was beaten back in the 1840 presidential race, and Whig support declined precipitously thereafter because they "never succeeded in developing an effective organization."[178] Democrats so dominated the state by 1846 that the anemic Whigs were rumored to have "concluded to run no one [in the gubernatorial contest] and to let the democrats for want of opposition quarrel among themselves."[179] The county was the primary unit of local government until 1848 because "there was no provision for township government."[180] This county orientation affected the abolition movement by giving county antislavery societies unusual prominence, but abolitionism in early Illinois was weak and scattered. The first settlers were Southerners, but the northeastern part of the state expanded rapidly during the 1830s with an influx of settlers from New England and New York. Controversy over slavery existed during debates over the state's first constitution, and abolitionists had been present in the state, but, as the killing of Elijah Lovejoy demonstrated, they sometimes encountered hostility.[181] They founded the Illinois Anti-Slavery Society in October 1837 and established several local organizations, "the strongest region being the seven or eight northeastern counties, which stand in relation to the rest of the State much as the Western Reserve did to Ohio."[182]

The move to independent nominations began modestly. Delegates to a September 1839 meeting of the Illinois Anti-Slavery Society urged abolitionists to make their antislavery feelings known at the polls, but they did not devise a questioning system or endorse a separate political organization.[183] Hampered by the lack of a state newspaper—Benjamin Lundy's *Genius of Universal Emancipation* ceased publication shortly after his death on August 22, 1839—there was little movement toward a third party until July 5, 1840. After a July 4 meeting of about one hundred members of the state society refused to endorse strong political resolutions, a group of fifteen third-party advocates met the next day and endorsed the Birney-Earle ticket, the first official endorsement of the new party in the Old Northwest. They also set up an electoral ticket and endorsed a platform that called for the abolition of slavery "by law at sacrifice of time and money but not blood" and recommended moving the national capital northwest of the Ohio River.[184] They did little campaigning in the state, and estimates ranged from 150 to 160 votes (about 0.2%) for the Birney-Earle ticket.

After the election, the move toward political abolition began in earnest. On December 19, the (Lowell, Ill.) *Genius of Liberty* began publishing under the auspices of the LaSalle County Anti-Slavery Society. Edited and published by veteran journalist Hooper Warren and Lundy's able assistant, Zebina Eastman, it initially expressed "a strict neutrality in regard to any denominational or party influence." Nonetheless, it carried information on the new party and served as the successor to Lundy's newspaper. It began to move toward independent politics by recommending that third-party abolitionists call a convention after the state society meeting on February 24 in order to select delegates to the May 1841 national convention in New York City.[185] This meeting of the Illinois Anti-Slavery Society thoroughly debated the political question and finally resolved that it was "inconsistent and suicidal, for abolitionists to vote for pro-slavery men," but they did not endorse a third party.[186] Convinced that "efficient political action . . . can be produced only by independent and united effort," the third-party advocates met the following day to set up a rudimentary organization. They decided not to send representatives to New York in May, but "measures were taken to have our sentiments duly made known to that body."[187] The group took no action on statewide nominations because there would be no election until 1842, but it encouraged county organization and district nominations in upcoming congressional races.

The state society continued to move closer to third-party action at its fourth annual meeting on June 9, but the approximately 125 members passed only a recommendation that votes only be given to antislavery candidates. The delegates moved in a more militant direction, however. They voted by a two-thirds margin to excise that part of their constitution that "admits that each State in which slavery exists has by the constitution of the United States, the exclusive right to *legislate*, in regard to its abolition in said State." A political antislavery convention again met the following day at the same place and nominated Frederick Collins, a Chicago lawyer, for Congress from the Third District, the strongest abolitionist district in the state.[188] He joined the Birney-Morris presidential ticket on the masthead of the June 26 issue of the *Genius of Liberty*.

A few rallies and organizational activities seem to have taken place during the summer and fall, and the *Genius of Liberty* could afford to publish only irregularly.[189] Nevertheless, Collins received 527 votes in the August election, a substantial increase from the 150 to 160 statewide ballots that Birney had received ten months earlier. That this total was more than the 354 Democratic plurality was more significant because the third party held the balance of power in the district. Also important, the increase from one to thirty-five votes in Cook County (which included Chicago) reflected the more central role that Chicago began to play in Liberty efforts.[190] The Illinois Liberty Party made major progress in 1842, and by the end of the year it developed its basic operational structure. The fifth anniversary meeting of the state society in Chicago on May 26 again did not specifically endorse the party but did resolve "[t]hat the Liberty Party had its origin . . . in the ordinance of heaven, enstamped upon our social being by the finger of Omnipotence, impelling its members to associated and efficient action."[191]

The next day 105 Liberty supporters met and made plans to put the party on a stable basis. They endorsed the stands and candidates of the 1841 national Liberty Party convention and added a call for the repeal of the Illinois black laws. They nominated Colonel Charles W. Hunter, a founding father of Alton and ally of Elijah Lovejoy, for governor and Frederick Collins for lieutenant-governor, set up a state central committee, and made plans to establish a state newspaper to replace the *Genius of Liberty*, which had ceased publication in April. The convention address was a combination of religious exhortation and practical political strategy. While it emphasized "Our Dependence on God" and the "Retribution of God" for the institution of slavery, it did not claim the constitutional power to abolish slavery in the slave states. Instead, "[w]e propose to go, where [Benjamin] Franklin said he would, to the very verge of the Constitution."[192] Perhaps the most important decision of the convention was to establish the *Chicago Western Citizen,* a newspaper that would attain a large circulation and great influence in the Old Northwest. A stock offering of two hundred shares at five dollars per share was to underwrite its startup costs. Zebina Eastman became the editor and promised a general sheet that not only espoused antislavery but also temperance, political reform, religion, agricultural matters, and general news. It had a dual motto: a quote from the Declaration of Independence and the biblical injunction that "This commandment we have from him; That he who loveth God, love his brother also," combined with the motto "The Supremacy of God and the Equality of Man."[193] This gathering also moved the organizational center of the state's antislavery movement to Chicago. Of those attending the convention, 28 out of 105 came from Cook County and many others from nearby areas. Rapidly growing Chicago was the rare urban center where the Liberty Party flourished. It had a talented and diverse leadership that created a model Liberty environment with interracial gatherings that included both men and women. The Chicago leadership centralized and energized the party statewide and locally. It made many of the statewide nominations and cajoled congressional districts and counties to set up local tickets, including running mayoral candidates every year in Chicago.[194]

Liberty men continued their efforts throughout the summer. They organized several county societies, but they were somewhat disappointed by the returns in the first statewide contest since the 1840 presidential election. Hunter managed only 382 more votes statewide (909—1.1%) than Frederick Collins had gotten in just one congressional district a year earlier.[195] Zebina Eastman confessed that the "Liberty vote was not so large as we expected," and he claimed that in Cook County many Liberty voters found the "polls were so crowded that it was impossible to get their names upon the poll book."[196] The centerpiece of Illinois activity was the *Chicago Western Citizen* with Eastman as its hardworking editor. Inheriting four hundred subscribers from the *Genius of Liberty,* he soon built a sizable subscription list and branched out into other antislavery publishing and distribution ventures. He eventually published a monthly magazine, tracts, almanacs, and a short-lived daily newspaper and served as a distributor of other abolitionist literature.[197] Eastman appointed agents throughout Illinois, Indiana, Iowa, Wisconsin, and even New York to take subscriptions, and the Illinois traveling agents, Reverends William T. Allan and Edward Mathews, solicited subscriptions in their far-flung journeys in Illinois and throughout the territories. Nonetheless, the paper never enjoyed true financial success. Eastman's biographer notes "[t]he lack of money was so chronic that virtually every issue of the *Western Citizen* contained pleas that subscribers pay what they owed and that readers donate funds."[198] Still, the newspaper outlived the Liberty Party by five years.

Liberty followers began to take an interest in regional and national Liberty affairs during 1843. The state central committee pushed for county and congressional district leaders to organize their own areas and make nominations. This seems to have been a conscious effort on its part to decentralize the Liberty movement in the state and develop more local involvement. Leaders did not think it "advisable to hold a State Convention [because there would not be a statewide vote in 1843], and the State Committee do not feel that they have any authority to take any step in reference to the district organization." The committee did urge the calling of a Northwest Liberty convention, the first such call for a regional meeting.[199] Local leaders responded by calling conventions, selecting local candidates, and nominating men for four of the seven congressional districts. They were rewarded when the total Liberty congressional vote exceeded the 1842 gubernatorial numbers by over one thousand. Still, the official totals disappointed Eastman. He complained that many abolitionists "made no effort at the last election; in these counties the Citizen was not circulated, and abolition was not *dying* away, but *sleeping*." He also believed "that the votes cannot have been all reported," a common complaint in many areas where the party was just getting established.[200]

Illinois representatives made their first appearance on the national Liberty scene at the 1843 National Liberty Party convention. The Illinois delegation included Dr. Charles V. Dyer, honored as a vice president; Owen Lovejoy, named a secretary; and James H. Collins, appointed to the national committee of correspondence. The Colored Citizens of Chicago selected a delegate and two alternates at their own meeting.[201] Afterward, there was a renewed sense of energy as the party prepared for the 1844 presidential election. One important move was Eastman's recruitment of Ichabod Codding from Connecticut to work as an antislavery lecturer and organizer. Codding, a Congregational clergyman and veteran antislavery lecturer, was a magnetic speaker who had been a vice president of the party's founding convention in Albany.[202] He joined John Cross, William T. Allan, Edward Mathews, Owen Lovejoy, and others as they lectured across the state, sometimes going into Southern counties where inhabitants rarely heard abolitionist appeals.[203] At the same time Eastman began publication of the *Liberty Tree*, a monthly antislavery magazine. He culled much of its material from Illinois writers—such as Allan, Mathews, and Lovejoy—as well as a variety of other antislavery writers. He included opposition abolition views, such as William Lloyd Garrison, and non-abolitionists, such as Henry Clay. The magazine suffered from the same financial problems as the *Chicago Western Citizen*, and finally ceased publication in 1846.[204]

At the same time the Illinois Anti-Slavery Society became an adjunct of the Liberty Party. The older organization was several hundred dollars in debt by the time of its semiannual convention on October 24. This meeting "virtually transformed that body into an arm of the Liberty Party."[205] The next day a "Meeting of Friends of the Liberty Party" established a committee to call a statewide convention for January 24, 1844, in Aurora that would devise a formal plan of organization, nominate presidential electors, and transact other party business.[206] Soon after these meetings most auxiliaries of the state society were subsumed in Liberty activities, although it and some of the local groups retained their organizations for a few more years. Meanwhile, some local societies were becoming Liberty Associations. The Chicago Liberty Association was the first such group in Illinois, and its constitution was to serve as a model for similar organizations throughout the state. The membership initiation fee was to be fifty cents and quarterly dues were twenty-five cents. The object of the organization was "to sustain a political party which shall be based upon the principle that 'all men are created equal.'" It will operate "in a faithful conformity to the fundamental principles of our government; and in doing which we will recognize the supremacy of God in all things, especially as a Ruler and a Lawgiver." Members would maintain a strong political focus, by pledging that "hereafter we will vote for no slaveholder, apologist for slavery, nor any person for any office, who will not make protection of the inalienable rights of man his first duty."[207] Most of the subsequent associations in the state took the place of an Illinois Anti-Slavery Society auxiliary.[208] Some of these associations served more than just a political purpose, welcoming women and carrying on general antislavery activities. In other areas older antislavery societies remained or women formed their own gender-specific groups, some of which maintained close ties with the local Liberty Party.

What Zebina Eastman called the "largest and best antislavery meeting ever held in the State" met at the state Liberty convention on January 24.[209] Ichabod Codding, whose organizational hand is apparent throughout the proceedings, reported that the roll of 111 missed many and did not include the spectators. The convention outlined a plan of organization for the state, including encouraging women to join the movement, and selected presidential electors for the fall. It reiterated its view that no voter could be viewed as an abolitionist who did not vote the Liberty ticket. Perhaps more important was authorizing three thousand dollars for the upcoming campaign, of which about eight hundred dollars was pledged at the meeting.[210] The 1844 campaigns began immediately after the meeting for the spring local elections, the summer congressional races, and the presidential contest. The indefatigable Codding traveled constantly during the year, setting up Liberty associations, raising funds and organizing conventions and rallies, reorganizing many antislavery groups to a more Liberty orientation, and setting up Liberty electoral tickets. Some of this local activity was rewarded as Ira Miltimore, a Chicago businessman, became the first successful Liberty candidate, winning the election for alderman in the Third Ward. In Chicago the average vote increased from the spring of 1843 (45) to August 1843 (100) to the spring of 1844 (206), although the Liberty candidate for marshal received 405 votes.[211] Codding intensified his efforts throughout the summer, by one count lecturing in eighteen counties.[212] Liberty men nominated congressional candidates in five of the seven districts and seem to have further intensified their efforts. They were rewarded by a total of 3,149 votes, an increase of 61.2% in one year.[213] Particularly impressive were advances in the highly organized Fourth District—which included abolition hotbeds DeKalb and Bureau counties as well as the Chicago vote—from 1,174 to 1,882 and in the Sixth District—including Knox and Winnebago—which almost doubled its vote from 254 to 505. These districts would remain key Liberty areas. Efforts continued into the presidential contest as Eastman sent free copies of the *Chicago Western Citizen* to individuals in weak Liberty areas "who will see that it is put to good use."[214] The presidential results, however, were disappointing.

Henry Clay (Whig)	45,931 (42.4%)
James K. Polk (Democrat)	58,982 (54.4%)
James G. Birney (Liberty)	3,433 (3.2%)

The Birney-Morris ticket increased its total from August to November by only 284 votes statewide, but it did receive votes in 50 out of 99 counties.[215]

Undoubtedly, heightened activity by Illinois Whigs hurt the Liberty vote. Contemporaries and subsequent analysts have acknowledged that most Liberty supporters had been Whigs, and, when Liberty candidates received endorsements from outside the party in local elections, they invariably came from Whigs.[216] After the August elections Eastman lamented that "[o]ur vote has been very much injured by some of the 'Abolition Whigs,' as they are called, voting for the Whig party."[217] Whig efforts to win back former members intensified during the presidential campaign. They spread the rumors of Birney's acceptance of a local Democratic nomination in Michigan and exploited the Garland Forgery.[218] Nonetheless, the Illinois Liberty Party made considerable progress in 1843–1844.

The Illinois experience after 1844 differed from Michigan and Ohio in that the Liberty Party both increased its vote and had few of the internal disputes that plagued its neighbors. While expanding the Liberty platform, working with the major parties in elections, and discussions on the antislavery nature of the U.S. Constitution were all debated, statewide gatherings were harmonious affairs that arrived at a consensus. They adhered to the one-idea platform, denounced fusion or coalition with the major parties, and usually reached an understanding on the relationship between slavery and the U.S. Constitution. The party appeared largely dormant in 1845 because there were no statewide or congressional races, but it continued to run candidates in local races.[219] It continued to promote the effort and built the *Chicago Western Citizen* circulation to 2,016 by September, "being a larger circulation by some hundreds than any other weekly paper in the city."[220] Zebina Eastman also printed and distributed a Liberty almanac with the help of agents throughout the state.[221]

In 1846 the Illinois Liberty Party made its greatest gains. Early in the year, Liberty followers held conventions and made nominations in local races and for all but one (in hostile southern Illinois) congressional seats.[222] After some encouraging results in the spring elections, Chicago Liberty leaders spearheaded a much more thorough organization of the state party.[223] They led the drive to set up a state central committee and leased a large meeting place, the City Saloon, as their base of operation.[224] A state Liberty convention at Princeton in late May followed this example and urged establishing committees all the way down to school districts and endorsed a tract system to print and distribute five thousand copies of four different tracts. It nominated Dr. Richard Eels, who had been tried and fined four hundred dollars by Judge Stephen A. Douglas in a famous fugitive slave case, for governor in the August election.[225]

The party efforts during the summer rivaled those in any state. Eastman offered campaign subscriptions to the *Chicago Western Citizen* that increased its circulation from 2,880 in April, to 3,072 in May, 3,288 in June, and 3,648 in July and reflected the intensity of the effort.[226] He also had the monthly magazine the *Liberty Tree*, and a new Liberty newspaper, the *Liberty Banner*, began publishing in the northwestern part of the state at Rock Island.[227] Liberty advocates held meetings in all areas, but the hub continued to be Chicago, where interracial, mixed-gender Liberty Association meetings and special lectures were enlivened by the Chicago Liberty Choir and Chicago Brass Band. The party made special efforts for Owen Lovejoy in the Fourth Congressional District. Lovejoy gave countless speeches between May and August, and Ichabod Codding, a particularly effective speaker, lectured widely in the district as he worked throughout the state. Certain parts of Illinois were rough places to work, and both Lovejoy and Codding received eggings and threats in the course of the campaign.[228] And the "Liberty Minstrel," George W. Clark, who came to perform at the regional convention in Chicago, wrote a song for Lovejoy and accompanied him on his campaign tour for a week in July.[229] The campaign received a further boost when Chicago hosted the North-Western Liberty Convention on June 24–26 that brought many of the leading abolitionists in the region together.[230] Rallies continued up to the eve of the election, and the unprecedented Liberty efforts were rewarded by a great increase in the party vote since 1844. Eels received a 50% (5,147—5.1%) increase over Birney's total of 3,433 less than two years before.[231] Even more encouraging were the results in the Fourth Congressional District, where Lovejoy (3,531—16.3%) exceeded Birney's statewide vote of 1844 and almost doubled the previous Liberty vote for Congress.[232] This success catapulted Lovejoy into the ranks of the leading Liberty politicians in the country. Massachusetts Liberty men recruited him to work in their fall campaign where he spoke fifty-five times in forty-one days and impressed his listeners with his abilities and informal manner.[233]

The enthusiasm generated in 1846 carried over into 1847 even though there were no statewide or congressional contests that year. The Fourth District was especially active. It was the heart and soul of the Liberty movement in Illinois and one of the leading concentrations of Liberty strength in the country. Virtually one of every six voters was a Liberty man, and Chicago was its headquarters. A large mid-1847 convention in Elgin set party philosophy and charted plans for the coming two years. After a particularly strong denunciation of Garrisonian anticlericalism and disunionism, delegates prepared "to carry the district in 1848" by making a special effort to elect local candidates in 1847.[234] A committee of three was to monitor progress and encourage meetings, and counties were to contribute toward supporting a permanent lecturer and an ambitious tract system. The committee brought in former slaves Henry Bibb, Lewis Washington, and others to lecture, held two large conventions and several smaller meetings, and encouraged the active and politically involved women's societies. It also subsidized campaign editions of the *Chicago Western Citizen*, appointed Alanson St. Clair as financial agent, and encouraged local nominations.[235] Another Liberty newspaper, the *Lake County Visitor*, appeared in April.[236] There was no doubt, however, that Chicago and its core of Liberty leaders remained its center as the home of the *Chicago Western Citizen* and the Chicago Liberty Association.[237]

The tone of the *Chicago Western Citizen*, the level of activity, and the optimism of correspondents indicated that the party was doing well. In Chicago the party did better than in 1846 by electing two aldermen, two street commissioners, and one or two "half-loaves."[238] It won local offices elsewhere and even helped send a true Liberty Party man, Hurlburt Swan, as a delegate to the upcoming 1847 Illinois Constitutional Convention, although he also received Whig votes.[239] The party was also spreading into the southern part of the state. A southern Illinois Liberty convention that met in mid-October in Eden resolved to do more work in coordinating the antislavery sympathizers in the southern counties. It decried the disabilities on African Americans under the proposed state constitution and resolved to explore the possibility of establishing a newspaper in the southern part of the state.[240] The Liberty Party in Illinois at the end of 1847 was the fastest growing and among the most united in the country.

A major incentive for Liberty followers as they began 1848 was their disdain for Article XIV of the proposed new Illinois Constitution that was being submitted to the voters. It recommended limiting citizenship to white people and prohibited free people of color from immigrating or slaveholders from freeing their slaves in the state.[241] The Liberty Party fought consistently for full citizenship rights for African Americans and included them in all their activities. They had devoted at least one widely distributed tract to the Illinois black codes and regularly passed resolutions opposing discrimination and favoring full civil rights.[242] Now the possibility of even more restrictive barriers galvanized them into action.[243] They opposed the discriminatory resolutions submitted on a separate ballot. Although they managed to help defeat the bill in fourteen northern counties, the bill passed easily statewide by a 49,063–20,884 margin, causing the *Chicago Western Citizen* to comment "[t]hus the devil has it all his own way."[244]

The party also began to prepare for the 1848 state and national elections. Unlike many other states, members were not sending or accepting overtures for coalition or fusion with other parties. They also did not endorse stronger antislavery constitutional interpretations, the Liberty League, or an expanded platform—although some local conventions and individuals approved of such choices. They held to an emphasis on the one-idea concept and a refusal to get involved in any coalition or fusion efforts. Liberty men campaigned into July as if the Liberty Party would be holding to its own candidates in the August state contests and the November presidential election. They started with Lovejoy's overwhelming renomination for the Fourth District in February.[245] He began a vigorous campaign tour with a popular Liberty singer financed by a subscription fund, but he soon found that he had to field questions on issues other than slavery. While declaring the paramount importance of antislavery, he explained his personal positions on various issues.[246] In general, Lovejoy's views were very close to many of those in the Foster-Beckley-Birney expanded platform and those espoused by the Liberty League, but some applied to specific Illinois situations. His willingness to speak on non-slavery-related matters was indicative of a subtle modification in the thinking of many in the Illinois Liberty Party. They did not want to abandon their organization and core positions but were interested in participating in a larger movement.

A key event was the state Liberty convention in Hennepin on July 4 and 5. Dissident Whigs and Democrats were present to discuss their views and to see what kind of accommodations the Liberty members might be willing to accept. While stating that members could not "lower their platform of action," they selected nine Liberty delegates to represent them at the Buffalo Free Soil convention. They also demonstrated that they did not automatically sign onto the new movement by nominating Charles V. Dyer and Henry Snow as a Liberty gubernatorial ticket for the August elections.[247] The Whigs did not even nominate a candidate for governor for the early August election. Liberty men held their own, again demonstrating the core loyalty that they had built up in their areas of strength with 4,748 votes (6.6%).[248] The heart of Liberty support continued to be the Fourth Congressional District, where Lovejoy's willingness to give his views on non-slavery issues did not hurt or help him substantially. His major-party opponents both took advanced antislavery ground in their own parties. John Wentworth was a powerful and popular Democrat who was the only Illinois Democrat in the U.S. Congress to support the Wilmot Proviso, and J. Young Scammon publicly declared himself a Free Soil Whig. Wentworth and Lovejoy received approximately the same vote that they had two years earlier, but Scammon increased the Whig total by over two thousand votes. Approximately two-thirds (3,159—13.5%) of the Liberty support in the state came from this one congressional district. This was the last election for the Liberty Party in Illinois.

Most Illinois Liberty delegates selected at the Hennepin convention in July remained loyal to Hale in the preliminary ballot for president at the Buffalo convention, but three Liberty (and four Whigs) threw their support to Van Buren. This indicated that at least some Liberty men were anxious enough to form the new coalition to accept Van Buren. Eventually, all of them endorsed the Van Buren–Adams ticket. When Eastman returned from Chicago, he put the new ticket on the masthead of the *Chicago Western Citizen* and joined in a call for an Illinois Free Soil convention for August 30.[249] Liberty men took enthusiastic roles in the presidential election, and some were designated presidential electors. Their efforts helped Van Buren to triple the third-party strength from the peak statewide vote.

Zachary Taylor (Whig)   52,853 (42.4%)
Lewis Cass (Democrat)   55,915 (44.9%)
Martin Van Buren (Free Soil) 15,791 (12.7%)

Historians differ over which party contributed most to the Free Soil vote, but the consensus is that former Democrats provided most of its support.[250] Sixty percent of Van Buren's support came from Lovejoy's Fourth Congressional District, including a plurality in seven counties and a clear majority of 58% in Lake County.[251] In a post-election analysis, Zebina Eastman noted the Van Buren strength among traditional antislavery constituencies and inroads into the "Pseudo Democratic Party," but he believed that Hale would have polled a much larger vote than Van Buren.[252]

Whatever the composition of the Illinois Free Soil coalition, it collapsed after the national election. Combined with an economic depression, antislavery leaders were unable to rally their forces. The *Chicago Western Citizen* limped on, and antislavery activity was neither as powerful nor united as during the Liberty years. Attempts to resuscitate the old Liberty Party met opposition from some former leaders, and it would be two years before former Liberty Party members made a concerted effort to reinvigorate antislavery politics. They would eventually reassemble in a strong Republican Party and help elect Owen Lovejoy to the U.S. Congress.

The Illinois Liberty Party began slowly, but by mid-1848 it was the strongest and most united in the Old Northwest. Its strength was concentrated in just a few areas, but in these areas it was a factor in politics. It was inclusive in its membership with significant female and African American participation in its events and auxiliaries. It did not have the internal strife of Liberty organizations in many states. Differences were present, but party followers were able to put them aside to unite on commonly accepted standards. The state organization adhered to one idea, plus temperance, although individual members expressed their opinions on other issues. It disapproved of fusion and coalition efforts until the Free Soil merger. The party was characterized by high moral standards. Most leaders and members were devout Christians, but no sect seems to have dominated. Religious differences never obstructed party effectiveness. By 1848, it was one of the strongest state parties in the country. Illinois may have been the most important Liberty state in the Old Northwest. Michigan developed more quickly and Ohio had more national influence, but for depth of antislavery political commitment and the spread of the Liberty message beyond the state's boundaries, the Illinois Liberty Party has been underrated. That the Liberty Party received less than 3.2% of the state's 1844 presidential vote masks the fact that Illinois produced 8 of the 28 counties nationwide that gave over 10% of their vote to the Birney-Morris ticket. Among these were 2 of the 3 banner counties in the nation (the top county, DeKalb—25.4%, and Putnam—23.1%).[253] In addition, Illinois Liberty men exerted a great influence on the Wisconsin and Iowa territories and, to a lesser extent, Indiana. The *Chicago Western Citizen* had agents and covered events in these places, sometimes becoming the official paper of record.[254] It supported the highly successful forays of Illinois agents Edward Mathews and Ichabod Codding into Wisconsin and William T. Allan and Alanson St. Clair into Iowa to organize the Liberty movement there.

WISCONSIN

When James K. Polk signed the bill admitting Wisconsin to the Union on May 28, 1848, the two-party system and political antislavery already existed in the state. Voters selected a Democrat as the territorial delegate to Congress in 1843 and 1845 and a Whig in 1847. The expanding electorate—from 8,454 votes in 1843 to 39,171 in the 1848 presidential contest—reflected the area's rapid growth.[255] Wisconsin attracted settlers from both the South and Northeast. Southerners were the earliest immigrants. They settled in the southwestern part of the territory and brought their institutions, distaste for abolitionists, and even some slaves with them. Large numbers of emigrants from New York and New England, however, began coming to central and southeastern Wisconsin during the late 1830s. They transplanted their architecture, lifestyles, and religious views and were the basis for the antislavery movement in the territory.[256] Abolitionists in Racine established a local society in 1840, but there appears to have been no further activity until 1842.[257] At that time 125 abolitionists issued a June 1842 call for a territorial antislavery convention for August 2, 1842, at which delegates set up the Wisconsin Territory Anti-Slavery Society.[258] The session included scriptural reading and had the religious and moralistic tone that would characterize Wisconsin abolitionism but did not mention political action. By the time of the next meeting of the state society in early February 1843, the state's abolitionists had founded at least one county antislavery society (for Walworth) and several local auxiliaries.[259]

Sixty delegates attended the first anniversary meeting of the Wisconsin Territorial Anti-Slavery Society on February 7, 1843. This gathering took strong antislavery positions, first resolving that "the Constitution of the United States does not recognize the idea that one man has the right to hold another in bondage." Another resolution, placed on the table until the next meeting, recommended the abolition of slavery in the slave states.[260] Still, nothing was done toward the formation of a third party, causing one Wisconsin abolitionist to wonder "whether any thing [was done] on the subject of political action. I trust there will be a 'Liberty Party' formed in Wisconsin."[261] The next semiannual meeting was small and still made no mention of political action, but soon voting abolitionists began laying the groundwork for a new party.[262]

Small numbers of territorial abolitionists had been casting antislavery ballots since at least 1840.[263] Abolitionist Edward D. Holton's April 1843 victory for sheriff of Milwaukee County over a Democrat was attributed to antislavery votes, although he may have been part of a fusion ticket.[264] The first appearance of the Liberty Party, however, was in the fall 1843 elections. A September 13 convention met in Madison and selected local candidates in addition to a statewide nomination for the territorial delegate to Congress.[265] The nominee, fervent Whig Jeduthan Spooner, not only refused the nomination but also campaigned against himself. Spooner received only about 152 votes.[266] Attempts to organize the party locally met with mixed results. While the party ran well in some races, other efforts were discouraging.[267]

After this inauspicious beginning, Liberty men moved quickly to put the party on a more solid footing. They made plans to publish a Liberty newspaper, the (Racine) *Wisconsin Aegis*, beginning in 1844.[268] Illinois encouraged them and subsidized two agents, Edward Mathews and Ichabod Codding. Mathews was a Baptist minister from England who represented both the Illinois Anti-Slavery Society and the American Baptist Home Mission Society in Wisconsin. He subsequently became an agent for Wisconsin and lectured across the territory, often meeting strong opposition from some residents. As well as establishing antislavery Baptist churches, he was a warm advocate of antislavery political action and the Liberty Party.[269] The arrival of the ubiquitous Ichabod Codding had a more immediate impact on the Liberty cause. He was a Liberty Party founder who had worked in Vermont, Maine, Connecticut, and Illinois. He came to Wisconsin in February 1844 as the agent of the Illinois Anti-Slavery Society and to help set up a Liberty Party in the state. He succeeded by convincing the delegates at a mid-February convention in Kenosha (then Southport) of the need to form a permanent Liberty Party and nominate candidates for all local offices.[270] He then lectured at several places and persuaded the annual meeting of the territorial antislavery society to identify with the Liberty Party. It unequivocally resolved "[t]hat the Liberty Party is the only one which aims at the entire extermination of the slave power through the constitutional agency of the General Government, and, therefore every freeman is under the highest political obligation to support it."[271] He also convinced Charles Clark Sholes, the editor of the

Milwaukee Democrat, to leave the Democratic Party, with which he had become disillusioned over the slavery issue, and to make his newspaper the state's Liberty sheet, the *American Freeman*.[272]

Early Liberty efforts emphasized male participation and local politics, with women forming their own gender-specific societies.[273] Abolitionists set up a Liberty Association for Milwaukee that produced "not far from one hundred and twenty names—all, or nearly all, legal voters." They set up Liberty tickets for the spring local election in several towns, and the elections revealed pockets of Liberty strength.[274] A Milwaukee correspondent reported that "[t]hree or four towns in the county have gone for us" and claimed that Liberty men won six of the twenty-three seats on the county board of supervisors.[275] In Milwaukee the party received about one hundred of over six hundred votes. The election also demonstrated a greater willingness for the two major parties to unite against the Liberty Party in Wisconsin than in many states. As elsewhere, Whigs seem to have suffered greater defections to the Liberty Party in these early elections.[276] A unique aspect of the Wisconsin Liberty Association was the presence of antislavery members who remained identified with the two major parties. In other states strong identification of antislavery organizations with the Liberty Party usually drove Democrats and Whigs out of Liberty activities. In Wisconsin some major-party supporters not only remained in the Liberty Association but also took leadership roles and contributed financially. Two of the best known were Asahel Finch and William Lynde. Finch was a Whig lawyer who had been a former member of the Michigan legislature before moving to Milwaukee. He was on the association's executive committee, but maintained his ties with the Whig Party. Lynde was Finch's law partner, but he was a Democrat who was territorial attorney general in 1844 and a U.S. district attorney in 1845 at the same time that he was a stockholder in the state's Liberty Association.[277]

Liberty men spent the remainder of the year working on putting the party on a financial and organizational footing. C. C. Sholes ceased publication of the *American Freeman* for three months during the summer and moved the newspaper to the more friendly environs of Prairieville, Waukesha County. In the meantime Liberty adherents set up the Wisconsin Territorial Liberty Association that was to be funded as a joint stock company with public offerings at five dollars per share. This new group then bought the *American Freeman* and hired C. C. Sholes to run it for three years.[278] Stock offerings were a continuing source of funds for the Liberty Association and made the newspaper and the party stronger financially.[279] The party contested local elections with some success and worked to recruit new members. Subsequent years would be more challenging, however, as Liberty men confronted statehood, black suffrage, and the desirability of coalition.

The centerpiece in the Wisconsin Liberty effort after 1844 was the Territorial Liberty Association. Its move into politics began immediately. First, the Wisconsin Territorial Anti-Slavery Society endorsed Edward D. Holton for territorial representative to the U.S. Congress. Then it revised its constitution to make it "the duty of every member of this Society to vote for none but Liberty men, when there are Liberty men of the requisite qualifications." No one withdrew from the society after the change, and then everyone automatically became a member of the Territorial Liberty Association. An editorial conceded, however, that "it may lessen our numbers somewhat."[280] At least one area had a meeting opposed to the new direction. Its criticism was that "[t]he self-styled Liberty Party [was] accustomed to unchristianize all who did not fall in with their views."[281] In particular, it appeared that Liberty nominations in local elections on the one-idea basis were causing disruptions in a previously harmonious town. The editor replied that minor offices were stepping-stones to larger offices, and the party continued to contest for local offices. They won some and held the balance of power in others, and major parties appear to have united against the new party more frequently in Wisconsin than in other states.[282] Liberty power concerned major parties because of its possible effect on selecting delegates to the upcoming constitutional convention for statehood.

Liberty candidate Holton did not receive a large vote for territorial representative in 1845, but, as in Illinois, the party was stronger than its statewide numbers might indicate because its strength was concentrated, in this case in the southeastern counties. As historian Theodore Clarke Smith has noted, these counties were "practically an appendage of Illinois" and were "contiguous with those worked over by [Owen] Lovejoy."[283] The Liberty Party managed to get 790 votes (5.9%).[284] These southeastern counties remained the center of the political antislavery strength until the formation of the Republican Party. There were no territory-wide elections in 1846, but elections of delegates to a convention to devise a state constitution, a requirement before the territory could become a state, caused Wisconsin Liberty voters to clearly define their state party. A major problem for them was how to most effectively promote the suffrage for African Americans. This was the same situation that was causing so much consternation in the New York Liberty Party. It was a basic question: Should Liberty voters join like-minded members of the Democrat and Whig parties who advocated unrestricted adult male suffrage, or should they maintain their party lines and not cooperate with parties that had slaveholding members? Wisconsin Liberty leaders struggled with the problem before arriving at a party position.[285] Initially, party members followed their policy of no cooperation, but they started to waver as they began to receive overtures from some major-party elements that wished to develop a pro-suffrage united front. The temptation to exert some influence not only on the suffrage question but also on the direction of its first state constitution intrigued many because the orientation of a new state could be greatly influenced by its first constitution. Although the February convention of the Wisconsin Liberty Association opposed cooperation with non-Liberty candidates, some Liberty men expressed a willingness to work on a ticket with like-minded pro-suffrage Whigs and Democrats, but these attempts quickly broke apart. Other Liberty men objected to cooperation.[286] Soon the organization made its policy clear. The author (probably C. C. Sholes) in the *American Freeman*, admitted, "For a short time we entertained the hope that the voters of Wisconsin . . . would be disposed to lay aside their partisan armor . . . This hope we no longer entertain."[287]

This view reflected the feelings of delegates to the important semiannual meeting of the territorial association in mid-July. They also heard an encouraging report on the expansion of the Liberty Party into new areas from its agent, Edward Mathews, as he reported that Liberty organizations were receiving a better public reception and now existed in at least ten counties. The convention also made plans to resuscitate the *American Freeman*, which had not published any issues since June 11.[288] Along with Mathews, Ichabod Codding and George W. Clark lectured and sang in the campaign for Liberty candidates. In the election itself, the Liberty vote seems to have increased very slightly, but it was more widespread. The party elected no candidates, but its presence seems to have influenced politicians to take more pro-suffrage stands in some areas.[289]

Democrats dominated the October 5 convention to form a state constitution by a 103–12 margin. The convention initially proposed a whites-only suffrage clause, then overwhelmingly rejected a pro-black-suffrage amendment, and then, after a lengthy debate, narrowly passed a provision for a separate referendum to be voted on at the same time as the constitution. In April the constitution went down to defeat 20,233–14,116, and the suffrage provision lost 15,959–7,704.[290] There were at least two significant factors for Liberty men in the suffrage vote. First, the Liberty Party was only a small percentage of the pro-suffrage sentiment. Even in the race for territorial delegate to Congress later in the year, the party could not get one thousand votes. The fact that a substantial number of voters was somewhat sympathetic to black rights could not have been lost on Wisconsin abolitionists. The strongest pro-suffrage areas were strong Liberty areas that would have potential for Liberty gains. And second, that barely two-thirds of the voters who voted on the constitution even bothered to vote on the suffrage issue indicated that black rights were not burning issues for many Wisconsin voters. Liberty followers were happy that the constitution failed, and they were pleased that they held their own in local races where they had some strength.[291]

A change in Liberty orientation also took place as the constitutional convention sat. The tone of the newspaper and Liberty meetings became even more moralistic and militant than they had been, and the party gave indications that it was going to broaden its scope. The most discernible changes took place between the fall 1846 elections and the end of the year. C. C. Sholes and Amnon Gaston resigned as editors of the *American Freeman* at the end of September. They were squeezed out in an internal power and philosophical struggle, "convictions now being entertained . . . that the interest of the press and the cause will be better served by change."[292] Part of the problem may have been financial, as the publisher notified the one thousand subscribers that the paper might have to be suspended unless they paid their bills.[293] Soon the tenor of the newspaper and the Wisconsin Liberty Party began to change. The rewording of the motto on the *American Freeman* as it began its third volume was significant and indicative of the party's move in a more expansive direction. It changed from "UNIVERSAL EQUALITY OF HUMAN RIGHTS" to the more specific "DEVOTED TO LIBERTY POLITICS, TEMPERANCE, EDUCATION, AGRICULTURE, MECHANICAL ARTS, AND GENERAL INTELLIGENCE."[294] The transformation became complete when Chauncey C. Olin and Ichabod Codding took over the paper after a transfer of stock took place at the semiannual meeting of the Wisconsin Liberty Association.[295] Changes in the newspaper were immediately noticeable. Temperance, never emphasized by Sholes, who even accepted advertisements from establishments that served intoxicating beverages, became pronounced in the newspaper and conventions, as did condemnations of some religious groups for their lack of antislavery principles.[296] Some abolitionists who achieved antislavery prominence outside the territory—Mathews, Codding, and Alanson St. Clair—frequently spoke at Liberty gatherings and emphasized third-party participation, the sinfulness of slavery, and the failure of some churches to respond appropriately.[297]

Liberty advocates continued to nominate and work for candidates where they had some strength. The semiannual meeting of the Wisconsin Liberty Association in mid-July 1847 selected Charles M. Durkee, a Milwaukee farmer-merchant, as their nominee for territorial delegate to Congress and made plans for the fall election.[298] Although he received 973 votes (4.5%), which increased the Liberty vote by 23.2%, the Liberty percentage declined because of an overall increase in turnout of 59.9%. Durkee received 599 of his votes from just 5 counties, all in the southeastern part of the state. Whig John Tweedy upset controversial Democrat Marshall M. Strong in an election in which 13,000 fewer voters participated than had voted on the constitution 6 months previously.[299] Whigs improved their minority status in the recently called second constitutional convention to 46–23. This new convention, anxious to come up with an acceptable document that would be approved so Wisconsin could become a state, compromised on many issues, including black suffrage. After a motion to remove the "white" qualifier failed by approximately a 2–1 margin, the convention passed an article that would only permit the expansion of the suffrage if a majority of voters approved it after passage by the state legislature. Despite strong opposition by the Liberty Party, the new constitution passed 16,759–6,384, and on May 28 James K. Polk signed the bill admitting Wisconsin to the Union.[300]

In the meantime, Wisconsin Liberty men transformed their party into the most uncompromising and militant state Liberty organization in the country. Although the semiannual meeting in July 1847 went on record as not approving the Liberty League, the Wisconsin Liberty Association moved toward an expanded platform and an antislavery interpretation of the U.S. Constitution.[301] They also made it clear that anti-annexation and the Wilmot Proviso were not sufficient grounds for party support. Shortly after taking control of the *American Freeman,* Codding added that the principles that make abolition the paramount interest "bind us also with hooks of steel to lay ourselves out against protective tariffs, LAND MONOPOLIES, RUIN and WAR." He said that Liberty men must look at all aspects of society using God as a guide.[302] The annual meeting of the Wisconsin Liberty Association in late January 1848 demonstrated the new Liberty direction. Participants approved with only one dissenting vote a resolution endorsing the comprehensive platform. Then a debate over approving the recent Buffalo convention's nomination of John P. Hale for president did not go smoothly. What was a pro forma decision in most states occasioned intense debate in Wisconsin over whether to endorse him because many believed that his views were not sufficiently orthodox Liberty doctrine. Hale finally won a 2–1 majority endorsement only after an anti-Hale resolution was softened to support his candidacy if he "be found heartily to espouse the great principle which is the basis of our organization."[303]

Although there were a few objections, the party reaffirmed this in subsequent meetings.[304] A state convention that met in April to select nominees for positions in the new state government not only reaffirmed the expanded platform but refused to endorse Hale for the presidency. The convention also endorsed the proposition that the U.S. Constitution "is antislavery in its character."[305] When veteran Liberty editor Sherman Booth arrived from the East to take over the editorial duties of the *American Freeman*, he expanded these sentiments. The Wisconsin Liberty Party was going in a different direction than other state parties elsewhere in the North, and its militant tone characterized it right up to the formation of the Free Soil Party.[306] Nonetheless, the results of the gubernatorial election in May made it apparent that the Liberty Party as then constituted would never be much of an electoral force statewide. Democrats returned to power and the Liberty vote declined another percentage point, although Charles Durkee attracted 16.5% more raw votes (1,134—3.2%) than he had 7 months before.[307] It was becoming apparent that something had to be done if the party was to survive as any more than a fringe element in the rapidly expanding state.

Soon a movement to become part of the Free Soil coalition was underway as Liberty men reconsidered the party's position. Edward D. Holton worried that the numerical weakness of antislavery voters might leave the way clear for slavery to enter recently acquired New Mexico and California.[308] Party chairman and recent gubernatorial candidate Durkee, arguably the leading Liberty man in the state, also pondered the likelihood of a wider political base. He finally issued a call in the *American Freeman* on June 28 for a convention in Southport on July 19 to consider how to respond to overtures from Free Soil elements in the major parties. They chose to participate in the wider group. Despite continuing objections from Booth and two days of debate, the convention selected thirteen delegates to represent them at the national convention in Buffalo. It made clear, however, that it would not support candidates who "are not only pledged against the extension of slavery, but are also committed to the policy of abolishing it."[309] Several Liberty men then attended the subsequent Free Territory convention that selected the official delegation for Buffalo that included several Liberty men.[310] In the informal vote at Buffalo, the Democratic orientation of the delegation was reflected in the informal vote of Van Buren over Hale 9–3 with one person casting a vote for a third candidate.[311]

Former Liberty men threw themselves wholeheartedly into the Free Soil campaigns. Most surprising was the about-face of Sherman Booth, who had served on the platform committee in Buffalo. Only a week before the national gathering, he declared that if there should be a Van Buren nomination, "we are out of the Liberty Party in a twinkling. We shall then run up the Independent Flag."[312] Two weeks later the Van Buren–Adams ticket was on the masthead of the *American Freeman* and Booth was a leading propagandist for the new movement. He changed the newspaper's name to the *Wisconsin Freeman* on August 24 and also began publishing a campaign newspaper, the *Barnburner*.[313] Free Soilers resumed their Janesville convention, set up their statewide organization, endorsed the Van Buren–Adams ticket, and then met on September 27 to select Van Buren electors. Democrats dominated these gatherings, but Liberty men also played important roles. Free Soilers ran candidates in local races, but the party's focus was on the presidential and congressional contests.[314] In the presidential race the Wisconsin Free Soil Party made the best showing of any state in the Old Northwest.

Zachary Taylor (Whig)	13,747 (35.1%)
Lewis Cass (Democrat)	15,001 (38.3%)
Martin Van Buren (Free Soil)	10,423 (26.6%)

Analysts agree that virtually all the former Liberty men voted Free Soil and that the bulk of the new party's support was from former Democrats.[315] Most of Van Buren's strength came from the southeastern part of the state, where the Liberty Party had been strongest. The antislavery nature of this area was demonstrated more clearly in the First Congressional District election, where Charles Durkee won a seat in the U.S. Congress.

Asahel Finch (Whig)	3,621 (27.7%)
William P. Lynde (Democrat)	4,436 (33.9%)
Charles Durkee (Free Soil)	5,038 (38.5%)[316]

Ironically, both of his opponents also had been members of the Wisconsin Liberty Association.[317] Free Soilers "also chose nearly twenty members of the state legislature, some of them by coalition."[318] The party and its successors would continue to be the backbone of antislavery agitation in the coming years, although its numbers would decline from the 1848 totals. Numbers were only part of the equation. As the party's early historian, Theodore Clarke Smith, has pointed out, "Both Whig and Democratic parties had been driven to take strong Free Soil ground, so that the State of Wisconsin, in November, 1848, was more nearly anti-slavery than any similar area in the Union."[319]

Unlike other states, Wisconsin's Liberty Association ran the party. Unlike most other areas, the Wisconsin party became more militant and moralistic as the Free Soil coalition developed. A major factor in this was the uncompromising tone that Ichabod Codding and, later, Sherman Booth brought into the area and points to the changes in party behavior that can result from strong leadership. Eventually, such leaders as Durkee, Holton, Lybrand, James H. Paine, Edward G.

Dyer, Joseph Trotter Mills, and others led the way into the Free Soil Party. They played important roles in later antislavery politics and the Republican Party, although only Durkee had a career in national politics. The Liberty Party in Wisconsin had a greater impact than its statewide numbers might indicate. Like Illinois, antislavery sentiment and activities were concentrated in a relatively small area, but there the antislavery feelings were clear. The party had capable leaders and a powerful Liberty Association that welcomed female participation. These individuals would continue to be very active throughout the 1850s, particularly in fighting fugitive slave legislation.

INDIANA

Indiana was a rapidly expanding state where a genuine two-party system did not emerge until 1840. Widely dispersed populations and poor communication systems hampered party development until the popular William Henry Harrison ran for the presidency in 1836 and 1840. Despite Whig success in the 1840 election, Democrats won every subsequent statewide election until the Republican Party triumph in 1860, but elections were competitive and produced a high voter turnout.[320] Abolition flourished only in scattered pockets of the state. Most of Indiana's early immigrants were poor whites from the South and only a few, such as Quaker North Carolinian Levi Coffin, showed antislavery leanings. Some sentiment began to appear during the 1830s.[321] Stephen S. Harding, whose family had moved to Indiana from Palmyra, New York, in 1820, began speaking in favor of immediate abolition and temperance in southern Indiana.[322] Abolitionists set up a few local antislavery societies in 1836 and 1837, but it was only in September 1838 that they finally established a state society. Still, before New England Quaker Arnold Buffum—founder and first president of the New England Anti-Slavery Society and a founder of the American Anti-Slavery Society—began to proselytize the eastern part of the state, "Indiana was the most backward of all the Northwestern States in anti-slavery matters," with only eight local societies by 1838.[323]

That so weak an antislavery environment produced little enthusiasm for the Birney-Earle ticket in 1840 was not surprising. Opponents overwhelmingly voted down an attempt by a few third-party abolitionists to set up an electoral ticket at a state antislavery convention.[324] After the 1840 election, however, antislavery voters moved to establish a third party. By early February 1841, they had gained control of the Indiana Anti-Slavery Society and endorsed the new party, but made few organizational efforts.[325] There would be no gubernatorial contest until 1843, but some areas made local and congressional nominations. The movement lacked statewide organization and support was light.[326] The year 1842 produced only a slight increase in the Liberty vote in scattered elections.[327] Statewide totals were small, but a few pockets of strength developed that would be the areas of Liberty strength in upcoming elections.

The Liberty Party became more energized statewide with the triennial gubernatorial election in 1843, the first statewide contest since 1840. Liberty advocates began early by nominating a state ticket in September 1842. Respected physician Elizur Deming and lawyer Stephen S. Harding headed the state ticket, and Jacob Bigelow, who later would gain fame as an Underground Railroad operator in Washington, D.C., was the candidate for the U.S. Congress. Party members made nominations for some local and county offices.[328] They also made organizational efforts in the mid-eastern portion of the state along the Ohio border where there was a strong Wesleyan Methodist and Quaker influence. Here Benjamin Stanton published his (New Garden) *Free Labor Advocate and Anti-Slavery Chronicle*, which was the healthiest and longest-lived Liberty newspaper in the state.[329] They also established mixed-gender Liberty Associations.[330] These efforts were rewarded with a Liberty vote of 1,684 (1.4%).[331] The greatest concentration of votes was in New Garden Township, Wayne County, the home of the *Free Labor Advocate*, where "the liberty vote was 155, while the Whig and Democratic vote together, was only 39."[332] This greater activity continued into the 1844 presidential contest.

Henry Clay (Whig)	67,866 (48.4%)
James K. Polk (Democrat)	70,183 (50.1%)
James G. Birney (Liberty)	2,108 (1.5%)

Although the Liberty Party increased its percentage of the total vote by just 0.1%, its actual vote grew by 25.2% because of higher turnout in the election. Sixty-five of 90 counties recorded Liberty votes, but party strength concentrated in only a few areas. Twelve counties gave over 50 Liberty votes, and these accounted for almost 70% (1,473 out of 2,108) of the party's total.[333] Nine counties gave over 5% of their votes for the third party, and 7 of these were in the central/east-central part of the state, which was the home of the *Free Labor Advocate* and where Quaker and Wesleyan Methodist influence was great.[334] Grant County's 20.2% made it the fourth highest Liberty county in the country. There was also considerable Liberty support in the north-central part of the state along the Michigan border. This area had a major Underground Railroad line that ran through it and even had a local editor, Asa Brown, of the *Chicago Western Citizen* at Michigan City, Indiana, before his untimely death in 1844.[335]

The Indiana Liberty Party stagnated after 1844 and was the weakest in the Old Northwest. If not for a few areas of intense activity and a handful of dedicated leaders, it would not have existed at all. The party lacked a strong central authority and developed different strategies in different areas. Benjamin Stanton, Quaker editor of the *Free Labor Advocate and Anti-Slavery Chronicle*, was an uncompromising abolitionist who believed that politics was part of an antislavery crusade that included an unequivocal religious opposition to slaveholding and support for the free produce movement. Arnold Buffum and his newspaper, the *Protectionist*, and Levi Coffin were similar Indiana Quaker Liberty men. The area in the northeastern part of the state also had a militant orientation that it took from its close association with the Illinois and Michigan abolitionists. Henry W. DePuy, editor of the (Indianapolis) *Indiana Freeman*, had a different approach. He was more willing to accept coalition and fusion politics even before the Free Soil movement took shape. In fact, he resigned his own congressional candidacy in 1847, at the behest of the nominating convention, when a Whig gave adequate answers to questions posed by Liberty representatives.[336] He worked in an antislavery environment very different from Stanton's closely knit, supportive community. Indianapolis was a dangerous place to be an abolitionist. Those who opposed slavery were more willing to soften their views in order to expand their small base.[337]

Nevertheless, at a May 30, 1845, state convention, the disparate elements managed to field candidates in congressional elections in 1845 and select a state gubernatorial ticket of respected jurist Stephen C. Stevens and Stephen S. Harding for the fall of 1846. The party does not seem to have made any gains in the local races in 1845, and some publications from outside the state commented on the lack of Liberty activity then and in 1846.[338] The lackadaisical approach was reflected in the 1846 gubernatorial election results in which the party added less than two hundred votes (2,301—1.8%) since 1844.[339] Reactions to the results varied. Benjamin Stanton was not willing to compromise his antislavery positions in order to achieve greater electoral strength. If this meant adhering to strict antislavery standards and refusing to vote for any but Liberty candidates, he was quite willing to do that. He disdained those who softened their beliefs or cooperated with the major parties. Some Indiana Liberty men had been flirting with such cooperation since at least 1845, and they were being enticed by a more aggressive antislavery approach by some in the major parties. For instance,

Caleb B. Smith, an antislavery Whig, solicited Liberty support in an 1847 congressional election and succeeded in persuading the Liberty candidate to withdraw.[340] When the aforementioned Henry DePuy and others showed a willingness to step aside for major-party candidates, Stanton announced that he would not compromise and would go it alone if necessary.[341]

That some Liberty men showed that they would break party ranks to support a major-party candidate whom they considered to be sufficiently antislavery (i.e., anti-extension) helped easily move the Liberty Party into the Free Soil coalition despite the active opposition of Stanton. A June 12, 1848, state Liberty convention passed an anti-extension resolution and approved the Hale-King presidential ticket, and it recommended participating in a national mass convention of those opposed to the further spread of slavery.[342] Stanton then rethought his position. He participated in a local free territory meeting that selected him as a delegate to a July 26 Free Territory convention that set up the Indiana Free Soil Party, and he attended the national convention in Buffalo. The Liberty gubernatorial ticket of the previous fall was also enthusiastic about the new movement. Both Judge Stevens and Stephen S. Harding sent letters of approval to the convention and served as official delegates to Buffalo, where Stevens called the national Free Soil convention to order and Harding served on a committee. Stanton swallowed his uneasiness over Van Buren and returned from Buffalo a Free Soil convert.[343]

Liberty men took important roles in a second Indiana Free Soil convention that set up a state electoral ticket. Stephen S. Harding gave a long speech at this convention designed to convince reluctant abolitionists to accept Van Buren. He admitted "that it was with some difficulty he got his own consent to go for him—but he finally concluded to do it."[344] The Free Soil Party only received slightly more than 5% of the vote.

Zachary Taylor (Whig)	70,300 (46.0%)
Lewis Cass (Democrat)	74,558 (48.8%)
Martin Van Buren (Free Soil)	8,060 (5.3%)

The top two Liberty counties of 1844, Grant (20.2%) and Randolph (11.2%), were the third and fourth Free Soil counties with 27.5% and 26.9% respectively. Its vote seems to have come at the expense of both the Democrats and Whigs in former areas of Liberty strength in the east-central counties and near Chicago.[345]

The Free Soil Party continued a successful operation in 1849 with the election of George W. Julian to Congress. It lost much of its support, because, "as their own systematic questioning of candidates soon made clear, most Indiana

Whigs and Democrats were as firmly committed to non-extension and the divorce of slavery from government as any Free Soiler."[346] By 1850, the party was virtually moribund. Julian and his followers and the core of old Liberty leadership kept political antislavery alive, but it did not become a major factor in state politics until the Republican Party.

Indiana was not an important state for the Liberty Party. It exerted no national or regional influence and only developed a small following in the state. Nonetheless, where it was strong it was very strong, as shown by three counties giving more than 10% of their vote to Birney in 1844. Nevertheless, it provided a political outlet for antislavery voters and furnished an organization for abolition sentiment in the state.

IOWA

When James K. Polk signed the document admitting Iowa to the Union on December 28, 1846, there was no statewide Liberty organization. Hawkeye Liberty Party sympathizers were the last group to establish a state or territorial society.[347] They operated in a environment that was unfriendly for abolitionists. Most of Iowa's early immigrants came from slave states, and a few brought their slaves with them. Slavery was not popular, however, but neither were blacks. Democrats dominated the territorial legislature and passed laws to discourage blacks from settling there. The first legislature passed the notorious Act to Regulate Blacks and Mulattoes that forced African Americans to have a court certificate of their freedom and post a five hundred-dollar bond to ensure their lawful behavior.[348] Hoping to win the two U.S. Senate seats, the national Whig Party poured resources into the new state and made it more competitive. It financed a partially successful challenge to Democratic hegemony in 1846 and temporarily won control of the lower house.[349]

Antislavery activity took place in a small number of towns in the southeastern part of the territory. The abolitionists who settled in these communities were usually from the Northeast or Ohio, but there were also a significant number of Quakers from the South. Often one religion dominated a particular township, but local societies were mixed. The most prevalent religious affiliation was Congregationalist, but there were also communities where Presbyterians, Seceder Presbyterians, and Methodists predominated.[350] They formed a few county and township societies beginning in 1840, but did not attempt to form a territorial society until late 1843.[351] Finally, in April 1843 Aaron Street issued a call for an October meeting to set up an Iowa Territorial Anti-Slavery Society.[352] Fifty-eight abolitionists, including twenty women, met at the Round Prairie Presbyterian Meeting House and set up the Iowa Territorial Anti-Slavery Society. Bible readings punctuated all sessions and religious discussions permeated the meetings, and the group quickly demonstrated a political orientation. Although not explicitly endorsing the Liberty Party, they adopted the Illinois Liberty newspaper, the *Chicago Western Citizen*, as their official newspaper. They unanimously passed a strong political resolution, Number 10, that declared "[t]hat no consistent abolitionist can support a political party, or vote for a man to any office, who is not found in active opposition to slavery."[353] Iowa abolitionists showed no tendency to embrace Garrisonian ideas on disunionism or nonresistance.

Nonetheless, Iowa abolitionists made no effort to establish a statewide Liberty Party until late 1847. Instead, they concentrated on petitioning the state legislature over black rights, establishing new antislavery societies, and making a few unsuccessful attempts at questioning candidates. Liberty proponents were active on the local level, however, and ran candidates in their pockets of strength as early as 1843, although their electoral impact was minimal. The Liberty platforms in these years emphasized the slavery issue and rarely mentioned black rights.[354] The party continued to run candidates in local races, for the territorial legislature and constitutional convention, but Liberty candidates usually received only a few dozen votes and rarely came close to winning contests in townships where they had some strength.[355] Nevertheless, the party provided an antislavery political outlet for those who refused to vote for either major party. Proceedings of Liberty meetings were similar to those of the state society and early abolition gatherings with their religious orientation, Bible readings, and prayers.[356]

These few Liberty voters seem to have come predominantly from former Whigs. Ward Robert Barnes has painstakingly researched the political antecedents of identifiable Liberty voters and has found that twenty-two of twenty-five Liberty supporters that he could trace were former Whigs.[357] Both major parties recognized this, and Whigs began to move toward more antislavery positions as the Mexican War and Wilmot Proviso controversies produced more public discussion and delineated notable differences between Whigs and most Democrats in Iowa.[358] Liberty efforts seem to have declined in the 1847 elections after Whigs made overtures to Liberty voters and the Whig-controlled assembly came out with a strong anti-extension resolution. Interest in the third party returned as the Whig Party turned to the slaveholding Mexican War hero Zachary Taylor as its likely presidential nominee for 1848.[359]

Plans to establish a state Liberty organization had been mentioned as early as the November 1846 fourth annual meeting of the Iowa Anti-Slavery Society,[360] but the movement did not gain momentum until Alanson St. Clair, an agent from Illinois, gave several speeches in the autumn of 1847. He was instrumental in calling a convention for December 14–15 in Denmark, where the Iowa Liberty Party was born. Not coincidentally, the fifth annual meeting of the Iowa Anti-Slavery Society was going on at the same, and the two meetings were apparently conducted as a single endeavor. The major decision was to employ St. Clair to lecture throughout the winter and raise funds for a state newspaper. He proposed the same type of plan that Wisconsin abolitionists had developed—raising one thousand dollars by selling shares at twenty-five dollars apiece while on his tour. Delegates immediately subscribed to half the shares, set up an Iowa central committee, and passed a series of resolutions.[361]

St. Clair's presence undoubtedly gave character to the party and changed the tone of Iowa antislavery. He had argued strategy and tactics with William Lloyd Garrison and worked in the Liberty Party from its beginnings in Massachusetts, New Hampshire, and Illinois. The convention's resolutions reflected this change, and most were similar to the positions taken by more outspoken conventions in other states. While not forsaking a highly moralistic tone, Iowa Liberty supporters now paid more attention to practical politics and constitutional issues than previously. After standard Liberty reference to the ideals of the Declaration of Independence, the delegates went beyond an anti-extension position to one in favor of the eventual destruction of the slave system. They came out against any fusion or coalition with either of the major parties, something that they had done at least occasionally. They also chided the recent October 1847 national Liberty convention for putting a Liberty opponent on its national committee, and replaced him with Dr. George Shedd, a Denmark physician and longtime Liberty supporter.

Probably most indicative of the new orientation was an interest in the powers of the U.S. Constitution over slavery. After much discussion, delegates endorsed the unique position that slavery existed legally only in the six original slave states and should be immediately abolished in the nine slave states that had subsequently legalized it. This put the Iowa party's constitutional construction far beyond that of many other Liberty organizations or the stance of the national party. They also came out strongly against Iowa's black laws, the most onerous in the North, particularly those that required African Americans to carry free papers and post a five hundred-dollar bond before being allowed to live in the state. The meeting concluded with an endorsement of John P. Hale, the presidential nominee of the national convention. For the first time, Iowa Liberty men were a part of the party.

Sparked by St. Clair's speaking tour in early 1848, party members showed unprecedented enthusiasm. On March 4 the *Iowa Freeman* began publishing with St. Clair as temporary editor. It was officially made the permanent organ of the state party in late May.[362] St. Clair remained in Iowa through the summer, and he used his time well. He organized local affiliates and tickets, distributed printed ballots, and attempted to extend Liberty influence beyond its core areas. His zeal sometimes exceeded his prudence, however, and one incident in particular embarrassed the party. He circulated ballots in the spring election for the Liberty candidacy of Samuel L. Howe for state superintendent of public instruction without Howe's knowledge. When Howe declined the nomination—supposedly at the behest of antislavery Whig candidate James Harlan, a fellow Mount Pleasant educator—and his letter was widely circulated, the Liberty Party still seemed to show itself willing to work with non-Liberty candidates despite pronouncements at the state meeting. Strictly speaking, this was not an endorsement of a non-Liberty man, but it nonetheless caused some Liberty uneasiness.[363]

This was an exceptional incident, however, as the state party progressed in its first six months. A state Liberty convention in late May nominated candidates for statewide offices and the two U.S. congressional seats for the August elections plus a slate of Liberty presidential electors. The two congressional candidates were veteran Iowa antislavery men—Samuel L. Howe and James Dawson, a Washington merchant and leading Seceder Presbyterian layman. The convention showed little public interest in the burgeoning anti-extension coalition movement and reiterated its support for John P. Hale. It continued to criticize the black laws and supported the almost axiomatic Liberty position on temperance. Again, St. Clair's influence was apparent, and the convention seemed almost a copy of pre-1844 Liberty gatherings in the Northeast.[364]

Liberty men picked up additional Whig support throughout the summer after Zachary Taylor was made the nominee, although they seem to have made few new converts among the Democrats despite the candidacy of Lewis Cass. The new party set up several county tickets for local races and continued to emphasize slavery and black rights issues. Whigs realized that they would suffer more by these efforts at a time when they were showing signs of becoming more competitive with the Democrats. Their stronger anti-extension stands and seeking Liberty support met with some success. Democrats used the tactic less frequently, but they coalesced with Liberty men in some races in Henry County, a Whig stronghold.[365]

Led by the traditional anti-coalition, anti-fusion Alanson St. Clair, Liberty men resisted these enticements in most areas and pressed forward with their candidates in the August congressional and statewide races. Nonetheless, Liberty candidates did poorly numerically, but some races were so hotly contested that Liberty votes almost made a difference. In the First Congressional District, Samuel L. Howe's 310 ballots (2.4%) came within 76 votes of holding the electoral balance. All of the Liberty support except 10 votes came from 3 out of 15 counties with Henry County leading the way with 10.5%. In the Second Congressional District, James Dawson did not do as well with only 178 votes (1.6%). All except 5 of Dawson's total came from 3 out of 17 counties, but Washington County's 12.6% of the vote made it the banner county in the state. These pockets of Liberty strength were relatively deep, but most of the state had no interest in the third party. In the other statewide races, the party averaged "526 votes, a little under two percent and short of a balance by more than 600 votes," although the Liberty Party may have held the balance in some local races.[366]

The Iowa Liberty Party soon became part of the Free Soil movement. The only representative at the Buffalo Free Soil convention from west of the Mississippi was Dr. William Miller, an Iowa physician who was a leader in the Liberty Party. Although he supported Hale in the vote at the convention, he quickly accepted the Van Buren–Adams ticket. So did the Iowa Liberty men, but they probably had no alternative. They had not been reluctant to coalesce with a major party in some areas already, and only the drive and energy of Alanson St. Clair may have held this tendency in check. By the time of the Free Soil convention, however, the indefatigable St. Clair was fatigued. Worn out and ill, he returned to Illinois, leaving the *Iowa Freeman* in the hands of another Illinois Liberty migrant, David M. Kelsey, who led the Liberty men into the Free Soil Party. Kelsey put the Van Buren–Adams ticket on the masthead of the newspaper and issued a call for an Iowa Free Soil convention to meet September 19–20. Former Liberty men dominated this meeting, but they made special efforts to include Whigs and the few like-minded Democrats in leadership positions.[367] Despite some efforts in the state, the Iowa Free Soil Party did more poorly in the presidential race than any other state that had a Liberty organization with the exceptions of Pennsylvania and New Jersey.

Zachary Taylor (Whig)	11,064 (43.3%)
Lewis Cass (Democrat)	12,093 (47.4%)
Martin Van Buren (Free Soil)	1,216 (4.4%)
Scattering	1,241 (4.9%)[368]

It appears that the new party received half of its strength from former Liberty voters. There is no evidence that any appreciable number of Liberty voters from the summer elections either sat out the presidential contest or defected to the major parties, although some may have ended up in the scattering column by error.

The two Free Soil banner counties—Washington (18.0%) and Henry (14.5%)—were the same as the banner Liberty counties during the summer congressional races. The scattering votes probably resulted from a number of factors. Free Soilers had difficulty distributing ballots in some areas, and errors on improvised tickets caused election officials to omit them from Van Buren's total.[369] Past elections had shown that the dominant Democrats had utilized questionable appeals to alter returns and the results of elections.[370] And probably some Whigs who could not support Taylor could not bring themselves to cast a ballot for the Barnburner Democrat Van Buren.[371] Whatever the reasons for the scattering votes, non–major-party voters held a precarious balance of power in the state. Yet the importance of this can be overemphasized. It would only be significant if one major party could coalesce with a high percentage of the disaffected voters, although there is no doubt that the disaffected faction could use its power as a pressure group to bring about changes in major parties' positions. Otherwise, a plurality was sufficient for election to office or to win the state's electoral votes.

In sum, the Iowa Liberty Party had a short life before it became part of the Free Soil movement. It served its major purpose by providing abolitionist voters with a vehicle to express their antislavery sentiments politically and drawing attention to the twin problem of slavery and Iowa's black laws. The Free Soil Party continued these functions, but it barely exceeded the numbers posted by the Liberty Party. Antislavery-oriented politics would have to wait for the advent of the Republican Party before making any electoral impact in Iowa.

VIRGINIA

During these early years there was even an attempt to establish the Liberty Party and set up an electoral ticket in a Southern state in time for the 1844 presidential election. In June 1844 antislavery citizens from Ohio County, Virginia—an area that would later become West Virginia—held a public meeting and appointed a committee to correspond with like-minded voters throughout the state.[372] Subsequently, antislavery men met in a barn, founded the Virginia Liberty Party, set up a slate of seventeen presidential electors, and held a Virginia Liberty Party convention. The resolutions were typical of early Liberty conventions, coupling a duty to God with the Declaration of Independence. It declared "[t]hat in organizing a Liberty Party in the State of Virginia, we do so from a sense of duty to God" and "[t]hat the principles we profess, are the principles of the Declaration of Independence." The convention made no local nominations, but it appointed a committee "to prepare an address, together with a ticket, and have published with the proceedings of this meeting, in pamphlet form."[373] Its address referred to Liberty vice presidential nominee Thomas Morris in particular as "a native of Western Virginia, who has been from his boyhood a consistent advocate of equal rights."[374] A later Ohio County Liberty convention met closer to the election to encourage voters to turn out for the presidential election.[375] One source that tabulated returns gives the Liberty Party sixty votes from Virginia, but most sources do not acknowledge any Liberty ballots.[376] Liberty sympathy undoubtedly existed in areas where it was too dangerous or impractical to set up a party. There were rumors in late 1845 that someone was going to try to establish a Liberty press in North Carolina, but little seems to have come of the effort.[377] And if the former Whig Quaker from North Carolina who claimed "to belong to the Liberty party, and am a whole souled opponent to all pro slavery parties" ever carried his convictions to the polls in his state, I can find no record of it.[378]

The emphases in these state studies have been on the political strategies and tactics of Liberty Party members. The party developed differently in the various states while sharing a belief in antislavery political action. The party was more than just a political machine, however. It had a unique appeal and encompassed groups not usually considered part of the political process in nineteenth-century America. The following chapters examine other aspects of the Liberty experience: its philosophical underpinnings; its propagandizing tools; its disparate membership, including African Americans and women; and its place in the larger antislavery movement during the 1840s.

8

THE LIBERTY PARTY APPEAL

> And first of all we wish distinctly, as a Party, to acknowledge our dependence on God and our amenability to Him. We firmly believe in the natural equality of man ... But we have seen so much of apparent Atheism in the political documents and action of the nation as such, almost from its existence, that we deem it highly proper at the outset to make the explicit avowal that we recognize God as the Most High, who ruleth among the nations of the earth, that he is Governor and Lawmaker, that he presides with high and undivided authority as Supreme over all. If we cannot succeed with these principles we welcome disappointment.
>
> OWEN LOVEJOY, "Address to the Liberty Party of Illinois, May 27, 1842"

The basis of the Liberty Party was its opposition to slavery and racial discrimination, and its rhetoric injected the moral fervor of the abolitionism of the previous decade into the political system. The most distinctive features of the Liberty Party were its high-toned moralism and religious orientation. After the Liberty Party merged into the Free Soil movement, a Liberty editor recalled that the "sentiment of liberty and humanity which compose the groundwork of the Liberty organization was deep toned *religious* sentiment ... a confidence in the righteousness of the cause ... a mingling of soul."[1] Liberty advocates freely used such words and phrases as "moral warfare," "our holy cause," "moral obligation," "sinfulness," and "righteousness" to describe aspects of their undertaking. The symbol of the party was the Cedar of Lebanon, the construction material of Solomon's home and temple (1 Kings 4:33; 7:2; 10:17, 21) and a biblical symbol of strength.[2] Liberty newspapers frequently had biblical quotes on their mastheads, and their columns were filled with religious imagery. The abolition movement had always been steeped in religious feeling, but never before had so much religious rhetoric appeared in American politics. Owen Lovejoy declared "first of all we wish distinctly, as a Party to acknowledge our dependence on God and our amenability to him."[3] Ohio Liberty man Dyer Burgess, in arguing for independent antislavery political action, declared that it was not only that "the world may see that some will vote right, but that God may see that I vote right."[4] A religious tone marked most party activities. Ministers played important roles in the party in all states throughout its existence, but especially in the early years. At the time of the split in the Massachusetts Anti-Slavery Society in 1839, Francis Jackson, president of the Old Organization, criticized the New Organization because "all (or nearly all) who are publicly engaged in its advocacy are clergymen. Messrs. Phelps, Torrey, St. Clair, Wise, Cummings, Scott, Allen &c. are all clergymen."[5] Nearly all these men became closely identified with the Liberty Party during its first few years.

No one religious group dominated the party in any state. Denominational affiliations were less important than a strong Christian, Protestant identification, usually with an evangelical orientation. At least one-third of all Liberty Party editors were ministers, and almost all the rest were active in religious enterprises. Liberty candidates were deeply religious. They belonged to both the main denominations and newer movements, such as evangelical and perfectionist sects. Richard Carwardine has pointed out that "[t]he exercise of the Christian conscience in politics was a basic obligation of every evangelical."[6] This was not a static situation, however, because many Liberty Party supporters changed their religious orientation during the 1840s. Some Congregationalists and Presbyterians broke away from their church structures to form independent antislavery congregations, and many antislavery Methodists joined Wesleyan Methodist groups in the early 1840s.[7] Additionally, many Liberty men made fundamental changes in their religious practice. Perhaps this was most prevalent in Upstate New York, where Liberty Party stalwarts Myron Holley, Gerrit Smith, Alvan Stewart, William Goodell, and others left established churches. Many joined Liberty editor Luther Myrick in forming antislavery Union churches that "were committed to supporting the Liberty Party" or broke away and formed their own antislavery congregations.[8] In fact, Douglas Strong maintains that "the entire leadership of the party in upper New York (with the possible exception of Henry B. Stanton) . . . were also ecclesiastical abolitionist (church reformers)."[9]

These ministers and pious laymen exemplified the high moral tone that characterized Liberty pronouncements. They were especially visible in the early years of the party and retained much influence even after some party leaders toned down moralistic rhetoric after 1845. Even in areas where party leaders were not as religiously demonstrative, most local meetings still had religious overtones. Most Liberty men believed "human governments are of divine appointment," and that there was a moral duty to vote.[10] Voting for pro-slavery candidates was considered a "heinous sin."[11] While many did not withdraw from churches that refused to condemn slavery, they censured passive ministers. These themes permeated all facets of the movement. Elizur Wright declared that the Liberty Party was "a party ruling its members by *truth* and the *fear of God*."[12] Sometimes members broke away to form strictly antislavery congregations while remaining within a larger church structure that tolerated slaveholders in its membership. For instance, the Reverend Edward Mathews established over fifty antislavery Baptist churches in Illinois and Wisconsin while remaining in the larger church structure, and many Presbyterians formed antislavery congregations while maintaining membership in the denomination. Others remained in churches and congregations that tolerated slaveholders or refused to take measures condemning slaveholding, choosing to work within their church organization rather than leaving it. Some would leave an established congregation to establish a more antislavery church within the same sect.

The diversity of religious sentiment within churches and the Liberty Party is noteworthy. Linda Jean Evans has shown that "by 1840 there were at least five competing theological viewpoints represented in the Presbyterian and Congregational churches of northern Ohio."[13] This variety is true for all the states, and intra-denominational differences were also significant. That religious convictions played an important part in Liberty affairs is almost axiomatic, but the party's effect on the churches is not so easily ascertained. Few religious groups went as far as the 1842 Free Will Baptist Yearly Meeting at Penobscot, Maine, that declared that it was every voter's duty "to give their suffrages *in favor of what is now politically called the Liberty Party of these United States.*"[14] Nonetheless, Liberty advocates were represented in every sizable religious denomination in the North except, with a few exceptions, Roman Catholics and Jews.[15] They were interested in the antislavery positions of their own and other denominations, and they often pushed for action in church meetings. The 1840s were crucial years in the fragmentation of the major denominations (except Episcopalians and Catholics) over the slavery issue. Local Liberty conventions urged the churches to take action, and many Liberty followers were also leaders in their own denominations. Tracing specific denominational influences on the religious orientation is even more difficult because a member might change denominational affiliation or become less spiritually committed. Even such a committed Liberty man as Edward Wade did not belong to any sect.[16] While Elizur Wright's path from evangelical belief to atheism or James G. Birney's growing antisectarianism may be extreme examples, there was denominational movement among many Liberty men.[17] The general tone of the party and some of its new members also became more secular in outlook as the decade progressed. This was particularly true among the younger members of the party. Important young Liberty leaders—William Birney, Stanley Matthews, Joseph Hawley, Martin Delany, and Henry DePuy—exhibited a less religious and more secular approach to party matters. Nonetheless, this change was only a matter of degree. The religious orientation of the party remained one of its salient characteristics.

The best examples of the Liberty Party's religious orientation were Liberty conventions, which were frequently held in conjunction with religious antislavery gatherings. Liberty meetings normally opened and closed with prayers. Women and children often attended meetings at which the political strategy took second place to religious antislavery rhetoric. Participants often sang hymns, frequently led by the prominent Hutchinson Family of New Hampshire, "Liberty Minstrel" George W. Clark, the Chicago Liberty Choir (an interracial group of both sexes), or a similar group.[18] Many Liberty Party conventions more closely resembled the abolition meetings of the 1830s in their revival tone than the standard political party convention of the 1840s. Nonetheless, Liberty speakers sometimes received criticism for preaching politics on the Sabbath. Gerrit Smith, Luther Lee, Charles T. Torrey, Luther Myrick, William Jackson, Edward Mathews, Ichabod Codding, and E. W. Goodwin did not hesitate to combine Liberty politics and their Sunday worship, although other Liberty men studiously avoided preaching politics or even traveling on the Sabbath.[19] It cannot be overemphasized, however, that Liberty Party activities were just part of a larger religious universe for many Liberty followers. One reading the Liberty newspapers or the voluminous writings of some of its important leaders is immediately struck by how much they deal with religious matters and how little space is devoted to practical politics.

Liberty conduct of political business and selection of candidates for state offices varied from state to state with no regional pattern. Some states—such as Vermont, Connecticut, and Illinois—were controlled by a small group that presented candidates and policies to the conventions. Their suggestions usually were adopted overwhelmingly. Sometimes, additional resolutions were added on the convention floor, but these normally had nothing to do with substantive policy or strategy. They were further condemnations of slavery, discrimination, Southern domination of the government or economy, or some other antislavery topic. In short, Liberty conventions in these states were political rallies that included little real debate over substantive party matters. A small, like-minded elite controlled the party in these states, and any disagreements were usually worked out beforehand. These states also had few acrimonious debates in their party press.

At the other end of the spectrum was New York, where party policies and tactics were debated heatedly in state conventions and the party press. New York had the most talented group of Liberty leaders in the nation, but most were strong-willed individuals who viewed issues from an unwavering moral base. Their inability to compromise led to serious disputes over multi-reform, endorsement of candidates to the state constitutional convention, and the selection of nominees for office. There was also a noticeable difference between the evangelical perfectionism of most Upstate New York leaders and the Downstate anti-come-outer orientation of William Jay and the Tappan brothers' group.[20] The situation in New York upset Liberty men outside the state. Zebina Eastman, editor of the *Chicago Western Citizen*, perceptively described the situation in New York in 1846 at the height of its intra-party turmoil: "The Liberty Party in the State of New York is in embarrassing circumstances—It is the only State where the Liberty party may be said to have *leaders*, and each leader has such an extraordinarily development of wisdom and self conceit, that he must lead in his own way, and pertinaciously refuse to make any concession for the common good."[21]

Disputes in other states rarely matched the vituperative nature of those in New York, but debates over policy in some states could become testy and revealed diverse opinions over the character of the party. On the whole, though, Liberty members in most states got along with each other. Outside of New York, Massachusetts, and, later, Michigan, serious intra-party bickering was unusual. Even where there were diverse views, Liberty men pulled together at election time to support party candidates. Most party regulars preferred to work on a consensus basis and avoid serious divisions. They realized their minority status was weak enough without any destructive situations. As a result, a state convention might not reflect some of the strong opinions in the state.

Most Liberty followers were involved in several reform movements. Liberty approval of temperance was almost universal, and most Liberty newspapers supported a variety of causes, although antislavery received the major emphasis. Joshua Leavitt is an example. Despite his adherence to the "one idea" of antislavery as party policy, he clearly stated in 1844 that his new Liberty daily newspaper, the *Boston Morning Chronicle*, supported many reforms and also refused to accept advertisements from theaters.[22] Governmental reforms received much attention from Liberty members, but other causes aimed at individual and societal regeneration were popular. Temperance was the most obvious, but there were others. For instance, Lewis and Arthur Tappan were closely identified with a myriad of activities. Massachusetts reformer Elihu Burritt and Ohioan Asa Mahan were leading figures in the peace movement. Liberty gubernatorial nominee and a former Maine state representative, James Appleton, was known as the "Father of Prohibition." James G. Carter of Massachusetts was a leading educational reformer.

Liberty candidates were held to high personal standards. Owen Lovejoy's claim that "[o]ur candidates are of impeachable integrity" was true.[23] When the party's 1841 Massachusetts gubernatorial candidate, Lucius Boltwood, was accused of owning buildings that were leased out as rum shops, a Liberty man defended him as "thorough-going-tea-total temperance," and added that all Liberty candidates were temperance men.[24] Presidential candidate Birney felt compelled to give a long, detailed account to an Ohio man who had a friend who claimed that Birney was "a public sabbath breaker, and therefore could not give you his vote."[25] Birney took great pains to assure the man that he believed in an "inseparable connection between a due observance of the Lord's day and the maintenance and propagation of Christianity."[26] These incidents were indicative of the demands that Liberty men placed on themselves. One would have difficulty maintaining any position of eminence in the Liberty hierarchy without having demonstrably high standards of personal morality.

The Liberty Party went beyond religious and moral appeals. Liberty theoreticians marshaled political and economic arguments for their antislavery positions. The previously discussed debates on the U.S. Constitution created turmoil in some Liberty circles, but there were other approaches that Liberty men used that became important propaganda pieces for the Liberty Party. Some of these were anti-Southern in character and appealed to political and economic reasoning. They did not emphasize the degradation and inhumanity to the enslaved or the moral evil of slavery—the major thrusts of much abolition literature—but concentrated on the disproportionate economic and political power that the South held over the rest of the nation.[27] Discussions of disproportionate Southern influence were not new and even antedated the Liberty Party. Seymour B. Treadwell outlined the basic arguments as early as 1838.[28] Whig journalist Richard Hildreth, who later became a Liberty candidate, wrote an extended treatise, *Despotism in America,* at the same time that he wrote a campaign biography for William Henry Harrison for president in 1840.[29] Perhaps more significant, Thomas Morris presented his criticism of the Slave Power on the Senate floor in 1839 in what historian Jonathan Earle has called "unquestionably his greatest speech."[30] William Jay's *A View of the Action of the Federal Government in Behalf of Slavery* (1839) emphasized the results of the three-fifths clause.[31] Other writers continued the Slave Power arguments in Liberty propaganda.[32] They remained staples of antislavery rhetoric up to the Civil War.

One of the most famous of these treatises was Joshua Leavitt's "The Financial Power of Slavery," which was frequently published in Liberty newspapers and received wide distribution as a pamphlet and tract.[33] Instead of discussing the effects of slavery on blacks, he detailed the effects of the peculiar institution on the economic well-being of the North. He complained that there was a steady drain of Northern capital to the South, and that slavery absorbed much of this capital. Leavitt presented a multitude of statistics to show how the South was maintaining its economic system at the expense of the North. This could only be changed through the ballot box, where the voters could change the system by electing those opposed to slavery. He went on speaking tours to promulgate these ideas, especially through industrial areas of Massachusetts, where he maintained that the Southern planter class was living extravagantly on Northern credit and was putting pressure on the Northern workingman. The South was taking the fruits of both slave and free labor and was a "vampyre which is drinking up the life blood of free industry" and "consumes faster than it pays." His solution was quite simple: free the slaves and pay them wages that they would promptly spend on Northern manufactures. They would become "steady and paying customers."[34] He also emphasized the disproportionate influence of the South in national politics, whereby "the South sends into the House of Representatives, some twenty-four members of Congress, chosen by virtue of its slave population [because of the three-fifths clause]."[35] Others developed similar arguments.[36] Two of the most widely distributed were those of Alvan Stewart and Charles Dexter Cleveland.

In a widely circulated tract, "The Cause of the Hard Times," New York's tart-tongued Alvan Stewart asked, "Why is this country in such deep Distress, without Famine, Pestilence, or War?" He had a ready answer: "It is because one third of this nation have lived in idleness, on the labor of the other two thirds, by means of credit, for the last twenty years." He indicted the South because "[l]abor, in the slave States, is regarded as disgraceful, when performed by white persons." He pointed out that the indebtedness of the South to Northern communities was a situation that would continue "until slavery is overthrown, and it is no longer disgraceful to the white man to earn his bread by the *sweat of his brow*."[37] Charles Dexter Cleveland's 1844 "Address of the Liberty Party of Pennsylvania"—which went through printings of sixty thousand copies—expanded on these arguments of Southern domination of the U.S. government and military and discussed the Slave Power as being "the Chief Cause of Our Financial Embarrassments." He argued that "the great majority [of commercial treaties with foreign nations] are made with reference to the products of slave labor."[38] Other Liberty men developed and published similar arguments. William Birney, the presidential candidate's son and a Cincinnati lawyer, also wrote on the political and economic threat of the Slave Power.[39] Part of Charles T. Torrey's series on the policy of the Liberty Party for the *Boston Free American* emphasized the contest between free and slave labor and its resulting favors for the South.[40] In fact, the leading Liberty newspapers in Indiana, Arnold Buffum's *Protectionist* and Benjamin Stanton's *Free Labor Advocate and Anti-Slavery Reporter,* highlighted the issue and made the free produce movement—whereby individuals would only use items produced by free labor—a cornerstone of their antislavery philosophy. Gerrit Smith was particularly hard on Liberty men who "come together ... with stolen clothes upon their backs and stolen food in their stomachs (for such are all slave labor-products)."[41]

As the party matured, these economic appeals were directed more specifically toward workingmen. This attitude was expressed at a workingmen's meeting in New England. The speaker, Liberty state senatorial candidate Abner L. Bayley, insisted that slavery "must degrade the free workingman" and that the slaves' "interests are identical to yours." He accused Southern politicians of subscribing to the belief that *"slavery is the natural state of the laborer."*[42] Sometimes Liberty men equated their position with a class struggle, claiming, for instance, that the Liberty struggle was "a contest between *labor* and *capital,* for the right of the laboring classes in opposition to the encroachment of the wealthy and aristocratic."[43] The Liberty Party in many areas became so closely involved with the labor movement that its candidates often received the nomination of a workingman's party or organization. In 1846 Henry Bradley, the Liberty candidate for governor of New York, and his running mate, William Chaplin, received the nomination of Henry Evans and the National Reform Association, as did the Liberty League and Gerrit Smith's National Liberty Party in 1848. Salmon P. Chase, who was running for Congress, sought the endorsement of the National Reformers, as did several Liberty candidates in Massachusetts.[44]

By 1846, the party in many areas "made the call to the urban worker a feature of its platform."[45] Liberty men used economic arguments and appeals to labor most frequently and effectively in New York, Massachusetts, western Pennsylvania, and Ohio. Local Liberty candidates sometimes came from the ranks of common men who were often artisans and mechanics in manufacturing locales.[46] As one Liberty agent recorded in his journal, "It is men that we want in the Liberty cause. We have comparatively occasion for that description of person whom society, by a shocking misnomer, calls *gentlemen.*"[47] The indications are that some workingmen responded with their votes.[48] A writer corresponding with Joshua Leavitt from Millbury complained that the 1843 Liberty vote in that town had suffered after some factories had closed and another burned down.[49] The relationship between the workingmen's movement and Liberty organizations grew even more cordial after 1844, especially in New York and western Pennsylvania.[50] This does not mean that the workingmen had the sympathy of all Liberty men. The Tappan brothers had been hostile to labor during the 1830s when Lewis was the editor of the New York *Journal of Commerce,* a strong opponent of trade unions.[51] Nevertheless, the Democratic drift of the third party could only have made it more appealing to workingmen. Certain leaders made the appeal to labor an important part of their Liberty program. Dr. William Elder, a Pittsburgh physician-lawyer, combined his work as a Liberty organizer with an interest in the workingmen's movement. He believed that the antislavery movement had to reach out to working men, and he was delighted when their local meetings endorsed the Liberty Party.[52] One of his allies in this appeal was Salmon P. Chase. Part of Chase's plan to move the Liberty Party in the direction of the Democratic Party was his appeal to Northern labor. He claimed that slavery "paralyzes your industry and enterprise" and "degrades and dishonors labor."[53]

Arguments against the South contained certain key points. The South was able to wield economic control over the country because it controlled the national government. Liberty writers and speakers were fond of pointing out the distribution of federal offices and appointments and detailing the preponderant Southern influence in the control of the presidency, vice presidency, Speaker of the House, ambassadors, and even West Point appointments. Southerners were able to achieve this imbalance because they received the three-fifths representation for slaves who could not vote. Until this minority control ended, the North would continue to suffer economically.[54] Some Liberty men, most notably Chase and the Cincinnati group, preferred "to direct all the energies of our political action against the unconstitutional encroachments of the Slave Power and against slavery wherever it may exist without constitutional sanction."[55] These individuals spoke only for a minority of the party until the Free Soil merger. Even in Ohio most opposed the tactics of the Chase faction, which wanted to redirect the party's strategy. William Birney declared that they were "a temporising, bargain and sale class of politicians" who were willing "to sacrifice our purity as a party." He further reported that in Ohio "the old stock of Abolitionists understand Mr. Chase and distrust him."[56] While the anti-Southern political and economic arguments figured prominently in Liberty rhetoric, few were willing to give them primacy in party dogma.[57] They continued to emphasize religious and moral arguments against slavery as the core party belief.

The Liberty Party operated very much like other political parties of the 1840s. After eschewing the open abolition convention of the 1830s, they moved toward representative gatherings on the national level and permitted a wider range of participation than other parties in all its meetings. Its basic methods were similar everywhere: a combination of the revival abolition techniques of the 1830s and the conventional political practices employed by the two major parties.

Party newspapers were central to the Liberty effort. One editor claimed that 66,000 copies of antislavery newspapers were coming out weekly by mid-1846.[58] Most newspapers of the 1840s were mouthpieces for political parties. Each major party had a press in every Northern state that was recognized as the party's newspaper and reflected that party's positions. These papers were not dispassionate and objective but fiercely and openly partisan. Indeed, a reader had to scan the newspapers of all parties to have a reasonably accurate grasp of the political situation. Editors made no effort to conceal their loyalties or biases. Whig papers commonly referred to the Democrats as "locos," or "locofocos," terms referring to the group of Democrats that struck new "locofoco" matches to light a meeting hall that had its gas lights extinguished by opponents. The Democrats often called Whigs "feds" or "federalists" after the long defunct political party that many felt was the antecedent to the current Whig Party. This was a derisory term because the former party had been tainted in many minds by aristocratic pretensions and disloyalty stemming from the Hartford convention and actions during the War of 1812. Major-party presses were sources for national, state, and local party news as well as means for party leaders to communicate with the party membership. They also served nonpolitical roles. For instance, the post office would run lists of persons who had received letters in the largest local newspaper. Some journals quoted stock prices, transportation schedules, and almost anything that might be useful to a reader. In addition, newspapers served as a source of entertainment by publishing stories, poems, serialized novels, and interesting bits of trivia from around the world.

Liberty journals did all these things. Yet they maintained the character of the reform-oriented abolition newspapers of the 1830s. Most Liberty papers grafted their political features onto what was a moralistic, antislavery journal. Often a Liberty Party sheet would do a very nonpolitical thing—not mention the Liberty Party by name in a whole issue—although much space was devoted to antislavery and, especially, religious matters. This was an indication that the Liberty cause was much more than merely everyday politics. An ebb and flow of political information existed in most Liberty presses. The usual pattern was for party information and communication to increase during the summer, when the annual meetings were usually held, or in the few months preceding important elections. When the event or election was over, political information took up much less space. These newspapers operated on a spectrum from highly moralistic and evangelical to more secular. More often than not, the character of a

Liberty newspaper revealed more about the editor than it did about the preferences of his constituency. A good example was when the (Wis.) *American Freeman* changed to a more moralistic, general reform publication after the more secular C. C. Sholes left the editorial chair and Ichabod Codding took over. And Gamaliel Bailey's selective editing of Liberty news and views in the *Philanthropist* has given many the incorrect impression that the majority of Ohio Liberty men were calculating politicos who substantially differed from party members in most states. Editors were powerful, and they sometimes omitted or delayed publication of views with which they disagreed or thought injudicious.

Liberty publications varied in quality and success. Newspapers of the 1840s exchanged copies with several other papers, and editors could ease the pressure of a tight schedule by freely borrowing, sometime without credit, from other presses. Liberty journalists were no exception. Besides copying stories from the general press, Liberty editors relied on each other for party news from other areas. Indeed, this was the way that the average Liberty member found out what was happening elsewhere. Even more Liberty Party history would be lost if editors had not reprinted articles from sources that are no longer extant. Only a handful of the more than thirty Liberty sheets that existed by the mid-1840s could be termed successful in having an impact outside Liberty circles and being self-supporting, but a few did have a wide circulation and much influence beyond their immediate area. The (Boston) *Emancipator* was the leading Liberty newspaper in the Northeast. Ably edited for much of the party's existence by Joshua Leavitt, its unyielding moral tone and righteous positions accurately reflected the character of most New England Liberty men. The *Philanthropist*, on the other hand, was an important Liberty paper, but it spoke primarily for a relatively small clique that was located near Cincinnati, well away from the state's main antislavery area along the Western Reserve. Editor Gamaliel Bailey produced a neat, widely distributed, readable sheet that had a more secular tone, but his exclusion of items and opinions that he believed harmful to the overall goals presented a slanted view of Ohio Liberty affairs.[59] Nonetheless, the *Philanthropist* enjoyed a wide circulation and carried Liberty news from several states. Similarly, Bailey's national newspaper, the *National Era*, did not reflect the general state of Liberty thinking at the time of its establishment in Washington, D.C., in early 1847, but it was an attractive, well-edited, influential national newspaper.

Zebina Eastman's *Chicago Western Citizen*, a newspaper with a large, wide circulation, was more influential at the grassroots in the Old Northwest. It printed much material from Wisconsin and, later, Iowa. It even had an assistant editor in Michigan City, Indiana, who produced a special Indiana section of the paper. It also welcomed contributions from women writers on political matters. Eastman's paper was similar to its counterparts in the East with its mood of Christian reform, but Eastman and most abolitionists of the region did not propose the same policies that were seen elsewhere, such as the attempt to make the U.S. Constitution an antislavery document. The *Chicago Western Citizen*, in spite of its impact on the abolition movement in many states and its large circulation, has probably been the most underrated Liberty, if not abolition, newspaper in the country.[60] These were the most important Liberty newspapers, although Theodore Foster and Guy Beckley's (Ann Arbor, Mich.) *Signal of Liberty*, Austin Willey's (Maine) *Liberty Standard*, Wesley Bailey's (Utica, N.Y.) *Liberty Press*, and the *Albany Patriot* also served their states well.

The Liberty press improved noticeably after 1844 as Joseph Poland's (Montpelier, Vt.) *Green Mountain Freeman*, the (Concord, N.H.) *Granite Freeman*, L. L. Rice's (Warren, Ohio) *Liberty Herald*, Francis Julius LeMoyne's *Washington* (Pa.) *Patriot*, and the (Pittsburgh) *Spirit of Liberty* more than adequately filled journalistic vacuums and aided the Liberty Party in organizing their areas. Normally, these newspapers were partially financed by the state Liberty organization or the state antislavery society, but some were private ventures. A few, such as the *Green Mountain Freeman*, became self-sufficient, but most had financial difficulties and were in danger of folding, usually because they could not get their subscribers to pay for their subscriptions.[61] The early *Philanthropist*, *Utica* (N.Y.) *Friend of Man*, (Wis.) *American Freeman*, the (Hartford, Conn.) *Christian Freeman*, and others had to close shop for a few weeks at a time until they could pay the printer. This put editors in a difficult position. If they struck subscribers off of their lists, then the effectiveness of the newspaper as a propaganda tool would be hampered.

Liberty journals regularly collapsed or were absorbed by other Liberty newspapers. None of the five Liberty dailies survived very long, and more newspapers went out of business in the first two years of the party than survived. The Liberty Party had more than sixty papers under its banner at one time or another during the 1840s. The American and Foreign Anti-Slavery Society published a list of extant abolitionist newspapers in 1846 and said thirty-six of these were sympathetic to the Liberty Party.[62] Most states were unable to support more than one newspaper at a time for long, but Ohio, New York, and Massachusetts often had four or five operating at the same time, and Maine was able to support two for much of its existence.[63] Some Liberty sheets lasted just a few weeks until after elections, many hung on for a couple of years, and a few existed from early in the party's history until well after the Free Soil merger. The *Green Mountain Freeman*, for instance, published continually until 1885. Many mediocre Liberty newspapers did not last very long. These journals usually reprinted much of their material from other publications, had minimal editorial work or comment, and largely neglected state and local Liberty affairs.[64] Similar sheets often supplemented them near election time. There was even a report of someone's attempting to establish a Liberty newspaper in North Carolina, but this venture does not seem to have materialized.[65]

The founding of the *National Era* in Washington, D.C., was a significant event in the history of the Liberty Party.[66] The North-Western Liberty Convention in Chicago in June 1846 set up a committee to explore the possibility of a national paper in Washington, and ultimately drew up a report outlining the project. It included a list of agents in the Northern states and some Southern states.[67] When the first issue appeared on January 7, 1847, the party had a truly national newspaper for the first time, and it was on the borders of slave states and in the nation's capital where slavery was still legal. Joshua Leavitt, who had experience lobbying in Washington and whose *Emancipator* probably had had the most national influence, was bypassed for the more amiable Gamaliel Bailey. Lewis Tappan, who remembered his disagreements with the less diplomatic Leavitt, expressed a preference for Bailey, helped finance the venture, and swung many members of the American and Foreign Anti-Slavery Society behind it.[68] Bailey and his backers assembled a talented group of contributing Liberty journalists—including Linnaeus P. Noble from New York, John Greenleaf Whittier and Amos A. Phelps from Massachusetts, Guy Beckley from Michigan, and William Elder from Pennsylvania. By September 1847, the *National Era* was publishing 11,000 issues, although many were given for free on its exchange list.[69]

Not all Liberty men welcomed the *National Era*. Several expressed concerns that the well-edited national newspaper would damage the subscription lists of financially troubled local presses. Leavitt, whose *Boston Morning Chronicle* had already failed and left him in debt, foresaw the national newspaper hurting the subscription list of the *Emancipator*. Within fifteen months he had severed all his connections with the newspaper that he had ably edited for so many years.[70] Other editors worried about the survival of their newspapers.[71] Some also questioned the milder antislavery tone of the new publication. Beriah Green called for "a little *bravery*" in its policies. And James G. Birney was having such a difficult time getting some of his outspoken views published that he requested "the *reason for not publishing*" and requested Linnaeus P. Noble to "be so good, as to make some special mark, like this + on the envelope of my national Era."[72] Nonetheless, the national newspaper was popular and fulfilled a real need. It collected and reprinted information on the party throughout the nation. It was the one publication that truly kept an eye on the party everywhere. At the same time, its editorial positions put it firmly in the wing of the party that was trying to soften Liberty positions and welcoming attempts at coalition.

Liberty journals were not the only reminders that the party had grown out of the abolition movement of the 1830s. Liberty groups took advantage of new printing technologies to publish tracts and almanacs. They financed traveling agents to give speeches for the party, especially near elections. These writings and speeches were not very different from their counterparts in the 1830s. The tracts included reprinted letters, speeches, and articles supporting Liberty positions. Leavitt's "The Financial Power of Slavery" became an antislavery classic because of its frequent reprinting and distribution. The state organization usually funded tract dissemination, relying on contributions when they could get them. Liberty men who could afford it often printed tracts at their own expense. Gerrit Smith became a virtual cottage industry of tracts and broadsides all by himself. He financed the publication and distribution of his carefully crafted position papers on a variety of topics.[73] Sometimes tracts emphasized the antislavery message almost exclusively, with little or no mention made of party.

Liberty men made genuine efforts to establish a tract system. Alvan Stewart, as chairman of the party's national committee, wrote a directive to Liberty organizations that urged them to develop a system for printing and distributing tracts.[74] The Liberty Party platform of 1844 recommended that "the friends of Liberty in each town form tract organizations, of men and women, to distribute tracts to every family in such towns." This goal did not come close to realization in most areas, but Liberty organizations were responsible for the publication of large numbers of tracts and reprints. As previously mentioned, Charles D. Cleveland was personally instrumental in the printing and distribution of sixty thousand copies of his own 1844 "Address to the Liberty Party of Pennsylvania" and another one hundred thousand copies of Chase's 1845 "Address to the Southern and Western Liberty Convention."[75] Chase described how the process worked in Ohio, but it could easily have referred to the system in other states.

> I do not know that you are acquainted with the plan of tract distribution. It is this. Dr. Bailey occasionally makes a selection of leading articles from the Philanthropist, such for example as the articles of Mr. Leavitt on the Financial Power of Slavery, and publishes them in pamphlet form, sometimes four, sometimes eight pages, and circulates them gratuitously through the city and country . . . The mode of distribution is this. A distributor takes a bundle of tracts and walks through a given district call-

ing at every shop & house. He asks those whom he meets if they are willing to read an Antislavery tract. If they answer yes: he gives one; if no: he quietly turns away. This plan of effort there is reason to believe, does a great deal of good; and it depends for support on voluntary contributions.[76]

The system had its pitfalls, however, especially before 1844. *Signal of Liberty* editor Theodore Foster later questioned its political effectiveness because some of the tracts exhibited a harsh tone and "loose and often extravagant statement of facts: their most important conclusions were unsupported by substantial and tangible data, and were often the mere assumptions of the writer."[77] As the tone of the party became more secular later in the decade, the tracts became more subdued and analytical.

Liberty almanacs were another heritage of the abolition movement of the 1830s. Liberty men in all areas of the country published them for their regions. They contained calendars highlighting important antislavery dates, information of local interest, and selections from important antislavery writings. The almanacs were an important propaganda tool. In 1845 a run of two thousand (fifty cents per dozen) quickly sold out in Illinois, and the *Chicago Western Citizen* announced that a new printing of several thousand more would soon be available.[78] A German-language publisher in Philadelphia even printed a fifty-four-page German Liberty Almanac in 1847 for distribution among the three hundred thousand estimated German-speaking citizens in the United States.[79] The Liberty Party made considerable effort to go into the German communities, even providing an interpreter in Wisconsin,[80] and most Liberty followers were opposed to "the insane and cruel 'Native American' folly."[81] Nonetheless, few of these foreign-born newcomers seem to have gotten deeply involved in Liberty affairs.

Newspapers, tracts, and almanacs were only a part of Liberty publishing endeavors. Books, songbooks, campaign volumes, and lengthy accounts of debates between Liberty supporters and opponents were churned out in large numbers and distributed widely. Perhaps the most popular, George Washington Clark's *The Liberty Minstrel*, went through seven editions and continued its life as *The Free Soil Minstrel* in 1848. This was a substantial publication that not only contained lyrics and music but also included works from such distinguished poets as John Greenleaf Whittier and John Pierpont.[82] And Beriah Green wrote a campaign biography of Birney for the 1844 election that was widely distributed along with the candidate's many writings.[83]

Liberty supporters also made use of traveling agents, another system that had its roots in the earlier reform and abolition movements. Usually state Liberty organizations or wealthy individuals, such as Gerrit Smith or the Tappans, hired men to travel in an area to conduct Liberty meetings, lecture on the party and the evils of slavery, circulate antislavery petitions, receive donations, and sell tracts and subscriptions for Liberty newspapers. The 1844 Liberty platform encouraged the use of these itinerant lecturers, who often took a fugitive slave or free black along with them as added attractions. These agents were effective, but they were an expensive luxury that the party could not usually afford. Occasionally, a state party would employ a full-time agent, but the more frequent pattern was to commission a few speakers in the months preceding an election. Massachusetts sometimes had five or more in the field at election time, and Gerrit Smith sometimes saturated his home area of Madison County, New York. Liberty newspapers sometimes had their own agents in their reading areas to take subscriptions. Agents could receive a salary, work on commission, or lecture for free. These usually were state or local endeavors. James G. Birney's subsidized trip before the 1844 election was an exception.

Generally, Liberty newspapers published an agent's itinerary, and local families often provided his food and lodging. He lectured at antislavery conventions, solicited subscriptions for the party's newspaper, sold and distributed tracts, conducted Liberty business, and attempted to establish a Liberty organization if one did not already exist. The similarity of resolutions and proceedings of the conventions on an agent's route indicated that most speakers followed a set formula of operations and dominated the local proceedings. Well-known agents often moved from state to state and region to region. Ichabod Codding, for example, worked in several eastern states before serving in both Illinois and Wisconsin. He was a superb speaker, editor, and organizer who invigorated the party wherever he went. Alanson St. Clair also worked in the East before moving to Illinois and then on to Iowa, where he was one of the founders of its Liberty Party.

Liberty followers also established Liberty Associations. These probably had their roots in the young men's associations that the major parties used as recruitment tools, but the function of a Liberty Association encompassed much more. These associations filled the void left by the demise of many state and local antislavery societies. The typical Liberty Association was more broadly based than the party itself, including nonvoters—women, young adults, disfranchised blacks, and even children—and the occasional major-party member as well as the Liberty Party men.[84] They operated differently from state to state, but the associations gradually became more important in the Liberty movement. The organization provided something for everyone to do, and it helped bring in much needed revenue. Membership was easy. Alvan Stewart recommended that males pay twelve and a half cents per week dues, females six cents, and children (male and female, 6–16) two cents. In Maine, anyone who paid one dollar annually (or ten dollars for a lifetime membership) received voting rights and one copy of its publication.[85] In most states the Liberty Association was an adjunct to the party, although the Wisconsin Liberty Association eventually became the controlling force in the state party.

Liberty men did not depend solely on the earlier abolition tactics, however, because they soon realized that additional strategies were necessary for achieving a modicum of political success. They borrowed tactics freely from the Democrats and Whigs. The first two national conventions in 1840 and 1841 were similar to the abolition conventions of the 1830s where everyone present was permitted to vote on convention business, but Liberty leaders adopted proportional representation for the national convention in 1843. This convention approved a platform, as the Democrats had done in 1840, and endorsed party organization at the national, state, and local levels (Resolutions 30, 31). The ideal was a set of interlocking committees. It began with a school district organization, which then sent a representative to the town committee, which sent a member to the county or congressional committee, whose chairman was a member of the state central committee, which maintained contact with the national committee.

Most states did not come close to achieving the ideal. The Massachusetts organization was most successful statewide, largely through the early efforts of Henry B. Stanton and some of his successors. Nevertheless, the 1847 chairman of the state central committee claimed that party losses in recent elections were due "to an apathy arising out of a want of systematic organization."[86] Lack of effective organization was a major problem in all the states. State conventions passed countless plans and resolutions for improving the state and local party machines, but real accomplishments were sporadic and usually temporary. Certain areas were well organized: Gerrit Smith's Madison County; Albany and Utica, New York; John G. Whittier's Amesbury, Massachusetts; Mercer County in Pennsylvania; parts of Ohio's Western Reserve; Chicago; Owen Lovejoy's Congressional District in Illinois; Ann Arbor, Jackson, Battle Creek, Marshall, and certain towns in Wayne County, Michigan; New Garden, Indiana; areas of Wisconsin; and other pockets of Liberty strength. These often had their own Liberty newspapers and held regularly scheduled meetings. Most places had only a rudimentary Liberty organization, however, and some leading Liberty men did not seem to place a very high premium on local organization. Presidential candidate

Birney admitted that there was no Liberty organization in his area of Michigan, and he does not appear to have made an effort to start one.[87]

Local hostility, lack of patronage, and little electoral success hampered Liberty efforts to organize, but the absence of any real national coordination was a great obstacle. Each state party conducted its affairs as local leaders saw fit, and they abrogated little of their power to the national committee. As early as 1842, Alvan Stewart complained that an Ohio state Liberty convention must have "forgotten there was a United States Executive Committee, of which I was chairman" when it recommended a national Liberty convention for the summer.[88] When national business came to the committee, however, Stewart encountered difficulty in contacting all the members.[89] His attempts to institute strategies for propagandizing and organizing the cause usually met with only lip service. Each state had a member on the national committee, but the position was more honorific than functional. An Ohio editor summarized the situation in mid-1847 when he wrote, "The Committee has never acted as such. It has had no meetings—no mutual consultation. Mr. Stewart has put forth some articles, which he signs as Chairman, but these were never passed upon by the Committee, and were probably not shown before publication to any member of it."[90]

Liberty men campaigned similarly to Whigs and Democrats. They distributed special campaign editions of newspapers, held political rallies, and made special efforts to get known Liberty sympathizers to the polls. It took courage to vote for the Liberty Party in some places, especially if an individual had been a staunch Whig or Democrat. Voting was not a secret affair. Parties distributed clearly identifiable ballots and there was even viva voce voting in some races. Political parties in most states printed and distributed easily identifiable political ballots that listed the party's candidates. These tickets were distinguishable from each other, so it was relatively easy to find out how someone voted. Since most people during the 1840s lived in small communities, Liberty men could receive social and economic reprisals from their neighbors. Most were not as blatant or well publicized as when some prominent members of the local school board visited a teacher in Worcester, Massachusetts, and advised him to decline a Liberty nomination for a local post. After he refused their request, the resultant publicity probably saved his job.[91] While instances of such harassment rarely appeared in the Liberty press, there were many accusations that Liberty votes were not being tallied. This was more prevalent in the early years when Liberty men were trying to organize their efforts in areas that had few Liberty votes to report. Liberty rallies and endorsements from some places were not reflected in the subsequent examinations of votes, particularly in upper-level elections. It is safe to conclude that Liberty totals were consistently under-reported, especially where their strength was minimal. Liberty presses sometimes suffered a loss of advertising revenue and did not receive governmental contracts to which they were entitled. Zebina Eastman complained that the *Chicago Western Citizen* did not receive the postal contract that its circulation warranted.[92]

Anti-party feelings are sometimes identified with the Liberty Party, and there is no doubt that this is reflected in some of its rhetoric.[93] This anti-partyism was as much a tactic as it was intellectual conviction for Liberty men. Working in the party-conscious atmosphere of the 1840s, when voter turnout was great, party loyalty high, and ticket splitting minimal, Liberty men had to advance arguments against staying with the major parties if they wished to have any hope for success. Austin Willey summed up the Liberty anti-party attitudes of many in his article on "Political Partyism—Its Evils and Remedy."[94] He argued that political parties were aristocratic and despotic, hostile to individual liberty and true democracy, instruments of crimes against minority groups, and a hindrance to progress and reform, and tended to become corrupt. Of course, Liberty men argued that the way to remedy all this was to vote the Liberty Party into power. Willey and most other Liberty leaders were vehement at election time in urging Liberty men to "hold the line" and not return to their old parties. They denounced backsliders, and opposed Liberty men giving support to non-Liberty men. While some party members were willing to work with Whigs and Democrats, a large number held to the traditional Liberty position of "no union with slaveholders or those in political fellowship with slaveholders." In fact, many Liberty men had a Janus-faced attitude toward the idea of party. A political party was bad unless it happened to be the Liberty Party. When Whigs in many states began to persuade former Whigs to return to their old party, Liberty men showed that they could appeal to party loyalty as well as any party-machine Democrat.

No two states' parties conducted their Liberty affairs in exactly the same way, but certain regional nuances distinguished parties in the Old Northwest from those in many eastern states. These regional differences have sometimes been misunderstood and given a much more important role in Liberty development than they deserve. The distinctions had more to do with intra-party relations within the states than any great policy disagreements. The ability and willingness of state party members in the Northwest to compromise on issues that caused problems in some eastern states clearly distinguished them from some areas in the East. Even though the overwhelming majority of Liberty men in the Old Northwest were transplanted New Englanders and New Yorkers, they did not bring moral absolutism in party affairs with them. Whether to vote for non-Liberty men as delegates to the state constitutional conventions brought about serious divisions in New York. The same issue brought about only long discussions in Illinois and Wisconsin before party members finally decided against the practice, thus ending the matter. Theodore Foster dropped his campaign for a multi-reform program when it became clear that only a small portion of the Michigan Liberty Party shared his ideas. Spirited gatherings of the Wisconsin Liberty organization rarely threatened the unity in the state. The only feud that had serious party repercussions in the Old Northwest was the dispute between Thomas Morris and some of the Ohio leaders, but its negative results were transitory and limited.

There was more internal bickering in the East. The most serious disputes were in New York, but Liberty men did not hesitate to deal with each other on less than friendly terms in some other states in the region. The general tone of debate was more vindictive and less compromising in the East, with many personal feuds developing. The conflict between Liberty editors Austin Willey and John Godfrey disturbed the situation in Maine for a few years.[95] Joshua Leavitt and Elizur Wright sniped at each other through their newspapers, resulting in Wright's estrangement from the main body of Massachusetts Liberty men.[96] Nonetheless, most easterners would still pull together at election time. Mounting intra-party disputes could reach a very personal level and hurt Liberty efforts. The normally mild-mannered John G. Whittier was frustrated by the drift of party affairs as early as 1845 because "for want of due energy at headquarters our election is going by default."[97] Zebina Eastman declared that disputes in the East showed that "[t]he slave has sunk almost out of sight, while some hair-split theory or problem in morals, dependency on some subtleties in the philosophy of reform, are all engrossing and all important."[98]

During its existence, the Liberty Party combined the general tone, style, and strategies of the abolition movement of the 1830s with the tactics and organizational techniques employed by the major political parties. In the beginning, the party was little more than an abolition organization that ran political candidates. As the party matured, it grew to resemble a traditional political party in modes of operation and the value put on electoral success. Other affiliated Liberty organizations began to deal with the nonpolitical aspects of the antislavery movement by the mid-1840s as the Liberty Party devoted itself more exclusively to electoral matters. This was accompanied by a less moralistic and more secular approach among many elements in the party. This process was part of the transition of the party from political protest to the political involvement that led to the Free Soil merger. Unlike other political parties, however, the Liberty Party had a larger constituency that encompassed disfranchised African Americans and women.

9

AFRICAN AMERICANS AND THE LIBERTY PARTY

> I could not and would not go to the polls again in support of either the Whig or Locofoco party... I denounced both of these parties, and rushed through their midst and found my way to the Liberty party—and they give me the right hand of fellowship—not the left hand as the other two parties do.
>
> HENRY JOHNSON, Maine African American voter

Most studies that deal in any detail with black involvement in the Liberty organization treat events and individuals only in a national context or about activities in New York State.[1] In fact, the most recent book-length study on the Liberty Party claims that "the northwestern Liberty party was necessarily a lily-white political organization."[2] And a book on black women abolitionists states that "[f]or women and most black men, who could not vote, the formation of political parties held little meaning."[3]

These assertions were not true for the northwestern states or any other state in which the Liberty Party existed. African Americans participated in Liberty activities from the party's inception. Liberty political conventions were racially mixed affairs where black men sometimes took leadership roles and black women occasionally attended, whether in the main meetings, in their own gatherings, or in Liberty Associations. Blacks increasingly identified with the Liberty organization as the decade progressed. They constantly reassessed and debated their political and ideological strategies during the 1840s.[4] They often worked in their own racially exclusive environment, but, at the same time, they continued to participate in interracial antislavery activities. The major institutional outlets for politically oriented blacks were the Liberty Party and its attendant activities. Even those political blacks who did not work exclusively within the Liberty Party usually gave it a substantial amount of support. This was the only realistic course open to them except in the few areas that the Whig Party provided consistent support for antislavery and black rights. Liberty organizations may not have been their only, or even primary, antislavery and equal rights vehicle, but it was an important element in the efforts of most activists. African American participation in the Liberty Party was widespread and important. They took on duties and played significant roles in the Liberty movement.

At the end of the 1830s, black and white abolitionists debated the desirability of an antislavery political party. Most blacks did not view themselves as part of the American political system. Having just lost the suffrage in Pennsylvania, they possessed an unrestricted vote only in the four upper New England states—Maine, Massachusetts, New Hampshire, and Vermont—and, with property restrictions, in New York.[5] Many feared reprisals if they voted in some areas of these states, some wanted nothing to do with an American political system that sanctioned slavery and discrimination, and others were apathetic.[6] Black voters were usually in the literate segment of the urban population that was professional or in private business. Almost all had identified with the Whig Party because it had been more forward in promoting African American interests and rights.[7] Only in Rhode Island, however, did Whigs make a genuine statewide effort to work for black rights and support. They endorsed black suffrage during the 1840s, and then made a direct appeal for black votes, "claiming their opposition to the expansion of slavery and their support of black suffrage."[8] When the Whigs won and delivered unrestricted black suffrage, their consistency gained them African American loyalty.[9]

It seems natural that a political party committed to ending slavery would appeal to politically oriented blacks and attract many others who might have been politically indifferent, but this was not always the case. The idea of an antislavery third party occurred in the late 1830s during a period of turmoil in abolitionist organizations. When political abolitionists finally set up a presidential ticket at an April 1, 1840, convention in Albany, New York, black reformers were confronted with some serious choices.[10] Within two months the American Anti-Slavery Society split into two factions with many abolitionists, including most of the advocates of independent political action, breaking away from the Garrison-dominated Old Organization to form a New Organization, the American and Foreign Anti-Slavery Society. Garrison's opposition to political parties in general and the new antislavery party in particular affected some blacks in the Northeast.

Garrison's early and uncompromising advocacy of black equality had won him the respect and affection of African Americans. They were early financial backers of his newspaper, the *Liberator*, and served as its agents. By 1834, almost three-fourths of the 2,300 subscribers to the paper were black, and many of these took part in the founding of early antislavery societies. A believer in an interracial society, Garrison was personally close to many blacks and mixed with them socially.[11] Many, especially in the Boston and Philadelphia areas, sided with him in the 1840 disputes in the American Anti-Slavery Society and in his vigorous opposition to the new political party.[12] Nevertheless, some were already becoming disenchanted with Garrison, especially because of his perceived anticlericalism. At least eight of the officers in the new American and Foreign Anti-Slavery Society were black clergymen, and African Americans enjoyed a much greater role in the leadership of the New Organization than they had in the Old Organization's American Anti-Slavery Society.[13] Some tried to maintain neutrality between the two factions, while others worked in harmony with members of both groups.[14]

Garrison's strong opposition to an antislavery political party was shared by a few of his black associates, such as Frederick Douglass and Charles Lenox Remond in Massachusetts and William Wells Brown in western New York. Douglass was an escaped slave and the most famous black lecturer during the antebellum period. Remond was a well educated, free mulatto who was an agent of the Massachusetts Anti-Slavery Society. And Brown, a fugitive slave, lived in western New York until he relocated to Massachusetts in early 1847 to serve as an agent for the Massachusetts Anti-Slavery Society. They were excellent orators who lectured internationally and throughout the North, and they vehemently opposed the Liberty Party for its entire existence.[15] There are other reasons why some blacks remained reluctant to support the Liberty Party, particularly in the early 1840s. Some undoubtedly believed that Garrison had been poorly treated by some Liberty men, and a few black voters were unwilling to break their major-party connections.[16]

Black Garrisonians had a limited and diminishing following, however, and were not indicative of African American opinion immediately before the Free Soil merger in 1848.[17] Garrison's influence among Philadelphia blacks also waned after 1840, not because they opposed him—he remained a cherished and admired figure—but because Philadelphia blacks took a unique course that left them out of mainstream civil rights movements. The Philadelphia black community of over twenty thousand persons was the largest in the North, and its leaders "were moving further and further from the center of black activism in the North." They became "an inward-looking community" that only became minimally involved in the black convention movement and other national black ventures.[18] A trend toward more black support for the Liberty Party developed as the decade progressed, however, in Massachusetts, New York City, and even eastern Pennsylvania, areas where Garrison was formerly strong and there had been some doubt among African Americans concerning the wisdom of independent antislavery political action.[19] By 1848, blacks in Boston were even discussing an attempt to establish a black auxiliary to the Liberty Party.[20]

Garrison was losing touch with blacks in other ways. One incident concerned a memorial to Charles T. Torrey, a founder of the Liberty Party and one of his adversaries during the 1839 and 1840 schisms, who became a martyr among blacks when he died of tuberculosis in a Maryland penitentiary after being jailed for helping runaway slaves. Torrey had worked closely with blacks in the North and South and was an admired figure in their communities. Garrison refused to be part of the committee of arrangements for the funeral, and he urged blacks not to erect a monument to Torrey.[21] Garrison also refused to participate in or encourage the purchase of slaves in order to give them their freedom because he believed that this acknowledged the legitimacy of the system. Many African Americans, desperate to rescue loved ones from slavery or to protect themselves against capture and re-enslavement, strongly disagreed.[22] In addition, the American and Foreign Anti-Slavery Society, besides including African Americans in responsible positions, had gradually become more supportive of the third party until it urged its members at its annual meeting in 1845 to "unite their efforts with the Liberty party."[23] As this was happening, blacks were assuming significant roles within the party itself.

Liberty gatherings at all levels encouraged African American involvement. Liberty men demonstrated these convictions most clearly at the National Liberty Party nominating convention at Buffalo in 1843, when blacks were admitted to a national political convention as fully accredited delegates for the first time. John J. Zuille, Theodore S. Wright, and Charles B. Ray sat on the party's nominating committee. Samuel Ringgold Ward, who had participated in the August 1840 New York state convention that had set up a presidential electoral ticket in 1840, opened the meeting with a prayer.[24] Ray, former editor and owner of the defunct *Colored American,* served as a convention secretary. Henry Highland Garnet, a Presbyterian clergyman from Troy, New York, delivered an impressive address. Other blacks were in attendance. A meeting of colored citizens of Chicago had selected one delegate and two alternates for the Illinois Liberty delegation.[25] Shortly before the Liberty convention, a Colored People's National Convention, which also met in Buffalo, and a New York State convention in Rochester, overwhelmingly adopted resolutions approving the Liberty Party. Not all black conventions agreed, however, and many preferred to take no partisan political position.[26]

Given the small and scattered number of black voters in New York and New England, it is impossible to estimate the black vote with any precision; but there is little doubt that the Liberty Party received a substantial portion of the total.[27] Soon after the independent slate was set up in April 1840, a black convention in Albany, New York, carried on a long debate over whether to support the new party before laying the motion on the table.[28] A smaller local meeting in Albany "called on all colored voters to sustain Birney and Earle in the coming election,"[29] and the *Colored American* urged support for the new party's presidential ticket.[30] An 1842 Convention of Colored People for Maine and New Hampshire in Portland, Maine, gave the Liberty Party an endorsement by 21–7, but many delegates abstained.[31] Outside these areas, however, there never had been much opposition to the Liberty Party among African Americans. Indeed, the importance of black abolitionists in the Liberty movements in Connecticut, Michigan, and western Pennsylvania has received scant attention. In these areas the Liberty Party welcomed black participation in Liberty affairs even though African Americans did not have the franchise, and in some of these states, blacks played crucial roles in party development.

In Connecticut, two black leaders, James W. C. Pennington and Amos Gerry Beman, were among the founders of the state's Liberty Party.[32] They were part of a talented group of African Americans who were involved in a variety of abolition and civil rights causes, especially the suffrage movement and the Underground Railroad. Blacks in Connecticut had a greater role in shaping the party than they did in most states because they filled a leadership vacuum because of their abilities, disparate political opinions among white abolitionists, and a smaller white Liberty leadership. In addition to the Garrisonian presence, Connecticut political abolitionists were divided between the Liberty Party and the Whigs, whose leader, Roger Baldwin, was a well known antislavery man who had been the chief lawyer for the *Amistad* slave captives. He became the Whig gubernatorial candidate as the Whigs attempted to halt defections to the Liberty Party after the 1842 gubernatorial election, the first Whig defeat in five years.[33]

Although Michigan blacks participated regularly in state antislavery conventions, their passage into the Liberty Party was a bit more difficult.[34] An 1841 Washtenaw County Liberty Party incident in which two blacks were not allowed to participate because they were not legal voters presaged the 1843 state Liberty convention that debated whether to accept two black delegates.[35] When the *Michigan Argus* criticized the Liberty men because the two blacks "were denied the privilege of voting because their complexions were a shade darker than the editors of the Signal," the antislavery editors quickly replied. They said that the blacks "were objected to, not on account of their color, but because they were not *legal voters* . . . Their nomination was rejected by only one majority, and at the evening meeting, the decision was reversed, and the colored gentlemen were admitted as members of the Convention by unanimous vote."³⁶ In fact, they worked closely with the party in several areas of the state. Some blacks in Michigan probably voted for the Liberty Party even though they did not have the legal franchise. An historian of the Detroit black community has found that "[o]ccasionally Negroes balloted by fraudulently swearing that they were eligible electors. In the 1844 presidential election, Negroes had openly voted, 'neither party having the hardihood to offer a challenge on the ground of color.' Aside from the 'open' election of 1844, Negroes were reported to have voted in Cass County [a heavily black area] in the late 1840s."³⁷ Sometimes this happened because they could pass for white or there had been no set standard to define what percentage of black blood was necessary to render one ineligible.³⁸ This is not surprising from the Detroit area where black activists William Lambert and George DeBaptiste worked with the Liberty Party and in their own organizations for the suffrage and against discriminatory practices. They supported and campaigned for the Liberty Party, had their own Vigilant Committee, and were a primary force behind the Underground Railroad terminal from which fugitives were taken across the Detroit River into Canada.³⁹

Western Pennsylvania produced a group of talented and energetic black leaders that worked effectively in the Liberty Party. As previously mentioned, Pennsylvania was the only state where both the Liberty Party and the state antislavery society actually were divided along regional lines, with the eastern and western areas having their own organizations. The same was true in the larger world of black activism. Eastern activities were much milder, with petitions to the legislature a chief form of protest. Westerners, on the other hand, were more likely to be involved in politics and the black convention movement, and they issued more harshly worded statements. Even influential blacks, such as Frederick Douglass and Pittsburgh's Martin Delany, declared that the Philadelphia black community was quiet and apathetic.⁴⁰ Delany was one of several vigorous workers who were prominent in the Pittsburgh black community and supported the Liberty Party. He had the assistance and advice of older black reformers in the community—his mentor Lewis Woodson, John B. Vashon, Henry Collins, and John C. Peck—and the help of young George Boyer Vashon who had graduated from Oberlin in 1844. Delany published the *Mystery*, a black antislavery newspaper, from 1843 until early 1848, and backed the Liberty Party. Its editorial committee not only worked in black organizations, but also took part in the very dynamic Pittsburgh Liberty Party.⁴¹ These leaders spoke at Liberty gatherings and invited Liberty men to speak at their black conventions. Dr. Francis Julius LeMoyne, the Liberty gubernatorial nominee and editor of the *Washington Patriot*, invited black speakers to local Liberty rallies in his home area, and they responded by inviting him to speak at their convention.[42] The African American community became a vibrant force in the Liberty Party of western Pennsylvania.

While African Americans' participation in the Liberty operations in some states did not reach the levels of New York, Connecticut, Michigan, Illinois, and western Pennsylvania—often because there were simply so few blacks in some areas of Liberty strength—blacks were welcomed at Liberty gatherings and took part in the myriad of activities that surrounded the political conventions.

Blacks occasionally were involved in intra-party disputes. The question over black suffrage in New York caused considerable debate in black circles and, ultimately, between some blacks and some white Liberty men. African Americans had been working to obtain the unrestricted suffrage in the state for years. They maintained that not having the vote was a political disability and an insult to their manhood. As they said in an 1840 address to the citizens of New York, "We base our claim upon the possession of those common and yet exalted faculties of manhood. WE ARE MEN."[43] The major point of contention was whether to endorse just the Liberty Party or to cooperate with sympathetic members of the major parties. Blacks had explored their options in the black conventions of the early 1840s, but the issue did not become divisive in the Liberty Party until Wisconsin, Illinois, and New York began electing delegates to conventions to write state constitutions.

Many black and white Liberty men believed that the Liberty Party should drop its candidates where the candidate of one of the major parties supported unrestricted black suffrage. They dreaded the possibility that a candidate in favor of restricting the suffrage to whites might be elected by a plurality because the remaining voters might be divided over which pro-suffrage candidate to support. This presented a difficult practical and philosophical situation for Liberty men. Some, particularly the many evangelical perfectionists in the movement, subscribed to a come-outer philosophy in which individuals left churches and political parties that countenanced slaveholders in their midst. Obviously, to support Whigs or Democrats would put them in alliance with men who tolerated slaveholders in their parties. On a more practical note, Liberty men who voted for major-party candidates would be ignoring or abandoning individuals who had courageously left their former parties to stand as Liberty candidates. Liberty followers in Wisconsin and Illinois discussed the matter and decided to hold their party lines, and there was little trouble over the decision. In fact, Liberty candidates were sometimes elected when one of the major parties threw its support to a Liberty candidate.[44]

A more volatile situation in New York led to a crisis in the party. Observers were aware that in September 1842 Rhode Island blacks had received the vote as a result of their support for the winning Whig faction in the election for a constitutional convention.[45] Despite the convoluted and idiosyncratic nature of Rhode Island politics in the early 1840s, some blacks saw how cooperation with major parties could work to their advantage. Intrastate differences had always been noticeable, however, among New York State African American leaders. New York City blacks were less willing to commit meetings and conventions to the Liberty Party than were those from Upstate and western New York.[46] The debate became acrimonious. At an 1844 black state convention, Liberty man Henry Highland Garnet referred to "the cunning of the delegates from New-York [City]" during debate over the propriety of endorsing the Liberty Party. A New York City delegate—after losing a vote on the issue in a poll in which all present could vote—lamented that an area "with a joint total colored population of less than 1,000 rejected the petition of New-York [City], containing 20,000 free colored people."[47] Then four New York City delegates resigned from the convention. This did not necessarily mean that those who wished to withhold official endorsement of the Liberty Party were opposed to it. Indeed, two New York City blacks who were against the endorsement made it clear that, if the convention endorsed any party, it should be the Liberty Party.

A group of New York African Americans, including several who had been active in Liberty affairs, questioned Gerrit Smith about whom he believed they should elect as delegates to the constitutional convention. They asked whether the "leading minds in the Liberty party would consent to vote for such men as delegates to the proposed convention, without distinction of party, as may be in favor of the extension of the suffrage right to colored citizens."[48] They clearly believed that they should. Smith strongly disagreed. Before long, many Liberty blacks were temporarily alienated from such strong black rights supporters as Gerrit Smith, who chided blacks who were willing to vote for non-Liberty candidates, telling them that they were casting their ballots for men "who think slaveholders fit to administer Civil Government."[49] These blacks were not alone, however, as many white New York Liberty men, including the national party chairman, Alvan Stewart, were willing to cross party lines to vote for major-party candidates who favored Negro suffrage.[50] A 1,200-person antislavery meeting in Herkimer, near Smith's home area, resolved that they were willing "to unite with our fellow citizens irrespective of previous party association . . . provided always that the object of *free suffrage* be made prominent in the call." If both major political parties refused this offer, they would "recommend strict Liberty party nominations."[51] In fact, Smith could not even hold his own bailiwick in Madison County.[52] He later complained that the party was "torn to pieces by our Convention question."[53]

Whatever tactics were used, black suffrage was soundly defeated in constitutional conventions and wherever it was put on the ballot except Rhode Island. The situation for black voting rights at the end of the 1840s was worse than it had been twenty years earlier. Blacks who could vote seem to have usually cast their ballots for the Liberty and Free Soil parties except in Rhode Island, where they remained Whigs, and in New York, where some led by Samuel Ringgold Ward supported the Liberty League in 1848.[54]

Far more valuable than the relatively few black votes that could be cast for the abolition party was the widespread use of African Americans for convention speakers. Sometimes these lecturers spoke without reimbursement, but often the party employed them as paid lecturers.[55] Former slaves were especially popular. Whites in many areas rarely saw a black person or one who had been enslaved, so the announcement that a former slave was going to speak at a public gathering was free publicity for the party. This often resulted in the Liberty gathering attracting many that normally would not have attended, sometimes making converts to the cause. White abolitionist leaders usually accompanied fugitive slaves. Michigan Liberty man Seymour Boughton Treadwell accompanied Henry Bibb on a frontier tour during the 1844 campaign and spent "two or three months in lecturing throughout the State of Michigan . . . in a section of the country where abolitionists were few and far between."[56] Whites also traveled with free blacks, especially if they were venturing into areas where they might not be entirely welcome.[57] Many African Americans developed into popular, well-known speakers for the Liberty Party. Henry Bibb, Milton and Lewis Clarke, Lunsford Lane, and others traveled through many states delivering countless emotionally charged lectures describing their lives in slavery.[58] The party employed runaways who were making national news, such as Lewis Washington, a slave who had escaped in a highly publicized effort led by Liberty men Charles T. Torrey and George Latimer, himself the subject of a famous Boston fugitive slave case in the early 1840s.[59] Pittsburgh's Lewis Woodson and Martin Delany consistently impressed the predominantly white audiences with their eloquence. Jehiel C. Beman traveled throughout New England black communities speaking for the party while he was the pastor of churches in Boston and Middletown, Connecticut. And Jermain W. Loguen, later to become famous in the "Jerry Rescue" incident, was an extremely effective speaker in Upstate New York, "and his efforts were credited with doubling Liberty Party votes there."[60]

Perhaps Henry Highland Garnet, Samuel Ringgold Ward, and Henry Bibb were the Liberty Party's most tireless black orators. Garnet was an uncompromising Liberty Party man who carried on a running feud with Frederick Douglass and Charles L. Remond on the proper role for the blacks in the abolition movement. From his pulpit at the Liberty Street Presbyterian Church in Troy, New York, and as a speaker throughout the region, he took stronger stands than many blacks were willing to accept. In his "Address to the Slaves of the United States" at the black convention before the 1843 Liberty Party national convention, he justified the use of slave violence.[61] When Garrisonian Maria Weston Chapman criticized him in the *Liberator* for his ideas and Liberty Party politics, he rebuked her for her views and patronizing manner. He declared that "it astonished me to think that you should desire to sink me again to the condition of a slave, by forcing me to think just as you do ... If it has come to this ... then I do not hesitate to say that your abolitionism is abject slavery."[62]

Samuel Ringgold Ward rivaled Garnet in ability and influence. Douglass later recalled that "[a]s an orator and thinker he was vastly superior, I thought, to any of us, and being perfectly black and of unmixed African descent, the splendors of his intellect went directly to the glory of race."[63] He was a founding member of the New York State Liberty Party and lectured for it across the North with such power that he was characterized as "the black Daniel Webster."[64] He later recalled that "[t]hat party was founded in August, 1840, at Syracuse. I then became for the first time, a member of a political party. With it I cast my first vote; to it I devoted my political activities; with it I lived my political life."[65] He continued this work for the Liberty Party as an official paid agent of the New York State Anti-Slavery Society, and as editor of the pro-Liberty Party and Liberty League's (Cortland, N.Y.) *True American*.

Henry Bibb was a fugitive slave who settled in Detroit in 1842. He began lecturing for the Liberty Party in 1844, speaking primarily in Michigan but also traveling to Illinois, Ohio, and New England. He participated in state and local conventions and was a main speaker at the North-Western Liberty Convention at Chicago in 1846. He was popular because he was an effective orator who would temper his serious message with some humor. The light-complected Bibb was fond of relating that the "American people have robbed me of my rights, of my friends, and three-fourths of my color besides."[66] The use of blacks could have its pitfalls, however, as listeners sometimes questioned a speaker's credentials.[67] There was enough concern over the authenticity of some black Liberty speakers that they were subject to special scrutiny. Henry Bibb's background received a close inspection from James G. Birney, who questioned the validity of some of Bibb's claims. Bibb was upset that Birney thought him an impostor and that "I had better go home and go to work and that I must stop or you would expose me." Bibb explained that "it is tru I have not been as carful in explaining dates and some other things as I should have been, which has led you and others to doubt my honesty . . . yet I hop I shall be able to prove to the world that I have told the truth and will be herd for my people."[68] Birney's concerns were proved groundless. An investigation by a committee from the Detroit Liberty Association concluded with its "conviction that Mr. Bibb is amply sustained, and is entitled to public confidence and high esteem."[69]

Blacks were welcomed in the total Liberty environment, not just as convention speakers. Races were treated equally and mingled freely at Liberty gatherings. On the day before Christmas 1846, a non-abolitionist farmer was taking a walk in Chicago when he heard music. When he asked a passerby what it was, he was told "[i]t is a niggar show." Going in, he came to a room of people where "it appeared a social meeting to all but me, every face lighted up with a friendly smile. I saw the white man shake hands of the African; females of all hues smiled together and nodded to each other in sisterly love." He had walked into a Liberty meeting. Songs were sung, probably by the integrated Chicago Liberty Choir, prayers were offered, and a speech by Ichabod Codding so moved him that he concluded that

> I have resolved never to vote for a slaveholder again, nor for any apologist for slavery, and farther, I will not patronize a pro-slavery newspaper, nor a pro-slavery minister. I must confess that I am almost an abolitionist. There is another scene that I have not alluded to on that memorable 24th Dec., which is this: —When the three slaves were presented to the audience, to you it might have no effect, but to me it was a thrilling moment, to see that father, that mother and daughter, raised from degraded slavery to the platform of liberty, and the appropriate song of the choir, which says: —
>
> "*The hounds are
> baying on my track,
> O! Christians will
> you send me back?*"[70]

This was the spirit that pervaded local, state, and national Liberty gatherings.

The party also articulated this belief in equality countless times in its conventions and platforms. The National Liberty Party Platform of 1844 spoke directly on this:

> 4. *Resolved*, That the Liberty party has not been organized merely for the overthrow of Slavery. Its first decided effort must indeed be directed

against slaveholding, as the grossest form and most revolting manifestation of Despotism; but it will also carry out the principles of Equal Rights, into all their practical consequences and applications, and support every just measure conducive to individual and social freedom . . .
35. *Resolved*, That this convention recommend to the friends of Liberty in all the free States where any inequality of rights and privileges exist on account of color, to employ their utmost energies to remove all such remnants and effects of the slave system.

And the party made clear its commitment to "cordially welcome our colored fellow citizens to fraternity with us in the *Liberty party*" in Resolution 36. This was also true on the state and local levels. The case of Henry Johnson, a former slave of New Bedford, Massachusetts, was not atypical. He had been a member of both major parties, but he finally concluded that "I could not and would not go to the polls again in support of either Whig or Locofoco party. I have been and still remain, an uncompromising advocate of the Liberty party principles . . . [T]hey give me the right hand of fellowship—not the left hand as the other two parties do."[71]

Demands for black rights were also an important part of the Liberty program in the state parties, but there were regional variations in a selection of goals. Blacks in five New England states had full legal rights by early 1843, so there was less emphasis on voting in these states. Here New England Liberty followers supported movements against racial injustice.[72] Liberty gatherings made clear their opposition to segregated schools, discrimination on boats and trains, and other prejudices blacks suffered. Lawyer Samuel Sewall, the Massachusetts gubernatorial candidate, was involved in several prominent fugitive slave cases, most prominently the case of Liberty speaker George Latimer.[73] Several Liberty men, including the Tappan brothers, Joshua Leavitt, and Henry B. Stanton, had been involved in the defense of the captives who had been involved in the famous mutiny aboard the *Amistad*.[74] While the case was in the courts, Sherman Booth, future Liberty editor in Connecticut and Wisconsin, spent part of his final year at Yale tutoring and helping the *Amistad* Africans until they returned home.[75] The situation in New York, where blacks had to meet an income qualification to vote, was similar to New England. An historian of New York abolitionism makes it clear that the party "directed as much of its effort to improving the condition of the free Negro as it did to emancipation."[76]

Liberty organizations also worked tirelessly against discrimination beyond suffrage and education. Liberty organizations in Illinois, Ohio, Michigan, Wisconsin, and Iowa were vociferous about eliminating the "black laws" from state constitutions. These laws imposed special disabilities on African Americans—

such as prohibiting blacks from testifying against whites, serving on juries, and sending their children to public schools. The first statewide Illinois Liberty Party convention in May 1842 demanded repeal of the state's black laws, and this remained a feature of the party throughout its existence.[77] When the new state constitution passed in 1848 with a recommendation for legislation to prevent black immigration, the *Chicago Western Citizen* lamented that "[t]hus the devil has it all his own way."[78]

Michigan Liberty men included the fight for equal rights as an important part of the party creed, not surprising considering the black activists from Detroit and elsewhere who played important roles in the party. William Lambert, an African American Liberty supporter from Detroit, declared "[t]hat an important duty rests on abolitionists to promote the elevation of the colored people at the North, and thus disprove the allegation of the natural inferiority of their intellect."[79] The *Signal of Liberty* declared that anyone, "whether white or black, rich or poor, learned or ignorant, he is entitled to *all* the civil and political rights which belong to *any*."[80] Liberty organizations in Michigan promoted petitioning the state legislature assiduously.[81] The state's Liberty Party stressed all rights, but the greatest effort was the unsuccessful fight for suffrage.[82] Wisconsin Liberty men worked for black rights and suffrage from the party's territorial beginnings. Despite the fact that blacks were not enfranchised, "[t]hey were allowed to accumulate property, serve on juries, hold public and private meetings, petition the legislature, testify against whites, send their children to public schools, pursue any occupation, and marry whom they chose."[83] Liberty groups continued to endorse black suffrage and personal liberty laws and to oppose formal and informal restrictions on black activities.

Such rights were not part of African American life in Ohio. Resolutions against Ohio's onerous black laws were regularly passed in Liberty conventions, but the statement that "Ohio Liberty leaders did not openly advocate granting the suffrage" is somewhat misleading.[84] The Southern and Western Liberty Convention of June 1845 in Cincinnati did not even mention black rights, nor did blacks participate in it in any meaningful way. The situation was different in other areas, especially on the Western Reserve, where conventions were more outspoken in behalf of black suffrage and legal rights.[85] In fact, the Ohio Liberty Party hired Walter C. Yancey, a local black minister, as an agent when it was preparing for the 1844 elections.[86] Ohio Liberty men worked closely with blacks in other ways. Ohio Liberty lawyers were probably the most organized group in the country in aiding the fugitive slaves, particularly in the Cincinnati area across from the slave state of Kentucky. Salmon P. Chase gained much of his early legal fame from the number of these cases that he took and his skill in handling them. His standing with blacks was very high because he not only worked in these fugitive cases but drew up wills and deeds, dispensed legal advice, and performed other legal services free or for small fees. In 1845 the African Americans of Cincinnati gave him a testimonial silver cup in appreciation of his work on their behalf, and his public responses in support of black rights and the suffrage were much stronger than most of his public stances on party policy.[87] James G. Birney's son, William, who was a lawyer and Liberty member in Cincinnati, assisted Chase in this work.[88] Thomas Morris, former U.S. senator and 1844 Liberty vice presidential nominee, also took and won a case in the Ohio Supreme Court against a judge who refused to grant a license to perform marriages to a black Methodist Episcopal clergyman.[89] In the Columbus area, African American leader Charles Langston combined his membership in the Liberty Party, writing for the (Columbus, Ohio) *Palladium of Liberty,* an African American newspaper, and the black convention movement in his work for repeal of the black laws and equal rights in education for black children.[90]

The fledgling Liberty Party in Iowa had to fight against the most onerous anti-black legislation in the North. An 1839 territorial law, which carried over into statehood, made it mandatory for a black person entering Iowa to post a five hundred-dollar bond against becoming a ward of the state and for good behavior. At both the organizing meeting for the state's Liberty Party in December 1847 and at a state Liberty convention in May 1848, delegates took strong positions against the black laws. They specifically targeted those "which forbid to the free man of color a settlement within our borders, to breathe the free air of our prairies and cultivate our soil without free papers and $500 bonds."[91]

That abolitionists believed blacks to be the moral and intellectual equals of whites was not necessarily a corollary to their working for antislavery causes or civil rights. To support legal equality for blacks was not an endorsement of intellectual equality, and blacks were considered intellectually inferior in most circles during the 1840s. It was well known that Thomas Morris had such serious reservations about the black person's capabilities during the 1830s that he had written an article opposing black suffrage, although he no longer opposed the black vote by the 1844 election.[92] Lewis Tappan, despite his tireless antislavery work and mixing with blacks socially and in reform causes, did not hire black clerks for his store, even when pressured to do so by Jehiel Beman. His biographer has pointed out that "the Tappans' failure—in good times as well as bad—to hire any Negro above the level of porter remains a matter of record."[93] In the mid-1830s William Jay opposed leadership roles for blacks in the state antislavery society and the plan to have Theodore S. Wright address the American Anti-Slavery Society. His biographer, Stephen P. Budney, points out that Jay believed "that neither the general public nor the abolitionists could countenance such a bold step."[94]

Few Liberty followers, however, subscribed to these beliefs, and most had abandoned them by the 1840s. Many African Americans in the North were illiterate, led lives of poverty, had high rates of alcoholism and disease, and had low life expectancies. Most Liberty men argued that this was a result of environmental conditions and discrimination. Henry B. Stanton had summed up these feelings as far back as the famous Lane Seminary debates on slavery in 1834. He asked, "[S]hall we make the *present* degradation of the free blacks, *which is the work,* of our hands the premises from which to draw the conclusion, that 'they can never rise in this country'?"[95] To correct this situation most Liberty theorists believed that blacks had to be integrated fully into the social system. James G. Birney expressed the sentiments of his party when he wrote that blacks should have the same kind of opportunities as everyone else "to use their faculties of whatever kind, as others do, for their own improvement." To do this, Birney stated, all laws discriminating on color or descent had to be repealed, blacks should not attend separate schools, and colonization would have to be abandoned as a solution to the race problem because of its demoralizing influence. He concluded that "[i]n proportion as you shut them out from a place in the social system, you degrade and ultimately destroy them. If you would do all that can be done towards making them virtuous and moral, *put them fully into it.*"[96]

Liberty writers attacked those who believed in the innate inferiority of blacks by emphasizing the achievements of illustrious blacks, including Frederick Douglass, Charles Remond, Henry Highland Garnet, Charles B. Ray, and many others. John G. Whittier remarked that a speech on this subject by Douglass, who "eight years ago was a slave toiling on a Maryland plantation," was a "noble refutation of the charge of natural inferiority urged against the colored man."[97] Liberty men demonstrated that many blacks had been patriots who had served their country in times of war and peace; and, therefore, they deserved to be accorded the rights of ordinary citizens.[98] Sometimes attitudes evolved. Certainly such men as James Birney, Thomas Morris, and others did not have the doubts about the capabilities of black people that they might have had years earlier. Liberty meetings frequently pointed out the need for more educational opportunities for blacks at all levels. At least two institutions of higher learning during this time that admitted blacks and encouraged black enrollments were headed by strong Liberty men: Beriah Green at Oneida Institute in Upstate New York and Asa Mahan at Oberlin. These schools were integrated institutions that admitted students regardless of color.

Founded by future Liberty man George Washington Gale in 1826, Oneida had its most important years with Beriah Green as president from 1833 to 1843. It was a manual labor school where students worked to help pay their expenses. It emphasized moral subjects and abolition, and it served as a stop on the Underground Railroad. Years later Josiah Grinnell, Liberty man, college founder, and Republican congressman from Iowa, recalled some of his fellow students at Oneida as

> object lessons related to the ludicrous. There were an emancipator's boys from Cuba; mulattoes removed from their sable mother—illegitimate (said to be), under an *alias;* the high tempered Spanish student, Slingerland his name, whose slinging an iron poker at me left an impression; then an Indian, with that inelegant name, Kunkapot, the calling of which created a laugh; black men who had served as sailors, or as city hackmen, also the purest Africans escaped from slavery, of a class like the eloquent Garnet, the protégé of Joseph Sturge, the English reformer; sons of the American radicals, Bible students scanning Hebrew verse with ease, in place of Latin odes; enthusiasts, plowboys and printers; also real students of elegant tastes, captured by the genius of President Green.[99]

In fact, Green could not be specific about the exact number of African Americans at his school. When a friend asked how many blacks attended the school, Green replied that "I know not what number of coloured students we have had. We have at this time, including those of Indian blood, about 20."[100] His biographer, Milton Sernett, says that this fact demonstrates the life at Oneida Institute.

> Beriah's inability to provide an exact tabulation of black students at Oneida is indicative of the philosophy with which he approached interracial education. He was not so much interested in numbers as creating an egalitarian community of youthful reformers. He welcomed fugitive slaves to his home and to the campus, where students hid them in their dormitory rooms. Interracial education was a self-authenticating right ... Oneida Institute became known as the "Negro school," not because black students ever outnumbered whites, but because blacks took their rightful place alongside students from all classes, races, and backgrounds.[101]

Students also printed the Liberty newspaper, the *Utica Friend of Man.* Among the blacks who attended Oneida Institute who became involved in Liberty Party activities were Alexander Crummell, Henry Highland Garnet, Jermain W. Loguen, Amos Gary Beman, and William G. Allen, black leaders of mid-nineteenth-century America.

Oberlin was the another school that had a great impact on antislavery. One historian has claimed that "[d]irectly and indirectly it was from Oneida Institute that Oberlin was mainly derived."[102] It was a school where manual labor and biblical studies were emphasized and the classics deemphasized. It was an important stop on the Underground Railroad, and antislavery action was considered axiomatic. Its faculty and male students believed in political action generally and in the Liberty Party in particular. While many women students later became Garrisonian abolitionists, the college's historian has stated that "[i]t is significant that not a single one of the male leaders of the Oberlin community was a Garrisonian."[103]

The faculty generally supported independent nominations and the Liberty Party. President Asa Mahan with Professor Charles Grandison Finney and lawyer Edward Wade attended and spoke for political action at the 1839 meeting of the American Anti-Slavery Society in Cleveland.[104] Oberlin became a bastion of third-party antislavery politics in Ohio. Mahan, Finney, Timothy Hudson, and James Fairchild worked in the party with many faculty members and college officers, including future congressmen Amasa Walker, James Monroe, and Norton S. Townshend. The Liberty Party regularly turned out a strong vote in the town. "Fully one half of the 1842 Liberty vote in Lorain County, Ohio, for example, came from the single township of Russia, home to the Oberlin colony and college."[105] The college even supplied its "Big Tent," free of charge, to Liberty Party and Liberty League conventions and the 1848 Free Soil gathering. The African Americans who became leaders of various movements in the nineteenth century were one of Oberlin's greatest legacies. Black students George Boyer Vashon, David Peck, William Howard Day, and John Mercer Langston were important figures during the Civil War era and after. They fondly remembered Oberlin as an institution where the famous faculty member and evangelist, Charles Grandison Finney, "might groan for the soul's salvation at one moment and pray for a Liberty party victory the next, while piling up evidence like the lawyer he had been."[106] Black students frequently lived in faculty households and ate in racially mixed settings and supported the Liberty Party. Liberty Party men founded other "color blind" colleges—the current Olivet, Adrian, and Hillsdale in Michigan; Knox in Illinois; and Beloit College in Wisconsin. They had a strong antislavery orientation to their evangelical perfectionism, and all were stops on the Underground Railroad.

In all of this, however, the question that most abolitionists, white or black, did not wish to approach was miscegenation. Their reasoning was practical: they believed that there was nothing to gain by publicly confronting the subject.[107] Miscegenation, or "amalgamation" as it was then called, was a volatile issue that the Liberty Party tried to avoid. No party member publicly opposed the repeal of the anti-miscegenation law in Massachusetts in 1843, but very little was said in the party press or surviving correspondence about it. The general approach was to deny that the party espoused amalgamation and leave it at that.[108] Occasionally, however, a Liberty speaker was forced to take a stand. A persistent interrogator refused to let Alvan Stewart avoid answering the question of whether he "would be willing to have a white man marry a 'nigger.'" Stewart calmly replied "to the gentleman that if he should fall in love with a colored girl, and should find that he could not be happy without her, *I should interpose no objection to the marriage.*"[109]

Unquestionably, the passage of the Fugitive Slave Law in 1850 resulted in an increase in the number of blacks fleeing to Canada, but escaped slaves had been going into the free states and on to Canada for decades. While it is difficult to put numbers on this illegal and clandestine enterprise, the movement of refugees from slavery to freedom was substantial during the 1840s. The Liberty Party platform for 1844 espoused repeal of the Fugitive Slave Act of 1793 "so that we may be delivered from the unconstitutional obligations to become kidnappers on our own soil" (Article 34). And it declared the "third clause of the section of the fourth article of that instrument, whenever applied to the case of a fugitive slave, as utterly null and void, and consequently as forming no part of the Constitution of the United States."

Liberty families everywhere were involved in the most racially integrated enterprise in the antislavery movement, the Underground Railroad.[110] The purpose here is not to trace every Liberty man involved. Virtually every serious abolitionist was in favor of the Underground Railroad and participated in it to some extent if given the opportunity. Despite the amount of anonymity surrounding participation in this activity, many of the main conductors on the routes were Liberty members. In some areas near the South, most notably Cincinnati, whites were discouraged from active participation because they were closely watched by slave hunters and authorities, but this was not true for most areas. Whites forged close working relationships with blacks in spiriting refugees through the free states.[111]

Possibly the most open and outspoken members of the Underground network were Liberty members in Illinois. They openly acknowledged being active in transporting slaves in the state, and the affiliated women's societies freely announced their goal of assisting the runaways. Liberty man and future U.S. congressman Owen Lovejoy, brother of the antislavery martyr Elijah Lovejoy, ran ads in the *Chicago Western Citizen*. As the general agent of the "CANADA LINE OF STAGES," he announced that he would "*very respectfully* inform the ladies and gentlemen of color of the South, who wish to travel North for the BENEFIT of their condition . . . that the above line of stages will be in action, and efficient operation during the summer."[112] The *Chicago Western Citizen* of July 13, 1844, ran a cartoon of the Underground Railroad that an Illinois historian has said "is perhaps Illinois' first political newspaper cartoon."[113] It was a bold and challenging piece of work. Under a picture of a locomotive going through a mountain, there is a daring and uncompromising announcement.

> The improved and splendid Locomotives, Clarkson and Lundy [two famous abolitionists from England and Illinois], ... will run their regular trips, during the present season, between the borders of the Patriarchal Dominion and Libertyville, Upper Canada.
>
> SEATS FREE, *irrespective of color.*
>
> Necessary Clothing furnished gratuitously to such as have *"fallen among thieves."*
>
> For seats apply at any of the trap doors, or to the conductor of the rain.
>
> J. CROSS, Proprietor.
>
> N.B. For the special benefit of Pro-Slavery Police Officers, an extra heavy wagon for Texas, will be furnished, whenever it may be necessary, in which they will be forwarded as dead freight, to the "Valley of Rascals," always at the risk of the owners.[114]

Some of these Illinois Liberty men suffered for their zeal. Owen Lovejoy came under indictment for being caught aiding two runaway black women. John Cross, who traveled the Old Northwest recruiting agents and setting up a more formal relay system in the early 1840s, spent time in jail in 1844. And Dr. Richard Eels was assessed a fine of four hundred dollars by Judge Stephen A. Douglas for helping a fugitive.[115] Illinois Liberty women were just as publicly identified with Underground Railroad work. The constitution of one local society, after declaring its support for the Liberty Party, stated that one of its goals was to provide clothes for the fugitives "who are escaping from bondage."[116]

Even some law enforcement officials in Illinois were part of its operation. A Scottish immigrant ran a cooperage in Dundee, Illinois, that was a major station on the "Liberty Line" even while he was a deputy sheriff in Kane County. The young Scotsman was defeated in his run for county sheriff on the Liberty ticket in 1847, but he had gained such a reputation as an effective lawman that he was offered the full-time job of a deputy sheriff for Cook County. At the urging of abolitionist friends, he accepted the appointment, sold his business, and moved his family to rapidly growing Chicago. He continued his Underground Railroad work while working as a deputy sheriff and later a police detective in Chicago, where he developed a close personal and working relationship with stationmaster and Liberty man John Jones, perhaps the wealthiest black in Chicago. Thus began the long career of the original "private eye," Allan Pinkerton.[117]

While some Underground Railroad activists were well known as operators in Illinois, the subject usually was not advertised so publicly elsewhere. Liberty men everywhere worked on this clandestine activity. These were difficult journeys in the 1840s for regular travelers and much more so for fugitives. In addition to Lovejoy and Cross, two of the most famous operators on the Underground Railroad during the 1840s were Levi Coffin in Indiana and later Cincinnati and Reverend John Rankin and a whole group of abolitionists in Ripley, Ohio. Coffin's home in New Garden (now Fountain City), Indiana, was called the "Grand Central Station of the Underground Railroad," and he reputedly sheltered over two thousand slaves before moving in 1847 to Cincinnati, where he continued his activities and became the model for Simeon Halliday in *Uncle Tom's Cabin*. He was also an ardent Liberty Party supporter, being a secretary at the national Liberty Party convention in 1841. Rankin's home in Ripley, Ohio, is also famous in Underground Railroad lore as being the place where Eliza ran across the ice in *Uncle Tom's Cabin*. For years it was one of the famous landmarks for slaves escaping across the Ohio River. After some initial hesitation, he became a strong Liberty Party supporter in the early 1840s. He joined his son Adam Lowry Rankin and former U.S. senator Alexander Campbell, both of whom had been party members since 1840.[118]

In Michigan, almost all the prominent stationmasters were important Liberty Party men. In fact, when Erastus Hussey was recounting his work on the Underground Railroad, he specifically pointed out when a man "was not specifically identified with the Liberty Party."[119] John Cross personally recruited Hussey, a future Liberty congressional candidate and editor from Battle Creek. Although a Quaker, he could adopt a militant stance, and he estimated that he aided over one thousand fugitives.[120] Jabez S. Fitch, the agent at Marshall, was the first Liberty Party gubernatorial nominee in Michigan, and Dr. Nathan Thomas, a Liberty Party organizer and its candidate for lieutenant-governor in 1845, was the agent in Schoolcraft. The two editors of the *Signal of Liberty*, Theodore Foster and Guy Beckley, were also well known agents.[121]

In the Northeast, the Underground Railroad activities of the prominent New York and New England Liberty men have been frequently chronicled. Less well-known is the participation of several other important party figures from the region. Francis Gillette of Connecticut, frequent Liberty party gubernatorial candidate and future U.S. senator, owned two stops on the Underground Railroad. He was perhaps Connecticut's most famous public figure working in the cause, and his homes were cultural centers where the civic and cultural leaders, including his relative, Harriet Beecher Stowe, gathered. Others who took shelter there "certainly less conspicuous—were the dark travelers who came in secrecy, found shelter and food in Gillette's barn, and went on their way never knowing that they had enjoyed the hospitality of a United States Senator."[122]

The home of Dr. Francis Julius LeMoyne, three times a Liberty candidate for governor of Pennsylvania and editor of the *Washington Patriot*, was a stop in western Pennsylvania. One of his daughters later recalled "the day when twenty-five slaves at one time were concealed in their mother's big room in the second story."[123] Titus Hutchinson, former chief justice of the supreme court of Vermont and a candidate for governor on the Liberty Party ticket, was another Liberty man who was very active on the escape routes. In 1976 "an Underground Railroad tunnel was discovered extending from the Hutchinson home to the Kedron River," a distance of four-tenths of a mile.[124] Many homes that were run by Liberty men on the Underground Railroad are still standing. Indeed, the burgeoning research recently on the Underground Railroad has revealed literally scores of homes of Liberty members that are historic sites.

It was not just white Liberty men who were involved in this illegal activity, as well-known black supporters of the party were probably more involved in urban areas and areas with higher concentrations of blacks than were whites. This was certainly true in Detroit, where escapees either fled across the Detroit River to Canada or melted into the Detroit black community.[125] In Cincinnati, the African Americans did much of the Underground Railroad work, in part because white abolitionists were so closely watched.[126] The strong black community in Pittsburgh under Lewis Woodson, Martin Delany, John C. Peck, Henry Collins, and George Vashon was active in moving fugitives north.[127] In Connecticut, J. W. C. Pennington associated with Talcott Street Congregational Church in Hartford, Jehiel C. Beman in Middletown, and Amos Gerry Beman in New Haven were Liberty African Americans who were important operatives on the Underground Railroad.[128] And, of course, black leaders such as Jermain Loguen, Samuel Ringgold Ward, and Henry Highland Garnet were major participants in the movement that worked closely with Gerrit Smith.

Party members' commitment to Underground Railroad work during the party's existence was well demonstrated by the importance of the aforementioned Oberlin College in Ohio and Knox College in Galesburg, Illinois. The faculties of both of these schools were almost all Liberty supporters and their communities were decidedly abolitionist. Former student and future president of Oberlin College, Edward Fairchild, recalled the perception that "Oberlin was a 'nigger' town."[129] The college and town were in constant danger because many Underground lines came and went from the town.[130] The college historian for those years has claimed that "all who came were hospitably received and cared for, and none was ever forcibly returned from Oberlin to the 'House of bondage.' Townsmen, students, college faculty, and officials were involved in the conspiracy."[131] The same was true at Knox College in Galesburg, Illinois, which was "probably the principal underground station in Illinois."[132] Some in nearby Quincy referred to it as "THE LITTLE NIGGER STEALING TOWN . . . a nest of nigger thieves."[133] Like Oberlin, the whole community was involved in the project from the college president down. It was no coincidence that these were two of the leading towns in the country for a Liberty vote. This was typical of the larger Liberty experience.[134]

The importance of African Americans to the whole Liberty enterprise cannot be overemphasized. White members reached across color lines, and they received positive responses from most black activists. Their approval was not merely lip service but involved true integration into all aspects of the movement. These whites, including women, had certain characteristics that differentiated them from the average Northerner during the 1840s.

10

THE LIBERTY PARTY MEMBERSHIP

> Although they were everywhere totally misunderstood and grossly misrepresented, they clearly comprehended their work and courageously entered upon its performance... They were anything but political fanatics, and history will record that their sole offense was the espousal of the truth in advance of the multitude, which slowly and finally followed in their footsteps.
>
> GEORGE W. JULIAN, *Political Recollections, 1840 to 1872*

Lack of information on grassroots abolitionism and lack of systematic methodology have hampered attempts to understand membership in antislavery organizations. Compared to the major parties, the Liberty Party had few adherents and its grassroots voters are difficult to identify. No poll books—contemporary lists of voters and their political leanings—have been found for any election that show the Liberty Party participation along with the other parties. Voter lists, which Liberty leaders constantly urged each other to maintain, were rarely kept or have been lost.[1] That its constituency changed, sometimes dramatically, during the eight years of the party's existence further complicates the situation. All these factors make the identification of a reasonable sample of Liberty voters very difficult. In fact, precise characteristics of the mass of Liberty voters may never be known because the data for reliable generalizations may not exist. Nonetheless, town-level voting returns, biographical details about more prominent Liberty members, and contemporary observations on the party provide sufficient information for some general statements on Liberty Party membership, especially the leadership.

While the lack of uniform data on individual party members prevents a precise analysis of the Liberty constituency, certain characteristics were common to large numbers of Liberty voters. There is also the problem of what exactly constitutes a Liberty voter because individuals varied in their commitment to the party. Some were undeviating, strong supporters of the party from its inception until it merged in the Free Soil coalition. Some early members left it in later years, and some early opponents of independent nominations joined it later. More difficult to classify are the borderline Liberty men—those who voted the Liberty ticket sporadically; those who would vote the Liberty ticket at one level and a major-party slate at another; or those who would split their national, state, or local tickets between Liberty and non-Liberty candidates. The constituency of the party changed during its eight-year existence, and so did its political tone. This analysis studies the Liberty membership in two general categories, leaders and the mass of supporters, and discusses the change in each over time.

Newspaper editors, party agents, state policymakers, strong local leaders, and the Liberty candidates for political office made up the Liberty elite. Once someone joined this group, he usually remained faithful to the party. These members were responsible for the important state and national decisions. Two relatively distinct groups made up this elite during the early years, the active day-to-day participants and the more passive supporters. The former group contained those who were working for the party on an ongoing basis, such as editors, agents, writers, and party organizers. They gave considerable time, usually without compensation. These activists made strategy decisions and established state party policies during the early years. They were widely recognized as the spokesmen for the party. Joshua Leavitt, Henry B. Stanton, Elizur Wright, Austin Willey, Alvan Stewart, Gerrit Smith, James G. Birney, Theodore Foster, Guy Beckley, Owen Lovejoy, Zebina Eastman, Gamaliel Bailey, Salmon P. Chase, Ichabod Codding, William Smyth, Sherman Booth, Russell Errett, William Elder, Charles D. Cleveland, and several others belonged to this group. They formed the core of the Liberty Party leadership.

The more passive group in the elite did not have as great a policymaking role but were important to the life of the party. They were recognizable figures who allowed their names to be put in candidacy for state and local offices. These men brought political experience and known reputations to their Liberty candidacies. For instance, New York Liberty leaders were very happy when they finally convinced William Jay to join the party and become a candidate. The son of founding father John Jay and an important jurist and antislavery exponent, he added considerable luster to the Liberty ticket. Many early Liberty candidates for governor and seats in the U.S. Congress did little campaigning and rarely participated directly in party affairs beyond the local level. Frequently, these men were not even present at the conventions that nominated them. At one time or another, the Liberty organization in almost every state found itself in the embarrassing position of having nominated someone who publicly disavowed any association with the party. Nonetheless, many Liberty candidates never figured prominently in any state or national Liberty Party meetings. Several exceptions to the early pattern—James G. Birney (Michigan), Daniel Hoit (New Hampshire), Francis Gillette (Connecticut), Samuel Fessenden (Maine), and Gerrit Smith (New York)—were among the powerful leaders of their state parties as well as candidates. This division in the leadership was less apparent in some areas or states, such as Michigan, in the early years.

This dichotomy between policymakers and candidates decreased as the party matured, especially as younger recruits began to assume more prominent roles. Policymakers became more interested in political office, and political figureheads took on a greater role in party management. By the time of the Free Soil merger, experienced and ambitious politicians had a much greater voice in party matters than they had five or six years earlier, undoubtedly contributing to the ease with which the Liberty Party slipped into the Free Soil coalition. This group included many future public figures. Over thirty men clearly identified with the Liberty Party became state governors, members of the U.S. House or Senate, or judges on the U.S. Supreme Court. Others were prominent in state politics or fields outside politics. These men achieved higher offices on the state and local levels later, usually as Free Soilers or Republicans. These included some of the younger members of the Liberty Party.

That the two groups had much in common is not surprising because they were part of a minority pushing antislavery action to lengths that most Americans thought excessive, but they also differed in several aspects. Both groups were about equal in terms of formal education, although the early policymakers tended to have more formal religious training while the candidates possessed medical, legal, and professional backgrounds. Members of both groups were involved in multiple reform activities. The previously mentioned commitment to temperance was probably the most universal example, but Liberty men were involved in nearly every contemporary reform.

The leaders were individuals of high character and moral integrity. Major-party newspapers sometimes criticized the Liberty Party in very strong terms, but they rarely attacked a member's morality. Instances of scandal among Liberty men were almost unheard of, and Liberty men generally led exemplary lives. The views of a contemporary historian of New York politics that "this party, in proportion to its numbers, probably contains more men of wealth, of talents, and personal worth, than any party in the state" were true wherever the party existed.[2] Liberty propagandists were aware that this played out well in the communities. One Liberty writer challenged the public: "Into their characters, and into the character of all whom the Liberty Party, now or hereafter, may nominate for office, we invite your strictest scrutiny."[3] Even when there was a basis for an unpleasant incident, it was not brought up because it did not reflect the true character of the man by the 1840s. For instance, no one brought up that Maine's Samuel Fessenden's son, future politician William Pitt Fessenden, was born out of wedlock due to a youthful indiscretion because even the elder Fessenden's opponents had great respect for his integrity.[4] In short, members of the Liberty elite were well educated men of high moral character who were imbued with a spirit of Christian reform. They assumed important roles in their communities and were respected and trusted by their neighbors. This was one reason the Liberty Party had so much local electoral success.

There were many differences in the Liberty elite, however, between policymakers and candidates in most states during the early years. The policymakers were younger than the candidates. Most of the policymakers were in their forties or younger, whereas the candidates were much more evenly divided across the age spectrum, several even having seen service in the War of 1812. In part this was a product of the backgrounds of the policymakers. They had come to abolitionism as young men, sometimes making reform a full-time profession during the 1830s as editors, agents, and lecturers. They had a certain freedom from responsibility that allowed them to move around with limited income. Later, some of them decreased their reform activities as familial obligations and other duties increased. The younger men grew up in the antislavery movement during the 1830s and had little inclination to go directly into politics. Such future Liberty leaders as Elizur Wright, Amos A. Phelps, Ichabod Codding, Alanson St. Clair, and the slightly older William Goodell and Joshua Leavitt were building up careers as reformers without personal political ambition. John G. Whittier, Thomas Earle, Myron Holley, and Francis Gillette were exceptional in that they worked as reformers and were involved in electoral politics, although not as professional politicians. As a result, many Liberty policymakers were new to political activism. They sought others who combined political experience and respect in their communities with sympathy to antislavery reform. Political veterans who did come over to the Liberty Party added an important element to the party. Willing candidates with political credentials gave the party a credibility that would have been lacking if the policymakers themselves had run for office. They brought political realism to the party, and many assumed more important roles as the party matured. Some came with extensive political experience on the local, state, and national levels. Two former U.S. senators from Ohio, Thomas Morris and Dr. Alexander Campbell of Ripley, became mainstays of the Liberty Party, as did former U.S. congressmen William Jackson of Massachusetts, David Potts of Pennsylvania, and, later, Seth Gates of New York. They were joined by a large number of men who had served in important capacities in state and local offices.

The candidate group, as a whole, was wealthier and more established than the policymaking group. While a few of the policymakers—Gerrit Smith, Charles D. Cleveland, C. V. Dyer, and, later, Arthur and Lewis Tappan—were wealthy men, the average member of the policymaking elite often struggled to make a living. Many were ministers who held a position at the whim of a congregation or newspaper editors who went into debt and whose papers foundered because they had little financial backing. Patronage positions did not exist for Liberty activists, and the few who depended on the party for their financial support often lived on the edge of poverty. For instance, three of the most prominent early leaders in Massachusetts who made many personal sacrifices for the party—Joshua Leavitt, Henry B. Stanton, and Elizur Wright—restricted their Liberty activities by the time of the Free Soil merger because of financial concerns. By 1847, Leavitt "felt the need to look elsewhere for means of providing for his sons and for his and Sarah's [his wife] old age."[5] Wright had little financial success as a newspaper editor and translator. In addition to serving as the editor of the *Boston Daily Chronotype*, he translated Jean LaFontaine's *Fables* and sold them door to door. He then began putting his considerable mathematical skills to work in the mid-1840s as an actuarial scientist to better provide for his family.[6] Stanton began practicing law in Boston in 1842 with Samuel Sewall in order to support a large family. Financial stress plus his work for the party exhausted him. The family eventually moved to Seneca Falls, New York, to enhance his economic and political prospects.[7]

Many who were very active on the local level were unable to afford wider involvement because of age, finances, or obligations in their professions. Financial and physical hardships accompanied Liberty representatives when they went on speaking tours. Even when they received local accommodations and a collection was taken up to help them defray expenses, speakers and participants at state, regional, and national conventions usually suffered loss of income because they were absent from their normal business obligations. These men took part in Liberty affairs and other reforms but were not professional reformers or politicians. They made their greatest impact on the state level and as opinion leaders in their local communities. In virtually every pocket of Liberty strength there was one or more of them working for the party.

A higher percentage of the candidates were financially secure professionals. Liberty nominees came from all walks of life, but educators, lawyers, and doctors were disproportionately represented on Liberty slates. When Edward Mathews asked a doctor why so many of them were abolitionists, his friend replied that "doctors are the best informed men in the world!"[8] They shared their tickets with small businessmen, merchants, as well as a few artisans, farmers, and clergymen. Although the average candidate lived comfortably, he was usually not rich, although there were exceptions. Among these, Joel Hayden of Williamsburgh, Massachusetts, a Liberty representative in the state legislature and one of the party's most successful candidates, was a large manufacturer of buttons whose factories gave work to "several hundred hands."[9] David Potts, former U.S. congressman and Liberty candidate, was owner and manager of Warwick Furnace near Pottstown, Pennsylvania. Liberty gubernatorial candidate Lawrence Brainerd was a wealthy St. Albans, Vermont, businessman with investments in steamboats and railroads. Charles V. Dyer was a pioneer Chicago physician who became a wealthy land speculator as the city boomed. Charles O. Shepard, a frequent Liberty candidate for lieutenant-governor, was a wealthy Upstate businessman with economic interests in steamships and railroads.

The Liberty elite was a highly educated group. In a time when formal education was limited, many had attended institutions of higher learning and worked in learned professions, such as law, the ministry, education, journalism, and medicine. Others were successful businessmen. Notably absent from the state and national leadership were working farmers and artisans, although these occupational groups often contributed locally.[10] Undoubtedly, financial constraints prevented many of them from being more involved in wider aspects of the party. Town artisans, small businessmen, and farmers usually could not afford the time and expense associated with the difficult journeys to national, state, and regional gatherings. Nonetheless, they participated in local meetings and sometimes served as candidates on town and county tickets.

More elusive are important Liberty men who moved, sometimes frequently, during their lives. Horace Greeley's exhortation to Liberty man Josiah Grinnell to "Go West, young man" reflected the restlessness of many Liberty men who carved out new lives on the frontier.[11] Many became leading citizens in their new locales. William Larimer founded Denver, Colorado, in 1858, and at least two Liberty Party founders had frontier towns named after them: Jacob Lybrand (Lybrand, Iowa) and Samuel Newitt Wood (Woodsdale, Kansas). Oscar L. Shafter, the Liberty congressional candidate in 1843 and Free Soil gubernatorial candidate in 1848, moved from Vermont to California in 1854 and eventually became an associate justice of the California Supreme Court. Many other leaders moved around the country seeking fulfilling lives and careers.[12]

Liberty candidates came from both Democratic and Whig backgrounds. While former Whigs predominated in the early years, an increasing number of Democrats joined the Liberty Party as the decade progressed. Liberty men always made special attempts to balance state and national tickets. James G. Birney, a former Whig, ran with two former Democrats, Thomas Earle and Thomas

Morris. Party candidates for lieutenant-governor often had a different political background than did the gubernatorial candidate. As Democrats made up a greater proportion of the Liberty support after 1844, more Democrats came into the party leadership and ran for office. These men became more involved in the political aspects of the party than the earlier candidates, particularly after John P. Hale's success in New Hampshire heightened the possibility for a broader-based movement. Lawrence Brainerd of Vermont, Charles C. Sholes and Charles Durkee of Wisconsin, and Amasa Walker of Ohio and Massachusetts were among those who became important to the party. In fact, both the candidates for governor and lieutenant-governor in Vermont during the late 1840s came from the Democratic Party. At the same time, the Liberty leadership suffered few defections back to the Whig Party. This party loyalty at the top obscured changes that were taking place among the mass of Liberty voters.

The Liberty Party's voter base changed during the mid-1840s. The party had a solid core of supporters who were loyal to Liberty candidates from the early years of the party. Nevertheless, much evidence shows that the average Liberty voter outside this core was neither as committed nor as consistent in his voting pattern. Close examination of the situation shows that Liberty voters often split their tickets and that the voter base of the party changed considerably in the elections in 1844 and afterward. Ticket splitting was difficult because party organizations normally supplied voters with party tickets that could be altered only with some difficulty. Whigs and Democrats used their party machines more to ensure a large turnout for themselves and sway the independent voter than to convert opposition regulars. Most Liberty ticket splitting took place between statewide and local elections or just in local elections. There was little ticket splitting among Liberty voters between the gubernatorial and presidential elections of 1844 in states where national and state balloting took place at the same time, and there was also little change in the Liberty vote when the elections were held on different days.[13]

The pattern changed between statewide and local contests. Many voters would cast their ballot for a Liberty man running in a township, county, or congressional district election, but refuse to vote for the statewide Liberty ticket. For instance, Liberty men won five seats in the General Court (lower house) of the Massachusetts legislature in the 1843 state elections. Each winning candidate had to receive over 50% of the votes. None of the towns cast over half its vote for Samuel Sewall, the Liberty candidate for governor in the same election. Only Georgetown, with 45%, came even close to casting the minimum required for its representative.

REPRESENTATIVE	TOWN	SEWALL %
H. P. Claflin	Georgetown	45
Dr. Sawyer	Berlin	24
Joel Hayden	Williamsburgh	14
Henry Donks	Springfield	6
Hinsdale Fisher	Medfield	4[14]

This was not an isolated case. The Liberty Party elected over two hundred town representatives to the lower houses of New England state legislatures, but only a handful of towns ever cast more than half of their votes for Liberty men in the annual gubernatorial contests.[15] This same pattern held in all other states in which the Liberty Party seriously contested local elections. Although the party had no success in placing its candidates in the state legislatures outside of New England, it won countless other races for boards of supervisors, aldermen, coroners, constables, school boards, and other local offices.[16] Many factors were responsible for the greater degree of success in local races. The personal popularity of an individual candidate counted for much in the small-town political environment, and party lines did not mean as much as they did in upper-level races. Local officeholders often affected people's daily lives more directly than national or state government, and voters were more inclined to vote person not party in these situations.

Endorsement of Liberty candidates by one of the major parties sometimes contributed to Liberty success in local races. Whigs or Democrat would endorse a former fellow party member who was running on the Liberty ticket, or they would not nominate a candidate, the tacit assumption being that party members were free to vote for the Liberty nominee. Again, this was particularly prevalent in runoff elections in New England towns that would not be represented in the state legislatures unless one candidate received a simple majority. These cross-endorsements seemed to be particularly prevalent when one party dominated a town.[17] The weaker major party would side with the Liberty Party in order to challenge the stronger party. Of course, these temporary accessions did not truly reflect Liberty strength or even antislavery sentiment. This was apparent in New Hampshire in the early 1840s when Whigs were faced with the strong Democratic machine. Ironically, as the Liberty Party developed strength in some areas, Democrats and Whigs would unite to defeat it in local races.[18]

Before 1846, the Liberty Party was steadfastly opposed to outright public fusion with one of the major parties in an election, and its voters generally held to this in local elections.[19] While Liberty men did not endorse major-party candidates in local elections, it appears that they sometimes reached an accommodation, such as the Liberty Party dropping its own nominee in some instances when one of the major parties selected a strong antislavery candidate. Indeed, many Liberty men voted for major-party antislavery candidates instead of the Liberty Party. These agreements and understandings did not extend to statewide and national races except for the Independent Democrat–Liberty union in New Hampshire. It was paradoxical that the Liberty Party had greater success in local races, which rarely had any direct effect on the slavery question, than in contests where the candidate could exert some influence in behalf of the antislavery cause.

After a review of the literature on the earlier affiliations of Liberty Party members, an historian observed that "William Goodell estimated that 80 per cent of the voting abolitionists had previously been affiliated with the Whigs. No contemporary estimate was less than 65 per cent, and modern research has generally borne this out."[20] These observers, however, did not take into account the changes over time that might have affected the party's constituency. They took it for granted that the Liberty Party had the same basic composition throughout its entire existence. This was not the case.[21]

The Liberty Party voter base changed significantly between the early and late 1840s. The Liberty Party was Whig-based in its early years, but by the time it merged into the Free Soil coalition in 1848, the Liberty Party in Massachusetts, Vermont, and New Hampshire was composed predominantly of former Democrats. These former Democrats joined the Liberty Party in great numbers after 1844, while many of the grassroots Liberty men returned to the Whig Party. In Maine, the Liberty Party retained much of its early Whig support, while the Democratic accessions after 1844 made Maine one of the most powerful state Liberty organizations in the nation. Despite the confused Liberty situation in New York after 1845, it seems likely that a similar occurrence took place there.[22] Historian Lex Renda's study that examines town-level returns in Connecticut claims that "Whigs cast roughly two-thirds" of the 1841 gubernatorial vote for the Liberty Party, and "four-fifths of the Liberty Party's vote [in the spring 1843 gubernatorial election] came from men who voted Whig in 1840."[23] He also notes the Democratic accessions between presidential contest in 1844 and the gubernatorial election in 1845.[24] Studies on Ohio have noted the Democratic support, not surprising given the increasingly Democratic orientation of the Chase-Bailey faction. Bailey's biographer states that "by 1844 Bailey could claim that the Ohio Liberty party drew support equally from both national parties."[25] Although no other states have been systematically been studied on this question using statewide township-level returns, there are reasons for suspecting that the trend in the Northeast might be true elsewhere.[26]

First, the Democratic Party fell under Southern control during the 1840s. The pro-slavery tone of the 1844 Democratic platform, the behavior of the Polk administration on slavery and the annexation of Texas, the Mexican War, and the diminishing influence of Northern Democrats in national party councils caused trouble for many state Democratic parties. Some disgruntled Democrats became Liberty voters.[27] Second, the Whig Party in the North was becoming more favorable to antislavery and anti-extension sentiments. Whigs began holding their own antislavery members and winning back some earlier defections. Whig antislavery spokesmen in national and state governments increased with the election of such men as Thaddeus Stevens in Pennsylvania, William Slade in Vermont, Charles Sumner and the Conscience Whig element in Massachusetts, Joshua Giddings in Ohio, William Seward in New York, and Roger Baldwin in Connecticut.[28] The tones of most state Whig parties were also changing. Third, much of the Liberty Party rhetoric consciously appealed to Democratic sentiments. Zebina Eastman's and Joshua Leavitt's editorials calling for Democrats to join the third party emphasized that the Liberty position on slavery was merely carrying Democratic principles to their logical conclusions.[29] Gerrit Smith and William Goodell's Liberty League and Theodore Foster's multi-reform package reflected long-held Democratic positions: antimonopoly, free banking, rights for the workingman, free land, reduced national expenditures, and a low tariff. The appeal of Liberty leaders to workingmen in western Pennsylvania, Massachusetts, and elsewhere tapped another source of Democratic support. And it was common knowledge that Salmon P. Chase had been making public and private overtures to the Democrats since the early 1840s. In his address to two thousand delegates at the 1845 Southern and Western Liberty Convention, he declared that "[p]rofoundly do we revere the maxims of the true Democracy." After criticizing the Whig Party because "[i]ts natural position is conservative," he concluded "we . . . must of necessity maintain our separate organization as the true Democratic Party of the country."[30] These attitudes were attractive to antislavery Democrats who were naturally reluctant to go over to the Whigs, with whom they had little in common beyond the slavery issue. These Democratic positions could drive some wavering, former Whigs back to their old party, which had become more tolerant and supportive of antislavery sentiment, as the Liberty Party made direct appeals to Democrats for support. The (Vt.) *Green Mountain Freeman* stated that the "Liberty Party, while it makes fewer pretensions and does not assume the name, yet is actually engaged in carrying out every Democratic principle which any honest Democrat would wish to secure."[31] Fourth, that Independent Democrat John P. Hale, who agreed with his old party on all issues except slavery, brought dissatisfied Democrats and Liberty men together in New Hampshire was not lost on numerous Liberty leaders. His willingness to work with Liberty men in other states had an effect. Former Whig Samuel Fessenden confessed that "two thirds of our gain this year [1846] has been from the democratic party [because] Mr. Hale's efforts told with much power on the Democratic party in this state [Maine]."[32] Hale soon became the favorite for the Liberty presidential nomination for 1848. Fifth, that the vast majority of Liberty men slipped so easily into the Free Soil coalition with its Democratic tone indicates that the new movement was amenable to many Liberty men for non-slavery-related reasons. And sixth, Liberty and non-Liberty reports in many states commented on former Democrats as the new source of Liberty strength.

An astute political observer for the *New York Express* accurately predicted the change in Liberty Party support that he thought would take place after 1844. Speaking about the Liberty voter base, he wrote, "now all those original Whigs, or nearly all, who entertain these extreme opinions, have left the party. And any future accessions of strength which the abolitionists may receive, will be from a similar class of men, who have, by one expedient or promise or another, been hitherto kept within the Democratic ranks."[33] Undoubtedly, a change in the Liberty base of support took place around 1844 with an infusion of formerly Democratic support. The rate and timing of this varied from state to state, but attempts to gauge the changes precisely are difficult because of a lack of survey data on individual voting behavior. It is difficult to assess the speed and degree of change since there does not seem to be any single event that triggered it.

There was no national pattern to the rise and fall of Liberty fortunes in the states. The party developed at varying rates from state to state. It continued to grow in some states, but modest declines were evident in New York, Pennsylvania, and Michigan by 1846. Nonetheless, the party reached its peak strength in that year with over seventy thousand votes nationally, almost eight thousand more than in 1844. And even these figures are somewhat misleading concerning Liberty strength vis-à-vis the major parties because the Liberty Party generally did not suffer as much as the major parties did from a drop in voter turnout. For instance, the party reached previously unmatched highs of nearly 15% of the 1846 gubernatorial vote in both Maine and Vermont. The party also made its best showing ever in Illinois. The party's slow growth in some states and stagnation or decline in others, however, made Liberty leaders generally more receptive to the fundamental changes in policy that caused Liberty men so much inner turmoil during the party's last few years. They had worked hard for a more efficient grassroots organization in 1845 and 1846 with limited success, so they began to look for candidates and policies that would appeal to a wider voting public.

An important factor in Liberty success was the quality of this leadership at both the state and local levels. Almost every township where the Liberty strength greatly exceeded that of its demographically similar neighbors contained one or more vigorous leaders who took it upon themselves to organize the party. This entailed calling meetings, setting up rallies, and perhaps printing some tracts and leaflets. Voting patterns often showed strong towns surrounded by other towns whose strength decreased as they became more removed from the centers of activity.[34] Many Liberty members participated in the activities of neighboring towns if their own did not have enough interested citizens to set up their own organization. Invariably, these Liberty hotbeds had strong local leadership. That the party did not do well in larger urban areas despite the presence of some strong leaders is more difficult to understand. For instance, in the 1844 presidential contest, New York City only gave 117 of 54,798 votes (0.002%), Philadelphia 22 of 42,368 votes (0.005%), and Cincinnati 298 of 16,482 votes (0.02%) to the Liberty Party. Despite the presence of leading antislavery leaders, these cities never generated a large Liberty vote.

The Liberty Party's greatest need throughout its whole existence was for more capable leadership at the grassroots level. Most Liberty sympathizers had neither much time nor money to give to the cause. The average Liberty man in the 1840s put in a hard day's work, six days a week, and devoted Sunday to worship. There was no national party treasury, and most state parties had barely sufficient funds to limp along. There was no patronage for a party with so little electoral success. Where financing and talented leadership existed—such as Gerrit Smith for Madison County, New York—efforts usually far outstripped neighboring areas with similar ecological profiles. Many potential grassroots leaders, though, were unwilling or not able to make the requisite sacrifices to mobilize the possible Liberty voters. James G. Birney, by all accounts well respected by his neighbors, received only two votes in 1844 from his home county in which there was no Liberty organization.[35]

This leadership factor helps explain many of the isolated pockets of Liberty strength. Party success in Bureau County, Illinois, Wyoming County, New York, and New Garden, Indiana, were largely results of the tireless efforts by Owen Lovejoy and William Goodell and Benjamin Stanton. It also helps to explain why the party suddenly took hold in areas where it had received little previous support. It was no coincidence that many local party organizations flourished in Indiana, Illinois, Wisconsin, and Iowa after an Ichabod Codding, Alanson St. Clair,

Edward Mathews, or some other activist settled there. These were often ministers or very pious laymen and they are the unsung heroes of the Liberty cause. They worked tirelessly for the party throughout its existence, and maps of their travels show significant increases in Liberty support almost everywhere that they went. Indeed, the role of antislavery ministers cannot be overemphasized. Strong Liberty locales almost always had an outspoken antislavery clergyman nearby. Some states had such weak leadership that their limited electoral successes are still surprising. The New Hampshire party lacked vigorous state leadership until its merger with the Independent Democrats. Its town organization lagged far behind neighboring states, and its central committee did little. Nevertheless, the Granite State produced a creditable state Liberty turnout year after year. There can only be speculation on how much better it or other seemingly fertile areas might have done if there had been some capable leaders.

Liberty membership did not comprise just white voting males. African American participation has been noted already, but women also took part in Liberty affairs, although usually more peripherally. Historians cite women's antislavery activities as the first major involvement of females in public affairs and in organizing gender-specific activities. What is less well documented is that women's participation in Liberty conventions and organizations was part of the whole process of the politicization of women activists. Few studies have examined the role of any women except elite Garrisonian activists. Studies of the abolition movement or the Liberty Party rarely mention the role of women in the party organization.[36] In fact, many studies view the party as hostile to women's rights and political participation. Those who hold this position argue that it was "the political abolitionists, whose more conservative views on gender roles were expressed in their 1839 and 1840 efforts to exclude women from equal participation in the AASS [American Anti-Slavery Society]."[37] In fact, many political abolitionists were women's rights advocates and most women abolitionists were sympathetic to the New Organization and, eventually, the Liberty Party.

That most women joined affiliates of the New Organization or set up their own independent societies has often been ignored. A majority of the women in the Boston Female Anti-Slavery Society, an Old Organization affiliate, voted 142–10 to dissolve the old society and form the Massachusetts Female Emancipation Society. This new society broke with the Old Organization and affiliated with the new Massachusetts Abolition Society because the "*no*-government *friends* . . . became so amazing in their movements, that it *was* found impracticable to continue united with them."[38] In fact, all twelve founders of the original society became members of the new society.[39] A committed Garrisonian, who had been a member of the Leominster (Mass.) Anti-Slavery Society, lamented that that society's affiliation with the New Organization by 1842 left her practically alone in opposition. Almost all of the thirty members abandoned the Garrisonians.[40] When the split took place in the American Anti-Slavery Society in 1840, members of the Ladies' New York City Anti-Slavery Society walked out with those seceding from the Old Organization. They resolved that "we deprecate the discussions . . . of topics foreign to the objects for the promotion of which the Society was organized" and "we are opposed to the public voting and speaking of women in said meeting, to their acting on Committee, or, as officers of the Society with men."[41] They left the old society and affiliated with the American and Foreign Anti-Slavery Society. In other words, these women went with the organizations that were supposedly opposed to rights for women. In eastern Pennsylvania, the Philadelphia Female Anti-Slavery Society remained affiliated with the Old Organization and its policies mirrored those of the eastern branch of the Pennsylvania Anti-Slavery Society: initial acceptance of political action with an eventual endorsement of the Garrisonian positions on disunionism and against voting. This resulted in substantial losses in membership by 1847 as women sympathetic to political action left the organization.[42]

After the Liberty Party became the primary vehicle for antislavery protest, many women's abolition groups worked closely with it. Some articulate and outspoken women—such as Maria Weston Chapman, Abby Kelley, Lucretia Mott, and Lydia Maria Child—continued to work in the Old Organization, but by the early 1840s, many women's antislavery groups worked and sympathized with Liberty Associations and groups. The level and style of female participation in Liberty affairs varied greatly from state to state and even within states. That the Liberty Party was a political organization would seem to preclude female participation because they did not yet have the vote, but this was not the case. This participation obviously took different forms than directly voting. Historians Mary P. Ryan and Lori Ginzburg have traced the involvement of women on the fringes of the political process, such as spearheading petition drives and their roles in molding public sentiment on a range of issues.[43] In general, direct female participation in Liberty affairs was most restricted in the upper four New England states, somewhat more apparent in the Middle States, and probably most pronounced in the Northwest. Nonetheless, pockets of activism existed across the North, but variations were significant. Even while women participated in Liberty meetings and associations, they often continued to work within their own gender-exclusive organizations.

Antislavery women in Massachusetts held bazaars to raise funds, and Liberty women sewed the Liberty Party banner that was given to the town with the highest percentage in the annual gubernatorial race. These women had no voice in the operation of the Liberty organization and usually did not participate in the main meetings, but they often were present.[44] Most Massachusetts women worked in their own sphere without any turmoil over their role. And one woman's interest in Liberty affairs may have been motivated by something other than abolitionist theory. Garrisonian Ann Weston confided to her siblings that Ida Russell, who was president of the Milton Anti-Slavery Society in Massachusetts, backed the Liberty Party "owing to Whittier with whom she is carrying on a desperate flirtation."[45]

The situation in Maine was similar, although female participation was an issue in the state in the early years. The eighth annual meeting of the of the Maine Anti-Slavery Society in January 1843 passed a resolution excluding women, whereupon a group withdrew to set up a new state society, but this group seems to have had few Garrisonian followers.[46] The situation changed a few years later when a convention at West Waterville declared that ladies "*always should be at anti-slavery meetings of all kinds.* The Liberty Party holds no meetings unsuitable for women, and at which they are not expected."[47] These women organized antislavery fairs, made banners, prepared food, and attended the conventions in sizable numbers, but they only seem to have participated directly in their own gender-exclusive societies and groups.[48] Nonetheless, they participated indirectly in Liberty politics, as when they raised money through a "Donation Party" to help sustain the publication of the *Liberty Standard*.[49]

Vermont women were leaders in the antislavery movement during the 1830s. With the advent of the Liberty Party women seem to have continued to participate. An early historian of the Vermont Liberty Party has claimed that "[w]omen were welcomed in the party councils although there seems to have been no sentiment in favor of women voting on party questions."[50] In fact, Vermont did not even organize a separate women's state society until 1847.[51] There were no attempts to organize New Hampshire ladies statewide until the mid-1840s, but there was still considerable activity in local groups. As Julie Roy Jeffrey has observed, "The collapse of a unified national antislavery effort in 1840 actually created a variety of individual and collective opportunities to work for the slave and encouraged different styles of activism."[52] Despite limited sources, Connecticut female participation in Liberty affairs seems to have taken place primarily through the Liberty Associations.[53] James C. Jackson, editor of the *Albany Patriot*, contrasted these situations with New York when he reported on a Boston Liberty convention in 1843.

> There has gathered already a fine body of Liberty men, but there is one thing lacking. It is the presence of women. How different from the Lib-

erty meetings of New York! The meetings of our state always wear the gleam of sunshine, but over the Liberty congregation now gathered there is a sombre hue, the body of the convention being a heavy background with *one woman* in relief . . . Is there a Liberty man in New York, who would not feel at a loss in a Liberty Convention in which there should be no women? Enough of this. Massachusetts has *her notions.* They are different from ours. We think one way—she another. I prefer ours.[54]

New York Liberty advocates established a Female Anti-Slavery Society affiliated with the Liberty Party at a mid-October 1843 Liberty Party convention in Rome. They aimed "to secure the *systematic* enlistment of every man, woman, and child, in some department of anti-slavery work," but Jackson later reflected that the party's neglect of the woman question had hurt it.[55] Endorsement of female participation was sporadic. Sometimes women were included in Liberty meetings, and sometimes there is no mention of their participation. It seems that women often had important roles in the meetings, although not necessarily in the political aspects. Historian Julie Roy Jeffrey describes an 1844 Liberty convention and picnic in Arcade, New York, at which "Liberty Party organizers anticipated earning enough from the picnic to replace the usual collection."[56] Gerrit Smith later took a definitely advanced position that women should be welcome in the Liberty camp because "[a]bolitionists are, so much more generally than anti-abolitionists, in favor of restoring to woman her natural right of suffrage."[57] These feminist attitudes were more likely to be formed Upstate than in the New York City area, where the attitudes of the Tappans and others precluded a more active female role.[58]

When Alvan Stewart helped design a model constitution for a Liberty Association, he explicitly included provisions for both men and women.[59] The 1843 Liberty Party state convention in Connecticut passed a resolution declaring "we recognize women as equally embarking, in the same organization with men," and they did in fact take part in many aspects of the Liberty organization, albeit in traditional female roles.[60] The same was even true in Philadelphia, no bastion of Liberty strength, where Liberty women participated in traditional antislavery fairs and bazaars. They made the mistake, however, of inviting William Lloyd Garrison to their Philadelphia Liberty Party Bazaar. He quickly responded, "I hope none who desire to be friendly to the American Anti-Slavery Society will aid the Philadelphia Bazaar, which is hostile to the very existence of that Society, and would rejoice at its extinction this hour."[61] Throughout the Northeast, women participated in antislavery affairs under the aegis of Liberty organizations, usually in Liberty Associations but sometimes in gender-specific societies. Even the small Liberty group in New Jersey made it a point to include female abolitionists in its Liberty Association.

Women enjoyed their fullest participation in Liberty affairs in the Old Northwest. Women were encouraged to attend Liberty conventions in all the states. Some hotels even offered special considerations for ladies and husband-wife travelers.[62] Again, the types of antislavery activities in which women took part in varied from state to state and sometimes even within states.[63] Linda Evans has noted, "Illinoisians manifested a variety of attitudes toward women's role in the crusade."[64] They were very involved in supplying fugitive slaves with clothing and blankets for their trips on the Underground Railroad.[65] They often worked locally, but they were also invited to and did attend the general Liberty conventions. Some Illinois women's antislavery societies either endorsed specific Liberty nominees or expressed their willingness "to exert their influence in favor of the Liberty Party."[66] In 1843 and 1844 a large number of women's societies were formed that were loyal to the Liberty Party. There was not a statewide meeting of the Illinois State Women's Anti-Slavery Society until May 1844, another meeting in 1845, and then there was talk of disbanding this loosely organized state society less than a year later.[67] This was also true, however, for the Illinois State Anti-Slavery Society, which had ceased to function as an independent agency in 1843 when it effectively became part of the Liberty Party. At least part of the reason for this lack of a female state agency was the warm welcome women received at the mixed-gender, interracial Liberty activities and the various antislavery religious conventions that immediately preceded or followed Liberty gatherings. Liberty Associations in Illinois seem to have been particularly well organized and active.[68] Illinois women in the Liberty areas of strength in the northeastern counties were more involved in Liberty activities than in any other state.

Michigan women's societies were formed as auxiliaries of the state society, but they generally maintained separate spheres of activity.[69] During the early 1840s, there is little evidence of much formal activity, although women continued to work in the Underground Railroad and church activities. Liberty men began to take a greater interest in female antislavery activities in the mid-1840s. Touring antislavery speakers, the state Liberty newspaper, and conventions encouraged women to form their own gender-specific societies and to begin taking a more active role in statewide meetings.[70] Liberty man Charles H. Stewart encouraged women "to use their influence in behalf of human rights . . . [because] [t]hey could accomplish almost any thing they would undertake."[71] Female leaders in Michigan were usually married to prominent Liberty Party men, but they do not seem to be as closely identified with the Liberty Party as in Illinois.[72] The situation was similar in Indiana, where the women's societies were formed as auxiliaries of the state organization, but females still participated in some local societies. These women were like those in Michigan, preferring more traditional roles.[73]

The same was true in Wisconsin, where women preferred to work in their own organizations as well as the Liberty Associations. As early as 1844, twenty-nine women in Prarieville and Milwaukee became members of the new Female Anti-Slavery Society of Prarieville and Milwaukee, a number that increased to fifty-four less than a year later.[74] They held monthly meetings, prepared clothes for fugitive slaves in Canada, maintained a library of thirty-five volumes, purchased publications and stationery, and subscribed to one share in the *American Freeman*. These societies were less political than those in Illinois. A contributor to the *American Freeman* felt that she should publish her support anonymously or under a pseudonym in the "Ladies Department."[75] Liberty organizations appealed to women, and the Wisconsin Liberty Association, which had taken over the Wisconsin Anti-Slavery Society in early 1845, declared that "[w]e shall see a large representation of ladies present" when it announced its annual meeting late in 1846.[76] A correspondent of the *American Freeman* reporting on Liberty conventions said that "there is to my mind something so similar in these gatherings, the large attendance of *the people*—the large proportion of women . . . [A]ll this seems to me to be common to Liberty Conventions."[77]

Ohio female abolitionists varied in their approaches to the cause. They actively participated in some early conventions that supported independent nominations. Shortly after the 1840 election the Ohio Anti-Slavery Society called a meeting "[t]o agree upon some rational, effective plan of antislavery political action." It passed a resolution 101–16, with both men and women participating, "that abolitionists nominate candidates for office in all places where they are not perfectly assured that one or both of the existing parties will nominate candidates, for whom they can consistently vote." Later in 1841, at the sixth annual meeting of the Ohio Anti-Slavery Society, women participated in the nomination of Leicester King for governor.[78] Most Ohio women remained independent or worked closely with the Liberty organizations. A Cincinnati area woman, originally from Massachusetts, reflected that "all nominal abolitionists here for the last nine years (since it has been my home) have either been *Liberty Party* . . . [or] so called *Christian* Abolitionists, meaning those who will labor for the slave in and with *their* church but not *out* of it."[79] Some women felt that they were not welcome at political meetings, but others attended, especially if there were concurrent church or women's antislavery activities.[80]

These antislavery women did not push for equal political rights. Women's rights questions occasionally reached the Liberty meetings of these states, but men controlled the main meetings and ran most of the aspects of the Liberty Associations. Women often attended, however, as silent spectators. In reporting on a Liberty Party convention in Detroit, James G. Birney noted that few women were in attendance because "the subject was *political.*"[81] Women were expected to be behind the Liberty men to give them encouragement and support. An announcement of an early Liberty Party meeting in Michigan urged women to "[c]ome to the meeting and cheer us, and nerve our arms . . . If you should hear its political aspects and bearings discussed, it will not harm you. 'Your tears may rust the captive's chains.'"[82] Liberty men wanted women involved in the antislavery struggle, but most did not mean equal or gender-blind participation. Abby Kelley spoke at the 1843 national Liberty nominating convention in Buffalo (the first woman to speak at a national political gathering) "until the patience of the members was exhausted, and the zealous Abby Kelly [sic] was with difficulty silenced."[83] Antislavery women who worked on the fringes of the Liberty Party did not resent the absence of equal rights. Even Elizabeth Cady Stanton, Henry B. Stanton's wife and future women's rights advocate, did not try to enhance women's roles in the Liberty organization. Nonetheless, in private correspondence she maintained that "I am in favor of political action, & the organization of a third party as the most efficient way of calling forth & *directing* action."[84] These women were content to take a different role than men.

The issue came up, however, in a few Liberty meetings. At the North-Western Liberty Convention in Chicago in June 1846, George W. Clark showed himself as a "[w]oman's rights man of the straightest kind, being an advocate of the absolute equality of the condition of the sexes."[85] His proposal to endorse women's suffrage met with little support.[86] In fact, even the women present seemed to show little enthusiasm for it, prompting *Signal of Liberty* editor Theodore Foster to comment sarcastically that these women "*were not disposed to accept their liberty even if it were offered to them!*" He commented that four women present "turned the cold shoulder to their warm hearted advocate."[87] Instead, the emphasis was on giving encouragement that "[l]adies might act out a prominent part in this work, in moulding the minds of children, and in persuading pro slavery husbands to act rightly."[88] Women's rights received more than a perfunctory nod with the coming of the Liberty League and Gerrit Smith's National Liberty Party, and women participated in the meetings. In Macedon Lock in 1847, Lydia Maria Child and Lucretia Mott each received a vote when the convention selected candidates. Mott received five votes for the vice presidential nomination in the initial balloting when the National Liberty Party (the Liberty League offshoot) set up its 1848 presidential ticket in June 1848.[89] This was unusual, and most women preferred to accept auxiliary roles.

An example of this was Antoinette Brown Blackwell, the first ordained female Congregational minister. She was a notable exception to the statement of Oberlin's historian that "all of the outstanding women abolitionists educated at Oberlin supported him [Garrison]."[90] Unlike other feminists at Oberlin—her friends Betsey Cowles, Lucy Stone, and Sallie Holley, daughter of Liberty Party founder Myron Holley—she did not convert to Garrisonian abolition. She came from a politically active Liberty family from Upstate New York and supported political antislavery. She rejected come-outerism in religion and the disunionist, nonresistant theories of Garrison. Even before becoming an ordained minister, she sought "to integrate orthodox Christianity with reform politics."[91] When Lucy Stone offered to have her expenses paid if Brown would speak before a Garrison-sponsored women's rights convention in 1850, Brown asked, "[W]hy should your Convention pay any portion of my expenses. I might go there and speak against them many things for I do not believe exactly with your party even on the subject of woman's rights and I would not be bought to silence."[92] She later worked in Gerrit Smith's 1852 congressional campaign, but she never felt comfortable in the political sphere in these years. The politics continued to be a male realm. Other women took more direct roles. One woman was an important writer for a Liberty newspaper. Two women served as editors of newspapers sympathetic to the Liberty Party. Jane Van Vleet published the *Star of Freedom* in Niles, Michigan, in 1845. It was a short-lived sheet, but it did receive a recommendation of support from the Michigan state Liberty convention.[93] Little is known about her and her political, antislavery, or feminist activities.

Two other women journalists, Mary Brown Davis and Jane Grey Swisshelm, were more important for their Liberty Party activities. Davis joined her husband, Samuel, in Peoria, Illinois, in 1837. The couple came from Virginia, where he still owned two slaves, and he became the editor of the Peoria *Register,* which became the Whig newspaper in the town. He continued his Whig affiliation until he joined the Liberty Party in the mid-1840s. While the husband lagged behind, Davis quickly became active in the antislavery movement and published articles in the *Genius of Universal Emancipation* as early as 1839.[94] She would eventually publish at least sixty antislavery articles there and in the *Chicago Western Citizen* under her M.B.D. byline. She was involved in several facets of the Liberty movement, particularly the fight against the black codes in Illinois and establishing local and state antislavery societies in 1843 and 1844, organizations closely allied with the Liberty Party. Davis wrote on many antislavery subjects, not hesitating to discuss political matters and encourage women's participation in Liberty functions.[95]

Jane Grey Swisshelm was a journalist for the Liberty cause in Pittsburgh.[96]

She was born there in 1815 but had lived part of her life in Louisville, Kentucky, where she saw slavery firsthand and was particularly bothered by "the degree to which the existence of slavery demeaned and degraded both black and white women." [97] Shortly after the (Pittsburgh) *Spirit of Liberty* was founded in 1844, she began to write antislavery articles for it. Like Mary Brown Davis, she wrote under her initials "for two reasons—my dislike and dread of publicity and the fear of embarrassing the Liberty Party with the sex question." In a perceptive observation, she noted that "[a]bolitionists were men of sharp angles. Organizing them was like binding crooked sticks in a bundle, and one of the questions which divided them was the right of women to take any prominent part in public affairs."[98] She was aware that in her area "[t]he political wing of the anti-slavery party had given formal notice that no woman need apply for a place among them. True, there was a large minority who dissented from this action, but there was division enough, without my furnishing a cause for contention. So I took pains to make it understood that I belonged to no party . . . [yet] [i]t seemed good unto me to support James G. Birney, for president, and to promulgate the principles of the platform on which he stood in the last election."[99] She left the *Spirit of Liberty* when she began to sign her name to articles that now encompassed women's rights (although not suffrage) as well as slavery.[100] For over two years she then wrote for the Whig (Pittsburgh) *Commercial Journal*, supporting women's rights and attacking the Democrats for the annexation of Texas.

In December 1847 she became the editor-publisher of the (Pittsburgh) *Saturday Visiter*, the only woman in the United States who owned and edited a political newspaper. In its inaugural issue Swisshelm made it clear that she believed in abolition by "no reasonable way except by a distinct third party."[101] She also viewed herself as a political realist. When the Free Soil Party was formed and nominated Martin Van Buren, she dropped Birney—whom she had supported—from her masthead and replaced him with the Free Soil ticket, for which she was criticized harshly by Garrisonians and Liberty Leaguers.[102] In many ways, however, Swisshelm was a loner and an atypical representative of even the segment of the Liberty movement that believed in women's rights. She was a vehement anti-Catholic nativist who could not abide labor unions. One historian sees her embracing a conspiracy theory wherein "[l]abor unions, the Catholic church, and slavery were all in an interlocking conspiracy to destroy enterprising men who worked alone."[103] These were positions that put her at odds with the appeals that such Liberty men as Russell Errett and William Elder were making to the workingmen's movement in Pittsburgh and elsewhere.

Swisshelm was similar to most other female activists in the Liberty camp in not pressing for complete equality and the suffrage. Those who did step out of the traditional sphere conceived of women's rights as something other than electoral politics. Swisshelm herself, reflecting problems in her personal life, pursued the cause of furthering the rights of married women. In fact, she was openly opposed to making claims for sexual equality and believed in distinctions between the sexes.[104] Antoinette Brown Blackwell emphasized economic and social rights, such as being permitted to speak in public and be ordained. She had been agitating for these since her days at Oberlin.[105] Mary Brown Davis talked little on women's rights, but in her valedictory column she referred to the subject and wished more could be done for "laws unfavorable to married women and to the father's exclusive legal rights to children."[106]

After assessing the effects of women on the Liberty movement, we are still left with the difficult question of whether it had any impact on women's rights activities. Answers are speculative, but it would seem that as antislavery and other reforms were taken into the political arena, the importance of female participation in public affairs was heightened, albeit within limits. As Alice Taylor points out, "At antislavery rallies female abolitionists honored their traditional roles as nurturers and benefactors of men; however, these they did so not in the home but rather within a very public, political space."[107] Women seeking the vote during the 1850s added to the progress of the preceding two decades. They saw that political strength was necessary for substantive change. As Lori Ginzburg has pointed out, "[T]hose men who turned increasingly to electoral work in the 1840s forced their female co-workers to examine more closely their own access to those in authority and the continuing viability of a nonvoting stance."[108] This is probably the most important result for the women's rights movement that came from involvement in Liberty affairs.

What happened to Liberty members politically after the party's demise? Initially, as Samuel May reported, "The 'Liberty Party' of this country has gone in solid phalanx, with only an exception here & there, into the ranks of the so-called Free Soil party."[109] As that party began to lose strength, they again went various ways. Some remained in the smaller Free Soil movement and a few joined the small Liberty League contingent. Others returned to Whig or Democratic allegiances, or became involved in the Free Democracy movement. Few were involved with the Know Nothing movement even though this group had a noticeable antislavery orientation in the North. Perhaps the most noteworthy was William Larimer of Pennsylvania, who had joined the Whig Party in the 1850s. After initially resisting the Know Nothings, he eventually became a formal member in June 1854.[110] Chauncy Knapp, former Vermont secretary of state and Massachusetts Liberty congressional candidate in 1846, was elected to the U.S. Congress in 1854 with American Party endorsement, but he does not seem to have been very active in its policies.[111] He was reelected as a Republican in 1856. Jane Grey Swisshelm made no secret of her anti-Catholicism.[112] Thomas Spooner of Ohio was a much more committed nativist who had been active in the Liberty Party. His uncle was Samuel Lewis, a respected educator and Liberty gubernatorial and congressional candidate in Ohio. Spooner was a full-fledged member of the Ohio Know Nothings and president of the Ohio Know Nothing council. He has been credited with convincing many antislavery Free Soilers to enter the nativist ranks, but he seems to have had little success with convincing former Liberty leaders to come over to the movement.[113] He did carry on a dialogue with Salmon P. Chase, who was running for governor and was intrigued by the possibility of Know Nothing support, but Chase was quite clear in his opposition to the movement by late 1854. He wrote, "Can Anti Slavery men especially join in the indiscriminate proscription of those Americans of foreign birth who stood shoulder to shoulder with us in the Anti-Nebraska struggle . . . I cannot take upon myself any secret political obligations . . . I cannot proscribe men on account of their birth . . . I cannot make religious faith a political test."[114] Elizur Wright was particularly vehement in his denunciations of the nativist American movement. He especially criticized Charles W. Denison, an early Liberty leader, who edited the *American Signal,* a nativist newspaper.[115] The Liberty Party of the mid-1840s had shunned the nativist movement, and few former Liberty men flirted with it in the 1850s. Another Massachusetts Liberty man, Caleb Swan, was so upset by the Know Nothing tinge to the regular Republican Party that he allowed himself to be run on the "Straight Republican" ticket for governor.[116]

By the late 1850s, most former Liberty adherents regrouped under the banner of the Republican Party.[117] They were not passive followers, but took active leadership roles in all national Republican conventions and in all the states where their former party existed. Most remained loyal to the Republican Party for the remainder of their lives. At the same time they carved out careers in a variety of fields.

A further question is, What did members of the Liberty Party do in subsequent years? Of course, some members died or had retired from active work. Party founders Myron P. Holley and Alvan Stewart from New York, vice presidential candidates Thomas Morris and Thomas Earle, Amos A. Phelps and Charles T. Torrey from Massachusetts, Orange Scott and Jonathan P. Miller from Vermont, Ebenezer Dole from Maine, Guy Beckley, Jabez Fitch, and Arthur L. Porter from Michigan, and David Nelson and Richard Eels from Illinois were only a few of those gone by 1850. Nevertheless, a large number of former Liberty men continued to take an active part in public life at the local, state, and national levels for the next several decades. Particularly noteworthy are many individuals whom one does not associate with the Liberty Party. This is especially true of many men who joined the party as young men and achieved a measure of national prominence later.

Many Liberty men became judges. While Salmon P. Chase and Stanley Matthews reached the U.S. Supreme Court, many others served on federal, state, and local benches. This reflected their high public esteem, their legal skills, and their political sensitivity. Many lawyers also flourished in private practice and made their marks in the legal profession, and many argued fugitive slave cases with no compensation.

Other Liberty Party members went on to serve in the U.S. Senate or House of Representatives or became governors. The ambitious Salmon P. Chase became a U.S. senator, governor of Ohio, secretary of the treasury under Lincoln, and the chief justice of the U.S. Supreme Court. While others may not have had such a full resume, many held high office. Liberty men who were U.S. senators, members of the house of representatives, or governors are listed on pages 288–289. The lists will probably grow longer as more intensive work is done on the Liberty Party and younger, low-level activists who would become prominent later are discovered. Included on the lists are men who held office before the advent of the Liberty Party. They brought their name recognition, political experience, and reputations into the new party. It can be argued that a few—such as Hale and Tuck from New Hampshire—were not real Liberty Party supporters but just temporarily allowed themselves to be identified with the third party. Most of the other men, however, were consistent, active Liberty Party participants. They were just the few who achieved a high degree of prominence in various aspects of public life. Many others were elected to state and local political offices or the judiciary, served in the diplomatic corps, or received appointive positions.[118]

Education was always a high priority for individuals in the Liberty Party, so it is not surprising that many made it their life's work. They served not only as teachers but also in the founding and administration of several institutions. Paul Goodman has discussed the involvement of abolitionists in the manual labor movement,[119] and Liberty men were deeply involved in this and the general field of higher education. Their schools were bastions of the Liberty Party and stations on the Underground Railroad. What is not so often noted is that many founders of institutions of higher education were party members. Liberty men who were founders or presidents of colleges are listed on page 290. Most were

Liberty Men Who Were U.S. Senators, U.S. Congressmen, Governors, or Lieutenant-Governors

U.S. SENATORS
Lawrence Brainerd (Vt.), 1854
Alexander Campbell (Ohio), 1809–1813
Salmon P. Chase (Ohio), 1849–1855, 1860–1861
Joseph Cilley (N.H.), 1846–1847
Charles Durkee (Wis.), 1855–1861
Francis Gillette (Conn.), 1855
John P. Hale (N.H.), 1847–1853
Joseph R. Hawley (Conn.), 1881–1905
Stanley Matthews (Ohio), 1877–1879
Thomas Morris (Ohio), 1833–1839

U.S. CONGRESSMEN
Charles Durkee (Wis.), 1849–1853
Russell Errett (Pa.), 1877–1883
Seth Merrill Gates (N.Y.), 1839–1843
Josiah Grinnell (Iowa), 1863–1867
John P. Hale (N.H.), 1842–1845
Joseph R. Hawley (Conn.), 1872–1875, 1879–1881
John Hutchins (Ohio), 1859–1863
William Jackson (Mass.), 1833–1837
Chauncy L. Knapp (Mass.), 1855–1859
John Mercer Langston (Va.), 1889–1891
Dewitt Clinton Leach (Mich.), 1857–1861
Owen Lovejoy (Ill.), 1857–1864
Daniel Fry Miller (Iowa), 1849–1851
James Monroe (Ohio), 1871–1881
Ralph Plumb (Ill.), 1885–1889
David Potts (Pa.), 1831–1839
Alvah Sabin (Vt.), 1853–1857
Gerrit Smith (N.Y.), 1853–1854
Norton S. Townshend (Ohio), 1851–1853
Amos Tuck (N.H.), 1847–1853
Edward Wade (Ohio), 1853–1861
Amasa Walker (Mass.), 1862–1863

GOVERNORS AND LIEUTENANT-GOVERNORS
John A. Andrew (Mass.), 1861–1865
Nathaniel S. Berry (N.H.), 1861–1863
James Birney (Mich.), Lieutenant-governor 1861–1863

Salmon P. Chase (Ohio), 1855–1859
Henry W. DePuy (Nebraska Territory), Secretary
Charles Durkee (Utah Territory)
Stephen S. Harding (Utah Territory)
Joseph R. Hawley (Conn.), 1866–1867
Joel Hayden (Mass.), Lieutenant-governor, 1863–1866
Charles K. Williams (Vt.), 1850

not just Liberty voters. They were active in antislavery and the operations of the party. These lists demonstrate the talent that enrolled in the Liberty Party.

Former Liberty men are sometimes unfairly criticized for leaving full-time reform work to make a living. Many struggled to support large families. For instance, a leading historian of antislavery has claimed that "Stanton did degenerate thereafter into the most ordinary of political hacks in the Free Soil and later Republican parties, displaying a loss of conviction that hardly surprised the Garrisonians who had warned the abolitionists of this dereliction for many years."[120] This is just not true. Stanton was an individual who sacrificed much of his youth to the antislavery cause, continued to work for the cause after becoming a lawyer in 1843, and showed his abolitionist principles for the rest of his life. He had a growing family to support and his wife, Elizabeth Cady Stanton, was taking a leadership role in the women's rights movement. One of the reasons that he moved to Seneca Falls, New York, from Boston was that his health was suffering because he was so overworked from the extra labors he was devoting to antislavery and the Liberty Party. Another historian has more accurately reported that "Stanton was as much an abolitionist at heart as ever, but he had lost some of his crusading zeal since the early days when he had been mobbed more than two hundred times."[121] Although he held some elective and appointive offices, he spent most of his life as a lawyer and journalist. Most Liberty men did not have the sponsorship of a Francis Jackson or have trusts and gifts as did Garrison. It is amazing that they stayed so active for so long, and that they never totally abandoned the struggle. Elizur Wright, Joshua Leavitt, Theodore Foster, James C. Jackson, and others left full-time Liberty work because of broken health or familial responsibilities.

Indeed, the energy, perseverance, and self-sacrifice of many Liberty Party workers over many years were truly remarkable. They traveled considerable distances, often at their own expense and unsure of what kind of reception might greet them, to spread the Liberty message. Others lectured, campaigned, and even just attended Liberty conventions and rallies closer to home. All of these activities required them to make financial sacrifices and take time from their

Liberty Men Who Were College Founders and College Presidents

COLLEGE FOUNDERS

Flavel Bascom: Chicago Theological Seminary; Beloit (Wisconsin) College (1846)
Jonathan Blanchard: Wheaton (Illinois) College
Daniel Branch: Michigan Central (now Hillsdale) College
James Gordon Carter: Framingham, Bridgewater, and Westfield (Massachusetts) colleges
Oren B. Cheney: Bates College (1863)
Nathaniel Colver: Colver Institute (now Virginia Union, Richmond)
Elizur Deming: (LaPorte) Indiana Medical College
George Washington Gale: Oneida Institute (1827); Knox College (1837)
Josiah Grinnell: Grinnell College (1856)
Cyrus Pitt Grosvenor: New York Central College (McGrawsville, 1849)
Hiram H. Kellogg: Knox College (1837)
Francis Julius LeMoyne: LeMoyne Normal Institute (Memphis, Tennessee, 1870)
Lucius Matlack: Wheaton (Illinois) College (1853)
John Monteith: University of Michigan (1817)
David Nelson: Marion (Missouri) College; Mission Institute (Quincy, Illinois, 1836)
Abraham Pennock: Haverford College (1833)
John Jay Shipherd: Oberlin College (1832); Olivet (Michigan) College (1844)

COLLEGE PRESIDENTS

Jonathan Blanchard: Knox College (1845–1857); Wheaton College (1862–1882)
Oren B. Cheney: Bates College (1863–1894)
John Payne Cleaveland: Marshall (Michigan) College (1837–1841)
James H. Fairchild: Oberlin College (1866–1889)
Charles G. Finney: Oberlin College (1851–1866)
George Washington Gale: Oneida Institute (1827–1834); Knox College (1837–1839)
Henry Highland Garnet: Avery College in Pittsburgh (1868–1870)
Beriah Green: Oneida Institute (1834–1843)
Cyrus Pitt Grosvenor: New York Central College (1849–1850)
Hiram H. Kellogg: Knox College (1838–1845)
John Mercer Langston: Howard University (acting president); Virginia Normal and Collegiate Institute (1885–1887)
Asa Mahan: Oberlin College (1835–1850); Cleveland University (1850–1855); Adrian (Michigan) College (1860–1871)
Lucius Matlack: Wheaton (Illinois) College (1853–1860)
John Monteith: University of Michigan (1817–1821)
George B. Vashon: Avery College (1864–1867)

busy lives. Birney, Smith, Goodell, Chase, Leavitt, Alvan Stewart, Beriah Green, George W. Clark, and others produced an output of writing and correspondence that is exhausting just to read.

Historians who have denigrated the Liberty Party and its members clearly have not examined the evidence. The Gilbert Hobbs Barnes characterization of Liberty men as "[t]he most pathetic residue of antislavery organization" is merely one in a string of denunciations by historians of antislavery.[122] Aileen Kraditor more recently has written that "[t]he Liberty party was conceived in frustration and self-delusion, acted out a farce, and died by betrayal" and that "[t]he Liberty Party had no grass-roots organization, no ward campaigners."[123] A cursory reading of the sources does not substantiate these conclusions. Even if the party had been totally impotent electorally, represented a small portion of the antislavery movement, and produced no leaders of lasting importance, it fully justified its existence. It provided an outlet for those who wished to be politically active but could not bring themselves in conscience to support a major-party candidate because of the slavery issue. It provided an organization for like-minded individuals that they saw as much more effective than scattering votes. It developed into much more. The Liberty Party and its attendant organizations became the vehicle for serious abolitionism during the 1840s. It began as an instrument for antislavery men to express themselves politically because felt they had no alternatives. Working in the major parties was fruitless; moral suasion, while good and noble in itself, was not coming close to ameliorating the condition of the slave; and William Lloyd Garrison was taking the American Anti-Slavery Society down a road that most of them did not wish to follow. They chose to experiment, and their major experiment in 1840 was the Liberty Party. Most new additions to the antislavery movement joined it, and it very quickly expanded its organizational structure to include all elements of the antislavery struggle.

11

THE GARRISONIANS, THE LIBERTY PARTY, AND THE ABOLITION MOVEMENT IN THE 1840S

> The influence of "the Garrisonians," so called, has always been overrated both by abolitionists and hunkers... Not they, but the political antislavery men, have done the great work of reforming the opinion of the country; and the man who, away back of 1840, first cast a vote against the proslavery parties, came nearer to the root of the matter than Garrison or Phillips... [T]he first man who ever cast a Liberty-party vote was the wisest politician of his time, because he was the first man to see the inevitable future, and to do all in his power to prepare for and hasten it.
>
> WILLIAM S. ROBINSON, *"Warrington" Pen Portraits*

William Lloyd Garrison is the most famous individual in the American abolition movement, so much so that he has overshadowed other important figures.[1] He and his followers criticized the Liberty Party from its inception through its entire existence. He had an impact on the party in Massachusetts, New York, eastern Pennsylvania, Ohio and, perhaps for a short time, New Hampshire. Nonetheless, his importance should not be exaggerated. Liberty newspapers and correspondence even in these states mention him only occasionally, especially after the early 1840s. His influence on the party in the other states was negligible. In fact, only in eastern Pennsylvania and in Massachusetts did Garrisonians have an effect on Liberty decisions. His limited following in New Hampshire, New York, and Ohio was visible but did not greatly influence the party.

Garrison was a forceful, dominating presence who exercised major control over what was left of the American Anti-Slavery Society during the 1840s.[2] While all these abolitionists may not have marched in step to Garrison's orders, most either marched to his general tune or left the organization.[3] Bad feelings between the Garrisonians and many of the men who became Liberty leaders developed from the time of the split in the Massachusetts Anti-Slavery Society in 1839 and the division in the American Anti-Slavery Society in 1840. Not all Garrisonians denounced the Liberty Party in the early 1840s or even disapproved of it. The harshest criticisms of the party and its adherents were made by a small group of people surrounding Garrison that included Edmund Quincy, Maria Weston Chapman, John A. Collins, Abby Kelley, and Stephen Foster. They not only denounced the Liberty followers but also those Garrisonians who were more moderate in their approaches.[4] Lydia Maria Child, the editor of the *National Anti-Slavery Standard* and a critic of the new party, bemoaned the harshness of this group. She believed that "Chapman and Quincy also had a covert agenda—to discredit 'new organization' once and for all and to ensure a crushing defeat for the Liberty party in the 1842 and 1844 elections."[5] Child was under pressure from this group because of her more tempered approach, and she finally resigned after a vituperative editorial in the *Liberator* by Quincy attacking Lewis Tappan and gloating over his recent bankruptcy. She left decrying the spirit of sectarianism that engulfed Massachusetts abolitionism.[6] In addition to personality and ideological clashes, Garrison was convinced that Joshua Leavitt and the New Organization had stolen the *Emancipator* from the old society. He hammered at this so steadily that four years later Elizur Wright suggested that the whole matter be sent to arbitration to be settled because it was causing Liberty men embarrassment.[7] Most abolitionists were upset by his attacks on the ministry, his nonresistance, and his later denunciations of the U.S. Constitution and government.[8]

In the Old Northwest Garrison had meaningful support only in Ohio. State societies in Michigan, Illinois, Indiana, western Pennsylvania, and Wisconsin Territory quickly went over to the Liberty Party and its attendant organizations.[9] Iowa Territory maintained both a Liberty and Garrisonian presence. But neither was very strong.[10] Even in Ohio, the movement had two distinct phases during the 1840s. The first took place before Garrison started pushing his disunionist doctrines. The second phase took place in the second half of the decade as the Garrisonians attempted to rebuild their base of support in Ohio. At the beginning of the first phase, opponents of the Liberty Party, nonvoters, and moral suasionists were welcomed at meetings of the Ohio Anti-Slavery Society and the Liberty Party, with women being allowed to enroll and participate. This was in a large part a result of Gamaliel Bailey's insistence on keeping the state society together and independent.[11] Nonetheless, there were some nonvoters, nonresistants, Quakers, and those who believed in the primacy of moral suasion. They continued to participate in the national affairs of the Old Organization American Anti-Slavery Society and remained close to Garrison. When the state society refused to consider a resolution to reaffiliate with the American Anti-Slavery Society, the dissidents withdrew to form a second state society, the Ohio American Anti-Slavery Society. There is also evidence that they were unhappy with the increased political orientation of the state society.[12] This society, however, continued to welcome and receive Liberty members and maintained a working agreement with Gamaliel Bailey and the *Philanthropist*.[13] In fact, many members continued to participate in both as well as the Liberty Party.[14] The relationship worked out well for the next two years until Garrison's pronouncements on the U.S. Constitution and government caused a crisis in the newer state society. Its decline was a part of the changing status of Garrison within the whole antislavery movement.

Garrison's influence had been declining rapidly everywhere during the 1840s, even in his home state of Massachusetts.[15] In part this was because he moved beyond nonresistance to the antigovernment philosophy of disunionism. In May 1842 the *Liberator* began to run the statement that "[a] repeal of the Union between northern liberty and southern slavery is essential."[16] Then, two years later, at the tenth annual meeting of the American Anti-Slavery Society, he said that "the time had come for the American Anti-Slavery Society to hoist the banner of 'Repeal,' and to declare the American Union at an end."[17] Soon a New England Anti-Slavery Society convention endorsed the same sentiments.[18] Garrison wanted to separate the liberty-loving North from the slaveholding South. "No Union with Slaveholders" became the cry of the Garrisonian movement.

This was too much for many who previously backed him and caused the Garrisonians to lose much of their support. Massachusetts Liberty Party gubernatorial candidate Samuel Sewall remained in the Old Organization, but strongly disagreed with Garrison, as did historian-journalist Richard Hildreth. Gerrit Smith, who had maintained a close relationship with both Old and New organizations plus the Liberty Party, resigned his membership in the American Anti-Slavery Society, as did Boston Lawyer Ellis Gray Loring, who resigned from the board of officers of the Massachusetts Anti-Slavery Society after its formal assent to disunionism.[19] Then George Bradburn, a former Massachusetts Whig legislator—and who had recently been an American Anti-Slavery Society lecturer in Ohio—joined the Liberty Party. This defection particularly stung Garrison because Bradburn had been a proselytizer who had lectured widely and effectively for the Old Organization despite his belief in political action. He explained his unhappiness with the new Old Organization policy in a letter announcing his support for the Liberty Party:

> But our old Society has grown more belligerent. It is no longer content with cannonading the Liberty party, for the alledged [sic] sins of a few of

its members. But, making voting itself, under this government, a crime against God, it now wars against that party, *per se*, . . . I now . . . regard the Liberty party as *the* most efficient anti-slavery instrumentality; as the grand instrument, indeed, by which slavery, in this country, is to be overthrown; while I consider all other abolition instrumentalities as chiefly useful, in so far only as they shall tend to establish a right system of political action; such a system, as it is the aim of that party to carry out.—Therefore, if I have not "joined the Liberty party," I shall certainly avail myself of the earliest opportunity of joining it.[20]

Garrison treated him as an apostate. "Poor man! there is more of the politician than of the Christian in his composition, and therefore he clings to political action, even if it must be at the expense of principle. To think of his now being a partisan of the pseudo 'Liberty party,' and in full fellowship with such men as Leavitt, Birney, Stanton, and the like! 'To such base uses do men come at last,' who are not prepared to sell all that they have, that they may follow Christ."[21] Hildreth received similar treatment from an 1845 meeting of the New England Anti-Slavery Society when he was prevented from giving a talk due to the unpopularity of his Liberty Party beliefs.[22]

These important defections reflected what was happening among the rank and file as Garrison became a peripheral element in the American antislavery movement. After Garrison had taken control of the American Anti-Slavery Society in 1840, its income fell from forty-seven thousand dollars to seven thousand dollars, and did not rise above twelve thousand dollars until 1865.[23] The *Liberator*'s subscription list, which "rose to almost fourteen hundred in 1837," lost nearly 500 subscribers and cut 200 to 300 delinquents by the end of 1840.[24] Additionally, from 1844 to 1846 the subscription list for the *National Anti-Slavery Standard*, the official newspaper of the American Anti-Slavery Society, dropped from 3,500 to 1,400.[25] At the same time, Garrison's *Non-Resistant* ceased publication in early 1845 with only 300 subscribers.[26]

Conversely, after a slow beginning the Liberty Party's *Emancipator* built its subscription list to "about 8,600" by 1844, according to its publisher.[27] The American and Foreign Anti-Slavery Society never attracted a large following. Its major backer, Lewis Tappan, admitted that the antislavery societies had "very little vigor" and "the great body of abolitionists in the land now belong to the 'Liberty Party' as it is called."[28] By 1845, the Liberty Party and its affiliated societies were the only organizations representing a sizable number of both male and female abolitionists in the United States.[29] Key Garrisonians lamented the diminution of their numbers and acknowledged that almost all abolitionists adhered to the Liberty Party.[30] As mentioned earlier, Garrison was even losing his African

American constituency. Overseas observers recognized the decline. Englishman Joseph Sturge told a friend "that G's [Garrison's] was a very small party, that the finest minds among the Abl's in the U.S. ranged themselves under the 'Liberty' banner. Mr. [John] Scoble said the same at a large public meeting . . . I heard a quaker describing to Mr. S. the bad character of the 'Liberator.'"[31]

Garrison's strictures against the churches and clergy hurt him as much as his stands on disunionism and Liberty Party politics. Another Englishman, Garrisonian sympathizer Dr. John Bishop Estlin, believed that Garrison was *"going out of his way* to make himself unpopular."[32] Eunice Dosman, an Old Organization stalwart, described a typical situation for Garrison when she wrote about abolitionism in Maine in 1843: "Last year I found thirteen persons in four towns who would receive the Liberator gratis; now I know of only two. The Standard of liberty [Austin Willey's *Liberty Standard*] is read by a few, and the Editor of the same has given the people in Kennebunk two lectures but old organized abolition is cast out and abhored [sic]. The people verily believe that Garrison is an infidel, and Quincy a blasphemer."[33] By 1845, Garrison himself realized that he had lost much of his support. When he announced to a friend that he was advocating "a total separation from Church and State, and a warfare upon both," he realized that "[i]t will cause further reduction of our numbers (though, thank Heaven! We have not many more to lose)."[34]

Not all Garrisonians left him. Samuel Joseph May, an ardent friend of Garrison, "had vigorously opposed the Liberty Party," but his position "had changed by February 1846. He informed Maria Weston Chapman that despite his rejection of 'political partyism' he would attend meetings of the Liberty party . . . The next year he began working closely with the party."[35] Still, he remained on good terms with Garrison. Nonetheless, Garrison and some of those who worked closely with him were regarded as extremists, cranks, and misfits even within the small abolition community. Liberty Party followers had to defend themselves constantly against charges that associated them with Garrisonian ideas. As Herman Von Holst wrote at the end of the nineteenth century, "[A]bolitionists generally were held responsible for every word uttered by Garrison, who, after all, was only the leader of the small extreme wing."[36]

Disunionism had a deep effect on the Garrisonian Ohio American Anti-Slavery Society. Shortly after the American Anti-Slavery Society had adopted Garrison's disunion position, the Ohio American Anti-Slavery Society held its anniversary meeting. Several members objected to their society's remaining affiliated with the parent society because of its disunionism. The critics were outnumbered, but in the end the society was weakened by losses of Liberty men and other voting abolitionists. The Garrisonian loyalists acknowledged that they were few, but they continued working under the stricter principles.[37] To bolster their numbers and morale, Abby Kelley arrived from the East in June 1845 ready to do battle with the Liberty Party and purge its influence from the Ohio American Anti-Slavery Society.[38] Within a year she succeeded in driving virtually all of the Liberty influence from the organization, including its president, who declined to run for reelection in 1846.[39] When Kelley came to Ohio, one of her stated purposes was to counteract the influence of the Liberty Party, and the trip did reignite Garrisonian and disunionist sympathies. She quickly helped establish Old Organization antislavery societies and aided in setting up a Garrisonian newspaper, the (Salem, Ohio) *Anti-Slavery Bugle*.[40]

She was later joined by another well-known lecturer from the East, Stephen S. Foster. They were a memorable pair, the outspoken Kelley and the striking Foster, whom one local paper described as "a fanatic, out and out. His forehead is small and contracted, the hair growing down almost to his eyes, and if we were traveling with him in a stage coach, we would be sure to keep our hands upon our pocketbook."[41] They were successful, however, in resuscitating Garrisonian ideals in much of Ohio, although their efforts around the Chase-Bailey stronghold in Cincinnati met with little success. They attempted to counteract the influence of the Liberty Party–oriented Ohio Anti-Slavery Society with a Southwestern Anti-Slavery Society, but the effort was virtually stillborn.[42] Nonetheless, Kelley and Foster hurt the Liberty Party in Ohio. They "overcame Bailey's influence and converted Ohio Garrisonians, who had previously opposed disunionism. They also converted significant numbers of Liberty men and half the executive committee of the Ohio Anti-Slavery Society."[43] They had less success on their two trips to Oberlin College. During the second one in September, they had a series of lively debates with its president, Asa Mahan, a strong Liberty supporter. The historian of the college has reported that the "Fosters were past masters in the art of public, oral abuse, and Mahan was no amateur at recrimination" and "that not a single one of the male leaders of the Oberlin community or alumni was a Garrisonian."[44] Neither side seems to have made any inroads with the other. After they left, the *Oberlin Evangelist* declared that "[t]he Faculty concur fully in regarding them as unsafe advocates of the slave."[45]

By the end of their stay in fall 1846, the Ohio American Anti-Slavery Society was renamed the Western Anti-Slavery Society at its annual meeting. Abby Kelley then discovered that she was pregnant, and the couple returned to the East. Their activities began the second phase of Garrisonian influence in Ohio, and it would be characterized by increasing strength. The tour also had another more humorous side that illustrated the tensions in the East between the Garrison group and the Liberty Party. When several Liberty newspapers announced that fiery Abby Kelley had married the uncompromising Stephen Foster—who frequently was bodily ejected from religious and abolition meetings where he attempted to speak—Old Organization newspapers cried foul.[46] The *Liberator* castigated Liberty editors for lack of taste in circulating the false rumor, and the *National Anti-Slavery Standard* declared that "[i]t was a lie, it seems, of some Liberty party paper, got up for the purpose of perpetuating a silly and witless joke."[47] Neither paper reacted when the happy couple announced their betrothal.

As the Liberty Party gained strength and the Garrisonians lost support in the Northeast during the 1840s, Liberty men paid less attention to their rivals. Garrison maintained only isolated pockets of strength—Boston, western New York in the Rochester area, and eastern Pennsylvania.[48] The *Liberator*, the *National Anti-Slavery Standard*, and the *Pennsylvania Freeman*—three newspapers friendly to Garrison and the Old Organization—continued to criticize the Liberty Party, but by the mid-1840s most Liberty men ignored them. Former Liberty vice presidential candidate Thomas Earle was an exception, as he continued to attend conventions of the Old Organization Eastern Pennsylvania Anti-Slavery Society and wrote articles denouncing the disunionists that the *Pennsylvania Freeman* eventually refused to publish.[49] He was definitely in the minority at these conventions. At the eighth annual meeting of the Eastern Pennsylvania Anti-Slavery Society in August 1845, a resolution espousing disunionism passed 442–188.[50] Nevertheless, he continued to attend, causing Garrison to comment on one occasion that "Thomas Earle was there to annoy us as usual."[51] He participated and contributed funds until his death in 1849, but held no office after 1844. No mention was made of his death, and, in the words of his biographer, he "had been completely ostracized and apparently forgotten by this Society which he had worked so hard to promote."[52] At the same time, Stephen S. Foster and some other Garrisonians continued to attend Liberty meetings, but were often given little chance to speak and sometimes had to be physically removed because of their disruptive behavior.[53]

Aside from Garrison's pique at some Liberty men, the major criticism that his group of abolitionists leveled at the party was that it was willing to recognize and work under the U.S. Constitution, which he characterized as a "covenant with death."[54] Conversely, a major criticism of Garrison by Liberty men was that he had forgotten about the slave. As David Grimsted has succinctly expressed it, "Yet had Garrison exerted controlling influence after 1840, slavery would not have been tied to politics, the North would have allowed (if not initiated) secession, and slaves would have had to take care of their own freedom as best they could."[55] Garrisonians preached that Liberty men were in error for working within a corrupt system. A resolution adopted at the twelfth annual meeting of the American Anti-Slavery Society in 1846 outlined his position "that no party in the country can be a Liberty party, except in name, but must, from the nature of the alliance, be a pro-slavery in fact, which seeks office and power under the present Constitution of the United States."[56]

Liberty men occasionally responded to such criticism, but they were more concerned with being identified with Garrisonian principles. Massachusetts Liberty men, weary of being tarred as disunionists, took a novel approach to the problem. Led by Samuel Sewall, Henry B. Stanton, Joshua Leavitt, and Joseph Lovejoy, they petitioned the Massachusetts legislature "asking that the residences and names of all petitioners for the dissolution of the Union may be printed 'in order that the whole people may know how many, and who they are.'"[57] Nevertheless, disunion arguments may have influenced the willingness of many of them to accept the constitutional theories that proclaimed the U.S. Constitution an antislavery document. Garrison's criticism of the clergy and churches, begun in the 1830s, also continued unabated. A Vermont correspondent wrote him that "[t]he name GARRISON is a dreadful name in the ears of the religious community."[58] Old Organization denunciations of Liberty men continued until the party was long out of existence, but the hostility was generally confined to the East. Garrisonians were convinced that Liberty men from the Old Northwest were very different from the eastern wing of the party.[59] The *National Anti-Slavery Standard* believed that western Liberty men were "always honest in the main," and were "learning the principle, or want of principle, of the eastern branch of the party is not in accordance with the idea of morality or expediency."[60] Garrison himself felt that Liberty Party members in Ohio were friendlier than in the East.[61] He was able to discover this firsthand the year after Abby Kelley and Stephen Foster returned from Ohio.

Garrison followed the newlyweds with a tour of his own in 1847.[62] He traveled with Frederick Douglass, and they reinforced the Kelley-Foster message as they toured Ohio. He arrived at Oberlin in time for the college commencement exercises before an "immense" audience. He reported that "[t]wo of the graduates took occasion in their addresses, to denounce 'the fanaticism of Come-outerism and Disunionism,' and to make a thrust at those, who, in the guise of anti-slavery, temperance, &c. are endeavoring to promote 'infidelity'!" Garrison then debated Asa Mahan in front of packed audiences of approximately three thousand people. They debated come-outerism and the U.S. Constitution, with Mahan taking the position that the Constitution was an antislavery instrument that was capable of eliminating slavery and Garrison affirming his belief in disunionism. The event was not marked by the hostility of the previous year, although these debates did not change the minds of any of the principles. Garrison commented that "[h]e [Mahan] was perfectly respectful, and submitted to our interrogations with good temper and courtesy." He found his adversary "adroit and plausible, but neither vigorous nor profound."[63] A Mahan sympathizer held a different view. "The reply of Prest. Mahan was masterly and dignified, overturning and scattering to the winds every position of his opponent, until we judged from his flushed countenance and agitated manner, Mr. Garrison himself might have truly said with Othello. 'My occupation's gone!'"[64]

The degree to which Garrisonian incursions into the antislavery movement in Ohio hurt the Liberty Party and cut into its strength is debatable, but it seems clear that it had a noticeable effect. Garrisonians came away from the Oberlin confrontations with female converts that included Sallie Holley, the daughter of Liberty Party founder Myron Holley, and Lucy Stone. They also enrolled many former Liberty followers, women, nonvoting Quakers, and others. Nevertheless, Ohio was an isolated example of some Garrisonian success in the Northwest during the Liberty Party's existence. With few exceptions, Liberty groups conducted most of the organized antislavery work in the region.

Even with the success in Ohio, the Old Organization made few new inroads and continued to lose support. While many who remained in the Old Organization refused to participate in politics and believed that the Union should be dissolved because the Constitution was a pro-slavery document, some members continued to vote non-Liberty tickets. Their reasons varied from a dislike of the Liberty leadership to the conviction that political action should play a secondary role to moral suasion. These abolitionists would either scatter their votes on write-in candidates, set up independent antislavery tickets that were not affiliated with the Liberty Party, or vote for a major party. Such tactics were not unusual in 1840 and 1841, but they declined as the 1840s progressed when the great majority of these voting abolitionists joined the Liberty Party, returned to their old parties, or gave up politics. The early tactics did not die out completely, however, as a small number of voters continued to scatter their ballots and some abolitionists in eastern Pennsylvania put independent non-Liberty slates into nomination as late as 1844.[65]

Much animosity existed between the Old Organization and the Liberty Party, but to say that there was bitter hatred between all members of both groups would be erroneous even in strife-torn Massachusetts. For instance, Samuel Sewall remained in the Old Organization for a number of years even though he was a member of the Liberty state central committee and was running for governor in Massachusetts on the Liberty ticket because he believed in the primacy of moral suasion. John G. Whittier maintained cordial relationships with most Old Organization members. And Old Organization newspapers had kind words for

Samuel Fessenden, claiming that there was "no man connected with the Liberty Party, for whom we entertain more respect and esteem."[66] There was also respect of a more material kind. Garrison and Wendell Phillips sent Gamaliel Bailey one hundred dollars on behalf of the Massachusetts Anti-Slavery Society to help replace the printing press for the *Philanthropist* after it had been destroyed by a mob in 1841, even though they "very seriously differed in opinion with the Philanthropist."[67] Garrison even seemed to enjoy some of the exchanges. After spending an evening in late 1842 discussing the third party with Alvan Stewart and James C. Jackson, a recent Liberty recruit from the Old Organization, Garrison wrote happily to his wife that he had "made them both rather uneasy; for poor James evidently felt that he stood on a sandy foundation."[68]

Nevertheless, the dominant feeling between the two groups was hostility, and mutual criticisms were often personal and biting. The strong opposition of the remaining Old Organization members to an antislavery political party virtually ceased with the Free Soil merger in 1848, but hard feelings for the Liberty Party remained. Edmund Quincy—whom Elizur Wright described as "the noble and gentle, the well descended and wealthy, the man who writes antislavery articles in a New England palace and lives on the interest of money earned by his ancestor"[69]—summed up the dominant Garrisonian feeling for the Liberty Party shortly after the Free Soil coalition:

> But throughout its course, and in all its various phases, it has shown none but a malign aspect to the Anti-Slavery cause. Its influence, as far as it has gone, has been evil, only evil, and that continually. What apparent good it may have done, has been incidental and accidental. It has retarded, not hastened, the very state of political feeling, which has now devoured it up. The Free Soil Party exists, not because, but in spite of it. We believe that an effective political opposition to Slavery would have been embodied, longsince, had not the ground been cumbered with this preposterous faction.[70]

To read this quote one would think that the Liberty Party was a small adjunct, and a hindrance at that, to the antislavery movement. This was just not true. What Dwight Lowell Dumond wrote in 1961 holds true today. "There has been a tendency among historians to belittle the political action of the antislavery men in 1839–40, just as there has been a tendency to think of William L. Garrison as the great leader of the antislavery movement after 1840. *Neither is true.* In fact, nothing could be farther from the truth . . . Only about one-tenth of the antislavery men paid any attention to Garrison."[71] His estimate may have been generous to Garrison and his followers, who were bit players in the abolition movement of the 1840s. His base shrunk to almost nothing, his newspaper readership declined precipitously, and he lived with the financial assistance of a few benefactors. Why his standing among current writers remains so high is somewhat puzzling. Perhaps the availability of abundant Garrisonian resources in pleasant surroundings and the four-volume history of his life by his children with its extensive—although highly selective—primary source documentation provide so much material for the researcher that the Garrisonians appear more important than they actually were.[72] Maybe writers are impressed that some of Garrison's basic positions were so clear-cut and uncompromising and that he followed these premises to their seemingly logical conclusions. There is an ideological purity in refusing to ransom slaves or work under a flawed constitutional system that is intellectually appealing for its consistency. This is certainly a valid approach when examining his positions as philosophical constructs, but to claim that these ideas were influential or had a positive impact on the antislavery movement does not necessarily follow. Many individuals had a far greater impact on the fight against slavery during the 1840s than Garrison did. His contemporaries knew it, but many subsequent historians have accorded him influence that he did not have.[73] In fact, a case can be made that he actually retarded the development of a slave-centered movement during these years.

AFTERWORD

The primary purpose of this book has been to present a comprehensive narrative of the institutional history of the Liberty Party. Nonetheless, the study would not be complete without some evaluation of the Liberty Party's place in both American politics before the Civil War and antislavery reform. Sometimes such reflections become theories that are not supported by the research, but I deliberately try to minimize such speculations even though some evidence points in certain directions. Thus I focus on politics and antislavery reform during the 1840s and only tangentially on later developments. This task is large enough.

As we have seen, few of the leading historians of American politics of the 1840s have paid much attention to the Liberty Party. The reader who examines the indexes of most of their studies finds few references to the party, and these are usually confined to its dismal performance in 1840, its causing Henry Clay's defeat in New York State in 1844, and perhaps its part in the Free Soil coalition in 1848. These historians spend little time assessing its influence on slavery's transformation from an issue that was off stage in 1840 to one at center stage in 1848. To a great extent, the same is true in antislavery studies. With a few exceptions, most make only scattered references to the Liberty Party and neglect the changes in it until the beginning of the Free Soil movement. Even many biographies of Liberty members treat their party experiences cursorily if at all. Indeed, a serious reader could fairly ask how the Liberty movement could be of much importance if it has been so marginalized by many historians of American politics and reform. As the leading historian of American abolition, James Brewer Stewart, has said, "[T]he two fields have lost contact with each other. To read in them simultaneously is to slip back and forth between alternate universes."[1] This study is an attempt to reconcile the two. I began studying the party as a political historian in the early 1970s by collecting town-level voting data and reading the secondary literature on party activities in the upper four New England states. Once

I began delving into the primary sources, I realized that I should have concentrated on just one state and that my dissertation was going to take considerably longer than I had anticipated. I was particularly surprised because the modern historian most directly linked to the party, Aileen Kraditor, consulted few of the rudimentary Liberty sources before writing her highly critical accounts of the party.

In fact, the Liberty Party had a significant role in the changes taking place in both the political and antislavery environments in the three decades before the Civil War. Snapshots of the country in 1830, 1840, 1850, and 1860 show a nation undergoing significant political and social changes. The two-party system that emerged by 1840 was fragmenting by the end of the decade and disintegrated by the 1850s primarily because of attitudes toward slavery and its expansion. While the Liberty Party was not solely responsible for these developments, it brought the slavery issue into national politics in 1840 because of the unwillingness of the major parties to even allow its discussion in Congress. Eight years later, discussion of slavery issues were such a part of national politics that the vast majority of Liberty adherents were willing to abandon their own organization and continue their efforts in less ideologically rigid parties. To quantitatively assess with any accuracy the contribution of the Liberty Party and its attendant organizations to this process is impossible, but it would be naïve to dismiss its role as inconsequential. Change undoubtedly would have come, but it would not have come so quickly.

The neglect by political historians is understandable, however, because they do their work in a large, complicated universe. Perhaps more puzzling is the degree to which the Liberty Party has been forgotten or derided by many historians of abolition. Many general studies or more specialized monographs on antislavery hardly mention the party at all. And few have married the political aspects of the party with its role in the larger abolition movement, almost as if political action tainted the purity of the cause. This minimizes the contributions of those who believed that their moral stewardship necessarily encompassed an involvement in public affairs and voting but could not tolerate their treatment that they were receiving in the political arena. Such voters who insisted on carrying their antislavery convictions to the polls were left with only two viable alternatives by 1840 after the failure of the questioning system and being ignored by the two major parties. They could either scatter their votes among a variety of write-in candidates or set up a formal organization to challenge Whigs and Democrats. Most abolitionists made neither choice in 1840. The death of William Henry Harrison and the elevation of John Tyler to the presidency, however, caused many of them to move to the new party, especially in areas that did not have someone like Joshua Giddings, William Slade, Roger Baldwin, or John Quincy Adams to vote for. At the same time, the Liberty movement moved beyond electoral politics to encompass other aspects of abolitionism.

As the 1844 election approached, Northern Whigs found it necessary both to accommodate their antislavery members and to win back former allies who had defected to the new party. These efforts met with some success, especially after Henry Clay's narrow defeat gave the presidency to hard-line Southerner James K. Polk. Party numbers did not suffer, however, as these Whigs were replaced by former Democrats who were disillusioned by their party's pro-slavery stands and encouraged by the Democratic orientation of some Liberty theorists. This smoothed the way for most party members to become part of the Free Soil coalition.

Party members also worked to expand the party's influence in the larger abolition movement. This effort began in the early years, and they were increasingly successful as the party matured among many of those reluctant to commit themselves to such an overtly political organization. William Lloyd Garrison's strident denunciation of the U.S. Constitution and embrace of a nonresistant philosophy alienated many from the American Anti-Slavery Society. This combined with the declining influence of the American and Foreign Anti-Slavery Society created a void that left abolitionists with no other effective national or statewide vehicle except Liberty-related activities. These appeals were particularly well received by women and African Americans. These parts of the Liberty movement suffered the most as the political segment of the party committed itself in the Free Soil movement, which did not have such auxiliary groups.

To generalize about the Liberty electorate is difficult because of its changes over time. The relative stability in its statewide numbers is deceptive because so many former Democrats entered the party as former Whigs returned to their old party. Statewide numbers changed little, but studies have shown that the components of the vote changed substantially as some towns suffered a serious decline in Liberty strength while others added significant new votes. This volatility in the Liberty electorate was often reflected when former Democrats served as candidates and in important positions. One major problem in many analyses of the party is that they are rooted at one point of time, usually the early 1840s. This does not take into account the changing membership and political philosophies as they became more Democratic and, in some areas, more oriented toward the workingmen's movement.

That a more secular orientation emerged, however, did not negate the religious strain in the party that existed from its inception. The overwhelming majority of Liberty men were churchgoers—itself unusual in the 1840s—and the overwhelming majority were evangelical, as were, according to Richard Carwardine, "well over 90 percent of all Protestants."[2] Most of these were liturgically indistinguishable from those who did not carry their antislavery convictions to the ballot box. Upstate New York abolitionists were not typical of the total Liberty environment with their unique approach to religion and politics. In fact, a substantial portion of identifiable Liberty men had mainline Protestant affiliations. Indeed, some party members changed their religious outlooks during the 1840s. Historians should be very careful in generalizing on the strains of Christian morality in the party because it varied widely among individuals and from area to area where local leaders often left their imprint on party affairs.

Some political abolitionists supported the Liberty Party because they saw it as a means to pressure a major party to adopt a less tolerant position on slavery. As the Whig Party became more receptive to the antislavery message, many rejoined it. Other political abolitionists made a more complete break and conceived of the abolition party as a permanent part of the American political system. They only abandoned it for an entirely new, albeit less rigid, political party that was unfriendly to slavery, the Free Soil Party. Even so, a small minority that considered themselves the "true" Liberty Party, the Liberty League, refused to participate in the new movement and continued as an independent, permanent entity. There was less movement away from the party among its leaders, whose stability masks the volatility of the mass electorate. This instability makes too precise generalizations on the character of the movement misleading.

The Liberty Party has been criticized for many things—political naïveté, ideological inconsistency, the election of an ardent slaveholder in 1844, paternalism, opportunism—but perhaps the greatest tragedy is not mentioned: the huge void it left in the antislavery movement after it became a part of the Free Soil coalition. Its many nonpolitical activities quickly ceased because there were no parallel auxiliary groups within Free Soil to match the all-inclusive Liberty Associations or women's support groups. Some of these local organizations labored on for a time, but they lacked the centralized state and national focuses that the Liberty organization afforded. The result was a much more multifaceted antislavery movement during the 1850s without any one group able to lay claim to speaking for a substantial portion of antislavery reform.

Appendix A

RESULTS BY PARTY OF MAJOR STATEWIDE RACES, 1840–1848

This appendix lists the number and percentage of votes garnered by each party in races for president, governor, and territorial delegate to Congress in states and territories where the Liberty Party had a significant presence. Data for gubernatorial territorial congressional delegate elections are from various sources. Data for Gubernatorial Elections are from W. Dean Burnham, *Presidential Ballots, 1836–1892* (Baltimore: Johns Hopkins Press, 1955).

Results for Massachusetts, Maine, and Vermont

	MASSACHUSETTS	MAINE	VERMONT
1840 Gubernatorial Elections			
Liberty Party	1,081 (0.8%)		
Whig Party	70,844 (55.6%)	45,574 (50.0%)	33,653 (59.4%)
Democratic Party	55,169 (43.3%)	45,507 (49.9%)	23,000 (40.6%)
Other	181 (0.1%)	98 (00.1%)	
1840 Presidential Election			
Liberty Party	1,618 (1.3%)	194 (0.2%)	319 (0.6%)
Whig Party	72,874 (57.6%)	46,612 (50.1%)	32,445 (63.9%)
Democratic Party	51,954 (41.1%)	46,201 (49.7%)	18,009 (35.5%)
1841 Gubernatorial Elections			
Liberty Party	3,488 (3.1%)	1,662 (1.9%)	3,039 (6.3%)
Whig Party	55,974 (50.4%)	36,780 (42.7%)	23,353 (48.7%)
Democratic Party	51,367 (46.3%)	47,354 (55.0%)	21,302 (44.4%)
Other	233 (0.2%)	347 (0.4%)	248 (0.6%)

Results for Massachusetts, Maine, and Vermont (continued)

	MASSACHUSETTS	MAINE	VERMONT
1842 Gubernatorial Elections			
Liberty Party	6,382 (5.4%)	4,080 (5.7%)	2,093 (3.9%)
Whig Party	54,939 (46.6%)	26,745 (37.3%)	27,167 (50.9%)
Democratic Party	56,491 (47.9%)	40,855 (56.9%)	24,130 (45.2%)
Other	180 (0.2%)	109 (0.2%)	35 (0.1%)
1843 Gubernatorial Elections			
Liberty Party	8,903 (7.3%)	4,962 (10.0%)	3,766 (7.5%)
Whig Party	57,899 (47.7%)	17,244 (34.6%)	24,465 (48.7%)
Democratic Party	54,242 (44.7%)	27,631 (55.4%)	21,982 (43.8%)
Other	246 (0.2%)		21 (0.04%)
1844 Gubernatorial Elections			
Liberty Party	9,734 (7.3%)	5,527 (7.0%)	5,618 (10.2%)
Whig Party	69,570 (51.8%)	33,342 (42.0%)	28,265 (51.5%)
Democratic Party	54,714 (41.0%)	40,540 (51.1%)	20,930 (38.2%)
Other	204 (0.2%)		34 (0.1%)
1844 Presidential Election			
Liberty Party	10,815 (8.3%)	4,836 (5.7%)	3,894 (8.0%)
Whig Party	67,521 (51.8%)	34,378 (40.4%)	26,770 (55.0%)
Democratic Party	52,146 (40.0%)	45,719 (53.8%)	17,994 (37.0%)
1845 Gubernatorial Elections			
Liberty Party	8,316 (7.9%)	5,592 (9.0%)	6,534 (13.5%)
Whig Party	51,638 (48.8%)	24,880 (40.2%)	22,770 (47.2%)
Democratic Party	37,427 (35.3%)	31,353 (50.7%)	18,594 (38.5%)
Other	8,543 (8.1%)		362 (0.8%)
1846 Gubernatorial Elections			
Liberty Party	9,997 (9.8%)	9,343 (13.0%)	7,118 (14.6%)
Whig Party	54,813 (53.4%)	28,986 (40.2%)	23,644 (48.5%)
Democratic Party	33,199 (32.6%)	33,805 (46.9%)	17,877 (36.7%)
Other	3,907 (3.8%)		64 (0.1%)
1847 Gubernatorial Elections			
Liberty Party	9,157 (8.7%)	7,517 (11.5%)	6,926 (14.4%)
Whig Party	53,742 (50.1%)	24,304 (37.2%)	22,455 (46.7%)
Democratic Party	39,398 (37.4%)	33,461 (51.3%)	18,601 (38.7%)
Other	3,110 (3.0%)		98 (0.2%)
1848 Presidential Election			
Free Soil Party	38,058 (28.3%)	12,096 (13.9%)	14,337 (29.6%)
Whig Party	61,070 (45.4%)	35,125 (40.3%)	23,122 (47.8%)
Democratic Party	35,281 (26.2%)	39,830 (45.8%)	10,948 (22.6%)

Results for New Hampshire, Connecticut, and Pennsylvania

	NEW HAMPSHIRE	CONNECTICUT	PENNSYLVANIA
1840 Presidential Election			
Liberty Party	126 (0.2%)	57 (0.1%)	343 (0.1%)
Whig Party	26,297 (44.4%)	31,598 (55.5%)	144,018 (50.0%)
Democratic Party	32,801 (55.4%)	25,283 (44.4%)	143,675 (49.9%)
1841 Gubernatorial Elections			
Liberty Party	1,273 (2.5%)		763 (0.3%)
Whig Party	21,178 (40.8%)	26,078 (56.0%)	113,473 (45.3%)
Democratic Party	29,453 (56.7%)	20,458 (44.0%)	136,504 (54.4%)
Other	10 (0.02%)		22 (0.009%)
1842 Gubernatorial Elections			
Liberty Party	2,756 (5.7%)	1,989 (3.8%)	
Whig Party	12,364 (25.7%)	23,700 (46.2%)	
Democratic Party	26,830 (55.8%)	25,564 (49.9%)	
Other	6,152 (12.8%)		
1843 Gubernatorial Elections			
Liberty Party	3,416 (7.7%)	1,872 (3.4%)	
Whig Party	12,561 (28.2%)	25,591 (46.6%)	
Democratic Party	23,052 (51.7%)	27,416 (49.9%)	
Other	5,530 (12.4%)	49 (0.09%)	
1844 Gubernatorial Elections			
Liberty Party	5,737 (11.7%)	1,971 (3.2%)	2,576 (0.8%)
Whig Party	14,794 (30.3%)	30,093 (49.4%)	156,040 (48.9%)
Democratic Party	26,155 (53.5%)	28,845 (47.4%)	160,322 (50.3%)
Other	2,158 (4.4%)		
1844 Presidential Election			
Liberty Party	4,161 (8.5%)	1,943 (3.0%)	3,152 (1.0%)
Whig Party	17,866 (36.3%)	32,832 (50.8%)	160,384 (48.4%)
Democratic Party	27,160 (55.2%)	29,841 (46.2%)	167,394 (50.6%)
1845 Gubernatorial Elections			
Liberty Party	5,464 (12.0%)	2,142 (3.7%)	
Whig Party	15,591 (34.4%)	29,508 (51.0%)	
Democratic Party	23,298 (48.6%)	26,258 (45.3%)	
Other	1,024 (2.3%)		
1846 Gubernatorial Elections			
Liberty Party	10,406 (18.8%)	1,750 (3.4%)	
Whig Party	17,704 (32.0%)	25,344 (49.0%)	
Democratic Party	26,914 (48.6%)	24,586 (47.6%)	
Other	368 (0.7%)		

Results for New Hampshire, Connecticut, and Pennsylvania (*continued*)

	NEW HAMPSHIRE	CONNECTICUT	PENNSYLVANIA
	1847 Gubernatorial Elections		
Liberty Party	8,531 (14.1%)	2,135 (3.6%)	1,861 (0.6%)
Whig Party	21,109 (34.9%)	30,137 (50.7%)	128,148 (44.6%)
Democratic Party	30,806 (50.9%)	27,135 (45.7%)	146,081 (50.8%)
Other	54 (0.1%)		11,253 (3.9%)
	1848 Presidential Election		
Free Soil Party	7,560 (15.1%)	5,029 (8.1%)	11,273 (3.1%)
Whig Party	14,781 (29.5%)	30,318 (48.6%)	185,423 (50.2%)
Democratic Party	27,763 (55.4%)	27,051 (43.4%)	172,704 (46.8%)

Results for New York, Michigan, and Ohio

	NEW YORK	MICHIGAN	OHIO
	1840 Presidential Election		
Liberty Party	2,943 (0.7%)	321 (0.7%)	903 (0.3%)
Whig Party	226,013 (51.2%)	22,933 (51.7%)	148,043 (54.3%)
Democratic Party	212,736 (48.2%)	21,096 (47.6%)	123,944 (45.4%)
	1841 Gubernatorial Election		
Liberty Party		1,223 (3.2%)	
Whig Party		15,449 (41.0%)	
Democratic Party		20.993 (55.7%)	
	1842 Gubernatorial Elections		
Liberty Party	7,264 (1.8%)		5,134 (2.1%)
Whig Party	186,089 (46.4%)		117,902 (48.5%)
Democratic Party	208,062 (51.8%)		119,774 (49.3%)
Other			40 (49.3%)
	1843 Gubernatorial Election		
Liberty Party		2,776 (7.1%)	
Whig Party		14,899 (38.1%)	
Democratic Party		21,392 (54.7%)	
	1844 Gubernatorial Elections		
Liberty Party	15,136 (3.1%)		8,898 (3.0%)
Whig Party	231,057 (47.4%)		146,333 (48.7%)
Democratic Party	241,090 (49.5%)		145,062 (48.3%)
Other			11 (0.004%)

Results for New York, Michigan, and Ohio (*continued*)

	NEW YORK	MICHIGAN	OHIO
1844 Presidential Election			
Liberty Party	15,814 (3.3%)	3,638 (6.5%)	8,083 (2.6%)
Whig Party	232,452 (47.8%)	24,185 (43.5%)	155,091 (49.7%)
Democratic Party	237,588 (48.9%)	27,737 (49.9%)	149,127 (47.8%)
1845 Gubernatorial Election			
Liberty Party		3,023 (7.7%)	
Whig Party		16,316 (41.3%)	
Democratic Party		20,123 (50.9%)	
1846 Gubernatorial Elections			
Liberty Party	12,844 (3.2%)		10,799 (4.4%)
Whig Party	198,878 (49.1%)		118,857 (48.3%)
Democratic Party	187,306 (46.2%)		116,554 (47.3%)
Other	6,306 (1.6%)		46 (0.02%)
1847 Gubernatorial Election			
Liberty Party		2,585 (5.6%)	
Whig Party		18,990 (41.1%)	
Democratic Party		24,639 (53.3%)	
1848 Presidential Election			
Free Soil Party	120,510 (26.4%)	10,393 (16.0%)	35,523 (10.8%)
Whig Party	218,603 (47.9%)	23,947 (36.8%)	138,656 (42.1%)
Democratic Party	114,320 (25.1%)	30,742 (47.2%)	154,782 (47.1%)
Liberty League	2,545 (0.6%)		
Other	73 (0.02%)		

Results for Illinois, Indiana, and Wisconsin

	ILLINOIS	INDIANA	WISCONSIN
1840 Presidential Election			
Liberty Party	159 (0.2%)		
Whig Party	45,576 (48.9%)	65,307 (55.8%)	
Democratic Party	47,443 (50.9%)	51,789 (44.2%)	
1842 Gubernatorial Election			
Liberty Party	909 (1.1%)		
Whig Party	38,308 (45.2%)		
Democratic Party	45,608 (53.8%)		

Results for Illinois, Indiana, and Wisconsin (*continued*)

	ILLINOIS	INDIANA	WISCONSIN
1843 Gubernatorial and Territorial Delegate to Congress Elections			
Liberty Party		1,684 (1.4%)	152 (1.8%)*
Whig Party		58,701 (48.5%)	3,360 (39.7%)
Democratic Party		60,714 (50.1%)	4,942 (58.5%)
1844 Presidential Election			
Liberty Party	3,433 (3.2%)	2,108 (1.5%)	
Whig Party	45,931 (42.4%)	67,866 (48.4%)	
Democratic Party	58,982 (54.4%)	70,183 (50.1%)	
1845 Territorial Delegate to Congress Election			
Liberty Party			790 (5.9%)
Whig Party			5,787 (43.3%)
Democratic Party			6,803 (50.8%)
1846 Gubernatorial Elections			
Liberty Party	5,147 (5.1%)	2,301 (1.8%)	
Whig Party	36,939 (36.7%)	60,138 (47.5%)	
Democratic Party	58,576 (58.2%)	64,104 (50.7%)	
1847 Territorial Delegate to Congress Election			
Liberty Party			973 (4.5%)
Whig Party			10,670 (49.9%)
Democratic Party			9,748 (45.6%)
1848 Gubernatorial Election			
Liberty Party	4,748 (6.6%)		1,134 (3.2%)
Whig Party			14,621 (41.0%)
Democratic Party	67,453 (93.4%)		19,875 (55.8%)
1848 Presidential Election			
Free Soil Party	15,791 (12.7%)	8,060 (5.3%)	10,423 (26.6%)
Whig Party	52,853 (42.4%)	70,300 (46.0%)	13,747 (38.3%)
Democratic Party	55,915 (44.9%)	74,558 (48.8%)	15,001 (38.3%)

*Wisconsin elected a territorial delegate to Congress in 1843 and 1845.

Appendix B

BANNER LIBERTY COUNTIES, 1844

This appendix lists, by region and state, counties in which the Liberty Party garnered more than 10% of the vote in the presidential election of 1844 or in which the Liberty Party received the highest percentage of the vote in that state.

	LIBERTY VOTE	TOTAL VOTE	LIBERTY %
New England States			
Massachusetts			
Essex	1,887	15,664	12.0%
Worcester	2,147	19,068	11.3%
Hampshire	626	5,956	10.5%
Maine			
Franklin	392	3,133	12.5%
Vermont			
Lamoille	411	1,655	24.8%
Orleans	245	2,270	10.8%
Chittenden	386	3,754	10.3%
New Hampshire			
Merrimack	628	6,038	10.4%
Connecticut			
Windham	363	5,529	6.7%
Middle States			
New York			
Madison	1,311	8,842	14.8%
Cortland	542	5,278	10.3%
Pennsylvania			
Mercer	604	5,313	11.4%

	LIBERTY VOTE	TOTAL VOTE	LIBERTY %
Old Northwest States			
Michigan			
Jackson	475	3,166	15.0%
Shiawassee	96	665	14.4%
Kalamazoo	276	2,036	13.6%
Genesee	183	1,592	11.5%
Ohio			
Lorain	473	4,222	11.2%
Ashtabula	537	5,048	10.6%
Illinois			
DeKalb	131	515	25.4%
Putnam	140	605	23.1%
Bureau	160	908	17.6%
DuPage	173	1,096	15.8%
Winnebago	159	1,074	14.8%
Kane	299	2,093	14.3%
Lake	131	1,137	11.5%
Knox	162	1,597	10.1%
Indiana			
Grant	197	973	20.2%
Randolph	206	1,833	11.2%
Marshall	54	509	10.6%

Appendix C

NATIONAL LIBERTY PARTY PLATFORM, 1844

From Kirk H. Porter and Donald Bruce Johnson (compilers), *National Party Platforms, 1840–1960* (Urbana: University of Illinois Press, 1961), 4–9.

PREAMBLE

Being assembled in general Convention, as the representatives of the Liberty party in the United States, and feeling it incumbent on us to set forth, clearly and fully, the principles which govern us, and the purposes which we seek to accomplish, and this, the rather because these principles and purposes have been much misunderstood, and either ignorantly or maliciously much misrepresented: be it therefore

1. *Resolved,* That human brotherhood is a cardinal doctrine of true Democracy, as well as of pure Christianity, which spurns all inconsistent limitations; and neither the political party which repudiate it, nor the political system which is not based upon it, nor controlled in its practical workings, by it, can be truly Democratic or permanent.

2. *Resolved,* That the Liberty Party, placing itself upon this broad principle, will demand the absolute and unqualified divorce of the General Government from Slavery, and also the restoration of equality of rights, among men, in every State where the party exists, or may exist.

3. *Resolved,* That the Liberty party has not been organized for any temporary purpose, by interested politicians, but has arisen from among the people, in consequence of a conviction, hourly gaining ground, that no other party in the country represents the true principles of American Liberty, or the true spirit of the Constitution of the United States.

4. *Resolved,* That the Liberty party has not been organized merely for the overthrow of Slavery. Its first decided effort must indeed be directed against slaveholding, as the grossest form and most revolting manifestation of Despotism; but it will also carry out the principles of Equal Rights, into all their practical consequences and applications, and support every just measure conducive to individual and social freedom.

5. *Resolved,* That the Liberty party is not a Sectional party, but a National party—has not originated in a desire to accomplish a single object, but in a comprehensive regard to the great interests of the whole country—is not a new party, or a third party, but is the party of 1776, reviving the principles of that memorable era, and striving to carry them into practical application.

6. *Resolved,* That it was understood in the time of the Declaration and the Constitution, that the existence of slavery in some of the States, was in derogation of the principles of American Liberty, and a deep stain upon the character of the country, and the implied faith of the States and the Nation was pledged, that slavery should never be extended beyond its then existing limits; but should be gradually, and, yet, at no distant day, wholly abolished by State authority.

7. *Resolved,* That the faith of the States, and the nation they pledged, was most nobly redeemed by the voluntary abolition of slavery in several of the States, and by the adoption of the ordinance of 1787, for the government of the Territory North West of the river Ohio, then the only Territory in the United States, and consequently the only Territory subject in this respect to the control of Congress, by which ordinance slavery was forever excluded from the vast regions which now compose the States of Ohio, Indiana, Illinois, Michigan, and the Territory of Wiskonsin, and an incapacity to bear up any other than freemen, was impressed on the soil itself.

8. *Resolved,* That the faith of the States and Nation thus pledged, has been shamefully violated by the omission, on the part of many of the States, to take any measures whatever for the abolition of slavery within their respective limits; by the continuance of slavery in the District of Columbia, and in the Territories of Louisiana and Florida; by the legislation of Congress; by the protection afforded by national legislation and negotiation to slaveholding in American vessels, on the high seas, employed in the coastwise slave traffic; and by the extension of slavery far beyond its original limits, by acts of Congress, admitting new slave states into the Union.

9. *Resolved,* That the fundamental truths of the Declaration of Independence, that all men are endowed by their Creator with certain inalienable rights, among which are life, liberty, and the pursuit of happiness, was made the fundamental law of our National Government, by that amendment of the Constitution which

declares that no person shall be deprived of life, liberty, or property, without due process of law.

10. *Resolved,* That we recognize as sound, the doctrine maintained by slaveholding Jurists, that slavery is against natural rights, and strictly local, and that its existence and continuance rest on no other support than State legislation, and not on any authority of Congress.

11. *Resolved,* That the General Government has, under the Constitution, no power to establish or continue slavery any where, and therefore that all treaties and acts of Congress establishing, continuing or favoring slavery in the District of Columbia, in the Territory of Florida, or on the high seas, are unconstitutional, and all attempts to hold men as property within the limits of exclusive national jurisdiction, ought to be prohibited by law.

12. *Resolved,* That the plea sometimes urged, in behalf of the constitutionality of slaveholding under the sanction of national legislation, that the continuance of slavery was secured in the District of Columbia, by stipulations in the deeds of cession by Virginia and Maryland, and in Florida by provisions of the Treaty with Spain is false in fact; and the other plea, sometimes urged to the same purpose, that Congress might constitutionally authorize slaveholding in the District under the power to legislate for the same in all cases whatsoever, and in Florida under the power to make needful rules and regulations for the government of national territories, and in American vessels on the seas under the power to regulate commerce, cannot be sound in law, so long as the great Interdict of the People against depriving *any person* of life, liberty, or property, without due process of law, remains unaltered.

13. *Resolved,* That the provision of the Constitution of the United States, which confers extraordinary political powers on the owner of slaves, and thereby constituting the two hundred and fifty thousand slaveholders in the slave States a privileged aristocracy; and the provision for the reclamation of fugitive slaves from service, are anti-republican in their character, dangerous to the liberties of the people, and ought to be abrogated.

14. *Resolved,* That the operation of the first of these provisions is seen in the growth of a power in the country hostile to free institutions, to free labor, and to freedom itself, which is appropriately denominated the slave power; this power has maintained slavery in the original States, has secured its continuance in the District and in the Territories, has created seven new slave States, has caused disastrous fluctuations in our national policy, foreign and domestic, has gradually usurped the control of our home legislation, has waged unrelenting war against the most sacred rights of freedom, has violated and set at naught the right of petition, has dictated the action of political parties, has filled almost all the offices

of the National Government with slaveholders, and threatens, if not arrested in its career, the total overthrow of popular freedom.

15. *Resolved,* That the practical operation of the second of these provisions, is seen in the enactment of the act of Congress respecting persons escaped from their masters, which act, if the construction given to it by the Supreme Court of the United States in the case of Prigg *vs.* Pennsylvania be correct, nullifies the habeas corpus acts of all the States, takes away the whole legal security of personal freedom, and ought therefore to be immediately repealed.

16. *Resolved,* That the peculiar patronage and support hitherto extended to slavery and slaveholding, by the General Government, ought to be immediately withdrawn, and the example and influence of national authority ought to be arrayed on the side of Liberty and free labor.

17. *Resolved,* That we cherish no harsh or unkind feelings toward any of our brethren of the slave States, while we express unmitigated abhorrence of that system of slaveholding which has stripped a large portion of their population of every right, and which has established an aristocracy worse than feudal in the midst of Republican States, and which denies to the poor non-slaveholder and his children the benefits of education, and crushes them in the dust, or drives them out as exiles from the land of their birth.

18. *Resolved,* That the impoverished and embarrassed condition of the slave States, so much deplored by their own statesmen, may be clearly traced to the fact that the coerced, reluctant, and ill-directed labor of slaves will not supply their own scanty subsistence, and also support their masters in the habits of wasteful extravagance which slavery generates.

19. *Resolved,* That the withering and impoverishing effect of slavery on the free States, is seen in the fact, among many others, that these States are taxed to the amount of about half a million dollars a year, to pay the deficits of the slave States, and that the slave States have received, for years past, to the amount, as it is estimated, of more than ten millions of dollars a year, for which no payment has ever been, or ever will be made.

20. *Resolved,* That we behold with sorrow and shame, and indignation, the dishonor brought upon the name of the country by the influence of the slave power upon our National Government—corrupting its administration at home—paralyzing all generous action and utterance in behalf of right and freedom abroad, and exhibiting the American people to the world in the ridiculous and contemptible character of patrons of the slave trade.

21. *Resolved,* That we are inflexibly opposed to that policy of the General Government, which plies every art, and strains every effort of negotiation, to se-

cure the markets of the world for the products of free labor, while the products of free labor are to a great extent, confined to the non-paying market of the slave States; and we insist that it is the duty of the Government, in its intercourse with foreign nations, to employ all its influence, and to exert its utmost energies to extend the markets for the products of free labor, and we do not doubt that if this duty be performed in good faith, the result will be most auspicious to the general and permanent prosperity of the country.

22. *Resolved,* That we are fully persuaded that it is indispensably necessary to the salvation of the union of the States, to the preservation of the liberties of the people, and to the permanent restoration of prosperity in every department of business, that the National Government be rescued from the grasp of the slave power; that the spirit and practice of slaveholding be expelled from our National Legislature, and that the administration of the Government be conducted henceforth in conformity with the principles of the Constitution, and for the benefit of the whole population.

23. *Resolved,* That the practice of the General Government, which prevails in the slave States, of employing slaves upon the public works, instead of free laborers, and paying aristocratic masters, with a view to secure or reward political services is utterly indefensible, and ought to be abandoned.

24. *Resolved,* That we believe intelligence, religion, and morality, to be the indispensable supports of good government, and are therefore in favor of general education; we believe, also, that good government itself is necessary to the welfare of society, and are therefore in favor of rigid public economy, and strict adherence to the principles of justice in every department of its administration.

25. *Resolved,* That freedom of speech and of the press, and the right of petition, and the right of trial by jury, are sacred and inviolable; and that all rules, regulations, and laws, in derogation of either are oppressive, unconstitutional, and not to be endured by a free people.

26. *Resolved,* That we regard voting in an eminent degree, as a moral and religious duty, which when exercised, should be by voting for those who will do all in their power for immediate emancipation.

27. *Resolved,* That we can never lose our vote, although in ever so small a minority, when cast for the slave's redemption; as each vote for the slave, whether in minority or majority, is a part of that great mass of means which will work out his final deliverance.

28. *Resolved,* That the Whig and Democratic parties always throw away their votes, whether in a majority or minority, and do worse than throw them away, as long as they cast them for binding the slave with fetters, and loading him with

chains, and for depriving him of himself, his wife, and his children, which these parties always have done, in bowing down to the slaveholding portions of said parties.

29. *Resolved,* That we especially entreat the friends of Liberty in the slave States to reflect on the vast importance of voting openly for Liberty, and Liberty men; and to remember and adopt the words of the illustrious Washington, who said, "There is but one proper and effectual mode by which the abolition of slavery can be accomplished, and that is by legislative authority; and this, as far as my suffrage will go, shall not be wanting."

30. *Resolved,* That we earnestly exhort the Liberty men everywhere, to organize for efficient action in their respective States, counties, cities, towns, and districts, and not to turn to the right side or to the left, until despotism shall have been driven from its last entrenchment, and thanksgivings for victory in the second great struggle for Liberty and Independence shall be heard throughout the land.

31. *Resolved,* That we most earnestly recommend that the Liberty party make efforts to secure the control of town power, so that every officer shall be a Liberty party man; and that our friends should not fail to nominate a Liberty ticket annually in their towns, and sustain the same, never yielding to a compromise with the other parties.

32. *Resolved,* That a county and State organization of the Liberty party should be faithfully maintained; and we also recommend that our friends employ some proper person to lecture, organize, and distribute tracts in each Congressional district, in the several States, for the space of at least three months in a year.

33. *Resolved,* That the friends of Liberty in each town form tract organizations of men and women, to distribute tracts in every family in such towns, by directing the labors of said tract distribution, so that no neighborhood or family be overlooked or unsupplied.

34. *Resolved,* That it be recommended that said tract distributors circulate petitions through the several towns, praying Congress to abolish the abominable act of Congress, of the 12th of February, 1793, so that we may be delivered from the unconstitutional obligation to become kidnappers on our own soil.

35. *Resolved,* That this Convention recommend to the friends of Liberty in all those free States where any inequality of rights and privileges exist on account of color, to employ their utmost energies to remove all such remnants and effects of the slave system.

36. *Resolved,* That we cordially welcome our colored fellow citizens to fraternity with us in the *Liberty party,* in its great contest to secure the rights of mankind, and the religion of our common country.

37. *Whereas,* The Constitution of these United States is a series of agreements, covenants, or contracts between the people of the United States, each with all, and all with each, and

Whereas, It is a principle of universal morality, that the moral laws of the Creator are paramount to all human laws; or in the language of an apostle, that "we ought to obey God, rather than men";—and

Whereas, The principle of Common Law—that any contract, covenant, or agreement, to do an act derogatory to natural right, is vitiated and annulled by its inherent immorality—has been recognized by one of the Justices of the Supreme Court of the United States, who in a recent case, expressly holds that "*any* contract that rests upon such a basis, is *void*";—and

Whereas, The third clause of the second section of the fourth article of the Constitution of the United States—when construed as providing for the surrender of a fugitive slave—*does* "rest upon such a basis," in that it is a contract to rob a man of a natural right—namely, his natural right to his own liberty; and is, therefore, absolutely *void.*

Therefore, Resolved, That we hereby give it to be distinctly understood, by this nation and the world, that, as abolitionists, considering that the strength of our cause lies in its righteousness—and our hope for it in our conformity to the LAWS OF GOD, and our respect for the RIGHTS OF MAN, we owe it to the Sovereign Ruler of the Universe, as proof of our allegiance to Him, in all our civil relations and offices, whether as private citizens or as public functionaries sworn to support the Constitution of the United States, to regard and treat the third clause of the section of the fourth article of that instrument, whenever applied to the case of a fugitive slave, as utterly null and void, and consequently as forming no part of the Constitution of the United States, whenever we are called upon, or sworn, to support it.

38. *Resolved,* That the power given to Congress by the Constitution, to provide for calling out the militia to suppress insurrection, does not make it the duty of the Government to maintain slavery, by military force, much less does it make it the duty of the citizens to form a part of such military force. When freemen unsheath the sword it should be to strike for *Liberty,* not for Despotism.

39. *Resolved,* That to preserve the peace of the citizens, and secure the blessings of freedom, the Legislature of each of the free States, ought to keep in force suitable statutes rendering it penal for any of its inhabitants to transport, or aid in transporting from such State, any person sought, to be thus transported, merely because subject to the slave laws of any other States; this remnant of independence being accorded to the free States, by the decision of the Supreme Court, in the case of Prigg *vs.* the State of Pennsylvania.

40. *Resolved,* That we recognize in Daniel O'Connell, a true patriot of the Liberty school, and admire his consistent devotion to freedom throughout the world. We thank him and the Irish people whom he represents, for their sympathy with us in our great struggle.

41. *Resolved,* That the thanks of this Convention are hereby tendered to Professor Taylor, for his kindness in furnishing the spacious tent, belonging to the Oberlin Collegiate Institute, which has been occupied by the Convention during its sitting.

42. *Resolved,* That the doings of the Convention be published, under the direction of the Secretaries.

43. *Resolved,* That the thanks of this Convention be tendered to the authorities of the County of Erie, and of the city of Buffalo, for the use of the Court House and the Park for its sitting.

44. *Resolved,* That the thanks of this Convention be presented to the President, Vice-President, and Secretaries, for their services during its sessions.

Appendix D

LIBERTY MEMBERSHIP

ALLAN, WILLIAM T. (1810–1882) was born in Tennessee, the son of a slaveholding Presbyterian minister. After being educated at Centre College in Kentucky, he became one of Theodore Dwight Weld's converts to immediate abolition. He was one of the Lane Rebels before finishing his theological studies at Oberlin. He was "One of the Seventy" antislavery lecturers before serving as a Presbyterian minister in Peoria, Illinois. He was instrumental in combining the Illinois Anti-Slavery Society with the Liberty Party and was an officer at the North-Western Liberty Convention in Chicago in 1846. He also worked in the early antislavery movement in Iowa before returning to Illinois.

ALLEN, WILLIAM G. (1820–1888) was a freeborn Virginia mulatto who graduated from Oneida (N.Y.) Institute in 1843. He edited a newspaper with Henry Highland Garnet and became active in the Liberty Party in Troy, New York, before studying law in Boston. After becoming a faculty member at New York Central College, he married a white woman and subsequently moved to England because of the furor. Allen made his living as a lecturer and tutor, and he published his autobiography, *A Short Personal Narrative* (1860). He and his wife continued to live in England, remained active in reform causes, and worked in schools for at least the next twenty years.

ANDREW, JOHN ALBION (1818–1867) moved to Boston in 1837 after graduating from Bowdoin College. He was admitted to the bar in 1840, left the Whig Party to become an active Liberty supporter, and was a founder of the Free Soil and Republican parties in Massachusetts. He was elected to the state legislature in 1857 and as governor in 1860, an office that he held until he declined to run again in 1866. He raised funds to support John Brown and initially supported Salmon P. Chase for the presidency in 1864. He was a Unitarian.

ANDREWS, STEPHEN PEARL (1812–1886) was the son of a Baptist minister in Massachusetts. He attended Amherst before going in 1830 to Louisiana, where he was admitted to the bar. In 1839 he moved to Houston, where he was mobbed in 1843 because of his abolitionist sympathies. After a trip to England to raise funds for the purchase of slaves, Andrews returned to Massachusetts, where he became a member of the Liberty Party's business committee and lectured widely for the party. Throughout his life he was more interested in reform movements than politics, including work in phonography, women's rights, economic theories, philosophy, communitarianism, and even support for Victoria Woodhull and her free love movement.

APPLETON, JAMES (1785–1862) was a silversmith who was born in Ipswich, Massachusetts. He was a Massachusetts Federalist and Whig who served in both the Massachusetts (1813–1814) and Maine (1836–1839) state legislatures and became a brigadier general during the War of 1812. He was a vice president in the American Anti-Slavery Society (1839–1840) and was the Liberty Party candidate for governor in Maine in 1842, 1843, and 1844. He was "a mechanic working daily at blow-pipe and watchspring" (*Liberty Standard,* February 9, 1842) who became a Liberty representative in the Maine legislature, where he gave a famous speech against the legislature's approval of the annexation of Texas. He was a Free Soil presidential elector in 1848. He was so active in the temperance movement that he became known as the "Father of Prohibition."

BAILEY, GAMALIEL (1807–1859) was born in New Jersey to an itinerant Methodist Episcopal preacher, moved to Philadelphia, and graduated from Jefferson Medical College in 1828. After teaching and working as a common sailor on a China trader, he went to Baltimore to edit a newspaper for a breakaway faction of the Methodist Church. The next year he moved to Cincinnati, where he served as a physician during a cholera epidemic. Soon he became one of the most influential antislavery and Liberty Party editors, first with the (Cincinnati) *Philanthropist* and later with the (Washington, D.C.) *National Era.* He was active in the Free Soil and Republican parties.

BAILEY, WESLEY (1808–1891) was born in Vermont and moved to New York, where he was an editor and publisher of Liberty Party newspapers, including the *Madison County Abolitionist* and the (Utica) *Liberty Press.* He was a founder of the Wesleyan Methodist connection and later was elected as an inspector of prisons in New York State. He moved to Iowa in 1860 and founded the *Decorah Republican.*

BARBER, EDWARD DOWNING (1806–1855) was born in Greenwich, New York. He was an attorney who was active in the Anti-Masonic Party as editor of the (Middlebury, Vt.) *Antimasonic Republican* and in the American Anti-Slavery Society, where he held various offices (1838–1841). He was a graduate of Middlebury College (1829) and was a member (1832–1833) and clerk (1834–1835) of the Vermont House of Representatives. He was the Democratic Party candidate for lieutenant-governor in 1841 before he joined the Liberty Party and became its candidate for the same office in 1842, when the Democrats also nominated him. He later became a leader in the state's Free Soil movement and became postmaster of Middlebury.

BASCOM, FLAVEL (1804–1890) was born in Connecticut and graduated from Yale (1828) and later attended its theological school. After being licensed to preach, he moved to Chicago (1839–1849) and later to Galesburg (1849–1856) as a Presbyterian minister. In 1857 he was a missionary for the American Missionary Association before becoming the minister of the Congregational Church in Princeton, Illinois. He was a founder of the Chicago Theological Seminary, a trustee of Knox College, and a founder and trustee of Beloit (Wis.) College. He was a leader of the Liberty Party in Chicago.

BAYLEY, ABNER LOWELL (1808–1870) was born in and was a hatmaker in Amesbury, Massachusetts. His small business expanded into the Merrimac Hat Corporation, which had more than fifty employees by 1860. He was a Liberty candidate for the U.S. Congress as well as both houses of the state legislature. He was a leader in the Amesbury and Salisbury Liberty Association and was very active in labor reform.

BECKLEY, GUY (1805–1847) was raised in Vermont and became a Methodist Episcopal clergyman and antislavery advocate, serving as "One of the Seventy." He relocated to Ann Arbor, Michigan, as pastor of its First Methodist Church as well as working as a merchant-farmer. Dissension within the church caused him to help found the more antislavery Wesleyan Methodist Church in June 1843. He was coeditor, with Theodore Foster, of the Liberty Party's *Signal of Liberty* (1841–1846) and was an early corresponding editor of the (Washington, D.C.) *National Era*. He became an advocate of supporting major-party antislavery candidates in 1847.

BEMAN, AMOS GERRY (1812–1874) was born to Jehiel C. Beman, the black pastor of the African churches in Middletown, Connecticut. He attended Oneida Institute (1835–1836) and later taught in Hartford while studying for the Congregational ministry. While he was the pastor of the Temple Street Colored Congregational Church in New Haven, he edited the *Zion Watchman*. After the 1840 split in the American Anti-Slavery Society, he helped found and served on the executive committee of the American and Foreign Anti-Slavery Society and was a founder of the Liberty Party in Connecticut. After the Civil War, he held several appointive offices and worked with freedmen in Tennessee and Washington, D.C. He was made chaplain of the state legislature in Connecticut in 1872.

BEMAN, JEHIEL C. (1789–1858) was born free in Connecticut to a former slave mother and Revolutionary War veteran father. He was a shoemaker and a minister of the African Methodist Episcopal Zion Church in Boston and Middletown, Connecticut, and was very active in temperance and was a founding member of the American Anti-Slavery Society. He was a manager in the American Anti-Slavery Society (1837–1839), but his conflict with William Lloyd Garrison caused him to join the Massachusetts Abolition Society and the new American and Foreign Anti-Slavery Society, where he served on its executive committee (1841–1843). Beman was involved in Liberty Party activities and was active in the black convention movement.

BERRY, NATHANIEL S. (1796–1894) was born in Maine and moved to New Hampshire, where he was in the tanning business. Before becoming a judge (1841–1856) he served numerous terms as a Democratic state representative (1828, 1833–1834, and 1837) and state senator (1835–1836). He was a delegate to the Democratic convention in Baltimore in 1840 but left it because of the slavery question. He worked for the Liberty Party from 1840 and ran for governor on the Liberty coalition ticket in the annual elections in 1846–1847 and the Free Soil ticket in 1848–1850. Berry was a probate judge before being elected governor (1861–1863) as a Republican.

BIBB, HENRY WALTON (1815–1854) was born a slave in Kentucky to a black slave mother and slaveholder father. He escaped from slavery in 1837, eventually settling in 1842 in Detroit, where he attended William Monroe's school. During the 1840s, he increasingly became involved in the antislavery movement, lecturing for the Michigan State Anti-Slavery Society and then for the Liberty Party in several states, including a speech at the North-Western Liberty Convention in Chicago in 1846. After the passage of the Fugitive Slave Act in 1850, he moved to Canada, where he was involved in the publication of the *Voice of the Fugitive*, a newspaper for emigrant blacks in Canada.

BIGELOW, JACOB (1790–1865) was born in Waltham, Massachusetts, and trained as a lawyer, He worked in his family business in Montreal and Indiana, where he was the Liberty candidate for the U.S. Congress in 1843. Shortly thereafter, he relocated to Washington, D.C., where he worked as a congressional reporter and was so active on the Underground Railroad and in other antislavery activities that he was called the "General Manager of the Underground Railroad." He was a contributor to the *National Era*, a member of the Washington Free Soil Association, and a delegate to the 1856 Republican convention.

BIRNEY, JAMES (1817–1888) was born in Kentucky, the firstborn son of Liberty Party presidential candidate James G. Birney. He attended Centre College and graduated from Miami University of Ohio in 1836. He taught school before enrolling at Andover Seminary and becoming a Congregational minister in Massachusetts, Connecticut, and New York. During the 1840s, he was active in antislavery work and support of his father. He later took a law degree from Yale and became active in Michigan politics, being elected to the state senate in 1859 and as lieutenant-governor in 1860. He was a circuit judge (1861–1865), delegate to the Michigan constitutional convention (1867), and resident minister to the Hague (1876–1882).

BIRNEY, JAMES GILLESPIE (1792–1857) was born in Kentucky to an aristocratic, slaveholding, plantation family. He graduated from Princeton in 1810, undertook legal training in Philadelphia, and was admitted to the bar in 1814. He returned to Kentucky, where he was elected a state representative in 1816, and eventually relocated to Alabama, where he served in the general assembly in 1819. He was a leader in the American Colonization Society before moving to immediate emancipation by the mid-1830s and freeing his own slaves. After moving to Cincinnati, he became editor of the *Philanthropist* and "One of the Seventy" and held other offices in the American Anti-Slavery Society. After the 1840 split in the society, he served on the executive committee of the American and Foreign Anti-Slavery Society. Birney was an early advocate of independent antislavery nominations and became the Liberty Party's most prominent national figure. Birney was its presidential nominee in 1840 and 1844 and its candidate for governor of Michigan in 1843 and 1845. A fall from a horse in 1845 incapacitated him, but he remained interested in the party and wished it to go into more general reforms. He supported the Liberty League in

1848. He eventually joined his old friend Theodore Dwight Weld in a reformist community in New Jersey.

BIRNEY, WILLIAM (1819–1907) was born in Alabama, the second son of James G. Birney. He was educated at Centre College, Miami, and Yale before studying law in Cincinnati. He joined Salmon P. Chase in giving representation to fugitive slaves, was very active in the Ohio Liberty Party, and became a proprietor of the *Philanthropist* in 1842. His joining the Masons caused a brief rift with his father, and he subsequently traveled to Europe as a journalist, where he became a leader in student organizations during the turmoil in 1848. He commanded black troops during the Civil War, rising to the rank of brigadier general. After the war, he practiced law in Washington, D.C.

BLANCHARD, JONATHAN (1811–1892) was born in Vermont and graduated from Middlebury College (1832). He studied for two years at Andover before graduating from Lane Seminary (1838). He was "One of the Seventy" and attended the World Anti-Slavery Convention in London in 1840. Blanchard was an anti-Mason and Whig, became a Presbyterian minister in Cincinnati, and was very active in the Liberty Party while he was president of Knox College (1845–1857). He was a Free Soil presidential elector in 1848. He subsequently was a founder and president of Wheaton College (1862–1882). He was a lifelong supporter of the temperance movement and was considered as a candidate for president for a small Christian Party in the 1880s.

BOLTWOOD, LUCIUS (1792–1872) was born in Amherst, Massachusetts. He was a graduate of Williams College (1814) who was admitted to the Massachusetts bar in 1817. He retired from business in 1836 and was appointed to the board of trustees of Amherst College. Originally a Whig, he was the Liberty Party candidate for governor (1841) and the U.S. Congress (1842 and 1844). He supported Lincoln and the Republican Party.

BOOTH, SHERMAN MILLER (1812–1904) was born in New York and was a temperance lecturer there before graduating from Yale at age twenty-nine. During his senior year, he tutored the *Amistad* captives. He edited the (Hartford, Conn.) *Charter Oak,* helped organize the Liberty Party in Connecticut, and was chairman of the state central committee. He was an editor and proprietor of the (Hartford) *Christian Freeman* before he moved to Wisconsin in mid-1848 to edit the *American Freeman*. He was a delegate to the Buffalo Free Soil convention in 1848 and was a founder of the Free Soil and Republican parties in Wisconsin. During the 1850s, he was arrested and went to prison for aiding a fugitive slave in the famous *Booth v. Ableman* court case. He received a pardon from James Buchanan shortly before Lincoln's inauguration. He was also a strong supporter of women's rights. After the Civil War, he lived in Philadelphia before returning to Chicago in 1879. He wrote for the Chicago *Tribune* and, in 1890, he was appointed U.S. deputy director of internal revenue for Chicago.

BOWDITCH, HENRY INGERSOLL (1808–1892) was born in Salem, Massachusetts, and graduated (1828) and studied medicine at Harvard, where he eventually became Jackson Professor of Clinical Medicine (1859–1867). During his career he made many contributions to medicine and public health, child welfare, and poor relief. Bowditch worked on the Latimer Committee and the Underground Railroad. Beginning in 1840, he was a Liberty Party candidate for state representative and state senator. He became an ardent Free Soiler and Republican. He was interested in public health and was a charter member and president (1877) of the American Medical Association.

BRADBURN, GEORGE (1806–1880) was born in Attleborough, Massachusetts, and became a Unitarian minister. Beginning in 1839, he was elected to three terms as a Whig in the Massachusetts legislature, where he was a leader in anti-miscegenation legislation. He was a delegate to the 1840 World Anti-Slavery Convention in London, and remained in the Garrisonian faction of the antislavery movement until he joined the Liberty Party in 1844. He was an editor of the *Lynn* (Mass.) *Pioneer* and the Liberty *Cleveland American* and *True Democrat*. A believer in many reforms, he was a vice president at the Liberty League–oriented national Liberty Party convention in mid-June 1848. He soon joined the Free Soil Party and became editor of the *Cleveland True Democrat*. He was an early member of the Republican Party, and he later had a position in the Boston Customs House until his retirement in 1875.

BRADLEY, HENRY (1794–1878) was born in Northville, New York, where he was the postmaster. He left in 1823 and became a respected and prosperous merchant of Penn Yan, New York. He was active in Presbyterian and Congregational churches. A longtime temperance proponent, antislavery advocate, and Underground Railroad agent, he was the Liberty Party and National Reform Association candidate for governor of New York in 1846.

BRAINERD, LAWRENCE (1794–1870) was born in East Hartford, Connecticut, and attended St. Albans (Vt.) Academy before entering the steamboat and railroad business there. Originally a Democrat, he was a member of the state legislature in 1834. He was a strong Anti-Masonic Party supporter who became a manager in the American Anti-Slavery Society (1839–1840) and kept a station on the Underground Railroad. He was the Liberty candidate for governor in 1846–1847 and resigned the 1848 nomination after the Free Soil merger. He was the Free Soil Democratic gubernatorial nominee in 1852, 1853, and 1854. He was elected to the U.S. Senate (1854–1855) to fill an unexpired term, and was a signer for the call of the first Republican nominating convention in Philadelphia in 1856. He was a Congregationalist who served as a president of the American Missionary Association during the 1850s.

BRANCH, DANIEL (1802–1895) was born in New York and taught at Oberlin before becoming the head of the Free Will Baptist Geauga Seminary of the Western Reserve Free Will Baptist Society, where he taught James A. Garfield. He was president of the 1844 Chester (Geauga County, Ohio) Liberty convention. He was a founder of Michigan Central (now Hillsdale) College. In 1859, he founded Prairie City (Ill.) Academy. He later moved to Iowa.

BREWSTER, JOHN M. (1789–1869) was born in Lenox, Massachusetts, and studied medicine with his father before graduating from medical school in Boston (1812). He practiced medicine in Lenox (1812–1837) and served as town clerk there for two years. In 1837 he moved to Pittsfield, Massachusetts, where his house was a stop on the Underground Railroad. He was active in the Liberty Party, serving as its nominee for lieutenant-governor in 1845, 1846, and 1847. He was one of Emily Dickinson's doctors.

BRIGGS, CHARLES C. (1817–1892) was a graduate of Dartmouth who became a Congregational minister, antislavery lecturer, and temperance advocate. He was an editor-publisher of the (Vt.) *Green Mountain Freeman* until 1846 and later edited the *Burlington (Vt.) Gazette*. He moved from Vermont to Illinois in 1853 and became a very successful businessman. He was a founder and president of the Briggs, Spafford and Penfield Bank in Rockford, which later became part of the Third National Bank. He also was involved in real estate investment and the insurance business. He became a Republican and was very active on the Underground Railroad.

BRISBANE, WILLIAM H. (1803–1878) was born in Beaufort, South Carolina, and was a wealthy cotton planter and slaveholder on the Sea Islands. After freeing his slaves, he moved to Cincinnati to practice medicine. Brisbane was a member of the executive committee of the American and Foreign Anti-Slavery Society and a strong supporter of the Ohio Liberty Party, for which he was a congressional candidate in 1844. In 1855 he moved to Wisconsin as a pastor of a Baptist church. During the Civil War, he became a tax commissioner in South Carolina before returning to Wisconsin.

BROWN BLACKWELL, ANTOINETTE (1825–1921) was born into the reform-minded Brown family in Henrietta, New York. She attended Oberlin, eventually finishing the theological course and being ordained in 1853. She worked as a pastor in South Butler, New York, and is best known for her long career in women's rights. Unlike many Oberlin women, she consistently followed her family's belief in antislavery politics and the Liberty Party, even taking an active effort in Gerrit Smith's successful 1852 congressional campaign.

BROWN, ABEL W. (1810–1844) was born in Springfield, Massachusetts, and was a Baptist minister and temperance preacher. He lectured for the American Antislavery Society in New York and the Pennsylvania Anti-Slavery Society in western Pennsylvania. While training antislavery agents, he lived along the Ohio River and participated on the Underground Railroad. In April 1841 he became the pastor of a Baptist church in the Albany, New York, area. He joined the Liberty Party and published the *Tocsin of Liberty* with Charles T. Torrey and Edwin W. Goodwin. He had an especially close relationship with the African American community, and Henry Highland Garnet preached at his funeral.

BROWN, ASA B. (1807–1844) was born in Vermont and eventually moved to Ohio in the early 1830s. He was a prosperous physician who was evangelized and moved to northern Indiana, where he was a corresponding editor for the *Chicago Western Citizen*.

BUFFUM, ARNOLD (1782–1859) was a Quaker businessman and hat manufacturer from Rhode Island who was a member of the Pennsylvania Abolition Society, founder and first president of the New England Anti-Slavery Society, and a founder of the American Anti-Slavery Society. He moved to Indiana, where he was a merchant, edited an antislavery newspaper, *The Protectionist,* and worked on the Underground Railroad. Originally an opponent of the Liberty Party, he became one of its greatest supporters.

BURGESS, DYER (1784–1872) was born in Vermont and moved to Ohio in 1816. He moved from Methodism through Congregationalism to Presbyterianism as a minister of the Chillicothe Presbytery in Constitution. He was an anti-Mason who was active on the Underground Railroad. He was one of the earliest Ohio supporters of antislavery political nominations and a founder of the Ohio Liberty Party. He served on the committee that founded the *National Era.*

BURLEIGH, WILLIAM H. (1812–1871) was born on a Connecticut farm but was apprenticed to a printer and became a writer for reform newspapers and a poet. He was "One of the Seventy" lecturers and a manager in the American Anti-Slavery Society (1840–1841) before becoming an editor of the Liberty Party (Hartford) *Christian Freeman* and (Hartford) *Charter Oak.* He worked in the temperance movement and campaigned for the Republican Party in 1860. His brother was the famous colorful antislavery (though not Liberty Party) lecturer and writer, Charles C. Burleigh.

BURRITT, ELIHU (1810–1879) was a self-educated scholar from Connecticut who was a blacksmith by trade but was best known as a translator and as the editor of his reform newspaper, *The Christian Citizen.* Originally a Whig, he became a member of the Massachusetts Liberty Party in 1843, but he directed his primary reform efforts to the peace movement. He turned down the Liberty League nomination for vice president in 1847. An early internationalist, he later became the U.S. consul in Birmingham, England.

CAMPBELL, ALEXANDER (1779–1857) was born in Virginia and studied medicine at Transylvania (Ky.) University. He practiced in Kentucky and was elected to the state legislature in Kentucky in 1803. After moving to Ohio and freeing his slaves, he was elected to the state legislature (1807–1809) and the U.S. Senate (1809–1813). He moved to Ripley, Ohio, in 1815, serving in the Ohio lower house (1819, and as Speaker, 1832–1833) and the Ohio Senate (1822–1824). He was a Jeffersonian Democrat presidential elector in 1820, Whig presidential elector in 1836, unsuccessful Ohio gubernatorial candidate in 1826, and mayor of Ripley (1838–1840). He was a vice president of the first Antislavery Society of Ohio (1835), a very active participant on the Underground Railroad in Ripley, and an early Liberty Party supporter, running for the U.S. Congress on the Liberty ticket in 1846.

CARPENTER, PHILO (1805–1886) was born in Massachusetts and moved to Chicago in 1832. He invested and lost money in real estate but regained solvency as Chicago's first pharmacist. He was a Liberty Party leader who remained a civic leader in Chicago, where he organized the Relief Aid Society after the 1871 fire and served on the school board and board of health. Originally an elder in the Presbyterian Church, he split with his church during the Civil War. He then organized and became a deacon in the First Congregational Church. He was the Liberty mayoral candidate in Chicago 1846–47.

CARTER, JAMES GORDON (1795–1849) was a Massachusetts-born educational reformer who championed theories of inductive reasoning instead of rote learning. He attended Groton, graduated from Harvard (1820), and taught for ten years before establishing three normal schools for teacher training (Framingham, Westfield, and Bridgewater), considered the beginning of the teacher's college movement. Between 1835 and 1840 he served as a Whig in both houses of the state legislature and was so responsible for drafting the bill establishing the state board of education that he is remembered as the "Father of the State Board of Education." Carter left the Old Organization and signed the call for the Liberty Convention of the Northeastern and Middle States in 1845 and was selected as the president of the North-Western Liberty Convention in 1846. He was a Liberty candidate for the U.S. Congress in 1846.

CHADBOURNE, THOMAS (1790–1864) was born in Conway, New Hampshire. He graduated from Dartmouth (1813) with his M.D. He began practice in Concord, New Hampshire, in 1813. He mixed practicing medicine with other activities, including operating a drugstore. He was an active Congregationalist who was a representative to the national Liberty Party convention in New York City in 1841.

CHAPLIN, WILLIAM L. (1796–1871) was born in Middlesex, Massachusetts, and raised in New York. His father was a Presbyterian minister, although William later became a Congregationalist. He was educated at Groton and Harvard and worked as a lawyer, reporter, and editor. He was a manager in the American Anti-Slavery Society (1839–1840) and a founder of the Liberty Party, for which he served as the editor of the *Albany Patriot* and as candidate for lieutenant-governor of New York in 1846. In 1850 he was arrested in Washington, D.C., and extradited to Maryland for aiding fugitive slaves. He was finally released on nineteen thousand-dollar bond, much of it furnished by Gerrit Smith. His health broken, he jumped bail, soon left the active antislavery movement, and retired with his new wife to a water-cure facility in Glen Haven, New York.

CHASE, SALMON PORTLAND (1808–1875) was born in New Hampshire, graduated from Dartmouth (1826), became a teacher in Washington, D.C., and was a student in William Wirt's law office before moving to Cincinnati. He was a colonizationist before becoming involved in immediate abolition in the mid-1830s. He was elected to the city council as a Whig and supported Harrison for the presidency in 1840, but he soon became involved with the Liberty Party and served as the Ohio member of its national committee. Chase was a tireless worker for the party and wrote most of its 1844 platform as well as several important Liberty documents. He was a congressional Liberty candidate in 1846 and was a prime architect of the Liberty participation in the Free Soil coalition in 1848. He was elected to the U.S. Senate as a Free Soil Democrat (1849–1855) and as a Republican

(1860–1861), served two terms as governor of Ohio (1855–1859), became Lincoln's secretary of the treasury (1861–1864), and was appointed chief justice of the U.S. Supreme Court (1864–1875). He was a deacon in the Episcopal Church.

CHENEY, OREN BURBANK (1816–1903) was born in Holderness, Grafton County, New Hampshire, the son of Moses Cheney, who was a member of the New Hampshire state legislature. Oren was educated at Brown and Dartmouth, where he took a B.A. in 1839 and an M.A. in 1842. He was a schoolteacher (1839–1844) before becoming a Free Will Baptist minister in 1845. He was influential in helping to put together the Free Soil coalition that elected John P. Hale to the U.S. Senate. Cheney moved to a pastorate in Augusta, Maine, in 1851 and was quickly elected to the Maine state legislature as a Free Soiler who was sympathetic to Prohibition. In 1852 he was a delegate to the Free Soil Party convention in Pittsburgh. He was the founding president of Bates College and served in that capacity for over thirty years (1863–1894).

CILLEY, JOSEPH (1791–1887) was born in New Hampshire, graduated from Atkinson Academy, and was wounded in the War of 1812. He turned down a Whig nomination for governor, but he was elected to the U.S. Senate by a coalition of antislavery Whigs, Democrats, and Liberty men after serving as a Liberty congressional candidate in 1846. While a U.S. senator (1846–1847), he returned to the Whig Party and received much abolitionist criticism for his support for the Mexican War. He was a Congregationalist.

CLARK, GEORGE WASHINGTON (1812–1893) was born in Bangor, Maine, but moved to Canada with his father. In 1837 he was arrested as a sympathizer with the 1837 rebellion. He escaped to Ann Arbor, Michigan, where he established the state's first temperance newspaper. He subsequently moved to Rochester, New York, where he worked in the antislavery movement, became the "Liberty Minstrel," and wrote a number of songbooks. He joined the Liberty League and served on the business committee of the June 1848 national Liberty convention in Buffalo. He returned to Michigan by 1877 and ran a music store. He was active in many reforms.

CLARKE, EDWIN W. (1801–1886) was born in Pompey Hill/Manlius, New York, and moved to Oswego, New York, in 1807. He was a founder of the Liberty Party, serving on the business committee at the Albany convention. He was a lawyer who became the first clerk of the Village of Oswego. He supported the Liberty Party in 1840 and was the 1842 president of the Oswego Anti-Slavery Society. He was very active on the Underground Railroad and participated in the famous "Jerry Rescue."

CLARKE, LEWIS GARRARD (1815–1897) was born a slave in Kentucky but escaped to Canada before moving to Ohio with his brother, Milton (1817?–1901). They were very popular antislavery lecturers for the Liberty Party in several states. He lived in Canada during the 1850s to escape the Fugitive Slave Law. After the Civil War, he returned to the United States and lived in Oberlin and Kentucky. He was the model for George Harris in *Uncle Tom's Cabin*.

CLEAVELAND, JOHN PAYNE (1799–1873) was born in Massachusetts and was a graduate of Bowdoin College. He was a pastor of New School Presbyterian churches in Detroit (1834–1837), Cincinnati (1841–1844), Providence, Rhode Island (1844–1851), and Northampton, Massachusetts (1853–1855). He was also president of Marshall (Mich.) College (1837–1841) and minister of the First Presbyterian Church of Marshall in addition to serving as an editor of the *American Intelligencer.* He was a manager in the American Anti-Slavery Society (1837–1840), a member of the executive committee of the American and Foreign Anti-Slavery Society (1840–1843), and president of the Michigan State Anti-Slavery Society (1841). He was a chaplain for the Thirtieth Massachusetts Regiment in the Civil War. He was also a strong temperance advocate.

CLEVELAND, CHARLES DEXTER (1802–1869) was born in Massachusetts and educated at Dartmouth. He taught classics at Dickinson College and the University of the City of New York before conducting a school for young ladies in Philadelphia (1834–1867). He was a Liberty leader in eastern Pennsylvania and author of the "Address of the Liberty Party of Pennsylvania," which went through sixty thousand copies. He was very active on the Underground Railroad and was a central figure in the attempted slave escape in the famous *Pearl* incident. He became U.S. consul in Cardiff, Wales (1861–1867).

COBB, SYLVANUS (1798–1866) was born in Norway, Maine, and became a minister in the Universalist Church in 1821. He served as a pastor in Waterville and Winthrop, Maine (1821–1828), and in Walden, Massachusetts (1828–1839). He was editor of the *Christian Freeman and Family Visitor* in Waltham, Massachusetts (1839–1862). He also served in both the Maine and Massachusetts state legislatures. He was an active supporter of the Liberty Party and served as its candidate for state representative in Massachusetts in 1847. He wrote extensively on religious matters.

CODDING, ICHABOD (1811–1866) was born in New York and attended Middlebury College. He was "One of the Seventy" and spent most of his life fighting slavery. He was a Congregational (and later Unitarian) minister who was one of the most effective and well-traveled Liberty Party proponents, working for the party in Vermont, New York, Maine, Connecticut, Illinois, and Wisconsin. He was a vice president of the 1840 Albany convention that established the party and founded the (Hartford, Conn.) *Christian Freeman.* In Wisconsin he successfully established the party in several communities, edited the *American Freeman,* ran for the U.S. Congress on the Liberty ticket in 1848, and was a delegate to the national Free Soil convention in Buffalo. He was active in the Republican Party in Illinois and participated in the 1856 national Republican convention in Philadelphia. He returned to Wisconsin as a Unitarian minister in Raraboo (1862–1866).

COFFIN, LEVI (1798–1877) was an Orthodox Quaker who was born in North Carolina and settled in Indiana in 1816. He was a merchant-businessman who became known as the "Father of the Underground Railroad." He was a manager with the American Anti-Slavery Society (1840–1842) and a leader in the movement to use only products produced by free labor. In 1847 he moved to Cincinnati, where he opened a free labor store and continued to aid escaped slaves. He was a supporter of the Liberty Party and was a secretary at its national convention in 1841.

COLLINS, FREDERICK (1804–1878) was born in Litchfield, Connecticut and studied law. He eventually moved to Chicago, where he ran for the U.S. Congress on the Liberty ticket in 1841 and was the Liberty nominee for lieutenant-governor in 1842. He was active in the Liberty Party and on the Underground Railroad.

COLLINS, HENRY (1819–1874) was born in Pittsburgh to a Methodist Episcopal clergyman. He invested wisely in real estate and became a leader in the Pittsburgh black community. He worked in the black convention movement, on the Underground Railroad, on the publishing committee of the (Pittsburgh) *Mystery,* in the suffrage movement, and in politics. In the early 1850s he moved to San Francisco, where he became a wealthy businessman and worked in the black state convention movement.

COLLINS, JAMES H. (1800–1854) was born in Cambridge, New York, and moved from Oneida County, New York, to Chicago in 1833. He became one of the city's most successful lawyers. He served as president of the Illinois Anti-Slavery Society, worked on the Underground Railroad, and defended Owen Lovejoy in a fugitive slave case. He was Chicago's representative at the first state Liberty convention and was a member of the Liberty Party national corresponding committee. He was one of the founders of the Illinois Free Soil Party, a delegate to the 1848 Buffalo convention, and an unsuccessful congressional candidate in 1850.

COLVER, NATHANIEL (1794–1870) was born and raised in frontier Vermont. He was a self-educated Baptist minister who was originally a tanner by trade. After his ordination in 1819, he was a minister in Vermont and New York before founding Boston Tremont Temple, an interracial congregation, in 1839 and serving as its pastor until 1852. He was later a minister in Detroit, Cincinnati, and Chicago (1861–1867) before founding Colver Institute (now Virginia Union) in Richmond, Virginia, for the training of black ministers. Originally "One of the Seventy" for the American Anti-Slavery Society, he eventually became one of Garrison's bitterest opponents. He worked for the Liberty Party in Massachusetts and Illinois and became famous as the one of the persons who purchased famous Boston African American George Latimer's freedom for four hundred dollars.

COVER, JOSEPH CARMAN (1819–1872) was born in Smithfield, Pennsylvania, but left the state and moved to Wisconsin in 1846 because of prejudice against him on account of his abolitionism. He was a member of the Liberty Party in Wisconsin, and in 1854 he joined the Republican Party and supported it with his newspaper, the *Grant County Herald,* which he ran (1851–1869). He was a regent of the University of Wisconsin (1866–1870) and served as U.S. consul to the Azores (1870–1872). He died in a shipwreck while returning to the United States.

CROCKER, WILLIAM A. (1793–1863) was an early Liberty supporter from Machias, Maine, serving as a Birney presidential elector in 1840 and president of the Maine Liberty Association in 1847. He was a Free Soil candidate for the U.S. Congress and a presidential elector in 1848.

CROSS, JOHN (1797–1885) was born in Ashfield, Massachusetts, and attended Oneida Institute. He was ordained a Congregational minister in 1836 and soon became "One of the Seventy" antislavery lecturers. He eventually became a Wesleyan Methodist. After working with the American Anti-Slavery Society, he became an early member of the Illinois Liberty Party and was the president of the state convention in 1844 and 1848. He served jail time for assisting escaped slaves and became known as the "Superintendant of the Underground Railroad" for his recruitment efforts in several midwestern states. He was a founder of Wesleyan Methodist Institute (now Wheaton College) in 1853 and Amity College (Iowa) in 1857.

CRUMMELL, ALEXANDER (1819–1898) was born in Brooklyn, New York, to a free black businessman who was active in the black community. After an excellent education in black schools in New York, he graduated from Oneida Institute in 1839. Crummel was ordained an Episcopal priest in 1844 and became pastor of the Church of the Messiah. Less directly involved in Liberty affairs, he still supported the party. He went to England in 1848, received an A.B. degree from Queen's College, Cambridge, in 1853, and went as a missionary to Liberia. He taught at Liberia College before returning to the United States. For the last twenty-five years of his life, he was pastor at St. Luke's Episcopal Church in Washington, D.C. He is most famous for his work in Black Nationalism and Pan Africanism.

CUMMINGS, HIRAM (1810–1887) was born in Concord, Vermont. He was a minister who served as a very effective Liberty agent in Massachusetts. He was a publisher and editor of the *Emancipator* and *The Liberty Man's Book* in 1847. He later moved to California and founded the First Congregational Church of Pescadero. He ran for railroad commissioner on the Prohibition Party ticket in 1882.

CURTIS, JEREMIAH (1804–1883) was born in Hampden, Maine. He was a former Democrat who was involved in banking and railroads in Calais, Maine. He was the Liberty candidate for governor (1841) and the U.S. Congress in Maine, and he was also a Free Soil congressional candidate in 1848. He was on the executive committee of the Maine Liberty Association. By 1850, he was a druggist who was one of the owners of the popular Winslow's Soothing Syrup. By 1870, he had become wealthy and moved the enterprise to Brooklyn, New York.

DAVIS, MARY BROWN (1799–1874) was born into a slaveholding Virginia family and moved to Illinois with her husband, SAMUEL, and children in 1837. She wrote for both the *Genius of Universal Emancipation* and the *Chicago Western Citizen*. She wrote the call and served as the secretary at the first convention of the Illinois Female Anti-Slavery Society. After her husband's death in 1849, she worked at a number of jobs before moving to Kansas.

DAVIS, SAMUEL (1792–1849) was born in New York City but was a former slaveholder and veteran of the War of 1812 from Virginia. He moved in 1837 with his wife, MARY BROWN DAVIS, to Peoria, Illinois, where he became publisher of the (Peoria) *Register*. Originally opposed to abolitionism and the Liberty Party and a supporter of Harrison in 1840, he nevertheless condemned the violence toward abolitionists. Finally, riots in Peoria in 1843 made an abolitionist out of him; and he himself received injuries in an 1846 attack over his antislavery principles. He became a leader of the Liberty Party in Illinois and served as the president of the Liberty Party state conventions in 1846 and 1848, as well as writing articles for the *Chicago Western Citizen*. He was one of the nine Liberty Party delegates to the Buffalo Free Soil convention in 1848, and then he supported the new party. He died of cholera in 1849 shortly after moving to the strong antislavery community of Galesburg. He was a Presbyterian.

DAVIS, WOODBURY (1818–1871) was a Maine native and former Whig lawyer in Portland, Maine, who was an agent for the Liberty Party (1846–1848). He later served as a justice on the Maine Supreme Court (1855–1856, 1857–1865) before resigning to become postmaster in Portland in 1866. He was an active Congregationalist, a temperance advocate, and a founder of the Republican Party in Maine.

DAWSON, JAMES (1808–1903) was born in Pennsylvania and later moved to Iowa Territory. He was a Seceder Presbyterian lay minister, who was a Liberty congressional candidate in the summer of 1848. He was on the Iowa Free Soil central committee and was a founder of the Iowa Republican Party. He was a banker and community leader in Washington County, Iowa.

DAY, WILLIAM HOWARD (1825–1900) was born in New York City to a veteran of the War of 1812 who became a sail maker and sailor. After his father died at sea in 1829, Day's mother worked hard to allow him to receive an education. She eventually allowed him to be adopted into the white family of J. P. Williston of Northampton, Massachusetts, where he excelled in his studies and learned the printer's trade. He entered Oberlin as the only black in a class of fifty and graduated in 1847. Later that year he was an Ohio delegate to the Liberty Party national convention in Buffalo, and he continued his support of antislavery politics with the Free Soil Party. He spent years during the 1850s working in the black convention movement, editing newspapers, and struggling for black suffrage and the elimination of the Black Laws in Ohio. He moved to Canada and Great Britain before returning to New York City in 1863. He was ordained a minister in the African Methodist Episcopal Zion Church, and worked in church affairs and the Freedmen's Bureau. He was intermittently involved in local Republican politics after moving to Pennsylvania in the 1870s.

DEBAPTISTE, GEORGE (1814–1875) was born into a free black Virginia family and was a barber and personal servant as a young man. He migrated to Indiana in 1838 and became the personal servant to William Henry Harrison in the White House. He was active on the Underground Railroad in Indiana, where he was saved from expulsion and possible sale by STEPHEN C. STEVENS, a member of the Indiana Supreme Court and future Liberty Party gubernatorial nominee. In 1846 he eventually moved to Detroit, where he was involved in a number of businesses, the Liberty Party, and black causes, especially the Underground Railroad station that operated out of his church, the famous Second Baptist Church. He was sometimes called the "President of the Detroit Underground Railroad." After the Civil War, he worked for the Freedmen's Aid Commission.

DELANY, MARTIN ROBINSON (1812–1885) was born free in Virginia and subsequently relocated to Pittsburgh, Pennsylvania, where he became an apprentice to a doctor. He founded and edited the *Mystery,* a black antislavery weekly, from 1843 to 1848. He later worked on Frederick Douglass's *North Star.* After being refused admittance to Harvard Medical School because of his color, he became a proponent of black emigration. He returned to the United States in 1863 to recruit black soldiers, and in 1865 he received a commission and became the first black field officer in the Civil War. After the war, he worked in the Freedmen's Bureau and in Republican politics in South Carolina, serving as a judge for a short time.

DEMING, ELIZUR (1798–1855) was a physician from Tippecanoe County, Indiana. Before joining the Liberty Party, he was elected to the state legislature in Indiana (1841–1842). He was the Liberty Party nominee for governor in 1843 and was briefly considered for the Liberty vice presidential nomination after the 1844 election. He was named to the national Liberty corresponding committee in 1843 and to the Buffalo convention in 1847. He founded the Indiana Medical College at LaPorte, where one of his students was William Worrall Mayo, who went on to found Mayo Clinic. He was a founder and junior warden of the St. John's Protestant Episcopal Church and a founder and master in the Montezuma Masonic Lodge (1849).

DENISON, CHARLES WHEELER (1809–1881) was born in Connecticut and became a Baptist clergyman who was an agent and manager in the American Anti-Slavery Society (1833–1840) as well as assistant editor to WILLIAM GOODELL on the early *Emancipator.* He was a member of the Liberty Party nominating committee in 1841. He was one of the few Liberty Party leaders to embrace nativism and he became an editor of a nativist newspaper, the *American Signal.* He later served as consul in British Guyana.

DEPUY, HENRY WALTER (1820–1876) was born in Pompey Hill, New York. Trained as a lawyer, he worked as an editor and printer of the *Indiana Freeman* (1845–1847), *Sandusky* (Ohio) *Chronicle* (1848), and the *Rockford* (Illinois) *Free Press* (1848–1850). He became secretary for Governor Horatio Seymour of New York (1853–1854) and wrote several history books. During the Lincoln administration, he served as consul to Carlsruhe and secretary of the legation to Berlin. He was appointed secretary to the Nebraska Territory, helped to organize it, and became the first speaker of the Nebraska legislature.

DEWOLF, CALVIN (1815–1899) was born in Brantrim, Pennsylvania, but moved to Ohio as a young man and attended the Grant River Institute in Ashtabula, Ohio. He moved to Illinois and spent many years as a schoolteacher. He was admitted to the bar in Chicago in 1843 and was a law partner of fellow Liberty man L. C. P. FREER. He was one of the founders of the first antislavery society in Chicago, the *Chicago Western Citizen,* and the Illinois Liberty Party. Beginning in 1854, he was elected to six consecutive terms as a justice of the peace in Chicago, where he also was elected an alderman. He was very active on the Underground Railroad. He was a Methodist.

DOLE, EBENEZER (1776–1847) was a distant cousin of William Lloyd Garrison. He was born in Massachusetts and became a wealthy merchant and philanthropist in Hallowell, Maine. He was active in founding the New England Anti-Slavery Society and the American Anti-Slavery Society, of which he was a vice president (1833–1835). He was a deacon in the Congregational Church and participated in both the Liberty Party and the peace movement. He was a Birney presidential elector in 1840.

DUFFY, JOHN was a correspondent of Salmon P. Chase and an editor-publisher of the *Columbus* (Ohio) *Freeman*. He was a Roman Catholic who believed he suffered discrimination in the antislavery movement because of his religion and the reticence of the Catholic Church to take stands against slavery. He was an early and strong supporter of the Liberty Party after switching his newspaper's allegiance from Henry Clay and the Whig Party.

DURKEE, CHARLES (1807–1870) was born in Vermont and went to Burlington Academy. He was a merchant-farmer who relocated to Kenosha, Wisconsin Territory, in 1836. He was a former Democrat who served in the territorial legislature (1836–1838, 1847–1848) and was an outspoken Liberty Party man in the legislature. He was named to the national Liberty corresponding committee at the Buffalo convention in 1847 and was nominated to be first governor of Wisconsin on the Liberty ticket in the 1848 elections. He was one of those who issued a call for the Buffalo Free Soil gathering in 1848, and he served as a delegate to the Buffalo Free Soil convention. He was subsequently elected to the U.S. Congress on the Free Soil ticket in 1848 and 1850. He was also elected to the U.S. Senate (1855–1861) as a Republican. President Johnson appointed him governor of the Utah Territory, where he developed friendly relations with the Mormons. He also invested in mining in Nevada and the Union Pacific Railroad. He was a convert to Methodism in 1832, but later took a great interest in Swedenborgianism. During the 1850s, he became involved in the peace movement.

DYER, CHARLES VOLNEY (1808–1878) was born in Vermont and graduated from Middlebury College and Medical School. He went to Chicago in 1835 and became a wealthy physician and real estate speculator in Illinois. He was originally a Democrat and was elected by the legislature as a judge of probate court for Cook County in 1837. He was one of the earliest abolitionists in Chicago, was a founder of the Chicago Anti-Slavery Society and the *Chicago Western Citizen*, and was very active in both the Liberty Party and the Underground Railroad. Dyer was chair of a committee to establish a national newspaper—which ultimately became the (Washington, D.C.) *National Era*—at the North-West Liberty Convention in Chicago in 1846, Liberty candidate for governor of Illinois in 1848, and a representative to the Buffalo convention to establish the Free Soil Party in 1848. During the Civil War, he was named by Lincoln to serve as the U.S. representative on the International Court to Suppress the Slave Trade. Dyer was a Swedenborgian in religion.

DYER, EDWARD GALUSHA (1806–1888) was born in Russia, Herkimer County, New York, and received his degree from Fairfield Medical School in New York. He began practicing in Trenton, New York, but soon moved to Ohio and then to Burlington, Wisconsin, in 1839. He was a leading citizen of the town, where he belonged to the local Baptist church and was an agent on the Underground Railroad. He organized the Burlington Liberty Association in 1844 and was active in Liberty politics. He eventually became a Republican and was elected to the state assembly of Wisconsin in 1858.

EARLE, THOMAS (1789–1849) was a Hicksite Quaker born in Leicester, Massachusetts, and he attended Leicester Academy. After moving to Philadelphia in 1817, he became a lawyer and involved in Democratic politics, from which he was proscribed for his antislavery views. He was a leader in the Pennsylvania Abolition Society during the 1820s. Earle was a manager in the American Anti-Slavery Society but eventually was shunned by the Old Organization because of his political stances. He was the Liberty Party vice presidential candidate in 1840 and continued to support the party. He is sometimes erroneously credited with the views of another Thomas Earle.

EASTMAN, ZEBINA (1815–1883) was a native of Massachusetts who became editor of the (Fayettville, Vt.) *Free Press* at age nineteen. He became an associate editor of the *Genius of Universal Emancipation* (1837–1840) and the *Genius of Liberty* (1840–1842). He was one of the most successful and influential Liberty Party editors with his *Chicago Western Citizen* (1842–1853). He moved into the Free Soil and Republican parties. Lincoln appointed him consul to Bristol, England (1861–1869), where he was a member of the Congregational Church.

EELS, RICHARD (1801–1846) was a medical doctor who was born in Connecticut and moved to Quincy, Illinois, in 1833. He established a medical practice and taught at Dr. David Nelson's Mission Institute. He worked on the Underground Railroad in Quincy, Illinois. Eventually he was caught aiding a fugitive slave and was fined four hundred dollars by Judge Stephen A. Douglas, whereupon he was elected president of the Illinois State Anti-Slavery Society (1843). He was unanimously nominated for governor in 1846. He was a Baptist.

ELDER, WILLIAM (1806–1885) was born in Somerset, Pennsylvania, and attended Jefferson Medical College. In his lifetime he worked as a physician, lawyer, editor, and writer. He was active in both the anti-Masonic and colonization movement after moving to Pittsburgh in 1838. He served as the county recorder of deeds as an anti-Masonic Whig in 1839. He was admitted to the bar in 1842 and opened a law practice. Elder was active in the workingmen's movement and tried to join it with the Liberty Party. He also sought to bring the Liberty Party closer to the Democrats. He was a Liberty Party leader in Pittsburgh, where he was a close friend of Martin Delany and, after moving to Philadelphia in 1845, was named to the national Liberty corresponding committee at the Buffalo convention in 1847. He was a Liberty presidential elector in 1844, the editor of the (Philadelphia) *Liberty Herald* (1847–1848), and a contributor to the (Washington, D.C.) *National Era*. He was a leader of the Free Soil movement in Philadelphia before working in the Republican Party. He wrote extensively on economic and political matters and was a follower and biographer of the economic theorist Henry Charles Carey.

ELLS, GEORGE W. (1809–1887) was born in Hartford, Connecticut, but grew up in Virginia. Ells was the only supporter of Thomas Morris in the 1840 Ohio state Democratic convention and, like Morris, was expelled from the party for his antislavery views. He was a lawyer who became a strong Liberty Party leader in Granville, Licking County, Ohio. He played an important role in the 1847 National Liberty Party convention. He eventually moved to Iowa and became a bookseller. He was a Republican delegate to the Iowa State Constitutional Convention in 1857 and was a signer of the document.

ERRETT, RUSSELL (1817–1891) was born in New York City and raised as a Campbellite (Disciples of Christ). In 1829 he moved to Pittsburgh, Pennsylvania, where he became a newspaper reporter during the 1840s and eventually the influential editor of the (Pittsburgh) *Daily Gazette* during the 1850s. He was chairman of the western Pennsylvania Liberty Committee and founded the *Washington* (Pa.) *Patriot* with Francis J. LeMoyne in 1845. After the demise of the Liberty Party, he was an important figure in the Whig Party and in the formation of the Republican Party in Pennsylvania. He served as comptroller of Pittsburgh in 1860, clerk of the state senate (1860–1861, 1872–1876), paymaster in the Union army during the Civil War, and a pension agent at Pittsburgh (1877–1883). He was elected to the U.S. Congress from Pittsburgh for three terms (1877–1883). He also did much theological writing as a member of the Disciples of Christ.

EVANS, GEORGE HENRY (1805–1856) was born in Bromyard, Herefordshire, England, and came to the United States in 1820. He was an apprentice to a printer. He was the founder of the National Reform Association, a land reform group, in 1846. This group endorsed the Liberty Party candidate for governor in New York in 1846, lieutenant-governor in 1847, and the Liberty League–National Liberty Party presidential ticket in 1848. Evans was a confirmed atheist who seems to have had little direct interest in the antislavery movement, his primary effort being expended on land and workingmen's reforms.

FAIRCHILD, JAMES HARRIS (1817–1902) was born in Stockbridge, Massachusetts, but his family moved to the Western Reserve of Ohio when he was one year old. In 1834 he was a member of the first freshman class at Oberlin, beginning a lifelong affiliation with the school. He graduated from the school in 1838 and the Theological Department in 1841. In 1841 he was given responsibility for the Department of Languages, subsequently was made professor of mathematics in 1847, and finally became an associate professor in moral philosophy in 1858. He served as president of Oberlin (1866–1889) before returning to the classroom. Fairchild was an active Liberty Party man and antislavery propagandist. He was an agent on the Underground Railroad and had a leading role in the Wellington slave rescue in 1858.

FARNSWORTH, DRUMMOND (1789–1866) was born in Norridgewock, Maine, and fought in the War of 1812. He was a Democrat who was an owner-founder of the *Democrat Som-*

erset Republican (1828). He was a former state senator and judge of probate in Maine. Farnsworth was very active in the Maine Liberty Party and Liberty Association, holding many offices in both organizations. He was a Liberty congressional candidate in 1844 and a Free Soil presidential elector from Maine in 1848.

FESSENDEN, SAMUEL (1784–1869) was born in Fryeburg, Massachusetts, which later became part of Maine. He was a graduate of Dartmouth (1806) who taught school in New Hampshire while studying law with Daniel Webster. He was a widely respected lawyer and ardent Federalist who served in the Massachusetts legislature (1813–1815) and state senate (1818–1819) and also supported calling the Hartford convention. He was a major general in the Massachusetts militia for fourteen years (the reason that he is sometimes referred to as "general"). After Maine became a state, he was elected to its state legislature (1825–1826). He was an early antislavery advocate, serving as president of the first meeting of the New England Anti-Slavery Society, vice president in the American Anti-Slavery Society (1833–1839, 1840–1844), and one of its managers (1839–1840). In 1844 Fessenden sponsored a black man for admission as an attorney to the U.S. Court. He was the Maine Liberty Party congressional (1842, 1844) and gubernatorial candidate (1845–1847) and Free Soil candidate (1848). He was named to the national Liberty corresponding committee in 1843 and as a delegate to the Buffalo convention in 1847. He was a Congregationalist.

FINCH, ASAHEL, JR. (1809–1883) was born in Genoa, Cayuga County, New York, and moved to Michigan in 1830. He worked as a merchant before being admitted to the bar in 1838. He served in the Michigan legislature as a Whig in 1839 before moving to Milwaukee. There he became a law partner with William Pitt Lynde. He was involved with the *Wisconsin Temperance Journal* and was an executive in the Wisconsin Territorial Liberty Association, although not a Liberty Party member. In 1848 he ran for the U.S. Congress as a Whig and lost to the Free Soil candidate, CHARLES DURKEE.

FINNEY, CHARLES GRANDISON (1792–1875) was born in Connecticut and educated at Hamilton Oneida Academy in Clinton, New York. He studied law privately before being admitted to the New York bar. In 1824 he was licensed to preach in the St. Lawrence Presbytery and became one of the great preachers of the Great Revival Movement. In 1836 he withdrew from the Presbyterian Church and became a Congregationalist. He established a Theology Department at Oberlin College (1836) and eventually became president of Oberlin (1851–1866). He preached the Liberty Party from the pulpit.

FITCH, JABEZ (1795–1843) was born in Unadilla, New York, and moved to Marshall, Michigan, in 1838. He became a well-known architect and builder, and some of his buildings still stand. He was the Liberty Party candidate for governor in 1841. He was an elder and founder of the First Presbyterian Church in Marshall. He died in an industrial accident while building the church in 1843.

FLEESON, REESE C. (1813–1863) was an antislavery and temperance advocate who founded the temperance *Washington Banner* with William H. Burleigh in 1840. In 1842 he founded the (Pittsburgh) *Spirit of Liberty*, which supported the Liberty Party. He continued his support of political abolition through the Free Soil and Republican parties. He co-owned and edited the (Pittsburgh) *Dispatch* from 1849 until his death.

FOOTE, CHARLES C. (1811–1891) was a Presbyterian and Congregational minister from New York who graduated from Oberlin and settled in Detroit by the mid-1840s. As well as working on the Underground Railroad, he was active in Liberty Party affairs and became the vice presidential nominee of the Liberty League and the National Liberty Party for the 1848 election. He was active in raising money for the Refugee Home Society, which aided blacks and escaped slaves in Canada, and was a close ally of Henry Bibb. He attended the meeting that founded the Republican Party in Michigan in 1854. During the early 1860s, he worked in Livonia, Michigan. He lived later in Philadelphia and Kansas. He preached at the memorial for Charles G. Finney at Oberlin in 1876.

FOSTER, THEODORE (1812–1865) was born in Rhode Island and was the son of U.S. Senator Theodore Foster. He went to sea as a young man, but he moved to Michigan in the family milling and lumbering business. He was a newspaperman for most of his life, first as the editor of the (Ann Arbor, Mich.) *Signal of Liberty* (1841–1847), and then was corresponding editor of the (Detroit) *Michigan Free Democrat*, and also the editor of the *Lansing State Republican* in 1864. He was an inspector of elections for Webster Township before 1840, and he was defeated as a Whig for the state senate (1840). He was a frequent officer in the Michigan State Anti-Slavery Society and was a delegate to the 1847 national Liberty Party convention. He worked for the Free Soil and Republican parties. Foster later became superintendent for the Michigan Industrial School for Boys (1856–1860). He was a Presbyterian Church elder.

FREER, LEMUEL COVELL PAINE (1813–1892) was born in New York, and eventually moved to Chicago, where he practiced law and was very active in the Liberty Party and Disciples of Christ Church, from which he eventually separated. He was also a prominent Chicago agent on the Underground Railroad and close friend of black activist John Jones.

GALE, GEORGE WASHINGTON (1789–1862) was born in New York and was a graduate of Union College (1814) and Princeton Theological Seminary. He became a Presbyterian pastor in Adams, New York (1819–1825). In 1827 he assisted in the founding of Oneida Institute and served as its president until 1834. He founded Knox College in Illinois in 1837, was its president until 1839, and was a professor of languages and moral philosophy there until 1857. He was a manager in the American Anti-Slavery Society (1837–1840), but he became a Liberty Party supporter and his town of Galesburg was one of its strongest areas. He left Knox in 1857 after a dispute with Jonathan Blanchard over New School Presbyterian beliefs. He also developed more mainstream political leanings at this time, supporting the Whig Orville Browning.

GALUSHA, ELON (1790–1856) was born in Shaftesbury, Vermont, and studied law before entering the Baptist ministry. He was pastor of Baptist churches in Whitesborough, Utica,

Rochester, and Perry, all in New York. His church at Rochester was the first to allow Negroes to occupy regular pews; during his pastorate in Perry (1839–1841), his church became a come-outer church. In 1844 he became an Adventist (also called Millerite). He was a manager for the American Anti-Slavery Society (1839–1840) and a delegate of the new American and Foreign Anti-Slavery Society to the World Anti-Slavery Convention in London (1840). He was a strong Liberty Party supporter and participated in the 1843 national convention in Buffalo. His father served two terms as governor of Vermont.

GARNET, HENRY HIGHLAND (1815–1882) was born a slave in Maryland and escaped with his family in 1824. After settling in New York, he attended various black schools before graduating from Oneida Institute in 1839. He moved to Troy, New York, where he was minister to the black Liberty Street Presbyterian Church, edited reform newspapers, opened a black school, and immersed himself in antislavery activities and the Liberty Party. He was an agent of the American Anti-Slavery Society until he delivered a keynote address at the national convention of the Liberty Party at Buffalo in 1843. He spoke at a black convention where his militant "Address to the Slaves of the United States" explored the justification for slave violence. He was perhaps the most tireless and outspoken African American in the Liberty Party. During the 1850s, he traveled to England and served as a missionary to Jamaica. He returned to the United States to recruit black soldiers during the Civil War. After the war he returned to the ministry in Washington, D.C., and New York and was president of Avery College. He died shortly after taking a post as U.S. minister to Liberia in 1881.

GASTON, AMNON (1809–1849) was born in Morrisville, New York. He was pastor of Congregational churches in Elkhorn, Sugar Creek, and Delavan, Wisconsin (1841–1845), after moving to Wisconsin in 1841. He was a very active abolitionist and a founder of the Wisconsin Territorial Anti-Slavery Association in 1842, an editor of the *American Freeman*, and a supporter of the Liberty Party. He moved to Illinois in 1846 and continued his Liberty affiliation.

GATES, SETH MERRILL (1800–1877) was born in New York and attended Middlebury Academy (Wyoming, N.Y.). He became an attorney in LeRoy, New York, and was the editor of the *Leroy Gazette*. During the mid-1820s, he served as both the inspector of common schools and sheriff of LeRoy. He then took a seat in the New York Assembly in 1832. During the revivals of the 1830s, Theodore Dwight Weld converted him to antislavery. Subsequently, he became an outspoken antislavery Whig in the U.S. Congress (1839–1843) and his house in Warsaw was a stop on the Underground Railroad. Originally opposed to the Liberty Party, he changed his mind in 1843, the same year that he relocated to Warsaw, New York. He was defeated as the Free Soil candidate for lieutenant-governor of New York in 1848. In addition to his legal work, he was involved in lumber, hardware, and dry goods businesses. He became postmaster of Warsaw, New York (1861–1870). He broke away from his original church over the slavery issue and was a founder of the Second Congregational Church in Warsaw, New York.

GAZZAM, EDWARD D. (1803–1878) was born in Pittsburgh, Pennsylvania, and graduated from the University of Pennsylvania Medical School and then studied law. He also became a newspaper editor. He was a delegate to the national Free Soil convention in Buffalo and a leader in the Free Soil Movement in Pennsylvania. Gazzam later served in the Pennsylvania state senate (1857–1859) as a Republican from Allegheny County.

GAZZAM, JOSEPH P. (1797–1863) was born in Philadelphia, Pennsylvania, and moved to Pittsburgh when he was five years old. He was a practicing physician in Pittsburgh (1817–1863) who was a graduate of the University of Pennsylvania. He was a manager of the American Anti-Slavery Society (1837–1840) and a strong Liberty Party supporter. He was nominated for the Pennsylvania state legislature on the Liberty Party ticket even though he was a Mason in an anti-Masonic area.

GIBBONS, JOSEPH (1818–1883) was born in Upper Leacock, Pennsylvania, and was a Quaker physician whose house was a stop on the Underground Railroad in Upper Leacock Township. He was a temperance advocate who moved from the Liberty to Free Soil Party and was a founder of the Republican Party in Pennsylvania. He was an officer in the customs house in Philadelphia (1861–1865). He married THOMAS EARLE's daughter. Later, he established the *Friends' Journal* in 1873.

GILLETTE, FRANCIS (1807–1879) was born in Connecticut and graduated valedictorian and Phi Beta Kappa from Yale (1829). Forced by illness to give up law, he became a well-to-do farmer and later invested in the insurance business. He was a Whig who was a member of the state legislature in 1832 and 1838 and spoke for a bill giving negroes the right to vote. He was the Connecticut member of the Liberty Party national committee named in 1843 and at the 1847 Buffalo convention. He served numerous times as the Liberty Party and Free Soil nominee for governor of Connecticut. He was elected to the U.S. Senate (1854–1855) to fill an unexpired term. His house was an important station on the Underground Railroad. He was a Congregationalist whose wife was from the famous Beecher family and sister of Harriet Beecher Stowe.

GODFREY, JOHN E. (1809–1884) was born in Hampden, Maine, and was educated in the local public schools and academies before being admitted to the Maine bar in 1832. Before joining the Liberty Party, he had been a Whig, and he subsequently joined the Free Soil and Republican parties. Godfrey had a long career in local politics, held many local offices, and was active in the temperance movement. He was founder and editor of the Liberty Party *Bangor Gazette* and served as chairman of the Maine Liberty Party central committee. He was so popular in his community that he was selected to give the oration on Bangor's centennial.

GOODELL, WILLIAM (1792–1878) was a self-educated man born in New York and lived in Connecticut and Rhode Island. He left the American Colonization Society in 1832 and was a founder and manager (1833–1839) of the American Anti-Slavery Society and editor of the (New York, N.Y.) *Emancipator*. He then edited the *Utica* (N.Y.) *Friend of Man* (1836–1842), *Perry Impartial Countryman,* and *Radical Abolitionist.* He was a founder and a major theoretician in the Liberty Party, Liberty League, Radical Abolition Party, and Prohibition Party. He was the author of many works on slavery, antislavery, and the U.S. Constitution. Later, he moved to Connecticut and Wisconsin.

GOODWIN, EDWIN W. (1800–1845) was born in Ovid, New York, and was editor of the (Albany, N.Y.) *Tocsin of Liberty* and *Albany Patriot*. He also was part of the Albany Vigilance Committee and a member of the first Liberty Party national committee. He was a talented artist.

GREEN, BERIAH (1795–1874) was born in Connecticut, graduated as valedictorian from Middlebury College (1819), and attended Andover Theological Seminary. He was pastor of numerous New England churches (1821–1831) before becoming professor of sacred literature at Western Reserve College (1830–1833). He then became president of Oneida Institute, a position he held until its closing in 1843. Green was the president of the convention that founded the American Anti-Slavery Society (1833) and one of its vice presidents (1833–1837) and managers (1837–1840). Green was a founder of the Liberty Party, a member of the first Liberty Party national committee, and an active supporter of the Liberty League. Later he became disillusioned with politics and what he saw as a less strenuous abolition movement. In religion he was a New School Presbyterian who later became a Congregationalist.

GRIMES, JOHN (1802–1875) was born into a Quaker New Jersey family and lived there and in nearby Boonton most of his life as a physician. He was editor of the *New Jersey Freeman*. He served on a committee at the 1847 National Liberty Party convention. His houses in Mountain Lakes and Boonton were stops on the Underground Railroad. He was active in many reforms, especially temperance.

GRINNELL, JOSIAH BUSHNELL (1821–1891) was born in Vermont and attended Oneida (N.Y.) Institute, where he made the acquaintance of several future Liberty Party men and worked on the publication of the (Utica, N.Y.) *Friend of Man,* which was printed at the institute. After graduation he represented the American Tract Society in Wisconsin Territory and worked in antislavery. He then graduated from Auburn (N.Y.) Theological Seminary and became a the pastor of a mixed race Congregational Church in Union Village, New York, that had come out of the Dutch Reformed Church over the slavery issue. Grinnell claimed that "[t]he liberal party, headed by John P. Hale, received, I think, the entire suffrage of the voters in our Society." He moved to Washington, D.C., and New York City before moving to Iowa, where he established and was president of what would become Grinnell College. He served as a Republican member of the Iowa State Senate (1856–1860) and was a member of the U.S. Congress (1863–1867).

GROSVENOR, CYRUS PITT (1792–1879) was born in Grafton, Massachusetts, and graduated from Dartmouth. After teaching for a few years, he attended Princeton Theological Seminary (1821–1822) and became a Congregational minister and then a Baptist minister while working in the South. He returned to Massachusetts, where he became a leader among antislavery Baptists and was "One of the Seventy" of the American Anti-Slavery

Society, for which he was also a vice-president (1834–1835) and a manager (1839–1841). He was active in both religious and political antislavery efforts as a founder of the American Free Baptist Society in 1840 and as a candidate for the state senate in Massachusetts as early as 1840. In 1849 he was a founder of New York Central College in McGrawsville, New York, served as its first president (1849–1850), and was a faculty member for several years. He retired to Albion, Michigan, in 1867.

GURNEY, CHESTER (1794–1869) was born in New York and later moved to St. Joseph County, Michigan, where he was a judge, lawyer, and strong temperance advocate. He was a Liberty Party presidential elector in 1844 and the Liberty candidate for governor in 1847.

GUTHRIE, ALBERT AUSTIN (1803–1874) was an abolitionist from Putnam, Ohio, who was the corresponding secretary for the Ohio State Anti-Slavery Society in the mid- to late 1830s and an important agent on the Underground Railroad. He was a vice president in the American Anti-Slavery Society (1840–1841), and he served as the Liberty Party nominee for the U.S. Congress from the Fourteenth District in 1842. He was a delegate and served on a committee at the national Free Soil convention in Buffalo in 1848. He was a grocer who served as superintendent of public schools for forty years in Putnam, Ohio. He was a New School Presbyterian.

HALE, JOHN PARKER (1806–1873) was born in New Hampshire and was a graduate of Bowdoin College. He was admitted to the bar in 1830, elected as a Democrat to the New Hampshire legislature in 1832, and served as the U.S. attorney for New Hampshire (1834–1841). Hale served in the U.S. Congress as a Democrat (1842–1845) before being elected to the U.S. Senate as a Liberty–Independent Democrat candidate in 1847. He was the Liberty Party presidential candidate (1847–1848) before withdrawing and supporting the new Free Soil Party, whose candidate he became in 1852. He eventually joined the Republican Party and was appointed minister to Spain in 1865 by Lincoln. Originally a Congregationalist, he became a Unitarian, although he worshipped at several churches.

HALE, JOSIAH WHEELOCK (1783–1851) was a physician who had been born in Jaffrey, New Hampshire, and eventually settled in Brandon, Vermont. He was a Methodist who was a manager in the American Anti-Slavery Society (1839–1840). Hale was a Whig before being elected to the lower house of the Vermont legislature on the Liberty ticket. He was named the Vermont member on the national Liberty Party corresponding committee at the Buffalo convention in 1847. He was a Methodist.

HALL, LAURISTON (1808–1875) was born in North Kingston, Rhode Island. He was a manager in the American Anti-Slavery Society (1839–1840). He was named to the National Liberty Party corresponding committee for Rhode Island at the Buffalo convention in 1847. He was the Liberty (1847) and Free Soil (1849 and 1851) candidate for the U.S. Congress.

HALLOCK, HORACE (1807–1892) was born in Long Island, New York, and moved to Detroit in 1831. He was a clothing merchant who was president of the Detroit Liberty Association and served as candidate for lieutenant-governor of Michigan in 1847. He was very active on the Underground Railroad and in working with fugitive slaves in Canada. He served as an elder in Detroit's First Congregational Church.

HARDING, STEPHEN S. (1808–1891) was born in Palmyra, New York, and became a self-educated teacher and lawyer after he moved to Indiana in 1820. He left the Whig Party in 1840 over the slavery issue and became one of the leaders of both the Liberty and Free Soil parties in Indiana. He was the Liberty Party candidate for governor in both 1843 and 1846. He attended the Free Soil convention at Buffalo in 1848 and was a Free Soil presidential elector. He was an 1860 member of the Republican central committee in Indiana. He had known Joseph Smith in Palmyra and, perhaps for that reason, was appointed the governor of the Utah Territory in 1862. He later became consul in Valparaiso, Chile, and chief justice of the territorial court of Colorado.

HARRISON, MARCUS (1795–1874) was born in Connecticut and was a graduate of Yale and Andover Seminary. He was a noted Presbyterian evangelical minister in Groton, New York, who moved to Jackson(burg), Michigan, in 1836 as its first resident minister. He was an active Liberty Party supporter who served as a vice president of the North-Western Liberty Convention (1846) in Chicago. He later moved to Decatur, Illinois.

HASTINGS, SAMUEL DEXTER (1816–1903) was born in Massachusetts, moved to Philadelphia, and became a merchant. He worked in the abolition movement after 1835, was a founder of the Liberty Party in Pennsylvania in 1840, and became chairman of the state central committee. He continued his work in antislavery politics after relocating to Milwaukee in 1846, eventually winning a seat in the 1849 state legislature, where he immediately delivered a strong antislavery speech. He was again elected to the state legislature as a Republican. He became the state treasurer (1858–1866). He was a strong temperance advocate, and late in life he ran on the Prohibition Party ticket in Wisconsin for the U.S. Congress (1882) and governor (1884). Originally a Presbyterian, he withdrew from the church because of his antislavery views and became prominent in the Free Congregational Church.

HAWLEY, JOSEPH ROSWELL (1826–1905) was born in North Carolina and moved to Connecticut when he was eleven. He attended Cazenovia (N.Y.) Seminary and graduated from Hamilton College. He then studied law in Hartford, Connecticut, where he and his father were active in the Liberty Party. He was a delegate to the 1852 Free Soil convention and was a founder of the Republican Party in Connecticut. He was in the Union army (1861–1866) and was a governor of Connecticut (1866–1867). He was a Republican presidential elector in 1868, served in the U.S. Congress (1872–1875, 1879–1881), and then served in the U.S. Senate (1881–1905).

HAYDEN, JOEL (1793–1873) was born in Haydenville, Massachusetts, and was a blacksmith who became a large manufacturer of buttons. He was a Birney elector in 1840, a Liberty Party state representative from Williamsburgh in the Massachusetts legislature, and the Liberty Party candidate for the U.S. Congress (1844). He was elected lieutenant-governor of Massachusetts (1863–1866) with another former Liberty man, Governor John A. Andrew, on the Republican and Union tickets.

HILDRETH, RICHARD (1807–1865) was born in Massachusetts , was educated at Phillips Exeter Academy, and graduated from Harvard (1826). He was a man of many intellectual interests as an attorney, journalist, historian, novelist, and philosopher. He was elected to the Boston Common Council for 1832–1833 and unsuccessfully ran for the lower house of the Massachusetts legislature as a Whig in 1839. He helped found the *Boston Daily Atlas* in 1832. He became the chief editorial writer for that Whig newspaper in 1837 and wrote a campaign biography for William Henry Harrison in 1840. Hildreth was a temperance and antislavery advocate and wrote *Archy Moore* (1836), the country's first antislavery novel, while living on a Southern plantation for his health and the nonfiction *Despotism in America* (1840), an antislavery work. He lived in British Guyana (1840–1843) for his health. He joined the Liberty Party shortly after his return and strongly opposed the Garrisonian disunion positions. He was placed on the Liberty ticket for the state legislature in 1846 and 1847 and served as an attorney on fugitive slave cases. He edited the Boston *Telegraph* and wrote for the New York *Tribune* in the 1850s. He wrote a multivolume history of the United States, works on philosophy, and an influential book on Japan. Lincoln appointed him to be consul to Trieste, and he died in Italy. He was a Unitarian.

HOES, SCHUYLER (1807–1853) entered Cazenovia (N.Y.) seminary in 1828 and became a Methodist Episcopal preacher who worked in New York, New Jersey, and Massachusetts. He was a member of the national central committee of the Liberty Party. He also did mission work in Texas for the American Bible Society. He eventually became a Wesleyan Methodist.

HOIT, DANIEL (1778–1858) was a War of 1812 hero from Sandwich, New Hampshire, who was elected to the state legislature as early as 1807. He served fifteen years in the lower house of the New Hampshire state legislature, four years in the state senate, and two years on the council of censors as a Federalist and Whig. He was the Liberty Party nominee for governor of New Hampshire (1841–1845) and was named a member of the Liberty Party national committee in 1843 and at the 1847 national Liberty convention at Buffalo. He was a Methodist Episcopalian who had been a longtime antislavery advocate as a manager of the American Anti-Slavery Society (1836–1840) and on the executive committee of the American and Foreign Anti-Slavery Society (1841–1843).

HOLLEY, MYRON (1779–1841) was born in Connecticut and was a graduate of Williams College (1799). He was a bookseller but eventually became a produce salesman. He was appointed clerk of Ontario County and served in the New York legislature, where he was very active in promoting the Erie Canal. He became acting commissioner of the Erie Canal, but financial difficulties involving mishandled funds caused him to return to Lyons, New York, where he became a successful produce salesman. He was also editor of the (Lyons, N.Y.) *Countryman* (1831–1834), (Hartford, Conn.) *Free Elector* (1834–1835), and

(Rochester, N.Y.) *Freeman* (1839–1840). He was a fervent anti-Mason and an early abolitionist, being an original member of the American Anti-Slavery Society. He is considered one of the founders of the Liberty Party and spearheaded the movement that culminated in the Albany convention of April 1, 1840. Originally a Congregationalist, he developed unorthodox religious views by the end of his life.

HOLMES, SILAS M. (1816–1905) was born in Connecticut. He became a successful dry goods merchant in Detroit and was a secretary of the Detroit Liberty Association. He was elected state treasurer on the state's first Republican ticket in 1854 and served until 1859, when he moved to California, where he was in business until the late nineteenth century. He also owned the Detroit *Advertiser* from 1856 to 1858. He was a Congregationalist.

HOLTON, EDWARD DWIGHT (1815–1892) was born in New Hampshire and moved to Milwaukee in 1840. Originally a farmer, he became a dry goods merchant with interests in railroads, trade, and insurance. He was a deeply religious man who left his Presbyterian church and joined a Congregational church over the slavery issue. He was an avid participant in the political antislavery movement as an organizer of the Liberty, Free Soil, and Republican parties in Wisconsin. He was elected sheriff of Milwaukee County on a People's coalition ticket in 1843 before running unsuccessfully for the Wisconsin territorial representative to Congress on the Liberty Party ticket in 1845. Holton was the party's candidate for secretary of state in its first election in May 1848. He was a delegate to the 1848 Free Soil convention in Buffalo and was an unsuccessful candidate for governor on a People's ticket in 1853. He was elected to the state legislature as a Republican in 1860. He served as a state allotment officer during the Civil War. After the war, he invested in real estate and became a vice president of the Northwest National Insurance Company.

HOOKER, JOHN (1816–1901) was a longtime resident of Farmington, Connecticut, who had dropped out of Yale because of poor health. He read law and was the court recorder for the Connecticut Supreme Court for thirty-six years. He was an outspoken antislavery man and an early supporter of the Liberty Party, on whose ticket he ran for the U.S. Congress in 1843. He carried his political antislavery into the Free Soil and Republican parties. He was an active participant in Underground Railroad activity and is remembered for buying and freeing the prominent black activist James W. C. Pennington.

HOWE, APPLETON (1792–1870) was born in Hopkinton, Massachusetts. He graduated (1815) and received his medical degree (1819) from Harvard before becoming a physician in Weymouth, Massachusetts. He was in the state militia (1822–1840), reaching the rank of major general, and served in the state senate (1840–1841). He was the Liberty Party (1844, 1846, and spring 1848 contest to fill John Quincy Adams's seat) and Free Soil (1848–1850) candidate for the U.S. Congress from Massachusetts. He supported public worship but never affiliated with a church.

HOWE, SAMUEL GRIDLEY (1801–1876) was born in Boston and graduated from Brown (1821) and Harvard Medical School (1824). He volunteered to work for the Greeks in their war against Turkey. After returning to Boston he helped establish what became known as the Perkins Institute for the Blind, where he gained worldwide fame for his work with Laura Bridgman. Howe and his wife Julia Ward were active in several reforms, including education and antislavery. He was a friend of John Brown and helped finance the raid on Harper's Ferry. He ran on the Liberty ticket for the U.S. Congress against Robert Winthrop in 1846 and received 15% of the vote.

HOWE, SAMUEL LUKE (1808–1877) was born in Swanton, Vermont, and moved to Ohio when he was young. After attending Athens College, he founded Lancaster Academy in 1835. Among his students were John and William Tecumseh Sherman. In 1841 he moved to Iowa, where he was a schoolmaster and founded Howe's Academy in 1841 as an early coeducational institution. He was an early women's rights and antislavery supporter. A former Whig, he was an officer in the Iowa Anti-Slavery Society and served as a Liberty Party congressional nominee for in the summer of 1848. He was on the Iowa Free Soil central committee in 1848 and later edited a Free Soil newspaper, the *Iowa True Democrat*.

HUDSON, TIMOTHY B. (1814–1858) was born in Chester, Ohio, and was an 1847 graduate of Oberlin even though he taught Latin and Greek there (1838–1841). He then became an agent of the Ohio Anti-Slavery Society before he returned to Oberlin as a professor of ancient languages from 1847 until his death. He served on Liberty committees and spoke at Liberty conventions, including the national Liberty convention at Buffalo in 1843 and Gerrit Smith's Liberty convention in 1851. He was active in many reforms, including the peace movement and coeducation. His wife, BETSY, was also a strong Liberty Party supporter.

HUNTER, CHARLES W. (1783–1862) was a native of Watertown, New York, who fought in the War of 1812 as a major before becoming a merchant in St. Louis. He was pioneer of Alton, Illinois, in 1820, part of which was originally called Huntertown after him. He was a hotel owner and the second largest landholder in the town. He donated the plot of ground where Elijah Lovejoy was buried after he was murdered in 1837. He was the Liberty Party candidate for governor of Illinois in 1842 and for the U.S. Congress in 1848. He was very active on the Underground Railroad. He was a Presbyterian.

HURLBUT, THADDEUS B. (1800–1885) was born in New York, graduated from Hamilton College, and became a Congregational minister. He was postmaster in Upper Alton, Illinois, and served on the national committee of the Liberty Party.

HUSSEY, ERASTUS (1800–1889) was a New York–born Quaker and a self-educated teacher who farmed in the summer. He moved to Michigan in 1824, became involved in local politics, and won several local elections. He moved to Battle Creek, Michigan, in 1838 in manufacturing as well as continuing to farm and teach. He was elected as town clerk on the Whig ticket and was later elected mayor. He was an officer in state and local antislavery societies and was nominated for state senate in 1843 and the U.S. Congress in 1846 on the Liberty Party ticket. He edited the (Battle Creek) *Michigan Liberty Press* (1848–1849) and served as a delegate to the Free Soil convention in Buffalo. He was subsequently elected to the state legislature in 1850 and was president of the Jackson convention that formed the Republican Party in 1854. He was an important agent on the Underground Railroad in Michigan.

HUTCHINS, JOHN (1812–1891) was born in Ohio and attended Western Reserve College. He was a Democrat who was admitted to the Ohio bar in 1837 and eventually became the law partner of David Tod, who was the Democratic gubernatorial candidate for Ohio in 1844 and 1846. He served as the clerk of common pleas for Trumbull County (1838–1843) and also as mayor of Warren for two years. He was a strong Liberty leader on the Western Reserve and Lake County. He was elected as a Free Soil Democrat to the lower house of the Ohio legislature (1849–1850) and succeeded Joshua Giddings in the U.S. Congress (1859–1863).

HUTCHINSON, TITUS (1771–1857) was born in Massachusetts and was a graduate of Princeton. He was admitted to the New Hampshire bar in 1798 and later moved to Vermont. He was U.S. attorney in Vermont (1813–1823), was elected as a judge on the state supreme court, and served as its chief justice (1830–1833). He was a former Whig who was the Liberty Party gubernatorial candidate (1841) and its congressional candidate (1842, 1844, and 1846). He was a member of the party's national corresponding committee in 1843. He was one of the early theorists of the unconstitutionality of slavery.

JACKSON, JAMES CALEB (1811–1895) was born in Manlius, New York. Originally a farmer, he became deeply involved in the temperance and abolition movements. He voted for Andrew Jackson in 1832 but left the party over the slavery issue. He lectured for the New York State Anti-Slavery Society (1839), was on its executive committee (1840–1841), served as a corresponding secretary (1840–1842) of the American Anti-Slavery Society, and was an associate editor of the (New York, N.Y.) *National Anti-Slavery Standard*. Originally strongly opposed to the formation of the Liberty Party, he became a party spokesman and editor in the early 1840s. He edited the (Cazenovia, N.Y.) *Madison County Abolitionist* and the (Utica, N.Y.) *Liberty Press*. He owned and edited the *Albany Patriot* (1844–1847) before undergoing a water cure for his failing health. This turned him toward the health field, and he operated a hydropathy institute at Skaneateles, New York (1847–1858). He then earned a medical degree at the medical college in Syracuse. He was a member of the come-outer Union Church and supported the Liberty League.

JACKSON, WILLIAM (1783–1855) was born in Massachusetts, the brother of Garrisonian Francis Jackson, and was a successful businessman who served in the Massachusetts legislature (1829–1832) and as an anti-Mason in the U.S. Congress (1833–1837). He refused a third term and then joined the Whig Party after the decline of anti-Masonry. He was an early member of the Massachusetts Liberty Party and one of its most popular candidates, running at various times for lieutenant governor (1842, 1843, and 1844), U.S. Congress (1842), and the state legislature. He was named to the national corresponding committee in 1847. He was on the executive committee of the American and Foreign Anti-Slavery Society (1840–1841). He was a strong and early promoter of railroads and served as a superintendent of construction on several lines. He was a temperance advocate and very active in the Congregational Church, as a deacon and president of the American Missionary Association (1846–1854). He was a Free Soil presidential elector in 1848.

JAY, WILLIAM (1789–1858) was born in New York City, the son of founding father John Jay. He graduated from Yale and studied law but went into farming. He was a corresponding secretary (1835–1838) and on the executive committee (1836–1837) of the American Anti-Slavery Society. Jay moved to the new American and Foreign Anti-Slavery Society, where he was on its executive committee (1840–1855) and its vice president. His writing and name were very important to the antislavery movement. He was a judge in Westchester County, New York (1818–1843), until he was removed by Democrats because of his views and rulings on slavery. He was a Whig who did not support the Liberty Party until 1843, but then became its candidate for the state senate in New York. He was also talked about as a replacement candidate for James G. Birney on the Liberty Party's presidential ticket. He supported the Liberty League in 1848. He was involved in several other reforms, serving as president of the American Peace Society (1848–1858) and as a founder of the American Bible Society. He was an Episcopalian who embraced evangelical religion after the Second Great Awakening.

JOHNSON, HENRY (b. 1812) was born a slave in Virginia. He joined the large New Bedford black community during the 1830s. He was a town crier and represented the town at many antislavery meetings and at least two black conventions during the 1850s. He attended the annual meeting of the Garrisonian American Anti-Slavery Society in 1843, but he became an outspoken advocate of the Liberty Party. He was involved in vigilance committee work, the Underground Railroad, and the black convention movement.

JONES, JOHN (1816–1879) was born in Greene County, North Carolina, to a German father and a free mulatto mother. He apprenticed as a tailor in Tennessee, married, and moved to Illinois in 1844. He settled in Chicago a year later, where Liberty man L. C. P. Freer taught him how to read and write and where he published some articles on the defense of blacks in the *Chicago Western Citizen*. Jones expanded his small tailor business, acquired valuable real estate in rapidly expanding Chicago, and became a successful businessman and black advocate. He socialized with the leading Chicago abolitionists, was active in the city's Liberty Association, was a mainstay on the Underground Railroad, and worked for abolition of the Illinois Black Laws. He also worked in the black convention movement where he was opposed to emigration. After the Civil War, he became an important member of the Republican Party, serving as the first black elected political official in Illinois as a member of the Cook County Commission.

JONSON, GEORGE WASHINGTON (1801–1880) was born in New Hampshire and came to East Aurora, New York, where he founded a classics academy. He read law in Millard Fillmore's office and moved to Buffalo in 1832. In 1835 he drafted the constitution of the Buffalo and Erie County Anti-Slavery Society. He made sixty thousand dollars in land investments in Buffalo, which allowed him to spend two years in Europe. Afterward he spent some time in Massachusetts, where he left the Whig Party to run as the Liberty Party nominee for governor (1840) and was a member of the state central committee. In the early 1840s he returned to Buffalo, where he worked in law and real estate while being the driving force in the city's Liberty Party. He was one of the main agents in Buffalo's Underground Railroad. He was an officer in Gerrit Smith's Liberty Party convention in Buffalo in 1851. His last name is sometimes spelled "Johnson."

KEEP, JOHN (1781–1870) was born in Longmeadow, Massachusetts. He was a graduate of Yale and a Congregational minister in Blandford, Massachusetts (1803–1821); Homer, New York (1821–1834); and Cleveland, Ohio, where he organized the First Congregational Church. He also preached at several other churches in Ohio and New York. In 1836 he became the financial agent president of the board of trustees for Oberlin and was instrumental in admitting blacks and raising funds. He also traveled to England raising funds. As a professor at Oberlin he was very influential in setting the antislavery tone of the college and the community. He was pastor of the Hartford Congregational Church and authored the Western Reserve Liberty convention report that condemned pro-slavery churches. He was a strong Liberty Party supporter and participated in the 1843 national convention in Buffalo. In 1850 he again became financial agent at Oberlin.

KELLOGG, HIRAM HUNTINGTON (1806–1881) was born in Clinton, New York, and graduated from Hamilton College. He was converted in the Great Revival and was a devoted follower of Charles Finney, for whom he preached in the Oneida (N.Y.) area and as a Presbyterian minister in Clinton. While working in the Burned-Over District he became a close friend of Gerrit Smith, Beriah Green, and Alvan Stewart. He founded a Young Ladies Domestic Seminary in Clinton, the first female manual labor school and one that admitted blacks. He worked with George Washington Gale in establishing Knox College, and he served as its president from 1838 until 1845. He also opened a hotel, the Galesburg House, in 1842. He had a deep involvement in the antislavery movement in Illinois. He supported Birney in 1840, was the delegate of the Illinois Anti-Slavery Society to the London World Anti-Slavery Convention in 1843, and was active on the Underground Railroad. He continued his antislavery activities in the 1850s as a member of the American and Foreign Anti-Slavery Society. Later he lived in Wisconsin, Illinois, and Iowa.

KELSEY, DAVID M. was born in New England. He was active in the Illinois Liberty Party before becoming editor of the *Iowa Freeman* in 1848. He returned to Illinois, was active in Republican politics, and was elected to the state house in 1856–1858.

KING, LEICESTER (1789–1856) was a wealthy Ohio businessman who served two terms as a Whig state senator in the Ohio legislature and was a member of the Ohio Supreme Court (1840–1842). He angered members of both parties with his attempts to change the Ohio's notoriously discriminatory Black Laws. He had been a manager (1837–1838) and vice president (1839–1840) of the American Anti-Slavery Society. He eventually supported the Liberty Party and chaired the first Ohio Liberty Party convention (December 29, 1841). He was chairman of the 1843 national Liberty Party convention in Buffalo and served as Liberty gubernatorial nominee for Ohio in 1842 and 1844. The 1847 national convention selected him as John P. Hale's running mate on its presidential ticket. He subsequently stepped aside and supported the Free Soil movement in 1848.

KINGMAN, ELIPHALET (1775–1856) was born in Plymouth, Massachusetts, and was elected selectman in North Bridgewater (1824–1828), to the lower house of the state legislature (1831), and justice of the peace (1827). He was a former Democrat who ran on the Liberty ticket for state senator in 1843. He caused a stir in party circles when he committed himself to support the Democratic candidate for governor if he was elected to the legislature.

KNAPP, CHAUNCY LANGDON (1809–1898) was born in Vermont and was an apprentice printer in Montpelier, Vermont, for seven years. He eventually edited the (Montpelier, Vt.) *State Journal* and the *Voice of Freedom*. He became reporter for the Vermont legislature in 1833 and served as the Vermont secretary of state. He was an anti-Mason who became a strong Whig supporter of William Henry Harrison in 1836, but he was stripped of his secretary of state position in 1841 because he had supported Liberty candidates James G. Birney in 1840 and Titus Hutchinson for Vermont governor in 1841. He promptly moved to Lowell, Massachusetts, where he was involved in the antislavery movement and the Liberty Party. He had been a manager in the American Anti-Slavery Society (1840–1841), but he served on the executive committee of the American and Foreign Anti-Slavery Society. He was a Liberty congressional candidate in 1846 and supported the Free Soil Party in 1848, eventually becoming clerk of the state's lower house in 1851. He was elected to the U.S. Congress on the American Party ticket (1855–1857) and the Republican ticket (1857–1859). He then edited the (Lowell, Mass.) *American Citizen* (1859–1882). He was a Congregationalist who was involved in the temperance movement.

LAMBERT, WILLIAM (1818–1890) was born into a free black family in New Jersey. After a Quaker education, he settled in Detroit by 1840 and became successful in the tailoring business. He was involved in temperance activity, but he spent most of his time working for black causes and the black convention movement. He was an early supporter of the Liberty Party and was directly involved in its deliberations and conventions. He was one of the leaders of the Vigilance Committee and the Underground Railroad in Detroit, for which he earned the title "Vice President of the Detroit Underground Railroad." During the 1850s, he supported black emigration, particularly to Haiti, through conventions and the Episcopal Church. After the Civil War, he unsuccessfully ran for local offices as a Republican.

LANE, LUNSFORD (1803–1879) was born a slave in Raleigh, North Carolina. He eventually purchased his family's freedom. He became an antislavery lecturer, including working for the Liberty Party. At various times he lived in Philadelphia, Boston, Worcester, and New York. He worked as a steward in a Union hospital during the Civil War. He went to postwar North Carolina before returning to Massachusetts and finally New York City.

LANGSTON, CHARLES HENRY (1817–1892) was born a slave in Virginia but was emancipated in 1834. He enrolled at Oberlin and joined the Congregational Church. He helped found and taught at an African American school in Chillicothe, Ohio. He was on the executive committee and worked for the (Columbus, Ohio) *Palladium of Liberty*, was active in many civil rights causes, was involved in the black convention movement, and was a member of the Liberty Party. He was a leader in the Oberlin-Wellington rescue in 1858, aided John Brown, and endorsed violent protest. He was a Midwest recruiter for the Massachusetts Fifty-fourth and Fifty-fifth Regiments during the Civil War. Langston was active in the temperance movement and helped found Wilberforce University. He later moved to Kansas. He was John Mercer Langston's brother.

LANGSTON, JOHN MERCER (1829–1897) was born in Louisa County, Virginia, to a planter and his freed slave. The children of this union were taken care of in his will, and they moved to Ohio after the deaths of the parents in 1834. Raised by white foster parents, Langston earned his bachelor degree in 1849 and an M.A. in 1852 at Oberlin. He passed the Ohio bar in 1854. During the 1850s, he went from supporting emigration to espousing integration. While establishing a lucrative law practice, he became involved in local politics to go along with the antislavery activities he had begun at Oberlin. When he was elected township clerk in 1855, he became the first black elected to public office in the United States. In 1858 he helped organize the black Ohio State Antislavery Society. He recruited African American troops during the Civil War. After the war, he had a long career in education and politics: first dean of the law school, and later acting president, at Howard University; president of Virginia Normal and Collegiate Institute; consul to Haiti; and in the U.S. Congress (1889–1891) from Virginia.

LARIMER, WILLIAM (1809–1875) was born in Westmoreland County, Pennsylvania, and in 1834 moved to Pittsburgh, where he became a banker, merchant, and treasurer of the Ohio and Pennsylvania Railroad. Originally a Whig, he assisted in the organization of the Liberty Party in Pennsylvania and supported Birney in 1840 and 1844. When he ran for canal commissioner, an important state office in Pennsylvania, he gave the party its highest statewide percentage ever. He moved into the Free Soil Party in 1848, but eventually became a leading member of the Whig Party during the 1850s. After initial reluctance, he joined a Know Nothing lodge to further Whig interests. In 1855 he moved to Nebraska Territory, where he served in the territorial legislature as a Republican in 1856. He speculated in land in Kansas during the 1850s before creating the Denver City Land Company in 1858. He founded Denver (named after the territorial governor). During the Civil War, he served as a colonel in the Colorado volunteers before resigning to become a captain in the Kansas cavalry. After the Civil War, he was U.S. commissioner and probate judge in Denver. He supported Horace Greeley for the presidency in 1872.

LATIMER, GEORGE (1819–1896) escaped with his wife and child from Norfolk, Virginia, to Boston in late 1842. His owner followed him and had him arrested. Blacks failed in their attempts to rescue him, but then joined with white abolitionists to petition and raise funds for his defense. Ultimately, he was bought through the Tremont Baptist Society and released. The incident led to the passage of the Massachusetts Personal Liberty Act. He was an antislavery lecturer with Frederick Douglass, the Hutchinson Family singers, and later for the Liberty Party. Latimer worked as a paperhanger in Boston and for forty-five years in Lynn, Massachusetts. One of his sons, Lewis, became a famous inventor.

LEACH, DEWITT CLINTON (1822–1909) was born in New York and later moved to Michigan. He was a Liberty Party member and propagandist who contributed poetry and essays to the *Signal of Liberty*. He was elected to the Michigan lower house on a ticket supported by the Free Soil and Whig parties in 1849, was a delegate to Michigan's constitutional convention in 1850, and was a delegate to the Jackson, Michigan, convention that founded the Republican Party in 1854. He was the Michigan state librarian (1855–1856) and later edited newspapers in Michigan and Missouri. He was elected to two terms in the U.S. Congress (1857–1861) from Michigan, and he then was appointed Indian agent for Michigan (1861–1865). In 1867 he moved to Traverse City, Michigan, where he was involved in politics, journalism, and business. He was active in the Presbyterian Church.

LEAVITT, JOSHUA (1794–1873) was born in Heath, Massachusetts, to Chloe and Roger Leavitt, a prosperous businessman and representative to both houses of the Massachusetts legislature. He received two degrees from Yale (a B.A. in 1814 and a divinity degree in 1825). He was admitted to the bar in 1819 and was ordained a Congregational minister in 1825. He soon became involved in several reforms, eventually becoming an editor of several publications. He was an early colonizationist, but he soon became a convert to immediatism and a founding member of the New York State Anti-Slavery Society in 1833. He held various positions in the American Anti-Slavery Society before the schism in 1840. He then joined the American and Foreign Anti-Slavery Society, where he served on the executive committee (1840–1844, 1849–1852). He was probably the most important figure in the Liberty Party in New England. In fact, Elizur Wright called him "The Father of the Liberty Party." He was an editor of the *Emancipator* until 1847 and the short-lived (1844–1845) *Boston Morning Chronicle*. He was named a member of the national Liberty Party corresponding committee in 1843. He wrote, lectured, and lobbied extensively for antislavery causes, especially with his pamphlet on "The Financial Power of Slavery." He was a leader in the move to the Free Soil Party and later supported the Republican Party. He spent most of the rest of his life working on the reform newspaper the (New York) *Independent*.

LEAVITT, ROGER (1771–1840) was born in Massachusetts and was a prosperous businessman in Heath, which his father founded. He had served as a state representative, as a state senator, and in many local capacities, including a colonel in the state militia. He was a Congregationalist and reformer who was an officer in the local antislavery society. He died while a running as the Liberty candidate for lieutenant-governor in 1840.

LEE, LUTHER (1800–1889) was born in New York. He was very poorly educated until he married a teacher in 1825. He joined the Methodist Episcopal Church in 1821 and became an itinerant missionary and in 1836 began preaching abolition. He urged the formation of the Liberty Party in 1840. He seceded from the Methodist Church in 1842 and became a Wesleyan Methodist. He worked for the Liberty Party in many capacities, including making several trips to New Jersey to attend Liberty affairs and help organize the party there. He served on the executive committee of the American and Foreign Anti-Slavery Society (1846). In 1852 he returned to his congregation in Syracuse. After the Civil War he was a professor at Adrian College (1864–1867), a Wesleyan College in Adrian, Michigan. In 1867 he returned to the Methodist Episcopal Church. He remained in Flint, Michigan, after he retired.

LEMOYNE, FRANCIS JULIUS (1798–1879) was born in Pennsylvania and was a graduate of Washington College (1815) and Jefferson Medical College. He was a wealthy physician and philanthropist who was interested in scientific farming. He was very active in the Pennsylvania abolition movement. He served as an agent on the Underground Railroad, a manager of the American Anti-Slavery Society (1837–1840), and a vice president of the American and Foreign Anti-Slavery Society. He was an important Liberty Party member, serving as its only Pennsylvania gubernatorial candidate (1841, 1845, and 1847), a congressional candidate, and the Pennsylvania member of the Liberty Party national corresponding committee. He founded the *Washington* (Pa.) *Patriot* with Russell Errett in 1845 as a Liberty newspaper for the western part of the state. He supported the Liberty League in 1848, but by 1851 he joined the Free Democracy, the successor of the Free Soil Party, and later voted Republican. LeMoyne left his New School Presbyterian Church over the slavery issue and joined a Union church. In 1870 he gave a gift of twenty thousand dollars to the American Missionary Association to endow LeMoyne Normal Institute for colored students in Memphis, Tennessee. He was also an early advocate of cremation.

LEWIS, SAMUEL (1799–1854) was born in Massachusetts and worked as a cabin boy, farm laborer, mail carrier, carpenter, and surveyor's assistant. Without formal education, he was admitted to the bar in 1822. Nonetheless, he had a lifelong interest in educational reform. A member of the Whig Party, Lewis was state superintendent of schools for Ohio (1837–1839). He was also a licensed in 1824 as a Methodist Episcopal preacher with a reputation as an excellent orator. He was an important member of the Liberty Party in Ohio, serving as its congressional (1843, 1848) and gubernatorial (1846) nominee. He was named on the national Liberty corresponding committee. He was twice elected to the Cincinnati city council, and supported the Free Soil Party after 1848, serving as its gubernatorial candidate in 1851 and 1853.

LOGUEN, JERMAIN WESLEY (1813–1872) was born a slave in Tennessee and in 1835 fled to Canada, where he learned to read and write. He settled in Upstate New York, attended Oneida Institute, and subsequently opened schools for black children in Utica and Syracuse. He was ordained into the African Methodist Episcopal Zion Church in 1842 and opened several churches in the Upstate area. He soon became the chief agent of the Underground Railroad in Syracuse. During the mid- and late 1840s, he lectured extensively and effectively for the Liberty Party. In 1851 he fled to Canada to escape indictment for his role in the "Jerry Rescue." He returned to Syracuse in 1852, became more militant, and continued his aid to fugitives. He supported the Liberty League and the Radical Abolition Party during the decade. After the Civil War, he worked with Southern freedmen and was elected a bishop of his church.

LOVEJOY, JOSEPH C. (1805–1871) was a native of Maine and graduated from Bowdoin College (1829) and Bangor Theological Seminary (1834). He became principal of Hallowell Academy and was a Universalist minister in Old Town, Maine, until 1843 before moving to a church in Cambridgeport, Massachusetts (1843–1853). He was the first editor of the (Hallowell, Maine) *Liberty Standard* (1841–1842), a Liberty Party newspaper. He was the brother of antislavery martyr, Elijah, and Liberty leader and future congressman, Owen. During the 1850s, he renounced his earlier reform activities.

LOVEJOY, OWEN (1811–1864) was born in Maine and attended Bowdoin College for three years. He studied law but never practiced. Instead, after being refused ordination in the Episcopal Church because of his abolitionism, he became a Congregational minister in Princeton, Illinois (1837–1854). Lovejoy was an early antislavery worker and was a manager (1838–1840) in the American Anti-Slavery Society. He was a participant in the Liberty Party from its inception, serving on the Liberty Party National Committee named at the Buffalo convention in 1847 and running for the U.S. Congress on its ticket. He was a delegate to the 1848 Free Soil convention in Buffalo. He was a strong supporter of Free Soil coalitions before becoming one of the founders of the Republican Party in Illinois. He was elected a state representative in 1856 and then quickly chosen for the U.S. Congress, where he served until his death from Bright's disease in 1864. He was a lifelong temperance advocate and very active on the Underground Railroad in Illinois. His brothers were antislavery martyr, Elijah, and early Liberty Party editor, Joseph.

LYBRAND, JACOB (c. 1805–1875) was born in Philadelphia and relocated to Wisconsin at least by 1836. He was very active in the Wisconsin Liberty Party and the Wisconsin Liberty Association. He was the party's nominee for the territorial legislature in 1845, lieutenant-governor in 1848, and a delegate to the 1848 Buffalo Free Soil convention. He was a merchant in both Wisconsin and Iowa, where he moved in 1849. He made it a business practice to charge one price and refuse to bargain, as was common at the time. He donated lands for public building in both states and founded and platted the towns of Knob Prairie (later West Union) and Lybrand, Iowa. He was a respected but somewhat eccentric man. He eventually moved to Minnesota.

LYNDE, WILLIAM P. (1817–1885) was born in Sherburne, New York, and graduated from Yale (1838) and Harvard Law School (1841). He was a Democrat who was a stockholder in the Wisconsin Liberty Association. He was a law partner of Asahel Finch, territorial attorney general in 1844, and U.S. district attorney in 1845. He was elected to the U.S. House of Representatives as a Democrat in the state's inaugural election, but he lost to Free Soiler CHARLES DURKEE later in 1848. He was a reform mayor of Milwaukee in

1860–1861, a member of the state assembly in 1866, and a state senator in 1869–1870. He spent two terms (1875–1879) in the U.S. House of Representatives, where he introduced a bill for women's suffrage.

MAHAN, ASA (1800–1889) was born in New York and graduated from Hamilton College (1824) and Andover Theological Seminary (1827). He was licensed by the Oneida Presbytery and was a minister in the center of the Burned-Over District. He moved to a church in Cincinnati in 1831 and was elected a trustee for Lane Seminary, a position he resigned when he sided with the students in the antislavery debates. He then began a long career as a college president at Oberlin (1835–1850), Cleveland University (1850–1855), and Adrian (Mich.) College (1860–1871). Mahan was an early proponent of immediatism, was a vice president (1834–1835) in the American Anti-Slavery Society, and was active on the Underground Railroad. He was one of the early members of the Liberty Party in Ohio, participated in the 1848 national Free Soil convention, and later supported both the Free Soil and Republican parties.

MARSH, RODNEY V. (1807–1872) was born in Clarendon, Vermont. He was a lawyer active on the Underground Railroad in Brandon, Vermont, and in the Vermont Liberty Party. He was among those who issued the call for the 1845 Great Eastern Liberty Convention at Boston. He was elected to the lower house of the state legislature as a Republican in 1856, 1857, and 1858. He was the head of the Dred Scott committee that outlawed slavery in the state.

MATHEWS, EDWARD (1808–1873) was born in Oxford, England. He came to the United States and attended Hamilton Theological Seminary. He was a Baptist minister who would only establish churches that refused to recognize the right of slaveholding. He was the Illinois State Anti-Slavery Society's agent for Wisconsin and became an enthusiastic Liberty Party supporter, writer, and worker for the *Wisconsin Freeman*. In 1850 he was seized by proslavery men and dunked in a pond while he was working in Kentucky. Matthews was the model for "Fr. Dickson" in Harriet Beecher Stowe's novel, *Dred*, and a distant relative of temperance crusader Theobald Mathew. He returned to England in 1851.

MATLACK, LUCIUS C. (1816–1883) was born in Baltimore, Maryland. He was a founder of the Wesleyan Methodist Church and supporter of the Liberty Party. He was editor of the eastern Pennsylvania Liberty Party newspaper, the (Philadelphia) *American Citizen* (1845–1846). He established Illinois Institute, which became part of Wheaton (Ill.) College, in 1853 and served as its president until Jonathan Blanchard assumed control in 1860. He served as a chaplain in the Illinois Cavalry during the Civil War. He was a strong supporter of the Liberty Party and the editor of Henry Bibb's slave narrative and the *True Wesleyan* newspaper. He also served as a minister in Maryland, New Orleans, and Delaware.

MATTHEWS, STANLEY (1824–1889) was born in Cincinnati, Ohio, and graduated from Kenyon College in 1840. He worked at Union Seminary in Tennessee and was admitted to the Tennessee bar in 1842. While in Tennessee, he edited the *Tennessee Democrat,* a newspaper supporting James K. Polk. In 1844 he returned to Cincinnati to practice law with Salmon P. Chase, was a prosecuting attorney, and edited the Liberty Party's *Cincinnati National Press and Weekly Herald.* Matthews was a delegate to the 1847 national Liberty Party convention and went with most Liberty men into the Free Soil–Democratic coalition; but, unlike most, he did not join the Republican Party until 1863. He was elected clerk of the Ohio House of Representatives (1848–1849) and the state senate (1856–1858). He also filled several judgeships and prosecuting attorney positions during the 1850s, angering many antislavery men with his willingness to prosecute fugitive slave cases—behavior many believe hurt him politically later. Nonetheless, after rising to the rank of colonel in the Civil War, he was an elector on the Lincoln-Johnson ticket in 1864 and the Grant-Colfax ticket in 1868. Matthews was elected to the U.S. Senate (1877–1879) and was then appointed an associate justice of the U.S. Supreme Court (1881–1889). He was a practicing Presbyterian.

MAY, SAMUEL JOSEPH (1797–1871) was born in Massachusetts and attended Harvard and Harvard Divinity School. He was ordained a Congregational minister in 1822 and eventually was pastor at several churches. He was a founder of the American Anti-Slavery Society and was a close friend of William Lloyd Garrison. Originally a Garrisonian and opposed to the Liberty Party, May voted for and eventually worked with it by 1846. He gave an invocation at the 1848 Free Soil national convention and later supported the Republican Party.

MAY, SETH (1802–1881) was born in Winthrop, Maine, and educated at Monmouth and Hallowell academies. He was an accountant before becoming a successful and wealthy lawyer. He was a state committeeman in the Liberty Party and was the party's candidate for the U.S. Congress (1842, 1844) and later a justice on the Maine Supreme Court (1855–1862). After retiring from the court, he was the state's register of bankruptcy (1867–1873).

MCGEE, THOMAS (1790–1869) was born in Colrain, Massachusetts, and became a lawyer. After working in New York, he came to Michigan in 1832. He was a former Democrat who was an early supporter of the Liberty Party. He served as a presidential elector for the Birney-Earle ticket in 1840. He was also prominent on the Underground Railroad. He was elected to serve as a judge of probate (1856–1860).

MCKIM, JAMES MILLER (1810–1874) was born in Pennsylvania and educated at Dickinson College, Princeton Theological Seminary (1831), Andover Theological Seminary (1831–1832), and the University of Pennsylvania Medical School (1838–1839). He was a Presbyterian minister who left his ministry in to work in the abolition movement, eventually becoming a come-outer from the church. He had been a founder of the American Anti-Slavery Society in 1833 and was "One of the Seventy" lecturers. He was active in the Pennsylvania Anti-Slavery Society and was a corresponding editor for the *Pennsylvania Freeman* for twenty-five years. McKim supported the Liberty Party in some elections during the early 1840s, but he soon backed the Garrisonian American Anti-Slavery Society, for which he was a manager (1843–1853). He was very active on the Underground Railroad, supported John Brown, and recruited black troops during the Civil War. After the war, he was a founder of the *Nation* periodical.

MCKINNEY, MORDECAI (1796–1867) was born in Carlisle or Middleton, Pennsylvania, and graduated from Dickinson College in 1814. In 1817 he was admitted to the bar and began a practice at Harrisburg. He became deputy attorney general for Miami County, and in 1827 he was an associate judge of Dauphin County. He was a legal scholar with many publications. He was a Birney presidential elector in 1844. McKinney was on the Liberty Party convention committee in Harrisburg in July 1847 and was appointed as the Pennsylvania representative on the National Liberty Party corresponding committee at the 1847 Buffalo convention. He was a strong supporter of F. J. LeMoyne for governor and later was a Free Soil Democrat organizer. He represented blacks and was active on the Underground Railroad, especially after the passage of the Fugitive Slave Act of 1850. McKinney worked closely with the African American community during the 1850s and 1860s and helped them found the Second Presbyterian Church.

MELLEN, GEORGE WASHINGTON FROST (1804–1875) was born in Worcester, Massachusetts. He was an eccentric Boston chemist who wrote the first book-length study of the unconstitutionality of slavery, *An Argument on the Unconstitutionality of Slavery* (1841). He has been identified with the Liberty Party. He died in a mental institution.

MILLER, JONATHAN PECKHAM (1796–1847) was born in Vermont and attended both Dartmouth and the University of Vermont. He was called "colonel" because of his reputation as "the American Daredevil" that he gained fighting alongside Lord Byron in the war for Greek Independence from 1824 to 1826. Originally a tanner, Miller was admitted to the Vermont bar after his return from overseas. He was elected to three terms (1831–1833) in the Vermont legislature, where he sponsored resolutions ordering the Vermont representatives in Congress to introduce resolutions abolishing slavery and the slave trade in the District of Columbia. He was also a manager (1835–1837) in the American Anti-Slavery Society and in 1840 was a delegate to the World Anti-Slavery Convention in London, where he spoke strongly in favor of seating women as delegates. Initially opposed to a third party, he left the Whigs and became an important Liberty spokesman. He was also a trustee of Norwich University from its founding to his death.

MILLER, WILLIAM H. was born in Pennsylvania and eventually settled in Union and Birmingham, Iowa, where he was a physician and farmer. A former Whig, he ran for secretary of state on the Liberty ticket in the summer of 1848. He was the only delegate from west of the Mississippi at the 1848 Free Soil national convention and also served as one of its presidential electors for Iowa in 1848. He was an elder in the Presbyterian Church in Birmingham.

MILLS, JOSEPH TROTTER (1812–1897) was born in Kentucky and moved to Illinois and attended Illinois College, after which he served as a tutor to Zachary Taylor's children. In 1840 he settled in Lancaster, Wisconsin, where he was admitted to the bar (1844). He was active in both the Liberty and Republican parties. He was a state assemblyman (1856, 1857, 1862, and 1879). In 1864 he was elected court judge of the Fifth Judicial District, where he served from 1865 to 1877.

MILTIMORE, IRA (1813–1879) was born in Windham, Vermont, and eventually moved to Chicago, where he was a machinist and builder. He was a founding officer in the Chicago Anti-Slavery Society in 1840. He was elected an alderman in 1839, 1840, and 1841, and on the Liberty ticket in 1844. He helped found Chicago's first public school. In the mid-1840s he moved to Janesville, Wisconsin, where he built a large mill and participated in local Republican politics. He enlisted as a captain in the Civil War and was a war hero. He returned from the war and continued his public service.

MONROE, JAMES (1821–1898) was born in Connecticut and was a Garrisonian abolitionist lecturer (1841–1844) before enrolling at Oberlin, where he was converted to political abolition and the Liberty Party. He received his B.A. (1846), finished his theological training (1849), became a minister, and received his M.A. (1850) from Oberlin. Monroe married Charles G. Finney's daughter and taught at Oberlin (1849–1862, 1883–1896). He turned down the Free Soil nomination for Ohio's lower house (1851, 1853) and tended to prefer the Liberty League. By 1855, he changed his mind, and was elected a state representative (1856–1862) as a Republican. Lincoln appointed him consul to Rio de Janeiro (1863–1869). Shortly after he returned, he was elected to the U.S. Congress (1871–1881).

MONTEITH, JOHN (1787–1868) was born in Pennsylvania and graduated from Jefferson College and Princeton Theological Seminary. He founded the first Protestant church in Detroit in 1816 and was a cofounder and the first president of the University of Michigan (1817–1821). He later became a professor of classical languages at Hamilton College (1821–1832) before becoming pastor of the First Presbyterian Church in Elyria, Ohio. Monteith was a manager in the American Anti-Slavery Society (1833–1837) and was "One of the Seventy" abolitionist lecturers. He was an early proponent of antislavery political action and a delegate to several Liberty conventions in Ohio. His house on the Underground Railroad had a tunnel that went from his basement to the Black River.

MORRIS, THOMAS (1776–1844) was born in Pennsylvania and grew up in a poor Baptist family, never went to a formal school, moved to the Cincinnati area in 1795, read law, and was admitted to the Ohio bar in 1804. He was in office for thirty-three consecutive years in Ohio: lower house of the state legislature (1806–1815); state senate (1820–1833); justice of the Ohio Supreme Court (1815–1820); and U.S. Senate (1833–1839). After his senate term, the Democratic Party proscribed him because of his outspoken antislavery views. He was of the opinion that the Fugitive Slave Law of 1793 was unconstitutional. He served on the executive committee of the American and Foreign Anti-Slavery Society (1840–1844) and was active in temperance work. He joined the Liberty Party and became its vice presidential candidate in 1844.

MYRICK, LUTHER (1784–1843) was born in Washington, New York, and became a Presbyterian minister and pastor for several Presbyterian churches in Upstate New York. He was put on trial and subsequently suspended for preaching perfectionist doctrines. Eventually, he was a founder of the come-outer Union Church movement. In September 1841 he and James C. Jackson established the (Cazenovia, N.Y.) *Madison County Abolitionist*. By 1842, he supported the Liberty Party despite being a manager in the American Anti-Slavery Society (1841–1842). He was also a strong supporter of women's rights. He died in Jackson, Michigan.

NELSON, DAVID (1793–1844) was born in Tennessee and graduated from Washington College (Tennessee) at the age of sixteen. He studied medicine and was a former army surgeon who had served with Andrew Jackson in the War of 1812. Originally a New School Presbyterian, he became a hard-drinking, pleasure-oriented, slaveholding Deist; but after marriage, he returned to the church. In 1825 he gave up medicine, was licensed to preach, and became an evangelist. He moved to Missouri and established a manual training school, Marion College, but he was driven out of Missouri for his abolitionist convictions and being an agent of the American Anti-Slavery Society. He opened another manual training school to provide theological training, Mission Institute, in Quincy, Illinois, in 1836. He was very active in the antislavery movement. He was a vice president of the American Anti-Slavery Society (1836–1840) and on the executive committee of the American and Foreign Anti-Slavery Society. He was a leader on the Underground Railroad and was an officer at the convention in Princeton, Illinois (July 5, 1840), that set up the first Liberty Party ticket in the Northwest. He continued to work for the party until his death from the effects of epilepsy in 1844.

NOBLE, LINNAEUS P. (1802–1873) was born in Hoosick, New York, and moved to Fayettville, New York, in 1829. He was a founding member of the Liberty Party, serving as a secretary at the Albany convention, and gave a speech at the state Liberty convention in January 1841. He was a founder and publisher of the *National Era* (1847–1860) with Gamaliel Bailey. He was a deacon in the Fayettville Baptist Church and a director of the Syracuse National Bank.

OLIN, CHAUNCEY C. (1817–1896) was born in Canton, New York, and went to Wisconsin to obtain land in 1836. He returned to Canton for two years of schooling at Canton Academy before going back to Wisconsin in 1839. He was a strong supporter of the Liberty Party and lectured extensively with the former slave LEWIS WASHINGTON. He also served as editor of the *Wisconsin Freeman*. He later moved to Indianapolis, Indiana.

PAINE, JAMES HARVEY (1791–1879) was born in Milford, Connecticut, and later moved to Painesville, Ohio, which had been founded by his family. He was a former Whig state senator in Ohio and a general in the state militia. After opposing abolitionism in the mid-1830s, he became a committed abolitionist and was one of the first to help set up an independent antislavery slate in a local election in 1839. He was one of the earliest and most fervent supporters of the Liberty Party in Ohio and served as the president of the Ohio Liberty Party convention in 1844. Paine remained active in the party after moving to Milwaukee in 1848. He was selected to be a Liberty presidential elector for 1848 before attending and participating in the Free Soil convention in Buffalo. He remained one of the elder statesmen of antislavery politics in both the Wisconsin Free Soil and Republican parties. He and his son, Byron, successfully argued the unconstitutionality of the Fugitive Slave Law of 1850 before the Wisconsin Supreme Court.

PARKHURST, JONATHAN (1779–1854) was born in New Jersey and became a director for the Morris and Essex Railway. He was a founder and manager of the American Anti-Slavery Society (1833–1840). He was the Liberty Party candidate for governor of New Jersey in 1844 and state assembly in 1846. He was named to the national corresponding committee at the national convention in 1847. He later moved to Illinois.

PAYNE, JOHN A. was a delegate from New Jersey at the founding of the Liberty Party at the Albany convention on April 1, 1840. He was also on the executive committee of the American and Foreign Anti-Slavery Society (1842–1844). He was a Liberty nominee for the U.S. Congress from New Jersey in 1846. His last name is sometimes spelled "Paine."

PECK, JOHN C. (1802–1875) was born in Hagerstown, Maryland, and grew up in northern Virginia. He moved to Carlisle, Pennsylvania, in 1821 and then to Pittsburgh in 1837. He was successful in many businesses and became a leader in the Pittsburgh black community. He was also a minister and established an African Methodist Episcopal church in the city. He was on the publishing committee of the (Pittsburgh) *Mystery*, was a major figure on the Underground Railroad, was on the executive committee of the Western Pennsylvania Anti-Slavery Society, worked for black voting rights, and was a supporter of Liberty Party activities. He eventually became so discouraged that he professed a belief in emigration, but he never left Pittsburgh. His son, Dr. David Peck, became a prominent physician and black activist.

PENNINGTON, JAMES WILLIAM CHARLES (1807–1870) was born a slave and trained as a blacksmith on a plantation on Maryland's Eastern Shore. He escaped in late 1827 and eventually made his way to Brooklyn, New York, where he worked as a coachman and teacher. In 1835 he moved to Hartford, Connecticut, where he worked in antislavery and temperance while sitting in on classes at Yale Divinity School. After his ordination in 1838, he served at the Talcott Street Congregational Church in Hartford (1840–1847), which became an important stop on the Underground Railroad. He was a founder of the Connecticut Liberty Party. After he attended the World's Anti-Slavery Convention in London in 1843, he returned to Hartford and worked for the Liberty Party, especially playing an important role in a national convention that took place in Albany, New York, in early December 1844. In 1848 he went to New York City as pastor of the First Colored Presbyterian Church. During the early 1850s, he was purchased and freed by former Liberty man, John Hooker. He made several trips overseas to solicit funds and do missionary work. On one of these he was awarded an honorary doctor of divinity degree from Heidelburg. He was on the executive committee of the American and Foreign Anti-Slavery Society (1848–1850), and he remained a committed integrationist and opposed to the emigration movement. He developed a drinking problem in the 1850s that hampered his work, although he seems to have overcome it later. He encouraged black enlistment in the Civil War and died while working among the freedmen in Florida.

PENNOCK, ABRAHAM LIDDON (1786–1868) was born in Marboro, Pennsylvania. He was a Hicksite Quaker who worked in a variety of reforms and on the Underground Railroad. He was a businessman and inventor who devised a hose and a mailbag that he sold to the U.S. government. He served as vice president in the American Anti-Slavery Society and became an active Liberty man who was a personal friend of the Birney family. He was a founder of Haverford College (1833).

PHELPS, AMOS AUGUSTUS (1805–1847) was born in Connecticut and graduated from Yale (1826) and Yale Divinity School (1830). He was a Congregational minister and a member of the American Colonization Society who unsuccessfully tried to get it to condemn white racism. His *Lectures on Slavery and Its Remedy* (1834) became an important part of antislavery discourse. He was an early member of the New England Anti-Slavery Society and a founder and officeholder in the American Anti-Slavery Society and "One of the Seventy." He broke with Garrison in 1840 and was a founder of the Massachusetts Abolition Society and of the American and Foreign Anti-Slavery Society, for which he was corresponding secretary (1845–1847) and a member of the executive committee (1844–1847). He wrote several abolition pamphlets and was a successful antislavery lecturer. He was an influential Liberty Party leader and propagandist in Massachusetts and an early correspondent of the *National Era*.

PIERPONT, JOHN (1785–1866) was born in Connecticut and graduated from Yale (1804). He taught four years in South Carolina before returning North to study law with Tapping Reeves. He was admitted to the bar in 1812 before leaving law in 1814 to go into the dry goods business. When the business failed in 1816, he spent a short time in jail for debts (which must have been somewhat of an embarrassment to his grandson, J. P. Morgan). Pierpont then decided on the ministry for a career and graduated from Harvard Divinity School (1818). He was a Unitarian minister for most of the rest of his life. He eventually moved to a church in Troy, New York, before returning to the Boston area. He achieved a reputation as a poet and writer, including antislavery material, and was a strong supporter of the Liberty Party. At the 1843 Buffalo national convention, he was the author of the resolution declaring that slavery was unconstitutional. He later supported the Free Soil and Republican parties. He was a chaplain at the beginning of the Civil War, but left because of bad health. He became a clerk in the Treasury Department in Washington.

PINKERTON, ALLAN (1819–1884) was born in Scotland and fled to the United States to escape imprisonment relating to his activities in the Chartist movement. He settled in Illinois, where he ran a cooperage and became a deputy sheriff in Kane County. He eventually became a deputy sheriff of Cook County and later became the first detective for Chicago. He was active on the Underground Railroad and in the Liberty Party and served as a party candidate for sheriff. He established his detective agency and became head of the secret service for the Union during the Civil War. After the Civil War he ran his famous detective agency.

PLUMB, RALPH (1816–1903) was born in Busti, New York, and moved to Ohio's Western Reserve where he and his brother, Samuel, were leaders of the Liberty Party. He was elected to the Ohio legislature in 1855. He subsequently studied law and relocated to Oberlin, where he participated in the Oberlin-Wellington Rescue. During the Civil War he served as captain and quartermaster of volunteers, eventually becoming a colonel. After the war he moved to Streator, Illinois, and worked in mining and railroad businesses. He was mayor of Streator (1882–1885) before serving two terms (1885–1889) in the U.S. Congress.

PLUMB, SAMUEL (1812–1882) was born in Littlefield, New York, and by 1820 moved to Lenox, Ashtabula County, Ohio, on the Western Reserve, where he and his brother, Ralph, were leaders of the Liberty Party. He was elected to the state legislature (1850–1854). He was active in the antislavery movement for many years, being elected a secretary of the Vernon (Trumbull County, Ohio) Anti-Slavery Society in 1836 and was one of the two explorers for the Kansas Emigrant Aid Society of Northern Ohio in 1854. He settled in Oberlin by the end of the decade. He served as mayor of Oberlin in 1864 and 1865, and was a delegate to the Republican state convention in 1865. He was a leader in calling for the impeachment of President Andrew Johnson. He moved to Streator, Illinois (1869), where he was a banker.

POLAND, JOSEPH (1818–1898) was the founder of the (Vt.) *Voice of Freedom* in 1839 and was the editor of the (Montpelier, Vt.) *Green Mountain Freeman,* the Liberty newspaper, which he built into the newspaper with the largest circulation in Vermont. He eventually entered politics in the Free Soil and Republican parties. He ran unsuccessfully for state treasurer on the Free Soil ticket in 1849 and 1850. In his long political career, he was elected both as a state representative and state senator. He also edited some Congregational newspapers, including the *Vermont Watchman,* the *Vermont Chronicle,* and the *New Hampshire Journal.*

PORTER, ARTHUR LIVERMORE (1798–1845) was a native of New Hampshire and a graduate of Dartmouth (1818) before studying in Europe at the universities of London, Dublin, and Edinburgh. He developed a reputation as a doctor and chemist. He moved to Detroit in 1828 and became involved in abolition work during the 1830s. He was a manager in the American Anti-Slavery Society (1837–1840), secretary of the Detroit Anti-Slavery Society, and vice president of the Michigan State Anti-Slavery Society. Porter was one of the early advocates of antislavery political action, being involved in questioning candidates during the late 1830s and in the founding of the Liberty Party in Michigan in 1840. He was nominated for the U.S. Congress on the Liberty Party ticket in 1843 and was an officer in the Detroit Liberty Association. He had a deep interest in history and was a member of the Michigan Historical Society.

PORTER, SAMUEL DRUMMOND (1808–1881) was born in what became Bristol, Maine. He moved to Rochester, New York, in 1827 as a bookseller and later became wealthy in land speculation. He was very active in the abolition movement in the Rochester area, serving as secretary of the corresponding secretary of the Rochester Anti-Slavery Society and as a member of the Western New York Anti-Slavery Society. He was a manager of the Garrisonian American Anti-Slavery Society (1843–1844) but was a strong Liberty supporter who ran for mayor of Rochester on the Liberty ticket and was a Birney elector in 1844. His barn was a stop on the Underground Railroad, and he worked with Frederick Douglass in the 1850s to open Rochester schools to blacks. He switched his New School Presbyterian Church membership at least twice over antislavery issues.

POTTS, DAVID (1794–1863) was born in Pennsylvania and became an iron master. He was the owner and manager of Warwick Furnace. He was elected to the Pennsylvania house of representatives (1824–1826) before sitting in the U.S. Congress for four terms (1831–1839). He was a Liberty congressional candidate in 1844. He was also the Free Soil candidate for governor in 1854 but withdrew.

POWER, NATHAN (1801–1874) was born in New York State and migrated to Michigan in 1826, where he was a schoolteacher and farmer. A Quaker, he was a founding member of the Michigan State Anti-Slavery Society and a strong Liberty Party supporter and candidate for lieutenant-governor in 1841. He served as a delegate to the national Free Soil convention in Pittsburgh (1852) and was elected to the state legislature in Michigan as a Republican in 1855. He was a well-known operator on the Underground Railroad.

RANKIN, ADAM LOWRY (1816–1895) was born in Tennessee son of Reverend John T. Rankin. He was one of the founders of the Ohio Liberty Party. He went to Iowa Territory (1841–1843) as a Presbyterian missionary of the American Home Missionary Society. He returned to Ohio in 1843 and preached and did other reform work, including acting as a publishing agent for Cassius M. Clay's (Ky.) *True American* and as an agent for the antislavery Western Reform Book and Tract Society. He served as a chaplain in the Civil War before moving to Tulare, California, in 1873 as the pastor of a Congregational church.

RANKIN, JOHN T. (1793–1886) was born in Tennessee and was a pioneer in the antislavery movement. He joined his first abolition society in 1815 and continued his work in the Kentucky Abolition Society. Having been licensed to preach in the Presbyterian Church (1817), he moved to Ripley, Ohio, where he was the pastor of the Presbyterian Church (1821–1865). During these years he was an influential writer and lecturer on antislavery, and was mobbed many times. He was an important member of the American Anti-Slavery Society, serving as "One of the Seventy" and holding many offices. A supporter of William Henry Harrison in 1840, he later became a fervent Liberty, Free Soil, and Republican party supporter. Perhaps he is most famous for his work on the Underground Railroad, where his part in the escape of a slave and her son became the model for Harriet Beecher Stowe's novel, *Uncle Tom's Cabin*. He later moved to Illinois and Kansas before returning to Ohio in 1881.

RAY, CHARLES B. (1807–1886) was born to a family of mixed white, Indian, and black heritage in Massachusetts. He attended both Wesleyan Academy and Wesleyan Theological Seminary, from which he withdrew after complaints from white students. He moved to New York City in the early 1830s and opened a shoe store, but he made his name as a reformer, journalist, and antislavery leader. He was the owner-editor of the *Colored American* until its demise in December 1841 and then became pastor of a Congregational church in New York City in 1845. Throughout his life he was active in black causes, especially in education. Ray was on the executive committee of the American and Foreign Anti-Slavery Society (1847–1851, 1853–1855). He was a committed to political action and was an early supporter of the Liberty Party. He served on the Liberty Party nominating committee at the 1843 national convention.

RICE, LEWIS LIPPETT (1801–1886) was born in Otsego, New York, and trained as a printer in New York City. He was a former Whig editor of the *Painesville* (Ohio) *Telegraph* that became a Liberty Party newspaper. He was editor of the Liberty Party (Warren, Ohio) *Liberty Herald,* the *Ohio American,* and its successor, the *Cleveland American.* He served as private secretary to Governor Salmon P. Chase before becoming editor of the *Lorain County News* (1864–1865). He then served as the superintendent for public printing in Ohio for the next twelve years. He lived in Oberlin before moving to Hawaii in 1879. He was a Congregationalist.

SABIN, ALVAH (1793–1885) was born in Vermont and graduated from Columbian College (now George Washington University). He studied theology in Philadelphia and became a Baptist minister, and then returned to Vermont in 1825 to become a pastor. During the 1830s, he became "One of the Seventy" band of antislavery lecturers. Sabin was politically active with the Anti-Masonic and Democratic parties before joining the Liberty Party as its nominee for lieutenant-governor in 1841. He was regularly elected to the Vermont legislature between 1826 and 1851, was Vermont secretary of state (1841–1842), and served in the U.S. Congress (1853–1857). He was an officer in the Vermont Anti-Slavery Society and did much lecturing. In 1867 he moved to Sycamore, Illinois, as a Baptist preacher.

SCOTT, JACOB (1800–1878) was born in Barre, Vermont. He was a former Democrat who was the Liberty Party candidate for lieutenant-governor of Vermont (1846–1847). He bought the *Green Mountain Freeman* in 1849.

SCOTT, ORANGE (1800–1847) was born in Vermont and was a Methodist circuit riding preacher by the time he was twenty-one, four years before he was ordained in the Methodist Episcopal Church. The bishop of Providence, Rhode Island, removed him as an elder because he had begun to preach immediate abolition. He lectured for two years in New England and New York as "One of the Seventy" of the American Anti-Slavery Society, for which he was a manager (1838–1840). He became a strong opponent of William Lloyd Garrison and was an original member and on the executive committee of the American and Foreign Anti-Slavery Society. He endorsed the Birney-Earle ticket in 1840 and continued to work for the Liberty Party, although his major effort was to abolitionize the Methodist Church. Failing in this, he was a presiding officer in the convention that founded the Wesleyan Methodist Church in 1843.

SEWALL, SAMUEL (1799–1888) was born in Massachusetts and was the direct descendant of Judge Samuel Sewall, who presided at the Salem witch trials and wrote "The Selling of Joseph," the first antislavery essay written in America. He was a graduate of Phillips Exeter Academy, Harvard (1817), and Harvard Law School (1820). He was an early immediate abolitionist who was a founder and board member of the New England Anti-Slavery Society and a manager in the American Anti-Slavery Society (1833–1837). Formerly a Whig, he maintained ties with the Old Organization until 1842 while serving on the Liberty Party's state central committee. He was the party's gubernatorial candidate (1842–1847) and editor of the (Boston) *Emancipator* for a short time after 1847. He joined the Free Soil coalition in 1848 and was elected as a Massachusetts state senator (1851–1852). He later supported the Republican Party. He was active on the Underground Railroad, served as counsel in many fugitive slave cases, and worked for women's suffrage. He was a lifelong Unitarian, but he had wide religious interests.

SHAFTER, OSCAR LOVELL (1812–1873) was born in Vermont and graduated from Wesleyan College (1834) and Harvard Law School (1836). He was a legal scholar who came from a long line of Vermont politicians. Shafter was a former Democrat who joined the Vermont Liberty Party and served as its candidate for the U.S. Congress in 1844. He joined the Free Soil coalition in 1848 and was the Free Soil candidate for governor in 1848. He moved to California in 1854 and eventually became an associate justice of the California Supreme Court. His father was William R. Shafter.

SHAFTER, WILLIAM R. (1786–1864) was born in Vermont and served as a representative in the Vermont Assembly (1831), a member of the Constitutional Convention of 1836, and a county judge. A former Democrat, he was the Liberty candidate for governor (1844–1845) and a temperance candidate for governor (1855). His son was Oscar L. Shafter.

SHAW, BENJAMIN F. (1789–1874) was a Methodist minister who was a vice president at the April 1, 1840, Albany convention that founded the Liberty Party and was a delegate to the party's national convention in New York City in 1841. He was involved in establishing the Liberty Party in Vermont. He later delivered a famous sermon on the "Illegality of Slavery."

SHEDD, GEORGE (1810–1892) was originally from New Hampshire, graduated from Dartmouth (1839), studied medicine in Ohio, and received his M.D. from the Medical Institute in Cincinnati. He was appointed Iowa's representative on the Liberty Party national committee in December 1847. He was also active on the Underground Railroad and in the Congregational Church. He became a Free Soil organizer and later became superintendent of the Iowa State Penitentiary.

SHEPARD, CHARLES O. (1806–1867) worked in Arcade, New York, and was a member of the senate in the New York legislature during the 1830s. He was an original organizer of the Liberty Party, was the Liberty Party candidate for lieutenant-governor of New York (1840, 1842, 1844, and 1847), and went into the Free Soil Party in 1848. He was an officer of the Attica and Albany Railroad and was prominent in the New York Republican Party. Originally a Congregationalist, Shepard moved into the Union Church but later gave up organized religion. He operated an Underground Railroad station in Arcade.

SHIPHERD, JOHN JAY (1802–1844) was born in Vermont, the son of Zebulon Rudd Shipherd, who was a Federalist in the U.S. House of Representatives and a trustee of Middlebury College. He became a Congregationalist minister who was greatly influenced by Charles G. Finney. In 1831 he went into northeastern Ohio on missionary work and became one of the cofounders of the coeducational Oberlin College, where he received support from the Tappans and welcomed the Lane rebels. He later moved to Michigan, where he founded Olivet College in the year of his death.

SHIRAS, CHARLES P. (1824–1854) was from an influential and wealthy family. He was known as the "Iron City Poet" and was a close friend and collaborator of Stephen Foster. The Hutchinson Family antislavery singing group sang some of his work. He began the (Pittsburgh) *Albatross* to replace the defunct *Spirit of Liberty* as the Liberty newspaper in Pittsburgh.

SHOLES, CHARLES CLARK (1816–1867) was born in Connecticut and trained as a printer in Pennsylvania. He moved to Green Bay, Wisconsin Territory, in 1836 and founded at least three Democratic newspapers. He was appointed clerk of the Territorial District Court and was elected to the lower house of the territorial legislature (1837–1838). Sholes became disgusted with the Democratic Party's positions on slavery and Texas annexation, so he changed his *Milwaukee Democrat* into the antislavery *Free American*, which he edited until 1846, and supported the Liberty Party. He served several terms as a mayor of Kenosha, in both houses of the state legislature, and as Speaker of the Wisconsin state Assembly (1855). He was the Republican candidate for lieutenant-governor for 1856 and a delegate to the 1860 Republican National Convention. He was a state senator (1866–1867).

SMITH, EDWARD (1797–1856), Virginia born, was a Methodist minister who eventually became a Wesleyan Methodist. He joined the Liberty Party and edited the (Pittsburgh) *Spirit of Liberty* (1841–1843), an official Liberty newspaper in western Pennsylvania, and wrote on antislavery subjects. He eventually moved to Ohio, where he continued his Liberty Party and Underground Railroad activities. He attended the Southern and Western Convention in 1848 and spoke at the Free Soil convention at Buffalo in 1848. Smith was the Free Soil candidate for governor of Ohio in 1850. He was very active in the Canada Mission for freedom.

SMITH, GERRIT (1797–1874) was born in Utica, New York, and graduated from Hamilton College (1818). He was a wealthy landowner and businessman in Upstate New York who participated in and generously financed many reforms. He renounced the colonization movement in the mid-1830s and became a strong leader for the immediate abolition of slavery. He left his New School Presbyterian Church and started the Union Church movement over the slavery issue. Smith was a founder of the Liberty Party and served as its candidate for governor of New York in 1840. He was also a founder of the National Liberty Party in 1848 and of the Radical Abolition Party of the 1850s. He was the presidential candidate of the Liberty League, National Liberty Party, and National Reform Association in 1848. He was elected to the U.S. Congress for 1853 but resigned the following year. He continued to support the Radical Abolition Party through the 1860 election—he was even its reluctant candidate—but he supported Lincoln in 1864. He was a friend of John Brown, to whom he gave material support, and suffered a breakdown after Harper's Ferry. He supported the Republican Party except for a brief flirtation with the Prohibition Party in the late 1860s and early l870s. After his Union Church declined, he attended a Methodist church in his old age.

SMITH, JAMES MCCUNE (1813–1865) was born free to former slaves in New York City. After he was unable to enter American colleges because of his race, he went to Glasgow University, where he eventually graduated as a medical doctor. He returned to New York and became a leader in the African American community, especially espousing integration and self-help proposals. Initially opposed to the Liberty Party, he became one of its supporters by early 1848. He was the nominee of the Radical Abolition Party for secretary of state in New York. He wrote extensively on race issues throughout his life.

SMYTH, WILLIAM (1797–1868) was born in Pittston, Maine, and fought in the War of 1812. He graduated as class valedictorian from Bowdoin College (1822) and from Andover Theological Seminary before taking up duties as a professor of mathematics, natural philosophy, and classics at Bowdoin, where he wrote many textbooks. He served as a manager in the American Anti-Slavery Society (1835–1837) before becoming a member of the executive committee of the American and Foreign Anti-Slavery Society. He was a temperance advocate and worked on the Maine Underground Railroad. He was the editor of the (Brunswick, Maine) *Advocate of Freedom* and an early leader in the move to establish the Liberty Party in the state. He was an officer of his Congregational church in Brunswick.

SNOW, HENRY H. (1791–1861) was originally from New Hampshire, but moved to Alton and then Quincy, Illinois. He was a town pioneer and served as a judge, justice of the peace, city clerk, surveyor, and several other offices. He was an officer in the Adams County Anti-Slavery Society and became the Liberty Party candidate for lieutenant-governor of Illinois in 1848. He was a Congregationalist deacon and very active on the Underground Railroad.

SPOONER, THOMAS (1817–1890) was born in Cincinnati, Ohio. He was a neighbor of Salmon P. Chase in Cincinnati and the nephew of Samuel Lewis. He was one of the few Liberty Party supporters who became an ardent Know Nothing. He was elected president of the Ohio Order of the Star Spangled Banner (Know Nothing). He later joined the Republican Party. He received a minor customs post through Chase's influence in the Lincoln administration after having been passed over for more lucrative positions.

ST. CLAIR, ALANSON (1804–1877) was born in Maine and was attracted to Unitarianism and Universalism before returning to Congregationalism and being ordained a minister when he was thirty-six. He had a long career in the antislavery movement and worked in many states. He was an agent for the American Anti-Slavery Society in Massachusetts before he broke away and became a charter member of the Massachusetts Abolition Society in 1839. For the next few years he lectured on abolition and for the Liberty Party in Massachusetts, Vermont, and New Hampshire. He moved to a farm outside Chicago in 1845, but he was drawn back into antislavery work by 1847 as the financial agent and corresponding secretary for the Liberty Party in northeastern Illinois. St. Clair successfully lectured in the southern part of the state before going to Iowa in December 1847, founding the Iowa Liberty Party, and spending the winter lecturing there. He later supported the Free Soil and Republican parties, even winning the post of township clerk in Orlando, Illinois, in 1850. In addition to his lecturing and organizing work, he worked as an antislavery journalist. He was one of the four founders of the *Massachusetts Abolitionist*, co-founder of the (New Hampshire) *Advocate of Freedom*, and founder of the *Iowa Freeman*.

STANTON, BENJAMIN (1808–1849) was born in Indiana. He was the influential antislavery editor of the (New Garden, Ind.) *Free Labor Advocate and Anti-Slavery Reporter* who came to Indiana from Ohio. He was an Orthodox Quaker who had served as a manager in the American Anti-Slavery Society (1837–1840). He worked on the Underground Railroad and promoted buying only items that had been produced without slave labor. Stanton was initially opposed to the Free Soil movement and any dilution of Liberty principles; but, after serving as a delegate to the Buffalo convention, he endorsed the Free Soil Party. He was a leader in the 1843 split of antislavery Quakers in Indiana.

STANTON, HENRY BREWSTER (1805–1888) was born in Connecticut, attended Rochester (N.Y.) Manual Labor Institute (1828–1830), and was a reporter for Thurlow Weed's newspaper, the *Monroe Telegraph*. After being converted by Charles G. Finney, he spent over ten years working in the antislavery movement. He was one of the Lane Rebels and an agent for the American Anti-Slavery Society in New York, Connecticut, Rhode Island, and Massachusetts. With John Greenleaf Whittier and Theodore Dwight Weld he selected "The Seventy" agents to lecture on abolition. Stanton was a financial secretary of the American Anti-Slavery Society (1837–1840), and he was a main organizer of the petition campaigns that marked the decade. He broke with the Old Organization in 1840 and joined the new American and Foreign Anti-Slavery Society, for which he was secretary (1840–1841) and on the executive committee (1840–1844). He was a delegate to the World Anti-Slavery Convention at London in 1840, the same year he married future women's rights advocate, Elizabeth Cady. He was involved in Liberty affairs through the life of the party, but he also was admitted to the Massachusetts bar in 1843 and began practicing law to support his growing family. The family relocated to Seneca Falls, New York, in 1847, and Stanton was an important player in the Free Soil merger. Subsequently, he was elected to the state senate for two terms beginning in 1849 and helped organize the Republican

Party in 1855. He later was a journalist for the *New York Tribune* and the *New York Sun*. He ultimately returned to the Democratic Party during the Grant administration.

STEVENS, LUTHER F. (1783–1846), born in Massachusetts, was a lawyer and temperance advocate who came to Michigan from Seneca Falls, New York, in the late 1830s. He ran on the Whig ticket for the U.S. House of Representatives and almost received the party's gubernatorial nomination. Stevens was active in public and religious affairs, serving as a district judge and a delegate to the Presbyterian General Assembly in Philadelphia in 1836 and 1837. He moved to Kalamazoo about 1840 and was the Liberty Party candidate for lieutenant-governor in 1843. He was named the Michigan representative on the corresponding committee of the national Liberty Party in 1843. He also served as a judge in St. Joseph County.

STEVENS, STEPHEN C. (1793–1870) was born in Kentucky and went to Indiana before the War of 1812. He was wounded in the head at the battle of New Orleans, an injury that troubled him later and may have led to his insanity. He was admitted to the Indiana bar in 1817 and served in the lower house (1817, 1823–1824) and senate (1826–1828) of the state legislature before serving on its supreme court (1831–1836). He opened a law office in Madison and amassed a fortune that he lost in railroad investments. Stevens was the Liberty Party gubernatorial candidate in 1846, and he served as a delegate to the Free Soil convention in Buffalo where he was chosen to call the meeting to order. He was a Presbyterian.

STEWART, ALVAN (1790–1849) was born in New York and attended both Burlington College and the University of Vermont. He passed the bar and moved to Cherry Valley, New York, where he was elected mayor when he was thirty-one. He later moved to Utica, New York, joined the American Anti-Slavery Society in 1834, and issued the call for and chaired the convention that founded the New York State Anti-Slavery Society in 1835. He was a vice president (1834–1835) and manager (1837–1840) of the American Anti-Slavery Society. He eventually left this group to join and serve on the executive committee of the American and Foreign Anti-Slavery Society. Stewart was one of the first theorists to develop the idea that slavery was unconstitutional and was a leader in political action against slavery. He later argued a famous slave case in New Jersey on the unconstitutionality of slavery. A former Whig, he took the lead in forming the Liberty Party and was the president of the 1840 Albany convention that formed the party. He was the chairman of the Liberty Party national corresponding committee and was nominated for governor of New York in 1842. He was a tireless writer and worker for the party, and he helped organize the state parties in New Jersey and Connecticut. He disagreed with many of his fellow New Yorkers on the necessity for the Liberty League, and he supported the Free Soil movement in the months before his death. He was a member of a come-outer Union Church.

STEWART, CHARLES HENRY (1800–1871) was born in Ireland, graduated from Trinity College in Dublin, and came to the United States in 1832. He became a Whig lawyer who was president of the Michigan State Anti-Slavery Society (1842–1843) and attended the

1843 National Liberty Party convention. He was an important Liberty spokesman, was very active in the Detroit Liberty Association, and was a Liberty Party candidate for the U. S. Congress. He later moved to San Francisco. He was an Episcopalian.

STORRS, GEORGE (1796–1879) was born in New Hampshire and became a Methodist minister who withdrew from that faith in 1840 to become an Adventist. He had been very active in the abolition movement during the 1830s and early 1840s, serving as a manager (1835–1836), "One of the Seventy," and vice president in the American Anti-Slavery Society (1835–1837) and later on the executive committee of the American and Foreign Anti-Slavery Society (1840–1841). He was influential in setting up the Birney-Earle ticket in Vermont in 1840.

STREET, AARON (1811–1871) was born in Salem, Ohio, and later lived in Indiana. He moved to Salem, Iowa, in the mid-1830s and was a farmer and the township's first postmaster. He was a Quaker who was a leading abolitionist in Iowa. He issued the call and was the chairman of the October 1843 meeting that set up the Iowa Territorial Anti-Slavery Society. He then served as the organization's first president in 1844 and its vice president in 1847. He was active in the Liberty Party. He later moved to Kansas.

SWAN, CALEB (1790–1872) was a physician in Easton, Massachusetts, who was a member of the Massachusetts Abolition Society. He was the head of the Liberty central committee in Massachusetts for 1847 and an organizer of the Free Soil and Republican parties. He was on the state's central Free Soil committee. He ran for governor in 1857 as a "straight Republican," a splinter group opposed to the Know Nothing movement. His brother-in-law was Liberty gubernatorial candidate George Washington Jo(h)nson.

SWAN, HURLBURT (1797–1878) was born in Millington, Connecticut, and moved from Haddam Connecticut to Fremont, Illinois. He was an Illinois Liberty Party member who was elected as a Lake County delegate to the Illinois constitutional convention in 1847.

SWISSHELM, JANE GREY CAMERON (1815–1884) was born in Pennsylvania and lived in Louisville, Kentucky (1838–1839), after marrying. She returned to Pennsylvania in 1839 to nurse her mother and teach at a girls' school. She was interested in the antislavery movement and stressed the need for political action. She began writing for the (Pittsburgh) *Spirit of Liberty* (1844–1845) but moved over to the Whig *Commercial Journal* to write for women's property rights. In December 1847 she founded the (Pittsburgh) *Saturday Visiter* as owner and editor. Her journal came down strongly for direct political action against slavery in the form of the Liberty and Free Soil parties. After moving to Minnesota, she supported the Republican Party.

TAPPAN, ARTHUR (1786–1865) was in born in Northampton, Massachusetts, and worked as a merchant in Boston, Montreal, and Portland, Maine, before settling in New York as a successful dry goods merchant. He was a member of the American Colonization Society before becoming an early advocate of immediate emancipation. He was a founder of both the American Anti-Slavery Society and the New York State Anti-Slavery Society, was a charter member of the American and Foreign Anti-Slavery Society, and worked in a multitude of other reforms. He was president of the American Anti-Slavery Society (1833–1840) and the American and Foreign Anti-Slavery Society (1840–1845). Although less visible than his brother, LEWIS, he was a supporter of the Liberty Party. He was also involved in many reforms and charitable activities through the Congregational Church.

TAPPAN, LEWIS (1788–1873) was born in Northampton, Massachusetts, left school at age fourteen, and a year later moved to Boston. Eventually he ended up in New York with his brother, Arthur, and they established themselves in the dry goods business and became wealthy. Both brothers were involved in numerous reforms and sponsored missionary activities within the Congregational Church, but Lewis is probably best remembered for his work in abolitionism. He was a founder, on the executive committee (1834–1840), and a manager (1833–1837) in the American Anti-Slavery Society. He was one of the founding members, and primary financial sponsor, of the American and Foreign Anti-Slavery Society, for which he held many offices. He originally opposed the Liberty Party, but his conversion added an influential figure, both because of his reputation and financial resources. He was a founder and prime backer of the (Washington, D.C.) *National Era*. He was named to the national Liberty Party corresponding committee at the Buffalo convention in 1847. He began his political involvement as a Federalist, supported the Anti-Masonic Party, and sympathized with the Whigs before entering antislavery politics. He supported the Liberty League in 1848, Fremont in 1856, Gerrit Smith and the Radical Abolition Party, and Lincoln in 1864 (the first time that he had voted for a presidential winner). He was a founder of the Dun and Bradstreet Company.

THOMAS, NATHAN (1803–1887) was born into a Quaker family in Mount Pleasant, Ohio, and taught school before entering the Medical College of Ohio at Cincinnati. He subsequently became a well-to-do physician after moving to Michigan about 1830. He and his wife, Pamela, were very active participants on the Underground Railroad. A former Whig, he was involved in establishing of the state's first antislavery newspaper, was a main organizer for the Liberty Party in the Kalamazoo area in 1841, and was the party's candidate for lieutenant-governor in 1845. He lectured widely and served as the vice president of the Michigan State Anti-Slavery Society (1844–1845). He was a founder of the Republican Party at the 1854 Jackson, Michigan, convention and served on the nominating committee of the Michigan Republican Party (1854).

TIFFANY, JOEL (1811–1893) was born in Connecticut and by 1835 had settled in Ohio. He was a lawyer who served as the prosecuting attorney for Elyria (1838–1839). He was the Liberty Party congressional candidate in 1844 and 1846. His *A Treatise on the Unconstitutionality of American Slavery* is a leading exposition of this interpretation of the U.S. Constitution. From 1863 to 1869 he lived in Albany, New York, where he wrote on New York law. His interest in spiritualism led him to publish *Tiffany's Monthly; Devoted to the Investigation of Spiritual Science* in the late 1850s and early 1860s. He later moved to Chicago.

TORREY, CHARLES TURNER (1813–1846) was born in Scituate, Massachusetts, and graduated from Yale (1833) and studied at Andover Theological Seminary. He was pastor of a Congregational church in Salem (1838–1839) and editor of the *Massachusetts Abolitionist*

(1838–1839). He also edited the (Albany, N.Y.) *Tocsin of Liberty* and the *Albany Patriot*. Torrey served as a vice president of the April 1, 1840, Albany convention that founded the Liberty Party and was one of its major workers. He was a candidate of the party in Boston in 1841. In 1844 he was seized in Baltimore for aiding fugitive slaves and sentenced to six years in prison. He died behind bars in 1846.

TOWNSHEND, NORTON STRANGE (1815–1895) was born in England and came to the United States to farm in the Western Reserve area of Ohio with his family in 1830. He changed his mind after a period of school teaching and began to take courses at Cincinnati Medical College (1837–1838), finally graduating from the College of Physicians and Surgeons in New York City in 1840. While in Cincinnati, he had made the acquaintance of Salmon P. Chase and James G. Birney. At the latter's urging, he was an Ohio delegate to the World Anti-Slavery Convention in London in 1840. Back in Ohio, he moved to Elyria and became involved in a number of reforms and was very active in the Lorain County Liberty Association. He was a delegate to the 1848 Free Soil convention in Buffalo, where he worked with Chase on the committee on resolutions. Townshend won a seat in the Ohio lower house in 1848 on the Free Soil ticket. He then was elected to the U.S. Congress as a Free Soil Democrat (1851–1853). After being defeated for reelection, he was quickly elected to a seat in the Ohio senate. He was a leader in the founding of the Republican Party in Ohio, and during the late 1850s he served on the State Board of Agriculture and eventually became its president. He supported Chase for president in 1860, was a medical inspector during the Civil War, and was a main supporter in establishing Ohio State University.

TRACY, FREDERICK PALMER (1815–1861) was born in Windham, Connecticut. He became a minister in the Methodist Church at the age of nineteen and was a popular minister and scholar at churches in Southbridge, Massachusetts, and Concord, New Hampshire. He was a New Hampshire delegate to the national Liberty Party convention in New York City in 1841 and was editor of the (Concord, N.H.) *People's Advocate*. He left Concord to go to San Francisco and the gold regions in 1849. He became a lawyer, was San Francisco city attorney (1857–1859), and served as a delegate to the Republican national convention in 1860.

TREADWELL, SEYMOUR BOUGHTON (1795–1867) was born in Bridgeport, Connecticut, grew up in Monroe County, New York, and taught in Ohio and New York before going to Michigan in 1837. He became an antislavery agent, writer, and editor. His *American Liberties and American Slavery, Morally and Politically* (1838) is an important early abolitionist document. Treadwell was editor of the (Jackson) *Michigan Freeman* (1839–1841) and was a Whig who initially opposed third-party political action, but by 1840 he admitted the failure of moral suasion and became a committed Liberty Party man. He frequently lectured throughout the state, sometimes accompanied by fugitive slave Henry Bibb. He was a Liberty candidate for the Michigan state senate, president of the Michigan State Anti-Slavery Society, and a delegate and committee member at the 1848 Buffalo Free Soil convention. After supporting Hale in 1852, he was one of the founders of the Republican Party in Michigan and one of its first successful candidates, being elected to the statewide office of commissioner of the state land office in 1854 and 1856. His writings are marked by a strong religious tone, and he served as a deacon in a Presbyterian church in Jackson.

TUCK, AMOS A. (1810–1879) was born in Parsonfield, Maine, and graduated from Dartmouth (1835). He taught school and studied law, finally being admitted to the bar in 1838. He was an active Democrat who was elected to the New Hampshire legislature in 1842. He broke with the Democrats over the Texas issue and issued the call for the Independent Democrats to support John P. Hale. Tuck himself was elected to the U.S. Congress (1847–1853) on the coalition ticket that included Liberty Party participation. He became a leader in the formation of the Republican Party and was a delegate to its national conventions in 1856 and 1860, where he gave his support to Lincoln. He was a prominent businessman and lawyer after the Civil War.

TUCKER, JOHN N. T. (1812–1869) was born in Marion, New York. He was a Baptist minister who left the church and became a Union Church member. He went to the first meeting of the New York Anti-Slavery Society in 1836 and was a founder of the Liberty Party as a delegate at the Albany convention. He was an agent for the New York State Anti-Slavery Society and a Syracuse printer who published Liberty songbooks, the (Syracuse, N.Y.) *Democratic Freeman,* and a famous *Liberty Almanac,* which reportedly ran to fifty thousand copies in 1844. He later edited the *Troy Whig* before he moved to Brooklyn, New York, where he edited the *Brooklyn Freeman.* Tucker worked in state government as a clerk in the state senate in the late 1840s and early 1850s. He became an alcohol and opium addict and was tried for the murder of his four-year-old son in 1854, but he was acquitted on grounds of insanity. He soon escaped from the asylum, lived in Indiana, and died in Ohio.

VAN VLEET, JANE (1804–1879) was born in New Jersey but moved to Ohio, where her father was a publisher. She eventually moved to Michigan, where she edited and published the short-lived (Niles, Mich.) *Star of Freedom* (1845), which supported the Liberty Party. She married in the late 1840s and late in life moved to Kansas and then California, where she died. She is the subject of Jean Ducey's children's book on the Underground Railroad, *Out of this Nettle* (1983).

VASHON, GEORGE BOYER (1824–1878) was born in Pennsylvania and was the son of noted abolitionist John B. Vashon. He graduated from Oberlin in 1844 as its first black graduate and returned to Pittsburgh, where the family had moved in 1829. He worked with Martin Delany in publishing the *Mystery,* which supported the Liberty Party, and read law but was not allowed to take the bar exam in Pennsylvania because of his color. He passed the bar in New York and became the state's first licensed black lawyer. He lived in Haiti and worked at various professions from 1848 to 1850. Returning to begin a law practice in Syracuse, New York, he worked on the city's vigilance committee and was nominated twice for attorney general on the Liberty League ticket. He taught at New York Central College and in Pittsburgh before becoming president of Avery College in 1864. Recognized as a writer and intellectual, Vashon published widely in history and literature. He as a solicitor with the Freedmen's Bureau after the Civil War before going on to faculty positions at Howard and Alcorn State in Mississippi.

VASHON, JOHN B. (1795–1853), born free to a Virginia slaveholder, moved from Carlisle, Pennsylvania, to Pittsburgh in 1829, where he was a barber and owned a bathhouse. He was one of the leading black reformers in the city from the 1830s until his death. He was a personal friend of William Lloyd Garrison and a manager in the American Anti-Slavery Society (1833–1837). He was active in the earlier and later black convention movements, an early anti-colonizationist, and a supporter of political action. He contributed financially and was an advisor on the (Pittsburgh) *Mystery*. He was the father of George Boyer Vashon.

WADE, EDWARD (1802–1866) was born in West Springfield, Massachusetts, and was admitted to the Ohio bar in 1827. He served as justice of the peace of Ashtabula County in 1831 and as its prosecuting attorney. He moved to Cleveland in 1837 to practice law and eventually became president of the Cuyahoga County Anti-Slavery Society. Although he supported William Henry Harrison in 1840, he soon joined the Liberty Party and remained one of its strongest spokesmen and candidates. He ran for Congress on the Liberty Party ticket against antislavery Whig Joshua Giddings in 1843, 1844, and 1846. He was named to its national corresponding committee at the Buffalo convention in 1847. He eventually was elected to the U.S. Congress (1853–1861) on the Free Soil and Republican tickets. He was unusual in Liberty circles because he did not belong to any organized religion.

WALKER, AMASA (1799–1875) was born in Woodstock, Connecticut, and never attended college because of his poor health. He opened a wholesale shoe business at Boston in 1825 and was involved in the business community until 1840. He had been a strong anti-Mason and Democrat, serving as their candidate for the U.S. Congress. At the same time he worked in various reforms, serving as president of the Boston Temperance Society in 1839 and as a manager in the American Anti-Slavery Society (1837–1841, 1843–1844). In 1842 Walker went to Oberlin, which he had helped found, as a lecturer in history and political economy, returning to Massachusetts in 1844. He eventually became an examiner in political economy at Harvard (1853–1860) and a lecturer at Amherst (1860–1869). He worked for the Liberty Party during the 1840s, but he continued to participate in Democratic politics, particularly when in Massachusetts. Walker was one of the founders of the Free Soil and Republican parties in Massachusetts. He was elected to the Massachusetts legislature on the Free Soil ticket in 1848, was a Massachusetts elector for Lincoln in 1860, and served in the U.S. Congress (1862–1863). He was an Orthodox Congregationalist.

WARD, SAMUEL RINGGOLD (1817–1866) was born a slave on Maryland's Eastern Shore. His parents escaped to New Jersey and relocated to New York. He taught school in New Jersey (1835–1839) before settling in Poughkeepsie, New York, where he taught and was accepted as a minister by the New York Congregational Association. He was an agent of the American Anti-Slavery Society and the New York State Anti-Slavery Society. At the time of the 1840 schism, he affiliated with the American and Foreign Antislavery Society. He was an early supporter of the Liberty Party and was the pastor of a white Congregational church in Cortland, New York (1846–1851). He opposed the Free Soil merger in 1848 and was selected as a candidate for the New York legislature and for vice president in 1850 on the Liberty League ticket. He took part in the "Jerry Rescue" in Syracuse in 1851 before fleeing to Canada, where he served as an agent of the Anti-Slavery Society of Canada (1851–1853) and founded the *Provincial Freeman* (1853). He went to England in 1853 to solicit funds for Canadian fugitive slaves and published his *Autobiography of a Fugitive Negro* (1855). He then settled in Jamaica as a minister.

WARREN, HOOPER (1790–1864) was born in New Hampshire, moved to Vermont, and eventually relocated to Illinois, where he became an editor and publisher. His antislavery inclinations went back to the 1820s as editor of the *Edwardsville Spectator* and *Galena Advertiser*. He was clerk of the circuit court in Putnam (1831) and Hennepin (1831–1835) counties. He became the publisher of the *Genius of Universal Emancipation* and edited and published the *Genius of Liberty* (1840–1842) with Zebina Eastman. He was a Liberty Party congressional candidate and a candidate for local offices. He moved through the Liberty, Free Soil, and Illinois Free Democratic and Republican parties and was an editor of the *Free West*.

WASHINGTON, LEWIS (1822–1898) was a former slave from Virginia who had been aided in his escape by Liberty men Charles T. Torrey and George Latimer. He lived in New Jersey, where he was tutored in English and public speaking by Abel W. Brown, before moving to Wisconsin in 1847. He lectured for the Liberty Party in Illinois and Wisconsin and canvassed for the (Wis.) *Free American*. He settled in Wisconsin, but moved to Nebraska by the late nineteenth century.

WHEATON, LABAN MOREY (1797–1865) was born in Norton, Massachusetts, to former U.S. Representative and Wheaton College (Mass.) founder Laban Wheaton. He graduated from Brown (1817) before returning to Norton, where he served as postmaster (1818–1845) and justice of the peace until his death. He was elected to the state legislature in 1827, 1828, and 1838. He served in many other town offices and positions at the school. He was the Liberty candidate for the U.S. Congress in 1844 and 1846.

WHIPPER, WILLIAM (1804–1876) was born in Lancaster, Pennsylvania, to a white businessman and a black servant. He moved to Philadelphia during the 1820s and opened a small business. In 1835 he moved to Columbia, Pennsylvania, and gradually became one of the richest blacks in the antebellum United States. His home in Columbia was one of the major stops on the Underground Railroad and he used a merchant ship he owned on Lake Erie to shuttle fugitive slaves to Canada. He was a founder of the American Moral Reform Society that encompassed a number of causes. He was prominent in the black convention movement, temperance, and antislavery. Whipper was a strong Garrisonian, but by 1848 he had come to support the Liberty Party. He gave up hope for abolition and gradually became an exponent of racial separation and emigration, but he encouraged black enlistment during the Civil War. After the war he was a vice president of the Pennsylvania Civil Rights League.

WHITTIER, JOHN GREENLEAF (1807–1892) was born in Massachusetts and spent two years at Haverhill Academy, but he was largely self-educated. He became one of the most famous poets in the United States and had a long career as an antislavery newspaper editor. He was an Orthodox Quaker who was elected to one term in the lower house of the Massachusetts legislature as a Whig, but he turned most of his energies to his poetry and antislavery work. He was a founder and manager (1833–1840) of the American Anti-Slavery Society before breaking with the Garrisonians and joining the executive committee of the American and Foreign Anti-Slavery Society. He was a Liberty candidate for the U.S. Congress in 1842 and the Massachusetts state senate in 1844. Perhaps Whittier's greatest contributions came as a Liberty journalist. At various times he edited the *Pennsylvania Freeman*, the *Emancipator*, the (Amesbury, Mass.) *Essex Transcript* (1845–1847), and the *Middlesex* (Mass.) *Standard* and served as a corresponding editor of the (Washington, D.C.) *National Era*. He worked in the founding of the Massachusetts Free Soil and Republican parties and served as a Republican presidential elector in 1860 and 1864.

WILLEY, AUSTIN (1806–1898) was born in New Hampshire and attended Bangor Theological Seminary. He was a Congregational minister and antislavery editor who was probably the most influential abolitionist in Maine. He edited both the (Brunswick, Maine) *Advocate of Freedom* and the *Liberty Standard* and was the chief organizer of the Liberty Party in the state. He subsequently worked in the founding of both the Free Soil and Republican parties in Maine. He later moved to Minnesota.

WILLIAMS, AUSTIN F. (1805–1885) was a longtime abolitionist and Underground Railroad operator from Farmington, Connecticut. He was on the defense committee in the *Amistad* case. Although he had supported Whig Roger Baldwin for governor, he was a Birney elector in the 1844 presidential election. He later served on the executive committee of the American and Foreign Anti-Slavery Society and was a vice president in the Connecticut Temperance Society. After the Civil War, he was a director of the Freedman's Bureau for New York and New England. He was a Congregationalist.

WILLIAMS, CHARLES K. (1782–1853) was born in Massachusetts and graduated from Williams College (1800). He moved to Vermont and was admitted to the Vermont bar (1803), beginning a long career that would mark him as one of the state's outstanding jurists. He represented Rutland in the lower house of the Vermont state legislature almost every year between 1809 and 1821, was a brigadier general in the state militia, and was on the Vermont supreme court from 1822 to 1849 except for four years (1825–1829) when he was collector of customs. He served as chief justice of the court (1842–1846) and was president of the council of censors (1847). He was the Liberty Party candidate for governor (1842, 1843, 1844, and 1845). He was elected to the lower house of the state legislature in 1849 and then governor (1850–1851).

WILSON, MARTIN (1794–1881) came to Michigan in 1838. He was named to the National Liberty corresponding committee for Michigan at the Buffalo convention in 1847. He was on the committee examining Henry Bibb. He was a deacon in the Congregational Church.

WOOD, SAMUEL NEWITT (1825–1891) was born in Mount Gilead, Ohio, and later moved to Oberlin. He was a Hicksite Quaker who became chairman of his county Liberty Party central committee at the age of nineteen. He supported the Free Soil ticket in 1848 and the Hale-Julian ticket in 1852. He was admitted to the Ohio bar in 1854, but went to Kansas with the Kansas Emigrant Aid Society of Northern Ohio after the passage of the Kansas-Nebraska Act. He was an operative on the Underground Railroad in Lawrence and participated in the Wakarusa War. Wood was a delegate to the 1856 Republican convention in Pittsburgh and campaigned in Ohio and elsewhere for Fremont. He started a newspaper, the *Council Grove Press*, in 1859 and was elected a member of the territorial legislature (1859–1860). He fought in the Civil War with the Kansas Rangers, eventually becoming a lieutenant-colonel. He was elected to the lower house of the Kansas state legislature (1864–1865) and to the state senate (1866). While in the lower house, he introduced a women's suffrage resolution. He broke with the regular Republican Party in 1872 to support Horace Greeley. He returned to the Kansas House of Representatives (1876–1877), where he was elected Speaker of the House. He was the founder of Woodsdale, Kansas. He was assassinated in 1891.

WOODSON, LEWIS (1806–1878) was born in Greenbriar County, Virginia, to a family that eventually purchased themselves and moved to a black settlement in Ohio. He was ordained a minister of the African Methodist Episcopal Church in 1828, but he also worked in an interracial True Wesleyan Church. Woodson moved to Pittsburgh in 1831 to work as a barber and teacher. He labored in many reforms, was involved in the struggle for black suffrage, was active in the black convention movement, and worked on the Underground Railroad. He was an early advocate of black separatism and eventually encouraged emigration to Canada and the Caribbean. During the 1840s, he assisted Martin Delany, one of his former students, with the Pittsburgh *Mystery* newspaper and lectured for the Liberty Party. Later, he became a trustee of Wilberforce University.

WORK, ALANSON (1799–1879) was born in Connecticut and lived in Middletown from the early 1820s to about 1840, when he moved to Quincy, Illinois, where he became involved in antislavery and Underground Railroad work at the Mission Institute. He was captured in Missouri and sentenced to twelve years in prison. He was released after three and a half years and returned to Connecticut, where he supported the Liberty Party. He eventually moved to New York City.

WRIGHT, ELIZUR (1804–1885) was born in Connecticut and graduated from Yale (1826). He was a professor of mathematics at Western Reserve College (1829–1833) before devoting himself full-time to his antislavery work. He was a founder and corresponding secretary of the American Anti-Slavery Society and helped organize "The Seventy" abolitionist agents who lectured across the North in the 1830s. After the break with Garrison in Massachusetts in 1839, he edited the (Boston) *Massachusetts Abolitionist* and left the American Anti-Slavery Society to join the American and Foreign Anti-Slavery Society. He was an early proponent of political involvement and was one of the founders of the Liberty Party at the April 1, 1840, convention in Albany. During the 1840s, he edited the Liberty Party *Boston Free American* and the *Boston Daily Chronotype*, which later became a Free Soil newspaper, the *Commonwealth*, in 1850. He was a candidate for state senator in Massachusetts in 1847. In 1848 he briefly supported the Liberty League before supporting the Free Soil ticket. During the 1850s, he continued his support of reform activities, although he lost his religious fervor. He eventually put his mathematical skills to good use as an actuarial scientist in the insurance business. He moved from evangelical faith to religious doubt to atheism.

WRIGHT, THEODORE S. (1797–1847) was born in Rhode Island to free parents. His father was an early abolitionist who worked in an 1817 black convention opposed to colonization. He became the first black graduate of a theological institution in the United States when he graduated from Princeton Seminary in 1828. He became the pastor of the First Colored Presbyterian Church in New York City. A friend of the Tappans, he was involved in several reform movements, but he dedicated himself especially to abolition. He was a founder and manager and served on the executive committee of the American Anti-Slavery Society (1834–1840), but he left it in 1840 to join the American and Foreign Anti-Slavery Society, where he also served on the executive committee (1843–1847). He was an early proponent of political action and the Liberty Party and was a member of the party's central nominating committee. He backed Henry Highland Garnet's statements on black violence and took a deep interest in African missions.

YALE, LEVI (1792–1872) was born and was a farmer and teacher in Meriden, Connecticut. He was active on the Underground Railroad, a selectman, and a representative in the state legislature. He was the Liberty candidate for lieutenant-governor (1843) and was a founder of the Center Congregational Church in Durham.

YANCEY, WALTER CLAIBORNE (1817–1903) was a freeborn black from Virginia who became a resident of Chillicothe, Butler County, and Hamilton, Ohio. He was an itinerant minister for the African Methodist Episcopal Zion Church who was active in setting up black schools and in abolition. He lectured for the Garrisonians in Ohio during the early 1840s, but began working for the Liberty Party by 1844. He was a chaplain in the 66th Colored Infantry during the Civil War.

ZUILLE, JOHN J. (1814–1894) was born in Bermuda and moved to New York City in the 1830s. He worked as a printer and writer, most notably on the *Colored American*, and as a schoolteacher. He served on the central nominating committee of the Liberty Party at the 1843 convention in Buffalo. During the 1850s, he was active in many black conventions and organizations, especially those opposed to the Fugitive Slave Law. During the

Civil War he left New York for Hartford, Connecticut, where he worked in a bank until 1874. Shortly after his death, a subscription was begun commemorating his work on the Underground Railroad in New York City. In fact, he is sometimes credited with being its originator.

NOTES

INTRODUCTION

1. Theodore Clarke Smith, *The Liberty and Free Soil Parties in the Northwest* (New York: Longmans, Green and Co., 1897 [reprinted New York: Russell & Russell, 1967]), was the only extensive study that dealt specifically with the party. A few journal articles were narrower in scope: Julian Bretz, "The Economic Background of the Liberty Party," *American Historical Review* 34 (January 1929): 250–264; R. L. Morrow, "The Liberty Party in Vermont," *New England Quarterly* 2 (April 1929): 234–248; Joseph G. Rayback, "Liberty Party Leaders of Ohio: Exponents of Antislavery Coalition," *Ohio State Archaeological and Historical Quarterly* 17 (April 1948): 165–176. Dwight L. Dumond, *Antislavery: The Crusade for Freedom in America* (Ann Arbor: University of Michigan Press, 1961 [reprinted New York: W. W. Norton & Co., 1966]), 291–304, devoted two short chapters to the party.

2. Among the exceptions were: Ralph V. Harlow, *Gerrit Smith: Philanthropist and Reformer* (New York: Henry Holt Co., 1939); Betty L. Fladeland, *James Gillespie Birney: Slaveholder to Abolitionist* (Ithaca, N.Y.: Cornell University Press, 1955); Philip G. and Elizabeth Q. Wright, *Elizur Wright: The Father of Life Insurance* (Chicago: University of Chicago Press, 1937); Margaret C. McCulloch, *Fearless Advocate of the Right: The Life of Francis Julius LeMoyne, M.D.* (Boston: Christopher Publishing House, 1941); Edwin B. Bronner, *Thomas Earle as a Reformer* (Philadelphia: International Printing Company, 1948); Albert Bushnell Hart, *Salmon Portland Chase* (Boston: Houghton Mifflin & Co. American Statesmen Series, 1899). A few articles examined party members: Reinhard Luthin, "Salmon P. Chase's Political Career before the Civil War," *Mississippi Valley Historical Review* 11 (March 1943): 517–540; John E. Kephart, "A Pioneer Michigan Abolitionist [Guy Beckley]," *Michigan History* 45 (March 1961): 34–42; James M. McPherson, "The Fight Against the Gag Rule: Joshua Leavitt and Antislavery Insurgency in the Whig Party, 1839–1842," *Journal of Negro History* 48 (April 1963): 177–195.

3. There were a few exceptions: Margaret Louise Plunkett, "A History of the Liberty Party with Emphasis Upon Its Activity in the Northeastern States" (Ph.D. dissertation, Cornell University, 1930); Joel Goldfarb, "The Life of Gamaliel Bailey Prior to the Founding of the *National Era*: The Orientation of a Practical Abolitionist" (Ph.D. dissertation, University of California, Los Angeles, 1958); John R. Hendricks, "The Liberty Party in New York State, 1838–1848" (Ph.D. dissertation, Fordham University, 1959); John E. Kephart, "A Voice for Freedom: The *Signal of Liberty*, 1841–1848" (Ph.D. dissertation, University of Michigan, 1960); Rosalie Margolin, "Henry B. Stanton, A Forgotten Abolitionist" (M.S. thesis, Columbia University, 1962).

4. I am only including works that highlight the subject's Liberty Party or antislavery activities. Richard H. Sewell, *John P. Hale and the Politics of Abolition* (Cambridge, Mass.: Harvard University Press, 1965); Edward Magdol, *Owen Lovejoy: Abolitionist in Congress* (New Brunswick, N.J.: Rutgers University Press, 1967). William F. Moore and Jane Ann Moore, eds., *His Brother's Blood: Speeches and Writings, 1838–1864: Owen Lovejoy* (Urbana and Chicago: University of Illinois Press, 2004), has helpful introductions to Lovejoy's writings, but all except one selection have been previously printed. Others are: Arthur H. Rice, "Henry Brewster Stanton as a Political Abolitionist" (Ed.D. dissertation, Columbia University, 1968); Paula Glassman, "Zebina Eastman: Chicago Abolitionist" (M.A. thesis, University of Chicago, 1968); Louis S. Gerteis, ed., "An Abolitionist in Territorial Wisconsin: The Journal of Reverend Edward Mathews," *Wisconsin Magazine of History* 52 (Autumn 1968–Summer 1969): 3–18, 117–131, 248–262, 330–343; Bertram Wyatt-Brown, *Lewis Tappan and the Evangelical War Against Slavery* (Cleveland, Ohio: The Press of Case Western Reserve University, 1969); Charles A. Jarvis, "John Greenleaf Whittier and the Anti-Slavery Movement, 1828–1860" (Ph.D. dissertation, University of Missouri at Columbia, 1970) and his "Admission to Abolition: The Case of John Greenleaf Whittier," *Journal of the Early Republic* 4 (Summer 1984): 161–176; Leon Perkal, "William Goodell: A Life of Reform" (Ph.D. dissertation, City University of New York, 1972); Joel Schor, *Henry Highland Garnet: A Voice of Black Radicalism in the Nineteenth Century* (Westport, Conn.; Greenwood Press, 1977); Martin Burt Pasternak, "Rise Now and Fly to Arms: The Life of Henry Highland Garnet" (Ph.D. dissertation, University of Massachusetts, 1981); Yvonne Tuchalski, "Erastus Hussey, Battle Creek Antislavery Activist," *Michigan History* 56 (Spring 1972): 1–18; Ronald Kevin Burke, *Samuel Ringgold Ward: Christian Abolitionist* (New York: Garland Publishing, 1995); Milton Sernett, *Abolition's Axe: Beriah Green, Oneida Institute, and the Black Freedom Struggle* (Syracuse, N.Y.: Syracuse University Press, 1986); Stanley Harrold, *Gamaliel Bailey and Antislavery Union* (Kent, Ohio: Kent State University Press, 1986); Frederick J. Blue, *Salmon P. Chase: A Life in Politics* (Kent, Ohio: Kent State University Press, 1987); Stephen Middleton, "Ohio and the Antislavery Activities of Salmon Portland Chase, 1830–1849" (Ph.D. dissertation, Miami University, 1987); John Niven, *Salmon P. Chase: A Biography* (New York: Oxford University Press, 1995); Hugh Houck Davis, *Joshua Leavitt: Evangelical Abolitionist* (Baton Rouge: Louisiana State University Press, 1990); Lawrence B. Goodheart, *Abolitionist, Actuary, Atheist: Elizur Wright and the Reform Impulse* (Kent, Ohio: Kent State University Press, 1990); Stephen P. Budney, *William Jay: Abolitionist and Anticolonialist* (Westport, Conn.: Praeger, 2005); Frederick Blue and Robert McCormick, "Norton S. Townshend: A Reformer for All Seasons," in Jeffrey P. Brown and Andrew R. L. Cayton, eds., *The Pursuit of Public Power: Political Culture in Ohio, 1787–1861* (Kent, Ohio: Kent State University Press, 1994), 144–154; Stanley Harrold, "On the Borders of Slavery and Race: Charles T. Torrey and the Underground Railroad," *Journal of the Early Republic* 20 (Spring 2000): 273–292; Andrew S. Barker, "Chauncy Langdon Knapp and Political Abolition in Vermont, 1833–1841," *New England Quarterly* 73 (September 2000): 434–462. Sylvia D. Hoffert, *Jane Grey Swisshelm: An Unconventional Life, 1815–1884* (Chapel Hill: University of North Carolina Press, 2004). Frederick J. Blue, *No Taint of Compromise: Crusaders in Antislavery Politics* (Baton Rouge: Louisiana State University Press, 2005), contains eleven biographical treatments, including seven of Liberty Party supporters: Alvan Stewart, John Greenleaf Whittier, Charles Henry Langston, Owen Lovejoy, Sherman M. Booth, Jane Grey Swisshelm, and Edward Wade.

5. Richard H. Sewell, *Ballots for Freedom: Antislavery Politics in the United States, 1837–1860* (New York: Oxford University Press, 1976), especially 47–169, surpasses Aileen S. Kraditor, "The Liberty and Free Soil Parties," in Arthur M. Schlesinger Jr., ed., *History of U.S. Political Parties*, vol. 1, *1789–1860, From Factions to Parties* (New York: Chelsea House Publishers, 1973), 741–882.

6. Among the most important are Alan M. Kraut, "The Liberty Men of New York: Political Abolitionism in New York State, 1840–1848" (Ph.D. dissertation, Cornell University, 1975); his "The Forgotten Reformers: A Profile of Third Party Abolitionists in Antebellum New York," in Lewis Perry and Michael Fellman, eds., *Antislavery Reconsidered: New Perspectives on the Abolitionists* (Baton Rouge: Louisiana State University Press, 1979), 119–145; and his "Partisanship and Principles: The Liberty Party in Antebellum Political Culture," in Alan M. Kraut, ed., *Crusaders and Compromisers: Essays on the Relationship of the Antislavery Struggle to the Antebellum Party System* (Westport, Conn.: Greenwood Press, 1983), 71–99; Reinhard O. Johnson, "The Liberty Party in New England, 1840–1848: The Forgotten Abolitionists" (Ph.D. dissertation, Syracuse University, 1976); his "The Liberty Party in New Hampshire, 1840–1848: Antislavery Politics in the Granite State," *Historical New Hampshire* 33 (Summer 1978): 123–165; his "The Liberty Party in Vermont, 1840–1848: The Forgotten Abolitionists," *Vermont History* 47 (Fall 1979): 258–275; his "The Liberty Party in Maine, 1840–1848: The Politics of Antislavery Reform," *Maine Historical Society Quarterly* 19 (Winter 1980): 135–176; and his "The Liberty Party in Massachusetts, 1840–1848: Antislavery Politics in the Bay State," *Civil War History* 28 (September 1982): 236–265; Edward Schriver, "Black Politics Without Blacks: Maine 1841–1848," *Phylon* 31 (Summer 1970): 194–201; Vernon L. Volpe, *Forlorn Hope of Freedom: The Liberty Party in the Old Northwest, 1838–1848* (Kent, Ohio: Kent State University Press, 1990); and his "The Liberty Party and Polk's Election, 1844," *The Historian* (Summer 1991): 692–710; Stanley Harrold, "The Southern Strategy of the Liberty Party," *Ohio History* 87 (Winter 1978): 21–36. John W. Quist, *Restless Visionaries: The Social Roots of Antebellum Reform in Alabama and Michigan* (Baton Rouge: Louisiana State University Press, 1998), emphasizes Washtenaw County, Michigan, but contains much useful information on the statewide party. Michael J. McManus, *Political Abolitionism in Wisconsin, 1840–1861* (Kent, Ohio: Kent State University Press, 1998), 1–65. On the relationship between the Liberty Party and religion, see Linda Jeanne Evans, "Abolitionism in the Illinois Churches, 1830–1865" (Ph.D. dissertation, Northwestern University, 1981), passim; John R. McKivigan, *The War Against Proslavery Religion: Abolitionism and the Northern Churches, 1830–1860* (Ithaca, N.Y.: Cornell University Press, 1984), chapter 8: "Vote as You Pray and Pray as You Vote: Church-Oriented Abolitionism and Antislavery Politics," 143–267; and his "The Antislavery 'Comeouter' Sects: A Neglected Dimension of the Abolitionist Movement," *Civil War History* 26 (June 1980): 142–160; Richard J. Carwardine, *Evangelicals and Politics in Antebellum America* (New Haven, Conn.: Yale University Press, 1993), passim; Douglas M. Strong, *Perfectionist Politics: Abolitionism and the Religious Tensions of American Democracy* (Syracuse, N.Y.: Syracuse University Press, 1999); and his "Partners in Political Abolitionism: The Liberty Party and the Wesleyan Methodist Connection," *Methodist History* 23 (January 1985): 99–115; Milton C. Sernett, *North Star Country: Upstate New York and the Crusade for African American Freedom* (Syracuse, N.Y.: Syracuse University Press, 2002). Mark Voss-Hubbard, *Beyond Party: Cultures of Antipartisanship in Northern Politics before the Civil War* (Baltimore: Johns Hopkins University Press, 2002); and his "Slavery, Capitalism, and the Middling Sorts: The Rank and File of Political Abolitionism" *American Nineteenth Century History* 4 (June 2003): 53–76; and Bruce Laurie, *Beyond Garrison: Antislavery and Social Reform* (New York: Cambridge University Press, 2005), examine the party on a local level in select industrial settings.

7. David Hackett Fischer, *Paul Revere's Ride* (New York: Oxford University Press, 1994), xv.

8. James Brewer Stewart, *Joshua R. Giddings and the Tactics of Radical Politics* (Cleveland, Ohio: The Press of the Case Western Reserve University, 1970), 95–96. Even the titles of Stewart's informative biography and Douglas A. Gamble, "Joshua Giddings and the Ohio Abolitionists: A Study in Radical Politics," *Ohio History* 88 (Winter 1979): 37–56, demonstrate the problem.

9. Smith, *The Liberty and Free Soil Parties in the Northwest*, 4.

CHAPTER 1

1. Louis Filler, *The Crusade Against Slavery, 1830–1860* (New York: Harper & Row, Harper Torchbook, 1963), 67. These figures are frequently cited, but I believe that they are much too high.

2. No one has yet done a truly systematic study on how the abolitionists were different from the average person, although many writers on antislavery make some generalizations.

3. James Brewer Stewart, *Holy Warriors: The Abolitionists and American Slavery*, rev. ed. (New York: Hill and Wang, 1997), 56. Chapter 3, "Moral Suasion," 51–74, traces its development throughout the various aspects of the early abolition movement.

4. Lawrence J. Friedman, *Gregarious Saints: Self and Community in American Abolitionism, 1830–1870* (New York: Cambridge University Press, 1982), 203.

5. Contemporaries differed on what led directly to the split between the Old Organization (Garrisonians) and the New Organization. Henry B. Stanton to James G. Birney, January 26, 1839, in Dwight L. Dumond, ed., *Letters of James Gillespie Birney, 1831–1857* (New York: D. Appleton-Century Co., 1938), 1:481–482, thought that it was the "no-government" issue of the nonresistants. Amos A. Phelps to Gerrit Smith, April 10, 1839, Gerrit Smith Collection, Syracuse University, blamed the division on "the attempt on the part of Garrison and his friends to bend and shape abolition to their own views on the subjects of government and women's rights." Martha V. Ball to Elizabeth Pease, May 6, 1840, Antislavery Collection, Boston Public Library, explains the dissolution of the Boston Female Emancipation Society (Old Organization—Garrisonian) and the formation of the Massachusetts Female Emancipation Society (New Organization) as resulting because the "no government friends . . . became so amazing in their movements that it *was* found impossible to continue *united* with them." Joshua Leavitt, though agreeing with the Old Organization on the woman question, joined the New Organization because he thought that it was more effective; see (Maine) *Advocate of Freedom*, May 28, 1840. The address of the New Organization American and Foreign Anti-Slavery Society justified the breakup because of the woman question and the packing of the Annual Meeting of the American Anti-Slavery Society in 1840 by Garrisonian sympathizers; see *Emancipator*, June 5, 1840. H. C. Wright to N. P. Rogers, February 5, 1842, in (N.H.) *Herald of Freedom*, February 25, 1842, reported that Alanson St. Clair believed the woman question was "the original cause of the division." William Birney, *James G. Birney and His Times: The Genesis of the Republican Party with Some Account of Abolition Movements in the South before 1828* (New York: D. Appleton Company, 1969 [reprinted New York: Negro Universities Press, 1969]), 313, believed that "[t]he real issue of Nihilism *versus* Government and Law was adroitly kept in the background." Historians have stressed various factors. Aileen S. Kraditor, *Means and Ends in American Abolitionism: Garrison and His Critics on Strategy and Tactics, 1834–1860* (New York: Pantheon Books, 1969 [Vintage edition, 1970]), 10, sees it as a "basic radical-conservative split." Gilbert Hobbs Barnes, *Antislavery Impulse, 1830–1844* (New York: D. Appleton Century Co., 1933; published for the American Historical Association [Harbinger Edition, 1964]), 161–170, believes the split resulted from Garrison's stubbornness; Filler, *The Crusade Against Slavery*, 134–137, says that it was a power struggle for control of the society.

6. See *Liberator*, June 4, 1839, and (Maine) *Advocate of Freedom*, June 27, 1839, for accounts of the 1839 Massachusetts convention. See *National Anti-Slavery Standard*, June 18, 1840, for more details on the Massachusetts Abolition Society.

7. For more details, see Johnson, "The Liberty Party in New England," 91–95. As the Liberty Party developed in Massachusetts, the Massachusetts Abolition Society declined in importance and

fell into debt. There were attempts as late as 1845 to resuscitate the society and liquidate its debts. See *Emancipator,* July 3, 1844, May 21, 1845; *Liberator* (from the *Boston Post*), June 6, 1845; *National Anti-Slavery Standard* (from the *Correspondence of the Religious Recorder*), June 26, 1845.

8. Garrison to Helen Garrison, May 15, 1840, in Louis Ruchames, ed., *The Letters of William Lloyd Garrison,* vol. 3, *A House Dividing Against Itself, 1836–1840* (Cambridge, Mass.: The Belknap Press of Harvard University, 1971), 611, states that "[i]t was our anti-slavery boat-load that saved our society from falling into the hands of the new organization, or, more correctly, *disorganizers.*" He also accused his opposition of packing the meeting. Also on chartering the *Rhode Island* and packing the meeting, see Wyatt-Brown, *Lewis Tappan,* 197–198; McCulloch, *Fearless Advocate of the Right,* 137; and Birney, *James G. Birney,* 312. For an account of the meeting from a Garrisonian perspective, see Wendell Phillips Garrison and Francis Jackson Garrison, *William Lloyd Garrison, 1805–1879, The Story of His Life Told by his Children* (Boston and New York: Houghton, Mifflin and Co., 1894), 2:346–353.

9. For accounts of the meeting, see *Pennsylvania Freeman,* May 21, 1840. See *National Anti-Slavery Standard,* June 23, 1840, for Lewis Tappan's article on the meeting and the break. The vote on Kelley's nomination was 557–451 in favor (with women voting). The rupture did not upset some abolitionists. Samuel T. Pickard, "John Greenleaf Whittier and the Schism of 1840," *New England Quarterly* 28 (June 1964): 253, quotes a letter of May 30, 1840, where Whittier writes that the breakup was not "a matter of very serious lamentation. The two divisions *could not* work together on any terms." *Philanthropist,* June 16, 1840, also includes the minutes of the meeting of the American and Foreign Anti-Slavery Society. Initially, the American and Foreign Anti-Slavery Society stayed aloof from party politics and maintained that "[t]he Constitution of the Society forbids any actual participation in the machinery of party political arrangements. But the committee would do injustice to their own convictions were they not to say that they regard the general policy of independent anti-slavery nominations as having become a permanent and integral part of the great movements by which slavery is to be overthrown." See *Emancipator,* May 20, 1841. Austin Willey, *The History of the Antislavery Cause in State and Nation* (Portland, Maine: Brown Thurston, 1882 [reprinted New York: Negro Universities Press, 1969]), 175–176, lists the major officers, most of whom became Liberty Party men.

10. *Liberator,* May 29, 1840. Birney, *James G. Birney,* 312–313, traces the number of Massachusetts delegates to the annual meeting between 1834 and 1840: 6 (1834), 22 (1835), 26 (1836), 18 (1837), 22 (1838), 118 (1839), 550 (1840). This indicates the extent of the packing of the meeting.

11. The heart of this group became known as "The Seventy," although the exact number of lecturers is not known. Most eventually supported the Liberty Party. John L. Myers, "Organization of 'the seventy': To Arouse the North Against Slavery," *Mid America* 48 (1966): 29–46.

12. Affiliation of prominent state societies were as follows: (1) split in two, Massachusetts, New Hampshire, and Pennsylvania; (2) became independent, Illinois, Ohio, Connecticut, Vermont (1841), and Maine (1841); (3) affiliated with the American and Foreign Anti-Slavery Society, New York and Michigan (1842).

13. *Liberator,* February 18, 1832; *First Annual Report by the Board of Managers of the New England Anti-slavery Society Presented January 9, 1833* (Boston: Garrison and Knapp, 1833). The constitution of the New England Anti-Slavery Society stated that "[t]he objects of the Society shall be to endeavor by all means sanctioned by law, humanity and religion to effect the abolition of slavery in the United States." Its first annual report declared that its people were "to use their moral and political powers to overthrow slavery in the United States." And the "Declaration of Sentiments" of the

group founding the American Anti-Slavery Society maintained that these were the "highest obligations resting upon the people of the free States to remove slavery by moral and political action, as prescribed in the Constitution of the United States," in *Liberator*, December 14, 1833.

14. *Philanthropist*, November 18, 1836.

15. Smith, *The Liberty and Free Soil Parties in the Northwest*, 33.

16. Frank J. Klingberg, *The Anti-Slavery Movement in England: A Study in English Humanitarianism* (Hartford, Conn.: Yale University Press, 1926 [Archon Books, 1968]), 255, 265. See especially Betty Fladeland, *Men and Brothers: Anglo-American Anti-Slavery Cooperation* (Urbana: University of Illinois Press, 1972), chapter 9, "The New Vigor of Immediatism: The British Example," 195–220.

17. Johnson, "The Liberty Party in New England," 14; Laurie, *Beyond Garrison*, 46.

18. *Philanthropist*, June 11, 1839.

19. Harlow, *Gerrit Smith*, 138–144; Budney, *William Jay*, 44. Gerrit Smith to William Goodell, November 11, 1839, in *Utica* (N.Y.) *Friend of Man*, November 20, 1839, traces the history of the questioning system in Madison County, New York. Gerrit Smith to William Goodell, February 8, 1840, in *Utica Friend of Man*, February 19, 1840, discusses the failure of the questioning system in New York. On some pre-Liberty independent tickets in New York, see *Utica Friend of Man*, December 4, 1839. See Edwin Clarke to Goodell, December 26, 1839, *Utica Friend of Man*, March 4, 1840, for Oswego. The Ohio and New York examples were the most publicized. For some of these and others, see the state studies in chapters 5, 6, and 7.

20. William Goodell, *Slavery and Anti-Slavery; A History of the Great Struggle in Both Hemispheres; with a View of the Slavery Question in the United States* (New York: Negro Universities Press, 1968 [reprint of the 1852 edition published by William Harned]), 469.

21. Stanton, Wright, and Birney to Smith, July 1838, Smith Collection, Syracuse University.

22. *Liberator*, June 7, 1839.

23. *Philanthropist*, December 10, 1839.

24. "Abolitionists and Politics," *National Anti-Slavery Standard*, August 13, 1840.

25. "Political Action," *Emancipator*, August 30, 1838.

26. Wright to Stanton, October 12, 1839, Wright Papers, Library of Congress. This letter became controversial when it fell into Garrison's hands under mysterious circumstances. He published it in the *Liberator*, January 4, 1840, and in several other issues with his critical commentary. Garrison and Garrison, *William Lloyd Garrison*, 2:315–319, give an account of how it fell into Garrison's hands. Elizur Wright, *Myron Holley and What He Did for Liberty and True Religion* (Boston: Published by the author, 1882), 253, says that it "was stolen from his hat while dining at a hotel." Garrison and Garrison, *William Lloyd* Garrison, 2:315–319 (copy of the letter and correspondence Lyman Crowl to Garrison, November 15, 1839), say that "it fell into the hands of the writer of the first page [an anonymous source] accidentally" (316). A copy of this important letter is also in Richard O. Curry and Lawrence B. Goodheart, eds., "The Complexities of Factionalism: Letters of Elizur Wright, Jr. on the Abolitionist Schism, 1837–1840," *Civil War History* 29 (September 1983): 257–259. For a short summary of its impact, see Goodheart, *Elizur Wright*, 110–111.

27. *Utica Friend of Man*, February 20, 1840.

28. Blue, *No Taint of Compromise*, 23–26; Sewell, *Ballots for Freedom*, 50–54.

29. Harlow, *Gerrit Smith*, 145; Goodell, *Slavery and Anti-Slavery*, 469.

30. See *Emancipator*, August 8, 15, 1839, for the proceedings, which are indicative of the confusion in the antislavery ranks over political action. *Utica Friend of Man*, August 7, 1839; *Liberator*, August 9, 1839; Goodell, *Slavery and Anti-Slavery*, 470; Smith, *The Liberty and Free Soil Parties in the Northwest*, 34–36; Sewell, *Ballots for Freedom*, 51–54.

31. Morris to the Convention, July 22, 1839, in B. F. Morris, ed., *Life of Thomas Morris: Pioneer and Long a Legislator of Ohio, and U.S. Senator from 1833 to 1839* (Cincinnati, Ohio: Moore, Wilstach, Keys & Overend, 1856), 230, and 191–192, for his proscription. Jonathan H. Earle, *Jacksonian Antislavery and the Politics of Free Soil* (Chapel Hill: University of North Carolina Press, 2004), 44–48.

32. *Utica Friend of Man*, August 7, 1839.

33. Wright, *Myron Holley*, 256; Goodell, *Slavery and Anti-Slavery*, 470; *Liberator*, October 11, 1839.

34. *Utica Friend of Man*, December 18, 25, 1839.

35. See *Philanthropist*, November 5, 1839, for the minutes of the meeting; and Henry B. Stanton to John Greenleaf Whittier, October 26, 1839, in *Pennsylvania Freeman*, November 7, 1839, for Stanton's comments and description on the meeting. *Emancipator*, November 17, 24, 1839; Stanton to Elizur Wright, October 28, 1839, in Garrison and Garrison, *William Lloyd Garrison*, 2:314–315. Stanton voted to lay the Holley resolution on the table because "[t]o have nominated candidates would have been a great surprise to the great mass of our friends." *Liberator*, November 15, 22, 1839; Wright, *Myron Holley*, 252–256; Sewell, *Ballots of Freedom*, 56–57; Smith, *The Liberty and Free Soil Parties in the Northwest*, 46–47.

36. *Emancipator*, November 18, 1839; Wright, *Myron Holley*, 256–258; Garrison and Garrison, *William Lloyd Garrison*, 2:319–320.

37. See LeMoyne's letter in *Pennsylvania Freeman*, January 2, 1840; see also LeMoyne to Birney, December 10, 1839, in Dumond, *Letters of J. G. Birney*, 1:511–514; Birney's letter declining the nomination to Holley, Joshua Darling, and Josiah Andrews, December 17, 1839, in ibid., 1:514–516. For more on their reasons for declining, see McCulloch, *Fearless Advocate of the Right*, 133–135; and Fladeland, *James G. Birney*, 180–187. Birney later offered to withdraw his letter of declination "so that your communication may remain unanswered" if Holley saw fit. See Birney to Holley, December 26, 1839, in Dumond, *Letters of J. G. Birney*, 1:516–517.

38. Leavitt to Gerrit Smith, March 10, 1840, Smith Collection, Syracuse University. On the conflict over the editorials in the *Emancipator*, see Friedman, *Gregarious Saints*, 90–91. Davis, *Joshua Leavitt*, 153–156.

39. Smith to William Goodell, November 12, 1839, in *Utica Friend of Man*, November 20, 1839; Smith to Seymour B. Treadwell, March 23, 1840, Treadwell Papers, Bentley Historical Collections, University of Michigan; Wright to Beriah Greene, October 10, 1839, Wright Manuscripts, Boston Public Library; *Massachusetts Abolitionist*, October 24, 1839, February 13, 1840; "Political Action," *Pennsylvania Freeman*, October 31, 1839; (Maine) *Advocate of Freedom*, March 7, 1840; *Utica Friend of Man*, April 1, 1840.

40. *Utica Friend of Man*, February 19, 1840. Gerrit Smith, *Report from the County of Madison: To Abolitionists*, Gerrit Smith Broadside and Pamphlet Collection, Syracuse University, says that Holley was "somewhat disheartened by our failure in the Bloomfield Convention . . . [and] asked me whether I still thought the Call for the National Meeting should be printed . . . [W]e agreed that Mr. Holley should forthwith send the call to the press." Harlow, *Gerrit Smith*, 146–147; Sewell, *Ballots for Freedom*, 69.

41. Wright, *Myron Holley*, 258–266. Wright's account and articles in the *Utica Friend of Man*, April 8, 15, 1840, are fairly complete accounts of the convention. Wright lists the officers of the convention and the roll call vote on the formation of the party. See also *Massachusetts Abolitionist*, April 9, 1840; (Maine) *Advocate of Freedom*, April 18, 1840.

42. Wright, *Myron Holley*, 260, reports that "[l]etters approving the proposed object of the Convention were read from J. P. Miller, of Vt., J. G. Whittier, of Mass., Gerrit Smith, H. N. Robinson and

Hiram Corliss, of N.Y., from B. F. Hoffman and Levi Sutliff and O. Clark, of Ohio, and from Thomas Earle, of Penn." Most of these later became Liberty leaders in their areas.

43. Wright, *Myron Holley,* 261.

44. Some historians have taken a jaundiced view of the Liberty Party and some of its members. Pulitzer Prize–winning historian William Freehling in his Owsley-award winning *The Road to Disunion,* vol. 1, *Secessionists at Bay, 1776–1854* (New York: Oxford University Press, 1990), delivers a particularly harsh verdict on Birney. He claims to base his account on Betty Fladeland's "excellent" *James Gillespie Birney,* and "especially on" Dumond, *Letters of J. G. Birney* (footnote 22, p. 582). He also cites Birney's own pamphlet on colonization. Freehling says that Birney was the "most notorious antebellum example of supposed forced exile" (113). He depicts him as "drab, unemotional, colorless—in a word, unhistoric" (113). He calls him a "dissimulating reformer," who "was paid "$1000 a year to publicize colonization of blacks" (114). After renouncing colonization, according to Freehling, "the careerist had at least not lost a career by renouncing colonization" because "he now cashed checks from the American Antislavery Society" (115). He portrays a Birney who drank and "gambled away his fortune" (114) and as a cowardly opportunist who "fled north upon intimations of possible lynchings" (466).

Where Freehling has gotten his information is not clear, but it is surely not from Fladeland's biography or the Birney letters, of which he cites none later than 1835. Certainly there is nothing in Fladeland's work to warrant his judgments. She writes in her biography: "James Gillespie Birney was a Southern aristocrat and slaveholder who, from, from firsthand experience, became convinced of the evils of slavery, gave up a lucrative law practice, a position of influence and respect in his community, his home, and his inheritance, to dedicate his life to the cause of freeing the slaves ... Driven from point to point, refused positions because of his views, threatened and mobbed, Birney stood firmly for what he believed and for the right to speak and print those views. His fight for civil liberty helped to maintain freedom of speech and press in a time when censorship and gag laws were threatening the North as well as the South" (Fladeland, *James G. Birney,* v).

Freehling depicts Birney as a devious sot, but the truth is quite different. When a campaign biography of him was prepared in 1844, Birney himself admitted "[t]ill I was 34 years old, I was wild—much inclined to dissipation—and ambitious" (Birney to Elizur Wright, March 4, 1844, in Dumond, *Letters of J. G. Birney,* 2:797). His son, William, also discusses these early failings in his biography of his father, but, unlike Freehling, he puts them in perspective: "In Kentucky he had fallen into the fashion, universal in those days among Southern gentlemen, of playing for stakes and laying wagers on horse-races ... Several heavy losses ... compelled him to borrow money on mortgage security given upon his plantation and slaves." This caused him to "never bet again" and "to pay off the mortgage upon his property by the more active practice of the law" (Birney, *James G. Birney,* 42–43).

In claiming that Birney sold his slaves, Freehling is resurrecting a charge that Birney answered in 1836 (see Birney, *James G. Birney,* Appendix D, 423–430, for the letter of James G. Birney to Colonel W. L. Stone [editor of the *New York Spectator*], May 2, 1836; the letter was reprinted in the *Signal of Liberty,* September 2, 1844, when the charges resurfaced during the 1844 election). See Fladeland, *James G. Birney,* 72–73, 82–84, for Birney's relationship with his slaves and his subsequent manumission of them in 1834 after his conversion to immediatism. See other references to his explanation and further details of his actions in Birney to Robert H. Folger, July 24, 1844, in Dumond, *Letters of J. G. Birney,* 2:823–827. He also claims that James K.(*sic*) Birney was a Democrat (438) when he was actually a Jackson opponent who supported Henry Clay. Freehling also neglects to mention that Birney's accepting the thousand-dollar salary as the agent of the American Colonization Society came "at a great sacrifice" (R. R. Gurley [corresponding secretary of the American Colonization Society] to Birney, June 12, 1832, in Dumond, *Letters of J. G. Birney,* 1:6) and was "only one-fourth his income from law" (Fladeland, *James G. Birney,* 52).

Certainly Birney is not immune from criticism, but to paint him as an opportunistic bounder is clearly incorrect. One is only left to wish that Freehling would share the sources for his statements because the listed sources (including footnote 32, p. 117, which leads to no citation) not only do not support his positions but contradict them. In fact, Birney had a good reputation. Ronald P. Formisano, *The Birth of Mass Political Parties: Michigan, 1827–1861* (Princeton, N.J.: Princeton University Press, 1971), 279, points out that as late as 1860 "Republicans capitalized on the late James Birney's name by nominating one of their hack legislators of the same name for Lieutenant Governor [of Michigan]." (Actually, the "hack" was Birney's eldest son, a Congregational minister who took a law degree from Yale. He won the election and later became minister to the Hague.)

45. *Massachusetts Abolitionist,* April 9, 23, 1840, give the minutes and some of the speeches; *Emancipator,* April 9, 1840; *Utica Friend of Man,* April 22, June 3, 1840; (Maine) *Advocate of Freedom,* April 18, 1840; *Pennsylvania Freeman,* April 23, 1840; Austin Willey, *The History of the Antislavery Cause,* 131–135. Birney's letter of acceptance to Holley, Leavitt, and Wright, May 11, 1840, in Dumond, *Letters of J. G. Birney,* 1:562–574; Earle's letter of acceptance to Holley, Leavitt and Wright, in *Pennsylvania Freeman,* June 25, 1840, and reprinted in Bronner, *Thomas Earle,* 56–58. Earle delayed until May 30 to be sure that the movement was not going to fail. Kraditor, *Means and Ends in American Abolition,* 230, incorrectly states that Earle "had declined the Liberty nomination for Vice-President in 1840."

46. *Utica Friend of Man,* April 8, 1840.

47. Gerrit Smith is usually credited with later coining the name Liberty Party. In his *Report from the County of Madison,* November 13, 1843, Gerrit Smith Broadside and Pamphlet Collection, Syracuse University, Smith recalls that he spoke "of the new party as the "Liberty Party" in a February 8, 1840, letter to William Goodell. See Smith to Goodell, February 8, 1840, in *Utica Friend of Man,* February 19, 1840. The *Utica Friend of Man,* by July 29, 1840, endorsed the Birney-Earle ticket and designated it as the "Liberty Party." Sernett, *North Star Country,* 113.

48. Whittier to Birney, April 16, 1840, in Dumond, *Letters of J. G. Birney,* 1:555; Bailey to Birney, April 18, 1840, in ibid., 1:556–558.

49. *Pennsylvania Freeman,* June 4, 1840. (Hartford, Conn.) *Charter Oak,* as quoted in *Utica Friend of Man,* April 29, 1840; Lawrence Bruser, "Political Antislavery in Connecticut, 1844–1858" (Ph.D. dissertation, Columbia University, 1974), 62. Some evidence points to efforts in a few areas. See the discussion on Connecticut in chapter 5.

50. *Pennsylvania Freeman,* September 10, 1840, reported that a convention of New Jersey political abolitionists met and voted 12–11 against an electoral ticket. The minority then set up a ticket, but at least one nominee had already declined. See Alexander H. Freeman to (New Jersey) *Freeman,* December 16, 1844, in *New Jersey Freeman,* February 28, 1845, for a retrospective account of the state's situation in 1840 and the development of the support for the third-party ticket.

51. (Hartford, Conn.) *Christian Freeman,* January 16, 1845. The antislavery activists that remained worked closely with the Garrisonians and Nathaniel P. Rogers. See also (Ann Arbor, Mich.) *Signal of Liberty,* May 1, 1843.

52. William Jackson to Elizur Wright, C. Nichols, and C. T. Torrey, May 24, 1840, Antislavery Collection, Boston Public Library.

53. Hiram Cummings to Amos A. Phelps, September 8, 1840; Cummings to Phelps, September 10, 1840; Sewall to Jonson, September 26, 1840; Jonson to Phelps, October 6, 1840, all in Antislavery Collection, Boston Public Library. Sometimes his name is spelled "Johnson."

54. *Emancipator,* August 6, 1840.

55. Johnson, "The Liberty Party in Massachusetts," 240–241; Arthur P. Darling, *Political Changes in Massachusetts, 1824–1848: A Study of Liberal Political Movements in Politics* (New Haven, Conn.: Yale University Press, 1925), 268–269; *Liberator,* October 16, November 6, 1840, report that the Garrisonians passed anti-third-party resolutions at the State Anti-Slavery Convention in Worcester and the Springfield convention for the western Massachusetts counties.

56. *Advocate of Freedom,* October 22, 1840; Augustus F. Holt, as cited in Willey, *The History of the Antislavery Cause,* 149, and followed by a list of the electors.

57. *Voice of Freedom,* as cited in Wilbur H. Siebert, *Vermont's Anti-Slavery and Underground Railroad Record* (Columbus, Ohio: The Spahr and Glenn Co., 1937), 35; J. P. Miller to *Emancipator,* March 27, 1840, in *Emancipator,* April 9, 1840.

58. Wright, *Myron Holley,* 262, names Benjamin Shaw of Weston and Charles Sexton of Burlington. Shaw was a vice president of the convention. See *Emancipator,* June 12, 1840, for the call; *Emancipator,* June 25, 1840, for the meeting. David M. Ludlum, *Social Ferment in Vermont, 1791–1850* (New York: Columbia University Press, 1939), 177. Barker, "Chauncy Langdon Knapp," 458, reports that Knapp, the antislavery Whig secretary of state, ridiculed the new party in *Voice of Freedom,* June 13, 1840.

59. J. G. Whittier to Gerrit Smith, August 30, 1840, Smith Collection, Syracuse University.

60. "A Friend" (from New Hampshire) to Joshua Leavitt, August 8, 1840, in *Emancipator,* August 13, 1840; *Liberator,* September 11, 1840.

61. Goodell's *Utica Friend of Man,* July 29, 1840, finally endorsed the movement.

62. *Utica Friend of Man,* August, 12, September 23, 30, 1840; Harlow, *Gerrit Smith,* 149–152.

63. *Pennsylvania Freeman,* May 14, September 10, 24, October 1, 1840; M. Theophane Geary, *A History of Third Parties in Pennsylvania, 1840–1860* (Washington, D.C.: Catholic University of America, 1938), 40–44. On F. J. LeMoyne's opposition, see McCulloch, *Fearless Advocate of the Right,* 138.

64. *Michigan Freeman,* July 15, 1840, from *Pennsylvania Freeman,* July 30, 1840; *Michigan Freeman* from *Utica Friend of Man,* May 27, 1840; *Pennsylvania Freeman,* July 30, September 10, 17, 1840; Maurice D. Ndukwu, "Antislavery in Michigan: A Study of Its Origin, Development, and Expression from Territorial Period to 1860" (Ph.D. dissertation, Michigan State University, 1979), 136–139.

65. See *Philanthropist,* September 8, 1840, for the minutes and comments on the convention.

66. *Philanthropist,* August 25, 1840; Smith, *The Liberty and Free Soil Parties in the Northwest,* 42–43; N. Dwight Harris, *The History of Negro Servitude in Illinois and of the Slavery Agitation in that State, 1719–1864* (New York: Haskell House Publisher, 1969 [reprint of Chicago: A. C. McClurg, 1904]), 146–148.

67. Wright to Gerrit Smith, March 20, 1840, Smith Collection, Syracuse University. Henry B. Stanton to Birney, March 21, 1840, in Dumond, *Letters of J. G. Birney,* 1:541, says over one thousand had already cancelled their subscriptions (and this was even before the Albany convention).

68. *Pennsylvania Freeman,* September 10, 1840; *Michigan Freeman,* as quoted in *Pennsylvania Freeman,* September 17, 1840, reports that the attempt "is null and void," not having been passed at a regularly scheduled meeting of the board. The paper, however, ceased publication shortly thereafter.

69. Stanton to Birney, March 21, 1840, in Dumond, *Letters of J. G. Birney,* 1:541–542.

70. Alvan Stewart, "An Address to the Friends of Liberty and the oppressed in the United States," November 1840, in (Lowell, Ill.) *Genius of Liberty,* January 23, 1841.

CHAPTER 2

1. Kraditor, *Means and Ends in American Abolitionism,* 150–152, catalogues various Liberty Party positions, many of which are contradictory, to show the "abolitionist political diversity." She is criticizing the party as a national entity, and it often appears pathetic in its inconsistency. Although this diversity was not entirely eliminated at the local level, it was much less glaring than from a national perspective. For instance, the Liberty men of western Pennsylvania were almost uniformly for a high tariff, while Birney and several others were for lowering it. Nonetheless, strong opposition to slavery was the fulcrum of the party.

2. (Lowell, Ill.) *Genius of Liberty,* February 27, 1841. This February 25 meeting "*Resolved,* That efficient political action, can be produced by independent and united effort."

3. *Utica Friend of Man,* May 25, 1841, and *Emancipator,* May 20, 1841, give the minutes, role of the convention, and the vote on the nominations. Willey, *The History of the Antislavery Cause,* 175–177.

4. *Emancipator,* May 20, June 10, 1841. Alvan Stewart was the primary architect of the plan.

5. The address was signed by Alvan Stewart (chairman) and Joshua Leavitt, L. P. Noble, and Levi Coffin (secretaries). Sewell, *Ballots for Freedom,* 108, reports that it was drafted by William Goodell.

6. These arguments are discussed more fully in chapter 8. The standard work on this subject, Leonard L. Richards, *The Slavepower: The Free North and Southern Domination, 1780–1860* (Baton Rouge: Louisiana State University Press, 2000), discusses the role of Thomas Morris in the evolution of this concept but does not examine many Liberty theorists or the concept's relation to the Liberty appeal.

7. "Address of the National Liberty Party Convention in A.D. 1841 'To the Citizens of the United States,'" *Boston Free American,* June 3, 1841; *Philanthropist,* June 16, 1841; *Genius of Liberty,* June 26, 1841.

8. Cincinnati *Daily Enquirer,* April 1, 1842, as quoted in Fladeland, *James G. Birney,* 227.

9. There was some scattered support for third-party candidates in New Jersey in 1841, but there seems to have been little formal organization. See *New Jersey Freeman,* February 28, 1845. There is no evidence of organized party activity in Rhode Island, beyond a few votes cast for Birney in 1840, until 1846.

10. Theodore Foster, "The Liberty Party," Foster Papers, Bentley Library, University of Michigan, 18–19, retrospectively details some of the problems for Whig abolitionists.

11. Michael F. Holt, *The Rise and Fall of the American Whig Party* (New York: Oxford University Press, 1999), 156, speculates that "[a]ntislavery men who had clung to Whiggery in order to achieve economic reform saw little reason to remain in the party once it failed to enact that reform." I have found no support in the Liberty sources for this position. The primary issue was slavery, not economics.

12. See especially, Smith to Friends of the Slave, May 3, 1843, in *Albany Patriot,* March 25, 1843; Harlow, *Gerrit Smith,* 169–172. Kraut, "The Forgotten Reformers: A Profile of Third Party Abolitionists in Antebellum New York," 119–145, uses various subscription and voting lists to determine the motives of Liberty voters. Although he concedes that the "Liberty Party's success in Smithfield must be attributed at least in part to Smith's efforts," he underestimates the roles of Smith's leadership and resources in producing the large Liberty vote in the area.

13. Treadwell to *Michigan Signal of Liberty,* in *Signal of Liberty,* June 13, 1842.

14. See *Liberator,* October 30, 1840; *National Anti-Slavery Standard,* December 30, 1841; *Signal of Liberty,* May 10, 1842, for a few examples.

15. *Boston Free American,* November 11, 1841, lists the following Liberty newspapers with their editors:

(New York, N.Y.) *Emancipator*—Joshua Leavitt
(Boston, Mass.) *Free American*—Elizur Wright
(Hallowell, Maine) *Liberty Standard*—J. C. Lovejoy
(Concord, N.H.) *People's Advocate*—F. P. Tracy
(Montpelier, Vt.) *Voice of Freedom*—Chauncy L. Knapp
(Hartford, Conn.) *Charter Oak*—S. S. Cowles
(New York, N.Y.) *Colored American*—C. B. Ray
(New York, N.Y.) *People's Press* (Colored)—Hamilton and Diers
(Albany, N.Y.) *Tocsin of Liberty*—E. W. Goodwin
(Utica, N.Y.) *Friend of Man*—S. P. Hough
(Cazenovia, N.Y.) *Madison County Abolitionist*—James C. Jackson
(Rochester, N.Y.) *American Citizen*—W. L. Chaplin
(Philadelphia) *Pennsylvania Freeman*—E. Smith and W. H. Burleigh
(Cincinnati, Ohio) *Philanthropist*—Gamaliel Bailey
(Indiana) *Protectionist*—Arnold Buffum
(New Garden, Ind.) *Free Labor Advocate* (Quaker)—Way and Stanton
(Ann Arbor, Mich.) *Signal of Liberty*—executive committee of the Michigan Anti-Slavery Society
(Lowell, Ill.) *Genius of Liberty*—H. Warren and Z. Eastman

A few of these, such as the *Pennsylvania Freeman,* denied that they were Liberty papers, and the list also omits Austin Willey's (Maine) *Advocate of Freedom,* the short-lived *Columbus* (Ohio) *Freeman,* the black-owned (Cleveland) *Palladium of Liberty,* as well as other nonpolitical newspapers, such as the *Oberlin Evangelist,* which supported the Liberty Party.

16. Wright to Gerrit Smith, November 18, 1842, Smith Collection, Syracuse University.

17. The Inter-university Consortium for Political Research at the University of Michigan (ICPR). For a discussion of the Massachusetts situation, see Johnson, "The Liberty Party in Massachusetts," 250–252.

18. *Liberator,* March 17, 1843. Sources disagree on the number of Liberty men elected, probably because some may have appeared on two tickets. The three figures that I have seen are eight, six, and five. I have used six because it is the most frequently cited and is consistent with some of the votes in the Lower House.

19. *Liberator,* March 17, 1843. Because this view is inconsistent with other sources, cited below, the *Liberator* seems to have been in error and possibly motivated by pique against the Liberty Party.

20. *Emancipator,* February 2, 1843; *Boston Daily Advertiser,* January 14, 1843; Darling, *Political Changes in Massachusetts,* 291–293.

21. *Boston Daily Advertiser,* December 31, 1842; Darling, *Political Changes in Massachusetts,* 291. Frank Otto Gatell, *John Gorham Palfrey and the New England Conscience* (Cambridge, Mass.: Harvard University Press), 100–101, subscribes to a similar view.

22. Whittier to his brother in Portland, February 7, 1843, in Samuel T. Pickard, *Life and Letters of John Greenleaf Whittier* (Boston: Houghton-Mifflin, 1894), 1:292.

23. J. G. W. (Whittier) to *Emancipator*, February 18, 1843, in *Emancipator*, February 23, 1843; "Middlesex" (Whittier) to *Emancipator*, in *Emancipator*, February 16, 1843. The reluctant former Democrat was Louis Williams of Eaton.

24. *Emancipator*, February 23, 1843. Laurie, *Beyond Garrison*, 80, presents a very different picture of the 1842 election than I do here. In short, he writes that the Liberty men "held out through four ballots before throwing the speakership to H. A. Collins, a Whig from the abolitionist wing of his party, in return for favorable action on civil rights bills." Darling, *Political Changes in Massachusetts*, Laurie's only secondary source for these statements, does not even mention any bargain on civil rights legislation and points out that Collins left his party to vote for Morton for governor (299), was appointed keeper of the Eastham Lighthouse as a reward (304), and was later reviled by the party newspaper as "'Collins Morton' in nearly every issue a month before the election [of 1843]" (308).

25. *Liberator*, January 27, 1843.

26. *Emancipator*, February 16, 23, 1843.

27. J. G. W. (Whittier) to *Emancipator*, February 18, 1843, in *Emancipator*, February 23, 1843.

28. "Middlesex" (Whittier) to *Emancipator*, in *Emancipator*, February 16, 1843.

29. McPherson, "The Fight Against the Gag Rule," 177–195; William Lee Miller, *Arguing About Slavery: John Quincy Adams and the Great Battle in the United States Congress* (New York: Knopf, 1996), 399–408; Howard Jones, *Mutiny on the* Amistad: *The Saga of a Slave Revolt and Its Impact on American Abolition, Law, and Diplomacy* (New York: Oxford University Press, 1987), 7–8, 41–45.

30. Rayback, "Liberty Party Leaders of Ohio," 165–176, discusses this group. See Volpe, *Forlorn Hope of Freedom*, 126–129, on the diversity of opinion within Ohio and a criticism of Rayback for attributing the views of this group to all of Ohio Liberty men. Earle, *Jacksonian Antislavery*, 152–160.

31. See William Birney (James's son in Cincinnati) to James G. Birney, February 28, April 29, 1843, in Dumond, *Letters of J. G. Birney*, 2:720–722, 736–738, for an indication of the dislike and distrust some Ohio Liberty men felt for one another.

32. Chase to Gerrit Smith, May 14, 1842, Smith Collection, Syracuse University.

33. *Philanthropist*, January 5, 1842.

34. Morris, (William) Birney, Bailey, and Brisbane to Leavitt, February 9, 1842, in *Emancipator*, June 16, 1842.

35. Chase did have scattered support in some other states. See Charles D. Cleveland (of Philadelphia) to J. G. Birney, March 8, 1842, in Dumond, *Letters of J. G. Birney*, 2:67.

36. Stanley Harrold, *The Abolitionists and the South, 1831–1861* (Lexington: University Press of Kentucky, 1995), 131–138.

37. Later the (Salem, Ohio) *Anti-Slavery Bugle* was founded in June 1845 as an antislavery newspaper opposed to the Liberty Party.

38. *Philanthropist*, March 10, 1842.

39. Rayback, "Liberty Party Leaders of Ohio," 171–172; Chase to J. G. Birney, January 21, 1842, in Dumond, *Letters of J. G. Birney*, 2:661–662; Blue, *Salmon P. Chase*, 47–49; Niven, *Salmon P. Chase*, 69–70. See John Niven, ed., *The Salmon P. Chase Papers*, vol. 2, *Correspondence 1823–1857* (Kent, Ohio: Kent State University Press, 1994), 99–100, for the draft of a letter soliciting Adams to run on the Liberty ticket; and ibid., 2:103–104, Chase to Lewis Tappan, September 12, 1843, for word of Adams's declining and Jay's urging Birney's candidacy. Budney, *William Jay*, 72–76.

40. Birney to Chase, February 2, 1842, in Niven, *The Salmon P. Chase Papers*, 2:671.

41. Leavitt to Birney, February 14, 1842, in Niven, *The Salmon P. Chase Papers*, 2:673. See H. B. Stanton to G. Smith. August 14, 1843, Gerrit Smith Collection, Syracuse University, on the range of opinions among Liberty leaders.

42. William Birney to J. G. Birney, February 28, 1843, in Niven, *The Salmon P. Chase Papers*, 2:721. William Birney, a Cincinnati lawyer, continued to keep his father informed of Liberty affairs in Cincinnati after J. G. Birney relocated to Michigan. See Morris, *Life of Thomas Morris*, 231–233, for the Morris withdrawal at the Ohio state Liberty convention of December 28, 1842. Also see Volpe, *Forlorn Hope of Freedom*, 112; Smith, *The Liberty and Free Soil Parties in the Northwest*, 69.

43. Leavitt to J. G. Birney, February 14, 1842, in Niven, *The Salmon P. Chase Papers*, 2:673.

44. (Hartford, Conn.) *Christian Freeman*, January, 6, May 19, 1843; *Chicago Western Citizen*, April 20, 1843.

45. See *Signal of Liberty*, May 8, July 3, 1843, on the postponing of the convention for weather and elections. Still, Willey, *The History of the Antislavery Cause*, 227–228, lamented about the new August date that "[i]t was the week preceding our election in Maine, and unfortunate for our work. Some of us appointed delegates felt it our duty to remain at home."

46. Smith to president of the Liberty Party Convention, August 10, 1843, Smith Collection, Syracuse University.

47. Foster, "The Liberty Party," 24, in Bentley Historical Collections, University of Michigan.

48. As quoted in Henry Wilson, *History of the Rise and Fall of the Slave Power in America* (Boston: R. Osgood and Company, 1872), 1:552.

49. Morris, *The Life of Thomas Morris*, 233; Smith, *The Liberty and Free Soil Parties in the Northwest*, 69; Volpe, *Forlorn Hope of Freedom*, 112.

50. Stanton to Gerrit Smith, August 4, 1843, Smith Collection, Syracuse University.

51. "Official Proceedings of the National Liberty Convention," in *Michigan Signal of Liberty*, September 25, 1843; *Emancipator*, September 14, 1843; Fladeland, *James G. Birney*, 224–225.

52. See Birney to Samuel Lewis, July 13, 1843, in Dumond, *Letters of J. G. Birney*, 2:743–748, for Birney's views on various issues.

53. For an example of O'Connell's views, along with those of temperance advocate Father Theobald Matthew, see their "Address from the People of Ireland" (signed by "SIXTY THOUSAND other inhabitants of Ireland"), in *Chicago Western Citizen*, September 21, 1843.

54. *Philanthropist*, September 27, 1843. Chase was so disturbed by the resolution that he included a clipping from the *Gazette* that erroneously attributed it to him in his Scrapbook, Chase Papers, Library of Congress. Foster, "The Liberty Party," 27, Bentley Collections, University of Michigan, reports that this was later brought up against him in a Senate debate in January 1850, but Chase claimed not even to have been present when it passed.

55. Stanton to Chase, February 6, 1844, in the *Annual Report of the American Historical Association for the Year 1902* (Washington, D.C.: Government Printing Office, 1903), 462–464; Foster, "The Liberty Party," 27, Bentley Historical Collections, University of Michigan.

56. Chase to Gerrit Smith, May 14, 1842, Smith Collection, Syracuse University.

57. Smith, *The Liberty and Free Soil Parties in the Northwest*, 70.

58. Dorothy Sterling, *Ahead of Her Time: Abby Kelley and the Politics of Antislavery* (New York: W. W. Norton, 1991), 179.

59. John Alden to Joshua Leavitt, in *Emancipator*, August 31, September 7, 1843; Joel Schor, *Henry Highland Garnet: A Voice of Black Radicalism in the Nineteenth Century*, Contributions in American History, 54 (Westport, Conn.: Greenwood Press, 1977), 61. See William W. Brown to

National Anti-Slavery Standard, September 20, 1843, in *National Anti-Slavery Standard,* October 5, 1843, for disagreement with Garnet's statement. It is also reprinted with comment in William Edward Farrison, *William Wells Brown, Author and Reformer,* Negro American Biographies and Autobiographies series (Chicago: University of Chicago Press, 1969), 78–80.

60. Wyatt-Brown, *Lewis Tappan,* 264, 269, discusses Tappan's being convinced to join the third party by English abolitionist friends and his views on the lack of effectiveness of other abolition measures. On gains among the Garrisonians, see chapter 11.

61. *Chicago Western Citizen,* December 14, 1843, lists the members as Alvan Stewart (N.Y.), Joshua Leavitt (Mass.), F. J. LeMoyne (Pa.), S. P. Chase (Ohio), Francis Gillett (*sic*) (Conn.), Titus Hutchinson (Vt.), Daniel Hoit (N.H.), Samuel Fessenden (Maine), Elizur Demming (*sic*) (Ind.), James H. Collins (Ill.), and Luther Stevens (Mich.).

62. Chase to Lewis Tappan, September 12, 1843, in Niven, *The Salmon P. Chase Papers,* 2:104.

63. Only Michigan, Massachusetts, and New York in the North held their state elections at the same time as the national elections. State elections were either held in the spring or usually preceded the national contests.

64. *Signal of Liberty,* November 13, 1843; *Christian Freeman,* November 2, 1843.

65. Stanton and Merril to Elizur Wright, July 4, 1843, Wright Papers, Library of Congress.

66. *Signal of Liberty,* October 16, 1843. The Liberty nominee, Jeduthan Spooner, campaigned against himself.

67. *Chicago Western Citizen,* November 30, 1843, March 7, 1844; *Signal of Liberty,* December 11, 1843; (Wis.) *American Freeman,* March 27, 1844; McManus, *Political Abolitionism in Wisconsin,* 4–5.

68. *Emancipator,* October 19, 1843.

69. *Chicago Western Citizen,* October 12, 1843, March 7, 1844.

70. For just a few examples, see *Emancipator,* March, 14, April 3, 10, 1844; (Maine) *Liberty Standard,* April 18, 1844; *Albany Patriot,* March 27, April 3, 1844.

71. For details on Birney's activities during the campaign, see Fladeland, *James G. Birney,* chapter 12: "The Campaign of 1844," 227–251. Bay City was then called Lower Saginaw.

72. Birney to Russell Errett, August 5, 1844, in Dumond, *Letters of J. G. Birney,* 2:829; Errett to Birney, July 13, 1844, in ibid., 2:820; see later problems in Errett to Birney, October 4, 1844, in ibid., 2:844–846.

73. Birney to the Hartford Committee, August 15, 1844, in ibid., 2:833–836.

74. *National Anti-Slavery Standard,* October 31, 1844; Kraditor, *Means and Ends in American Abolitionism,* 38; Rice, "Henry Brewster Stanton as a Political Abolitionist," 249.

75. Birney to Charles H. Stewart and Joshua Leavitt, August 17, 1843, in Dumond, *Letters of J. G. Birney,* 2:754–758.

76. See William Birney to J. G. Birney, February 24, 1844, in ibid., 2:794, for more details on the Ohio split.

77. William Birney to J. G. Birney, March 28, 1844, in ibid., 2:802. Morris's opinions may have been only "ultra" vis-à-vis the Cincinnati standards.

78. See Blue, *Gamaliel Bailey,* 64–69, for the charges of racism against Morris and their mutual dislike.

79. George W. Clark, *The Liberty Minstrel,* as quoted in Wright and Wright, *Elizur Wright,* 146.

80. James Gillespie Birney, *Headland in the Life of Henry Clay* (Boston: Leavitt & Alden, 1844). See also *Emancipator,* September 17, 1844.

81. Beriah Green, *Sketches of the Life and Writings of James Gillespie Birney* (Utica, N.Y.: Jackson & Chaplin, 1844).

82. Fladeland, *James G. Birney*, 238–240.

83. Ibid., 241–244.

84. Birney to editor of the (New York) *Tribune* (Horace Greeley) October 10, 1844, in Dumond, *Letters of J. G. Birney*, 2:852.

85. Arthur L. Porter to Birney, October 4, 1844, in ibid., 2:847.

86. *New York Tribune*, October 10, 1844.

87. Arthur L. Porter and others (from Detroit) to Birney, October 3, 1844, in Dumond, *Letters of J. G. Birney*, 2:843–844; Joshua Leavitt (from Boston) to Birney, October 8, 1844, in ibid., 2:847–848; James M. Brown (from Trumbull County, Ohio) to Birney, October 9, 1844, in ibid., 2:849–850; Zebina Eastman (from Chicago) to Birney, October 17, 1844, in ibid., 2:853–854; Samuel D. Porter (from Rochester, N.Y.) to Gerrit Smith, October 7, 1844, in ibid., 2:861; W. F. Brayton (from Cleveland, Ohio) to Gerrit Smith, October 9, 1844, in ibid., 2:863–864. Smith sent Birney these letters.

88. A. W. Bentley (from De Ruyter, N.Y.) to Gerrit Smith, October 21, 1844, in ibid., 2:867, discusses the loss of votes, including his "nearest neighbor, who voted the Liberty Ticket as early as 1840, formerly a Whig, now a grey-headed old man, has come out for Clay" and a Seventh-Day Baptist deacon, who was going to sit out the election. The letter was forwarded to Birney.

89. As reported in Henry B. Stanton to Gerrit Smith, December 2, 1844, Smith Collection, Syracuse University.

90. Foster, "The Liberty Party," 62, Bentley Historical Collections, University of Michigan.

91. *Cortland County Whig—Extra*, October 31, 1844. This issue is reproduced between pages 868 and 869 in Dumond, *Letters of J. G. Birney*, vol. 2.

92. Fladeland, *James G. Birney*, 247–251, presents the details of the investigation.

93. James H. Duncan to J. T. Buckingham (the owner) of the *Boston Courier*, October 23, 1844, in *Liberator*, November 1, 1844, lists sixteen Haverhill men returning to the Whig Party; *Emancipator*, November 6, 1844, replies that these were never real Liberty Party men. Floyd B. Streeter, *Political Parties in Michigan, 1837–1860* (Lansing: Michigan Historical Collections, 1918), 68–69; *Signal of Liberty*, October 14, 1844.

94. William Birney to J. G. Birney, November 25, 1844, in Dumond, *Letters of J. G. Birney*, 2:886.

95. Stanton to Gerrit Smith, November 12, 1844, Smith Collection, Syracuse University.

96. Henry B. Stanton to Gerrit Smith, December 2, 1844, Smith Collection, Syracuse University.

97. Vernon L. Volpe, "The Liberty Party and Polk's Election, 1844," *The Historian* 23 (January 1991): 697.

98. Lee Benson, *The Concept of Jacksonian Democracy: New York as a Test Case* (New York: Atheneum, 1969), 133–135. Daniel Walker Howe, *The Political Culture of the American Whigs* (Chicago: University of Chicago Press, 1979), 19, statement that if African Americans had had universal manhood suffrage in New York "Henry Clay would have been elected president in 1844" neglects the fact that Liberty Party support among African Americans in New York State was very strong among those who did meet the property qualification for the franchise. There is no reason to think that the others would have gone over to the slaveholder Clay in sufficient numbers to change the results. Thomas B. Alexander, "The Dimensions of Voter Partisan Constancy in Presidential Elections from 1840 to 1860," in Stephen E. Maizlish and John J. Kushma, eds., *Essays on American Antebellum Politics, 1840–1860* (College Station: Texas A&M University Press, 1982), 78, 116, minimizes the Liberty impact and believes "the election of Polk must be attributed to numerous unknown and possibly irrelevant circumstances."

99. Benson, *The Concept of Jacksonian Democracy*, 136.

100. Volpe, "The Liberty Party and Polk's Election, 1844," 695. Lex Renda, "Retrospective Voting and the Presidential Election of 1844: The Texas Issue Revisited," *Presidential Studies Quarterly* 24 (Fall 1994): 849, makes the same argument with an emphasis on the Texas issue in Connecticut, which Clay won. Interestingly, neither historian mentions the Garland Forgery.

101. See further reactions in the state studies, especially those on New York and Michigan.

102. See chapter 8.

103. J. G. Birney to Abraham Pennock, March 31, 1844, in Dumond, *Letters of J. G. Birney*, 2:806.

CHAPTER 3

1. *Philanthropist*, December 2, 1844.

2. Ronald G. Walters, *American Reformers, 1815–1860* (New York: Hill and Wang, 1978), 93.

3. W. (Whittier ?) to editor of the *Philanthropist*, December 7, 1844, in *Philanthropist*, December 18, 1844. Resolutions and "Address of the Convention" in (Hartford, Conn.) *Christian Freeman*, December 12, 19, 1844; *Albany Patriot*, December 18, 1844. This was one of the few major conventions where Connecticut Liberty men had a significant role. Francis Gillette, Sherman Booth, and James W. C. Pennington participated. Davis, *Joshua Leavitt*, 221–222; Harlow, *Gerrit Smith*, 172; Fladeland, *James G. Birney*, 253.

4. Birney to editors of the *Albany Patriot*, January 31, 1845, in *Signal of Liberty*, March 10, 1845; Dumond, *Letters of J. G. Birney*, 2:923–924.

5. Fladeland, *James G. Birney*, 255–256. Birney, *James G. Birney*, 373–377, was with his father at the time of the fall. He reports that "[f]or the rest of his life . . . he was an invalid," although "[t]he clearness and vigor of his mind did not perceptibly diminish."

6. This was true for all parties. As Holt, *The Rise and Fall of the American Whig Party*, 238, says, "During the off-year elections of 1845, 1846, and 1847, every state in the nation had special peculiarities that influenced the precise shape of political developments within it."

7. *Niles National Register*, August 30, 1845.

8. Harrold, "The Southern Strategy of the Liberty Party," 29–31, is one of the few studies that recognizes the significance of these and briefly discusses all three meetings.

9. Salmon Portland Chase and Charles Dexter Cleveland, *Anti-Slavery Addresses of 1844 and 1845* (New York: Negro Universities Press, 1969 [originally published by Sampson Low, Son, and Marston, 1867]), "Appendix," note 1, 129–130. Estimates that total attendance at the sessions was in the 2,500 to 4,000 range have been generally accepted. See *Herald and Philanthropist*, April 23, 1845, for the call. A copy of the circular can be found in Dumond, *Letters of J. G. Birney*, 2:934–935.

10. Short accounts of the meeting are given by Earle, *Jacksonian Antislavery*, 155–157; Blue, *Salmon P. Chase*, 50–52; Harrold, *Gamaliel Bailey*, 73–74; and his "Southern Strategy of the Liberty Party," 28–30; Birney (a participant]) *James G. Birney*, 364–365; Fladeland, *James G. Birney*, 253–255; Rayback, *Free Soil*, 105–106; Volpe, *Forlorn Hope of Freedom*, 116–117; Smith, *The Liberty and Free Soil Parties in the Northwest*, 88–89; Willey, *The History of the Antislavery Cause*, 279–280. Contemporary accounts of the convention are in *Emancipator*, June 18, 25, July 2, 9, 1845; *Cincinnati Weekly Herald and Philanthropist*, June 25, 1845.

11. Harrold, *The Abolitionists and the South*, 139.

12. Birney, *James G. Birney*, 364. William Birney was a member of the executive committee of

the Ohio Liberty Party that reviewed Chase's address. He "strongly disapproved certain [of these] passages."

13. Ibid., 365; Volpe, *Forlorn Hope of Freedom*, 116–117; Smith, *The Liberty and Free Soil Parties in the Northwest*, 88–89; Chase and Cleveland, *Anti-Slavery Addresses*, 124.

14. Chase and Cleveland, *Anti-Slavery Addresses*, 72.

15. Hart, *Salmon Portland Chase*, 59; Michael William Pfau, *The Political Style of Conspiracy: Chase, Sumner, and Lincoln* (East Lansing: Michigan State University Press, 2005), 47–69. Pfau, a rhetorician, analyzes Chase's speech. He sees the speech as bringing political antislavery closer to mainstream politics by employing more secular arguments and rhetoric. While his analysis of Chase's speech is useful, he errs in maintaining that "[o]rganizationally, the Liberty Party usually relied on the church as the basic unit, and this church-centered organization overlay an unwillingness on the part of many Liberty men to engage in conventional political tactics" (51).

16. Chase and Cleveland, *Anti-Slavery Addresses*, passim.

17. Blue, *Salmon P. Chase*, 16–17; Niven, *Salmon P. Chase*, 74; Volpe, *Forlorn Hope of Freedom*, 120–121.

18. See *Emancipator and Weekly Chronicle*, August 20, 1845, for the call that was signed by 122 men from nine states.

19. *Emancipator*, October 8, 1845; *Granite Freeman*, October 23, 30, 1845; *Chicago Western Citizen*, October 23, 1845. Willey, *The History of the Antislavery Cause*, 282–284, gives the crowd estimate. Henry B. Stanton to Salmon P. Chase, October 6, 1845, Chase Papers, Library of Congress, estimates that there were two thousand delegates and three thousand present with every Liberty state represented except Indiana.

20. Willey, *The History of the Antislavery Cause*, 283. These non-Liberty men, however, declined to participate. See S. C. Phillips to Committee, September 29, 1845; W. H. Seward to Henry Brewster Stanton, Elizur Wright, Samuel Sewall, S. N. Barbour, and M. S. Scudder, September 25, 1845; T. Sedgwick to Elizur Wright, September 15, 1845, all in Wright Papers, Library of Congress.

21. Harlow, *Gerrit Smith*, 174.

22. Stanton to Chase, October 6, 1845, Chase Papers, Library of Congress. He also says that he opposed the adoption of the address, which was prepared by Gerrit Smith after John Greenleaf Whittier took ill. Rice, "Henry Brewster Stanton," 264. Stanton was beginning to move closer to the less moralistic ideas of Chase and Bailey.

23. Stanton to Chase, October 6, 1845, Chase Papers, Library of Congress, reported that the Spooner interpretation of the antislavery nature of the U.S. Constitution was referred to committee and thus "[t]he resolutions are safe on the constitutional question." "Diary and Correspondence of Salmon P. Chase," in the *Annual Report of the American Historical Association for 1902*, 2:465–466. Smith, *The Liberty and Free Soil Parties in the Northwest*, 89, mistakenly says that the interpretation of the Constitution as an antislavery document was adopted at the meeting. The convention only voted to refer them to the committee on publication to be printed with the proceedings "for the deliberate consideration of the Liberty party, and of the whole American people."

24. "Official Report of the Proceedings," in *Chicago Western Citizen*, June 30, 1846; *Emancipator*, July 15, 1846. *Chicago Western Citizen*, July 7, 14, 1846, sketch the debates and discuss the convention further. For an account from one of the participants, see Edward Mathews, *The Autobiography of the Rev. E. Mathews: The "Father Dickson," of Mrs. Stowe's "Dred"* (New York: Baptist Free Mission Society, 1866 [reprinted Miami, Fla.: Mnemosyne Publishing Co., 1969]), 217–226.

25. Magdol, *Owen Lovejoy*, 72, believes "Ohio's absence possibly was due to the influence of Chase, who was disappointed by his failure to swing the Cincinnati convention to his way of think-

ing." Chase did send a letter to the convention urging a decentralization of party decisions. Instead, he advocated localities discussing the issues and taking positions as they saw fit. See S. P. Chase to the Chicago Convention, June 13, 1846, in *Albany Patriot,* August 6, 1846. The newspaper did not approve of Chase's position.

26. Hamlin was exploring the possibility for an independent reform party if the Whigs did not nominate antislavery men for president and vice president. In the convention he broached the possibility of forming a committee "for the purpose of corresponding with Anti-slavery men of all parties throughout the United States." See details of his confidential conversation with Theodore Foster at the convention in Foster to James G. Birney, August 1, 1846, in Dumond, *Letters of J. G. Birney,* 2:1024–1026.

27. Kephart, "A Voice for Freedom," 178, states that "the number of persons who supported the Foster program was small."

28. Foster to Birney, August 1, 1846, in Dumond, *Letters of J. G. Birney,* 2:1025. This Michigan plan is discussed more fully in chapter 7 in the section on Michigan. *Chicago Western Citizen,* July 7, 1845; Magdol, *Owen Lovejoy,* 72–73.

29. Although the term *fusion* was loosely used in the 1840s, I use *fusion* to mean the uniting of various parties, on whatever level, on a candidate(s) while maintaining the parties' separate identities. By *coalition* or *merger,* I mean that the various elements became united in one party with a single organization. Fusion was a temporary alliance, whereas coalition or merger meant the formation of a new political entity (as in the case of the Free Soil Party).

30. The standard book on the subject is William Wiecek's excellent *The Sources of Antislavery Constitutionalism in America, 1760–1848* (Ithaca, N.Y.: Cornell University Press, 1977), especially chapters 7–11; Kraditor, *Means and Ends in American Abolitionism,* 185–217, has a discussion of many of the theories. Also see Staughton Lynd, " The Abolitionist Critique of the United States Constitution," in Martin Duberman, ed., *The Antislavery Vanguard: New Essays on the Abolitionists* (Princeton, N.J.: Princeton University Press, 1965), 209–239.

31. Stanton to Chase, February 6, 1844, in the *Annual Report of the American Historical Association for 1902,* 2:463.

32. Chase to Gerrit Smith, May 14, 1842, Smith Collection, Syracuse University; Blue, *Salmon P. Chase,* 49.

33. "Maine Liberty Party Address," *Liberty Standard,* May 24, 1843.

34. Morris, Birney, Bailey, and Brisbane to Joshua Leavitt, February 9, 1842, in *Emancipator,* June 16, 1842. This is the letter that Leavitt held for four months because of its views before publishing it.

35. Gerrit Smith to president of the Liberty Party, August 8, 1843, Smith Collection, Syracuse University, advised that the question be avoided by the party because of the variety of views.

36. *Cleveland True Democrat,* as quoted in *National Anti-Slavery Standard,* June 17, 1847.

37. Goodell to Luther R. Marsh, undated, in Luther R. Marsh, ed., *Writing and Speeches of Alvan Stewart on Slavery* (New York: Haskell House, 1970 [1860]), 27; Goodell, *Slavery and Anti-Slavery,* 475–476.

38. Goodell, *Slavery and Anti-Slavery,* 476; Fladeland, *James G. Birney,* 178; Wiecek, *The Sources of Antislavery Constitutionalism,* 254–255. Stewart had actually originated these ideas a year earlier. See "Address to the Abolitionists of the State of New York. *As Reported by a Committee appointed by the first Annual Meeting of the New York State Anti-Slavery Society, of which Committee Alvan Stewart, Esq., was Chairman, and was unanimously adopted, October 1836,*" in Marsh, *Writings and Speeches of Alvan Stewart,* 99, 103–104. Blue, *No Taint of Compromise,* 20–21. On the opposition of

many to these ideas in the late 1830s, including many who later supported the antislavery nature of the Constitution, see Wiecek, *The Sources of Antislavery Constitutionalism in America*, 254–256.

39. Budney, *William Jay*, 41–44. Blue, *No Taint of Compromise*, 21, says that Jay believed Stewart's position "should bring his expulsion from the New York abolition society."

40. Many arguments are in Donald E. Fehrenbacher (completed and edited by Ward M. McAfee), *The Slaveholding Republic: An Account of the United States Government's Relation to Slavery* (New York: Oxford University Press, 2001), passim. McAfee, in his "Preface," x–xi, states that "Fehrenbacher argues that the Constitution was neither proslavery nor antislavery in intent" and that "the fundamental law had been established upon a cultural assumption that slavery would remain only temporarily."

41. (Lowell, Ill.) *Genius of Liberty*, January 1, 1842.

42. Morris to Committee for the Erection of Pennsylvania Hall, May 11, 1838, in Morris, *Life of Thomas Morris*, 217.

43. James Appleton to J. C. Lovejoy, Simon Paige, Calvin Spaulding, William Stickney, and Washington Wilcox, February 17, 1842, in (Maine) *Liberty Standard*, February 23, 1842. See Gerrit Smith's complimentary letter sent six years later to Appleton, June 6, 1848, Smith Papers, Syracuse University. By then Smith had changed his earlier views and espoused an antislavery interpretation of the Constitution.

44. Reported in (Montpelier, Vt.) *Green Mountain Freeman*, August 20, 1846.

45. G. W. F. Mellen, *An Argument on the Unconstitutionality of Slavery, Embracing an Abstract of the Proceedings of the National and State Conventions on this Subject* (Boston: Saxton & Pierce, 1841 [reprinted New York: AMS Press, 1970]).

46. Wiecek, *The Sources of Antislavery Constitutionalism in America*, 256. Mellen often appeared at gatherings in the American Revolution era garb of his namesake.

47. Seventh Congressional District Liberty Convention, July 25, 1843, in *Liberty Standard*, August 2, 1843.

48. William Goodell, *Views of American Constitutional Law, in Its Bearing Upon American Slavery*, 2nd ed. (Utica, N.Y.: Lawson and Chaplin, 1845), 114.

49. Lysander Spooner, *The Unconstitutionality of Slavery* (Boston: Bela Marsh, 1846), 114. On his non-Liberty Party status, see Goodell, *Slavery and Anti-Slavery*, 476.

50. For instance, Gerrit Smith to *Emancipator*, April 6, 1847, in *Albany Patriot*, April 14, 1847, in which he endorses the Goodell-Spooner approaches. The *Cleveland American*, from *Albany Patriot*, April 14, 1847, reports George Bradburn's endorsement of Spooner's views.

51. Alvan Stewart (as chairman of the Liberty Party executive committee to the Liberty Press in the United States), June 1, 1844, in *Albany Weekly Patriot*, June 19, 1844.

52. "Argument, on the Question Whether the New Constitution of 1844 Abolished Slavery in New Jersey," in Marsh, *Writings and Speeches of Alvan Stewart*, 272–367; the case is summarized in Paul Finkelman, *Slavery in the Courtroom: An Annotated Bibliography of American Cases* (Washington, D.C.: Library of Congress, 1985), 150–155. *New Jersey Freeman*, June 1, July 1, 1845. An extensive legal analysis is presented in Daniel Ernst, "Legal Positivism, Abolitionist Litigation, and the New Jersey Slave Case of 1845," *Law and History Review* 4 (Fall 1986): 339–365. Blue, *No Taint of Compromise*, 31–33, summarizes Stewart's argument. Robert M. Cover, *Justice Accused: Antislavery and the Judicial Process* (New Haven, Conn.: Yale University Press, 1975), 56, comments that Stewart's "position was steadfastly held despite a Supreme Court decision holding the Fifth Amendment inapplicable as a restraint on state action, and despite the four clauses of the Constitution, which, by any candid construction, at least acknowledged the lawful existence of slavery in some states."

Later Cover maintains (157) that it "requires nothing more than a suspension of reason concerning the origin, intent, and past interpretation of the clause." Wiecek, *The Sources of Antislavery Constitutionalism*, 265–268, also gives a criticism of Stewart's ideas, but explains why Stewart may have taken some of his stands.

53. "Argument, on the Question, Whether the New Constitution of 1844 Abolished Slavery in New Jersey," in Marsh, *Writings and Speeches of Alvan Stewart*, 354.

54. On Birney, see his articles in *Albany Patriot*, May 12, 19, 26, 29, June 16, 1847; see Fladeland, *James G. Birney*, 262–265, on his "about-face." Gerrit Smith to J. G. Whittier, July 18, 1844, as quoted in Octavius Brooks Frothingham, *Gerrit Smith: A Biography* (New York: G. P. Putnam's Sons, 1878 [reprinted New York: Negro University Press, 1969]), 175, declares that "the constitution is an antislavery instrument." See Gerrit Smith, *Letter of Gerrit Smith to S. P. Chase, on the Unconstitutionality of Every Part of American Slavery* (Albany, N.Y.: S. W. Green, 1847); Harlow, *Gerrit Smith*, 279–283, on the evolution of his constitutional thought. On Wright, see Goodheart, *Elizur Wright*, 90–91. On Leavitt's move toward this constitutional interpretation, see Davis, *Joshua Leavitt*, 227–231.

55. *Emancipator*, July 23, 1845; (Maine) *Liberty Standard*, July 31, 1845.

56. *Emancipator*, October 8, 1845. See details of the convention earlier in this chapter that show it did not endorse the antislavery interpretation but merely presented it for consideration.

57. *Herkimer Freeman*, from *Signal of Liberty*, October 23, 1847.

58. *Albany Patriot*, November 10, 1847, comments on this.

59. Joel Tiffany, *A Treatise on the Unconstitutionality of American Slavery; Together with the Powers and Duties of the Federal Government in Relation to That Subject* (Cleveland, Ohio: J. Calyer, 1849).

60. *National Era*, January 7, 1847.

61. Elizabeth Cady Stanton, *Eighty Years and More: Reminiscences 1815–1897* (Boston: Northeastern University Press, 1993 [originally published by T. Fisher Unwin, 1898]), 88, discusses attending the 1840 World Anti-Slavery Convention in London with her husband Henry and how "[o]ur English friends were amazed that none of us drank wine. Mr. Gurney said he had never before seen such a sight as forty ladies and gentlemen sitting down to dinner and none of them tasting wine."

62. Cummings to *Emancipator*, in *Emancipator*, March 1, 1847.

63. *Boston Free American*, October 21, 1841.

64. *Bangor Gazette*, March 4, 1843.

65. The (Wis.) *American Freeman* did accept them in its early years. This policy changed when Ichabod Codding took over as editor from former Democrat C. C. Sholes. I have only found a few objections. J. N. T. Tucker (a publisher from Syracuse, N.Y.) to editor of *Utica Friend of Man*, July 1, 1840, objects to the emphasis on temperance that "we must just as properly make temperance &c. test questions, as abolition." He was told in no uncertain terms that "[i]n our view, temperance *should* be made a test question . . . Wine drinkers and hard cider drinkers will not be 'just ruling in the hand of God,' nor can human liberty ever be safe, for a moment, in their hands." The *Cincinnati Weekly Press and Weekly Herald* (which took the place of the *Philanthropist*), September 1847, declared that a temperance resolution was "entirely out of place in a Liberty Convention." The (Hartford, Conn.) *Christian Freeman*, April 7, 1843, criticized Austin F. Williams because "the objections to his Political Abolitionism, not that he urges a *scattering*, rather than an organized concentrated vote, but that he would have Abolitionists vote for those who are not 'Teetotal' Abolitionists." Williams was a Birney elector in 1844.

66. *Signal of Liberty*, March 2, 1842.

67. The party in Massachusetts had more luck working with temperance advocates than it did

in Maine or New York, where some temperance men were hostile to the Liberty Party. See *Emancipator*, April 10, 1844; *Albany Patriot*, March 2, 1843, April 17, 1844; *Bangor Gazette*, March 16, 1844.

68. *Boston Morning Chronicle*, March 22, 1844.

69. *Liberty Standard*, February 5, 1846.

70. Foster to Birney, July 7, 1845, in Dumond, *Letters of J. G. Birney*, 2:952.

71. Ibid., 2:950.

72. Gerrit Smith to William Goodell, April 15, 1845, in *Liberty Press*, April 26, 1845, as quoted in *Albany Patriot*, May 7, 1845. On the evolution of Goodell's thought, see Goodell, *Slavery and Anti-Slavery*, 472–475; Perkal, "William Goodell," 197–200.

73. Foster to Birney, September 12, 1845, in Dumond, *Letters of J. G. Birney*, 2:969.

74. William Birney to J. G. Birney, November 25, 1844, in ibid., 2:887; Volpe, *Forlorn Hope of Freedom*, 116–117; Blue, *Salmon P. Chase*, 50–52; Harrold, *Gamaliel Bailey*, 45–54.

75. Elder wrote a series of articles for the *National Era* in 1851 that were collected in pamphlet form in William Elder, *Third Parties* (Philadelphia: Merrihew and Thompson, 1851), 4, 28. Louis S. Gerteis, *Morality and Utility in American Antislavery Reform* (Chapel Hill: University of North Carolina Press, 1987).

76. *Spirit of Liberty*, as quoted in *Signal of Liberty*, May 18, 1846.

77. *Perry Impartial Countryman*, as quoted in *Albany Patriot*, June 24, 1846. Daniel J. McInerney, "'A Faith for Freedom': The Political Gospel of Abolition," *Journal of the Early Republic* 11 (Fall 1991): 373–374, discusses how abolitionists from the 1830s to the Civil War "commonly framed their understanding of faith in the vocabulary, values, and expectations of republican thought" and "pointed repeatedly to the harmony that they believed existed between Christianity and republicanism."

78. George W. Clark to William Chaplin, August 22, 1846, in *Albany Patriot*, September 16, 1846.

79. *Signal of Liberty*, March 30, April 20, May 11, 18, 1846. Stewart later relented on most of the positions but continued to oppose a low tariff.

80. "Address of the State Central Committee, To the Liberty Party of Michigan, March 23, 1846," in *Signal of Liberty*, April 6, 1846.

81. *Albany Patriot*, August 27, 1845.

82. *Albany Patriot*, July 23, 1845.

83. *Albany Patriot*, July 23, 1845.

84. Tappan to Gerrit Smith, July 29, 1845, Smith Collection, Syracuse University.

85. *Albany Patriot*, June 24, 1846.

86. *Liberty Party, National Convention, 1847, Macedon, N.Y.* (Albany, N.Y.: S. W. Green, 1847); *Albany Patriot*, June 16, 23, July 7, 1847. H. Witcher to Wesley Bailey, June 11, 1847, from the *Liberty Press*, as reported in the *Liberator*, July 2, 1847, gives a capsule description of the proceedings. Goodell, *Slavery and Anti-Slavery*, 475–479; Perkal, "William Goodell," 202–206; Harlow, *Gerrit Smith*, 177–180; Fladeland, *James G. Birney*, 262–265; McCulloch, *Fearless Advocate of the Right*, 164–165. William Goodell to James G. Birney, April 1, 1847, in Dumond, *Letters of J. G. Birney*, 2:1047–1057, offers Birney the nomination and encloses the call for the convention.

87. See Burritt's letter declining the nomination, June 19, 1847, in *Cincinnati National Press and Weekly Herald*, August 18, 1847.

88. Bailey to Gerrit Smith, June 5, 1847, Smith Papers, Syracuse University.

89. *Boston Daily Chronotype*, January 29, June 19, 1847; Goodheart, *Elizur Wright*, 133. See *Boston Daily Chronotype*, September 6, 1847, for a long article of support from Ichabod Codding, who was in Wisconsin.

90. Samuel Pickard, ed., *John Greenleaf Whittier as a Politician, Illustrated by His Letters to Professor Elizur Wright, Jr.* (Boston: Charles Goodspeed, 1900), 2–3; Jarvis, "John Greenleaf Whittier and the Antislavery Movement," 135; Rosalie Margolin, "Henry B. Stanton, A Forgotten Abolitionist," 66–67; Rice, "Henry Brewster Stanton as a Political Abolitionist," 258–275; Stanton to Salmon P. Chase, August 6, 1847, in *Annual Report of the American Historical Association for 1902*, 2:467–468. Stanton was not publicly consistent on this point; see "Stick to Our Candidates," in *Emancipator*, October 28, 1846; Harrold, *Gamaliel Bailey*, x–xiii; Blue, *Salmon P. Chase*, 45.

91. Whittier to Samuel Sewall, February 23, 1841, in *Boston Free American*, March 25, 1841.

92. Pickard, *Life and Letters of J. G. Whittier*, 1:284–285.

93. Wright's editorial, " Line Upon Line," *Boston Free American*, April 8, 1841.

94. Rayback, "Liberty Party Leaders of Ohio," passim. Rayback overemphasizes Ohio unity toward this goal. See Volpe, *Forlorn Hope of Freedom*, x–xxi, 108–114, 124–128.

95. William Birney to J. G. Birney, November 25, 1844, in Dumond, *Letters of J. G. Birney*, 2:887.

96. The term is a biblical reference to Revelation 18:4–5: "And I heard another voice from heaven, saying, Come out of her, my people, that ye be not partakers of her sins, and that ye receive not of her plagues. For her sins have reached unto heaven, and God hath remembered her iniquities."

97. *Emancipator*, August 27, 1840. See Davis, *Joshua Leavitt*, 226–227, 240–242, for Leavitt's position and the pressures on him to change after 1847.

98. *Emancipator*, November 9, 1843. Eliphalet Kingman was the nominee who made the commitment.

99. *Emancipator*, February 15, 22, 1844.

100. *Bangor Gazette*, March 7, 1846; apparently the strategy worked in this instance because the *Bangor Gazette*, March 13, 1846, reports that temperance men swept the city.

101. *Herkimer Freeman*, February 17, 1846, gives a good capsule summary of both sides of the issue; also see *Albany Patriot*, February 4, 1846.

102. *Albany Patriot*, February 11, 1846.

103. *Albany Patriot*, March 4, 1846.

104. Smith to Nodiah Moore, August 6, 1846, in *Albany Patriot*, August 12, 1846.

105. Smith to Salmon P. Chase, September 9, 1846, Smith Collection, Syracuse University.

106. The progress of this movement is outlined in Sewell, *John P. Hale*, 52–86; Johnson, "The Liberty Party in New Hampshire," 137–153; Lex Renda, *Running on the Record: Civil War-Era Politics in New Hampshire* (Charlottesville: University Press of Virginia, 1997), 25–31.

107. "The Execution of John P. Hale," in *Granite Freeman*, February 20, 1845.

108. John L. Hayes, *A Reminiscence of the Free Soil Movement in New Hampshire, 1845* (Cambridge, Mass.: J. Wilson & Son, 1885), 7–9.

109. "Stand Firm," in *Granite Freeman*, February 27, 1845.

110. Whittier to Hale, January 24, 1845, in Pickard, *Life and Letters of J. G. Whittier*, 1:306–307; John Greenleaf Whittier, *The Works of John Greenleaf Whittier* (Boston: Houghton-Mifflin, 1892), 3:101–102.

111. Sewell, *John P. Hale*, 64.

112. *Belknap* (N.H.) *Gazette*, as quoted in (Maine) *Liberty Standard*, December 4, 1845.

113. *Granite Freeman*, January 15, 1846; *Emancipator*, January 21, 1846; the anti-Liberty Party *National Anti-Slavery Standard*, January 29, 1846, approved the New Hampshire situation.

114. *Emancipator*, June 17, 1846; Sewell, *John P. Hale*, 80–81.

115. *Granite Freeman*, June 16, 1846.

116. Amos Tuck to John L. Carleton, September 16, 1846, Tuck Papers, New Hampshire His-

torical Society, Concord, N.H.; *Granite Freeman,* September 8, 1846; *Emancipator,* September 16, 1846.

117. Hale to Henry Ingersoll Bowditch, October 9, 1846, in Vincent Y. Bowditch, *Life and Correspondence of Henry Ingersoll Bowditch* (Boston: Houghton-Mifflin, 1902), 1:186.

118. *Letter of Gerrit Smith, to the Liberty Party of New Hampshire,* March 18, 1848 (Peterboro, N.Y.: Chaplin, 1848), Gerrit Smith Broadsides and Pamphlet Collection, Special Collections Research Center, Syracuse University.

119. *Liberty Standard,* September 3, 1846.

120. *Bangor Gazette,* July 4, 1846. For a detailed treatment, see Johnson, "The Liberty Party in Maine," 152–154.

121. Smith, *The Liberty and Free Soil Parties in the Northwest,* 115; Sewell, *Ballots for Freedom,* 132.

122. (New Garden, Ind.) *Free Labor Advocate,* April 1, 1847, as quoted in Volpe, *Forlorn Hope of Freedom.* I believe that Volpe, *Forlorn Hope of Freedom,* 118–120, overemphasizes the effect of the internal disputes in the churches on Liberty policy toward coalition politics. While there is no doubt that the come-outer philosophy influenced some Liberty men, he neglects the effects of the coalition successes in New Hampshire and the increasingly antislavery positions of the Whigs and Democrats in Indiana.

123. *Congressional Globe,* 29th Congress, 1st session, 1217.

124. Harrold, *Gamaliel Bailey,* 81–93, chapter 7, "*The National Era,*" treats its founding and early history in detail.

125. *Signal of Liberty,* February 9, 1842, reports on an abolitionist meeting in Cadiz, Harrison County, Ohio, that recommended that the *Emancipator* be moved to Washington, D.C., and agreed to subscribe to one hundred copies.

126. Wyatt-Brown, *Lewis Tappan,* 279.

127. On the support for Leavitt, his ultimate disappointment, and Tappan's influence, see Davis, *Joshua Leavitt,* 236–237.

128. For more on the *National Era,* see chapter 8.

129. *Albany Patriot,* July 1, 1846. Even here a core of voters remained plus accessions from the National Reform and anti-rent movements (see chapter 6). There also seems to be some movement in the voter base with some areas of former strength declining at the same time that the party was gaining new adherents. This was happening in many other states as well.

130. See more on the newspapers in chapter 8.

CHAPTER 4

1. *Cincinnati Free Press and Weekly Herald,* June 23, 1847.

2. *Emancipator,* June 23, 30, 1847.

3. He wrote to his sister "that in six months I have travelled not less than 6,000 miles in running to and fro on the earth pleading for the slave." Quoted in Marsh, *Writings and Speeches of Alvan Stewart,* 11.

4. On his illness, see Stewart to James G. Birney, April 14, 1842, in Dumond, *Letters of J. G. Birney,* 2:689; and on Mrs. Stewart's condition, James C. Jackson to Birney, April 15, 1844, in ibid., 2:810. Blue, *No Taint of Compromise,* 33–35, reports that his declining health forced him to move Downstate to live with his daughter.

5. Cilley was criticized severely by several antislavery papers. *National Era*, February 18, March 18, 1847; *National Anti-Slavery Standard*, February 25, 1847; *Emancipator*, February 3, March 17, 1847. *Granite Freeman*, February 19, April 2, 1847, attempted to defend Cilley. The *National Anti-Slavery Standard*, March 4, 1847, quickly attributed Cilley's actions to the Liberty Party in general. This myth continued with some writers hostile to the Liberty Party. See Garrison and Garrison, *William Lloyd Garrison*, 3:185, which discusses "the Liberty Party endorsement of the Mexican War." The overwhelming majority of Liberty men, but not all, opposed the Mexican War. Many criticized Gamaliel Bailey for advocating the annexation of all Mexico as a moral duty. See Harrold, *Gamaliel Bailey*, 94–96. Unlike Cilley, Amos A. Tuck, who had been elected to the U.S. Congress, cast independent ballots or did not vote in organizing Congress. See *Emancipator*, December 15, 1847.

6. His support was substantial. Joshua Leavitt to Birney, January 25, 1845, in Dumond, *Letters of J. G. Birney*, 2:922–923, urged him not to withdraw, proposed giving him a salary, and recommended that he relocate to the Boston area. William Goodell to Birney, April 1, 1847, in ibid., 2:1047, tried to recruit him as the presidential candidate for the Liberty League. So did James C. Jackson to Birney, April 23, 1847, in ibid., 2:1067–1070. It appears that many did not fully realize the extent of his physical disabilities after mid-1845 because he still retained his mental acuity.

7. *Liberty Standard*, January 14, 1847; *Chicago Western Citizen*, May 11, 1847; *Emancipator*, April 14, 1847; *Albany Patriot*, April 14, 1847; *Cincinnati National Press*, April 21, 1847. The *National Era*, September 23, 1847, errs in claiming that the *Chicago Western Citizen* was the first Liberty paper to endorse Hale.

8. *Emancipator*, January 27, 1847; Davis, *Joshua Leavitt*, 227, 240–241. Leavitt had trained as a lawyer as well as a minister.

9. Sewell, *John P. Hale*, 88.

10. Sewell, *Ballots for Freedom*, 137.

11. Stanton to Hale, July 6, 1847, Hale Papers, New Hampshire Historical Society.

12. Stanton to Salmon P. Chase, August 6, 1847, Chase Papers, Library of Congress.

13. *Emancipator*, September 21, 1847; Davis, *Joshua Leavitt*, 240–241. By summer Leavitt was sharing editorial duties with Stanton and Whittier, and he resigned as coeditor of the paper in August. See *Emancipator*, August 18, 1848. Davis, *Joshua Leavitt*, says Leavitt "ended his connection with the *Emancipator* in March 1848." Sewell, *Ballots for Freedom*, 134–135.

14. See especially, Harrold, *Gamaliel Bailey*, 111–121; Niven, *Salmon P. Chase*, 102–108; Blue, *Salmon P. Chase*, 54–64. They were particularly interested in Supreme Court Justice John C. McLean.

15. *National Era*, May 6, 1847.

16. *Emancipator*, June 23, 30, 1847. The poll showed eight (excluding Leavitt) in favor of the fall of 1847: Alvan Stewart (N.Y.), Schuyler Hoes (N.J.), Samuel Fessenden (Maine), Francis Gillette (Conn.), Titus Hutchinson (Vt.), F. Julius LeMoyne (Pa.), Owen Lovejoy (Ill.), and T. B. Hurlburt (Ill.). Those in favor of the spring of 1848 were S. P. Chase (Ohio), Daniel Hoit (N.H.), and C. H. Stewart (Mich.). The fact that Leavitt, who was substituting for the ailing Alvan Stewart, had difficulty reaching all the members shows the communication problem.

17. *National Era*, July 1, 1847; see *Emancipator*, July 7, 1847, for a reprint of the article with a rejoinder by J. C. Lovejoy. Response in *National Era*, July 15, 1847.

18. Pennsylvania state convention in Harrisburg, June 3, 1847, in *Signal of Liberty*, June 26, 1847; Michigan state Liberty Party convention in Jackson, June 23, 1847, in *Signal of Liberty*, July 3, 1847.

19. See *National Era*, July 1, 1847, for Whittier's appeal and *National Era*'s response.

20. Smith, *The Liberty and Free Soil Parties in the Northwest*, 115; Sewell, *Ballots for Freedom*,

132; *Green Mountain Freeman*, September 16, 1847. Also see the various state studies in chapters 5, 6, and 7.

21. Beckley to J. G. Birney, April 17, 1847, in *Signal of Liberty*, April 24, 1847. Beckley was responding to a lengthy letter from Birney questioning this position. See Birney to Beckley, April 6, 1847, in Dumond, *Letters of J. G. Birney*, 2:1057–1061. Ibid., 2:1057–1059, reprints Beckley's position. Quist, *Restless Visionaries*, 395–396.

22. Stanton to Chase, August 6, 1847, in *Annual Report of the American Historical Association for 1902*, 468.

23. Sewell, *Ballots for Freedom*, 132.

24. Crowd estimate is from the *Buffalo Daily Courier* (a Democratic paper), as reported in *National Era*, October 28, 1847. See *National Era*, November 11, 1847; *Emancipator*, November 10, 1847; and *Signal of Liberty*, November 20, 1847, for the official report and minutes of the convention. See *Cincinnati National Press*, November 10, 17, 1847; (N.H.) *Freeman and Independent Democrat*, November 11, 1847; *Chicago Western Citizen*, December 7, 1847; and *Washington Patriot*, October 30, 1847, for reports and the proceedings. Sewell, *Ballots for Freedom*, 136–138.

25. The pro–Liberty League *Albany Patriot*, November 10, 1847, complained that "a secret caucus decided against debate, and every effort was made to stave it off." Moore and Moore, *Owen Lovejoy*, 77.

26. *National Era*, November 4, 1847, lists the members of the National Liberty corresponding committee: Samuel Fessenden (Maine); Daniel Hoit (N.H.); Josiah W. Hale (Vt.); William Jackson (Mass.); Francis Gillette (Conn.); Lauriston Hall (R.I.); Lewis Tappan and Alvan Stewart (N.Y.);William Elder and Francis Julius LeMoyne (Pa.); Samuel Lewis and Edward Wade (Ohio); Elizur Deming (Ind.); Owen Lovejoy (Ill.); Martin Wilson (Mich.); Charles Durkee (Wis.); and W. W. Woods (Iowa). The Iowa Liberty Party disowned W. W. Woods and replaced him with a true Liberty man, Dr. George Shedd.

27. These are more fully detailed in chapters 5, 6, and 7.

28. *American Freeman*, November 10, 1847.

29. *American Freeman*, February 2, April 26, 1848.

30. *National Era*, October 21, 1847.

31. *Signal of Liberty*, February 5, 1848.

32. *Liberator*, November 5, 1847.

33. *Boston Daily Chronotype*, January 24, 1848.

34. *American Freeman*, April 26, 1848; Birney to Lewis Tappan, July 10, 1848, in Dumond, *Letters of J. G. Birney*, 2:1108–1109. See chapter 6 for more on the Liberty League in New York.

35. William L. Chaplin to Birney, February 10, 1848, in Dumond, *Letters of J. G. Birney*, 2:1091. Elizur Wright to Gerrit Smith, April 7, 1848, Smith Collection, Syracuse University, urges Smith to come to Boston to speak on Liberty League issues. See *Boston Daily Chronotype*, February 22, 1848, for Wright's criticism of Hale's principles.

36. See particularly, *Gerrit Smith to the Liberty Party of New Hampshire* on the party's "treason to liberty party principles"; the ongoing battle between Wright's *Boston Daily Chronotype* and the *Emancipator* through the spring and summer over issues that included the unconstitutionality of slavery and multi-reform; and Smith to Lewis Tappan, February 10, 1848, Smith Collection, Syracuse University.

37. Blue, *Free Soilers*, 16–80; Rayback, *Free Soil*, 202–221; David Herbert Donald, *Charles Sumner and the Coming of the Civil War* (Chicago: University of Chicago Press, 1960 [Phoenix Edi-

tion, 1981]), 130–177; Martin B. Duberman, *Charles Francis Adams, 1807–1866* (Boston: Houghton-Mifflin, 1961), 110–147; Frank Otto Gatell, *John Gorham Palfrey and the New England Conscience* (Cambridge, Mass.: Harvard University Press, 1963), 138–159. Stewart, *Joshua Giddings* 111, 155–158, discusses Giddings's attempts to coordinate with the Liberty Party after 1845 and his work in northern Ohio in 1848. Sewell, *Ballots for Freedom*, 139–142, gives an excellent, concise summary of the situations in Ohio and Massachusetts.

38. Blue, *The Free Soilers*, 47–54, and Rayback, *Free Soil*, chapter 11, "Baltimore & Philadelphia," 186–200, provide good discussions of the two conventions.

39. Porter and Johnson, *National Party Platforms*, 11.

40. Herbert Donovan, *The Barnburners: A Study of the Internal Movements in the Political History of New York State and of the Resulting Changes in Political Affiliation, 1830–1852* (New York: New York University Press, 1925), the standard history of the movement, mentions the antislavery issue only briefly.

41. Kinley J. Brauer, *Cotton Versus Conscience: Massachusetts Whig Politics and Southwest Expansion, 1843–1848* (Lexington: University of Kentucky Press, 1967), 230–233. For an overview of the Cotton Whig faction in Massachusetts, see Thomas J. O'Connor, *Lord of the Loom: The Cotton Whigs and the Coming of the Civil War* (New York: Charles Scribner's Sons, 1968), 58–80.

42. Whittier to Sumner, June 23 1848, in John Albree, ed., *Whittier Correspondence from the Oak Knoll Collection, 1830–1892* (Salem, Mass.: Essex Book and Print Club, 1911), 98. Also see J. Welfred Holmes, "Whittier and Sumner: A Political Friendship," *New England Quarterly* 30 (1957): 58–72.

43. *Cincinnati Weekly Herald*, June 28, 1848; *National Era*, July 6, 1848.

44. *American Freeman*, June 28, 1848; *Green Mountain Freeman*, July 20, 1848, came out against accepting mere anti-extension, but urged participation in the Free Soil convention.

45. "Address to the Friends of Liberty," in *Emancipator*, July 12, 1848. *Emancipator*, July 5, 1848, believed that "[o]ut of New York State, Mr. Van Buren cannot carry *half* as large a vote as *John P. Hale* and *Joshua Giddings*." (Maine) *Liberty Standard*, July 27, 1848.

46. Whittier to William Channing, July 1, 1848, in Pickard, *Life and Letters of J. G. Whittier*, 1:333. Whittier was ill and could not attend the convention. He favored John Van Buren for the nomination.

47. Stanton to Whittier, July 1, 1848, in Allbree, *Oak Knoll Collection*, 103.

48. Samuel Tilden to Chase, July 29, 1848, in *Annual Report of the American Historical Association for 1902*, 469.

49. *Cincinnati Weekly Herald*, July 12, 1848.

50. Again, see chapters 5, 6, and 7 for the variety of Liberty contributions.

51. *Albany Patriot*, June 7, 14, 1848.

52. The New York situation is discussed in more detail in chapter 6.

53. Analyses of the proceedings are Blue, *Free Soilers* 70–80, 218–230; Rayback, *Free Soil*, 218–230; Sewell, *Ballots for Freedom*, 156–165. John Mayfield, *Rehearsal for Republicanism: Free Soil and the Politics of Antislavery* (Port Washington, N.Y.: Kennikat Press, 1980), does not deal with Liberty contributions to the movement. Detailed contemporary accounts that are most accessible are in *National Era*, August 17, 24, 1848; and Oliver Dyer, *Phonographic Report of the Proceedings of the National Free Soil Convention at Buffalo, N.Y., August 9th and 10th, 1848*, as quoted in Kraditor, "The Liberty and Free Soil Parties," 871–882. *Liberator*, September 8, 1848, contains the Proceedings and Van Buren's letter of acceptance, and lists the committee members.

54. *Madison* (County, N.Y.) *Observer*, August 1, 1848, as quoted in Harlow, *Gerrit Smith*, 186.

55. Blue, *Free Soilers*, 73–79, and Blue, *Salmon P. Chase*, 60–66, give summaries of the negotiations. On Chase's role, also see Niven, *Salmon P. Chase*, chapter 8, "Free Soil, Free Labor and Free Men," 99–113.

56. Dyer, *Phonographic Report of the National Free Soil Convention*, in Schlesinger, *The History of U.S. Political Parties*, 871–872.

57. Blue, *Free Soilers*, 73, believes that "[i]t is safe to presume that Chase promised Liberty help in nominating Van Buren in return for Barnburner support for the [Leicester] King proposals [on the platform]." I agree that it is logical that some understanding was reached.

58. Stanton to Hale, August 20, 1848, Hale Papers, New Hampshire Historical Society.

59. *Emancipator*, August 16, 1848.

60. See *National Era*, August 31, 1848, for the Van Buren and Adams letters of acceptance; Duberman, *Charles Francis Adams*, 150, for the Dana comments on the reaction to Leavitt's speech; *Emancipator*, August 23, 1848, for Joshua Leavitt's endorsement in "Joshua Leavitt to the Liberty Party Members in the United States."

61. *Boston Daily Chronotype*, September 20, 1848.

62. *Wisconsin Freeman*, August 30, 1848.

63. *Liberator*, August 11, 1848. Garrison to Quincy, in *Liberator*, August 25, 1848, disagreed. He maintained "[o]ur Disunion ground is invulnerable . . . I hear it said that a number of those who have hitherto acted with us, think they can now vote, even for Martin Van Buren! What infatuation."

64. *National Era*, October 10, 1848, published the state tickets for presidential electors.

65. Alice Elizabeth Smith, *The History of Wisconsin*, vol. 1, *From Exploration to Statehood* (Madison: State Historical Society of Wisconsin, 1973), 638.

66. *Green Mountain Freeman*, September 14, 1848.

67. Johnson, "The Liberty Party in Vermont," 273; Ludlum, *Social Ferment in Vermont*, 197.

68. Johnson, "The Liberty Party in Maine," 163.

69. See Blue, *Free Soilers*, 162–166; Blue, *Salmon P. Chase*, 68–73; Smith, *The Liberty and Free Soil Parties in the Northwest*, 162–175; Niven, *Salmon P. Chase*, 114–122; Holt, *The Rise and Fall of the American Whig Party*, 398–401; and Stephen E. Maizlish, *Triumph of Sectionalism: The Transformation of Ohio Politics, 1844–1856* (Kent, Ohio: Kent State University Press, 1983), 124–143, all for the details of the complicated maneuver that would subsequently haunt Chase.

70. J. G. Birney to John J. Crittenden, January 8, 1849, in Dumond, *Letters of J. G. Birney*, 2:1124; Wyatt-Brown, *Lewis Tappan*, 281; McCulloch, *Fearless Advocate of the Right*, 164–165; Sernett, *Abolition's Axe*, 123–124. Some Liberty League votes undoubtedly were not tallied, a situation not uncommon for minor parties. For instance, in this letter, Birney reports voting for Gerrit Smith, but Michigan returns show no votes for Smith nor does Pennsylvania (LeMoyne's state) show any Liberty League votes. Clayton S. Ellsworth, "Oberlin in the Anti-Slavery Movement up to the Civil War" (Ph.D. dissertation, Cornell University, 1930), 114, reports that Russia Township, which contained Oberlin, gave sixty-one votes for Gerrit Smith.

71. *Albany Argus*, November 23, 1848.

72. Ray M. Shortridge, "Voting for Minor Parties in the Antebellum Midwest," *Indiana Magazine of History* 74 (March 1978): 128, statement for the Midwest that "[t]he rank and file Liberty men apparently recognized the Free Soil party as a legitimate antislavery organization because the evidence suggests that they followed their leaders into the new party" is true for the overwhelming majority of cases.

73. Johnson, "Liberty Party in New England," 182–194, 263–274, 354–356, 433–441. Massachusetts was the only upper New England state where the Free Soilers picked up substantial Whig support over what the Liberty Party already had. For Connecticut, see Lex Renda, "The Polity and the Party System: Connecticut and New Hampshire, 1840–1876" (Ph.D. dissertation, University of Virginia, 1971), vol. 1, pt. 1, 164–165, 218–219. For other analyses, see Blue, *Free Soilers*, 144–151, and Rayback, *Free Soil*, 281–287. Renda, *Running on the Record*, 30–31.

CHAPTER 5

1. Richard P. McCormick, *The Second American Party System: Party Formation in the Jacksonian Era* (Chapel Hill: University of North Carolina Press, 1966), 47–49; Ronald P. Formisano, *The Transformation of Political Culture: Massachusetts Parties, 1790s-1840s* (New York: Oxford University Press, 1983), 250–267; Darling, *Political Changes in Massachusetts*, 173–359.

2. The only work that deals with the party in detail is Johnson, "The Liberty Party in Massachusetts," although there are several biographies of prominent Liberty leaders. Voss-Hubbard, "Slavery, Capitalism and the Middling Sort," is a study of the middle-class base in two communities. Laurie, *Beyond Garrison*, 17–152, gives a different perspective on the party than is presented here. As will be seen, I question some of Laurie's evidence.

3. Samuel Sewall to Elizur Wright, September 9, 1840, Wright Papers, Library of Congress, calls for local conventions and town and county organization. Sewall, then an Old Organization member, was determined to keep the dispute between the two organizations separate from the party. He noted that "neither the old nor the new Abolition Societies have anything to do with this movement; nor will either be favored by it."

4. Davis, *Joshua Leavitt*, 167–168; Darling, *Political Changes in Massachusetts*, 268; *Boston Free American*, August 5, 1841.

5. Rice, "Henry Brewster Stanton," 247–248, details Stanton's efforts after he became chairman of the Liberty Party State Central Committee. Stanton to Gerrit Smith, November 12, 1844, Gerrit Smith Collection, Syracuse University, reported that he was lecturing almost every evening and most days and that "Leavitt, Pierpont, Andrews, [Hiram] Cummings, and [Joseph] Lovejoy have done herculean tasks."

6. ICPR returns. Unless noted, all state elections and congressional returns are from this source.

7. Scattering votes could be anything from protest votes to misspelled or irregular ballots.

8. *Liberator*, January 27, 1843, noted that support for Sewall among Old Organization voting abolitionists accounted for so few scattering votes.

9. See chapter 2.

10. Johnson, "The Liberty Party in New England," 120.

11. *Emancipator*, December 1, 1842.

12. Darling, *Political Changes in Massachusetts*, 290. See chapter 2 for details on the particularly complicated 1842 election.

13. Ibid., 289–291; Johnson, "The Liberty Party in Massachusetts," 252–253. Formisano, *The Transformation of Political Culture*, 299, implies a much greater drift from the Democrats than existed at this time.

14. *Emancipator*, November 6, 1844.

15. Rice, "Henry Brewster Stanton," 255–256. Stanton detailed many of his efforts in a series of letters to Gerrit Smith. See Stanton to Smith, July 6, November 12, 23, 1844, Gerrit Smith Collection, Syracuse University.

16. Davis, *Joshua Leavitt*, 217–220.

17. Burnham, *Presidential Ballots*, 510.

18. "Great Annexation Meeting, January 29, 1845," in *Emancipator*, February 5, 1845.

19. Peter Tolis, *Elihu Burritt: Crusader for Brotherhood* (Hamden, Conn.: Archon Books, 1968), 105, discusses Burritt's reluctance to be drawn into partisan politics.

20. Whittier to Elizur Wright, October 19, 1845, in Pickard, *John Greenleaf Whittier as a Politician*, 36–37.

21. Henry B. Stanton to Gerrit Smith, November 23, 1844, Smith Collection, Syracuse University, does mention that a man who had been a former Liberty candidate for mayor and state senator had presided over a nativist meeting and now distanced himself from the Liberty Party. It is likely that the few Liberty men sympathetic to nativism ceased their Liberty activities. In fact, many were hostile to nativism, and Richard Hildreth even published a pamphlet against it. See chapter 8 for more discussion of nativism vis-à-vis the Liberty Party.

22. Stanton to Smith, December 18, 1845, Smith Collection, Syracuse University.

23. *Emancipator*, March 4, 1846; Johnson, "The Liberty Party in Massachusetts," 243.

24. "Report of the Chairman of the State Central Committee [Caleb Swan]," in *Emancipator*, February 3, 1847. This system was similar to those employed by the major parties.

25. Candidates in this and subsequent elections included several cultural figures and intellectuals, including Samuel Gridley Howe, Chauncy L. Knapp, James G. Carter, and Laban M. Wheaton for the U.S. Congress and well-known Universalist minister Sylvanus Cobb, Henry Ingersoll Bowditch, and Richard Hildreth for the state legislature.

26. Several historians have examined these developments. Darling, *Political Changes in Massachusetts*, 312–359, emphasizes Democrats; Brauer, *Cotton Versus Conscience*, 206–258, deals with the Whigs; William G. Bean, "The Transformation of Parties in Massachusetts, with Special Reference to the Antecedents of Republicanism, from 1844–1860" (Ph.D. dissertation, Harvard University, 1922), chapters 1–3; Johnson, "The Liberty Party in Massachusetts," 258–264; Kevin Sweeney, "Rum, Romanism, Representation, and Reform: Coalition Politics in Massachusetts, 1847–1853," *Civil War History* 22 (June 1976): 116–137.

27. Goodheart, *Abolitionist, Actuary, Atheist*, 132–133. *Bangor* (Maine) *Gazette*, 21 November 1846, approved Wright's course. Gatell, *John Gorham Palfrey*, 136–138, discusses a Liberty committee's discussion with Palfrey and the election of 1846 in several congressional districts.

28. "Objects of Political Antislavery Action," in *Emancipator*, July 15, 1841. Leavitt was a lawyer as well as an editor and clergyman. On his changing opinion, see Davis, *Joshua Leavitt*, 227–231.

29. *Boston Free American*, July 1, 1841; "Can an Abolitionist Take an Oath to Support the Constitution of the United States?" in *Emancipator*, July 6, 1843; Wright and Wright, *Elizur Wright*, 109; Goodheart, *Abolitionist, Actuary, Atheist*, 90–91.

30. "State Liberty Convention at Faneuil Hall, January 20, 1847," in *Emancipator*, January 27, 1847. It abandoned this interpretation with its acceptance of John P. Hale as its national titular head later in 1847.

31. *Boston Daily Chronotype*, January 22, June 19, 1847. See *Boston Daily Chronotype*, June 17, 1848, on the report and proceedings of the national Liberty convention. *Boston Daily Chronotype*, June 17, 20, 21, 26, 1848, contain articles by Elizur Wright. Wright was still looking for a better alternative. He hedged somewhat in *Boston Daily Chronotype*, June 26, 1848, declaring that "though we

heartily support the ticket, *till we find a better one,* we do not place the names of the nominees at the head of our editorial column."

32. *Boston Daily Chronotype,* November 1, 1847.

33. Wright to Birney, February 8, 1847, in Dumond, *Letters of J. G. Birney,* 2:1038–1040, acknowledges the criticism of Leavitt and Beriah Green, but claims he "thought him [Palfrey] fairly a Liberty man, notwithstanding his ostensible Whiggism . . . I am sure we missed a figure by not nominating Palfrey ourselves without asking him any question." See Leavitt's comments critical of Wright in "The New Elizur Wright," in *Emancipator,* December 16, 1846.

34. On Whittier's early willingness to participate in coalition politics, see Pickard, *Life and Letters of J. G. Whittier,* 1:284–285; Jarvis, "John Greenleaf Whittier and the Antislavery Movement," 135–136.

35. See "J. G. W. [Whittier] on the Liberty Convention at Worcester," in *National Era,* September 23, 1847; and an account of the Suffolk Liberty Party Meeting, October 7, 1847, in *Emancipator,* October 13, 1847. Wright continued to support the Liberty League. *Boston Daily Chronotype,* January 6, 1848. George Bradburn, a former Garrisonian and Liberty candidate from western Massachusetts, was also sympathetic.

36. *Emancipator,* April 25, 1847; *The Liberty Man's Book* (Boston: Cleary & White, 1847). This book included information on the progress of the party, the encroachment of slavery on the political process, and pages for recording Liberty voters.

37. See *Boston Daily Chronotype,* June 30, 1848, for the "Proceedings of the Worcester Convention." Whittier to Sumner, June 23, 1848, in Allbree, *Whittier Correspondence from the Oak Knoll Collection,* 98.

38. *Emancipator,* July 12, 1848. *Emancipator,* July 5, 1848, expresses the *Emancipator*'s preference for Hale or Giddings. Henry Stanton, who had recently moved to New York, criticized the flip flops in the Massachusetts leadership in his letter to Whittier, July 31, 1848, in Allbree, *Whittier Correspondence from the Oak Knoll Collection,* 103. "I don't like the Emancipator folks. They pass resolutions against go[ing] to Buffalo as delegates, in State Committees, and then all hands turn out, attend Free Soil meetings called to appoint delegates, make speeches, and get appointed delegates themselves. I don't see the joke."

39. Hale received eleven out of thirty-five of the delegation's votes. See chapter 4.

40. On Leavitt's problems with Van Buren, see Davis, *Joshua Leavitt,* 248–249. The *Emancipator* refused to put Van Buren's name on its masthead, until Van Buren accepted the platform. See Lewis Tappan to Whittier, August 22, 1843, in Allbree, *Whittier Correspondence from the Oak Knoll Collection,* 106.

41. Unlike some other states, Liberty men received few major nominations. Only Appleton Howe and Chauncy L. Knapp received congressional nominations.

42. *Boston Daily Chronotype,* September 20, 1848. On his enthusiasm for coalition politics despite his multi-reform interests, see Goodheart, *Abolitionist, Actuary, Atheist,* 132–134. Wright and Wright, *Elizur Wright,* 183–185, discuss the irony of his enthusiastic support for Free Soil.

43. I have greatly condensed the analysis of the Massachusetts Free Soil roots found in Johnson, "The Liberty Party in New England," 182–194, which employs inter-election correlation coefficients, elementary linkage analysis, scatterplots, and banner town lists. Darling, *Political Changes in Massachusetts,* 354–358, is cautious and admittedly contradictory in his two methods of voter analysis. Other analyses are Bean, "Party Transformation in Massachusetts," 32–35; Rayback, *Free Soil,* 300–301; Blue, *Free Soilers,* 144–145.

44. Darling, *Political Changes in Massachusetts,* 355.

45. McCormick, *The Second American Party System*, 52–54; Louis Hatch, *Maine A History* (New York: American Historical Society, 1919), 1:1–275.

46. Willey, *The History of the Antislavery Cause*, 43. This is a very useful contemporary source on the antislavery movement and the Liberty Party in Maine. Schriver, "Black Politics Without Blacks," 194–201, is a short overview mostly from the pages of the *Liberty Standard*. The only extensive treatment of the party is Johnson, "The Liberty Party in Maine," 135–176.

47. Ichabod Codding to William Lloyd Garrison, December 1838, Anti-slavery Collection, Boston Public Library, reports on this as early as 1838; for another condemnation of Garrison by the state society, see (Maine) *Advocate of Freedom*, May 10, 1838.

48. Willey, *The History of the Antislavery Cause*, 113. Schriver, "Black Politics Without Blacks," 132, discusses the ineffectiveness of questioning in the 1838 gubernatorial race.

49. *Advocate of Freedom*, February 15, 22, 1840.

50. *Advocate of Freedom*, March 7, 1840; see the long editorial criticizing this stand in *Liberator*, March 13, 1840.

51. *Advocate of Freedom*, March 21, 1840; C. T. Torrey to editor, March 16, 1840, in *Advocate of Freedom*, March 28, 1840.

52. Wright, *Myron Holley*, 259, 262. Ichabod Codding to Willey, April 6, 1840, in *Advocate of Freedom*, May 7, 1840, clarifies that Codding went as a private individual and his votes in the open convention had "no connexion with abolitionists of Maine."

53. *Advocate of Freedom*, September 3, 1840; Willey, *The History of the Antislavery Cause*, 145.

54. *Advocate of Freedom*, October 22, 1840; Augustus F. Holt, as cited in Willey, *The History of the Antislavery Cause*, 149, followed by a list of electors. See James M. Dodge to Willey, January 1, 1841, in *Advocate of Freedom*, January 7, 1841, in which he complains that all votes for the Birney-Earle ticket were not reported.

55. "Meeting of the Piscataquis Antislavery Society," January 6–7, 1841, as reported in *Advocate of Freedom*, January 28, 1841; *Liberator*, February 19, 1841; *Advocate of Freedom*, February 16, March 11, 1841; *Emancipator*, June 10, 1841. See Willey, *The History of the Antislavery Cause*, 156–158, for details of the Sixth Annual Convention of the Maine Anti-Slavery Society.

56. Willey, *The History of the Antislavery Cause*, 159–161; *Advocate of Freedom*, March 11, 1841.

57. Edward O. Schriver, "The Antislavery Impulse in Maine, 1833–1853" (Ph.D. dissertation, University of Maine, 1967), 27, 76, reports that sixty-six individuals signed the original call in February, with the list gradually growing to 292. Willey, *The History of the Antislavery Cause*, 177, gives a partial breakdown by town of about four hundred delegates.

58. *Liberty Standard*, July 12, 1841; *Emancipator*, July 22, 1841; Willey, *The History of the Antislavery Cause*, 177–179; Schriver, "The Antislavery Impulse in Maine," 27.

59. See *Liberty Standard*, September 29, 1841; *Emancipator*, October 7, 1841; Willey, *The History of the Antislavery Cause*, 179, for Liberty town returns.

60. *Kennebec Journal*, as cited in *Liberty Standard*, November 3, 1841. On the base of the Liberty vote, see Johnson, "The Liberty Party in New England," 399–423; and "The Liberty Party in Maine," 163–165.

61. See Willey, *The History of the Antislavery Cause*, 183–186, 208–209, for the state leadership of both groups in 1842 and 1843.

62. Willey, *The History of the Antislavery Cause*, 196; "Annual Meeting of the Piscataquis County Anti-Slavery Society," January 5, 1842, as reported in *Liberty Standard*, February 2, 1842.

63. For details of the *Seventy-Six* project to publish and distribute tracts, see Willey, *History of the Antislavery Cause*, 232, and *Liberty Standard*, May 10, 1843. "J. L. [Joshua Leavitt] Editorial Cor-

respondence," September 2, 1842, in *Emancipator*, September 15, 1842, reports on the "most encouraging Liberty Association I ever attended . . . They have never been divided by the melancholy contests of Massachusetts and New York."

64. For an articulation of this position, see *Bangor Gazette*, May 28, 1842, June 23, 1843.

65. Willey, *The History of the Antislavery Cause*, 236–242.

66. *Bangor Gazette*, February 17, 1844, lists the three representatives elected in 1843.

67. *Liberty Standard*, January 18, 1843.

68. See *Bangor Gazette*, April 28, 1842, for the opening prospectus for the paper; *Liberty Standard*, May 31, 1843, for additional details on the daily.

69. Willey, *The History of the Antislavery Cause*, 224–225; quoted from *Liberty Standard*, February 9, 1842.

70. *Bangor Gazette*, March 4, 1843.

71. From the "Manuscript Journals," September 30–October 12, 1843, as quoted in Tolis, *Elihu Burritt*, 94; for a typical Willey editorial stressing this, see "Is the Law of God Paramount to Human Enactments? Shall He Govern the Nation?" in *Liberty Standard*, September 28, 1843.

72. Willey, *The History of the Antislavery Cause*, 262–263.

73. Ibid., 282.

74. *Liberty Standard*, February 5, 1846.

75. Johnson, "The Liberty Party in Maine," 148–154.

76. James Appleton to J. C. Lovejoy, Simon Paige, Calvin Spaulding, William Stickney, and Washington Wilcox, February 17, 1842, in *Liberty Standard*, February 23, 1842; "State Liberty Party Address," in *Liberty Standard*, May 24, 1843. There were exceptions to this general position. A July 25, 1843, convention in the Seventh Congressional District declared that "under that [U.S.] Constitution according to its letter and spirit no person can be born or held a slave" (*Liberty Standard*, August 2, 1843).

77. See Cumberland County Antislavery Convention, April 14, 1844, in *Liberty Standard*, May 23, 1844; Wilton District Liberty Convention, July 13, 1844, in *Liberty Standard*, August 1, 1844; State Liberty Convention in Portland, July 3, 1845, in *Liberty Standard*, July 10, 1845; Somerset Mass Convention, in *Liberty Standard*, July 16, 1845; Kennebec Liberty Convention, August 21, 1845, in *Liberty Standard*, November 6, 1845.

78. *Liberty Standard*, November 6, 1845.

79. Seth May to Austin Willey, February 13, 1844, in *Liberty Standard*, February 29, 1844; "Aggressions of Slaveholders, and Duty of Citizens" (editorial by Willey), in *Liberty Standard*, November 16, 1845.

80. "State Liberty Convention," January 6, 1846, in *Liberty Standard*, January 15, 1846.

81. Johnson, "The Liberty Party in Maine," 152.

82. For instance, see a long article on the 1843 Bangor local election in *Liberty Standard*, March 22, 1843; for New Sharon and Blanchard, see *Emancipator*, November 16, 1843; for New Sharon in 1845, see J. C. to Willey, October 10, 1845, in *Liberty Standard*, November 6, 1845; general comments from L. Harmon to Willey, January 12, 1846, in *Liberty Standard*, January 22, 1846.

83. *Bangor Gazette*, July 4, 1846.

84. *Bangor Gazette*, July 25, 1846. See *Bangor Gazette*, November 21, 1846, for its approval of Elizur Wright and the *Boston Daily Chronotype*'s endorsement of Whig John Gorham Palfrey over Liberty man James G. Carter for Congress in neighboring Massachusetts even though Carter is superior in "*political*, not to say moral firmness."

85. *Liberty Standard*, September 3, 1846.

86. *Bangor Gazette*, September 12, 1846.

87. *Liberty Standard*, January 12, 1847.

88. *Liberty Standard*, February 22, 1844, and Willey, *The History of the Antislavery Cause*, 241, discuss the founding and success of the Kennebec Liberty Association. See Willey, *The History of the Antislavery Cause*, 288, for an account of the founding of the Maine Liberty Association in January 1846. Schriver, "Black Politics Without Blacks," 198–199.

89. "First Annual Report of the Maine Liberty Association," in *Liberty Standard*, January 21, 1847; "Maine Liberty Association," in *Liberty Standard*, February 11, 1847. On the success of the associations, see Willey, *The History of the Antislavery Cause*, 290–292, 313.

90. "The Election, by W.[oodbury] Davis," in *Liberty Standard*, October 1, 1846. *Liberty Standard*, April 22, 1847, lists eight of the ten representatives. Willey, *The History of the Antislavery Cause*, 305, gives slightly different totals. The results were noticed outside the state. See (N.H.) *Granite Freeman*, September 25, 1846, which views it as a great triumph achieved with the help of John P. Hale.

91. Johnson, "The Liberty Party in New England," 395–423, does a quantitative analysis of the vote for 355 Maine towns for the period 1840–1848. He uses inter-election correlation coefficients, elementary linkage analysis, scatterplots, banner town lists, and a voting map. A detailed summary of his findings and the map are in Johnson, "The Liberty Party in Maine," 164–169.

92. *Liberty Standard*, October 22, 1846; Samuel Fessenden to John Keep, October 28, 1846, in *Liberty Standard*, January 21, 1847; Willey to readers, May 10, 1847, in *Liberty Standard*, May 13, 1847; *Liberator*, September 25, 1846; Willey, *The History of the Antislavery Cause*, 305–306.

93. "First Annual Report of the Maine Liberty Association," in *Liberty Standard*, January 21, 1847; "Maine Liberty Association," in *Liberty Standard*, February 11, 1847. Willey, *The History of the Antislavery Cause*, 306–307, lists the agents and their terms of service, which ranged from five weeks to one year. Former slaves Lewis Clark and Lunsford Lane also toured the state.

94. Willey, *The History of the Antislavery Cause*, 299.

95. Ibid., 318.

96. Ibid., 319.

97. *Liberty Standard*, September 16, 23, 1847.

98. See the two-part article, "Mission of the Liberty Party," in *Liberty Standard*, June 3, 24, 1847.

99. Willey, *The History of the Antislavery Cause*, 307–308. This sentiment appeared continuously in the *Liberty Standard*, dominated all the state conventions, and was reflected in most of the local gatherings.

100. Edward O. Schriver, "Antislavery: The Free Soil and Free Democratic Parties in Maine, 1848–1855," *New England Quarterly* 42 (March 1969): 82–83, discusses the changes in the coalition one-idea attitudes of Fessenden and Willey. There never seems to have been Liberty League sentiment in Maine, possibly because the religious pronouncements of many of its participants were too extreme.

101. Willey, *The History of the Antislavery Cause*, 319; Sewell, *John P. Hale*, 90.

102. *Emancipator*, October 6, 1847.

103. The rivalry between the *Liberty Standard* and the *Bangor Gazette* continued until the Free Soil coalition.

104. Richard A. Westcott, "A History of Maine Politics, 1840–1856: The Formation of the Republican Party" (Ph.D. dissertation, University of Maine), 101; *Liberty Standard*, July 13, 20, 1848. Willey to Salmon P. Chase, July 10, 1848, Chase Papers, Library of Congress, reported that "[w]e cannot support Mr. [Martin] Van Buren—it would destroy us." He preferred a Hale-Giddings ticket.

105. Westcott, "A History of Maine Politics," 107, notes that Liberty men dominated this confer-

ence even though it was called by Jabez Woodman, a Whig unhappy at the prospect of a Taylor administration.

106. *Liberty Standard,* August 17, 1847. This commentator was convinced that "[s]o far as its fundamental principles are concerned, therefore, the Free Soil party and Liberty party are one."

107. *Free Soil Republican,* August 31, 1848; Willey, *The History of the Antislavery Cause,* 361.

108. *Liberty Standard,* August 24, 1848. See the Free Soil ticket in Willey, *The History of the Antislavery Cause,* 61. At least three of the seven Free Soil congressional candidates—Fessenden, Jeremiah Curtis, and William A. Crocker—were former Liberty men.

109. Willey, *History of the Antislavery Cause,* 343–346. At least three former Liberty men—James Appleton, Drummond Farnsworth, and William A. Crocker—were among the nine selected.

110. Willey, *The History of the Antislavery Cause,* 344–345. See *Liberty Standard,* May 18, 1848, on the new law.

111. McCormick, *The Second American Party System,* 75; Walter Crockett, *Vermont: The Green Mountain State* (Burlington: Vermont Farm Bureau, 1938), 304; David M. Ludlum, *Social Ferment in Vermont, 1791–1850* (New York: Columbia University Press, 1939), 134–136, 197–198. The Liberty Party has been examined in two articles: Morrow, "The Liberty Party in Vermont," 234–248, and Johnson, "The Liberty Party in Vermont," 258–275.

112. John L. Meyers, "The Beginnings of Antislavery Agencies in Vermont, 1832–1836" *Vermont History* 36 (Summer 1958): 126–141, and his "The Major Efforts of Anti-Slavery Agents in Vermont, 1836–1838," *Vermont History* 36 (Fall 1968): 214–229, discuss the strength of antislavery. For a broad overview, see Neil A. McNall, "Anti-Slavery Sentiment in Vermont, 1777–1861" (M.A. thesis, University of Vermont, 1938).

113. Wilbur H. Siebert, *Vermont's Anti-Slavery and Underground Railroad Record* (Columbus, Ohio: The Spahr and Glenn Co., 1937), 23.

114. Ibid., 46–47; Crockett, *Vermont,* 169–171; Ludlum, *Social Ferment in Vermont,* 148.

115. James G. Birney to *Liberator,* November 4, 1837, in *Liberator,* November 9, 1837.

116. A list of the Vermont chapters can be found in the *Fourth Annual Report of the American Anti-Slavery Society* (New York: American Anti-Slavery Society, 1837).

117. *Liberator,* April 27, 1837; Stanton, *Random Recollections,* 55.

118. Ludlum, *Social Ferment in Vermont,* 168; Morrow, "The Liberty Party in Vermont," 237.

119. "Report of the Sixth Anniversary of the Vermont Anti-Slavery Society," in (Brandon) *Vermont Telegraph,* January 22, 1840.

120. (Montpelier) *Voice of Freedom,* June 6, 1840, as cited in Ludlum, *Social Ferment in Vermont,* 174.

121. After the New York split, the executive committee of the Vermont Anti-Slavery Society charged "that the editor of the Voice of Freedom and our own agents be instructed to take no part or side in relation to the recent division at the late anniversary in New York" (*Emancipator,* July 9, 1840). The *Emancipator* approved this course. On the independent course, see *Advocate of Freedom,* February 4, 1841; *Vermont Telegraph,* January 20, 1841; Ludlum, *Social Ferment in Vermont,* 180.

122. *Vermont Telegraph,* January 20, 1841.

123. See *Emancipator,* September 24, 1840; *National Anti-Slavery Standard,* September 24, 1840, for folding of the *Banner of Liberty.*

124. *Vermont Telegraph,* January 20, 1841. This was different from a November meeting. *Vermont Telegraph,* November 11, 1840, reports no resolutions on politics at the semiannual meeting of the Vermont Anti-Slavery Society at Montpelier in October, but *National Anti-Slavery Standard,* November 12, 1840, says that a resolution on political action was tabled.

125. Call for the convention in *Vermont Telegraph*, February 17, 1841. See *Vermont Telegraph*, March 10, 1841, and *Boston Free American*, March 25, 1841, for details of the convention. The delegates to New York were Homer Fiske (Waterville), Benjamin Shaw (Weston), Martin H. Seymour (Burlington), Henry Y. Barnes (Montpelier), and James Dean (Burlington).

126. See *Emancipator*, June 10, August 12, 1841; *Boston Free American*, June 24, July 15, August 19, 1841, for the progress through the summer.

127. Vermont Archives: http://vermont-archives.org/govinfo/elect/stoff1.htm. This is the source for Vermont returns in this section. Crockett, *Vermont*, 3:320; *Boston Free American*, October 28, 1841; *Vermont Telegraph*, October 20, 1841. The Liberty Party claimed nine representatives, and Hutchinson received nine (of 250) votes in the tally of the joint assembly for governor. It should be noted that the party lost three of these votes to the Whigs when the lieutenant-governor's race was decided, and it lost six of the Hutchinson votes to the Whigs in the treasurer's race. Therefore, it can be argued that there were only three "pure" Liberty representatives elected. *Emancipator*, November 25, 1841, lists eight "antislavery" members in the legislature who met and appointed a committee of correspondence on antislavery matters: J. W. Hale (Brandon), A. L. Beach (Charlotte), Oramel Sawyer (Royalston), John G. Chandler (Derby), J. M. Shafter (Townshend), Cornelius Lynds (Johnson), E. Bascom—chairman, T. H. Safford—secretary.

128. For Knapp's editorial supporting Hutchinson, see *Voice of Freedom* as reprinted in *Emancipator*, August 26, 1841. On Knapp's removal, see *Boston Free American*, November 18, 1841. Barker, "Chauncy Langdon Knapp," 460–461, discusses the removal but says Knapp continued as acting secretary of state until 1843. Laurie, *Beyond Garrison*, 136–137. This type of proscription did not continue in subsequent elections. See *Chicago Western Citizen*, November 25, 1842, which discusses the unsuccessful attempt "by a portion of the whig members to defeat his election." *Emancipator*, November 16, 1843, discusses C. K. Williams's election as chief justice by acclamation.

129. Unsigned letter from West Brookfield, Vt., to William Lloyd Garrison, September 21, 1845, in *Liberator*, October 10, 1845.

130. See *Emancipator*, June 9, August 11, 18, 1842, for the nomination and candidates' acceptances.

131. *Emancipator*, September 29, 1842.

132. See a report of J. P. Miller's remarks at a Liberty convention in Syracuse, New York, in E. D. Hudson to William Lloyd Garrison, October 20, 1842, in *Liberator*, November 11, 1842.

133. "Report of the Whig State Convention at Montpelier," in *National Anti-Slavery Standard*, November 16, 1843.

134. See Johnson, "The Liberty Party in New England," 228–257, for a quantitative analysis of the Liberty vote using data from 237 Vermont towns.

135. *Green Mountain Freeman*, as reprinted in *Emancipator*, September 11, 1844.

136. Unlike most Liberty newspapers, the *Green Mountain Freeman* had a long existence. It continued until 1885 and even published a daily edition during the 1860s.

137. *Green Mountain Freeman*, May 21, 1846.

138. Siebert, *Vermont's Anti-Slavery and Underground Railroad*, 92–93.

139. Morrow, "The Liberty Party in Vermont," 267–268. The "Records of the Green Mountain Liberty Association, 1845–1847," Vermont Historical Society, Montpelier, Vermont, contain only about 250 names and a few operational details, leading one to question the overall success of the organization.

140. *Green Mountain Freeman*, August 6, 13, 1846; *Emancipator*, July 22, 1846; Siebert, *Vermont's Anti-Slavery and Underground Railroad*, 39.

141. *Green Mountain Freeman*, December 28, 1848.

142. The address is reprinted in the *Green Mountain Freeman*, August 20, 1846.

143. *Emancipator*, July 23, 1845.

144. *National Era*, July 8, 1847.

145. *Green Mountain Freeman*, July 13, 20, 1848.

146. Ludlum, *Social Ferment in Vermont*, 189. Morrow, "The Liberty Party in Vermont," 241, suggests that the party did broaden its scope, although it remained basically a one-idea party.

147. *Green Mountain Freeman*, April 16, 1846.

148. *Green Mountain Freeman*, April 23, 1846, June 17, 1847, May 4, 1848.

149. *Green Mountain Freeman*, July 19, 1846. *Green Mountain Freeman*, February 2, 1848, reports a disagreement with the *Ludlow Journal of Liberty*. I have been unable to find the *Ludlow Liberty Journal*, but a copy of the *Burlington Liberty Gazette*, March 9, 1848, shows it to have had a less moralistic tone than did the *Green Mountain Freeman*.

150. *Green Mountain Freeman*, May 7, 1846.

151. *Green Mountain Freeman*, September 10, 1846; *Emancipator*, September 23, 1846.

152. Johnson, "The Liberty Party in New England," 234–236, shows the high Pearsonian inter-election correlation coefficients for the town vote for all three parties between 1846 and 1847— Whigs (0.9552), Democrats (0.9313), and Liberty (0.9200).

153. *Green Mountain Freeman*, May 4, 1848.

154. *Burlington Liberty Gazette*, as quoted in *National Era*, July 20, 1848.

155. *Green Mountain Freeman*, July 20, 1848.

156. *Green Mountain Freeman*, July 13, 1848.

157. Ludlum, *Social Ferment in Vermont*, 192–193; Crockett, *Vermont*, 368–370.

158. *Green Mountain Freeman*, August 10, 1848.

159. "Proceedings of the State Convention," in *Green Mountain Freeman*, August 10, 1848.

160. In fact, Jacob Scott, the Liberty nominee for lieutenant-governor, was also a former Democrat. For a quantitative analysis tracing the movement of Democratic areas into the Liberty Party after 1844, see Johnson, "The Liberty Party in New England," 244–253.

161. Ludlum, *Social Ferment in Vermont*, 194.

162. *Green Mountain Freeman*, August 17, 31, 1848.

163. *Green Mountain Freeman*, September 14, 1848.

164. *Green Mountain Freeman*, September 14, 1848. Crockett, *Vermont*, 370, reports that the combined legislative vote for governor was: Coolidge (122), Shafter (65), Dillingham (54), Scattering (2) This leaves some doubt as to whether the *Green Mountain Freeman* was too exuberant in reporting the Free Soil legislative results.

165. www.vermont-archives.org. House of Representative Races, 1848, note 20.

166. Ludlum, *Social Ferment in Vermont*, 197.

167. Johnson, "The Liberty Party in New England," 263; Blue, *Free Soilers*, 146.

168. Renda, *Running on the Record*, 5, 17–20; McCormick, *The Second American Party System*, 55, 61; Donald B. Cole, *Jacksonian Democracy in New Hampshire, 1800–1850* (Cambridge, Mass.: Harvard University Press, 1970), 185–187.

169. See Miller, *Arguing About Slavery*, 341–345, on the importance of Atherton's actions.

170. See Cole, *Jacksonian Democracy in New Hampshire*, 178, for the quote; ibid., 177–180, for some incidents.

171. John L. Myers, "The Beginnings of Antislavery Agencies in New Hampshire," *Historical New Hampshire* 25 (Fall 1970): 8.

172. Robert Adams, "Nathaniel Peabody Rogers: 1794–1846," *New England Quarterly* 20 (September 1947): 365–376.

173. Parker Pillsbury to John A. Collins, November 1839, Antislavery Collection, Boston Public Library.

174. Jonathan P. Curtis to Nathaniel P. Rogers, November 6, 1839, in *Herald of Freedom*, December 26, 1839.

175. (Maine) *Advocate of Freedom*, June 18, 1840; *Herald of Freedom*, June 13, 1840; *Emancipator*, June 25, 1840; *National Anti-Slavery Standard*, June 18, 1840.

176. *Emancipator*, June 25, 1840.

177. Julie Roy Jeffrey, *The Great Silent Army of Abolitionism: Ordinary Women in the Antislavery Movement* (Chapel Hill: University of North Carolina Press, 1998), 3–4.

178. Isaac Colby (for the executive committee of the New Hampshire Abolition Society) to the executive committee of the Massachusetts Abolition Society, June 6, 1840, Antislavery Collection, Boston Public Library.

179. As quoted in an article by "P" [probably Parker Pillsbury] in *Herald of Freedom*, August 7, 1840.

180. *Abolition Standard*, as quoted in *Liberator*, September 11, 1840.

181. *Herald of Freedom*, December 18, 1840. The call was signed by fifty men.

182. *Emancipator*, January 7, 1841, and (Maine) *Advocate of Freedom*, January 11, 1841, give fragmentary details of the convention. For an article denigrating the proceedings and giving a lower estimate of Liberty Party support, see *National Anti-Slavery Standard*, January 28, 1841, which characterizes it as a movement "of our Reverend political friends." Sewell, *John P. Hale*, 27–28.

183. *Herald of Freedom*, January 29, 1841, gleefully reported that at the January 14 meeting in Hillsborough County only seven persons were present.

184. ICPR returns. Unless otherwise noted, returns for the state elections are from this source.

185. *Herald of Freedom*, January 8, 1841; *Herald of Freedom*, January 15, 1841, reported that its subscription list dropped from 1,700 to 900. This did not translate into success for the *Abolition Standard*, however, because it was forced to discontinue publication in the spring.

186. *Emancipator*, May 20, 1841; F. P. Tracy (Concord), Thomas Chadbourne (Concord), and S. W. Buffum (Winchester) were the three.

187. *Emancipator*, June 17, 1841. The June nominating convention followed major-party practice in New Hampshire. Both parties traditionally nominated candidates a full nine months before the spring elections.

188. I have been able to locate only a few scattered issues in the New Hampshire Historical Society and the Library of Congress. The editors seem to have used their exchange list to cull most of their material.

189. (Maine) *Liberty Standard*, May 3, 1843.

190. *Emancipator*, April 13, 1843.

191. Roy F. Nichols, *Franklin Pierce: Young Hickory of the Granite Hills* (Philadelphia: University of Pennsylvania Press, 1931), 127, discusses this for the Concord local election.

192. *People's Advocate*, as reprinted in *Emancipator*, November 30, 1843.

193. Johnson, "The Liberty Party in New Hampshire," 134; Renda, *Running on the Record*, 23–24.

194. *Granite Freeman*, June 20, September 26, 1844.

195. *Herald of Freedom*, June 14, 1844.

196. *Liberator*, April 11, 1845.

197. See "Political Abolitionism," *New Hampshire Patriot*, October 31, 1844, for a particularly strong editorial denouncing political abolitionists as tools of the "Federalists" (Whigs). Renda, *Running on the Record*, 24, incorrectly identifies Birney as a former Jacksonian.

198. Sewell, *John P. Hale*, 48–49.

199. J. E. Hood to *Granite Freeman*, January 1, 1845, in *Granite Freeman*, January 9, 1845, was skeptical that the Grafton County Liberty Convention's resolution for school district meetings would be put into practice.

200. *New Hampshire Patriot*, March 19, 1846, lists the progress of the various elections.

201. (Maine) *Liberty Standard*, March 26, 1846.

202. *Emancipator*, April 1, 1846. Both of the above totals reflect the general composition. Because of coalition in some elections, two parties would sometimes claim a victorious candidate.

203. Sewell, *John P. Hale*, 80–81.

204. See Renda, *Running on the Record*, 27, for some of the differences.

205. See W. (J. G. Whittier) to *Emancipator*, in *Emancipator*, July 22, 1846, in which he writes about the New Hampshire Whig commitment to antislavery. Sewell, *John P. Hale*, 83.

206. *Albany Patriot*, as reprinted in *Granite Freeman*, April 6, 1846.

207. For a Liberty retrospective account, see *Emancipator*, January 5, 1848.

208. See *New Hampshire Patriot*, October 29, 1846, November 5, 12, 19, 1846, for similar editorials.

209. On the whole process, see Nichols, *Franklin Pierce*, 139–144.

210. See the Town Map for Governor in 1847 in Johnson, "The Liberty Party in New Hampshire," 157.

211. See Johnson, "The Liberty Party in New England," 322–352, for a quantitative analysis.

212. On the elections, see *Emancipator*, July 14, 1847.

213. For John Greenleaf Whittier's reasons for the defeat, most included here, see J. G. W. to *National Era*, March 12, 1847, in *National Era*, March 18, 1847. The national impact is treated in chapter 4.

214. *Emancipator*, October 6, 1847.

215. *Independent Democrat and Granite Freeman*, October 7, 1847; *National Anti-Slavery Standard*, October 28, 1847; *Emancipator*, November 3, 1847.

216. *Independent Democrat and Granite Freeman*, March 14, 1848, gives the state ticket.

217. *Independent Democrat and Granite Freeman*, March 23, 1848, implies the Whigs were at fault because they "place party capital above liberty."

218. Renda, "Retrospective Voting and the Election of 1844," 841–844; McCormick, *The Second American Party System*, 68–69; Jarvis Morse Means, *A Neglected Period of Connecticut History, 1818–1850* (New Haven, Conn.: Yale University Press, 1933), 193–197.

219. Bruser, "Political Antislavery in Connecticut," 50–51, 60.

220. John Hooker, *Some Reminiscences of a Long Life with a Few Articles on Moral and Social Subjects of Present Interest* (Hartford, Conn.: Belknap & Warfield, 1899), 342.

221. Utica (N.Y.) *Friend of Man*, January 15, 1840.

222. *Pennsylvania Freeman*, June 4, 1841; Sterling, *Ahead of Her Time*, 107–109.

223. Wright, *Myron Holley*, 263. The lone representative was M. G. Pierce of Middletown.

224. As quoted in the *Utica Friend of Man*, April 29, 1840.

225. Burnham, *Presidential Ballots*, 318, 320, reports 57 votes. The "Liberty Record for Connecticut," *Christian Freeman*, January 9, 1845, claims 401 Liberty votes in 1840 and 409 for governor in 1841. Renda, "Retrospective Voting and the Election of 1844," 844–845, believes "Connecticut's abo-

litionists abstained from the presidential race of 1840, and in the subsequent gubernatorial contest of 1841, an informal candidate with no party apparatus won less than one percent of votes cast." On the other hand, Yale University's obituary for Sherman Miller Booth claims that he organized the Liberty Party in New Haven during the summer and fall of 1840. See the *Obituary Record of Graduates of Yale University Deceased During the Academical Year Ending in June 1905. Presented at the Meeting of Alumni, June 27, 1905. No. 5 of Fifth Printed Series. No. 64 of Whole Record* (http://mssa.library.yale.edu/obituary_record/1859_1924/1904-05.pdf). *The American Liberty Almanac for 1846* (Hartford, Conn.: W. H. Burleigh), 32, reports 401 Liberty votes in 1840 and 409 in 1841. The almanac is in the Samuel J. May Anti-Slavery Collection, Cornell University.

226. *Pennsylvania Freeman*, May 26, 1841.

227. The best treatment of the early party is John J. O'Connell, "The Abolitionist Movement in Connecticut, 1830–1850" (M.A. thesis, Trinity [Conn.] College, 1971), 46ff. Means, *The Neglected Period of Connecticut History*, 360.

228. On Whig movement to a more antislavery stance, see (Hartford, Conn.) *Christian Freeman*, March 10, 1843. On Baldwin's popularity with abolitionists, see (Hartford, Conn. *Christian Freeman*, April 18, 1844; (Mich.) *Signal of Liberty*, April 20, 1842.

229. *Signal of Liberty*, July 4, 1842.

230. *Signal of Liberty*, July 3, 1843.

231. See *Christian Freeman*, January 22, for the December 21, 1842, meeting of the Fairfield Anti-Slavery Society that endorsed the Liberty Party.

232. *Christian Freeman*, January 6, March 17, 24, 1843.

233. *Christian Freeman*, January 20, 1843. See a reply of Booth to a letter of Collins to the *National Anti-Slavery Standard*, in *Christian Freeman*, January 20, 1843. The issue did not go away. See William Burleigh's article criticizing Maria Weston Chapman (interim editor of the *Liberator*) and Charles L. Remond in *Christian Freeman*, September 14, 1843.

234. *Christian Freeman*, February 24, 1843. This society never seems to have been very active. See *Christian Freeman*, April 7, 1843, which claims that there were only five or six "who do not believe in the expediency of the Liberty Party."

235. *Christian Freeman*, June 1, 8, 1843.

236. *Albany* (N.Y.) *Weekly Patriot*, March 9, 1843.

237. *Christian Freeman*, January 27, 1843, discusses Whig maneuvers to get Liberty voters and prevent defections. *Christian Freeman*, March 31, 1843, demands that the editors of the *Palladium* name the Liberty men defecting to the Whigs.

238. Town returns for governor are in *Christian Freeman*, April 28, 1843. The banner Liberty town was Woodstock, Windham County, with 116 votes (21.6%) (Democrats—217; Whigs—204).

239. *Christian Freeman*, May 12, 1843. *Hartford Courant*, April 21, 1843, for official vote.

240. On Liberty claims that they cost Baldwin the election, see "What the Whigs Might Have Saved," *Christian Freeman*, March 10, 1843.

241. *Christian Freeman*, April 25, 1844, gives the totals for 1843 and 1844.

242. Renda, "Retrospective Voting and the Election of 1844," 846–847. The Democrats also nominated a candidate for lieutenant-governor who was unfriendly to abolitionists. "On Our Late Election" by William Burleigh, in *Christian Freeman*, April 18, 1844, complains of "professed Liberty men, who strangely neglected to take their antislavery principles to the ballot box" and the popularity of Baldwin.

243. *Christian Freeman*, April 4, 25, 1844.

244. Renda, "The Polity and the Party System," 135, argues that "those accretions antedated the presidential election."

245. Ebenezer Disbrow to Birney, February 17, 1845, in *Albany Patriot,* April 30, 1845, and Dumond, *Letters of J. G. Birney,* 2:924–925.

246. On the financial problems in the society, see "Report of the Executive Committee of the Connecticut Anti-Slavery Society," in *Christian Freeman,* June 8, 1843; on the newspaper's own difficulties, see *Christian Freeman,* August 17, 1843.

247. See chapter 3.

248. *Charter Oak,* June 8, 1846.

249. *Christian Freeman,* December 25, 1845.

250. "Our State Liberty Convention," in *Christian Freeman,* November 6, 1845.

251. *Christian Freeman,* June 19, 1845.

252. Bruser, "Political Antislavery in Connecticut," 68. Renda, "Retrospective Voting and the Presidential Election of 1844," 845, maintains that in the Liberty Party's first gubernatorial race in 1842 "Whigs cast roughly two-thirds" of the Liberty vote. Ibid., 853, claims that a year later "[e]cological regression analysis shows that four-fifths of the Liberty's party vote came from men who had voted Whig in 1840." Between the spring 1844 gubernatorial contest and the fall presidential race, ibid., 849, says, "Whig and Liberty crossovers negated each other." This does not seem to me to be a logical progression. Why would former Whigs return to their old party because it became more antislavery while antislavery party members who remained Whigs would now desert it? As I suggest above, perhaps unhappy Democrats were going to the Liberty Party as former Whigs were leaving it. More intense town-level analysis is needed.

253. Connecticut State Liberty Convention, September 15, 1847, in *Charter Oak,* as cited in *Cincinnati National Press,* October 6, 1847; *National Era,* October 7, 1847.

254. *Charter Oak,* July 13, 1848, maintained that "Martin Van Buren is committed against our most cherished purposes; and for the Liberty Party to abandon its own candidates to support him, would be suicidal. In our own opinion there is not the most remote probability that it would do so."

255. Bruser, "Political Antislavery in Connecticut," 93–98. Renda, "The Polity and Party System," 164, somewhat unconvincingly sees much more movement between the parties than seems warranted and believes that "[m]ost Whigs and Democrats who voted for Van Buren were men who had already deserted their respective parties by 1844." The history of the antecedents of the Free Soil vote in Connecticut is yet to be written. Perhaps, Blue, *The Free Soilers,* 147, is correct in his assessment that in Connecticut "the Free Soil vote was too small to be indicative of any clear trend."

256. These did not approach the top towns in the upper four New England states in the level of their support. For instance, Woodstock, Windham County, was usually the top Liberty town, but it only received only 21.6% (217—Democrats; 204—Whigs; 116–Liberty) of the vote. See the town vote for 1843 in *Christian Freeman,* April 28, 1843.

257. "The 'Underground Railroad' and those who operated it," in *Springfield Union,* March 25, 1900 (www.bjmjr.com/spl_report/springfield_pt2.htm).

258. *National Era,* February 10, 1848.

259. Morse, *The Neglected Period in Connecticut History,* 330; Renda, "The Polity and the Party System," 154–156. Ibid., 152, believes Baldwin's strong stand hurt the Whigs.

260. *The American Liberty Almanac for 1846,* 32, reports that "[i]n Rhode Island the Liberty Party has no organization. But 4 or 5 votes were given for Birney in 1844." Edward Field, *The State of Rhode Island and Providence Plantation at the End of the Century: A History* (Boston and Syracuse: Mason Publishing Co., 1902), 351, says that there were 107 Liberty votes.

261. *Albany Patriot,* February 25, 1846, reports on the February 11 convention and lists the candidates for statewide office.

262. *New Jersey Freeman,* May 12, 1846; *Emancipator,* September 15, 1847, reports 162 votes.

263. "Proceedings of the Liberty Convention in Rhode Island. Providence. January 27, 1847," in *National Era*, February 18, 1847; "Rhode Island Liberty Convention. Mechanics Hall in Providence. March 9, 1848," in *National Era*, March 6, 1848.

264. *New Jersey Freeman*, February 16, 1847. I have been unable to locate any copies of this newspaper.

265. Three Rhode Island delegates attended the October 1847 Buffalo convention, and Lauriston Hall was made a member of the national Liberty corresponding committee.

266. Three members of the Rhode Island delegation supported Hale and three supported Van Buren on the preliminary ballot.

267. Blue, *The Free Soilers*, 147.

CHAPTER 6

1. McCormick, *The Second American Party System*, 104.
2. Friedman, *Gregarious Saints*, 68–126, compares the two groups.
3. Harlow, *Gerrit Smith*, 120–124.
4. *Emancipator*, October 5, 1837. See Harlow, *Gerrit Smith*, 138–145, on this and other disappointing questioning attempts in New York. Sewell, *Ballots for Freedom*, 16–18; Budney, *William Jay*, 44.
5. Smith to Goodell, November 12, 1839, in *Utica Friend of Man*, November 20, 1839, discusses in detail the history of abolitionists' going to the polls in Madison County. *Utica Friend of Man*, December 4, 1839. See Edwin W. Clarke to Goodell, December 26, 1839, in *Utica Friend of Man*, March 4, 1840, for Oswego.
6. See Smith to William Goodell, February 8, 1840, in *Utica Friend of Man*, February 19, 1840; Smith to Seymour B. Treadwell, March 23, 1840, Treadwell Papers, Bentley Historical Collections, University of Michigan. Smith had dropped his opposition to a third party after the fall 1839 elections. Smith to Goodell, November 12, 1839, in *Utica Friend of Man*, November 20, 1839.
7. Chapter 1 discusses the crucial roles of Stewart and Holley in the founding of the party.
8. *Utica Friend of Man*, Spring 1841, passim.
9. Friedman, *Gregarious Saints*, 100–101. *Utica Friend of Man*, March 9, 1841, shows Jackson still holding onto his Garrisonian nonresistance, but this changed by September 1841, when the new paper, largely bankrolled by Smith, was founded. He soon was lecturing enthusiastically for the Liberty Party and writing articles strongly supporting it. Garrison and Garrison, *William Lloyd Garrison*, 3:64. See his long argument in favor of the Liberty Party in *Emancipator*, December 2, 1841.
10. *Utica Friend of Man*, September 21, 1841.
11. Benson, *The Concept of Jacksonian Democracy*, 135; Kraut, "Liberty Men of New York," 161. *Tocsin of Liberty—Extra*, November 24, 1841, claims the abolitionists held the balance of power in Tompkins, Cattaraugas, Allegany, and Cortland counties.
12. Holt, *The Rise and Fall of the American Whig Party*, 158.
13. See William Jay to Gerrit Smith, September 6, 1843, in *Albany Weekly Patriot*, September 19, 1843, for his support of the Liberty Party. See also Bayard Tuckerman, *William Jay and the Constitutional Movement for the Abolition of Slavery* (New York: Dodd, Mead and Co., 1893), 117–118; Budney, *William Jay*, 72–77.
14. See *National Anti-Slavery Standard*, December 2, 1841, for a reprint of Tappan's arguments against a third party from a November 1839 *Emancipator*.

15. Smith to Lewis Tappan, June 19, 1840, Smith Collection, Syracuse University. See their earlier exchange over the issue in *Utica Friend of Man,* January 8, 1840.

16. Tappan to John Scoble, October 19, 1843, in Abel and Klingberg, *A Side-Light on Anglo-American Relations,* 149. Lewis's brother, Arthur, also joined but was less publicly involved.

17. Smith, *Report from the County of Madison: To Abolitionists,* 2. John Stauffer, *The Black Hearts of Men: Radical Abolitionists and the Transformation of Race* (Cambridge, Mass.: Harvard University Press, 2002), 106, in his discussion of the evolution of Smith's political thought and activity, inaccurately claims that "[a]lthough he [Smith] was one of the founders of the Liberty Party in 1840, save for his role in its founding he did not become an active member until 1844, when William Miller's prophecy of a new world failed to materialize." Despite occasional periods of unhappiness with the party, he was intimately involved in party affairs throughout its history. Harlow, *Gerrit Smith,* details his continuous activity and notes (169) that "[d]uring the state and local elections of 1843 the Liberty Party put on an impressive though unsuccessful demonstration in Madison County. Thanks to the extraordinary efforts of Gerrit Smith and his friends, the party vote in the country was raised from the mere 580 of 1842 to 1,785." Harlow devotes a whole chapter, "Religion and the 'Free Church' Movement" (193–217), to Smith's religious thought and activities during these years. Not only does Harlow not mention the Millerites, but he also describes (202–203) two series of Sunday meetings in the summers of 1842 and 1843 "in order to win converts to the Liberty Party." Strong, *Perfectionist Politics,* 111–113, discusses the Millerites and former Baptist Elon Galusha in discussing the "'complex relationship' that existed between Millerism and social reforms such as abolitionism" (112).

18. (Hartford, Conn.) *Christian Freeman,* April 7, 1843; Gerrit Smith, "Liberty Triumphant in Smithfield," March 5, 1843, in (Hartford, Conn.) *Christian Freeman,* May 5, 1843. Harlow, *Gerrit Smith,* 169–170, discusses the intensity of the Liberty effort in Madison County.

19. Harlow, *Gerrit Smith,* 168, discusses Smith's efforts but errs in claiming that "[i]n accordance with plans settled in advance, Judge William Jay was nominated for the governorship."

20. See *Albany Weekly Patriot,* July 13, 1843, for the endorsement.

21. *Signal of Liberty,* October 16, 1843. It maintained "[i]n our opinion this was a valid objection."

22. *Albany Weekly Patriot,* September 26, 1843; Kraut, "Liberty Men of New York," 122–123. Budney, *William Jay,* 61–63, discusses the history of bad feelings between Jay and Stewart, especially over interpretations of the U.S. Constitution vis-à-vis slavery.

23. Smith, *Report from Madison County: To Abolitionists,* 3. Some other prominent New York abolitionists were also unhappy. See Sernett, *Abolition's Axe,* 116. Others thought differently. See J. C. DeLong to Smith, November 25, 1843, Smith Papers, Syracuse University, for a complaint about Smith's overbearing attitude at the convention.

24. Computed from data in Kraut, "Liberty Men of New York," 161. The high percentage counties were Madison (26.1%), Clinton (22.2%), Wyoming (11.4%), Cortland (10.6%), Oswego (10.2%), and Oneida (10.0%). Those with rapid growth rates were Clinton (491.7%), Herkimer (457.5%), Wayne (207.3%), Madison (205.7%), Cattaraugus (173.7%), Jefferson (172.6%), and Cortland (105.6%).

25. *Christian Freeman,* November 2, 1843; *Signal of Liberty,* November 13, 1843.

26. Smith, *To the Friends of the Slave in the Town of Smithfield, 12 May 1844,* Gerrit Smith Broadside and Pamphlet Collection, Syracuse University. On Whigs and Democrats uniting against the Liberty Party, also see *Albany Weekly Patriot,* April 24, 1844. See *Albany Weekly Patriot,* March 20, 27, April 3, 24, 1844, for lists of some Liberty candidates who won local offices.

27. Stewart, *Joshua R. Giddings,* 97, quotes Gates as writing of Clay that "[h]e is as rotten as a stagnant fishpond, on the subject of slavery and always has been." Glyndon Van Deusen, *Horace*

Greeley: Nineteenth Century Crusader (New York: Hill and Wang, 1953), 94, concludes that the Alabama Letters "were fatal in New York, where they alienated many antislavery Whigs."

28. *Albany Weekly Patriot*, October 16, 1844, reports on a coalition of Whigs and former Liberty men in Albany.

29. (Wis.) *American Freeman*, October 5, 1844, reports Curtis and 105 Democrats of Madison County published an address in which they repudiated Polk and threw their support to Birney. *Bangor Gazette*, September 21, 1844; Harlow, *Gerrit Smith*, 170–171.

30. Holt, *The Rise and Fall of the American Whig Party*, 201. By contrast, the Whig numbers increased by 61,313 and the Democrats by 44,853.

31. Benson, *The Concept of Jacksonian Democracy*, 136; Volpe, "The Liberty Party and Polk's Election, 1844," 695. See chapter 2 for more on the 1844 election in New York and its national ramifications.

32. See Kraut, "Liberty Men of New York," 182, for the 1843 data; Burnham, *Presidential Ballots*, 632–646, for the 1844 data. Some decline was normal when moving from more local races to statewide races, but the drop here is very significant.

33. *Albany Patriot*, September 25, 1844.

34. Jabez Hammond, *The Political History of the State of New York*, vol. 3, *From January 1841 to January 1847* (Syracuse, N.Y.: Hall and Dickson, 1848), 503. Birney ran almost seven hundred votes ahead of the Liberty gubernatorial candidate, Alvan Stewart. Before Wright's untimely death in 1847, Salmon P. Chase, ever searching for candidates with electoral appeal, thought that Wright would have been an excellent addition on an antislavery ticket. See Blue, *Salmon P. Chase*, 54.

35. Van Deusen, *Horace Greeley*, 95; Birney, *James G. Birney*, 355.

36. (Hartford, Conn.) *Christian Freeman*, December 12, 19, 1844, give the resolutions and print the "Address of The Convention," which looks ahead to 1848 and 1852. Correspondent to *Philanthropist*, in *Philanthropist*, December 19, 1844, gave an account of the meeting and wrote "we could only regret our *Western* friends were unrepresented." Harlow *Gerrit Smith*, 172; Davis, *Joshua Leavitt*, 221–222.

37. Jefferson County Merchant to the editor, in *Albany Patriot*, April 9, 1845, lists the *Albany Patriot*, the (Utica) *Liberty Press*, the (Syracuse) *Democratic Freeman*, the *Perry Countryman*, the (Cortland) *True American*, and the *Herkimer Freeman*. He is against starting any more newspapers even though local needs might suffer because some of those already established might die. He claims that the *Albany Patriot* and the *Liberty Press* need three thousand subscribers and the others two thousand to break even, but "[t]here is not a paper in the State that has 3,000 and but two that have got over 1,000."

38. Perkal, "William Goodell," 191–225, traces the development and implementation of Goodell's ideas.

39. Alvan Stewart to editor, March 1845, in *Albany Patriot*, April 10, 1845, believed that nothing should matter as a test of a Liberty Party man except antislavery. Gerrit Smith to William Goodell, April 15, 1845, in *Liberty Press*, April 26, 1845, and *Albany Patriot*, May 7, 1845, believed that the Liberty Party was a temporary party and "would shut its doors against ten thousands of voting abolitionists were it to multiply its objects." On Jackson's view that it was not a temporary party and should expand its principles to other matters, see *Albany Patriot*, May 7, June 18, 1845; Wyatt-Brown, *Lewis Tappan*, 279. Tuckerman, *William Jay*, 120–121, reports that Jay explained his position in his acceptance letter after he "was unanimously nominated as a candidate for Senator [in 1845]." Jay wrote "attempts are making to render the Liberty party subservient to other objects than the overthrow of slavery and the elevation of the coloured people . . . [T]he Liberty party should not permit

itself to be distracted by the other questions which agitate the community, and which in truth are of but little moment compared with the great evil with which we are struggling."

40. Goodell, *Slavery and Anti-Slavery*, 475. He devotes less than one page of this lengthy book to this convention and the formal organization of the Liberty League in Macedon Lock two years later. *Albany Patriot*, July 9, 1845, contains much discussion on the convention, and *Albany Patriot*, July 23, 1845, contains Goodell's address. Among the principles, he declared the U.S. Constitution to be an antislavery document, called for the free distribution of public lands, advocated a weak central government, and endorsed a multitude of electoral reforms that would give voters more direct control over public institutions. Other Liberty leaders at the convention were Samuel Ringgold Ward and Lewis Tappan. Tappan made the motion to indefinitely postpone action and strongly opposed expansion of the platform.

41. *Albany Patriot*, August 27, 1845.

42. See Alan M. Kraut and Phyllis F. Field, "Politics Versus Principles: The Partisan Response to 'Bible Politics" in New York State," *Civil War History* 25 (June 1979): 104, for the vote compiled from the *Albany Argus*. The Liberty vote was usually higher in lower-level elections.

43. Phyllis F. Field, *The Politics of Race in New York: The Struggle for Black Suffrage in the Civil War Era* (Ithaca, N.Y.: Cornell University Press, 1982), 46–51; John L. Stanley, "Majority Tyranny in Tocqueville's America: The Failure of Negro Suffrage in 1846," *Political Science Quarterly* 84 (September 1969): 412–415.

44. "Liberty Party Politics," in *Albany Patriot* March 4, 1846. The article over-optimistically maintained that the Whigs would fall apart if the Liberty Party held firm.

45. J. C. Jackson to Readers of the Patriot, February 2, 1846, in *Albany Patriot*, February 11, 1846, describes the conflict among several of these. *Albany Patriot*, April 8, 1841, gives the "Oneida Resolution," which expressed a willingness to work with other parties.

46. Field, *The Politics of Race in New York*, 50, notes that "[e]ven in Madison County, Gerrit Smith's home, the vote declined to one-quarter of its level six months before." Kraut and Field, "Politics Versus Principle," 109–110. John Roberts to James C. Jackson, May 1, 1846, reports from Lockport that most Liberty men voted with the Whigs in the election.

47. *Smith to Messrs. E. S. Bailey of Brookfield, A. Raymond of Eaton, and F. Rice of Cazenovia*, April 10, 1846, Syracuse University Special Collections Research Center, Gerrit Smith Broadside and Pamphlet Collection.

48. *Albany Patriot*, July 1, 1846.

49. *Albany Patriot*, November 10, 1847, correctly described the mood of the state's Liberty men after hearing of the party's restrained official position of the party at the October 1847 national Liberty Party convention in Buffalo: "Our readers will be astonished at the decision on the Constitutional question. In our meetings, large and small, in this State, for three years past, the vote has uniformly and almost unanimously been against the constitutionality of slavery."

50. Goodell to Curtis, April 20, 1846, in the *Impartial Countryman*, reprinted in the *Albany Patriot*, May 20, 1846, begins a series of Goodell's exposition of his positions. See also *Albany Patriot*, May 6, June 4, 1846.

51. *Albany Patriot*, June 24, 1846. This issue contains the constitution of the Liberty League.

52. *Albany Patriot*, July 1, 1846. This was similar to Birney's call to pay attention to the white as well as black rights.

53. *Albany Patriot*, July 15, 1846.

54. *To the Liberty Party, 7 May 1846*, Syracuse University Library, Special Collections Research Center, Gerrit Smith Broadsides and Pamphlet Collection. Harlow, *Gerrit Smith*, 178, confuses the

Farmington convention and the convention in Macedon Lock, which took place a year later. At the time of the Farmington convention, Liberty Leaguers still considered themselves part of the Liberty Party. Tuckerman, *William Jay*, 121–122, quotes Jay as writing in 1846 that "I shall leave the Liberty party whenever it makes abolition a packhorse to carry favourite measures unconnected with slavery, whether those measures are of whig or democratic origin."

55. Smith to the Convention, September 8, 1846, in *Albany Patriot*, September 23, 1846. Ironically, Jay had sided with Stewart in the controversy over delegates to the Constitutional Convention. Smith seemed to have come out of the doldrums of the summer. In Gerrit Smith to the Liberty Party of Madison County, September 15, 1846, in *Albany Patriot*, September 30, 1846, and Syracuse University Library, Special Collections Research Center, Gerrit Smith Broadsides and Pamphlet Collection, he declared that the "New York State Liberty Car is again upon the track." He included a warm endorsement for Henry Bradley, although "I do not know his sentiments on the various questions of economy and finance."

56. "State Nominating Convention of the Liberty Party," September 9, 1846, in *Albany Patriot*, September 23, 1846, has the proceedings and the vote for the candidates. Votes on the first ballot showed the range of philosophies: Bradley—48; Stewart—40; Jay—32; Chaplin—19; Arthur Tappan—6; Goodell—6. Although Bradley urged his friends to transfer his votes to another candidate, he increased his tally to 83 and then 105 before it was made unanimous. Obviously, no one stage-managed this convention.

57. Kraut, "The Liberty Men of New York," 135; *Philanthropist*, October 21, 1846.

58. Kraut and Field, "Politics Versus Principle," 104. Holt, *The History of the Whig Party*, 239–243, gives a good summary of the major parties but does not even acknowledge that there was a Liberty Party vote. His Table 21 (on p. 218) shows the Democratic and Whig vote as comprising the total vote.

59. Kraut and Field, "Politics Versus Principle," 115–116.

60. *Albany Patriot*, December 23, 1846. Only ten counties passed it.

61. George W. Clark [the Liberty Minstrel] to William Chaplin, April 14, 1847, in *Albany Patriot*, April 21, 1847, reports that in Ontario County "[m]any of the Abolitionists forgot the bleeding slave, and turned aside 'this once' for the sake of giving temperance a 'boost' and voted with the party who have their heels upon the neck of the crushed poor men!"

62. Smith explains his thinking in *Gerrit Smith, To the Editors of the Emancipator, Boston: Peterboro, August 23, 1847*, in Syracuse University Library, Special Collections Research Center, Gerrit Smith Broadsides and Pamphlet Collection.

63. *Albany Patriot*, February 10, 1847.

64. *Albany Patriot*, April 14, 1847, preferred Birney (but he had a "health problem") or Gerrit Smith ("far too wise to be anybody's candidate"), but settled on Chase and Samuel P. Fessenden of Maine (another one-idea proponent) for vice president.

65. *Albany Patriot*, April 28, 1847. William Goodell to James G. Birney, April 1, 1847, in Dumond, *Letters of J. G. Birney*, 2:1047–1057, includes the extensive call for the convention and outlines its positions.

66. Goodell to Birney, April 1, 1847, in Dumond, *Letters of J. G. Birney*, 2:1047–1057; Jackson to Birney, April 23, 1847, in ibid., 2:1067–1070; Birney to Goodell, April 26, 1847, in ibid., 2:1071–1074, cites his health, stating "[s]o great do I consider my disability, that I do not much expect, ever again, to be outside the county." He supported Goodell and said, "I freely give you my name to be signed to the call." Birney to Jackson, May 17, 1847, in ibid., 2:1073–1074, added that he "will cheerfully support the persons that may be nominated by the convention for the highest office."

67. See *National Era*, June 27, 1847; *Albany Patriot*, June 16, 23, 1847, for details and the proceedings. Women were allowed to vote, and Lydia Maria Child and Lucretia Mott each received a vote. *Albany Patriot*, June 23, 1847, contains the address and corrections from the earlier issue. The address is also in Syracuse University Library, Special Collections Research Center, Gerrit Smith Broadsides and Pamphlet Collection.

68. *Albany Patriot*, June 23, 1847, reported that the *Hamiltonian Student*, the student newspaper of Hamilton College, endorsed alumnus Gerrit Smith.

69. *Young America* (the organ of the National Reform Association), March 11, 1848, lists the five members of the National Committee of the Liberty League: E. S. Gilbert, William D. Babbitt, William R. Smith, A. Pernell, and William Pitts. *Young America*, February 19, 1848, endorsed Gerrit Smith as "Free Soil candidate" for president in 1848.

70. Green to Birney, April 23, 1847, in Dumond, *Letters of J. G. Birney*, 2:1063–1067. Green and Stewart had a troubled relationship dating back to the early 1840s over control of the *Friend of Man* and Stewart's failure to contribute financially to Oneida Institute. See Sernett, *Abolition's Axe*, 101–102, 114–117, for this and Green's unwillingness to support Stewart's gubernatorial candidacy. Blue, *No Taint of Compromise*, 34–35.

71. James G. Carter to Beriah Green, March 30, 1847, in *Albany Patriot*, April 7, 1847, in response to Green to Carter, February 1847, in *Albany Patriot*, February 24, 1847.

72. D. Plumb to *Albany Patriot*, in *Albany Patriot*, July 21, 1847.

73. *National Era*, October 7, 1847.

74. Kraut, "Liberty Men of New York," 141, notes the decline in some previous areas of Liberty strength. Totals from Kraut and Field, "Politics Versus Principle," 104. *Liberty Press,* from (Mich.) *Signal of Liberty,* January 15, 1848, notes that Shepard ran two thousand votes ahead of the other state totals and concludes "[t]he diminished Liberty vote of the State generally is attributed to the disaffection and opposition of the Leaguers." There also may have been some change in the base of Liberty support.

75. Harlow, *Gerrit Smith*, 181–185, traces some of his actions.

76. Smith to James Appleton, January 6, 1848, Smith Papers, Syracuse University.

77. Smith to Lewis Tappan, February 10, 1848, Smith Papers, Syracuse University.

78. *Gerrit Smith, to the Liberty Party of New Hampshire,* March 18, 1848, in Syracuse University Library, Special Collections Research Center, Gerrit Smith Broadsides and Pamphlet Collection.

79. *Albany Patriot*, June 7, 14, 1848, reported the proceedings and endorsed the candidates. The newspaper did not even know the first name that it endorsed for lieutenant-governor (someone named Anderson from Orlean County), showing the loose and haphazard structure of the League.

80. *Proceedings of the National Liberty Convention Held at Buffalo, N.Y., June 14th & 15th, 1848; Including the Resolutions and Addresses Adopted by That Body, and Speeches of Beriah Green and Gerrit Smith on That Occasion* (Utica, N.Y.: S. W. Green, 1848), in Syracuse University Library, Special Collections Research Center, Gerrit Smith Broadsides and Pamphlet Collection, gives a complete account of the proceedings and votes. *Boston Daily Chronotype*, June 17, 20, 21, 26, 1848, contain articles by editor Elizur Wright, who was a participant. *Liberator*, June 23, 1848. Charles H. Wesley, "Participation of Negroes in Anti-Slavery Political Parties," *Journal of Negro History* 29 (January 1944): 51, says that this was the first political convention Frederick Douglass ever attended.

81. Harlow, *Gerrit Smith*, 182–183, shows that Gerrit Smith was unsuccessful in most of his efforts to get many important abolitionists to attend.

82. *Boston Daily Chronotype*, June 20, 1848.

83. Goodell, *Slavery and Anti-Slavery*, 482.

84. Their vote was also swelled by an endorsement from the National Reformers.

85. *Buffalo Commercial Advertiser*, September 16, 1848, as quoted in Kraut, "The Liberty Men of New York," 147.

86. *National Era*, September 21, 1848; Rice, "Henry Brewster Stanton," 309–310; Kraut, "The Liberty Men of New York," 147. Stanton was made a Free Soil presidential elector for Seneca County. Blue, *No Taint of Compromise*, xiii, states that Alvan Stewart "refused to abandon Liberty party with Free Soil party formation," but later in his book (35) accurately reports the ailing Stewart's enthusiasm for the new movement.

87. Blue, *The Free Soilers*, 143, believes that Van Buren "probably received support from at least 8,113 former Whigs," a number that was only slightly more than half of the 1844 Liberty vote.

88. Ibid., 264.

89. McCormick, *The Second American Party System*, 144–147; Charles McCool Snyder, *The Jacksonian Heritage in Pennsylvania Politics, 1833–1848* (Harrisburg: The Pennsylvania Historical and Museum Commission, 1958), 223–224.

90. Richard S. Newman, *The Transformation of American Abolitionism: Fighting Slavery in the Early Republic* (Chapel Hill: University of North Carolina Press, 2002), especially chapters 1–4, traces the development and strategies of the Pennsylvania Abolition Society, which was a definite presence in eastern Pennsylvania. Perhaps its restrained and limited approach to abolition activity at least partially explains the subsequent different development of the cause in the eastern and western parts of the state.

91. Robert S. Hochreiter, "The *Pennsylvania Freeman*, 1836–1854" (Ph.D. dissertation, Pennsylvania State University, 1980).

92. "Political Action," in *Pennsylvania Freeman*, October 31, 1839.

93. See "Proceeding of the Kennet (Chester County) Anti-Slavery Society," in *Pennsylvania Freeman*, November 21, 1839; and a resolution for the Bucks County Anti-Slavery Society in *Pennsylvania Freeman*, March 16, 1840.

94. LeMoyne to James G. Birney, December 10, 1839, in Dumond, *Letters of J. G. Birney*, 1:513; McCulloch, *Fearless Advocate of the Right*, 134–136. See the *Pennsylvania Freeman*, January 2, 1840, for his letter declining the nomination.

95. *Pennsylvania Freeman*, March 26, 1840.

96. Wright, *Myron Holley*, 260; Bronner, *Thomas Earle*, 53.

97. Bronner, *Thomas Earle*, 56–58; Earle to Myron Holley, Joshua Leavitt, and Elizur Wright Jr., May 30, 1840, in *Pennsylvania Freeman*, June 25, 1840. His problems with the Old Organization are detailed later.

98. *Pennsylvania Freeman*, May 14, 1840; see also the strong disapproval of the Lundy Anti-Slavery Society of Schuykill Township in *Pennsylvania Freeman*, May 7, 1840.

99. Benjamin S. Jones, *Abolitionrieties*, as quoted in Bronner, *Thomas Earle*, 64. Earle had been on the cutting edge of abolition strategy in the eastern part of the state for many years. See Newman, *The Transformation of American Abolitionism*, 30, 41, 51, 53–54, 116, 119–120.

100. See *Pennsylvania Freeman*, June 11, 1840, for the Philadelphia meeting; *Pennsylvania Freeman*, September 10, 1840, for a county convention in Montrose, Susquehanna County, for September 9; G. F. Horton to C. C. Burleigh, September 25, 1840, about a Freeman's convention in Terrytown, Bradford County, in *Pennsylvania Freeman*, October 1, 1840.

101. *Pennsylvania Freeman*, September 24, October 15, 1840.

102. On the questioning, see *Pennsylvania Freeman*, October 1, 1840; on McKim's support, see *Pennsylvania Freeman*, September 24, 1840; on the Philadelphia activity, see *Pennsylvania Freeman*, October 22, 29, 1840.

103. This is the number given by Wright, *Myron Holley,* 265, and Geary, *A History of Third Parties in Pennsylvania,* 44, who also gives the independent vote by county; Burnham, *Presidential Ballots,* 704, shows only votes for the two major parties.

104. *Pennsylvania Freeman,* December 31, 1840.

105. McCulloch, *Fearless Advocate of the Right,* 139.

106. McKim to *Pennsylvania Freeman,* August 20, 1841, in *Pennsylvania Freeman,* August 25, 1841.

107. See a reply to the *Boston Free American,* which had stated that it was Liberty Party newspaper, in *Pennsylvania Freeman,* November 17, 1841.

108. See *Pennsylvania Freeman,* October 6, 1841, on attempts to question legislative candidates. None replied.

109. On Philadelphia blacks, see Julie Winch, *Philadelphia's Black Elite: Activism, Accommodation, and the Struggle for Autonomy, 1787–1848* (Philadelphia: Temple University Press, 1988), 152–153.

110. *Pennsylvania Freeman,* May 12, July 21, 1841.

111. *Pennsylvania Freeman,* October 6, 1841. Smith later became a Wesleyan Methodist.

112. C. Peter Ripley et al., *The Black Abolitionist Papers,* vol. IV, *The United States, 1847–1858* (Chapel Hill: University of North Carolina Press, 1991), 128–129. These contributions are more fully discussed in chapter 9 on African American participation in the Liberty Party.

113. *Pennsylvania Freeman,* February 29, 1844, commenting on the Liberty Party convention for eastern Pennsylvania, said, "A meeting is seldom seen of any kind showing so large a proportion of gray heads."

114. Returns are cited in Charles McCool Snyder, *The Jacksonian Heritage in Pennsylvania Politics, 1833–1848* (Harrisburg: The Pennsylvania Historical and Museum Commission, 1958), 224; see Theophane M. Geary, *A History of Third Parties in Pennsylvania, 1840–1860* (Washington, D.C.: Catholic University of America, 1938), 46–47, for its growth in the West.

115. See *Pennsylvania Freeman,* February 29, 1844, for the eastern meeting at Philadelphia; *Christian Freeman,* February 29, 1844, for the western gathering.

116. *American Intelligencer,* September 1844; Charles D. Cleveland, "Address of the Liberty Party of Pennsylvania to the People of the State," in Chase and Cleveland, *Anti-Slavery Addresses of 1844 and 1845,* 11–68; on the number printed, see Chase and Cleveland, *Anti-Slavery Addresses of 1844 and 1845,* 11.

117. Chase and Cleveland, *Anti-Slavery Addresses of 1844 and 1845,* 46–47.

118. *Christian Freeman,* May 30, 1844.

119. *Pennsylvania Freeman,* September 19, 1844.

120. *Chicago Western Citizen,* July 4, 1844, comments on the level of party organization in the West.

121. *Chicago Western Citizen,* July 4, 1844; Joseph Gazzam to Birney, February 7, 1843, in Dumond, *Letters of J. G. Birney,* 2:712–713, reported that the *Spirit of Liberty* "has heretofore been a heavy tax on us" but now would be printed for free by the publisher, who would take the responsibility to make the operation profitable.

122. "Liberty Convention for Allegheny County," June 12, 1844, in *Christian Freeman,* July 4, 1844.

123. Errett to Birney, July 13, 1844, in Dumond, *Letters of J. G. Birney,* 2:820.

124. Birney to Errett, July 13, 1844, in ibid., 2:829; Errett to Birney, August 27, 1844, in ibid., 2:837.

125. Gerteis, *Morality and Utility in American Antislavery Reform,* 76.

126. Errett to J. G. Birney, August 27, 1844, in Dumond, *Letters of J. G. Birney*, 2:836; McCulloch, *Fearless Advocate of the Right*, 139–145.

127. "Addenda to the County Address Oct. 1844," in McCulloch, *Fearless Advocate of the Right*, 145.

128. Errett to J. G. Birney, August 27, 1844, in Dumond, *Letters of J. G. Birney*, 2:839.

129. Gubernatorial totals are from the Pennsylvania *Senate Journal, 1845*, vol. 1, 68–69, cited by Snyder, *The Jacksonian Heritage*, 224. There were only a total of four scattering votes cast.

130. *Public Ledger*, February 24, 1845, as quoted in Geary, *A History of Third Parties in Pennsylvania*, 116.

131. Geary, *A History of Third Parties in Pennsylvania*, 115.

132. See McCulloch, *Fearless Advocate of the Right*, 160; Gerteis, *Morality and Utility*, 76, on Elder. See Snyder, *The Jacksonian Heritage*, 185, on the nativist inability to make progress in the interior of Pennsylvania.

133. *Public Ledger*, February 24, 1845, in Geary, *A History of Third Parties in Pennsylvania*, 116–117. Three hundred subscriptions were received at the convention. *Pennsylvania Freeman*, April 10, 1845, suggests that most of the writing was done "from the pen of a *professor* [probably Charles C. Cleveland]."

134. Stewart to Gamaliel Bailey, February 28, 1845, from the (Utica, N.Y.) *Liberty Press*, as cited in the *Pennsylvania Freeman*, March 27, 1845.

135. "Thomas Earle to the Abolitionists of Pennsylvania" and a response from Burleigh, in *Pennsylvania Freeman*, June 17, 1845. For the refusal to publish the responses of Earle and Gibbons, see *Pennsylvania Freeman*, July 31, 1845. From this time on, the *Pennsylvania Freeman* became more hostile to the Liberty Party.

136. *Pennsylvania Freeman*, August 28, 1845.

137. Totals from Geary, *A History of Third Parties in Pennsylvania*, 117.

138. *Emancipator*, September 15, 1847.

139. Liberty Meeting at Pittsburgh, February 22, 1847, in *National Era*, March 11, 1847.

140. *Washington Patriot*, quoted in *Emancipator*, April 15, 1846, feared that "the great original object would soon be forgotten." *American Citizen*, cited in *Signal of Liberty*, May 23, 1846, wanted to maintain the present position.

141. *Spirit of Liberty*, quoted in *Signal of Liberty*, March 23, 1846. Gerteis, *Morality and Utility in American Antislavery Reform*, 75, attributes some of these positions to Salmon P. Chase, who was working to have the party adopt Democratic principles.

142. *Emancipator*, March 31, 1847; on the Pittsburgh convention that set up the interrogation, see *National Era*, March 11, 1847.

143. An account and the proceedings of the Harrisburg convention are in *National Era*, July 1, 1847; *Cincinnati National Press and Weekly Herald*, June 23, 1847; and *Signal of Liberty*, June 26, 1847.

144. Snyder, *The Jacksonian Heritage*, 199–203; Holt, *The Rise and Fall of the American Whig Party*, 228–289, passim.

145. Snyder, *The Jacksonian Heritage*, 225.

146. *National Era*, July 1, 1847; *Cincinnati National Press and Weekly Herald*, July 14, 1847.

147. Swisshelm, *Half a Century*, 91–92. She discusses the failed newspapers, including the *Spirit of Liberty*'s predecessor, *The Christian Witness*, which had had Liberty men William Burleigh, William Elder, and Edward Smith as editors, and how "all anti-slavery matter was carefully excluded from both religious and secular press." *National Era*, October 21, 1847.

148. Lester B. Shippee, "Jane Grey Swisshelm: Agitator," *Mississippi Valley Historical Review* 7 (December 1920): 211–212; Walker, *Moral Choices*, 137. See chapter 10 for more on Swisshelm.

149. John F. Coleman, *Disruption of the Pennsylvania Democracy, 1848–1860* (Harrisburg: The Pennsylvania Historical and Museum Commission, 1975), 26–29; Holt, *The Rise and Fall of the American Whig Party*, 364–365.

150. The vote is from the *Pennsylvania Senate Journal, 1849*, cited in Snyder, *The Jacksonian Heritage*, 226.

151. Burnham, *Presidential Ballots*, 704. As in many other states, a Liberty League vote is not listed despite some evidence of support for Gerrit Smith.

152. McCulloch, *Fearless Advocate of the Right*, 164.

153. "The Present Crisis," in *Pennsylvania Freeman*, September 7, 1848. On similar feelings at the eleventh annual meeting of the Anti-Slavery Society of Eastern Pennsylvania, New Jersey, and Delaware, see *Pennsylvania Freeman*, August 17, 1848.

154. McCormick, *The Second American Party System*, 124–125, 132–133.

155. Slave estimate from "Seventh Annual Report of the New Jersey Anti-Slavery Society," January 28–29, 1846, in *New Jersey Freeman*, February 14, 1846.

156. *Pennsylvania Freeman*, September 10, 1840.

157. Alexander H. Freeman to the (New Jersey) *Freeman*, December 16, 1844, in *New Jersey Freeman*, February 28, 1845, discusses Liberty voting in Passaic County and the state: "In 1840, this county gave Birney and Earle 17 votes, one fourth of the Liberty votes, one fourth of the Liberty vote of the State; in 1841 Patterson polled 38 votes, and the County Passaic 55 votes within about a dozen of what the state gave a year before.—This was a fine increase, and was the result of a few meetings and some agitation."

158. *New Jersey Freeman*, June 15, 1844. John Cudd, "The Unity of Reform: John Grimes and the *New Jersey Freeman*,' *New Jersey History* 97 (Winter 1979): 197–212.

159. "New Jersey Anti-Slavery Convention," May 10, 1844, in *New Jersey Freeman*, June 15, 1844. Weld, a New Jersey resident, participated in this meeting but his name does not appear in any of the Liberty gatherings.

160. *New Jersey Freeman*, July 15, August 15, 1844.

161. *New Jersey Freeman*, October 1, 1844.

162. *New Jersey Freeman*, October 26, 1844.

163. *New Jersey Freeman*, November 28, 1844, made the complaint, but the totals were later revised and 131 seems to have been the agreed-upon number. See *New Jersey Freeman*, February 28, 1845. Ninety of the votes came from just 3 (Essex—29, Gloucester—27, and Morris—34) of the 19 counties in the state.

164. *New Jersey Freeman*, November 28, 1844.

165. See *New Jersey Freeman*, December 31, 1844, May 14, 1846, for the first and last announcements of the meetings. There are no more references to this organization after the latter date. A. (lexander) H. Freeman to Dr. Grimes, 15 October 1845, in *New Jersey Freeman*, November 1, 1845, announced the formation of an "Anti-Slavery Association of Orange, New Jersey," signed by nine men. He added that "when the women write their names there will be about twice that number."

166. "The State Society," in *New Jersey Freeman*, January 31, 1845. The same issue also contains the resolutions and minutes.

167. These cases and arguments are discussed in detail in Marsh, *Writings and Speeches of Alvan Stewart*, 272–367. "Quarterly Meeting of the New Jersey Anti-Slavery Society," May 13, 1845, in *New Jersey Freeman*, June 1, 1845, unanimously approved Stewart's interpretation on the antislavery na-

ture of the U.S. Constitution, in *New Jersey Freeman*, June 1, 1845. *New Jersey Freeman*, July 1, 1845, reported that Stewart offered his services at the New Jersey state convention. *New Jersey Freeman* gave extensive coverage to the cases. Stewart's approach is discussed more fully in chapter 3.

168. *New Jersey Freeman*, September 9, 1845. At least five New Jersey men attended: John Grimes, Almon Underwood, Henry Belden, John A. Paine (Payne), and Thomas V. Johnson.

169. *New Jersey Freeman*, December 9, 1845.

170. See *New Jersey Freeman*, October 1, 1845, on the leaders' unhappiness. *New Jersey Freeman*, November 1, 1845, lists the tickets for Essex and Morris counties down to sheriff and coroner. *New Jersey Freeman*, December 9, 1845, provides returns from four counties. I have put the 1844 presidential returns in parentheses. Morris—35 (34), Hudson—17 (8), Gloucester—26 (27), Essex—45 (29).

171. *New Jersey Freeman*, November 28, 1846; *New Jersey Freeman*, April 8, 1847, gives the statewide Liberty total as 185 votes.

172. "Annual Meeting of the New Jersey Anti-Slavery Society," January 29, 1847, in *New Jersey Freeman*, February 16, 1847.

173. *New Jersey Freeman*, September 4, 1847.

174. *New Jersey Freeman*, November 1, 1847.

175. *New Jersey Freeman*, February 5, 1848.

176. John Grimes signed the call for the state convention in *New Jersey Freeman*, July 18, 1848.

177. *New Jersey Freeman*, October 25, 1848. The three were Benjamin B. Griswold, John D. Mills, and George W. Esten.

178. *New Jersey Freeman*, August 24, 1848. Cudd, "The Unity of Reform," 208, discusses Grimes's unhappiness.

179. *New Jersey Freeman*, October 25, 1848. Cryptically, he mentioned that he might say more in the future. He did not.

180. Blue, *The Free Soilers*, 147. Holt, *The Rise and Fall of the American Whig Party*, 376, agrees "that statistical analysis would be fruitless." Burnham, *Presidential Ballots*, 932, labels the "other" vote as "abolitionist."

CHAPTER 7

1. Streeter, *Political Parties in Michigan*, 18–22; Formisano, *The Birth of Mass Political Parties*, 22–25.

2. A highly detailed discussion of the early movement is Arthur Raymond Kooker, "The Anti-Slavery Movement in Michigan, 1796–1840: A Study in Humanitarianism on an American Frontier" (Ph.D. dissertation, University of Michigan, 1941). Steven J. Harold, "The Influence of New England in Michigan," *Michigan History* 19 (Autumn 1935): 321–353; Streeter, *Political Parties in Michigan*, 43–44. Laura S. Haviland, *A Woman's Life Work: Labors and Experiences* (Cincinnati, Ohio: self published, 1881), 32, says that the state's first immediatist society was a Quaker female society at Logan (now Adrian) that was spearheaded by Elizabeth Chandler. On Chandler's work in these early years, see Merton L. Dillon, "Elizabeth Margaret Chandler and the Spread of Antislavery Sentiment to Michigan," *Michigan History* 39 (December 1955): 481–494. For some of the other early local societies, see Ndukwu, "Antislavery in Michigan," 16, 25–26, 48.

3. *Michigan Freeman*, October 21, 1840.

4. Quist, *Restless Visionaries*, 364–376, emphasizes Washtenaw County but gives a fine sum-

mary of state developments. For another summary of questioning, see Ndukwu, "Antislavery in Michigan," 87–96.

5. Streeter, *Political Parties in Michigan*, 58–59; Smith, *The Liberty and Free Soil Parties in the Northwest*, 32; Volpe, *Forlorn Hope of Freedom*, 32; Kooker, "The Anti-Slavery Movement in Michigan," 287–301; *Emancipator*, November 14, 1839.

6. Theodore Foster, "The Liberty Party," 122–123, Foster Papers, Bentley Historical Collection, Ann Arbor, Michigan. For another contemporary expressing the same feelings, see Nathan M. Thomas, "Manuscript History of the Anti-Slavery Movement in Michigan," 24–26, Nathan M. Thomas Papers, Bentley Historical Collection, Ann Arbor, Michigan.

7. *Michigan Freeman*, March 4, 1840; A. L. Porter to Treadwell, April 23, 1840, is in favor of the Birney-Earle ticket but in Detroit "not more than one in ten [abolitionists] will go for it being nearly all Whigs."

8. See *Michigan Freeman*, July 15, 1840, for the call and Treadwell's endorsement.

9. *Michigan Freeman*, August 12, 1840. The electors were Jabez S. Fitch and Arthur L. Porter (former Whigs) and Thomas McGee (a former Democrat).

10. *Michigan Freeman*, July 15, 1840; *Pennsylvania Freeman*, September 10, 17, 1840; Smith, *The Liberty and Free Soil Parties in the Northwest*, 43. The *Michigan Freeman* appeared irregularly during this period.

11. J. B. Barnes to Stanley Hough, March 21, 1841, in *Utica* (N.Y.) *Friend of Man*, April 27, 1841; "Proceedings of the Ninth Anniversary of the Michigan State Anti-Slavery Society," in *Signal of Liberty*, April 28, 1841.

12. From this point forward I see no basis for Formisano's, *The Birth of Mass Political Parties*, 74–75, statement that "antiorganization and antiparty attitudes flourished among Libertyites . . . Even after Michigan abolitionists reluctantly organized, their antipolitical attitude retained a firm hold."

13. *Michigan Freeman*, September 16, 23, October 7, 1840.

14. Nathan M. Thomas to Treadwell, September 8, 1840, in *Michigan Freeman*, October 7, 1840.

15. Totals vary depending on the sources. I have used those in Smith, *The Liberty and Free Soil Parties in the Northwest*, 46. Burnham, *Presidential Ballots*, records no Liberty vote.

16. *Signal of Liberty*, April 28, 1841; *Utica Friend of Man*, April 27, 1841; *Emancipator*, June 3, 1841; Ndukwu, "Antislavery in Michigan," 151–152; Smith, *The Liberty and Free Soil Parties in the Northwest*, 52; Kephart, "A Voice for Freedom" (which is essentially a biography of the newspaper), 8–10. Kephart, "A Pioneer Michigan Abolitionist," 34–42, deals with Beckley's role in the newspaper, the Michigan Liberty Party, and the dispute within Methodism.

17. *Michigan Manual* (1913), 422, as cited in Streeter, *Political Parties in Michigan*, 62. See Theodore Foster to Birney, December 14, 1841, in Dumond, *Letters of J. G. Birney*, 2:644, for the quote.

18. "Report of the Executive Committee of the Michigan State Anti-Slavery Society," February 8, 1843, in *Signal of Liberty*, February 13, 1843. For the adultery editorial, see *Signal of Liberty*, April 10, 1843.

19. See *Signal of Liberty*, March 9, 1842, for the ticket. *Signal of Liberty*, March 13, 1843, claims that Detroit Liberty totals were low because "[m]oral questions never thrive in a city." Detroit gave just 8 of 1,476 Liberty votes in 1840 and 42 of 1,435 in 1841. Volpe, *Forlorn Hope of Freedom*, 61, notes that "[i]n Wayne County [which includes Detroit], Michigan, 61.5 percent of the 1843 third party vote was collected in just two townships (Plymouth and Livonia), which contained just 16.6 percent of the county's votes."

20. *Signal of Liberty,* April 6, 1842. *Signal of Liberty,* April 25, 1842, reports that most of the Liberty ticket in Adams, Hillsdale County, was elected despite the old parties [being] united against the abolitionists." The Liberty opposition in Flint and Genesee used the same tactic.

21. S. B Treadwell to Lucian H. Jones, April 14, 1842; "to the Friends of Liberty in Jackson County," September 14, 1842, both in the Lucian H. Jones Papers, Bentley Historical Collections, University of Michigan. John W. Quist, "'The Great Majority of Our Subscribers are Farmers': The Michigan Abolitionist Constituency of the 1840s," *Journal of the Early Republic* 14 (Fall 1994): 330, lists the towns where he has found victorious Liberty candidates. Admitting that the *Signal of Liberty* did not get reports on all of the elections, *Signal of Liberty,* May 15, 1843, reports on Liberty tickets being elected in Adams and Genesee townships.

22. Kephart, "A Voice of Freedom," 159, claims that "May, 1843, saw the last pronouncements in the *Signal* about political action versus moral suasion." Quist, *Restless Visionaries,* 376–377, discusses a few subsequent references. The *Signal of Liberty* occasionally did continue to refer to William Lloyd Garrison. See *Signal of Liberty,* June 17, 1844, June 2, 1845. *Signal of Liberty,* November 11, 1844, called for a truce in the quarrel between the Old and New organizations.

23. Report of the Executive Committee of the Michigan State Anti-Slavery Society, in *Signal of Liberty,* February 16, 1842, also reports on the loss of subscriptions to its newspaper.

24. *Signal of Liberty,* February 5, 1844.

25. Editorial: "State Politics," in *Signal of Liberty,* July 17, 1843. For comments on the Whig base, see the *Western Statesman* (a Whig newspaper), cited in *Signal of Liberty,* May 29, 1843, which claimed that 90% of the Liberty vote was former Whig. Holt, *The Rise and Fall of the American Whig Party,* 152; Quist, *Restless Visionaries,* 373, 386–388; Kephart, "A Voice for Freedom," 155. Ndukwu, "Antislavery in Michigan," 52, says that those with Liberty sympathies were formally expelled by the Whigs. Formisano, *The Birth of Mass Political Parties,* 120–121, claims that "the Liberty Party formed a splinter group of the Whig-Presbyterian-evangelical subculture" and that "voting for the Liberty Party undoubtedly was political suicide within Whiggery." Gerald Sorin, "The Historical Theory of Political Radicalism: Michigan Abolitionist Leaders as a Test Case" (M.A. thesis, Wayne State University, 1964), 76, says that he found no former Democrats among the Liberty leaders that he examined. Kephart, "A Voice for Freedom," 154–156.

26. *Signal of Liberty,* November 14, 1842. As Holt, *The Rise and Fall of the American Whig Party,* 1015, points out, "this weakness was largely attributable to representation based on at-large county tickets, rather than single member districts." This, as in New Hampshire, facilitated one-party dominance.

27. *Signal of Liberty,* December 11, 1843. Smith, *The Liberty and Free Soil Parties in the Northwest,* 325, gives it as 1,665; Willey, *The History of the Antislavery Cause,* 239, reports 2,130 votes.

28. *Signal of Liberty,* February 13, January 9, 1843.

29. "The State Central Committee to the Liberty Party of Michigan," in *Signal of Liberty,* January 9, 16, 23, February 6, 1843.

30. The *Signal of Liberty* reported many of these, including a July 4 Liberty celebration at Schoolcraft that drew an estimated 1,000 to 1,500 people. See *Signal of Liberty,* August 14, 1843.

31. Numbers vary slightly from source to source. I have used Formisano, *The Birth of Mass Political Parties,* 24. *Signal of Liberty,* November 20, 1843, gives the returns by county for 1841 and 1843.

32. Burnham, *Presidential Ballots,* 532, for Wayne County (which includes Detroit) shows the competitiveness of the two major parties. He shows the Democrats winning by fifty-one votes in

1836 and the Whigs triumphing by nine votes in 1840. In Detroit itself, the balance changed considerably between the 1840 presidential and 1841 gubernatorial races:

	1840	1841
Democrat	691	692
Whig	777	694
Liberty	8	42
Other		1

It would seem that the Liberty Party hurt the Whigs while leaving the Democrats virtually untouched. Manuscript state returns, Lansing, Michigan.

33. See the objections of Rufus Mathews over Guy Beckley's putting his name in nomination, *Signal of Liberty,* May 16, 1842; see also Jesse Thomas to *Signal of Liberty,* November 1842, in *Signal of Liberty,* December 5, 1842, where he complains of a loss of votes because of "the convention not making themselves sufficiently acquainted with the standing of one of the nominees."

34. *Signal of Liberty,* October 17, 1842.

35. Quist, *Restless Visionaries,* 386–392, discusses this in detail for Washtenaw County, emphasizing the efforts of the Whig newspaper, the (Ann Arbor) *Michigan State Journal.* Formisano, *The Birth of Mass Political Parties,* 212–215, discusses increased Whig denunciation of the South and slaveholders.

36. Streeter, *Political Parties in Michigan,* 68–69. *Signal of Liberty,* October 14, 1844, in an example of strong party spirit, says that these were not real Liberty men because of their backsliding.

37. *Emancipator,* August 14, 1844. Platt was unusual for being one of the few Garrisonians in Michigan, but it was also an anomaly in the Old Organization in the mid-1840s for one of its prominent members to be so politically active. He was a Congregationalist who served as a vice president in the American Anti-Slavery Society (1840–1850). A brief summary of the debate is in Fladeland, *James G. Birney,* 237.

38. *Detroit Advertiser,* as quoted in Smith, *The Liberty and Free Soil Parties in the Northwest,* 81, 74.

39. See chapter 2 on the Garland Forgery, other problems for Birney, and the election in Michigan.

40. Formisano, *The Birth of Mass Political Parties,* 212–213, reports the depth of future Republican leader Austin Blair's anger. Among other things, Austin declared, "I hate a Birneyite worse than a massasauga [rattlesnake] and want to throw eggs at them in the streets."

41. Theodore Foster to Birney, September 12, 1845, in Dumond, *Letters of J. G. Birney,* 2:967–970. See Foster to Birney, October 16, 1845, in ibid., 2:979, for the *Detroit Advertiser*'s referring to Birney's health to "indirectly prevent persons from voting for you."

42. Foster to Birney, September 29, 1845, in ibid., 2:972; Quist, *Restless Visionaries,* 391–393.

43. Foster to Birney, September 12, 1845, in Dumond, *Letters of J. G. Birney,* 2:968. On his ideas, see Fladeland, *James G. Birney,* 260–266.

44. See Formisano, *The Birth of Mass Politics,* 24, for the election data.

45. Foster to Birney, December 7, 1845, in Dumond, *Letters of J. G. Birney,* 2:982.

46. Foster to Birney, July 7, 1845, in ibid., 2:951–952.

47. Birney to Lewis Tappan, September 12, 1845, in ibid., 2:970–971. Birney's stroke did not affect his mental capacities. In fact, his confinement may have given him time to work out his ideas.

48. Foster to Birney, September 29, 1845, in ibid., 2:973; *Signal of Liberty,* October 6, 1845.

49. Foster to Birney, December 7, 1845, in Dumond, *Letters of J. G. Birney,* 2:983; Birney to the president of the Michigan State Anti-Slavery Society, January 1, 1846, in ibid., 2:990–996 (also in *Signal of Liberty,* February 23, 1846); Fladeland, *James G. Birney,* 257–259.

50. *Signal of Liberty,* February 23, 1846. The reference is to Mark 1:3—"The voice of one crying in the wilderness."

51. *Signal of Liberty,* February 16, 1846, is an account of the proceedings. On Foster's views of the meeting, see Foster to Birney, February 13, 1846, in Dumond, *Letters of J. G. Birney,* 2:1002–1004. For an extensive account, see Kephart, "A Voice for Freedom," 172–174. Foster to Birney, September 29, 1845, in Dumond, *Letters of J. G. Birney,* 2:973, was "inclined to think it [the expanded platform] will be adopted in Michigan with very little opposition."

52. Five of the most prominent abolitionists in the state—Charles H. Stewart, Seymour B. Treadwell, Horace Hallock, Nathan M. Thomas, and Chester Gurney—were the committee.

53. Beckley and Foster to Birney, February 9, 1846, in Dumond, *Letters of J. G. Birney,* 2:1000, unhappily writes, "The brethren generally were so thoroughly wedded to the '*one idea*' . . . even our most sensible friends."

54. Foster to Birney, February 13, 1846, in ibid., 2:1002–1004. Stewart to Birney, February 19, 1846, in ibid., 2:1004–1006, explains that they were surprised by the proposals at the convention that "came without a previous word of intimation . . . [S]omehow we all got a wrong conception of the subject" because of just hearing it at the public reading. After reading Birney's letter "in the seclusion and quiet of my chamber . . . I was startled to find it contained little more than propositions I have advocated invariably for the last 4 years . . . I have seen some of our friends—Treadwell—Gurney—Hammond—and they coincide in my present view." This last statement was not entirely accurate.

55. *Signal of Liberty,* March 30, May 11, 18, 1846; Kephart, "A Voice for Freedom," 174–176.

56. Kephart, "A Voice for Freedom," 176; *Signal of Liberty,* June 6, 13, 1846.

57. Foster, "History of the Liberty Party," 81, Foster Papers, Bentley Historical Collections, University of Michigan.

58. Foster to Birney, March 30, 1846, in Dumond, *Letters of J. G. Birney,* 2:1007–1009; *Albany Patriot,* April 8, 1846, in approving the circular says "[o]ur reform, we take it, has reached a point in its progress when it must be *reformed* or die."

59. Tappan to Birney, March 10, 1846, in Dumond, *Letters of J. G. Birney,* 2:1007.

60. Gerrit Smith, *To the Liberty Party, May 7, 1846,* Gerrit Smith Broadside and Pamphlet Collection, Syracuse University.

61. *Signal of Liberty,* March 23, 1843.

62. Foster to Birney, May 5, 1846, in Dumond, *Letters of J. G. Birney,* 2:1014–1016.

63. "Official Report of the Proceedings," in *Chicago Western Citizen,* June 30, 1846. See *Chicago Western Citizen,* July 7, 1846, for a report on the discussion at the convention on expanding the platform. *Signal of Liberty* July 4, 11, 1846.

64. Foster to Birney, August 1, 1846, in Dumond, *Letters of J. G. Birney,* 2:1025; Sewell, *Ballots for Freedom,* 114–117.

65. "Central Committee Address," October 13, 1846, in *Signal of Liberty,* October 17, 1846. Foster was much more easygoing than many leaders, and his personal preferences did not prevent him from reporting ideas other than his own. Besides, the *Signal of Liberty* was subsidized by the state society.

66. *Signal of Liberty,* February 13, 1847; Kephart, "A Voice for Freedom," 188–189.

67. Jeffrey G. Charnley, "'Sword into Plowshares' A Hope Unfulfilled: Michigan Opposition to the Mexican War, 1846–1848," *The Old Northwest* 8 (Fall 1982): 202–207, traces the Whig opposition to the war.

68. Foster to Birney, August 1, 1846, in Dumond, *Letters of J. G. Birney,* 2:1026.

69. *Signal of Liberty,* August 29, 1846.

70. *Signal of Liberty,* January 9, 1847. These principles were almost identical to those of Guy Beckley dealt with below.

71. "Report of the State Liberty Convention at Kalamazoo," in *National Era,* March 11, 1847.

72. Kephart, "A Pioneer Michigan Abolitionist," 34–42.

73. Beckley to *Signal of Liberty Signal of Liberty,* March 16, 1847, in *Signal of Liberty,* March 20, 1847.

74. The following are from Birney to Beckley, April 6, 1847, in Dumond, *Letters of J. G. Birney,* 2:1057–1061. *Signal of Liberty,* April 17, 1847.

75. Beckley to Birney, April 17, 1847, in *Signal of Liberty,* April 24, 1847.

76. *Signal of Liberty,* May 1, 1847.

77. *Signal of Liberty,* May 15, 1847.

78. "State Liberty Party Convention at Jackson," June 23, 1847, in *Signal of Liberty,* July 3, 1847; Silas M. Holmes to the *National Era,* June 30, 1847, in *National Era,* July 8, 1847.

79. *Signal of Liberty,* October 2, 1847.

80. Party totals cited in Formisano, *The Birth of Mass Political Parties,* 24.

81. *Signal of Liberty,* February 5, 1848.

82. Fladeland, *James G. Birney,* 244–246.

83. *Signal of Liberty,* February 5, 1848; *National Era,* February 24, 1848.

84. *Michigan Liberty Press,* April 13, 1848.

85. *Michigan Liberty Press,* April 21, 1848.

86. *Michigan Liberty Press,* August 18, 1848.

87. *Michigan Liberty Press,* August 25, 1848.

88. See the call for a Free Soil meeting in Battle Creek in *Michigan Liberty Press,* July 28, 1848. On the development of Free Soil in Michigan, see Ronald E. Seavoy, "The Organization of the Republican Party in Michigan, 1846–1854," *The Old Northwest* 6 (Winter 1980–1981): 347–350. Streeter, *Political Parties in Michigan,* 93–103; Smith, *The Liberty and Free Soil Parties in the Northwest,* 156; Formisano, *The Birth of Mass Political Parties,* 212–214; Quist, *Restless Visionaries,* 397–401; Blue, *The Free Soilers,* 141, 148–149.

89. There were some who did. James G. Birney's son, James Jr., was elected lieutenant–governor of Michigan, Silas M. Holmes served as state treasurer, Dewitt Clinton Leach served two terms in the U.S. Congress, Erastus Hussey served as a state representative and state senator, and Nathan Powers was a state legislator. Former Liberty members were more likely to have an elective or appointive impact in lower level positions.

90. McCormick, *The Second American Party System,* 267–269.

91. Maizlish, *Triumph of Sectionalism,* 17; Hart, *Salmon P. Chase,* 29.

92. Earle, *Jacksonian Antislavery,* 37–48.

93. Ann Hagedorn, *Beyond the River: The Untold Story of the Heroes of the Underground Railroad* (New York: Simon & Schuster, 2002), 33. She focuses her account on Rankin and the Ripley abolitionists. The quote, an inscription in a book to Rankin, was made in 1853. See Garrison and Garrison, *William Lloyd Garrison,* 1:306. For Garrison's appreciation of Rankin in 1835, see Garrison

to Henry E. Benson, December 10, 1835, in Walter M. Merrill, ed., *The Letters of William Lloyd Garrison*, vol. 1, *I Will Be Heard, 1822–1835* (Cambridge, Mass.: The Belknap Press of Harvard University, 1971), 574–575. Birney, *James G. Birney*, 169, writes that Rankin was "one of the five most prominent advocates in this country [in 1827] of immediate abolition." Weld to Birney, January 23, 1835, in Dumond, *Letters of J. G. Birney*, 1:170–173; Weld to Elizur Wright, March 2, 1835, in Gilbert Hobbs Barnes and Dwight Lowell Dumond, eds., *The Letters of Theodore Dwight Weld, Angelina Grimke Weld and Sarah Grimke, 1822–1844* (Gloucester, Mass.: Peter Smith, 1965 [originally published by the American Historical Association, 1934]), 1:205–208; Barnes, *The Anti-Slavery Impulse*, 82–83; Robert H. Abzug, *Passionate Liberator: Theodore Dwight Weld and the Dilemma of Reform* (New York: Oxford University Press, 1980), 124.

94. *Philanthropist*, January 8, December 30, 1836; Fladeland, *James G. Birney*, 175–177; Birney, *James G. Birney*, 232–233, 341.

95. *Philanthropist*, June 12, October 2, 1838; Stewart, *Joshua Giddings*, 32–33; Birney, *James G. Birney*, 341.

96. Hagedorn, *Beyond the River*, 153–179, discusses the case. A Kentucky court ultimately freed Mahan.

97. Bailey to Birney, October 28, 1838, in Dumond, *Letters of J. G. Birney*, 1:473. See positive comments in *Emancipator*, November 1, 1838. Volpe, *Forlorn Hope of Freedom*, 27–30, judiciously comments that historians have been too quick to credit the Whig defeat to the abolitionists.

98. Earle, *Jacksonian Antislavery*, 42–46, traces the situation and concludes, "There is no evidence as to who gave the official order, but on December 2, 1838, Ohio's legislators voted to replace Morris." See the correspondence leading to Morris's proscription and his reply in Morris, *The Life of Thomas Morris*, 191–203. Ironically, Benjamin Tappan, the brother of the ardent abolitionists Arthur and Lewis, succeeded Morris in the Senate. He obviously did not share the same type of evangelical antislavery convictions as did his brothers. Daniel Feller, "A Brother in Arms: Benjamin Tappan and the Antislavery Democracy," *Journal of American History* 88 (June 2001): 54–57, argues that his subject had an "Enlightenment-driven outlook [that] shaped his hatred of slavery" that included a "deep-seated loathing for Christian doctrine." He "baldly denied any connection with modern abolitionism," although Thomas Morris is quoted as claiming Tappan was "'a more strenuous opposer [of slavery]' than himself." The only support Morris received came from future Liberty man George Ells, who was also expelled from the party.

99. Ellsworth, "Oberlin and the Anti-Slavery Movement," 103–104, details the case of the Whig legislator, William Andrews, who reneged on his promises. Robert S. Fletcher, *A History of Oberlin College From Its Foundations Through the Civil War* (Oberlin, Ohio: Oberlin College, 1943), 2:386–387; Smith, *The Liberty and Free Soil Parties in the Northwest*, 27, 31.

100. See Vernon Volpe, "Benjamin Wade's Strange Defeat," *Ohio History* 97 (Summer–Autumn, 1988): 131. Blue, *No Taint of Compromise*, 216–217. See *Liberator*, October 11, 1839, on an antislavery ticket in Geauga County.

101. Wilbur Greeley Burroughs, "Oberlin's Part in the Slavery Conflict," *Ohio History* 20 (July 1911): 278.

102. Details of the late May 1840 meeting of the Ohio Anti-Slavery Society are in *Emancipator*, June 11, 18, 1840, and *Utica* (N.Y.) *Friend of Man*, June 17, 1840. *Utica Friend of Man*, July 8, 1840, criticized the convention for its unwillingness to back a resolution against supporting the two major parties' presidential candidates. "No wonder they are not ready for independent nominations."

103. Volpe, *Forlorn Hope of Freedom*, 42–47.

104. For a long article opposing the third party concept in late 1839, see *Philanthropist*, No-

vember 12, 1839. For his opposition shortly after the Albany convention, see Bailey to James G. Birney, April 18, 1840, in Dumond, *Letters of J. G. Birney*, 1:556–558. Harrold, *Gamaliel Bailey*, 34–36, 227, traces the evolution of Bailey's position and convincingly argues that "Bailey fully embraced third party action"; see also his earlier "Forging an Antislavery Instrument: Gamaliel Bailey and the Formation of the Ohio Liberty Party," *The Old Northwest* 2 (Summer 1976): 371–387. Goldfarb, "Gamaliel Bailey," chapter 14, on the other hand, argues that Bailey was less willing and was driven ineluctably to third-party action. See Bailey's editorial blasting Harrison for "doubledealing" in *Philanthropist*, June 30, 1840.

105. See details on a nominating convention for the Sixteenth District at Akron in *Utica Friend of Man*, August 26, 1840. Seventy-three individuals signed the call, including Elizur Wright Sr.

106. Proceedings in *Philanthropist*, September 8, 1840.

107. Speer, "Autobiography of Adam Lowry Rankin," 41.

108. Davis, *Joshua Leavitt*, 168–169. Leavitt would continue to refine the core of this speech into his work on the "Influence of the Slave Power." Bailey subsequently printed and distributed one thousand copies of the speech throughout the state.

109. *Philanthropist*, September 8, 1840. Most historians accept this figure. Speer, "Autobiography of Adam Lowry Rankin," 40, puts the vote at 57–34, while Rankin himself says it passed by a majority of seven. Dyer Burgess suggested the party name.

110. See their views in *Philanthropist*, September 22, 1840.

111. See a summation of his views in *Philanthropist*, December 9, 1840. He changed his views in early 1842.

112. Smith, *The Liberty and Free Soil Parties in the Northwest*, 42.

113. *Philanthropist*, September 15, 1840.

114. Volpe, *Forlorn Hope of Freedom*, 47; Ludlum, "Joshua Giddings," 108; L. D. Butts to Bailey, November 18, 1840, in *Philanthropist*, December 9, 1840. Hagedorn, *Beyond the River*, 205, reports that only five men in John Rankin's hometown of Ripley voted the Liberty ticket. This number included former U.S. senator Alexander Campbell and Adam Lowry Rankin. The latter's position caused some family tension.

115. Sewell, *Ballots for Freedom*, 76.

116. *Philanthropist*, January 13, 1841. Volpe, *Forlorn Hope of Freedom*, 53, accepts the figure of almost one thousand signatures, including Edward Wade's, on the call.

117. *Philanthropist*, December 16, 1840; Harrold, *Gamaliel Bailey*, 37.

118. *Philanthropist*, January 27, 1841; Smith, *The Liberty and Free Soil Parties in the Northwest*, 50–51; Harrold, *Gamaliel Bailey*, 37–40.

119. See Chase's entreaties to Harrison in Chase to William Henry Harrison, February 13, 1841, in Niven, *The Salmon P. Chase Papers*, 2:72–74.

120. Volpe, *Forlorn Hope of Freedom*, 52–54. See Blue, *Salmon P. Chase*, 41–44, and Hart, *Salmon P. Chase*, 87–89, on Chase's disappointment with Harrison, with whom he enjoyed a personal relationship. On his and other Whigs' reaction to his death, see Niven, *The Salmon P. Chase Papers*, 1:159–160.

121. See Blue, *Salmon P. Chase*, 42–46, on Chase's political journey. Hart, *Salmon P. Chase*, 87, dates his conversion to a May Liberty Party meeting in Cincinnati. Niven, *Salmon P. Chase*, 67, from "sometime in the fall of 1841." On Oberlin, see Ellsworth, "Oberlin and the Anti-Slavery Movement," 104–108.

122. Smith, *The Liberty and Free Soil Parties in the Northwest*, 55.

123. See *Philanthropist*, January 5, 1842, for the proceedings.

124. Blue, *Salmon P. Chase*, 47–48; Niven, *Salmon P. Chase*, 67–68; Blue and McCormick, "Norton S. Townshend," 146, says the this was the future congressman's "first political anti-slavery convention."

125. Stewart, *Joshua Giddings*, 73–76, is a good brief account of the incident. See also Ludlum, "Joshua Giddings," 120–124; Barnes, *Antislavery Impulse*, 185–189.

126. Smith, *The Liberty and Free Soil Parties in the Northwest*, 112; Volpe, *Forlorn Hope of Freedom*, 83; *Philanthropist*, April 6, 13, 1842.

127. *Liberator*, April 1, 1842.

128. Chase to Giddings, February 9, 1843, Julian Papers, Indiana Historical Society, as quoted in Volpe, *Forlorn Hope of Freedom*, 179.

129. By mid-summer there were at least seven in Cincinnati and the surrounding area. See Niven, *The Salmon P. Chase Papers*, 2:89, note 4.

130. ICPR returns. All Ohio returns are from this source unless noted. Maizlish, *Triumph of Sectionalism*, 35; Volpe, *Forlorn Hope of Freedom*, 84–88. Smith, *The Liberty and Free Soil Parties*, 56, shows a slightly larger Liberty vote of 5,405, and calculated that 11 Western Reserve counties contributed 2,433 King votes to the other 67 county totals of 2,972.

131. Using county returns, Volpe, *Forlorn Hope of Freedom*, 87, calculates King's percentage correlating at +0.41 with those of Harrison in 1840 and concludes that "Liberty votes can be safely attributed to the Whig defeat." Ellsworth, "Oberlin and the Anti-Slavery Movement," 108–109, cites this and other elections to show the Whig antecedents of Liberty strength.

132. Smith, *The Liberty and Free Soil Parties in the Northwest*, 57, discusses the results and the Liberty charges of under-reporting the Liberty vote.

133. For instance, see Smith to Lewis Tappan, June 19, 1840, Smith Collection, Syracuse University; Smith to Bailey, September 13, 1842, in *Philanthropist*, October 15, 1842; Harrold, *Gamaliel Bailey*, 43. Harlow, *Gerrit Smith*, 151; Ellsworth, "Oberlin and the Anti-Slavery Movement," 111; and (Warren, Ohio) *Liberty Herald*, October 26, 1843, show that some Ohioans agreed with Smith. Ironically, in 1844 Smith admitted that he had supported a temperance ticket "composed of proslavery as well as anti-slavery names" in 1842. See "Gerrit Smith to the Friends of the Slave in the Town of Smithfield," March 12, 1844, Gerrit Smith Broadsides and Pamphlets Collection, Syracuse University. Bailey to James G. Birney, November 16, 1842, in Dumond, *Letters of J. G. Birney*, 2:709.

134. Ellsworth, "Oberlin and the Anti-Slavery Movement," 110–111, reports that the "one exception" to strong Liberty support from the community after 1840 was the 1843 election in the Nineteenth District, where antislavery Whig Edward S. Hamlin received much Liberty support over the Liberty candidate (Francis D. Parish). On Edward Wade's race, see Smith, *The Liberty and Free Soil Parties in the Northwest*, 112–113; Blue, *No Taint of Compromise*, 218.

135. Harrold, *Gamaliel Bailey*, 51–52; Hagedorn, *Beyond the River*, 125.

136. Chase to Birney, January 21, 1842, in Dumond, *Letters of J. G. Birney*, 2:661–662; Harrold, *Gamaliel Bailey*, 62–67, deals with the Morris dispute.

137. William Birney to James G. Birney, January 12, 1844, in Dumond, *Letters of J. G. Birney*, 2:774, for the immediate rupture. William Birney to James G. Birney, February 26, 1844, in ibid., 2:794–795, summarizes the dispute for which he saw as having "no particular cause." He attributed the disagreement to the fact that "both aspired to lead the Liberty party," that they were "almost totally different in character. Neither will consent to follow is the only point of similarity." The younger Birney is critical of both sides.

138. Chase to Gerrit Smith, May 14, 1842, in Niven, *The Salmon P. Chase Papers*, 2:97–98.

139. Chase to William Ellery Channing, May 3, 1842, in ibid., 95.

140. *Philanthropist*, February 14, 1844; *Liberty Herald*, February 22, 1844.

141. Maizlish, *Triumph of Sectionalism*, 27–39, deals with issues leading up to the election. He believes that "1844 marked a turning point in Ohio politics" and "established the direction of politics for nearly a generation" (27).

142. David T. Disney to James K. Polk, October 21, 28, 1844, as quoted in Maizlish, *Triumph of Sectionalism*, 34. Volpe, *Forlorn Hope of Freedom*, 92, discusses the Hamilton County Democrats' secret circular's trying to persuade former Democratic Liberty men to support the Democratic presidential ticket.

143. Birney, *James G. Birney*, 355. For problems over the Garland Forgery for Liberty men in Ohio, see James H. Paine to James G. Birney, October 31, 1844, from Fairport, in Dumond, *Letters of J. G. Birney*, 2:868–869; and Francis D. Parish to Birney, November 2, 1844, from Sandusky, in ibid., 2:873–874.

144. Maizlish, *Triumph of Sectionalism*, 34–39; Stewart, *Joshua Giddings*, 104–106; Smith, *The Liberty and Free Soil Parties in the Northwest*, 85; Volpe, *Forlorn Hope of Freedom*, xiii, 97–100. The Ohio Liberty Party's dislike for Giddings continued. See the exchange between Birney and Edward Wade over a speech in which Liberty men believed Giddings substituted the views of Cassius Clay for Henry Clay during the 1844 campaign. Wade believed Giddings was "but little understood I regret to say, by the body of Liberty party in the country at large and has duped many at home. . . ; Mr. Giddings [sic] unquestionable deception with his C.M. Clay letter is but one among the many bits of duplicity from him which has made him the great enemy of the Anti Slavery cause in this region. They are indeed 'too numerous to mention—'." Birney to Edward Wade, March 15, 1847, and Wade's reply, March 27, 1847, in Dumond, *Letters of J. G. Birney*, 2:1040, 1044–1046. See chapter 3 for the Great Southern and Western Convention.

145. *Herald and Philanthropist*, January 7, 1846; Smith, *The Liberty and Free Soil Parties in the Northwest*, 91. For an example of Lewis's frenetic speaking schedule, see the list of his speaking engagements in the *Herald and Philanthropist*, August 19, 1846.

146. Stewart, *Joshua Giddings*, 118.

147. Smith, *The Liberty and Free Soil Parties in the Northwest*, 92. For the election and Liberty influence, see Leonard Erickson, "Politics and Repeal of Ohio's Black Laws, 1837–1849," *Ohio History* 82 (Summer–Autumn 1973): 156–157.

148. *Cincinnati National Press and Weekly Herald*, March 24, 1847.

149. On dropping the name, see *Weekly Herald and Philanthropist*, December 9, 1846; on the subscription list before and after the name change, see *Cincinnati National Press and Weekly Herald*, March 24, 1847.

150. Volpe, *Forlorn Hope of Freedom*, 193.

151. Blue, *Salmon P. Chase*, 56, describes the party at this time as "highly diverse and decentralized." Volpe, *Forlorn Hope of Freedom*, 112–114, also discusses the diversity. Chase to John P. Hale, May 12, 1847, Chase Papers, Library of Congress, expresses discouragement at the progress at the Liberty Party in Ohio and believes that it can go no further.

152. *Cincinnati National Press and Weekly Herald*, September 22, 1847; *National Era*, September 30, 1847. On his opposition to the antislavery interpretation of the U.S. Constitution in a criticism of the *Emancipator* and the Massachusetts Liberty Party, see *Cincinnati National Press and Weekly Herald*, May 5, 1847, and *National Era*, May 13, 1847. There is a long editorial criticizing Lysander Spooner in the *Cincinnati National Press and Weekly Herald*, November 24, 1847. In *Cincinnati National Press and Weekly Herald*, March 8, 1848, he takes on Elizur Wright and the *Boston Daily Chronotype* on the same issue. A future U.S. Supreme Court justice, Matthews later angered many

with his willingness to enforce the Fugitive Slave Law as a prosecuting attorney and judge. William R. Wantland, "Jurist and Advocate: The Political Career of Stanley Matthews, 1840–1889" (Ph.D. dissertation, Miami University, 1994), chapter 1.

153. See *Cincinnati Press and Weekly Herald*, September 1, 8, 15, 22, 1847, for meetings before the 1847 local elections. In general, the meetings closer to Cincinnati had less moralistic pronouncements, did not embrace other reforms, and were less likely to view the U.S. Constitution as an antislavery document.

154. Smith, *The Liberty and Free Soil Parties in the Northwest*, 99, 118–119. The motion was tabled.

155. Joel Tiffany, *A Treatise on the Unconstitutionality of American Slavery; Together with the Powers and Duties of the Federal Government in Relation to That Subject* (Cleveland, Ohio: J. Calyer, 1849).

156. Fletcher, *A History of Oberlin College*, 2:269–270; Ellsworth, "Oberlin and the Anti-Slavery Movement," 120–121; Garrison and Garrison, *William Lloyd Garrison*, 3:202–204.

157. *National Era*, October 28, 1847.

158. *Cincinnati Weekly Herald*, February 10, 1847; *National Era*, February 18, 1847.

159. *Cincinnati National Press and Weekly Herald*, October 20, 1847; Volpe, *Forlorn Hope of Freedom*, 129.

160. Bradburn to Chase, June 25, 1848, Chase Papers, Library of Congress; Erwin H. Price, "The Election of 1848 in Ohio," *Ohio Archaeological and Historical Society* 36 (April 1927): 235.

161. For an overall approach to the situation, see Maizlish, *Triumph of Sectionalism*, chapter 5, 99–120.

162. Luthin, "Salmon P. Chase's Political Career," 518, discusses how Chase's correspondence by 1846 "reveals how strongly he became convinced that the natural refuge for anti-slavery men was the Democratic party." Hart, *Salmon P. Chase*, 97–98; Harrold, *Gamaliel Bailey*, chapter 4, "True Democracy in the Shadow of Slavery," 41–54.

163. Harrold, *Gamaliel Bailey*, 67, believes that by 1844 "Bailey and Chase and their allies had not only lost their two year struggle to impose their concept of political antislavery action on the entire Liberty party but also weakened their control of the Ohio party in the process."

164. Price, "The Election of 1848 in Ohio," 229.

165. *Cincinnati Weekly Herald*, May 17, 1848. There were four and one half columns of signatures. Hart, *Salmon P. Chase*, 96, and Niven, *The Salmon P. Chase Papers*, 2:170, say that one thousand people signed the call.

166. For the change, see *Cincinnati Weekly Herald*, June 7, 1848.

167. Chase to John P. Hale, June 25, 1848, in Niven, *The Salmon P. Chase Papers*, 2:173–175.

168. "Proceedings of the People's Convention," June 20–21, 1848, in *Cincinnati Weekly Herald*, June 28, 1848.

169. *National Era*, July 6, 1848; "Proceedings of the Ohio State Liberty Convention," June 22, 1848, in the *Cincinnati Weekly Herald*, June 28, 1848; Price, "The Election of 1848 in Ohio," 239–241; Smith, *The Liberty and Free Soil Parties in the Northwest*, 133–134; Hart, *Salmon P. Chase*, 96–98.

170. *Cincinnati Weekly Herald*, July 12, 1848. The ticket was removed in the July 19 issue.

171. Price, "The Election of 1848 in Ohio," 249; Smith, *The Liberty and Free Soil Parties in the Northwest*, 142; Hart, *Salmon P. Chase*, 99–100, gives the reminiscences of his father, Dr. Albert Gaillard Hart, who was an Ohio delegate.

172. *National Era*, September 14, 1848.

173. Chase to John Van Buren, September 30, 1848, in Niven, *The Salmon P. Chase Papers*, 2:191.

174. Maizlish, *Triumph of Sectionalism*, 115. Smith, *The Liberty and Free Soil Parties in the Northwest*, 153, says that "[t]he effect of this Whig vote in Ohio was terrifying." Holt, *The Rise and Fall of the American Whig Party*, 362–363.

175. Blue and McCormick, "Norton S. Townshend," 146.

176. Burnham, *Presidential Ballots*, 676. As in many elections during the Liberty years, all ballots may not have been reported. Ellsworth, "Oberlin and the Anti-Slavery Movement," 114, note 25, reports sixty-one votes for Gerrit Smith.

177. Maizlish, *Triumph of Sectionalism*, 271, note 43; Holt, *The Rise and Fall of the American Whig Party*, 373; Blue, *The Free Soilers*, 147–148; Rayback, *Free Soil*, 286; Smith, *The Liberty and Free Soil Parties in the Northwest*, 155.

178. McCormick, *The Second American Party System*, 286–287.

179. Theodore Calvin Pease, *The Frontier State, 1818–1848* (Urbana and Chicago: University of Illinois Press, 1987 [reprint of vol. 2 of the Centennial History of Illinois, 1918]), 302.

180. McCormick, *The Second American Party System*, 279.

181. Merton L. Dillon, "Abolitionism Comes to Illinois," *Journal of the Illinois State Historical Society* 53 (Winter 1960): 389–403.

182. Smith, *The Liberty and Free Soil Parties in the Northwest*, 14.

183. *Philanthropist*, November 26, 1839; Hermann R. Muelder, *Fighters for Freedom: The History of Anti-Slavery Activities of Men and Women Associated with Knox College* (New York: Columbia University Press, 1959), 158; Harris, *Negro Servitude in Illinois*, 147; Smith, *The Liberty and Free Soil Parties in the Northwest*, 33; Magdol, *Owen Lovejoy*, 56.

184. (Peoria, Ill.) *Register and Northwestern Gazeteer*, July 17, 1840, as quoted in Muelder, *Fighters for Freedom*, 159–161, which is the best summary of the meeting and lists officers and the presidential electors. For a retrospective view of the meeting, see *Genius of Liberty*, February 6, 1841.

185. *Genius of Liberty*, December 19, 1840, January 23, February 6, 1841.

186. *Genius of Liberty*, February 27, 1841; *Pennsylvania Freeman*, April 14, 1841.

187. *Genius of Liberty*, February 27, 1841. For the sentiments of the convention in favor of the Liberty Party, see John Cross's letter to the May 1841 national convention in *Emancipator*, June 10, 1841.

188. *Genius of Liberty*, June 19, 1841. For the minutes and members at the meeting, see *Genius of Liberty*, July 3, 1841. The fact that Eastman and Warren were two-thirds of a committee to select another candidate if Collins declined showed the sympathies of the two editors to third-party politics. See *Genius of Liberty*, July 17, 1841, for the Collins letter of acceptance. Harris, *Negro Servitude in Illinois*, 147, and Magdol, *Owen Lovejoy*, 60, incorrectly place this convention in January 1841.

189. Smith, *The Liberty and Free Soil Parties in the Northwest*, 55–56.

190. *Genius of Liberty*, November 6, 1841; *Emancipator*, December 10, 1841.

191. *Chicago Western Citizen*, August 5, 1842.

192. *Chicago Western Citizen*, July 26, 1842. The valedictory issue of the *Genius of Liberty*, April 2, 1842, outlined the positions that the editors believed the Liberty Party should (and actually did) follow. Moore and Moore, *Owen Lovejoy*, 48–55, reprint Owen Lovejoy's address at the convention.

193. *Chicago Western Citizen*, July 26, 1842 (the inaugural issue); Glassman, "Zebina Eastman," 20. Harris, *Negro Servitude in Illinois*, 148–150, claims that only one-half the amount was actually

collected. In his valedictory issue, *Chicago Western Citizen,* October 18, 1853, Eastman wrote that the "press was bought, but not all paid for—and the balance of over six hundred dollars was left for us to pay."

194. Glassman, "Zebina Eastman," 62, terms this group the "Chicago Phalanx—of [L. C. P.] Freer, [Dr. Charles V.] Dyer, [James H.] Collins, [Calvin] DeWolf, and [Philo] Carpenter." They were joined later by a young Chicago detective, Allan Pinkerton. Robin L. Einhorn, *Property Rules: Political Economy in Chicago, 1833–1872* (Chicago: University of Chicago Press, 1991), 34, notes that the party ran a mayoral candidate each year between 1842 and 1847, using them "as opportunities to build party strength."

195. See Smith, *The Liberty and Free Soil Parties in the Northwest,* 57, for totals.

196. *Chicago Western Citizen,* August 5, 1842.

197. In *Chicago Western Citizen,* August 26, 1842, Eastman had hoped for one thousand subscribers, but the reception of the paper was so good that he aimed for a circulation of 1,500. The *Western Citizen* carried more local, state, and territorial Liberty Party news than any other newspaper.

198. Glassman, "Zebina Eastman," 20.

199. *Chicago Western Citizen,* April 20, 1843.

200. *Chicago Western Citizen,* October 12, 1843, gives the district totals by county from the secretary off state's office. The state's rapidly increasing population had expanded the state's congressional delegation from four to seven.

201. *Chicago Western Citizen,* July 27, September 7, 1843.

202. Zebina Eastman, "History of the Anti-Slavery Agitation, and the Growth of the Liberty and Republican Parties in the State of Illinois," in Rufus Blanchard, ed., *Discovery and Conquests of the Northwest with the History of Chicago* (Chicago: R. Blanchard, 1879), 666, describes the recruitment and states that "Chief Justice [Salmon P.] Chase has described Mr. Codding as being the most eloquent speaker he ever heard from a platform." On his role in Albany, see Wright, *Myron Holley,* 259–260. Hannah P. Codding, "Ichabod Codding," in *Proceedings of the State Historical Society of Wisconsin* (1897), 169–196, covers his career (177–185) and deals with Illinois activities. His wife wrote it before her death in 1884.

203. (Mich.) *Signal of Liberty,* October 16, 1843, noted approvingly the progress being made by its neighbor and that there were twenty-two upcoming meetings on various speakers' agendas.

204. *Chicago Western Citizen,* October 12, November 16, 1843; Glassman, "Zebina Eastman," 27–30.

205. *Chicago Western Citizen,* June 15, 1843, discussed the indebtedness of the society. The quote is from Muelder, *Fighters for Freedom,* 167. Muelder, *Fighters for Freedom,* 148, claims that William T. Allan had "the leading role . . . that transformed that organization into a machine for the Liberty Party." Codding's role also should not be underestimated. See *Chicago Western Citizen,* November 2, 1843, for a report of the meeting.

206. *Chicago Western Citizen,* December 21, 1843.

207. "Liberty Association of Chicago. Constitution," in *Chicago Western Citizen,* October 12, 1843.

208. Evans, "Abolitionism in the Illinois Churches," 78; Harris, *Negro Servitude in Illinois,* 152–153.

209. As quoted in Harris, *Negro Servitude in Illinois,* 153.

210. "Ichabod Codding on the State Convention at Aurora" and "Proceedings of the State Liberty Party Convention at Aurora," in *Chicago Western Citizen,* February 1, 1844.

211. *Chicago Western Citizen*, February 29, March 14, 28, 1844.

212. Harris, *Negro Servitude in Illinois*, 154.

213. *Chicago Western Citizen*, September 5, 1844. A justice of the peace was also elected in West Joliet.

214. *Chicago Western Citizen*, April 25, 1844.

215. Harris, *Negro Servitude in Illinois*, 155, using other sources, has fifty-five counties giving Liberty votes, ten of them for the first time. I have computed my numbers from Burnham, *Presidential Ballots*, 368–390.

216. I have not found any instances during this time frame of Democratic fusion with Liberty candidates in Illinois. *Chicago Western Citizen*, July 11, August 15, 1844, discuss the beginnings of some Democratic movement toward the Liberty Party.

217. *Chicago Western Citizen*, August 15, 1844.

218. *Chicago Western Citizen*, November 14, 1844; *Emancipator*, December 7, 1844.

219. *Chicago Western Citizen*, March 6, 1845, reports the party did elect one of twelve aldermen in Chicago despite its refusal to participate in a union ticket. Smith, *The Liberty and Free Soil Parties in the Northwest*, 87, 343, is only partially correct in characterizing 1845 as a "relapse." He found "no general returns accessible" because there were no general elections. He is correct, however, in that there is less political material in the newspapers.

220. *Chicago Western Citizen*, September 18, 1845.

221. *Chicago Western Citizen*, November 26, 1845, reports that two thousand had already been printed and distributed with plans to print another edition of several thousand.

222. *Chicago Western Citizen*, passim; Harris, *Negro Servitude in Illinois*, 156–158; Smith, *The Liberty and Free Soil Parties in the Northwest*, 95–96; Codding, "Ichabod Codding," 184–85.

223. *Chicago Western Citizen*, March 11, 1846, remarks on the Liberty improvement in the state.

224. *Chicago Western Citizen*, May 20, 1846, reports that in order to get the lease, the Liberty Association had to pledge that "it shall not be let for the purpose of giving what are called 'Ethiopian Concerts.'"

225. *Chicago Western Citizen*, June 3, 10, 1846. *Chicago Western Citizen*, June 17, 1846, lists the county committees. Three of the five members of the state central committee were from Chicago.

226. *Chicago Western Citizen*, April 8, May 6, June 3, July 14, 1846. *Chicago Western Citizen*, July 21, 1846, says 1,400 were campaign or free editions. Eastman's comment that he could not afford to carry subscribers who had not paid shows that the paper's finances were not as healthy as the subscription numbers might indicate.

227. *Chicago Western Citizen*, April 29, 1846.

228. Lovejoy to editor, June 1, 1846, in *Chicago Western Citizen*, June 10, 1846, describes the egging in Lexington. See Codding to Eastman, May 9, 1846, in *Chicago Western Citizen*, May 20, 1846, which describes how a planned attack upon Codding in Peoria, a particularly hostile place, was foiled by forewarning and preparation. On Lovejoy's campaigning, see Magdol, *Owen Lovejoy*, 75–78.

229. Magdol, *Owen Lovejoy*, 76.

230. See chapter 3 for details of the North-Western Liberty Convention.

231. *Chicago Western Citizen*, September 8, 1846.

232. Theodore C. Pease, *Illinois Election Returns, 1818–1848* (Springfield: Collections of the Illinois State Historical Library, 1923), 18:156. This sixteen-county district contained six of the eight counties that gave Birney more than 10% of their vote in 1844.

233. Magdol, *Owen Lovejoy*, 78–79.

234. *Chicago Western Citizen*, February 23, 1847. *National Era*, March 18, 1847, reports that the convention was so large that it had to be divided in two.

235. Harris, *Negro Servitude in Illinois*, 159–161.

236. *Chicago Western Citizen*, May 4, 1847.

237. See *Chicago Western Citizen*, February 23, 1847, for an account of one of these meetings.

238. *Chicago Western Citizen*, March 2, 1847. "Half-loaves" were those who were on two ballots. The *Chicago Western Citizen* admitted, "Local matters so affected the vote, that the election is no fair test of the strength of the parties—the Liberty men dividing as well as others—bridges and streets having the precedence over human liberty."

239. *Chicago Western Citizen*, April 19, 1847. *Chicago Western Citizen*, May 4, 1847, reported that Lovejoy lost when Whigs and some Democrats combined against him (Liberty—328, Whig—362, Democrat—235).

240. *Chicago Western Citizen*, November 2, 1847. They endorsed a presidential ticket of John P. Hale and Samuel (*sic*) P. Chase.

241. *Chicago Western Citizen*, February 22, 1848.

242. *Chicago Western Citizen*, June 3, 1846; Harris, *Negro Servitude in Illinois*, 157, 161–162.

243. Smith, *The Liberty and Free Soil Parties in the Northwest*, 334–335, traces various resolutions in the state constitutional convention and the ensuing legislation. *Chicago Western Citizen*, February 15, 1848, reports that the Liberty state convention at Chicago, February 9–10, 1848, voted almost unanimously that it could not support the new constitution.

244. *Chicago Western Citizen*, March 14, 1848. The state legislature did not act immediately, but in 1853 it passed some of the most discriminatory legislation in the North.

245. *Chicago Western Citizen*, February 15, 1848.

246. Magdol, *Owen Lovejoy*, 83–86, gives his positions on the issues: exempting homesteads for seizure for debt; the inalienability of land without the consent of one's wife; open public lands in limited quantities at no charge to actual settlers; free trade; federal appropriations for river and harbor improvements; reduction in postal rates; and direct election of the president. See Lovejoy's explanation of his positions in Owen Lovejoy to the *Chicago Western Citizen*, July 15, 1848, in *Chicago Western Citizen*, July 18, 1848. Moore and Moore, *Owen Lovejoy*, 82–86.

247. *Chicago Western Citizen*, July 11, 1848. The recently adopted state constitution had simplified the complex Illinois electoral schedule by setting the time for several types of election at the first Tuesday after the first Monday in November. The summer 1848 elections were the last under the old formula.

248. Smith, *The Liberty and Free Soil Parties in the Northwest*, 135.

249. *Chicago Western Citizen*, August 22, 1848.

250. Rayback, *Free Soil*, 250, believes "Democrats dominated." Blue, *The Free Soilers*, 140–141, states that "most of the Free Soil support was drawn from the Democratic stronghold in the northeastern part of the state and only the refusal of the most prominent anti-extension Democrat, John Wentworth, to renounce his party prevented the defections from being much larger." Smith, *The Liberty and Free Soil Parties in the Northwest*, believes Illinois Free Soil support "was drawn almost entirely from Democratic ranks." On the other side, Harris, *Negro Servitude in Illinois*, 173, argues less convincingly that the "great gain in Illinois on the national ticket . . . was due in large parts to accessions from the Whigs."

251. Raw data from Burnham, *Presidential Ballots*, 368–390. Rayback, *Free Soilers*, 287, also notes that the counties containing Chicago and Cleveland were the only "urban" centers to give pluralities to Van Buren. Both had been Liberty strongholds.

252. "The Retrospect and Prospect," in *Chicago Western Citizen*, November 14, 1848.

253. Lamoille County, Vermont, came in second at 24.8%. See Appendix B for a banner county list.

254. See *Chicago Western Citizen*, November 23, 1843, for its adoption as the official organ of the Iowa Territorial Anti-Slavery Society.

255. This growth was remarkable. In statewide elections the total vote was: 1843—8,454; 1845—13,380; 1847—21,391; 1848 (May gubernatorial election)—32,421; 1848 (presidential)—39,171.

256. Lois K. Mathews, *The Expansion of New England: The Spread of New England Settlement and Institutions to the Mississippi River, 1620-1865* (Boston: Houghton-Mifflin, 1909), 236-260. Smith, *The History of Wisconsin*, 1:196-197, 467-473; Gerteis, "Antislavery Agitation in Wisconsin," ii-v, 1-2; Theodore Clarke Smith, "The Free Soil Party in Wisconsin," *Wisconsin State Historical Society Publications* 42 (December 1894): 99-100; Gerteis, "An Abolitionist in Territorial Wisconsin," Part 1, 17.

257. *Philanthropist*, July 7, 1840. I have found no other societies before 1842.

258. *Chicago Western Citizen*, September 23, 1842, contains the "Proceedings of the Convention." This newspaper is a valuable source for Wisconsin antislavery activities, especially before the *American Freeman* became the state antislavery newspaper in 1844. See also Gerteis, "An Abolitionist in Territorial Wisconsin, Part III," 259. McManus, *Political Abolitionism in Wisconsin*, 4, dates the founding in June; but Amnon Gaston to James G. Birney, July 6, 1842, in Dumond, *Letters of James G. Birney*, 2:701-702, invites him to the convention at Delavan that was set for August 2. Birney was unable to attend, but the fact that he was invited reveals the political orientation of some. Mathews, *Autobiography*, 170, has a very short discussion of some of the proceedings.

259. On the Walworth County Anti-Slavery Society (founded on December 24, 1842), see *Chicago Western Citizen*, January 13, 1843. *Chicago Western Citizen*, April 20, 1843, reports local auxiliaries in Pewaukee and Lisbon, Prarieville, Waukeshe, Delavan, Yorkville, and Watertown and on Sauk Prairie.

260. *Chicago Western Citizen*, April 20, 1843; William J. Maher, "The Antislavery Movement in Milwaukee and Vicinity, 1842-1860" (M.A. thesis, Marquette University, 1954), 14-15.

261. Letter from Racine to the *Chicago Western Citizen*, in *Chicago Western Citizen*, April 27, 1843.

262. *Chicago Western Citizen*, June 22, 1843. The editor blamed poor weather for the small turnout.

263. Chauncy C. Olin, *Reminiscences of a Busy Life*, in *The Olin Album, 1893: The John Olin Family History, 1678-1893* (Indianapolis, Ind.: Baker Randolph Co., 1893 [printed for the Olin family]), 13, says that he cast one of the two abolition votes in Prairieville in an 1840 local election. The *Reminiscences* is contained in the larger work. This is an informative work by a former Liberty editor/publisher and Underground Railroad operative, but he is sometimes slightly inaccurate on his dates.

264. Smith, "The Free Soil Party in Wisconsin," 102.

265. *Signal of Liberty*, October 16, 1843.

266. Smith, "The Free Soil Party in Wisconsin, 102-103; Smith, *The Liberty and Free Soil Parties in the Northwest*, 59; Gerteis, "Antislavery Agitation in Wisconsin," 40. *Chicago Western Citizen*, November 30, 1843, has the county Liberty totals with Liberty man Jacob Lybrand receiving an additional nineteen votes. *Signal of Liberty*, December 11, 1843, also has the county returns.

267. Jacob Lybrand to Editor, April 3, 1844, in (Milwaukee, Wis.) *American Freeman*, April 10, 1844, reports only four people attended the first county Liberty convention the previous fall.

268. *Chicago Western Citizen*, January 4, 1844. The State Historical Society of Wisconsin has the only known issue of this publication. *Chicago Western Citizen*, March 21, 1844, announces that it shut down operations when the *American Freeman* became the party newspaper. Codding, "Ichabod Codding," 185–186

269. *Genius of Liberty*, October 23, 1841; *Chicago Western Citizen*, October 7, 14, 21, 1842; Gerteis, "An Abolitionist in Territorial Wisconsin, Part I," 17; Gerteis, "Antislavery Agitation in Wisconsin," 47–49; Harris, *Negro Servitude in Illinois*, 139.

270. Gerteis, "Antislavery Agitation in Wisconsin," 12; McManus, *Political Abolitionism in Wisconsin*, 5–6.

271. *Chicago Western Citizen*, March 7, 1844.

272. *Chicago Western Citizen*, March 21, 1844, urges its support "even if it hurts our subscription list"; Gerteis, "An Abolitionist in Territorial Wisconsin, Part III," 256; Gerteis, "Antislavery Agitation in Wisconsin," 31–33.

273. *American Freeman*, March 20, 1844, announced the formation of the "Ladies' Milwaukie [sic] Anti-Slavery Society" with forty-one signatures. *American Freeman*, September 18, 1844, reported that a women's society had been formed in Prairieville by eighteen women on July 16 and had several subsequent meetings. Genevieve G. McBride, *On Wisconsin Women: Working for Their Rights from Settlement to Suffrage* (Madison: University of Wisconsin Press, 1993), 13, reports that women were invited to the men's meeting but "declined, courteously, continuing to meet on their own and contributing a 'Ladies Department'—decorously unsigned or under pseudonyms, of course—to the *Freeman*."

274. *American Freeman*, March 27, 1844.

275. *Chicago Western Citizen*, April 11, 1844.

276. *American Freeman*, April 4, 1844. See Jacob Lybrand to editor, April 3, 1844, in *American Freeman*, April 10, 1844, for Racine; *Chicago Western Citizen*, April 11, 1844, claims Whig-Democratic coalitions "in many towns" cost the Liberty Party two seats on the Milwaukee County Board of Supervisors. McManus, *Political Abolitionism in Wisconsin*, 11, cites some instances of Whig-Democratic cooperation. *American Freeman*, September 28, 1844; Smith, *The Liberty and Free Soil Parties in the Northwest*, 75.

277. *American Freeman*, September 18, 1848; Gerteis, "An Abolitionist in Territorial Wisconsin, Part III," 260; Gerteis, "Antislavery Agitation in Wisconsin," 63–64.

278. *American Freeman*, September 18, 1844, describes the whole process. The newspaper did not publish between June 15 and September 18. Olin, *Reminiscences of a Busy Life*, 21, says each share was ten dollars; Gerteis, "An Abolitionist in Territorial Wisconsin," 256, footnote by W. (William) C.(Converse) H. (Haggod).

279. Olin, *Reminiscences of a Busy Life*, 21, on the continual sale of shares.

280. *American Freeman*, February 12, 1845. The objections did not cease particularly from committed Whigs. See "Liberty Voters—Prepare for Whig Coaxing," in *American Freeman*, September 16, 1845. Also see unsigned note in the *American Freeman*, November 17, 1846, that an attempt will be made at the annual meeting to rescind the resolution whereby the Wisconsin Anti-Slavery Society was changed to the Wisconsin Liberty Association. Editorial and an address of the Lisbon Liberty Association in *American Freeman*, November 24, 1846, opposing the proposed change. Mathews, *Autobiography*, 183, places the meeting in 1846 and says "[t]o show its identification with the political Anti-slavery party, its name was changed to the Liberty Association."

281. "Public Discussion in Reference to the Liberty Party," in *American Freeman*, March 19, 1845.

282. *American Freeman*, March 5, 12, 19, 26, April 2, 9, 1845, show Liberty successes and several major-party coalitions against them.

283. Smith, *The Liberty and Free Soil Parties in the Northwest*, 327.

284. *American Freeman*, November 10, 1847, gives the retrospective tally of several races. Smith, *The Liberty and Free Soil Parties in the Northwest*, 87, has wildly inaccurate totals (probably because of a transcription error), although those in his earlier "The Free Soil Party in Wisconsin," 103, are correct.

285. McManus, *Political Abolitionism in Wisconsin*, 22–53, covers the events leading up to the elections and the subsequent conventions and votes. The ability of Liberty advocates to reach a consensus was hampered by the inability of the *American Freeman* to publish for much of the time before the election.

286. See McManus, *Political Abolitionism in Wisconsin*, 24–25, on some of these. Matthew Smith to C. C. Sholes, in *American Freeman*, June 11, 1846.

287. "Duty of Liberty Men," in *American Freeman*, August 4, 1846.

288. "Semi-Annual Meeting of the Territorial Liberty Association," July 15, 1846, in *American Freeman*, August 4, 1846. Gerteis, "An Abolitionist in Territorial Wisconsin, Part 4," 340; Mathews, *Autobiography*, 240. Reporting on possible cooperation with the major parties, George W. Clark to William L. Chaplin, August 22, 1846, in *Albany Patriot*, September 16, 1846, describes a Milwaukee convention where "every one came to the right conclusion at last, and unitedly and with the best spirit made out their independent nominations on the spot."

289. McManus, *Political Abolitionism in Wisconsin*, 27–28; Maher, "Antislavery in Milwaukee," 23–24.

290. Sources vary on the vote. I have used figures from McManus, *Political Abolitionism in Wisconsin*, 29.

291. *American Freeman*, April 14, 1847. It also reports that Liberty candidates won two out of sixteen seats and held the balance of power on the Milwaukee County Board of Supervisors.

292. C. C. Sholes's letter of resignation, in *American Freeman*, September 29, 1846.

293. *American Freeman*, October 27, 1846, claims the newspaper was seven hundred dollars in debt.

294. The change took place between the October 27 and November 3, 1846, issues.

295. *American Freeman*, December 8, 1846; *Chicago Western Citizen*, December 29, 1846.

296. Gerteis, "An Abolitionist in Territorial Wisconsin, Part 4," 338, discusses several groups.

297. See Gerteis, "Antislavery Agitation in Wisconsin," 72–78, on religious questions in Liberty Associations and Edward Holton's leaving his Presbyterian church to join a Congregational church over slavery. See Mathews, *Autobiography*, 259–260, for his very strong statement "on the duty of voting for Anti-slavery rulers." Codding, "Ichabod Codding," 185.

298. "Our Semi-Annual Meeting," in *American Freeman*, July 21, 1847; Proceedings in *American Freeman*, July 28, 1847.

299. *American Freeman*, November 10, 1847, December 15, 1847. McManus, *Political Abolitionism in Wisconsin*, 30–31, recounts how the first election of a Whig in a territorial election was so unexpected that, "[a]nticipating defeat, Tweedy had absented himself from the territory on personal business."

300. The annual state Liberty Association convention on January 27, 1848, passed a resolution against the new constitution. See *American Freeman*, February 2, 9, 23, 1848.

301. *American Freeman*, July 28, 1847.

302. *American Freeman*, December 22, 1847.

303. *American Freeman,* February 2, 1848.

304. For one letter objecting to the expanded platform, see E. G. Dyer to Codding, March 20, 1848, in *American Freeman,* March 29, 1848. Codding replied that it had been passed at the state convention in January with only one dissenting vote. Codding criticized Owen Lovejoy of Illinois for voting against Gerrit Smith in Buffalo, and he devoted much press space in the *American Freeman* to national reform and the National Reform Party. See *American Freeman,* February 9, 1848.

305. "Proceedings of the State Liberty Convention," Waukesha, April 19, 1848, in *American Freeman,* April 26, 1848. McManus, *Political Abolitionism in Wisconsin,* 38, points out that a later Liberty convention in the northern counties endorsed Hale.

306. As late as the issue of the *American Freeman,* June 28, 1848, Booth aired his disagreement with the *Chicago Western Citizen*'s position that the Wilmot Proviso was sufficient ground upon which to stand.

307. Smith, "The Free Soil Party in Wisconsin," 160.

308. McManus, *Political Abolitionism in Wisconsin,* 39.

309. *American Freeman,* July 26, 1848.

310. Proceedings in *American Freeman,* August 9, 1848. Ichabod Codding to Booth, in *American Freeman,* August 2, 1848, says the Janesville meeting was one-half Democrats, one-third Liberty, and the rest Whig. Jacob Lybrand, Booth, Codding, and Durkee were among the Liberty leaders selected. There were eighteen Democrats, two Whigs, and five Liberty men—probably an accurate mirror of the grassroots support.

311. Dyer, *Phonographic Report of the Proceeding of the National Free Soil Convention,* in Schlesinger, *History of U.S. Political Parties,* 881.

312. *American Freeman,* August 2, 1848; Blue, *No Taint of Compromise,* 121–122. See Gerteis, "Antislavery Agitation in Wisconsin," 125–134, on Booth's transformation and a vignette from his 1897 dispute with historian Theodore Clark Smith.

313. *Wisconsin Freeman,* August 30, 1848; Smith, "The Free Soil Party in Wisconsin," 114.

314. Smith, "The Free Soil Party in Wisconsin," 117.

315. Smith, *The Liberty and Free Soil Parties in the Northwest,* 156–157; Blue, *The Free Soilers,* 149. McManus, *Political Abolitionism in Wisconsin,* 49, calculates that over 5,000 former Democrats, about 3,300 former Whigs, all the former Liberty men, and 600 voters of unknown backgrounds made up the Free Soil totals, but his analysis is dependent on the ecological fallacy. Rayback, *Free Soil,* 300, calculates 7,000 former Democrat, 1,400 former Whigs, and 2,000 former Liberty, but grossly overestimates previous Liberty strength.

316. Smith, "The Free Soil Party in Wisconsin," 118.

317. Smith, *The History of Wisconsin,* 1:638; Smith, "The Free Soil Party in Wisconsin," 116–117

318. Smith, *The Liberty and Free Soil Parties in the Northwest,* 158.

319. Smith, "The Free Soil Party in Wisconsin," 118.

320. McCormick, *The Second American Party System,* 271–277.

321. Marion C. Miller, "The Antislavery Movement in Indiana" (Ph.D. dissertation, University of Michigan, 1938), surveys the movement and emphasizes the religious roots.

322. French, "Stephen S. Harding," 212.

323. Smith, *The Liberty and Free Soil Parties in the Northwest,* 44, 14.

324. *Emancipator* September 24, 1840; French, "Stephen S. Harding," 220.

325. Smith, *The Liberty and Free Soil Parties in the Northwest,* 51–52, says that major-party abolitionists left the organization and the third-party group, "finding no opposition, gained courage to go on by themselves."

326. It appears that at least some voters had to use handwritten ballots because no printed ones were available. See Aaron Richardson to S. S. Harding, 1870, as quoted in French, "Stephen S. Harding," 216.

327. Smith, *The Liberty and Free Soil Parties in the Northwest*, 156, estimates the Liberty vote "to be between 800 and 900." Willey, *The History of the Antislavery Cause*, 239, and French, "Stephen S. Harding," 220, report nine hundred Liberty votes.

328. See *Chicago Western Citizen*, July 20, 1843, for the Indiana ticket. For Bigelow's later activities in Washington, see Stanley Harrold, *Subversives: Antislavery Community in Washington, D.C., 1821–1865* (Baton Rouge: Louisiana State University Press, 2003).

329. Miller, "The Antislavery Movement in Indiana," 95–99.

330. *Free Labor Advocate and Anti-Slavery Chronicle*, May 20, 1843.

331. *Chicago Western Citizen*, September 21, 1843, gives the totals by county. The Liberty total of 1,684 is most often cited, although French, "Stephen S. Harding," 220, claims the vote "increased to 2,050."

332. (Mich.) *Signal of Liberty*, September 25, 1843. The results were obtained through the newspaper's exchange list. *Chicago Western Citizen*, September 21, 1843, gives the 1843 returns by county. Letter to the *Chicago Western Citizen*, in *Chicago Western Citizen*, August 31, 1843, claims that a Liberty man was elected to the lower house of the state legislature, but I can find nothing to corroborate this.

333. These were Wayne (319), Randolph (206), Grant (197), Henry (188), Hamilton (139), Ripley (89), Decatur (68), Union (60), Marshall (54), LaPorte (53), Dearborn (50), and Jefferson (50).

334. Grant (20.2%), Randolph (11.2%)—the two highest percentage counties—and Wayne (319 votes)—most numerous—were in this area.

335. See Brown's obituary in *Chicago Western Citizen*, March 21, 1844.

336. *National Era*, July 1, 19, 1847. Smith, *The Liberty and Free Soil Parties in the Northwest*, 116, claims these "answers were not very strong."

337. C. Peter Ripley et al., eds., *The Black Abolitionist Papers*, vol. 3, *The United States, 1830–1846* (Chapel Hill: University of North Carolina Press, 1991), 423, reports that Charles L. Remond (an African American Garrisonian antislavery speaker of proven bravery) cancelled his Indianapolis appearance in September 1843, "believing that the intensity of racist and antiabolitionist feeling there endangered his life."

338. *Cincinnati Herald and Philanthropist*, November 12, 1845, August 12, 1847; *National Era*, April 29, July 29, 1847; *Emancipator*, October 28, 1846; Volpe, *Forlorn Hope of Freedom*, 118–119. For instance, in the 1845 congressional election, Wayne County, only increased its Liberty total by 14 votes from the 1844 presidential contest, 333–319, and 129 of these votes came from New Garden, the home of the *Free Labor Advocate*, which gave the third party 67.9% of its vote.

339. Smith, *The Liberty and Free Soil Parties in the Northwest*, 221.

340. *National Era*, July 29, 1847.

341. *Free Labor Advocate and Anti-Slavery Chronicle*, May 3, 10, 1845, April 1, 29, 1847. He declared that if nobody met his standards, "I will vote for myself." Sewell, *Ballots for Freedom*, 132.

342. *National Era*, July 13, 1848; *Cincinnati Weekly Herald and Philanthropist*, June 21, July 5, 1848.

343. French, "Stephen S. Harding," 222; Volpe, *Forlorn Hope of Freedom*, 132–133; Smith, *The Liberty and Free Soil Parties in the Northwest*, 134; Patrick W. Riddleberger, "The Making of a Political Abolitionist: George W. Julian and the Free Soilers, 1848," *Indiana Magazine of History* 51 (September 1955): 233–234.

344. *Indiana State Journal,* August 30, 1848, as quoted in French, "Stephen S. Harding," 223.

345. Blue, *The Free Soilers,* 148; Rayback, *Free Soil,* 285.

346. Sewell, *Ballots for Freedom,* 214.

347. Robert R. Dykstra, *Bright Radical Star: Black Freedom and White Supremacy on the Hawkeye Frontier* (Cambridge, Mass.: Harvard University Press, 1993), especially 68–83, plus scattered references, deals with the Liberty Party. Ward Robert Barnes, "Anti-Slavery Politics in Iowa, 1840–1856" (M.A. thesis, University of Iowa, 1968), chapter III, 53–105, plus scattered references, is an M.A. thesis that is superior to many Ph.D. dissertations in its depth and utilization of primary sources. Smith, *The Liberty and Free Soil Parties in the Northwest,* 76, 87, 96–97, 137, devotes only a few sentences to antislavery and the Liberty Party in Iowa; Volpe, *Forlorn Hope of Freedom,* does not deal with Iowa at all. A good part of the reason for the neglect is a lack of sources. Dykstra, *Bright Radical Star,* 69, comments that "less than 10 percent of its official newspapers, and a mere handful of letters to and from participants, have survived." Barnes, "Anti-Slavery Politics in Iowa," 103, could find no copies of the Liberty newspaper, the *Iowa Freeman.* The *Chicago Western Citizen* is a major source of Iowa articles, and the *Philanthropist,* and, later, the *National Era* also have some material. Barnes scoured local Iowa newspaper files for much of his information.

348. Barnes, "Anti-Slavery Politics in Iowa," 8–15, 61–62.

349. Holt, *The Rise and Fall of the American Whig Party,* 237–238; Dykstra, *Bright Radical Star,* 71; Barnes, "Anti-Slavery Politics in Iowa," 79–80. The Whigs failed to get a U.S. Senate seat.

350. Barnes, "Anti-Slavery Politics in Iowa," has a map of these counties in the southeastern part of Iowa. He has mapped towns that he estimated had more than ten abolitionists during the 1840s. He also has classified individual known Liberty Party supporters by county, township, nativity, profession, religion, and former political affiliation (292–296). He estimates that no more than one thousand out of one hundred thousand Iowa residents were abolitionists at the time of statehood. The religious affiliations in the towns are used here. *Chicago Western Citizen,* December 7, 1843, reports an antislavery society in Johnson County of mostly Methodists, "though not of the True Wesleyan denomination."

351. Barnes, "Anti-Slavery Politics in Iowa," 17, claims that the first society was founded in Denmark in January 1840. *Emancipator,* April 8, 1841, and *Chicago Western Citizen,* April 2, 1842, report that Quakers set up an antislavery society in Salem. These first two societies remained a vital core of Iowa antislavery.

352. Aaron Street Jr. to Zebina Eastman, April 27, 1843, in *Chicago Western Citizen,* May 18, 1843.

353. See *Chicago Western Citizen,* January 18, 1844, for the proceedings of the convention; Street to Eastman, November 3, 1843, in *Chicago Western Citizen,* November 23, 1843, for a letter on the meeting. Dykstra, *Bright Radical Star,* 43, identifies Illinois Anti-Slavery Society agent William T. Allan with Garrisonian positions here and later in his work, but Muelder, *Fighters for Freedom,* 148, sees Allan as having assumed "the leading role in the semi-annual meeting of the Illinois Anti-Slavery Society that transformed that organization into a machine of the Liberty Party." The *Chicago Western Citizen* frequently refers to Allan's Liberty activities. Moore and Moore, *Owen Lovejoy,* 366, detail his support for Lovejoy.

354. Barnes, "Anti-Slavery Politics in Iowa," 26ff. Samuel Luke Howe of Mount Pleasant led the Liberty ticket with 117 votes for a seat in the territorial legislature in this race. Whether positions on black rights were deliberately omitted for some reason or whether they were just taken for granted is uncertain.

355. Barnes, "Anti-Slavery Politics in Iowa," 68–75.

356. For instance, see the account of the Liberty Society of Big Greene and Cedar townships in *Chicago Western Citizen*, April 12, 1847.

357. Barnes, "Anti-Slavery Politics in Iowa," 80–81, 292–296. He found political backgrounds for only 25 out of 148 Liberty voters, but 88% is a large percentage, especially when one considers that many Liberty voters may not have had a consistent political background or had recently moved to Iowa.

358. Correspondent in Iowa City to *Chicago Western Citizen*, in *Chicago Western Citizen*, April 22, 1846, writes, "One year ago an abolitionist would have been subject to a malevolent mob . . . We have now discussions of slavery in our streets and public places unmolested."

359. Barnes, "Anti-Slavery Politics in Iowa," 80–81, and Dykstra, *Bright Radical Star*, 70–71, discuss the likelihood of some Liberty voters backing antislavery major-party candidates. Dykstra claims that Liberty men did not run candidates in the summer 1847 elections.

360. *National Era*, February 4, 1847.

361. The partial convention proceedings are in *Chicago Western Citizen*, January 25, 1848, and *National Era*, February 10, 1848. They imply Denmark as the convention site. Barnes, "Anti-Slavery Politics in Iowa," 84, and Dykstra, *Bright Radical Star*, 73–76, utilize additional primary sources to discuss the convention, but both place it in Yellow Springs.

362. *National Era*, July 13, 1848.

363. Barnes, "Anti-Slavery Politics in Iowa," 86–88. Harlan was later a Republican U.S. senator and secretary of the interior under Andrew Johnson.

364. *Chicago Western Citizen*, June 20, 1848; *National Era*, July 13, 1848.

365. Barnes, "Anti-Slavery Politics in Iowa," 90–92.

366. Ibid., 308, breaks down both district votes by county.

367. Dykstra, *Bright Radical Star*, 80–87; Barnes, "Anti-Slavery Politics in Iowa," 110–118.

368. Returns from Barnes, "Anti-Slavery Politics in Iowa," 310. Burnham, *Presidential Ballots*, 412, does not take into account the scattering votes. He has Whig—11,238; Democrat—9,930; Free Soil—1,103.

369. Dykstra, *Bright Radical Star*, 84, quotes David M. Kelsey to this effect.

370. Barnes, "Anti-Slavery Politics in Iowa," 86, attributes an 1847 Whig vote to "a dubious legal procedure."

371. Dykstra, *Bright Radical Star*. 84. His analysis is subject to the ecological fallacy. It concludes that "[c]omputer-aided analysis of the returns supports this logic by suggesting that the scattering of November 1848 consisted wholly of ballots cast by men who had voted Whig in August's congressional election . . . Despite a strong turnout—approximately 95 percent of the Whigs of August voted again in November—less than half supported Taylor." Blue, *The Free Soilers*, 149, says the Free Soil Party "attracted most of their small total from the Whig Party."

372. (Conn.) *Christian Freeman*, June 13, 1844; Harrold, *The Abolitionists and the South*, 131.

373. *New Jersey Freeman*, October 12, 1844, has an account of the convention, its resolutions, and a list of the seventeen presidential electors. *Christian Freeman*, August 1, September 12, 24, 1844; (Maine) *Liberty Standard*, August 22, 1844; Albany (N.Y.) *Patriot*, September 18, 1844.

374. Morris, *Life of Thomas Morris*, 322. Burnham, *Presidential Ballots* shows no votes from Ohio or any other Virginia county. Willey, *The History of the Antislavery Cause*, 259, discusses this convention and claims it "adopted sound resolutions, nominated a full electoral ticket, and issued an able address." *Christian Freeman*, September 26, 1844, reprints the "Address to the People of Virginia by the Virginia Liberty Party" from the *Cincinnati Herald and Philanthropist*; "To the People of Virginia," Samuel J. May Anti-Slavery Collection, Cornell University; "Liberty Convention of

Ohio County, Virginia," Samuel J. May Anti-Slavery Collection, Cornell University, lists seventeen electors.

375. *New Jersey Freeman,* October 26, 1844.

376. *New Jersey Freeman,* February 28, 1845. The rest of their tabulations are very close to other sources. Burnham, *Presidential Ballots,* shows nothing but returns for the two major parties for Virginia and West Virginia, including Ohio County. *Emancipator,* September 15, 1847, in a retrospective "Liberty Role" shows no Liberty votes from Virginia 1840–1847. That votes were cast for the Liberty electors but not counted is, as in some other areas, probable.

377. *New Jersey Freeman,* December 9, 1845. *The American Liberty Almanac for 1846,* 32, reports that "[i]n Virginia, there was a small Liberty vote in two counties—estimated at 100."

378. *New Jersey Freeman,* December 9, 1845.

CHAPTER 8

1. (Vermont) *Green Mountain Freeman,* December 28, 1848.

2. Psalm 92:12: "The righteous shall flourish like the palm tree: he shall grow like a cedar in Lebanon." Psalm 104:16: "The trees of the LORD are full *of sap;* the cedars of Lebanon, which he hath planted"; Foster, "The Liberty Party," 58, Foster Papers, Bentley Historical Collections, University of Michigan, says that Joshua Leavitt originated the symbol.

3. *Chicago Western Citizen,* July 26, 1842.

4. Dyer Burgess to Gamaliel Bailey, June 13, 1840, in *Philanthropist,* June 30, 1840.

5. "Address to the Abolitionists of Massachusetts," in *Liberator,* July 19, 1839.

6. Carwardine, *Evangelicals and Politics in Antebellum America,* 142.

7. On Wesleyan Methodists, see Strong, "Partners in Political Abolitionism," 99–115. Contrast that with Chris Padgett, "Hearing the Antislavery Rank-and-File: The Wesleyan Methodist Schism of 1843," *Journal of the Early Republic* 12 (Spring 1992): 63–84, which rarely mentions the Liberty Party.

8. Strong, *Perfectionist Politics,* 56. On Holley's unconventional views, see Wright, *Myron Holley,* 207–212, 314–315, and Harry S. Douglas, "Myron Holley, Abolitionist," *Historical Wyoming* [County, N.Y.] 13 (January 1960): 48–50. On Smith, see Ralph V. Harlow, "Gerrit Smith and the Free Church Movement," *New York History* 23 (July 1937): 269–287, and Harlow, *Gerrit Smith,* 193–217. On Goodell, see Perkal, "William Goodell," chapter 6: "Christian Abolitionist." On Stewart and the movement in Upstate New York, see Strong, *Perfectionist Politics,* 85–86. On a survey of several religious groups from a contemporary, see Goodell, *Slavery and Anti-Slavery,* 487–508. John L. Hammond, *The Politics of Benevolence: Revival Religion and American Voting Behavior* (Norwood, N.J.: Ablex Publishing, 1979), attempts to quantify the religious influences on voting. Whitney R. Cross, *The Burned-Over District: The Social and Intellectual History of Enthusiastic Religion in Western New York, 1800–1850* (Ithaca, N.Y.: Cornell University Press, 1950), is an older standard work on the Upstate New York abolitionists. Sernett, *North Star Country,* is a more recent account. Judith Wellman, *Grassroots Reform in the Burned-over District of Upstate New York: Religious Abolitionism and Democracy,* Studies in African American History and Culture (New York: Garland Publishing, 2001), closely examines select communities. Lewis Perry, *Radical Abolitionism: Anarchy and the Government of God in Antislavery Thought* (Ithaca, N.Y.: Cornell University Press, 1973), 92–128, discusses the origin and development of the come-outer philosophy.

9. Strong, *Perfectionist Politics*, 221–222. This was not necessarily true in other Liberty areas.

10. "Line Upon Line," *Boston Free American*, April 8, 1841.

11. "Liberty Party Convention at Amherst," October 6, 1841, in *Boston Free American*, October 14, 1841.

12. Wright to Gerrit Smith, March 20, 1840, Smith Collection, Syracuse University.

13. Evans, "Abolitionism in the Illinois Churches," 221. While she notes that the situation in Illinois was simpler, she chronicles the religious varieties in the Liberty camp.

14. (Maine) *Liberty Standard*, November 16, 1842. Daniel Branch, who was the head of the Free Will Baptist Geauga Seminary of the Western Reserve Free Will Baptist Society, was a vocal Liberty supporter who served as president of the 1844 Chester (Geauga County, Ohio) Liberty convention.

15. Volpe, *Forlorn Hope of Freedom*, 122, reports that John Duffey, editor of the short-lived *Columbus Freeman*, was an exception, and that he felt anti-Catholic bigotry in the movement. Except for an occasional Irish workingman, nonetheless, there are few Catholics in the movement despite the mutual Liberty approval between the party and Irish patriot Daniel O'Connell. In fact, a Catholic's participation in a Liberty meeting was often noted in the minutes or report of the meeting.

16. Blue, *No Taint of Compromise*, 215.

17. Goodheart, *Elizur Wright*, is subtitled "*Abolitionist, Actuary, Atheist.*" Wright and Wright, *Elizur Wright*, chapter 16, "Religion: Calvinism to Atheism." Ronald G. Walters, *The Antislavery Appeal: American Abolitionism After 1830* (Baltimore: Johns Hopkins University Press, 1976), 45, notes "[i]n the 1840s and 1850s, Birney evolved into an antisectarian in one of the most interesting transformations undergone by an abolitionist." As can be seen in Appendix D in the present study, many Liberty followers changed their religious outlooks over time.

18. These could be dangerous for the performer. George W. Clark traveled widely and was subject to the same abuse as many Liberty lecturers, especially in the hostile areas of the Northwest. Danger was not limited to the rougher, rural areas. As late as 1847, the Hutchinsons were requested not to perform in Philadelphia because of the possibility of violence. See *Cincinnati Weekly Herald*, March 3, 1847; Gac, *Singing for Freedom*, 213.

19. Foster, "The Liberty Party," 32–34, Bentley Collections, University of Michigan.

20. Budney, *William Jay*, 83, says Jay "felt compelled to excoriate the come-outers." Strong *Perfectionist Politics*, only mentions Tappan once (206), and that is in a footnote. Contrast this to Friedman, *Gregarious Saints*, 88–94, which deals with the full scope of Tappan's work in the Liberty Party. On Lewis Tappan's views on churches, see Wyatt-Brown, *Lewis Tappan*, 321–322.

21. *Chicago Western Citizen*, November 24, 1846.

22. "Prospectus," *Boston Morning Chronicle*, March 22, 1844.

23. *Chicago Western Citizen*, July 26, 1842.

24. Hiram Cummings to Joshua Leavitt, December 8, 1841, in *Emancipator*, December 24, 1841.

25. Harmon Kingbury to Birney, March 1, 1842, in Dumond, *Letters of J. G. Birney*, 2:678.

26. Birney to Kingsbury, March 8, 1842, in ibid., 2:678–681.

27. Bretz, "The Economic Background of the Liberty Party," 250–264, traces but overemphasizes these.

28. For example, see future Liberty leader Seymour Boughton Treadwell's pre–Liberty Party *American Liberties and Slavery: Morally and Politically* (New York: Negro Universities Press, 1968 [originally published by John S. Taylor, 1838]), 307–311, on the disproportionate Southern influence in Congress because of the three-fifths clause. Leonard L. Richards, *The Slave Power: The Free North and Southern Domination, 1780–1860* (Baton Rouge: Louisiana State University Press, 2000),

2, claims that making "the Slave Power thesis popular . . . lay mainly with the Free Soil Party of the late 1840s and early 1850s and the Republican Party thereafter." He makes only oblique references to Liberty Party theorists and the many works discussed in the present study that were written before the advent of the Free Soil Party. David Brion Davis, *The Slave Power Conspiracy and the Paranoid Style* (Baton Rouge: Louisiana State University Press, 1969), 72, characterizes much of the literature as having "hard grains of truth connected with a mucilage of exaggeration and fantasy. But the central theme, which is so central to the paranoid style, is the conviction that an exclusive monolithic structure has imposed a purposeful pattern on otherwise unpredictable events." This is not the approach taken in the present study.

29. Richard Hildreth, *Despotism in America: An Inquiry into the Nature, Results and Legal Basis of the Slave-holding System in the United States* (Boston: John P. Jewett & Company, 1854, First Edition, 1840 [reprinted New York: Augustus M. Kelley, Publishers, 1970]). Donald E. Emerson, *Richard Hildreth* (Baltimore: Johns Hopkins University, 1946), 68.

30. Earle, *Jacksonian Antislavery*, 46. See the background of the speech and the speech in Morris, *Life of Thomas Morris*, 107–165.

31. Budney, *William Jay*, 44–51.

32. For instance, see James Appleton (Maine Liberty candidate), "Tract No. 3: The Missouri Compromise and the Extension of the Slave Power" (1843), and Rev. Edward Smith, "Principles, Objects and Measures of the Liberty Party," *The Documents*, vol. 1, no. 1 (Pittsburgh: n.p., March 1845). Both of these documents are in the Samuel J. May Anti-Slavery Collection, Cornell University.

33. *Emancipator*, October 22, 1840; *Boston Free American*, August 19, 1841; *Emancipator Extra*, September 21, 1843, Tract No. 3 in *The Influence of the Slave Power with Other Anti-Slavery Pamphlets* (New York: Negro Universities Press, 1970 [originally published in 1836–1848]).

34. *Boston Free American*, August 19, 1841.

35. "The Influence of the Slave Power," *Emancipator Extra*, September 21, 1843.

36. Harrold, *Gamaliel Bailey*, 29, discusses pre-Liberty origins of the pro-slavery conspiracy theories.

37. Alvan Stewart, "Tract No. 4: The Cause of the Hard Times [1843]," in *The Influence of the Slave Power and Other Anti-Slavery Pamphlets*.

38. Cleveland, "Address of the Liberty Party of Pennsylvania," in Chase and Cleveland, *Antislavery Addresses of 1844 and 1845*, 38.

39. William Birney, "Statistics of the Distribution of the Offices of the Federal Government," in *Chicago Western Citizen*, July 6, 1843.

40. *Boston Free American*, September 30, 1841.

41. *Letter of Gerrit Smith to the Liberty Party of New Hampshire*, March 18, 1848, Gerrit Smith Broadside and Pamphlet Collection, Syracuse University.

42. A. L. Bayley to the Workingmen of Essex, October 6, 1846, in the (N.H.) *Herald of Freedom*, October 23, 1846. For more on the speech and Bayley, see Voss-Hubbard, "Slavery, Capitalism and the Middling Sort," 68–69. See Edmund Quincy to Caroline Weston, September 16, 1844, Antislavery Collection, Boston Public Library, on a Liberty Party shoemaker answering Quincy's speech proposing the dissolution of the Union.

43. "Liberty Party Meeting at Albany City Hall," in (Albany, N.Y.) *Tocsin of Liberty*, November 10, 1842.

44. *Philanthropist*, October 7, 21, 1846. Niven, *The Salmon P. Chase Papers*, 1:181–182, says that Chase failed to get the endorsement. Elizur Wright often ran the names of both Liberty and Workingman's Party candidates (some of whom appeared on both ballots). See *Boston Daily Chro-*

notype; November 2, 1847. Johnson, "The Liberty Party in Massachusetts," 256, reports that workingmen's meetings often endorsed Liberty candidates. Magdol, *The Antislavery Rank and File,* 108–113; Laurie, *Beyond Garrison,* especially chapter 4, 125–152, "'To Favor the Poorest and Weakest': Libertyism and Labor Reform." Laurie's treatment (136–140) is especially good on Chauncy L. Knapp, a Liberty congressional candidate who received labor backing.

45. Lofton, "Abolition and Labor," 259. Ibid., 282, sees some success in these efforts.

46. *Boston Free American,* November 4, 1841, printed the Liberty Party slate for Boston with the candidates' professions. There was one clergyman, with the rest being mechanics and artisans. Voss-Hubbard, "Slavery, Capitalism and the Middling Sorts," 53–76.

47. *Emancipator,* June 9, 1847.

48. Johnson, "The Liberty Party in Massachusetts," 255–256; Magdol, "Antislavery Petitions," 48–51; Voss-Hubbard, "Slavery, Capitalism and the Middling Sorts," 56–58.

49. *Emancipator,* November 30, 1843.

50. Norman Ware, *The Industrial Worker, 1840–1860* (Boston: Houghton Mifflin, 1924 [reprint Chicago: Quadrangle Books, 1964]), 234–235; Bernard Mandel, *Labor Free and Slave: Workingmen and the Anti-Slavery Movement in the United States* (New York: Associated Authors, 1955), 138–140; Gerteis, *Morality and Utility in American Anti-Slavery Reform,* 76–79.

51. Sean Wilentz, *Chants Democratic: New York City and the Rise of the American Working Class, 1788–1850* (New York: Oxford University Press, 1984), 265. Paradoxically, Lewis Tappan ended up voting for Gerrit Smith and the workingman-friendly Liberty League in 1848.

52. Gerteis, *Morality and Utility in American Antislavery Reform,* 75–79.

53. "The Address of the Southern and Western Liberty Convention," in Chase and Cleveland, *Anti-Slavery Addresses of 1844 and 1845,* 115–116. Harrold, *Gamaliel Bailey,* 97, discusses appeals to workingmen.

54. For example, see the list of federal offices by William Birney and C. T. Torrey in *Signal of Liberty,* July 10, 1843; see also "Influence of the Slave Power," in *Signal of Liberty,* October 16, 1843.

55. Salmon P. Chase to Gerrit Smith, May 14, 1842, Smith Collection, Syracuse University.

56. William Birney to J. G. Birney, November 25, 1844, in Dumond, *Letters of J. G. Birney,* 2:887.

57. Harrold, "Southern Strategy of the Liberty Party," 21–36, believes that Ohio Liberty men "sought to expand the Liberty Party into the southern states." I believe that he overstates his case and perhaps this might only be applied to the Chase-Bailey faction of the party. Of course, Liberty men would welcome Southern support, but to tie a constitutional interpretation protecting slavery in the slave states and the establishment of a national newspaper at Washington, D.C., so closely to a southern strategy gives undue importance to Liberty rhetoric and the efforts of a few. Most Liberty pronouncements in the press and conventions were decidedly hostile to the South and Southern influence. While sympathetic to Southern antislavery, few direct efforts were made to expand the party into the South (with the noteworthy exception of some efforts in western Virginia for the 1844 election), and no Southerners were involved on the Liberty Party national central committee. Bailey's *National Era,* however, had agents in several southern states.

58. *Chicago Western Citizen,* June 30, 1846.

59. William Birney and Thomas Morris found this irritating. For examples, see Birney to J. G. Birney, February 28, 1843, in Dumond, *Letters of J. G. Birney,* 2:720–722, on Bailey's use of the elder Birney's material without attribution and on his selective editing of local news; and Birney to J. G. Birney, February 26, 1844, in ibid., 2:794–795, on the Morris unhappiness with Bailey. Nonetheless, his biographer, Harrold, *Gamaliel Bailey,* 140, praises "Bailey's willingness to tolerate views in conflict with his own."

60. Evans, "Abolitionism in the Illinois Churches," 40, states that "he suppressed information about the dissidents from third-party strategy when he published accounts of state anti-slavery conventions." This may be so, but I have not noticed it in my reading of the sources.

61. *Chicago Western Citizen,* October 9, 1845, in commenting on the failure of the *Boston Morning Chronicle,* discusses the *Emancipator* and its own difficulties in getting subscribers to pay.

62. *Signal of Liberty,* June 18, 1846, lists the newspapers from the Annual Report of the American and Foreign Anti-Slavery Society that listed all the antislavery newspapers in the country:

Maine:	(Bangor) *Bangor Gazette* (weekly)
	(Hallowell) *Liberty Standard* (weekly)
	(Hallowell) *Flag of Freedom* (monthly)
New Hampshire:	(Concord) *Granite Freeman* (weekly)
Vermont:	(Montpelier) *Green Mountain Freeman* (weekly)
Massachusetts:	(Boston) *Emancipator* (weekly)
	(Worcester) *Worcester County Gazette* (weekly)
	(Northampton) *Hampshire Herald* (weekly)
	(Taunton) *Beacon of Liberty* (weekly)
Connecticut:	(Hartford) *Charter Oak* (weekly)
New York:	(Honeoye) *Christian Investigator* (monthly)
	(New York) *Anti-Slavery Reporter* (monthly)
	(Albany) *Albany Patriot* (weekly)
	(Utica) *Liberty Press* (weekly)
	(Little Falls) *Herkimer Freeman* (weekly)
	(Cortland) *The True American* (weekly)
	(Syracuse) *The Liberty Intelligencer* (weekly)
	(Perry) *Impartial Countryman* (weekly)
New Jersey:	(Boonton) *New Jersey Freeman* (monthly)
Pennsylvania:	(Philadelphia) *American Citizen* (weekly)
	(Washington) *Washington Patriot* (weekly)
	(Mercer) *Mercer Luminary* (weekly)
	(Pittsburgh) *Spirit of Liberty* (weekly)
	(Indiana) *Clarion of Freedom* (weekly)
Ohio:	(Cincinnati) *Morning Herald* (daily)
	(Cincinnati) *Philanthropist* (weekly)
	(Cleveland) *Cleveland American* (weekly)
	(Cadiz) *Liberty Advocate* (weekly)
	(Warren) *Liberty Herald* (weekly)
	(Lisbon) *Aurora* (weekly)
Indiana:	(Indianapolis) *Indiana Freeman* (weekly)
	(New Garden) *Free Labor Advocate* (weekly)
Illinois:	(Chicago) *Western Citizen* (weekly)
	(Chicago) *Liberty Free Press* (monthly)
Michigan:	(Ann Arbor) *Signal of Liberty* (weekly)
Wisconsin:	(Prairieville) *American Freeman* (weekly)

Five New Organization and twelve other antislavery newspapers "incapable of classification" are also listed. See also *Liberty Standard,* May 21, 1846, on the report.

63. Schriver, "Black Politics Without Blacks," 197, discusses the difficulties of doing this in Maine.

64. Of course, these short-run newspapers are difficult to find. For an example of the poor quality, see (Concord, N.H.) *People's Advocate* (there are a few copies of it in the Library of Congress).

65. *New Jersey Freeman*, December 9, 1845.

66. Harrold, *Gamaliel Bailey*, chapter 7, "The National Era," 81–92, is an excellent summary of the founding of the *National Era* and the selection of Gamaliel Bailey as its editor.

67. The complete committee report is published in the *New Jersey Freeman*, November 28, 1846. The committee was made up of Charles V. Dyer, Zebina Eastman, Charles Durkee, J. J. Deming, and Guy Beckley. One can only wonder whatever happened to agents Hugh M. Nisbet (South Carolina) and John Caughey (Mississippi) in their communities.

68. Wyatt-Brown, *Lewis Tappan*, 278–279.

69. Harrold, *Gamaliel Bailey*, 90; *National Era*, February 24, 1848, announced that it was greatly reducing its exchange list because it contained one-third of all the newspapers in the Union.

70. Davis, *Joshua Leavitt*, 236.

71. The *National Era* even reprinted some of these concerns from various states and tried to alleviate them. See *National Era*, February 11, May 6, 1847.

72. Beriah Green to James G. Birney, August 2, 1847, in Dumond, *Letters of J. G. Birney*, 2:1078. Birney to L. P. Noble, September 13, 1847, in ibid., 2:1082–1083.

73. The Syracuse University Library Special Collections Research Center has collected many of these and made them available on the Internet through a Gilder-Lehrman grant and the New York State Library. See http://libwwww.syr.edu/.

74. Alvan Stewart to Liberty Party Abolitionists of the United States, October 1843, in *Signal of Liberty*, November 13, 1843. For details of the *Seventy-Six* project to publish and distribute tracts, see Willey, *The History of the Antislavery Cause*, 232, and (Maine) *Liberty Standard*, May 10, 1843.

75. Chase and Cleveland, *Anti-Slavery Addresses*, 11, 72.

76. Chase to Charles D. Cleveland, May 18, 1841, in Niven, *The Salmon P. Chase Papers*, 2:74–75.

77. Foster, "The Liberty Party," 31, Bentley Historical Collections, University of Michigan.

78. *Chicago Western Citizen*, November 20, 1845.

79. *New Jersey Freeman*, September 18, 1846, contains the prospectus for *Freibeits-Calender fur das Jabr 1847* that would be issued by C. L. Rademacher of Philadelphia and would include a forty-page "An Address to the Germans in the United States on the Abolition of Slavery" by "W.F. Carove, Doctor of Philosophy at Frankfurt." See *Chicago Western Citizen*, August 4, 1847.

80. (Wis.) *American Freeman*, August 4, 1846.

81. Elizur Wright to Beriah Greene, November 11, 1844, Antislavery Collection, Boston Public Library. He criticizes Charles W. Denison, who had been a member of the National Liberty Nominating Committee in 1841, and his nativist newspaper, *The American Signal*, in a strong editorial in the *Boston Daily Chronotype*, June 17, 1847. Richard Hildreth, a polymath and Liberty candidate, published a pamphlet, "Native Americanism, Detected and Exposed by a Native American," reprinted in Martha M. Pingel, *An American Utilitarian: Richard Hildreth as a Philosopher* (New York: Columbia University Press, 1948), 177–198, that attacks the early manifestations of the party in Massachusetts in 1845. A July 1844 Liberty convention in Rochester, New York, "*Resolved*, That we repudiate the proscriptive principles on which the 'Native American Party' is founded which excludes persons from the enjoyment of all our political privileges and rights, on account of the place of their nativity," in *Albany Weekly Patriot*, July 3, 1844. (Hartford, Conn.) *Christian Freeman*, December 12, 1848, reports on the anti-nativism resolution at the national Liberty convention in Al-

bany, December 4, 1844. *Albany Patriot*, December 18, 1844, comments on Gerrit Smith's strong speech against nativism at the same convention. Geary, *The History of Third Parties in Pennsylvania*, 115–116, discusses the hostility of Liberty men to nativism at a Liberty convention for eastern Pennsylvania on February 21, 1845. McCulloch, *Fearless Advocate of the Right*, 160–161, details Pennsylvania's gubernatorial candidate F. Julius LeMoyne's disdain for nativism. (Mich.) *Signal of Liberty*, March 23, 1846, editorial against the movement. In Wisconsin, the editor of the *American Freeman*, September 28, 1844, rejoiced that "with not a single exception, that we know of, the expression is decidedly against [nativism]." A few prominent exceptions were Thomas Spooner, Jane Grey Swisshelm, and Denison. Others, such as Chauncy L. Knapp and William Larimer, seem to have been more reluctant fellow travelers. There may have been more at the local level. See Henry B. Stanton to Gerrit Smith, November 23, 1844, Smith Collection, Syracuse University, where he expresses concern about nativism. He admits "[a]t their first meeting, a gentleman presided whom we run [sic] for Mayor two years ago, & for State Senator last fall. However, for a year past, he has been rather cool toward us." Gerrit Smith, "To the Liberty Party," May 7, 1846, Syracuse University Library, Special Collections Research Center, Gerrit Smith Broadside and Pamphlet Collection, wrote that "[e]very Liberty man sees also, that the patriotism, which would exclude foreigners from the ballot-box and from office, is a sentiment unworthy of every just and generous heart, and contrary to all teachings of this great principle of Liberty Party action." Foner, *Free Soil, Free Labor, Free Men*, 233, notes that "[t]hose who had participated in the Liberty and Free Soil parties had long believed that the nation should cordially welcome immigrants and had always opposed efforts to abridge their rights."

82. See Dumond, *A Bibliography of Antislavery in America*, 39, for the publication history of several editions.

83. Beriah Green, *Sketches of the Life and Writings of James Gillespie Birney* (Utica, N.Y.: Jackson & Chaplin, 1844).

84. *Albany Patriot*, March 9, 1843, details a model association that Alvan Stewart helped devise for Hartford, Connecticut. See also a model Liberty Association and Constitution in *Emancipator*, September 21, 1843, and *Chicago Western Citizen*, October 12, 1843. Voss-Hubbard, "Slavery, Capitalism and the Middling Sorts," 57, discusses the vibrant local Amesbury and Salisbury (Mass.) Liberty Association and its merger into a Free Soil organization.

85. "Maine Liberty Association Constitution," *Liberty Standard*, January 15, 1846; Willey, *The History of the Antislavery Cause*, 288–289.

86."Report of the Chairman of the State Central Committee," *Emancipator*, February 3, 1847.

87. Birney to the Liberty Party, October 15, 1844, in Dumond, *Letters of J. G. Birney*, 2:856. The Liberty Party was almost nonexistent in frontier areas similar to where Birney lived.

88. Alvan Stewart to J. G. Birney, April 14, 1842, in Dumond, *Letters of J. G. Birney*, 2:689.

89. Alvan Stewart to Liberty Party Abolitionists of the United States, October 1843, in *Signal of Liberty*, November 13, 1843.

90. *Cincinnati National Press and Weekly Herald*, June 23, 1847.

91. *Emancipator*, November 6, 1844.

92. *Chicago Western Citizen*, May 4, 1847.

93. Formisano, *The Birth of Mass Political Parties*, 74–76.

94. (Maine) *Liberty Standard*, April 16, 1846.

95. When he wrote *The History of the Antislavery Cause*, 192, Willey had complimentary things to say about Godfrey.

96. Johnson, "The Liberty Party in Massachusetts," 244–250.

97. Whittier to Elizur Wright, October 19, 1845, in Pickard, *J. G. Whittier as a Politician*, 36–37.

98. *Chicago Western Citizen*, December 7, 1847.

CHAPTER 9

1. Wesley, "Participation of Negroes in Anti-Slavery Political Parties," 33–74; James Oliver Horton and Lois E. Horton, *In Hope of Liberty: Culture, Community and Protest Among Free Northern Blacks, 1700–1860* (New York: Oxford University Press, 1997), 242–252; George E. Walker, *The Afro-American in New York City, 1827–1860* (New York: Garland Press, 1993), 136–140; Benjamin Quarles, *Black Abolitionists* (New York: Oxford University Press, 1969 [Da Capo paperback]), 183–188. Jane H. Pease and William H. Pease, *They Who Would Be Free: Blacks' Search for Freedom, 1830–1861* (Urbana and Chicago: University of Illinois Press, 1990 [originally published Atheneum press, 1974]), 195–200, acknowledge "[a]s the Liberty Party sought and won black endorsements, so too they made sure that Negroes played active roles in its organization" (196), but they examine the party only in New York and for national meetings.

2. Volpe, *Forlorn Hope of Freedom*, 2. The title of Schriver's "Black Politics Without Blacks" on Maine is indicative of how blacks have been neglected just because they did not have leadership roles in some states.

3. Shirley J. Yee, *Black Women Abolitionists: A Study in Activism, 1828–1860* (Knoxville: University of Tennessee Press, 1992), 128.

4. James Brewer Stewart, "Modernizing 'Difference': The Political Meanings of Color in the Free States, 1776–1840," *Journal of the Early Republic* 19 (Winter 1999): 710, goes beyond the chronological boundaries of his essay to conclude that "abolitionists also opened path-breaking ideological debates during the 1840s and 1850s that sustained the movement's vitality, deepened its radicalism, and documented its transformation into a recognizably modern enterprise." See also Howard H. Bell, "National Negro Conventions of the Middle 1840s: Moral Suasion vs. Political Action," *Journal of Negro History* 42 (October 1957): 247–260; Jane H. Pease and William H. Pease, "Black Power—The Debate 1840," *Phylon* 29 (Spring 1968): 19–26. For debates on this during the 1830s, see Tunde Adeleke, "Afro-Americans and Moral Suasion: The Debate in the 1830s," *Journal of Negro History* 83 (Spring 1998): 127–142.

5. Ripley et al., *The Black Abolitionist Papers*, 3:19, claims that "[b]y 1840 some 93 percent of northern blacks were completely or practically denied the franchise."

6. Wesley, "The Participation of Negroes in Anti-Slavery Political Parties," 36. This general apathy continued. Pease and Pease, *They Who Would Be Free*, 192, state that only one thousand of three thousand eligible black voters bothered to register in New York State in 1846, and they point out similar apathy in Pennsylvania and Massachusetts before 1838. James Oliver Horton and Lois E. Horton, *Black Bostonians: Family Life and Community Struggle in the Antebellum North* (New York: Holmes & Meier Publishers, 1979), 86, estimate that "about 50 percent of the eligible black voters [in Boston] paid their poll tax in preparation for the exercising of their right."

7. Wesley, "The Participation of Negroes in Antislavery Political Parties," 36; Leon F. Litwack, *North of Slavery: The Negro in the Free States, 1790–1860* (Chicago: University of Chicago Press, 1961), 74–93; Paul Finkelman, "Prelude to the Fourteenth Amendment: Black Legal Rights in the Antebellum North," *Rutgers Law Journal* 17 (Spring–Summer 1986): 416–482, is a careful state-by-state analysis of changing black voting rights before the Civil War. For New York, see Field, *The Politics of Race in New York*, for a book-length state study.

8. Ripley et al., *The Black Abolitionist Papers*, 3:44. The Whigs needed the black votes in the closely contested strife-ridden races of 1840s Rhode Island politics.

9. Wesley, "The Participation of Negroes in Anti-Slavery Political Parties," 57–58, discusses the situation and claims it continued into 1848 when African Americans "almost unanimously supported the Taylor ticket."

10. I have not found any evidence of black participation in these early debates and meetings, although Horton and Horton, *In Hope of Liberty,* 242, report that John T. Raymond, a black Albany minister, attended the April 1 convention. He may have been an observer, but Wright, *Myron Holley,* 258–265, does not show him participating in the proceedings.

11. Ripley et al., *Black Abolitionist Papers,* 3:7–8. Donald M. Jacobs, "William Lloyd Garrison's *Liberator* and Boston's Blacks, 1830–1860," *New England Quarterly* 44 (June 1971): 260–265.

12. On the loyalty from Boston blacks, see Horton and Horton, *Black Bostonians,* 87. Horton and Horton, "The Affirmation of Manhood: Black Garrisonians in Antebellum Boston," in Donald Jacobs, ed., *Courage and Conscience: Black and White Abolitionists in Boston* (Bloomington: Indiana University Press, 1993), 138–142, deals with both Boston and Philadelphia. On Philadelphia, see Winch, *Philadelphia's Black Elite,* 81–82. Stauffer, *The Black Hearts of Men,* 153–154, discusses Garrison's increasingly patronizing attitude toward African Americans.

13. McKivigan, *The War Against Proslavery Religion,* 78; Horton and Horton, *Black Bostonians,* 87. For the signers and constitution of the American and Foreign Anti-Slavery Society, see *Philanthropist,* June 16, 1840.

14. John W. Lewis to the Executive Committee of the New Hampshire Anti-Slavery Society, December 28, 1840, in Ripley et al., *Black Abolitionist Papers,* 3:352–353, resigned as agent of this Garrisonian society to maintain his neutrality between the two factions. James Oliver Horton, *Free People of Color: Inside the African American Community* (Washington, D.C.: Smithsonian Institution Press, 1993), 49–50, discusses Walker Lewis, a Boston and Lowell barber, who worked for the Liberty Party while remaining a committed Garrisonian.

15. On their work with the Garrisonians, see William S. McFeely, *Frederick Douglass* (New York: W. W. Norton & Company, 1991), 86–145; Miriam L. Usrey, "Charles Lenox Remond, Garrison's Ebony Echo: World Antislavery Convention, 1840," *Essex Institute Historical Collections* 106 (April 1970): 113–125; Farrison, *William Wells Brown,* 69–133. On some concerted efforts by the Garrisonians to counteract Liberty influence, see William E. Farrison, "William Wells Brown in Buffalo," *Journal of Negro History* 39 (October 1954): 305, on a series of anti-Liberty Party meetings in Buffalo, Rochester, and Syracuse in 1847. I am here referring to the original Liberty Party; the situation changed after the Free Soil merger in 1848 and the emergence of the Liberty League.

16. See this complaint from T. S. Wright (a black) to Joshua Leavitt, October 19, 1844, in *Emancipator,* October 30, 1844. One of these may have been multi-reformer Stephen Myers, editor of the (Albany, N.Y.) *Northern Star and Watchman,* who irritated both Liberty and Garrisonian supporters whose independent course included supporting Whigs. See William H. Pease and Jane H. Pease, *Bound with Them in Chains: A Biographical History of the American Antislavery Movement* (Westport, Conn.: Greenwood Press, 1972), 197; and Ripley et al., *Black Abolitionist Papers,* 3:378. Patrick T. J. Brown, "'To Defend Mr. Garrison': William Cooper Nell and the Personal Politics of Antislavery," *New England Quarterly* 70 (September 1997): 415–442.

17. Quarles, *Black Abolitionists,* 168, maintains that Garrison's theories were "maintained by only a handful of black leaders." A major theme of Adam Dewey Simmons, "Ideologies and Programs of the Negro Antislavery Movement, 1830–1861" (Ph.D. dissertation, Northwestern University, 1983), 165, is that "the black Garrisonians seemed to be less independent intellectually than any of the black abolitionists."

18. Winch, *Philadelphia's Black Elite,* 152–153. Part of the reason for this may also have been the unique relationship that existed between the African American community and the Pennsylvania Abolition Society. See Newman, *The Transformation of American Abolitionism,* 60–64 and passim.

19. Several commentators have noted this, often when dealing with other matters. Carol V. R.

George, "Widening the Circle: The Black Church and the Abolitionist Crusade," in Perry and Fellman, *Antislavery Reconsidered*, 81, sees "these prominent black abolitionists . . . can trace their tortuous paths through Garrisonianism and, for the most part, into the Liberty Party." Horton, *Free People of Color*, 90, comments that "New York's *Colored American* attempted to remain neutral, but many black New Yorkers sided with the political abolitionists." Winch, *Philadelphia's Black Elite*, 164, observes that "[t]he full extent of the denial of the Garrison position on politics became evident when William Whipper, possibly the most apolitical of all the Philadelphians endorsed the Liberty party." Stauffer, *The Black Hearts of Men*, 153, notes the claim of James McCune Smith, an influential black New York physician, in May 1848 that he was a "late convert" to political abolitionism. Schor, *Henry Highland Garnet*, 68, sees increasing black support in the Liberty Party as the decade progressed. Ripley et al., *Black Abolitionist Papers*, 3:468, observes that "New York black leaders were drawn to the Liberty Party." Horton and Horton, "Affirmation of Manhood," 142, conclude that early reluctance to join the Liberty Party was ending and "even Boston blacks were taking part in electoral politics by the mid-1840s." Howard H. Bell, "Expressions of Negro Militancy in the North; 1840–1860," *Journal of Negro History* 45 (January 1960): 11, says "many Negroes, by 1840, were moving slowly away from Garrisonian leadership. Many began associating with Liberty Party adherents and came shortly to advocate the viewpoint of that party as opposed to the moral."

20. Horton, *Free People of Color*, 91; Brown, "'To Defend Mr. Garrison,'" 434.

21. On the refusal to serve on the committee, see Garrison to Samuel E. Sewall, May 15, 1846, in Merrill, *The Letters of William Lloyd Garrison*, 3:338. On his opposition to the monument, see *Liberator*, July 10, August 7, 1846. See also Quarles, *Black Abolitionists*, 164–165. On Torrey, see Harrold, "On the Borders of Slavery and Race," 273–292. See Samuel Ringgold Ward to Frederick Douglass, March 1855, in C. Peter Ripley et al., *The Black Abolitionist Papers*, vol. 1, *The British Isles, 1830–1865* (Chapel Hill: University of North Carolina Press, 1985), 417–421, on Ward's longstanding criticisms of the Garrisonians.

22. Harrold, *Subversives*, 56–57, 63, discusses the declining influence of Garrison among blacks and the Garrisonian opposition to slave purchases by abolitionists. Laurie, *Beyond Garrison*, 78–79, discusses this with regard to George Latimer's purchase.

23. *American and Foreign Anti-Slavery Reporter*, July 1845; (Maine) *Liberty Standard*, May 22, 1845.

24. See "Freeman State Convention at Syracuse," August 5, 1840, in the *Friend of Man*, August 12, 1840.

25. *Chicago Western Citizen*, July 27, 1843.

26. *Emancipator*, August 31, 1843; William Wells Brown to editor, September 26, 1843, in *National Anti-Slavery Standard*, October 5, 1843, argues that Garnet was incorrect in an assertion that only Douglass and Remond opposed the resolution. Quarles, *Black Abolitionists*, 184, says the vote was about 50–7 at the national convention. Wesley, "The Participation of Negroes in Anti-Slavery Political Parties," 44–47; Schor, *Henry Highland Garnet*, 61.

27. Quarles, *Black Abolitionists*, 182, states that New York City had 250 eligible black voters in 1838; New York State 1,000 in 1844, a number that grew to 1,985 after Gerrit Smith gave land to black farmers so that they would qualify for the suffrage.

28. *Colored American*, August 29, 1840, reported that "[t]he third party as some call it, had in the Convention warm friends, and some of its ablest men; it also had some dissenters, and also some not opposed, but opposed to identifying the Convention with that measure."

29. Quarles, *Black Abolitionists*, 183.

30. *Colored American*, May 23, 1840; *Emancipator*, May 15, 1840; Quarles, *Black Abolitionists*,

183–184. The operators of the *Colored American* later differed on the correct political approach. See Horton, *Free People of Color,* 90.

31. (Maine) *Liberty Standard,* October 19, 1842; Willey, *The History of the Antislavery Cause,* 90.

32. Ripley et al., *Black Abolitionist Papers,* 1:118, 128. Pennington was also involved in convention work outside the state. See (Conn.) *Christian Freeman,* December 12, 19, 1844; *Albany Patriot,* December 18, 1844.

33. Bruser, "Political Anti-Slavery in Connecticut, 1844–1858," 68–74; Lex Renda, "The Polity and Party System," 1:132–135.

34. *Signal of Liberty,* April 28, 1841, October 24, 1842, February 20, 1843.

35. *Signal of Liberty,* September 1, 1841.

36. *Signal of Liberty,* July 31, 1843. Smith, *The Liberty and Free Soil Parties in the Northwest,* 58, discusses the political capital the Democrats made of this. Ronald P. Formisano, "The Edge of Caste: Colored Suffrage in Michigan, 1827–1861," *Michigan History* 61 (Spring 1972): 24, sketches the incident, but he incorrectly documents it by referring to *Signal of Liberty,* February 27, 1843. No issue was published that week because the paper was moving its offices. The newspaper does not mention the incident until it answered the party's critics in *Signal of Liberty,* July 31, 1843.

37. David M. Katzman, *Before the Ghetto: Black Detroit in the Nineteenth Century* (Urbana: University of Illinois Press, 1973; Illini Books edition, 1975), 33.

38. Formisano, "The Edge of Caste," 27–28.

39. Katzman, *Before the Ghetto,* 33–38; Ripley et al., *Black Abolitionist Papers,* 3:397; Siebert, *The Underground Railroad,* 70.

40. Winch, *Philadelphia's Black Elite,* 125–126, 152.

41. (Conn.) *Christian Freeman,* September 5, 1844, reported that L. [Lewis] Woodson, "an eloquent colored man," addressed the Mass Liberty Party Meeting at Pittsburgh on August 21–22, which was the largest antislavery meeting held in the city.

42. McCulloch, *Fearless Advocate of the Right,* 139, on black participation in Liberty affairs; ibid., 261, for Daniel Arnett et al. to F. J. LeMoyne, October 23, 1843, requesting that LeMoyne speak at a black convention in Canonsburg, Pennsylvania.

43. "Convention of the Colored Inhabitants of the State of New York, August 18–20, 1840," in Philip S. Foner and George E. Walker, eds., *Proceedings of the Black State Conventions, 1840–1865* (Philadelphia: Temple University Press), 23.

44. McManus, *Political Abolitionism in Wisconsin,* 24–25, points out that Liberty men originally were going to cooperate, but later changed their minds. On Illinois, see *Chicago Western Citizen,* April 5, 1847, for list of Liberty candidates to the Constitutional Convention; *Chicago Western Citizen,* April 19, 1847, that a Liberty candidate was elected in Kane County with Whig votes and *Chicago Western Citizen,* May 4, 1847, that Democrats and Whigs united to defeat a Liberty candidate; *Albany Patriot,* May 26, 1847, reports "several" Liberty delegates won in Illinois.

45. A very good account of the black and abolitionist efforts in Rhode Island is in Frederick Douglass, *The Life and Times of Frederick Douglass* (1893 edition) in Frederick Douglass, *Autobiographies* (New York: Library of America, 1994), 665–668. Garrisonians Douglass, James Monroe, Abbey Kelley, and Stephen Foster worked in the campaign and the Rhode Island Anti-Slavery Society hired Douglass as an agent. See also Litwack, *North of Slavery,* 79–80; George M. Dennison, *The Dorr War: Republicanism on Trial, 1831–1861* (Lexington: University of Kentucky Press, 1976), 220, reports that the constitution passed by a 3–1 margin and four thousand blacks were enfranchised. For a summary of the Dorr struggle, see Chilton Williamson, *American Suffrage from Property to Democracy, 1760–1860* (Princeton, N.J.: Princeton University Press, 1960), 242–259. J. Stanley

Lemons and Michael A. McKenna, "Re-enfranchisement of Rhode Island Negroes," *Rhode Island History* 30 (Winter 1971): 3–13.

46. See *Albany Weekly Patriot*, July 13, 1843, on how the colored population of Albany "have on all occasions manifested the most unwavering confidence in the Liberty Party, and gave it their hearty support."

47. "Minutes of the Fifth Annual Convention of the Colored Citizens of the State of New York, Schenectady, September 18–20, 1844," in Foner and Walker, *Proceedings of the Black State Conventions*, 1:34. After he was called to order, Garnet retracted the word *cunning*.

48. Ransom F. Wake, John Peterson, Alexander Crummell, Henry Williams, Daniel Elston, George Montgomery, Benjamin Stanly, and John J. Zuille to Gerrit Smith, June 13, 1845, in Ripley et al., *Black Abolitionist Papers*, 3:469. There was also great sentiment for this among other Liberty supporters, see *Albany Patriot*, January 28, February 4, 1846; Harlow, *Gerrit Smith*, 174–176.

49. Gerrit Smith to the Colored Citizens of Albany, March 13, 1846, in *Albany Patriot*, April 1, 1846. For maneuvering among the political parties, see Field, *The Politics of Race in New York*, 46–51; for an overall view of the issue, see Stanley, "Majority Tyranny in Tocqueville's America," 412–435.

50. Sewell, *Ballots for Freedom*, 98; *Albany Patriot*, January 26, 1846, reports that the (Utica, N.Y.) Liberty Press says: "We can vote for a Whig or Democrat of *common honesty*, who is pledged to the enfranchisement of the colored man."

51. *Albany Patriot*, February 4, 1846.

52. Smith to Dr. E. S. Bailey, April 27, 1846, Smith Papers, Syracuse University, complained that Liberty men voting for Whigs and Democrats for convention seats "had ruined the Liberty Party in this county."

53. Smith to Salmon P. Chase, September 9, 1846, Smith Collection, Syracuse University; Walker, *The Afro-American in New York City*, 140, sees black support for the party waning after 1844 "attributable in part to internal dissensions." I have not seen evidence of this in my research. Unless they considered the Whigs a viable alternative (and I have found few that did), they had nowhere else to go if they wished to remain politically active. My impression is that they were becoming more involved in Liberty Party affairs.

54. Wesley, "The Participation of Negroes in Anti-Slavery Political Parties," 52–58.

55. This could sometimes cause problems for the impoverished Liberty Party. The (Montpelier, Vt.) *Green Mountain Freeman*, February 25, 1847, chided party members in Washington County because they had not paid Lewis Clarke for his labors and were doing little to collect the money.

56. Lucius Matlack, ed., *Narrative of the Life and Adventures of Henry Bibb, An American Slave, Written by Himself* (New York: By the Author, 1849), in *Slave Narratives* (New York: Library of America, 2000), 546–547.

57. See *Chicago Western Citizen*, February 13, 1844, on the a free black lecturer, William Jones, whom Ichabod Codding accompanied on a Liberty campaign tour after he had been robbed and kidnapped in Chicago.

58. Stauffer, *The Black Hearts of Men*, 155, incorrectly identifies Lewis and Milton Clarke as Garrisonians. They were Liberty supporters who lectured often for the party.

59. (Wis.) *American Freeman*, June 23, 1847; *Emancipator*, November 12, 1845. Joshua Leavitt to the editor of the *Anti-Slavery Reporter*, April 1, 1843, in Abel and Klingberg, *A Side-Light on Anglo-American Relations*, 130, reported George Latimer lecturing in Massachusetts, Lewis Clarke in Maine, and Milton Clarke in New York. *Emancipator*, November 12, 1845, reported that George Latimer was still working for the Liberty Party in Chelsea. Laurie, *Beyond Garrison*, 78–80.

60. Horton and Horton, *In Hope of Liberty*, 242. On his Liberty Party campaigning, also see

Charles H. Wesley, "The Negroes of New York in the Emancipation Movement," *Journal of Negro History* 24 (January 1939): 96.

61. See especially, Schor, *Henry Highland Garnet*, 28–87. The speech can be found in Ripley et al., *Black Abolitionist Papers*, 3:403–411. Garnet was a very impressive person. Shortly before his death in 1882, Garnet met Arthur Conan Doyle, who was so impressed by him that he inspired three of his stories, including two Sherlock Holmes mysteries. See Christopher Roden, "Introduction," in *The Memoirs of Sherlock Holmes* (New York: Oxford University Press, 1993), xxii.

62. *Liberator*, December 8, 1843; Garnet to Maria Weston Chapman, November 17, 1843, in *Journal of Negro History* 10 (July 1925): 378–379.

63. Douglass, *The Life and Times of Frederick Douglass* (1893 edition) in Douglass, *Autobiographies*, 721.

64. *Dictionary of American Biography* (New York: Scribner, 1943), 19:440. On the convention, see "Freeman State Convention at Syracuse," August 5, 1840, in *Utica Friend of Man*, August 12, 1840.

65. Samuel Ringgold Ward, *Autobiography of a Fugitive Negro* (Eugene, Ore.: Wipfe and Stock Publishers, 2000 [reprint of London, England; John Snow, 1855]), 74–76.

66. "State Liberty Party Convention at Hallowell [Maine]," February 1, 1848, in (Maine) *Liberty Standard*, February 10, 1848.

67. Larry Gara, "The Professional Fugitive in the Abolition Movement," *Wisconsin Magazine of History* 26 (Spring 1965): 196–204, discusses the development, pitfalls, and benefits of this strategy.

68. Bibb to Birney, February 25, 1845, in Dumond, *Letters of J. G. Birney*, 2:928.

69. See the official Liberty exoneration of Bibb in "Report of the Undersigned, Committee Appointed by the Detroit Liberty Association to Investigate the Truth of the Narrative of Henry Bibb, a Fugitive from Slavery," in Matlack, *Narrative of the Life and Adventures of Henry Bibb, An American Slave*, 429 for the quote, 428–437 for the document.

70. *Chicago Western Citizen*, February 23, 1847.

71. Henry Johnson to Austin Willey, August 31, 1843, in (Maine) *Liberty Standard*, September 14, 1843; reprinted in Ripley et al., *Black Abolitionist Papers*, 3:413–414.

72. Laurie, *Beyond Garrison*, 115–116, 121–124, discusses transportation and civil rights in Massachusetts.

73. Nina Moore Tiffany, *Samuel E. Sewall: A Memoir* (Boston and New York: Houghton, Mifflin and Company, 1898), 69–70. On the Latimer case in general and Sewall's role in particular, see William M. Wiecek, "Latimer: Lawyers, Abolitionists, and the Problem of Unjust Laws," in Perry and Fellman, *Antislavery Reconsidered*, 226–234. Laurie, *Beyond Garrison*, 78–79, discusses the rivalry between Liberty efforts and more futile Garrisonian strategies over how to deal with the Latimer issue.

74. Jones, *Mutiny on the Amistad*, passim.

75. Gerteis, "Antislavery Agitation in Wisconsin," 116; *Obituary Record of Graduates of Yale University*.

76. Gerald Sorin, *The New York Abolitionists: A Case Study of Political Radicalism* (Westport, Conn.: Greenwood Publishing Corporation, 1971), 114.

77. "Address to the Electors of Illinois," in *Chicago Western Citizen*, July 26, 1842. On the ongoing struggle over black laws during the Liberty years, see Harris, *The History of Negro Servitude in Illinois*, 233–236.

78. *Chicago Western Citizen*, March 14, 1848.

79. *Signal of Liberty*, February 20, 1843.

80. *Signal of Liberty*, July 17, 1843.

81. Kephart, "A Voice for Freedom," 220, states that the first petition in the newspaper appeared on December 15, 1841. Another sample petition can be found in *Michigan Signal of Liberty*, December 9, 1844. They appeared irregularly.

82. Volpe, *Forlorn Hope of Freedom*, 104, says that in fighting the black codes the "[m]ost advanced were Michigan Liberty advocates."

83. McManus, *Political Abolitionism in Wisconsin*, 35.

84. Volpe, *Forlorn Hope of Freedom*, 104. This statement is perhaps accurate only when applied to some of the Cincinnati leadership. Also see Erickson, "Politics and Repeal of Ohio's Black Laws," 156–157.

85. For an example outside the Western Reserve, see the Franklin and Madison Counties Liberty Party Convention, in *Philanthropist*, August 19, 1846. There was an increase in material on the Black Laws during the summer and fall of 1846 in the *Philanthropist*.

86. William Cheek and Aimee Lee Cheek, *John Mercer Langston and the Fight for Black Freedom, 1829–1865* (Urbana: University of Illinois Press, 1989), 45, 145.

87. Blue, *Salmon P. Chase*, 39; Niven, *Salmon P. Chase*, 85–86.

88. Niven, *Salmon P. Chase*, 83–85; Fladeland, *James Gillespie Birney*, 154. In one of these cases, they persuaded an unfriendly judge that slavery was an artificial, local condition that inflicted a moral wrong on the victim. See Paul Finkleman, *An Imperative Union: Slavery, Federalism, and Comity* (Chapel Hill: University of North Carolina Press, 1981), 109–172; William E. Baringer, "The Politics of Abolition: Salmon P. Chase in Cincinnati," *Cincinnati Historical Society Bulletin* 29 (Summer 1971): 79–99.

89. Morris, *The Life of Thomas Morris*, 339–340.

90. Blue, *No Taint of Compromise*, 66–68. Website of the William Still Underground RR Foundation Inc. (http://www.undergroundrr.com/abol.html).

91. *Chicago Western Citizen*, January 25, 1848. For the May convention, see the *National Era*, July 13, 1848. Barnes, "Anti-Slavery Politics in Iowa," 62, underestimates the degree of Liberty sentiment in favor of black rights. More accurate is Dykstra, *Bright Radical Star*, 72–77.

92. Gamaliel Bailey to James G. Birney, March 31, 1843, in Dumond, *Letters of J. G. Birney*, 2:276; and Birney to Bailey, April 16, 1843, in ibid., 2:732. On this problem among abolitionists in general, see Leon F. Litwack, "The Abolitionist Dilemma: The Antislavery Movement and the Northern Negro," *New England Quarterly* 34 (March 1961): 50–73; William H. Pease and Jane H. Pease, "Antislavery Ambivalence: Immediatism, Expediency, Race," *American Quarterly* 17 (Winter 1965): 682–695, and their "Ends, Means, and Attitudes: Black-White Conflict in the Antislavery Movement," *Civil War History* 18 (June 1972): 117–128.

93. Wyatt-Brown, *Lewis Tappan and the Evangelical War Against Slavery*, 180.

94. Budney, *William Jay*, 40.

95. Henry B. Stanton, *Debates at Lane Seminary* (Boston: Garrison and Knapp, 1834), 7.

96. Birney to William Wright, June 20, 1845, in Dumond, *Letters of J. G. Birney*, 2:945–947.

97. *National Era*, June 3, 1847.

98. *National Era*, July 22, 1847.

99. Josiah Bushnell Grinnell, *Men and Events of Forty Years: Autobiographical Reminiscences* (Boston: D. Lothrop Company, 1891), 30. Grinnell was the person to whom Horace Greeley said, "Go West, young man, go West."

100. Green to Amos Phelps, July 21, 1840, as quoted in Sernett, *Abolition's Axe*, 51.

101. Sernett, *Abolition's Axe*, 51.

102. Muelder, *Fighters for Freedom*, 59.

103. Fletcher, *A History of Oberlin*, 2:266. Ironically, Sallie Holley, daughter of Liberty Party founder Myron Holley, was converted to Garrisonian abolition while at Oberlin.

104. Fletcher, *A History of Oberlin College*, 2:387, reports that on independent nominations "all three spoke for it." Louis Filler, *Crusade Against Slavery: Friends, Foes and Reforms, 1820–1860* (Algonac, Mich.: Reference Publications, Inc., 1986) 187, on the other hand, reports that Myron Holley's move for independent nominations was "opposed by Mahan of Oberlin, who favored moral action." Holley's motion for independent nominations was tabled.

105. Volpe, *Forlorn Hope of Freedom*, 61.

106. Cheek and Cheek, *John Mercer Langston*, 91.

107. Pease and Pease, *They Who Would Be Free*, 104, maintain that among blacks "[t]he issue generated neither any commonly accepted solutions nor even very much clear-cut debate."

108. *Philanthropist*, September 22, 1841. Laurie, *Beyond Garrison*, 11, 109–113, argues unconvincingly that a deal between Liberty men and Democrats was responsible for the repeal of Massachusetts miscegenation laws.

109. Marsh, *Writings and Speeches of Alvan Stewart on Slavery*, 30.

110. Siebert, *The Underground Railroad*, is still the most accurate and comprehensive treatment, although his county-by-county list of operators omits many blacks. He indicates, however, the black operators that he has found and discusses many of them.

111. On African American control of the Underground Railroad in Cincinnati, see Fladeland, *James G. Birney*, 151. Many persons in Appendix D have been identified as major agents on the Underground Railroad.

112. *Chicago Western Citizen*, June 1, 1843.

113. Pease, *The Frontier State*, 380.

114. *Chicago Western Citizen*, July 13, 1844.

115. Pease, *The Frontier State*, 379–380; Magdol, *Owen Lovejoy*, 40–44.

116. Constitution of the Female Anti-Slavery Society of Princeton, Bureau County, Illinois, in *Chicago Western Citizen*, November 9, 1843. Elizabeth Lovejoy to Zebina Eastman, January 14, 1845, in *Chicago Western Citizen*, January 30, 1845, notes how the Bureau County Female Anti-Slavery Society has declined since "the Underground Railroad has taken a different trunk, and runs on the other side of the river."

117. James MacKay, *Allan Pinkerton, The Eye Who Never Slept* (Edinburgh, Scotland: Mainstream Publishing, 1996), 60–65, 81–85. Pinkerton's activities upset some of his fellow citizens in Kane County. See his defense of his character in Allan Pinkerton to the *Chicago Western Citizen*, August 9, 1847, in *Chicago Western Citizen*, August 22, 1847.

118. Hagedorn, *Beyond the River*, the story of Rankin and the Ripley abolitionists, discusses their Liberty Party activities. Speer, "Autobiography of Adam Lowry Rankin," 42.

119. Charles E. Barnes, "Battle Creek as a Station on the Underground Railway," *Michigan Pioneer and Historical Collection* 38 (1912): 281. For more details, see Tuchalski, "Erastus Hussey," 1–18.

120. Barnes, "Battle Creek as a Station on the Underground Railway," 280–284. This figure is consistent with that given by the wife of another agent, Dr. Nathan Thomas of Schoolcraft, on the same line. See Alexis A. Praus, "The Underground Railroad at Schoolcraft," *Michigan History* 37 (June 1953): 177–182, which contains Pamela S. (Mrs. Nathan) Thomas, "A Station on the Underground Railroad" (written in 1892), 182, which states "[i]t has been estimated that during the twenty years that our house was a station, between one thousand and fifteen hundred received our aid."

121. Barnes, "Battle Creek as a Station on the Underground Railway," 282.

122. Strother, *The Underground Railroad in Connecticut*, 144.

123. McCulloch, *Fearless Advocate of the Right*, 159.

124. Charles L. Blockson, *Hippocrene Guide to the Underground Railroad* (New York: Hippocrene Books, 1994), 213.

125. Wilbert H. Siebert, "The Underground Railroad in Michigan," *Detroit Historical Monthly* 1 (March 1923): 14, reports that after the Fugitive Slave Law of 1850, "84 members disappeared forthwith from the African Baptist Church of Detroit."

126. Fladeland, *James Gillespie Birney*, 151, reports that "[u]sually the fugitives were taken care of by the colored people, " only informing Birney "of the escape only when it was safely accomplished."

127. R. J. M. Blackett, "Freedom, or the Martyr's Grave: Black Pittsburgh's Aid to the Fugitive Slave," *Western Pennsylvania Historical Magazine* 61 (April 1978): 117–134.

128. Strother, *The Underground Railroad in Connecticut*, 145–148 for Pennington, 153–154 for Jehiel C. Beman, and 111–112, 119–120 for Amos Gerry Beman.

129. As quoted in Nat Brandt, *The Town that Started the Civil War* (New York: Dell Publishing, a Laurel Book, 1991[reprinted from Syracuse University Press, 1990]), 45.

130. Siebert, *Underground Railroad*, 97.

131. Fletcher, *A History of Oberlin College*, 396–397. Siebert, *Underground Railroad*, 97, says " [s]o notorious did the place become that a guide-board in the form of a fugitive running in the direction of the town was set up . . . and the sign of a tavern . . . 'was ornamented on its Oberlin face with a representation of a fugitive slave pursued by a tiger.'"

132. Siebert, *Underground Railroad*, 97.

133. Muelder, *Fighters for Freedom*, 191.

134. Jeffrey, *The Great Silent Army of Abolitionism*, 268, states that so often the man in "underground railroad couples was active in abolition politics." Siebert, *The Underground Railroad*, 100, after reviewing his "mass of correspondence," concludes that "[a]t that time [1840], and again in 1844, many underground operators voted for the candidates of the Liberty party, and subsequently for the Free Soil nominee." I strongly disagree with the position enunciated by Larry Gara, *The Liberty Line: The Legend of the Underground Railroad* (Lexington: University of Kentucky Press, 1961), 18, that the "relatively few slaves who did escape were primarily dependent on their own resources. The Abolitionists play a less important part." I believe that he greatly underestimates white involvement and the level of organization in the 1840s, and these only grew in the 1850s. Filler, *Crusade Against Slavery*, 341, criticizes James Brewer Stewart's position that "Gara documents the blacks' self-sufficiency in aiding fugitive slaves." Filler, who sarcastically characterizes these historians as "anti-abolitionist," responds "Self Sufficiency; so much for [Wilbur] Siebert's 40 years of study in the field, William Still's labors, and the library of fugitive slave cases and publications." The errors in the Gara position continue to be documented by the recent surge in research on the Underground Railroad. Tuchalski, "Erastus Hussey," 6, believes that "the Underground Railway was more than a hit-or-miss operation." Harrold, "On the Borders of Slavery and Race," 287–288, remarks that when white Liberty man Charles T. Torrey crossed into the South, he "embarked on an antislavery strategy that was explicitly biracial" and there was "an extensive biracial support network stretching from Virginia to Pennsylvania." See also Barnes, "Battle Creek as a Station on the Underground Railway," 280, on Erastus Hussey's close relationship with Samuel Strauther, a black Battle Creek businessman. No one should question the black commitment to the Underground Railroad, but it would have been impossible for escaping blacks to move North without an extensive white network, especially through areas where there were few or no African Americans.

CHAPTER 10

1. The only lists that I have found are one for some voters in Boston in *Emancipator*, October 27, 1847, and a few lists—graciously brought to my attention by Marshall Blake of the Syracuse University Archives—of Liberty voters for Gerrit Smith's area in the Smith Collection at Syracuse University. Later Alan M. Kraut used these lists in his essay "The Forgotten Reformers," 119–148, but the sample is so small and Smith's influence and resources in this area so great that it is not methodologically sound to apply these lists to the larger Liberty universe.

2. Hammond, *Political History of the State of New York*, 3:479.

3. Cleveland, "Address of the Liberty Party of Pennsylvania," 62.

4. For a discussion of the illegitimacy, see Charles Jellison, *Fessenden of Maine: Civil War Senator* (Syracuse, N.Y.: Syracuse University Press, 1962), 3–5.

5. Davis, *Joshua Leavitt*, 236.

6. Goodheartt, *Abolitionist, Actuary, Atheist*, 143–145; Wright and Wright, *Elizur Wright*, chapter 13, "The Father of Life Insurance," 220–239.

7. Elisabeth Griffith, *In Her Own Right: The Life of Elizabeth Cady Stanton* (New York: Oxford University Press, 1984), 42, 48–49.

8. Mathews, *Autobiography*, 81.

9. (Conn.) *Christian Freeman*, November 13, 1845.

10. Voss-Hubbard, "Slavery, Capitalism and the Middling Sorts," passim; Laurie, *Beyond Garrison*, 61–62.

11. Internet resources and the work of state and local historians have made it easier to trace many individuals who seem to have dropped out of sight. During the years I have been working on this project, I have come across local Liberty leaders who just disappeared. Trying to trace them can be maddening. What happened to them? Many of them simply relocated and became important citizens in their new areas, invariably taking their antislavery beliefs with them. As state and local web sites proliferate and search engines become more effective, historians will be able find more about them, but I have no doubt that new links will aid us in developing a more accurate picture of the Liberty leadership and membership. Indeed, Appendix D at the end of this study and other lists that I have been compiling are constantly expanding as I collect more information. Many of these people were less likely to have accumulated and saved collections of personal records as they moved. We know little of them except what is in the public record. This does not diminish the impact or influence that they had. Contrast them with Garrison, Gerrit Smith, Salmon P. Chase, and James G. Birney, who either moved little or were able to keep their records. Sometimes a person's reputation does not survive because his personal papers do not.

12. Again, I encourage the reader to consult Appendix D at the end of the study when curious about the life of someone who is mentioned in the main body of the text.

13. Only voters in Massachusetts, New York, and Michigan (of the states in which there was a Liberty presence) voted in state and national elections at the same time.

14. *Emancipator*, November 16, 1843. The votes for governor are computed from town returns, Massachusetts Archives, Boston. Numerical results of races for local offices are difficult to find, especially on a statewide basis. One can verify party affiliation by noting how many votes the Liberty candidate for speaker would receive in lower houses of state legislatures.

15. Johnson, "The Liberty Party in New England," tracks the township vote for over 1,100 towns in Massachusetts, Maine, Vermont, and New Hampshire for the annual gubernatorial elections and the presidential races. The Liberty Party rarely approached 50% of the vote.

16. Charles Durkee was elected to a seat in the Wisconsin Territorial Legislature.

17. I. Washburn to *Boston Free American*, November 11, 1841, in *Boston Free American*, November 25, 1841, describes the tactic.

18. On the situation in Georgetown, Massachusetts, perhaps the strongest Liberty town in the state, see *Emancipator*, December 1, 1842; on Wisconsin, see McManus, *Political Abolitionism in Wisconsin*, 11. On Indiana, see Volpe, *Forlorn Hope of Freedom*, 100–101.

19. For the Old Northwest, see Smith, *The Liberty and Free Soil Parties in the Northwest*, 111. There were exceptions, however. See the *Emancipator*, August 24, 1844, for a situation in Indiana; and the *Philanthropist*, November 8, 1843, for one in Ohio.

20. Gerald Sorin, *Abolitionism: A New Perspective* (New York: Praeger, 1972), 134. For some of the studies, see Benson, *Concept of Jacksonian Democracy*, 213; Formisano, *Birth of Mass Political Parties*, 74; Smith, *The Liberty and Free Soil Parties in the Northwest*, 39. Using county data and multivariate analysis, Ray M. Shortridge, "Voting for Minor Parties in the Antebellum Midwest," *Indiana Magazine of History* 74 (March 1978): 126, suggests for the Midwest "that in 1844 the Liberty party drew some support from 1840 Democratic voters and significant support from 1840 Whig voters and 1840 non-voters." Darling, *Political Changes in Massachusetts*, 290–291, does an intensive town-level analysis for the gubernatorial election of 1842 and concludes that the Liberty support overwhelmingly had a Whig base.

21. Johnson, "The Liberty Party in New England," 127–157 for Massachusetts, 228–257 for Vermont, 322–347 for New Hampshire, 395–419 for Maine. Elementary linkage analysis, inter-election correlation coefficients, scatterplots, and banner town lists are used in these analyses, along with town maps of the states. The data sets aggregate the data at the town level for over 1,100 New England towns.

22. Kraut, "The Liberty Men of New York," 141, insists that the Liberty Party remained Whig based even though "its electoral support continued to dwindle in areas where it had received the support of abolitionists in the early 1840s." Some of his data and inter-election correlation tables lead me to believe that more of a change was taking place toward a greater Democratic base. Kraut's "The Forgotten Reformers: A Profile of Third Party Abolitionists in New York State," in Perry and Fellman, *Antislavery Reconsidered*, 127, presents a chart for Smithfield, New York, that shows substantial former Democratic support going to the Liberty Party, although the process began in 1843.

23. Renda, "Retrospective Voting and the Election of 1844," 845, 853.

24. Renda, The Polity and the Party System," vol. 1, part 1, table 2.9, 213; and Renda, *Running on the Record*, 24.

25. Harrold, *Gamaliel Bailey*, 62. Maizlish, *Triumph of Sectionalism*, 33–34, notes the contemporary awareness of the movement back to the Whig Party of some former Liberty voters while Liberty men with Democratic antecedents remained faithful to the third party.

26. Some preliminary work that I have done on Michigan seems to show that it was not as pronounced as in the upper New England states.

27. Even before the 1844 election some Democrats were protesting their party's course. Nineteen Democrats in Chelsea, Massachusetts, called for an October 24, 1844, meeting that expressed strong disapproval of their party's course; see *Emancipator*, November 6, 1844. *Emancipator*, November 13, 1844, reports an increase in the Chelsea Liberty vote from 47 to 92 in a single year. Volpe, *Forlorn Hope of Freedom*, 167, states "that an unusually large proportion of [Liberty] party support in 1840 came from antislavery Democrats" in Ohio, but he does not say whether he believed this continued. Earle, *Jacksonian Antislavery*, 65–66.

28. See Joel H. Silbey, *Shrine of Party Congressional Voting Behavior, 1841–1852* (Pittsburgh: University of Pittsburgh Press, 1967), for roll call analysis of congressional behavior on slavery issues.

29. For examples, see *Chicago Western Citizen*, July 11, 1844, and *Emancipator*, December 31,

1845. These continued after Leavitt left his editorial chair at the *Emancipator*. See *Emancipator*, December 1, 1847.

30. Chase, "Address of the Southern and Western Convention," in Chase and Cleveland, *Anti-Slavery Addresses*, 104, 123–124; Pfau, *The Political Style of Conspiracy*, 58.

31. "A Talk with Honest Democrats," in *Green Mountain Freeman*, February 13, 1846.

32. Fessenden to John Keep, in *Liberty Standard*, January 21, 1847.

33. *New York Express*, as reprinted in the *Boston Morning Chronicle*, August 23, 1844.

34. See township maps of Massachusetts, New Hampshire, Maine, and Vermont in Johnson, "Liberty Party in New England," 167, 348, 422, 254, or in the state articles "The Liberty Party in New Hampshire," 157; "The Liberty Party in Vermont," 266; "The Liberty Party in Maine," 168.

35. And neither of the votes was from Birney himself. See, Birney to Moses Pierce, August 4, 1848, in Dumond, *Letters of J. G. Birney*, 2:1110, where he admits to not voting because he was detained at home until the day after the election. Birney probably was the only man nominated for the presidency twice that never voted for himself. He was at the World Anti-Slavery Convention in London in 1840.

36. Jeffrey, *The Great Silent Army of Abolitionism* is a notable exception. She presents a thoughtful and insightful survey of the many activities of less well-known women. Michael D. Pierson, *Free Hearts and Free Homes: Gender and American Antislavery Politics* (Chapel Hill: University of North Carolina Press, 2003), 17, acknowledges that "[a]ntislavery women supported the Liberty Party," but his chapter 1, "Liberty Party Gender Ideologies," 25–46, is a forced attempt to analyze the gender ramifications of Liberty Party politics with a selective use of atypical sources.

37. Chris Dixon, *Perfecting the Family: Anti-Slavery Marriages in Nineteenth Century America* (Amherst: University of Massachusetts Press, 1997), 190–191.

38. Martha V. Ball to Elizabeth Pease, May 6, 1840, Antislavery Collection, Boston Public Library. See also (Maine) *Advocate of Freedom*, June 18, 1840. *National Anti-Slavery Standard*, October 29, 1840, contains the "Seventh Report of the Boston Female Anti-Slavery Society." *Massachusetts Abolitionist*, June 4, 1840. Debra Gold Hansen, *Strained Sisterhood: Gender and Class in the Boston Female Anti-Slavery Society* (Amherst: University of Massachusetts Press, 1993), 27–28, cites only a *Liberator* Extra in her account of the meeting, in which she sees conspiratorial designs. Her main contention that "it soon became clear that the society had divided along class and denominational lines" (97) deemphasizes the intrusion of the nonresistance philosophy as an important ideological cause of the break.

39. "First Annual Report of the Massachusetts Female Emancipation Society," in *Boston Free American*, August 12, 1841.

40. Jeffrey, *The Great Silent Army of Abolitionism*, 114.

41. "Extract from the Minutes of the Soc.," in New York Ladies Anti-Slavery Society to James G. Birney (no date), in Dumond, *The Letters of J. G. Birney*, 1:580. Amy Swerdlow, "Abolition's Conservative Sisters: The Ladies' New York City Anti-Slavery Societies, 1834–1840," in Jean Fagin Yellin and John C. Van Horne, eds., *The Abolitionist Sisterhood: Women's Political Culture in Antebellum America* (Ithaca, N.Y.: Cornell University Press, 1994 [2nd printing, 1995]), 32–44, examines "Who were these women who opposed their own rights?" (32).

42. Jean R. Soderland, "Priorities and Power: The Philadelphia Female Anti-Slavery Society," in Yellin and Van Horne, *The Abolitionist Sisterhood*, 79–81. For reports of an 1847 resignation from the society because of Liberty sympathies, see Jeffrey, *The Great Silent Army of Abolitionism*, 164–165.

43. Mary P. Ryan, *Women in Public: Between Banners and Ballots, 1825–1880* (Baltimore: Johns

Hopkins University Press, 1990), 132–141; Lori D. Ginzburg, *Women and the Work of Benevolence: Morality, Politics, and Class in the 19th-Century United States* (New Haven, Conn.: Yale University Press, 1990), 67–72; Carwardine, *Evangelical and Politics in Antebellum America*, 30–35.

44. See Griffith, *In Her Own Right*, 41, on lack of female participation at Liberty political gatherings.

45. A.W. Weston to C. and D. Weston, September 9–12, 1843, Antislavery Collection, Boston Public Library. Albert Mordell, *Quaker Militant: John Greenleaf Whittier* (Cambridge, Mass.: The Riverside Press, 1933), 192, reports that they were engaged briefly during the summer of 1846.

46. (Maine) *Liberty Standard*, January 25, March 8, 1843.

47. (Maine) *Liberty Standard*, March 25, 1845.

48. See Willey, *The History of the Antislavery Cause*, 187, 281–282, 290–292, for the manner of women's participation in Maine.

49. Alice Taylor, "From Petition to Partyism: Antislavery and the Domestication of Maine Politics in the 1840s and 1850s," *New England Quarterly* 77 (March 2004): 73.

50. Morrow, "The Liberty Party in Vermont," 242.

51. *Emancipator*, February 17, 1847.

52. Jeffrey, *The Great Silent Army of Abolitionism*, 3–4. She was commenting on the formation of a non-Garrisonian sewing circle in Dover, New Hampshire, in 1840.

53. *Christian Freeman*, October 24, 1844, reports that the Meriden Liberty Association had fourteen male and five female members.

54. *Albany Patriot*, January 15, 1843.

55. *Liberty Press*, October 24, 1843; Jackson to C. C. Foote, in *Albany Patriot*, July 15, 1846.

56. Julie Roy Jeffrey, "'No Occurrence in Human History Is More Deserving of Commemoration Than This': Abolitionist Celebrations of Freedom," in Timothy Patrick McCarthy and John Stauffer, eds., *Prophets of Protest: Reconsidering the History of American Abolitionism* (New York: The New Press, 2006), 211–212.

57. Gerrit Smith to the Liberty Party, May 7, 1846, in *Albany Patriot*, June 10, 1846. Smith consistently made statements supporting women's right and women's suffrage.

58. Friedman, *Gregarious Saints*, 144.

59. *Albany Patriot*, March 9, 1843.

60. *Christian Freeman*, May 19, 1843. See *Christian Freeman*, November 9, 1843, October 24, 1844, January 30, 1845, for some examples. The last, "Liberty Women," emphasizes traditional roles.

61. Garrison to John B. Estlin, September 8, 1846, in Merrill, *The Letters of William Lloyd Garrison*, 3:400.

62. *Chicago Western Citizen*, June 3, 1846.

63. Stacey Robertson, "'Ladies, Will You Meet With Us?' Women Abolitionists in the Old Northwest, Gender, and Third-Party Politics" at http://www2.h-net.msu.edu/~shear/s2000.d/pa/RobertsonStacey.htm describes her work in progress and has found "that many Western women abolitionists were politically knowledgeable and interested in third party politics." Also see her "Remembering Antislavery: Women Abolitionists in the Old Northwest," *Proteus: A Journal of Ideas* 19 (Fall 2002): 65–72.

64. Evans, "Abolitionism in the Illinois Churches," 66.

65. *Chicago Western Citizen*, November 9, 1843. Bureau County ladies made this a part of their constitution.

66. See *Chicago Western Citizen*, November 9, 1843, for the meeting of the Putnam County Female Anti-Slavery Society, which "*Resolved*, That as the *Liberty Party* makes the unchanging

principles of truth and justice their object, we will use our influence to further their progress." For an endorsement of Owen Lovejoy for Congress, see "Address of the Ladies' Antislavery Association of Dundee. To the Electors of the Fourth Congressional District." in *Chicago Western Citizen*, March 25, 1846. Sixty women signed the convention roll, and they also made a silk banner for the district producing the most votes for Lovejoy.

67. *Chicago Western Citizen*, April 25, May 23, June 20, 1844, April 24, 1845. On the possible dissolution, see Lydia S. Lewis to Zebina Eastman, in *Chicago Western Citizen*, March 25, May 27, 1846. Muelder, *Fighters for Freedom*, 180, has noted "[t]he circumstances that several local female societies were formed in Illinois about this time suggests some concerted action from a central impulse, but whence it came is not apparent."

68. Muelder, *Fighters for Freedom*, 176–183, discusses various women's access to the pages of the Liberty newspaper, the *Chicago Western Citizen*. Evans, "Abolitionism in the Illinois Churches," 71, discusses the state Liberty organization's encouragement for women's participation.

69. Dumond, *Antislavery*, 280.

70. Quist, *Restless Visionaries*, 424.

71. "Liberty Meeting at Grass Lake," in *Signal of Liberty*, May 18, 1846.

72. The wives of Nathan Thomas, Theodore Foster, Erastus Hussey, and Nathan Powers were among them.

73. Dumond, *Antislavery*, 280; Robinson, "'Ladies Will You Meet with Us?'" Gwendolyn J. Crenshaw, *"Bury Me in a Free Land": The Abolitionist Movement in Indiana, 1816–1865: The Catalog* (Indianapolis, Ind.: Indiana Historical Bureau, 1986), www.in.gov/history/3757.htm states that "the Henry County Female Anti-Slavery Society was by far the most overtly political female organization in the state. These women . . . resolved to persuade their male relatives to use their voting privileges to elect men 'who will remove these evils by the introduction of righteous and just laws.'"

74. E. to the editor, September 14, 1844, in *American Freeman*, September 18, 1844; "Minutes of the First Annual Meeting of the Female Anti-Slavery Society of Prarieville and Milwaukee," June 3, 1845, in *American Freeman*, June 12, 1845.

75. McBride, *On Wisconsin Women*, 11–13.

76. *American Freeman*, December 1, 1846; "To the Liberty Men and Women of Wisconsin," in *American Freeman*, September 16, 1845.

77. J. V. Smith to Eastman and Wheeler, January 28, 1847, in *Chicago Western Citizen*, February 2, 1847.

78. *Philanthropist*, December 16, 1840, January 27, 1841, June 23, 1841.

79. Sarah Ernst to Miss Weston, July 28, 1850, quoted in Jeffrey, *The Great Silent Army of Abolitionism*, 134.

80. Jeffrey, *The Great Silent Army of Abolitionism*, 164.

81. Birney to the *Signal of Liberty*, September 29, 1841, in *Signal of Liberty*, October 6, 1841. Also printed in Dumond, *Letters of J. G. Birney*, 2:633–636.

82. Joseph Morrison, Wm. S. Page, Alonzo Frost to People of Oakland County, June 28, 1842, in *Signal of Liberty*, July 18, 1842.

83. Smith, *The Liberty and Free Soil Parties in the Northwest*, 70. Nonetheless, A. W. Weston to ?, September 2, 1843, Antislavery Collection, Boston Public Library, reports that Kelley was pleased with the opportunity to speak at the meeting. Gerrit Smith tried to hire her to lecture for the Liberty Party in his area, but she refused. Sterling, *Ahead of Her Time*, 174, states that "[s]ince antislavery agents were paid no more than two hundred dollars a year, Abby could easily have construed Smith's offer of one hundred dollars for two months' lecturing as a bribe." Harlow, *Gerrit Smith*, 164–165, discusses the offer and some harsh words that ensued between the two of them.

84. Elizabeth Cady Stanton to Elizabeth Pease, February 12, 1842, Antislavery Collection, Boston Public Library.

85. Theodore Foster describes the convention in *Signal of Liberty*, July 4, 1846.

86. *Chicago Western Citizen*, June 30, July 4, 14, 1846.

87. *Signal of Liberty*, July 4, 1846. Foster later became outspoken in favor of women's rights. Quist, *Restless Visionaries*, 427, notes that "the slow conversion of this political outcast to women's suffrage underlines the extent to which this question was deemed radical by many contemporaries who were active in politics."

88. *Chicago Western Citizen*, June 30, 1846.

89. *Albany Patriot*, June 16, 23, 1847; *Proceedings of the National Liberty Convention at Buffalo, N.Y., June 14th & 15th*.

90. Fletcher, *A History of Oberlin College*, 2:266. Another exception in the area was faculty wife Betsy Hudson, wife of Liberty supporter Timothy B. Hudson, who maintained that "I have yet to be convinced that the Liberty party is not the heaven-appointed means for the overthrow of that most vile and heaven-insulting system of slavery." Betsy Hudson to Betsy Cowles, February 27, 1846, in Jeffrey, *The Great Silent Army of Abolitionism*, 168.

91. Elizabeth Cazden, *Antoinette Brown Blackwell: A Biography* (Old Westbury, N.Y.: The Feminist Press, 1983), 42.

92. Antoinette Brown to Lucy Stone, August 13, 1850, quoted in ibid., 55–56. She did attend and spoke on a woman's right to speak in public.

93. Quist, "'The Great Majority of Our Subscribers Are Farmers,'" 333, 337; Quist, *Restless Visionaries*, 424. He spells her last name "Van Fleet." No copies of this newspaper seem to be extant.

94. Much of this background on the Davises is from Muelder, *Fighters for Freedom*, 174–188. Also see Robertson, "'Ladies Will You Meet with Us?'"

95. For articles emphasizing women's activities, see *Chicago Western Citizen*, July 25, 1844, July 27, 1847.

96. Hoffert, *Jane Grey Swisshelm*, 105–108, deals with her work for the Liberty Party. Also see Walker, "Jane Swisshelm: Emancipated Woman," 87–205; Shippee, "Jane Grey Swisshelm: Agitator," 206–227.

97. Hoffert, *Jane Grey Swisshelm*, 137; Michael D. Pierson, "Between Antislavery and Abolition: The Politics and Rhetoric of Jane Grey Swisshelm," *Pennsylvania History* 60 (July 1993): 262–266.

98. Jane Grey Swisshelm, *Half a Century* (Chicago: n.p., 1880), 91.

99. Ibid., 112.

100. Walker, *Moral Choices*, 127.

101. *Saturday Visiter*, December 20, 1847, as quoted in Walker, *Moral Choices*, 137.

102. Swisshelm, *Half a Century*, 121.

103. Walker, *Moral Choices*, 165; Blue, *No Taint of Compromise*, 153.

104. Walker, *Moral Choices*, 127, 139.

105. Cazden, *Antoinette Brown Blackwell*, 68. Ibid., 27, reports that "[o]f all the professors at Oberlin in the late 1840s, only President Asa Mahan fully supported proposals to allow women to participate in discussions and debates, and he was consistently outvoted by the faculty."

106. Muelder, *Fighters for Freedom*, 183.

107. Taylor, "From Petitions to Partyism," 75.

108. Ginzburg, *Women and the Work of Benevolence*, 86.

109. Samuel May to J. B. Estlin, September 19, 1848, in Taylor, *British and American Abolitionists*, 327.

110. Holt, *The History of the Whig Party*, 883–884.

111. John R. Mulkern, *The Know-Nothing Party in Massachusetts: The Rise and Fall of a People's Movement* (Boston: Northeastern University Press, 1990), does not even mention Knapp. On the American Party attempts to woo established political figures in the state, see ibid., 69–71.

112. Walker, *Moral Choices*, 165; Hoffert, *Jane Grey Swisshelm*, 25–31.

113. Tyler Anbinder, *Nativism and Slavery: The Northern Know Nothings and the Politics of the 1850s* (New York: Oxford University Press, 1992), 174–175; Maizlish, *The Triumph of Sectionalism*, 214–215.

114. Chase to John Paul, December 27, 1854, in Niven, *The Salmon P. Chase Papers*, 2:393–394; Blue, *Salmon P. Chase*, 97–103, 110–111, discusses Chase's concern with Know Nothing support; on his personal opposition, see, Niven, *Salmon P. Chase*, 169–170. On his Know Nothing support and his willingness to try to involve them in a coalition, see William E. Gienapp, *The Origins of the Republican Party, 1852–1856* (New York: Oxford University Press, 1987), 200, 252–253. See also chapter 8.

115. *Boston Daily Chronotype*, June 17, 1847.

116. Kenneth M. Stampp, *America in 1857: A Nation on the Brink* (New York: Oxford University Press, 1990), 242–243; Mulkern, *The Know Nothing Party*, 164, 168. Swan only received 216 votes.

117. A notable exception to this among Liberty leaders, and one of the few true Liberty backsliders that I have found, was Joseph Lovejoy. His brothers were the martyred Elijah and the Illinois Liberty leader and future U.S. congressman Owen Lovejoy. He himself had been a temperance spokesman and energetic Liberty Party editor and organizer in Maine and Massachusetts who had gone over to the other side and become a spokesman for the liquor interests and an apologist for the South and slavery. See Magdol, *Owen Lovejoy*, 225–226. Moore and Moore, *Owen Lovejoy*, 166, relate how Joseph Lovejoy regretted his earlier antislavery views after several slaveholders financed a trip for him to the South. He published a controversial open letter in the *New York Union* to Owen "scolding him for his mistaken views." Nonetheless, "by 1862 Joseph was in Washington working at the U.S. Patent Office, tutoring students, and assisting Owen with constituent concerns."

118. I have identified the following with their diplomatic posts:

James Birney (son)	Resident Minister to the Hague
Elihu Burritt	Consul at Birmingham, England
Charles Dexter Cleveland	Consul at Cardiff, Wales
Joseph Carmen Cover	Consul to the Azores
Charles W. Denison	Consul at British Guyana
Henry W. DePuy	Consul to Carlsruhe, Secretary of Legation to Berlin
Charles Volney Dyer	U.S. Representative on the International Court to Suppress the Slave Trade
Zebina Eastman	Consul at Bristol, England
Henry Highland Garnet	Minister to Liberia
John P. Hale	Minister to Spain
Stephen S. Harding	Consul at Valparaiso, Chile
Richard Hildreth	Consul to Trieste
John Mercer Langston	Consul to Haiti
James Monroe	Consul to Rio de Janeiro

119. Paul Goodman, "The Manual Labor Movement and the Origins of Abolitionism," *Journal of the Early Republic* 13 (Fall 1993): 355–388.

120. Wyatt-Brown, *Lewis Tappan*, 280–281.

121. James M. McPherson, *The Struggle for Equality: Abolitionists and the Negro in the Civil War and Reconstruction* (Princeton, N.J.: Princeton University Press, 1964), 22. On Stanton's declining health, see Griffith, *In Her Own Right*, 46.

122. Barnes, *The Anti-Slavery Impulse*, 176.

123. Kraditor, "The Liberty and Free Soil Parties," 759.

CHAPTER 11

1. Louis Filler, "Garrison Again and Again: A Review Article," *Civil War History* 11 (March 1965): 69–75; James Brewer Stewart, "Garrison Again and Again and Again," *Reviews in American History* 4 (December 1976): 539–545.

2. For the workings of Garrison's immediate circle, see Friedman, *Gregarious Saints*, 43–67.

3. While many historians have maintained an almost worshipful tone toward Garrison, others have not been so sympathetic. Describing an earlier conflict that split the society, Hansen, *Strained Sisterhood*, 23, notes that "[t]o fight this defection, Garrison used the same tactics with which he fought all enemies—untempered accusation and denunciation." Garrison eventually had disputes with most of those close to him, with the exception of his largest financial backers, such as Francis Jackson and Edmund Quincy. Perry, *Radical Abolition*,10, writes, "[i]n 1831 he published the first issue of *The Liberator*, the newspaper through which he would denounce enemies or false friends of the slave and broadcast the gospel of immediate abolition; however, his reading of that gospel changed every week until 1865." John T. Cumbler, *From Abolition to Rights for All: The Making of a Reform Community in the Nineteenth Century* (Philadelphia: University of Pennsylvania Press, 2007), 42, quotes William Bowditch, who was a member of the Massachusetts Anti-Slavery Society and rejected the U.S. Constitution in 1846, as believing that Garrison "was essentially an unlovable man. He was utterly intolerant even of the smallest dissent from his views."

4. John L. Thomas, *The Liberator: William Lloyd Garrison: A Biography* (Boston: Little, Brown and Company, 1963), 324–325, discusses Garrison's "smoldering hatred for Birney, Leavitt and other 'apostates' who walked out of the old society in 1840 taking the *Emancipator* with them. The object of the Liberty Party, he implied more than once, was not the abolition of slavery but the overthrow of William Lloyd Garrison ... Lamentations like these were pure hokum."

5. Carolyn L. Karcher, *First Woman in the Republic: A Cultural Biography of Lydia Maria Child* (Durham, N.C.: Duke University Press, 1994), 288.

6. Ibid., 290–291.

7. Wright to Birney, February 6, 1844, in Dumond, *Letters of J. G. Birney*, 2:277; Wyatt-Brown, *Lewis Tappan*, 194–196, concludes that both sides were culpable. Davis, *Joshua Leavitt*, 158–161. The matter was never settled.

8. *Chicago Western Citizen*, January 12, 1847.

9. Pease's, *The Frontier State*, 372, statement for Illinois could characterize the situation in most of the Old Northwest. "The new wine of Garrisonian abolition, however, was a little too strong to be safely introduced into bottles of Illinois antislavery effort; a nonresistance and the alleged infidelity of Garrison were usually eschewed as stumbling blocks to antislavery men."

10. See Douglas A. Gamble, "Moral Suasion in the West: Garrisonian Abolitionism 1831–1861" (Ph.D. dissertation, Ohio State University, 1973), 219–227 and 299–300 for the period after 1844.

11. Ibid., 228–232. On Bailey's attempts to keep it together, see Harrold, *Gamaliel Bailey*, 35–36, 43–44.

12. Gamble, "Moral Suasion in the West," 247–249. William Birney to James G. Birney, June 9, 1842, in Dumond, *The Letters of J. G. Birney*, 2:698, attributes the move to "the wily arguments and plausible sophistry of [Garrisonian] J.[ohn] A. Collins, of Massachusetts, a gentleman sent out, it appears, expressly for the purpose of fomenting our dissensions. He has succeeded to his hearts content."

13. *Philanthropist*, July 9, 1842, provides a report on the arrangements.

14. Gamble, "Moral Suasion in the West," 252.

15. Jesse Macy, *The Anti-Slavery Crusade: A Chronicle of the Gathering Storm*, Chronicles of America Series, vol. 28 (New Haven, Conn.: Yale University Press, 1920), 57, states that "[p]robably not one in a hundred of even the New England abolitionists ever accepted the special views which the Garrisonian organization adopted after 1843." Russell B. Nye, *William Lloyd Garrison and the Humanitarian Reformers* (Boston: Little, Brown and Company, 1955), 129–130, believes that "Garrison's capture of the American Antislavery Society destroyed it as an effective abolitionist instrument . . . [T]he national society after 1840 counted no more than six hundred members, probably less than half of them active." Birney, *James G. Birney*, chapter 38, "The Small Extreme," 314–331, also makes a convincing case that contemporaries were aware of Garrison's declining influence. More recently, Laurie, *Beyond Garrison*, 5, notes that Garrison engaged in a "seemingly endless pursuit of self-purification that mistook the avoidance of politics for progress even as political abolitionism eclipsed his own movement." Cumbler, *From Abolition to Rights for All*, 44, errs in saying "most of the state's female and male members" supported the Massachusetts Anti-Slavery Society. He also equates the small group he examines with all of New England abolitionism.

16. *Liberator*, May 13, 1842, and after.

17. Garrison to James B. Yerrinton, May 7, 1844, in Merrill, *The Letters of William Lloyd Garrison*, 3:256. Thomas, *The Liberator*, 332–333, discusses the meeting and Garrison's waning influence in the larger antislavery movement.

18. Garrison and Garrison, *William Lloyd Garrison*, 112. Professor Amasa Walker of Harvard, historian Richard Hildreth, and poet John Pierpont were present and voiced their strong opposition.

19. On Sewall, see Tiffany, *Samuel E. Sewall*, 94. The mild-mannered Sewall left the Old Organization earlier than the others as it grew "more ultra and fanatical." See Sewall to James G. Birney, August 2, 1842, in Dumond, *Letters of J. G. Birney*, 2:207–209. The editors mistakenly identify him as "Stephen." On Hildreth, see Donald E. Emerson, *Richard Hildreth* (Baltimore: Johns Hopkins University Press, 1942), 128, and Garrison and Garrison, *William Lloyd Garrison*, 3:111–112; on Smith, see Walter M. Merrill, *Against Wind and Tide: A Biography of Wm. Lloyd Garrison* (Cambridge, Mass.: Harvard University Press, 1963), 209; on Loring, see Garrison and Garrison, *William Lloyd Garrison*, 3:134.

20. Bradburn to John B. Swanton, August 9, 1844, in *Chicago Western Citizen*, September 5, 1844. See the letter also in *Liberator*, August 16, 1844, and *Emancipator*, August 21, 1844, and *Boston Morning Chronicle*, August 17, 1844. On Bradburn's work for the Old Organization, see details of a speaking tour that covered Ohio, Indiana, Pennsylvania, and New York, in *Signal of Liberty*, July 24, 1843.

21. Garrison to Henry C. Wright, October 1, 1844, in Merrill, *The Letters of William Lloyd Garrison*, 3:266. See also Garrison and Garrison, *William Lloyd Garrison*, 3:212. Letter from Bradburn to the editors in *National Anti-Slavery Standard*, November 28, 1844, defends his decision against the claim of the newspaper that Liberty members in Massachusetts "are the sheerest political demagogues, and broken-down politicians."

22. (Concord, N.H.) *Herald of Freedom*, June 13, 1845, a non-Liberty abolition newspaper, claimed that this resulted from "the persons who control this convention, carried away by the priestley [*sic*] idea that they are alone and especially called and appointed of God, to have the leadership in this matter." Cumbler, *From Abolition to Rights for All*, 193, note 64, believes "the split was less significant in new England than is often depicted."

23. The decline of the American Anti-Slavery Society has been acknowledged in some historical writing, although many historians still overestimate its importance numerically and ideologically. The figures quoted are from Richard Hofstadter, "Wendell Phillips: The Patrician as Agitator," in *The American Political Tradition and the Men Who Made It* (New York: Random House, 1948 [Vintage Paperback]), 147.

24. The first figure is from Albert Bushnell Hart, *Slavery and Abolition, 1831–1841* (New York: Haskell Publishing House, 1968 [first published 1906]), 181–182; the latter figure is from Garrison to G. W. Benson, January 7, 1841, in Garrison and Garrison, *William Lloyd Garrison*, 3:40. For the *Liberator*'s continuing difficulties, despite lowering the subscription price in 1847, see Garrison and Garrison, *William Lloyd Garrison*, 3:72, 215. For Wendell Phillips's and other Garrisonians' awareness of this, see James Brewer Stewart, *Wendell Phillips: Liberty's Hero* (Baton Rouge: Louisiana State University Press, 1986), 141–143.

25. Martin Duberman, *James Russell Lowell* (Boston: Beacon Press, 1966 [Beacon Press Edition, 1968]), 86. Lowell was a Garrisonian, but he refused to excoriate the Liberty Party. In fact, there was a rumor that he had voted for it. See ibid., 408. Karcher, *The First Woman in the Republic*, 288, reports that the subscriptions plunged from 5,300 to 1,300.

26. *Liberator*, April 18, 1845.

27. J. W. Alden to Elizur Wright, July 1, 1844, Wright manuscripts, Library of Congress.

28. Tappan to John Beaumont, January 30, 1844, in Klingberg and Abel, *A Side-Light on Anglo-American Relations*, 174. He also commented that the "Garrison party" was dwindling every day" and would be insignificant if not for the membership of Hicksite Quakers.

29. The American and Foreign Anti-Slavery Society was resuscitated a few years later, largely through the efforts of Arthur and Lewis Tappan, but it was never a great force and was finally disbanded in 1855.

30. J. Stafford to Francis Jackson, July 25, 1843, for Cummington; William Bates to Francis Jackson, July 22, 1843, for Waltham; Abijah Allen to Francis Jackson, July 21, 1843, for Millbury, all in Antislavery Collection, Boston Public Library. Lucretia Coffin Mott to Nathaniel Barnes, as quoted in McFeely, *Frederick Douglass*, 114, in commenting on Douglass's being depressed by the lack of antislavery fervor in Chester County, Pennsylvania, explains that "this political party movement is taking some of our most active members from us."

31. J. B. Estlin to W. (R. D. Webb), November 13, 1845, Antislavery Collection, Boston Public Library, partially excerpted in Clare Taylor, *British and American Abolitionists. An Episode in Transatlantic Understanding* (Edinburgh, Scotland: Edinburgh University Press, 1974), 241–242. J. H. Treadgold to James A. Collins, January 2, 1841, in *National Anti-Slavery Standard*, March 25, 1841, discusses his failure to get a vote of confidence from the British and Foreign Anti-Slavery Society and "since the division which took place in May last [1840]: that cause in the United States the Committee now consider as more truly represented by the American and Foreign Anti-Slavery Society."

32. J. B. Estlin to Samuel May, October 1, 1846, in Taylor, *British and American Abolitionists*, 291.

33. Eunice Dosman to "Respected Friend" F. J. (Francis Jackson), March 19, 1843, Antislavery Collection, Boston Public Library.

34. Garrison to James Miller McKim, July 19, 1845, in Merrill, *Letters of William Lloyd Garrison*, 3:307. Elaine Brooks, "Massachusetts Anti-Slavery Society," *Journal of Negro History* 30 (January 1945): 327–328, notes that "abolitionists generally rallied to support the new party forsaking Garrison's fold" and that the Massachusetts Anti-Slavery Society after the split "was, in fact, a brand new society proclaiming doctrines and advocating policies in direct contradiction to those of the original organization."

35. Donald Yacovone, *Samuel Joseph May and the Dilemma of the Liberal Persuasion, 1797–1871* (Philadelphia: Temple University Press, 1991), 132.

36. As quoted in Birney, *James G. Birney*, 314. Birney has assembled a collection of quotations from his correspondence to buttress this argument. Volpe, *Forlorn Hope of Freedom*, 189. On Wisconsin, Smith, "The Free Soil Party in Wisconsin," 106, reports that he found "absolutely no trace [of Garrisonism] in the Territory or State," although "[Wendell] Phillips and Garrison's utterances were continually being cast up against the Wisconsin Liberty men by the *Sentinel, Democrat, Courier,* and other papers." Pfau, *The Political Style of Conspiracy*, 58, notes that Salmon P. Chase crafted his 1845 address at the Southern and Western Convention to avoid any tinge of Garrisonian ideas because "[i]n the filiopietistic atmosphere of nineteenth-century political discourse, Garrison's radical critique of the Republic's foundation was impolitic."

37. Gamble, "Moral Suasion in the West," 295–296.

38. Sterling, *Ahead of Her Time*, 213–233, deals with her trip to Ohio.

39. Gamble, "Moral Suasion in the West," 321. Cyrus McNeely had resigned the year before after just two days because of his Liberty Party orientation, but he had agreed to serve when reelected. See ibid., 303–304.

40. Sterling, *Ahead of Her Time*, 215. I believe Sterling overstates the number of subscribers (one thousand).

41. (Cadiz, Ohio) *Sentinel*, as quoted in *Liberator*, October 17, 1845.

42. Gamble, "Moral Suasion in the West," 316.

43. Harrold, *Gamaliel Bailey*, 72.

44. Fletcher, *A History of Oberlin College*, 269, 266. The debates are summarized in "Oberlin and the Anti-Slavery Movement," 118–121, and Burroughs, "Oberlin's Past in the Slavery Movement," 279–280.

45. *Oberlin Evangelist*, September 30, 1846, as quoted in Ellsworth, "Oberlin and the Anti-Slavery Movement," 119; the Garrisonian side can be found in *Anti-Slavery Bugle*, October 9, 1846.

46. See one announcement in the *Chicago Western Citizen*, September 1, 1845.

47. *Liberator*, October 3, 1845; *National Anti-Slavery Standard*, September 25, 1845.

48. Wellman, *Grassroots Reform in the Burned-over District*, 154, notices in her community studies that "[b]etween 1840 and 1842, political abolitionists took over many local, county and state societies." There was also some activity in New York City centered around the *National Anti-Slavery Standard*.

49. *Pennsylvania Freeman*, June 7, July 31, 1845.

50. *Pennsylvania Freeman*, August 28, 1845.

51. Garrison to Helen Garrison, August 3, 1847, in Merrill, *The Letters of William Lloyd Garrison*, 3:504.

52. Bronner, *Thomas Earle*, 41. So forgotten that Garrison and Garrison, *William Lloyd Garrison*, 3:450, has him participating in a call for a disunion convention in 1856, seven years after his death.

53. See *Liberator*, January 29, February 12, 1847, *National Anti-Slavery Standard*, January 28,

1847, *Emancipator*, January 27, 1847, for assorted accounts of the January 20, 1847, Massachusetts state Liberty Party convention where Foster was not allowed to speak. See *Emancipator*, February 17, 1847, for Abby Kelley Foster's being carried out of an antislavery meeting. The article refers to her as a "lunatic." Parker Pillsbury to Edmund Quincy, November 3, 1846, in *Liberator*, November 13, 1846, complains about his ill treatment at a Liberty meeting in Marlborough.

54. Garrison to unknown recipient, November 3, 1846, in Merrill, *Letters of William Lloyd Garrison*, 3:448–449. The quote is from Isaiah 28:15. They believed that the U.S. Constitution sanctioned slavery and that the only alternative for the free North was to break off from the South.

55. David Grimsted, *American Mobbing, 1828–1861: Toward Civil War* (New York: Oxford University Press, 1998), 69. Perry, *Radical Abolitionism*, 166–187, discusses the intellectual underpinnings that he claims "were shared by the nonresistants and the leaders of the Liberty Party" (167).

56. *National Anti-Slavery Standard*, May 21, 1846.

57. *National Anti-Slavery Standard*, March 25, 1847.

58. *Liberator*, October 10, 1845.

59. Gamble, "Moral Suasion in the West," surveys the subject. He has condensed some of his speculation in "Garrisonian Abolitionists in the West: Some suggestions for Future Study," *Civil War History* 23 (March 1977): 52–68. See also *Liberator*, February 2, 1844, which comments "that many of its [Liberty Party] supporters, especially at the Far West, were in heart good and true men."

60. *National Anti-Slavery Standard*, May 22, 1845.

61. W. L. Garrison to H. E. Garrison, August 20, 1847, Antislavery Collection, Boston Public Library.

62. Henry Mayer, *All on Fire: William Lloyd Garrison and the Abolition of Slavery* (New York: St. Martin's Press, 1998), 368–374. Mayer's hagiographic biography neglects some of Garrison's less attractive aspects. Merrill, *Against Wind and Tide*, 230–239; *The Liberator*, 347–350; Garrison and Garrison, *William Lloyd Garrison*, 196–198; Burroughs, "Oberlin's Past in the Slavery Conflict," 279–280.

63. Garrison to Helen E. Garrison, August 28, 1847, in Merrill, *The Letters of William Lloyd Garrison*, 3:522–523.

64. Letter from Oberlin signed D. McB., August 25, 1847, in the (Cleveland) *True Democrat*, September 3, 1847, as quoted in Ellsworth, "Oberlin and the Anti-Slavery Movement," 121.

65. *Pennsylvania Freeman*, May 23, 1844. Smith, *The Liberty and Free Soil Parties in the Northwest*, 116, points out that Indiana Liberty men were using a questioning system in Indiana in 1847 in a move toward coalition politics; see also *National Era*, July 29, 1847.

66. *Pennsylvania Freeman*, July 2, 1847.

67. Garrison and Phillips to Bailey, September 27, 1841, in Merrill, *The Letters of William Lloyd Garrison*, 3:35; Harrold, *Gamaliel Bailey*, 43; *National Anti-Slavery Standard*, December 21, 1841, reports that the Essex County Anti-Slavery Society (Old Organization) "took up a contribution of $27 toward re-establishing the press of the Philanthropist; and sent it to Dr. Bailey with a cordial letter of encouragement and sympathy."

68. Garrison to Helen E. Garrison, November 21, 1842, in Merrill, *The Letters of William Lloyd Garrison*, 3:108.

69. *Emancipator*, September 1, 1847.

70. See Q., in *Liberator*, September 15, 1848. Quincy had an intense hatred for the Liberty Party. See his spoof of it in *Liberator*, January 6, 1843. When he was in doubt or error, he never seems to have corrected himself. For another Quincy editorial declaring that Birney was the "MOST OBJECTIONABLE CANDIDATE" in 1844, see *Liberator*, July 25, 1844; his criticism of Birney for the Garland

statement and Morris's old views on black suffrage in *National Anti-Slavery Standard,* October 31, 1844.

71. Dumond, *Antislavery,* 299.

72. Jeffrey, *The Great Silent Army of Abolitionists,* 259, notes that "[i]ronically, though the Garrisonians were the smallest abolitionist group, they are probably the most studied. The availability of records for the Garrisonians has drawn historians to document their views and activities in some detail." Many also follow Garrison and Garrison, *William Lloyd Garrison.* Theodore Clarke Smith, *Parties and Slavery* (New York: Harper & Row, 1968 [J. & J. Harper Edition. First published by Harper & Brothers, 1906]), 312, characterizes this work as "written in the spirit of unqualified filial eulogy." Most anthologies on abolition reflect the same trend.

73. There are exceptions among recent historians to this general statement in addition to the ones already cited. Pease and Pease, *Bound with Them in Chains,* 36, believe that "Garrisonianism was a thirty-year tribute to endless discourse, to interminable exhortation, to limitless verbiage. Garrisonians largely avoided direct action, whether in politics or on behalf of free Negroes." Or, it might be added, on behalf of those still in slavery.

AFTERWORD

1. James Brewer Stewart, "Reconsidering the Abolitionists in an Age of Fundamentalist Politics," *Journal of the Early Republic* 26 (Spring 2006): 5.

2. Carwardine, *Evangelicals and Politics in Antebellum America,* 4. He also believes that full church membership was 15%.

INDEX

Abolition Standard (Concord, N.H.), 122
Act to Regulate Blacks and Mulattoes (Iowa), 215
Adams, Charles Francis, 85–87, 91, 99, 119
Adams, John Quincy, 6, 31, 34, 82, 181, 187, 305, 349
Address of the National Liberty Party Convention in A.D. 1841 "To the Citizens of the United States," 24–25
Address of the Liberty Party of Pennsylvania (1844), 228
Address to the People of the United States (1845), 52–54, 402n15
Address to the Slaves of the United States (1843), 251, 343
Adrian College, 258, 290, 357, 359
Advocate of Freedom (Augusta, Maine), 15, 101, 103, 371
African Americans, 3, 38, 54, 68, 130–135, 143–144, 149, 151, 153–154, 158–159, 166–167, 177, 199, 201, 205, 215, 217, 221, 241–263, 278, 295–296, 329, 334, 343, 355, 361, 371 400n98
Alabama Letters, 141
Albany Convention (April 1, 1840), 15–18, 152, 332, 349, 363–364, 373, 376–377, 379, 382
Albany (N.Y.) *Patriot*, 65, 68, 77, 127–128, 140, 143–147, 171, 233, 331, 345, 351, 378
Albatross (Pittsburgh, Pa.), 158, 370
Allan, William T., 193–195, 323, 448n205, 456n353
Allen, William G., 257, 323
Almanacs, 43, 235–236, 377
Amalgamation. *See* Miscegenation

American and Foreign Anti-Slavery Society: founding of, 8, 9–10, 112, 121, 243, 277; mentioned, 48, 73, 81, 84, 165, 233–234, 245, 295, 305, 325–326, 329, 333, 343, 348, 351–354, 356–357, 362–365, 368, 371–375, 380, 382, 389
American Anti-Slavery Society: attempts to turn toward politics, 14–16; founding of, 5, 7, 100–101, 111, 137, 151, 211; Garrisonian control of, 38, 47–48, 289, 291–299, 315; loss of members in, 47–48, 298, 292–295, 315; split of, at the May 1840 national meeting, 8–12, 112, 130, 165, 244, 276–277, 388n5; mentioned, 57, 168, 255, 258, 324–326, 330–331, 333–334, 337–339, 342–346, 348–349, 351–354, 356–360, 362–363, 365–369, 371–375, 378, 381–382
American Baptist Home Mission Society, 203
American Citizen (Philadelphia, Pa.), 156–158, 357
American Colonization Society, 326, 344, 365, 374
American Freeman (Waukesha and Milwaukee, Wis.), 81, 84, 88, 204–209, 233, 281, 327, 343
American Party, 286, 354
American Peace Society, 352
American Republican Party, 96
American Signal, 286, 337
Amistad case, 31, 131, 246, 253, 327, 380
Andrew, John Albion, 288, 323, 348
Andrews, Stephen Pearl, 323–324, 413n5
Anticlericalism, 10, 101, 121, 156, 198, 244
Anti-Masonry, 2, 17, 92, 111, 294, 109, 258, 324, 327–328, 330, 339, 344, 349, 351, 354, 368
Anti-rent movement, 76, 142, 145, 147

Anti-Slavery Bugle (Salem, Ohio), 297
Appleton, James, 58, 103–105, 226–267, 324, 404*n*43
Arcade (N.Y.) Anti-Slavery Convention (January 28–29, 1840), 15
Ashtabula County (Ohio), 184, 189–190, 314, 337, 366, 378
Atherton, Charles, 120

Bailey, Gamaliel: on annexation of Texas, 409*n*5; biography, 324; on coalition politics in 1847, 76–78, 149; as editor of *Philanthropist*, 12, 186, 232; on 1840 presidential election, 12, 15, 16, 18, 178, 179, 180; on 1844 nomination of Morris for vice president, 41–42, 182–183; on Great Western Convention, 52; and the *National Era*, 29, 61, 72–73, 262, 264–265; and Ohio Liberty organization, 180–186; on Ohio politics in the late 1830s, 178; political and constitutional theories of, 32–33, 37, 61, 63, 66, 266; mentioned, 29, 50, 62, 72, 76, 186, 265, 293–294, 297, 301, 363
Bailey, Wesley, 65, 144–145, 324
Baldwin, Roger, 131–134, 246, 273, 305, 380
Bangor (Maine) *Gazette*, 67, 71, 104, 106–108, 344
Banner of Liberty (Montpelier, Vt.), 17, 112
Baptist Church, 101, 203, 224
Barber, Edward D., 113, 324
Barnburner Democrats, 76, 83, 84, 88, 91, 118–119, 148–149, 188, 220, 411*n*40
Barnburner (Milwaukee, Wis.), 219
Barnes, Gilbert Hobbs, 5, 291
Barnes, Ward Robert, 216, 456*n*47
Bascom, Flavel, 290, 324–325
Bayley, Abner L., 229, 325
Bebb, William, 185
Beckley, Guy: biography, 325; on expanded Liberty platform, 55, 79, 145, 157, 171–175, 200; mentioned, 166, 233–234, 261, 265, 286
Beliot (Wis.) College, 258, 290, 325
Belknap (N.H.) *Gazette*, 69
Beman, Amos Gerry, 133, 246, 257, 262, 325
Beman, Jehiel C., 250, 255, 262, 325
Beman, S. S., 15–16
Benson, Lee, 47, 141

Berry, Nathaniel S., 70, 126, 128–129, 188, 325–326
Bibb, Henry W., 55, 172, 198, 250–252, 326, 342, 359, 366, 391
Bible politics, 3, 25, 138, 149
Bigelow, Jacob, 212, 326
Birney, James (son), 288, 393, 480, 326
Birney, James Gillespie: on Beckley, 173–175; on Bibb, 250–252; biography, 326–327; early opposition to third party, 11, 26; Freehling's assessment of, 392–393*n*44; 1840 presidential candidacy of, 16–20; 1844 presidential candidacy and campaign of, 23–49, 168–169, 181–182; on expanding Liberty appeal and support for the Liberty League, 55, 62–65, 81, 90, 145–146, 170–176; interpretation of U.S. Constitution by, 60; nominated for governor of Michigan, 166, 169; in Ohio, 177–179; at the Southern and Western Convention, 152; stroke and illness of, 50–52; mentioned, 9–10, 76–77, 94, 111,125, 132, 141, 152, 155, 227, 234, 237, 256, 265–266, 275, 282, 291, 307
Birney, William, 45, 142, 182, 184, 186, 225, 228, 230, 327, 398*n*42
Black convention movement, 244–245, 249, 325, 334, 336, 352, 355, 378–379
Black laws, 177, 185, 192, 215, 217–218, 230, 254–256, 326, 352–353
Blanchard, Jonathan, 290, 342, 327
Blue, Frederick, 135
Boltwood, Lucius, 93, 227, 327
Booth, Sherman Miller, 131, 133, 209–210, 233, 253, 327
Boston Daily Advertiser, 30
Boston Daily Chronotype, 65, 81, 98, 268, 382
Boston Female Anti-Slavery Society, 276, 476*n*38
Boston Free American, 93, 229, 382
Boston Morning Chronicle, 62, 93, 226, 234, 356
Bowditch, Henry Ingersoll, 327–328, 414*n*25
Bradburn, George, 81–82, 187, 294, 328
Bradley, Henry, 145, 147, 229, 328
Brainerd, Lawrence, 117, 119–120, 269–270, 288, 328
Branch, Daniel, 290, 328
Brewster, John M., 95–96, 328–329
Briggs, Charles C., 117, 329

INDEX 489

Briggs, George, 96–97
Brisbane, William H., 329
British model of abolition, 10, 22
British West Indies, 5
Brown Blackwell, Antoinette, 283, 285, 329
Brown, Abel W., 379, 329
Brown, Asa B., 213, 329
Brown, William Wells, 39, 244
Budney, Stephen P., 255
Buffum, Arnold, 209, 211, 229, 329–330
Bureau County (Ill.), 196, 275, 314
Burgess, Dyer, 180, 222, 330
Burleigh, Charles C., 153, 156, 330
Burleigh, William H., 133–134, 341, 330
Burned-Over District, 40, 85, 137–138, 156, 353, 359
Burritt, Elihu, 65, 95, 146, 226, 330, 480
Butler, Benjamin, 162
Butler, William O., 82

Campbell, Alexander, 27, 180, 261, 267, 288, 330
Carpenter, Philo, 330–331, 448*n*194
Carter, James Gordon, 55, 97, 147, 227, 290, 331
Carwardine, Richard, 223, 306
Cass, Lewis, 82, 89, 99–100, 109, 118, 129, 164, 176, 218
Cass County (Mich.), 247
Catholicism, 41, 42, 155, 156, 224, 284, 286, 338, 459*n*15
Cause of Hard Times, The, 228
Cedar of Lebanon, 222, 458*n*2
Chadbourne, Thomas, 331, 422*n*186
Charter Oak (Hartford, Conn.), 16, 130–131, 134, 327, 330
Chaplin, William, 15, 138, 140, 145–146, 229, 331
Chapman, Maria Weston, 251, 277, 293, 296
Chase, Salmon P.: *Address to the People of the United States* (1845), 52–54, 235; biography, 331–332; attempts to replace Birney as Liberty presidential candidate for 1844, 34, 36, 52, 182; efforts to merge into the Free Soil coalition, 77–79, 81, 83–86, 90 149, 272–273; as lawyer for African Americans, 254–255; Ohio activities of, 182–189; political philosophy of, 32–34, 38–39, 41, 52–54, 57, 60, 63, 66, 230; mentioned, 26, 56, 72, 90, 119,
134, 146, 155, 189, 229, 277, 286–289, 292, 297, 323, 327, 338, 360, 368, 371, 376
Chase-Bailey group, 3, 32–33, 66, 78, 183–184, 187–188, 230, 272, 297
Cheney, Oren B., 290, 332
Chicago Brass Band, 197
Chicago Liberty Choir, 55, 197, 225, 252
Chicago Western Citizen, 29, 46, 73, 77, 195–202, 213, 218, 220, 225, 232–233, 236, 240, 254, 259–260, 283, 329, 335–339, 352
Child, Lydia Maria, 277, 282, 293
Christian Freeman (Hartford, Conn.), 131, 133, 233, 327, 330, 333
Christian Investigator (Honeoye, N.Y.), 147
Cilley, Joseph: biography, 332; criticisms of stance of, on the Mexican War, 409*n*5; mentioned, 70–71, 76, 127, 128, 288
Cincinnati National Press and Weekly Herald, 77, 84, 186, 188, 360
Cincinnati Weekly Globe, 188–189
Clark, George Washington, 55, 198, 225, 282, 291, 236, 332
Clarke, Edwin, 332, 390*n*19
Clarke, Lewis G., 250, 332
Clarke, Milton, 332
Clarkson, Thomas, 260
Clarion of Freedom (Indiana, Pa.), 154
Clay, Cassius M., 34, 52, 367
Clay, Henry, 42, 52–57, 141–142, 154–155, 168–169, 184, 195, 303, 305, 338
Cleaveland, John Payne, 290, 332–33
Cleveland, Charles Dexter, 52, 153–154, 228, 268, 333, 480
Cleveland American, 186–187, 328, 368
Cleveland Convention of the American Anti-Slavery Society (October 23, 1839), 14
Coalition, 2–3, 52, 61, 66, 68, 70, 72–73, 75–84, 87–88, 90–91, 98–99, 106–109, 116–117, 124–130, 146, 149, 158, 162, 173, 176, 187–188, 197, 199–202, 205, 209–210, 213, 217–218, 235, 264, 266, 272, 274, 403*n*29
Cobb, Sylvanus, 333
Codding, Ichabod, 101, 131, 133, 194–196, 198, 202–203, 207–208, 210, 225, 232, 237, 252, 265, 267, 275 333
Coffin, Levi, 211, 213, 261, 333
Colby, Anthony, 70, 126–129

Collins, Frederick, 192–193, 334
Collins, Henry, 247, 262, 334
Collins, James H., 194, 334
Collins, John A., 131, 293
Colonization movement, 5, 111, 137, 256, 326, 331, 339, 344, 356, 365, 370, 374, 378
Colored American (New York, N.Y.), 245, 382
Colored People's National Convention in Buffalo, 245
Colver, Nathaniel, 290, 334
Come-outer philosophy, 3, 66–67, 71, 143, 226, 248, 283, 299, 343, 360, 363, 373
Commercial Journal (Pittsburgh, Pa.), 284
Congregational Church, 101, 130, 223, 283
Connecticut Anti-Slavery Society, 130–133
Conscience Whigs, 76, 82–83, 85, 88, 98–99, 273, 291
Conservative Democratic Party (N.H.), 4, 123
Convention of Colored People for Maine and New Hampshire, 246
Cook County (Ill.), 192–193, 260, 338, 352, 365
Cortland (N.Y.) True American, 65, 147, 251
Cover, Joseph Carman, 334, 480
Cowles, Betsey, 283
Crocker, William A., 334
Crandall, Prudence, 130
Cross, John, 194, 260–261, 335
Crummell, Alexander, 257, 335
Cummings, Hiram, 61, 96, 98, 223, 335
Curtis, Jeremiah, 102, 103, 335
Curtis, John G., 141
Curtis, Jonathan, 121–122
Cushing, Caleb, 100

Dana, John, 107
Dana, Richard Henry, 88
Darling, Arthur P., 100
Davis, Mary Brown, 283–285, 335
Davis, Samuel, 283, 335–336
Davis, Woodbury, 107, 336
Dawson, James, 219, 336
Day, William Howard, 258, 336
DeBaptiste, George, 247, 336–337
Declaration of Independence, 53, 58, 193, 217, 220, 316
DeKalb County (Ill.), 46, 114, 196, 202, 314

Delany, Martin, 153–154, 225, 247, 250, 262, 337, 377, 381
Deming, Elizur, 212, 290, 337
Democratic Party: members of, moving to the Liberty Party, 272–274; national convention of 1844, 42; national convention of 1848, 82–83; in the New Hampshire coalition, 69–70, 125–129; opposition to antislavery in, 14, 69, 178; proscription of Thomas Morris by, 14, 178
Denison, Charles W., 286, 337, 480
Denver, Colorado, 269
DePuy, Henry W., 213–214, 225, 289, 337, 480
Despotism in America (1840), 227
Detroit Advertiser, 168, 349
Detroit Liberty Association, 252, 346, 349, 366, 374
Detroit Vigilant Committee, 247, 254
DeWolf, Calvin, 337–338
Dillingham, Paul, 112
District of Columbia, 10, 37, 57, 77, 81, 84, 101, 174, 178, 316–317, 361
Disunionism, 56, 128, 156, 159, 198, 216, 277, 283, 294–299, 348
Dodge, Henry, 83
Dole, Ebenezer, 48, 286, 338
Dorr War, 16, 135
Dosman, Eunice, 296
Douglas, Stephen, 197, 260, 339
Douglass, Frederick, 39, 244, 247, 251, 256, 299, 337, 356, 367
Downstate New York, 138, 226
Duffy, John, 338
Dumond, Dwight Lowell, 301
Durkee, Charles, 90, 207–211, 288–289, 338, 341
Dyer, Charles V., 55, 194, 200, 268–269, 338, 480
Dyer, Edward G., 210–211, 339

Earle, Jonathan, 227
Earle, Thomas: biography, 339; Pennsylvania activities of, 152–153, 156, 298; as vice presidential candidate in 1840, 16–19, 152; mentioned, 267, 269, 286
Eastern Pennsylvania Anti-Slavery Society, 156, 277, 298
Eastman, Zebina: as antislavery editor, 191, 193–

197, 202–203, 232–233, 240, 275; mentioned, 241, 265, 339, 480
Eels, Richard, 197–198, 260, 286, 339
Elder, William, 63, 66, 153–154, 158, 161, 230, 234, 265, 284, 339–340
Ells, George, 181, 340, 442n98
Emancipator (New York and Boston), 12, 15, 29–31, 61, 77, 88, 93, 95–96, 98, 116, 149, 157, 232, 234, 293, 295, 345, 347, 344, 356, 369, 380
Episcopal Church, 53, 337, 352, 374
Errett, Russell, 154–155, 265, 284, 288, 340, 357
Estlin, John Bishop, 296
Evangelicalism, 1, 5, 37, 77, 172, 223–226, 231, 248, 258, 305–306, 347, 352, 382, 438n25
Evans, George Henry, 145, 340
Evans, Linda Jean, 224, 280
Everett, Horatio, 118

Fairchild, James H., 258, 262, 290, 340
Fairfield, John, 103
Farmington (N.Y.) Liberty Party convention (1846), 144, 146
Farnsworth, Drummond, 340–341
Federalist Party, 103, 121, 125, 231, 224, 341, 348, 370, 375, 423n197
Fee, John, 52
Female Anti-Slavery Society of Prairieville and Milwaukee, 281
Fessenden, Samuel, 26, 54, 77, 89, 98, 105–107, 109–110, 266–267, 274, 301, 341
Fessenden, William Pitt, 267
Fifth Annual Convention of the Colored Citizens of the State of New York, 249
Fillmore, Millard, 83, 150, 352
Financial Power of Slavery, The, 227–228, 235–236, 356
Finch, Asahel, 204, 210, 341, 358
Finney, Charles G., 268, 290, 341–342, 353, 362, 370, 372
First Wisconsin Territorial Anti-Slavery Convention, 202
Fischer, David Hackett, 2
Fitch, Jabez, 166, 261, 286, 341
Flag of Freedom, 107
Fleeson, Reese C., 153, 341–342
Foote, Charles C., 65, 81, 85, 145, 148–149, 342

Fort Hamilton (Ohio) antislavery convention (1840), 18
Forward, Walter, 155
Foster, Stephen S., 36, 66, 293, 297–299
Foster, Theodore: biography, 342; as editor of the *Signal of Liberty*, 165–166, 180–181, 169; on expanding the Liberty platform, 55, 62–63, 66, 145, 157, 170–175, 241, 273; mentioned, 37, 44, 60, 212, 233, 236, 261, 265, 282, 289, 325
Fourth congressional district (Ill.), 197–201
Franklin, Benjamin, 68, 151
Free Democratic Party, 150
Free Labor Advocate and Anti-Slavery Chronicle (New Garden, Ind.), 72, 212–213, 229, 372
Free produce movement, 213, 229
Free Soil Campaigner (Battle Creek, Mich.), 176
Free Soil League, 118
Free Soil Minstrel, The, 236
Free Soil movement: in Connecticut, 134; in Illinois, 200–201; in Indiana, 214–215; in Iowa, 219–220; in Maine, 89, 109–110; in Massachusetts, 98–100; in Michigan, 176; overview, 75–91; national Free Soil convention in Buffalo, 85–88; in New Hampshire, 89–90, 129–130; in New Jersey, 162–163; in New York, 149–150; in Ohio, 184–189; in Pennsylvania, 158–159; in Rhode Island, 135–136; in Vermont, 89, 118–119; in Wisconsin, 89, 209–210
Free Soil Party platform, 85–86
Free Soil Republican (Hallowell, Maine), 110
Free Will Baptist Church, 101, 224, 328–329, 332
Freehling, William, 392–393n44
Freer, Lemuel Clovell Paine, 337, 342, 352
Fugitive Slave Act of 1793, 80–81, 86, 259, 320, 362
Fugitive Slave Act of 1850, 259, 326, 332, 361, 364, 382
Fusion, 66–68, 71, 77–79, 106–107, 116, 199, 201, 203, 213, 217–218, 403n29

Gag rule, 6, 31, 35, 76, 84, 120, 124–125, 168
Gale, George Washington, 256, 342, 353
Galusha, Elon, 342–343, 427n17
Garland, Jerome, F., 45

Garland Forgery, 43–45, 47, 94, 105, 132, 141, 168–170, 184, 196
Garnet, Henry Highland, 38, 138, 161, 245, 249–251, 256–257, 262, 290, 323, 329, 343, 382, 470n61, 480
Garrison, William Lloyd: background, 7–8; declining influence of, 482n15; disunionism of, 56, 128, 156, 159, 198, 216, 277, 283, 292–299, 348; on the 1840 split in the American Anti-Slavery Society, 8–10, 121–122, 388n5; enmity of, with the Liberty Party, 3–4, 7, 17, 292–306; nonresistance of, 7, 10, 13, 22 38, 66, 101, 216, 282–283, 293–294, 305; mentioned, 17, 22, 47–48, 112–113
Gaston, Amnon, 207, 343
Gates, Seth M., 89, 139, 141, 150, 267, 288, 343, 335, 339, 379
Gazzam, Edward D., 158, 344
Gazzam, Joseph P., 153, 344
Genesee County (Mich.) *Democrat*, 44–45
Genius of Liberty (Lowell, Ill.), 191–193, 339, 379
Genius of Universal Emancipation (Hennepin, Ill.), 7, 191, 283, 335, 339, 379
Georgetown, Mass., 94, 270–271
Germans, 236, 463n79
Gibbons, Joseph, 156, 344
Giddings, Joshua, 4, 18, 31, 66, 87, 168, 178, 181–182, 185–189, 273, 305, 351, 378, 445n144
Gillette, Francis, 131–135, 261–262, 266–267, 288, 344
Ginzburg, Lori, 277, 285
Godfrey, John E., 61, 67, 104, 241, 344
Goodell, William: constitutional theories of, 57–59; as editor, 13–15, 337; and Liberty League, 62–65, 142–147, 273; mentioned, 16, 18, 36, 85, 90, 138, 223, 267, 272, 275, 291, 334–345
Goodman, Paul, 287
Goodwin, Edwin W., 225, 329, 345
Granite Freeman (Concord, N.H.), 69–70, 124–129, 233, 276
Grant County (Ind.), 46, 212, 214, 324
Great Convention of the Friends of Freedom in the Eastern and Middle States, 51, 54–55, 60, 95
Greeley, Horace, 43, 142, 269, 355, 381

Green, Beriah, 16, 42, 65, 90, 131, 147, 234, 236, 256–257, 290–291, 345, 353
Green Mountain Freeman (Montpelier, Vt.), 73, 89, 115–118, 233, 273, 329, 345, 366, 368
Grimes, John, 159, 162, 345
Grimsted, David, 298
Grinnell, Josiah B., 257, 269, 288, 290, 345
Grosvenor, Cyrus P., 290, 345–346
Gurney, Chester, 175, 346
Guthrie, Albert Austin, 188, 346

Hale, John P.: biography, 346; insurgency of, in New Hampshire Democratic Party, 68–70, 124–130; Liberty Party presidential candidacy of, 62, 65–87, 96–99, 109–110, 118, 134–135, 148–150, 158, 162, 175–176, 187–188, 201, 208–209, 214, 217–219; work of, for the Liberty Party, 106–108; mentioned, 90–91, 96, 146, 173, 270, 274, 287, 288, 332, 345, 354, 377, 381, 480
Hale, Josiah W., 346
Hall, Lauriston, 346
Hallock, Horace, 175, 346–347
Hamlin, Edward S., 55, 403n26
Harding, Stephen S., 211–212, 214, 289, 347, 480
Harlan, James, 218
Harrison, Marcus, 172, 347
Harrison, William Henry, 14, 18, 26, 102, 139, 151, 165, 179–181, 211, 227, 304
Harrold, Stanley, 461n57
Hastings, Samuel D., 153, 347
Hawley, Joseph R., 135, 225, 288–289, 347
Hayden, Joel, 48, 269, 271, 289, 347–348
Headlands in the Life of Henry Clay (1844), 42
Herald of Freedom (Concord, N.H.), 17–18, 34, 121–122, 124–125
Herkimer (N.Y.) *Freeman*, 68, 144
Hildreth, Richard, 227, 294–295, 348, 463n81, 480
Hill, Isaac, 4, 120–121
Hillsdale College, 258, 290, 328
Hoes, Schuyler, 348
Hoit, Daniel, 70, 122–128, 266, 348
Holley, Myron, 13–18, 138–139, 223, 267, 283, 300, 348–349
Holley, Sallie, 283, 300

Holmes, Silas M., 349
Holton, Edward D., 203, 205, 209–210, 349, 453n297
Hooker, John, 130, 349
Howe, Appleton, 349
Howe, Samuel Gridley, 349–350
Howe, Samuel Luke, 218–219, 350
Hudson, Timothy, 258, 350
Hunter, Colonel Charles W., 192–193, 350
Hurlbut, Thaddeus B., 350
Hussey, Erastus, 175–176, 261, 350–351
Hutchins, John, 180–181, 189, 288, 351
Hutchinson, Titus, 58, 112–113, 116, 262, 351
Hutchinson family, 115–116, 225

Illinois Anti-Slavery Society, 18–19, 191, 195, 204, 323, 334, 339, 353
Illinois Constitutional Convention, 199
Illinois Female Anti-Slavery Society, 335
Illinois State Women's Anti-Slavery Society, 280
Indiana Anti-Slavery Society, 211
Indiana Free Territory Convention, 214
Indiana Freeman (Indianapolis), 213, 337
Independent Democrat and Granite Freeman (Concord, N.H.), 70, 129
Independent Democrats, 69–72, 98, 106, 126–130, 274, 276, 377
Iowa Territorial Anti-Slavery Society, 215–217
Iowa Freeman, 218, 219, 353, 372

Jackson, Francis, 223, 289
Jackson, James C., 15, 27, 31, 65, 68, 138–139, 142–146, 278–279, 289, 301, 351, 363
Jackson, William, 17, 27, 52, 95, 225, 267, 288, 351–352
Jackson County (Mich.), 165–167, 313
Jay, William, 34, 36, 51, 57, 90, 139–140, 145, 226–227, 255, 265, 352
Jeffrey, Julie Roy, 278–279
Jerry Rescue, 250, 332, 358, 379
Jewish faith, 224
Johnson, George Washington. *See* Jonson, George Washington
Johnson, Henry, 242, 253, 352
Jones, John, 261, 342, 352

Jonson, George Washington, 17, 93, 352–353
Journal of Commerce (New York, N.Y.), 230
Julian, George W., 214–215, 264, 371

Kane County (Ill.), 260, 314, 365
Keep, John, 353
Kelley, Abby, 8, 38, 277, 282, 293, 297–299, 478n83
Kellogg, Hiram Huntington, 290, 353
Kelsey, David, 219, 353
Kent, Edward, 102–103
King, Daniel P., 30–31
King, Leicester, 36, 39, 48, 81, 179–180, 183, 281, 353–354
King, Preston, 83
Kingman, Eliphalet, 354
Knapp, Chauncy L., 113, 120, 285–286, 288, 354
Knox College, 258, 262–263, 290, 325, 327, 342, 353
Know Nothing movement. *See* Nativism
Kraditor, Aileen S., 22, 75, 291, 304

Ladies' New York City Anti-Slavery Society, 277
Lake County (Ill.) *Visitor*, 198
Lambert, William, 247, 254, 354
Lamoille County (Vt.), 46, 114, 313, 335
Land reformers, 85, 145
Lane, Charles, 69
Lane, Lunsford, 103, 250, 354
Lane Seminary, 9, 256, 323, 327, 359, 370, 372
Langston, Charles H., 255, 355, 480
Langston, John Mercer, 189, 258, 288, 290, 355
Larimer, William, 156, 269, 285, 355
LaSalle County (Ill.) Anti-Slavery Society, 191
Latimer, George, 250, 253, 334, 355–356, 379
Leach, Dewitt Clinton, 288, 356
Leavitt, Joshua: biography, 356; as editor 15, 32, 62, 77, 93, 226, 232, 234, 273; *The Financial Power of Slavery*, 226–227, 235–236; as Liberty Party leader, 16–17, 25, 31–32, 34–36, 66–67, 77, 79, 87–88, 93, 99, 119, 135, 179, 265; relationship of, with Elizur Wright 66–67, 97–98, 241; relationship of, with William Lloyd Garrison, 8, 293, 295, 309; mentioned 60, 85, 229, 253, 267–268, 289, 291

Leavitt, Roger, 17, 356
Lee, Luther, 161, 225, 356–357
Lemoyne, Francis J., 14, 41, 65, 81, 90, 151–158, 233, 247–249, 262, 290, 340, 357
Leominster (Mass.) Anti-Slavery Society, 276–277
Lewis, Samuel, 52, 149, 179–181, 185, 188, 286, 357, 371
Liberator, 7, 30, 34, 88, 111, 181, 243, 251, 293–298
Liberty Advocate (Providence and Woonsocket, R.I.), 135
Liberty almanacs, 43, 193, 207, 235–236, 377
Liberty associations: Boonton (N.J.) Liberty Association, 160–161, 280; Chicago Liberty Association, 195, 198, 352; Detroit Liberty Association, 252, 337, 366, 374; in Connecticut, 132, 278; in general, 237–238, 306, 464n84; Green Mountain Liberty Association, 115; in Illinois, 195–196; in Indiana, 212; in Lorain (Ohio), 376; in Maine, 107–108, 111, 115, 335, 341; in Massachusetts, 325; Milwaukee Liberty Association, 40, 204; Northern Ohio Liberty Association, 187; Wisconsin Liberty Association, 81, 89, 99, 204–206, 208, 210–211, 238, 238, 281–282, 341, 343, 358; mentioned, 242, 277, 279
Liberty Banner (Rock Island, Ill.), 197
Liberty Choir of Chicago, 55, 197, 225, 252
Liberty Herald (Philadelphia, Pa.), 154, 158, 339
Liberty Herald (Warren, Ohio), 154, 158, 183, 186, 233, 368
Liberty League, 2, 4, 61, 65–66, 68, 72–91, 98–99, 116–117, 143–150, 162, 175, 186, 199–200, 208, 229, 250–251, 258, 273, 282, 284–285, 306, 326, 328, 330, 332, 340, 342, 345, 351–352, 357–358, 362, 371, 373, 375, 377, 379, 382, 429n40
Liberty Man's Book, The, 98, 335
Liberty Minstrel. *See* Clark, George Washington
Liberty Minstrel, The, 236
Liberty Party: in Connecticut, 130–135, 423–424n225; debates over expanding the platform of, 61–66, 68, 76–78, 80–81, 97–98, 116–117, 144–149, 226, 241, 273; debates over fusion and coalition tactics of, 66–73, 97–98, 106–107, 116; in Detroit, 438–439n32; first national nominating convention of (1841), 23–25, 182; in Iowa, 213–220, 232, 237, 253, 255, 326, 350, 353, 361, 369, 372, 374; in Illinois, 190–202; in Indiana, 71–72, 211–215; interpretation of the U.S. Constitution by, 56–61, 97, 105–106, 116, 144, 187, 299–300, 404–405n52; in Iowa, 28, 52, 55, 73, 80, 193, 202, 215–220; in Maine, 67–68, 71, 100–111; in Massachusetts, 83, 92–100; membership of, 264–291; in Michigan, 164–177; national corresponding committee of, 22, 24, 39, 81, 334, 337, 338, 339, 341, 346, 351, 356, 357, 361, 364, 369, 373, 375, 378, 381, 410n26, 426n265; national platform of, in 1844, 2, 4, 37–38, 42, 80, 86, 235–237, 252–253, 259, 315–322, 331; newspapers of, 29, 61–62, 77–79, 88–89, 93–94, 142–143, 147, 158, 160–161, 171, 189, 231–234, 396n15, 462n62; in New Hampshire, 68–71, 120–130; in New Jersey, 159–163; in New York, 68, 137–151; in Ohio, 177–190; in Pennsylvania, 151–159; in Pittsburgh, 64, 153–155, 157–158, 230, 247, 250, 283–284, 334, 337, 340, 342, 344, 355, 364, 370, 374, 378; position of, on Mexican War, 47, 72, 76, 82, 97, 108, 127–128, 149, 157, 173, 209, 216, 273, 332, 421n5; post-1844 election convention of, in Albany, 50, 142; in Rhode Island, 73; second national nominating convention of (1843), 35–40, 75, 79, 124, 194, 245; third national nominating convention of (1847), 79–81, 109, 134, 149; in Vermont, 40, 111–120, 162; in Virginia, 220–221; in Wisconsin, 84, 202–211; women's participation in, 38, 276–285

Liberty Party state conventions: in Connecticut, 131 (1841–1842), 133 (1846); in Illinois, 18–19 (1840), 191 (1840), 191–192 (1841), 192–193 (1842), 195–196 (1844), 197 (1846), 200 (1848); in Indiana, 212 (1842), 213 (1845), 214 (1848); in Iowa, 216; in Maine, 17 (1840), 102 (1841), 107 (1847); in Massachusetts, 17 (1840), 96 (1846), 77, 97 (1847); in Michigan, 18, 165 (1840), 166 (1841), 167–168 (1843), 169 (1845), 175 (1847), 175–176 (1848); in New Hampshire, 18 (1840), 113 (1843), 126–127 (1846); in New Jersey, 160 (1844); in New York, 18 (1840), 138–139 (1842), 139–140 (1843), 145 (1846); in Ohio, 18, 179 (1840),

180–181 (1841), 183 (1844), 185 (1845), 188 (1848); in Pennsylvania, 18, 152 (1840), 154 (1844), 157 (1847); in Vermont, 17 (1840), 112 (1841), 113–114 (1843), 115, 116 (1845 and 1847); in Virginia, 220–221; in Wisconsin, 203 (1843), 203–204 (1844), 204–205 (1845), 105–106 (1846), 207–208 (1847), 208–209 (1848)
Liberty Press (Utica, N.Y.), 31, 65, 68, 144, 147, 233, 324, 351
Liberty Standard (Hallowell, Maine), 67, 71, 77, 102, 107–110, 233, 288, 324, 358, 380
Locofocos. *See* Democratic Party
Loguen, Jermain W., 250, 257, 262, 357–358
Lorain County (Ohio), 60, 178, 184, 187, 189–190, 258, 314, 368, 376
Lorain County Anti-Slavery Society, 178
Loring, Ellis Gray, 294
Lovejoy, Elijah, 7, 102, 191–192, 259, 350, 358
Lovejoy, Joseph, 102–103, 299, 358
Lovejoy, Owen, 119, 194–201, 205, 222, 227, 238, 259–261, 265, 275, 288, 334, 358, 450n246
Lundy, Benjamin, 7, 191, 260
Lybrand, Iowa, 269
Lybrand, Jacob, 210, 269, 358
Lynde, William P., 204, 210, 341, 358–359

Macedon Lock Liberty League Convention (1847), 65, 78, 98, 146, 282
Madison County (N.Y.), 27, 37, 49, 138–141, 144, 237–238, 250, 275, 313
Madison County (N.Y.) *Abolitionist*, 27, 138, 324, 351, 363
Mahan, Asa, 187–188, 256, 258, 290, 297, 299–300, 359
Mahan, John, 178
Maine Anti-Slavery Society, 100–103, 278
Maizlish, Stephen, 189
Majority election laws, 10–11, 27, 29–31, 69–70, 89, 92, 94, 96, 100, 103–104, 107–108, 112, 131–133, 271
Marsh, Rodney, 359
Massachusetts Abolition Society, 8, 15, 122, 276, 325
Massachusetts Abolitionist, 8, 15, 19, 93, 372, 375, 382
Massachusetts Anti-Slavery Society, 5, 8, 69, 121, 244, 293–294, 301, 365, 372, 374

Massachusetts Female Emancipation Society, 276, 388n5
Massachusetts Plan, 115
Mathews, Edward, 193–195, 202–203, 206–207, 224, 268, 276, 359
Matlack, Lucius, 156, 290, 359
Matthews, Stanley, 61, 149, 186, 187–188, 189, 225, 287, 288, 359–360, 457n152
May, Samuel Joseph, 285, 296, 360
May, Seth, 48, 106, 360
McGee, Thomas, 360
McKim, James Miller, 152–153, 360–361
McKinney, Mordecai, 361
McLean, John, 86
Mellen, George Washington, 58, 361
Mercer (Pa.) *Luminary*, 154
Mexican War, 47, 72, 76, 82, 97, 108, 127–128, 149, 157, 173, 216, 273, 332, 409n5
Michigan Argus (Ann Arbor), 246–247
Michigan Circular, 157, 171–172
Michigan Freeman (Jackson), 15, 18–19, 165–166, 376
Michigan Liberty Press (Battle Creek), 176, 350
Michigan State Anti-Slavery Society, 19, 165–166, 175, 326, 333, 342, 366–367, 373, 375
Miller, Jonathan P., 17, 286, 361
Miller, William H., 219, 361
Mills, Joseph Trotter, 211, 361–362
Miltimore, Ira, 196, 362
Milton (Mass.) Anti-Slavery Society, 278
Milwaukee Democrat, 203–204
Miscegenation, 258–259, 328
Monroe, James, 189, 258, 288, 362, 480
Monteith, John, 290, 362
Moral suasion, 6, 9, 159, 291–293, 300, 376, 388n3
Morris, Thomas: biography, 362; difficulties of, with Bailey, 34–36, 41, 182–183, 241; as Liberty vice presidential candidate, 23, 36–37, 41, 269–270, 286; as U.S. senator, 14, 27, 178, 227, 288; mentioned, 50, 57, 180–181, 198, 233, 255–256, 267 340
Morse, Freeman H., 108
Morton, Marcus, 29–30, 67
Mott, Lucretia, 149, 277, 282
Murray, Orson, 112–113
Myrick, Luther, 223, 225, 362–363

Mystery (Pittsburgh, Pa.), 153–154, 158, 247, 334, 337, 364, 377, 378, 381

National Anti-Slavery Convention at Albany (1839), 14
National Anti-Slavery Standard (New York, N.Y.), 12, 34, 72–73, 293, 295, 298–299, 351
National Convention of Colored People in Rochester, 38–39, 245
National Era (Washington, D.C.), 29, 55, 61, 72–73, 76, 89, 98, 149, 173, 186, 232–235, 324–326, 330, 338–339, 363, 365, 375, 380
National Liberty Party. *See* Liberty League
National Reform movement, 145, 147, 239, 328, 340, 371
Native American Party, 156, 158
Nativism, 96, 142, 145, 156, 236, 284–286, 337, 463–464n81
Nelson, David, 286, 290, 339, 363
New England Anti-Slavery Society, 5, 7, 10, 121, 292, 295, 330, 338, 341, 365, 369, 414n21, 463–464n81
New Garden Township, Ind., 212, 238, 251, 275
New Hampshire Abolition Society, 17, 121–124
New Hampshire Anti-Slavery Society, 121, 125
New Hampshire Patriot (Concord, N.H.), 128
New Jersey Anti-Slavery Society, 160–162
New Jersey Freeman (Boonton, N.J.), 159–160, 162–163, 345
New Jersey slave cases, 59–60, 161–162
New Market (N.H.) Convention (1846), 70, 127–128
New Organization, 122–123, 153, 223, 243–244, 276–277, 294, 341. *See also* American Anti-Slavery Society
New York Female Anti-Slavery Society, 279
New York State Anti-Slavery Society, 14, 60, 251, 351, 356, 374, 377, 378
New York State Colored Convention in Rochester, 245
Niles' National Register, 51
Noble, Linnaeus, 73, 234, 363
Nonresistance, 7, 10, 13, 22 38, 66, 101, 124–125, 216, 282–283, 293–295, 305
Non-Resistant, 295
North-Western Liberty Convention in Chicago (1846), 51, 55, 157, 172, 194, 198, 234, 323, 331, 338, 347

Oberlin College, 180, 183, 199, 247, 256–258, 262–263, 283, 285, 290, 297, 299–300, 332, 333, 328–329, 332, 336, 340–342, 350, 353–355, 359, 362, 366, 377–378, 380, 381
Oberlin Evangelist, 48, 297
O'Connell, Daniel, 37, 322, 398n53
Ohio American Anti-Slavery Society, 294, 296–297
Ohio Anti-Slavery Society, 177–178, 180, 281, 293, 297, 346, 350
Ohio County (Va.) Liberty Convention, 221
Old Organization, 9–10, 73, 82, 93, 122, 124–125, 130, 153, 156, 223, 243–244, 276–277, 293, 294, 297–301, 331, 339, 341, 369, 372, 388n5. *See also* American Anti-Slavery Society
Olin, Chauncey C., 207, 363
Olivet College, 258, 290, 370
Oneida Institute, 16, 42, 147, 256–257, 290, 323, 325, 334–335, 342–343, 345, 357
Oregon, 42

Paine, James H., 180–181, 188, 210, 363–364
Paine, John A. *See* Payne, John A.
Palfrey, John G., 97–98, 148, 417n84
Palladium of Liberty (Columbus, Ohio), 255, 355
Parkhurst, Jonathan, 160, 364
Payne, John A., 364
Peace movement, 65, 95, 226, 330, 338, 350, 352
Peck, David, 258, 364
Peck, John C., 247, 262, 364
Pennington, James W. C., 133, 246, 262, 349, 364
Pennock, Abraham L., 66, 290, 365
Pennsylvania Abolition Society, 151, 329, 339
Pennsylvania Anti-Slavery Society, 18, 151–153, 329, 360, 432n90
Pennsylvania Freeman, 15, 18, 34, 151–153, 298
People's Advocate (Concord, N.H.), 123–124, 376
People's Convention in Columbus, Ohio (1848), 83, 188
Perfectionism, 223, 226, 248, 258, 363
Perry (N.Y.) Impartial Countryman, 64–65, 344
Phelps, Amos A., 54, 73, 93, 122, 223, 234, 267, 286, 365
Philadelphia Female Anti-Slavery Society, 277

Philadelphia Liberty Party Bazaar, 279
Philanthropist (Cincinnati, Ohio), 10, 12, 19, 29, 32, 50, 77, 182, 186, 232–233, 301, 324, 326–327
Phillips, Stephen C., 110
Phillips, Wendell, 56, 93, 192, 301
Pierce, Franklin, 68
Pierpont, John, 37–38, 52, 93, 147, 236, 365
Pillsbury, Parker, 66, 125
Pinkerton, Allan, 261, 365
Platt, Zephanah, 168
Plumb, Ralph, 189, 288, 365–366
Plumb, Samuel, 366
Poland, Joseph, 115–119, 233, 366
Polk, James K., 42–43, 47, 69, 75, 125, 140–142, 154, 168, 183–185, 202, 208, 212, 215, 273, 305, 260
Port Byron (N.Y.) Liberty meeting (1845), 63–65, 142–144, 429*n*40
Porter, Arthur L., 286, 366
Porter, Samuel D., 366–367
Potts, David, 27, 154, 267, 269, 288, 367
Power, Nathan, 367
Presbyterian Church, 215–216, 224
Prigg v. Pennsylvania, 318, 321
Prohibition Party, 111
Protectionist (New Garden, Ind.), 213, 229, 330
Putnam County (Ill.), 46, 202, 314

Quakers, 33, 151, 178, 212, 215, 293, 300
Questioning system, 10–15, 18, 22, 101–102, 111, 130, 138, 151, 157, 164–165, 178–180, 191, 215–216, 304, 366, 390*n*19
Quincy, Edmund, 81, 88, 293, 296, 301, 485–486*n*70

Radical Abolition Party, 4, 344–345, 358, 371, 375
Rankin, Adam L., 261, 367
Rankin, John T., 177, 179, 182, 261, 367
Rantoul, Robert, 100
Ray, Charles B., 245, 256, 367–368
Register (Peoria, Ill.), 283, 325
Remond, Charles L., 39, 244, 251, 256
Renda, Lex, 272
Republican Party, 48, 91, 111, 120, 129, 135, 150, 159, 166, 190, 201, 206, 211, 215, 257, 266, 286, 289
Rice, Lewis Lippert, 183, 186, 233, 368

Ripley (Ohio) abolitionists, 33, 177, 190, 261, 267, 330, 367
Robinson, William S., 292
Rogers, Nathaniel P., 11–12, 17, 121, 124–125
Roosevelt, Theodore, 50
Root, Joseph, 189
Russell, Ida, 278
Ryan, Mary P., 277

Sabin, Alvah, 112, 120, 288, 368
Saturday Visiter (Pittsburgh, Pa.), 158, 284, 374
Scammon, J. Young, 200
Scattering of votes tactic, 19–20, 93, 101, 113, 122, 291, 413*n*7
Scoble, John, 296
Scott, Jacob, 368
Scott, Orange, 223, 286, 368
Seceder Presbyterians, 215, 218, 336
Sernett, Milton, 257
Seventy, the, 323, 325–327, 330, 333–335, 345, 360, 362, 365, 367–368, 381, 389*n*11
Sewall, Samuel, 9, 29–30, 36, 54, 93–97, 253, 268, 271–272, 294, 299–300, 369
Seward, William, 34, 52, 63, 150, 181, 187, 273
Sewell, Richard H., 1, 126
Shafter, Oscar L., 89, 114, 118–119, 269, 369
Shafter, William R., 114–115, 369
Shaw, Benjamin, 369
Shedd, George, 217, 369
Shepard, Charles O., 18, 139–140, 147, 150, 269, 369–370
Shipherd, John Jay, 290, 370
Shiras, Charles P., 158, 370
Sholes, Charles C., 203–207, 232, 270, 370
Signal of Liberty (Ann Arbor, Mich.), 62–63, 79, 157, 166–175, 233, 236, 246, 254, 261, 282, 286, 325, 354, 356
Slade, William, 31, 114–115, 118, 273, 305
Slave Power theories, 24–25, 32–33, 37, 40, 53–58, 179, 182–183, 227–230, 236, 459*n*28
Smith, Caleb, 214
Smith, Edward, 153, 188, 370
Smith, Gerrit: biography, 370–371; financial resources of, 235, 237–238, 275, 331; and the Liberty League, 63, 65, 68, 71, 80–81, 85, 90, 98, 172, 229, 273, 282–283, 279; participation of, in the Liberty Party, 11, 15, 18, 27, 36–37, 39, 46, 48–49, 54, 137–151, 265–268; on the U.S.

Smith, Gerrit *(continued)*
　Constitution, 60; mentioned, 4, 77, 91, 108, 119, 137, 162, 182, 223–225, 229, 249, 262, 288, 294, 329, 353, 375
Smith, James McCune, 371
Smith, Theodore Clarke, 1, 4, 168, 205, 210
Smyth, William, 265, 371
Snow, Henry, 200, 371
Somerset County (Maine) Anti-Slavery Society, 17
Southern and Western Convention of the Friends of Constitutional Liberty at Cincinnati (1845), 51–54, 185, 273, 370
Southern Illinois Liberty Convention, 199
Southwestern Anti-Slavery Society, 297
Spirit of Liberty (Pittsburgh, Pa.), 64, 153–154, 157–158, 171–172, 233, 284, 342, 370, 374
Spooner, Lysander, 59
Spooner, Jeduthan, 203
Spooner, Thomas, 286, 371
St. Clair, Alanson, 122, 124, 198, 202, 207, 217–219, 223, 237, 267, 274, 353, 381 372
Stansbury, Edward A., 118
Stanton, Benjamin, 72, 212–214, 229, 275, 372
Stanton, Elizabeth Cady, 268, 282, 289, 372
Stanton, Henry Brewster, 8, 11, 14, 16, 20, 31, 36, 39, 45, 54–56, 66, 70, 77–79, 84–86, 93–98, 111, 148, 223, 238, 253, 256, 265, 268, 282, 289, 295, 299, 372–373
Stauffer, John, 427n17
Stevens, Luther F., 373
Stevens, Stephen, 213–214, 336, 373
Stevens, Thaddeus, 158, 273
Stewart, Alvan: biography, 373; constitutional theories of, 57–60, 161; Liberty Party activities of, 13–20, 24–25, 36, 76, 131–132, 138–147 passim, 156, 161–163, 172, 235, 238–239, 265, 279–280, 291; mentioned, 80, 119, 223, 228, 249, 259, 286, 301, 353
Stewart, Charles Henry, 64, 168, 171, 280, 373–374
Stewart, James Brewer, 303
Stone, Lucy, 283, 300
Storrs, George, 374
Stowe, Harriet Beecher, 262, 344, 359, 367
Straight Republican ticket, 286
Street, Aaron, 215–216, 374

Strong, Douglas, 223
Strong, Marshall M., 208
Sturge, Joseph, 357, 296
Suffrage: for African Americans, 68, 86, 134, 143–145, 156, 166, 170–171, 173, 199, 205–208, 242–243, 246–250, 253–255, 315–317, 320, 334, 336, 364 381, 400n98; for women, 55, 149, 156, 279, 284, 359, 369, 381, 476n36
Sumner, Charles, 99, 110, 273
Swan, Caleb, 96, 286, 353, 374
Swan, Hurlburt, 199, 374
Swisshelm, Jane Grey, 158, 283–286, 374

Talcott Street Congregational Church (Hartford, Conn.), 262, 364
Tappan, Arthur, 7–8, 46, 48, 138, 226, 230, 237, 253, 255, 268, 279, 370, 374–375, 382
Tappan, Lewis, 8–9, 39, 46, 48, 65, 73, 77, 80, 84, 90, 138–139, 145, 148, 161, 171, 226, 230, 237, 253, 255, 268, 279, 293, 295, 370, 375, 382
Tariffs, 24–25, 41, 62–65, 85, 153–155, 171, 208, 273
Taylor, Alice, 285
Taylor, Zachary, 82–83, 89–90, 99, 118, 129, 150, 162, 187, 189, 216, 218–219, 361
Temperance, 21, 61–62, 67, 94–95, 103–106, 111, 116, 161, 163, 166, 186, 193, 201, 207, 211, 218, 226–227, 266, 299, 324–325, 327, 329–330, 333, 336, 341, 345, 347–348, 351–352, 354–355, 359, 362, 364, 369, 378–380, 405n61, 405n65
Texas annexation, 35, 38, 42, 47, 54, 68, 72, 95–96, 101, 124–125, 140, 168, 183–185, 208, 273, 284, 324, 370, 377
Thomas, Nathan, 261, 375
Tiffany, Joel, 60, 185–187, 375
Tod, David, 185, 351
Torrey, Charles T., 61, 93, 101, 223, 225, 229, 245, 250, 286, 375–376, 473n134
Townshend, Norton S., 181, 188–189, 258, 288, 376
Tract system, 93, 102–104, 123, 132, 155, 193, 197–199, 228, 235–237, 275, 320, 345
Tracy, Frederick P., 123, 376
Treadwell, Seymour B., 19, 28, 64, 164–165, 172, 250, 376–377
Treatise on the Unconstitutionality of American Slavery; Together with the Powers and Duties

of the Federal Government in Relation to That Subject (1849), 187
True Democracy, 52–53, 63, 66, 273
Tuck, Amos, 90, 128–129, 148, 287–288, 377
Tucker, John N. T., 377
Tweedy, John, 208
Tyler, John, 14, 25–26, 45, 165, 180, 304–305

Uncle Tom's Cabin, 261, 332, 367
Unconstitutionality of Slavery, The (1845), 59
Underground Railroad, 3, 65, 115, 133, 224, 246–247, 257–262, 280, 287, 326–383 passim, 473n134
Union Church, 143, 223, 351, 357, 363, 370–371, 373, 377
Upstate New York, 2, 13, 85 91, 111, 137–138, 142–143, 147, 150, 161, 163–164, 177, 223, 226, 249–250, 256, 268, 279, 283, 306, 357, 362, 370
Utica (N.Y.) *Friend of Man,* 13, 19, 64, 233, 257, 344–345

Van Buren, John, 83, 110, 188
Van Buren, Martin, 15, 18, 42, 83–91, 99–100, 110, 117–119, 129, 134–135, 150, 158–159, 162–163, 200–201, 209–210, 214, 284
Van Fleet, Jane. *See* Van Vleet, Jane
Van Vleet, Jane, 283, 377
Vance, Joseph, 178
Vashon, George B., 247, 258, 262, 290, 377–378
Vashon, John B., 247, 378
Vermont Anti-Slavery Society, 111–112, 115
Vermont Telegraph (Brandon), 34, 112–113
View of the Action of the Federal Government in Behalf of Slavery (1839), 227
Views of American Constitutional Law (1844), 59
Voice of Freedom (Montpelier, Vt.), 17, 115, 354, 366
Volpe, Vernon, 1, 47
Von Holst, Herman, 296

Wade, Benjamin, 178
Wade, Edward, 179, 182, 185, 189, 224, 258, 288, 378
Wadsworth, L. L., 108
Walker, Amasa, 258, 270, 288, 378
Walters, Ronald G., 50

Ward, Samuel Ringgold, 65, 138, 149, 245, 250–251, 262, 378–379
Warren, Hooper, 191, 379
Warsaw (N.Y.) antislavery convention (1839), 14–15, 151
Washington, Lewis, 250, 363, 379
Washington (Pa.) *Patriot,* 233, 247, 262, 340, 357
Washingtonian Abolitionists, 62
Washtenaw County (Mich.) Liberty convention, 170
Wayne County (Mich.), 66, 168, 238, 437n19
Wayne County (Mich.) Liberty convention, 168
Weld, Theodore Dwight, 9, 160, 177, 323, 327, 343
Wentworth, John, 200
Wesleyan Methodist Church, 166, 173, 212, 223, 324–325, 356–357, 359, 368, 470n7
Western Anti-Slavery Society, 297
Western Pennsylvania Anti-Slavery Society, 153, 364
Western Pennsylvania Liberty Committee, 41
Western Reserve, Ohio, 4, 18, 27, 60, 66, 82, 177–178, 181, 183–185, 187, 189–191, 232, 238, 254, 328, 340, 346, 353
Western Reserve College, 8, 345, 351, 365–366, 376, 393
Wheaton, Laban M., 379
Whig Party: antislavery attitudes in, 17–19, 35, 168, 177–178; Conscience Whigs, 76, 82–83, 85, 88, 98–99, 273, 291; national convention (1839), 14–15; national convention (1848), 83, 118; in the New Hampshire coalition, 69–70, 125–129; opposition of, to the Liberty Party, 26, 42–45; reaction of, to the presidential election of 1844, 46–48, 142, 169–170; as voter base for early Liberty Party, 19, 133
Whipper, William, 379–380
Whittier, John Greenleaf, 15–17, 30–31, 36–37, 44, 66–67, 69–70, 73, 77–79, 83–84, 93, 95–96, 98–99, 148, 151, 234, 236, 238, 241, 256, 278, 300, 327, 380
Willey, Austin, 15, 25, 60, 67, 71, 101–109, 120, 233, 240–241, 265, 296, 380
Williams, Austin, 380, 406n65
Williams, Charles K., 112–114, 120, 289, 380
Williams, Jared, 129
Wilmot, David, 72, 158

Wilmot Proviso, 79, 82–86, 96, 98, 118, 173, 200, 208, 216
Wilson, John, 128
Wilson, Martin, 381
Wisconsin Aegis (Racine), 203
Wisconsin Free Territory Convention, 209
Wisconsin state constitutional conventions, 205–206, 208
Wisconsin Territorial Anti-Slavery Society, 40, 202, 205
Wise, Daniel, 223
Women's rights movement, 8, 10, 101, 121, 149, 276–277, 281–285, 289, 323–324, 327, 329, 350, 363, 374
Wood, Samuel Newitt, 269, 381
Woodbridge, William, 165
Woodbury, Levi, 70, 127
Woodsdale, Kans., 269
Woodson, Lewis, 247, 250, 262, 381

Woolman, John, 151
Worcester, Mass., 83, 239, 313, 354, 361
Work, Alanson, 133, 381
Workingman's Party, 96
Workingmen's movement, 53, 64, 76, 96, 155, 228–230, 272, 305, 339–340
World Anti-Slavery Convention in London (1840), 19, 327–328, 343, 353, 361, 364, 372, 376
Wright, Elizur, 8, 11, 13, 15–16, 19, 29, 60, 65–66, 81, 88, 93, 97–99, 224, 241, 265, 267–268, 286, 289, 293, 301, 356, 381–382
Wright, Silas, 82, 142, 428*n*34
Wright, Theodore, 245, 255, 382
Wyoming County (N.Y.), 141, 275

Yale, Levi, 134, 382
Yancey, Walter C., 254, 382

Zuille, John, 245, 382–383

www.ingramcontent.com/pod-product-compliance
Lightning Source LLC
Chambersburg PA
CBHW031948290426
44108CB00011B/729